Mark Twain
and the Colonel

Mark Twain and the Colonel

Samuel L. Clemens,
Theodore Roosevelt, and the
Arrival of a New Century

Philip McFarland

ROWMAN & LITTLEFIELD PUBLISHERS, INC.
Lanham • Boulder • New York • Toronto • Plymouth, UK

Published by Rowman & Littlefield Publishers, Inc.
A wholly owned subsidiary of The Rowman & Littlefield Publishing Group, Inc.
4501 Forbes Boulevard, Suite 200, Lanham, Maryland 20706
www.rowman.com

10 Thornbury Road, Plymouth PL6 7PP, United Kingdom

Distributed by National Book Network

British Library Cataloguing in Publication Information Available

Library of Congress Cataloging-in-Publication Data

McFarland, Philip James.
  Mark Twain and the Colonel : Samuel L. Clemens, Theodore Roosevelt, and the arrival of a new century / Philip McFarland.
    pages cm
  Includes bibliographical references and index.
  ISBN 978-1-4422-1226-8 (cloth : alk. paper) — ISBN 978-1-4422-1228-2 (electronic)
  1. United States—Civilization—1865–1918. 2. Twain, Mark, 1835–1910—Influence.
  3. Roosevelt, Theodore, 1858–1919—Influence. I. Title.
  E169.1.M1616 2012
  973.8—dc23

                                                                    2011051861

♾™ The paper used in this publication meets the minimum requirements of American National Standard for Information Sciences—Permanence of Paper for Printed Library Materials, ANSI/NISO Z39.48-1992.

Printed in the United States of America

for

PATRICIA

again, always

Do not all these things interest you? Isn't it a fine thing to be alive when so many great things are happening?
—*Theodore Roosevelt, 1903*

These are sardonic times. . . . But I am not sorry to be alive & privileged to look on.
—*Mark Twain, 1897*

Contents

Illustrations

Preface

One dominated the culture of his era, the other its politics: two towering Americans alive at the beginning of the twentieth century who, more than a hundred years later, are still vital, still known worldwide. Mark Twain and Theodore Roosevelt were often in New York City at that period of their lives; and because both were gregarious, their paths were bound to cross. Each was a prolific writer, and on a wide variety of subjects. In addition, each filled other professional roles besides authorship, Mark Twain principally as a lecturer, Roosevelt as a politician. They had first met in the mid-1880s. In their many appearances before the public thereafter, neither was heard to speak ill of the other; but in private they unburdened their minds more candidly, Roosevelt on one occasion volunteering that he would like to skin Mark Twain alive, and Mark Twain—or, to give him his name in the census, Samuel L. Clemens—setting down that Roosevelt, in addition to sometimes acting like a lunatic, was "far and away the worst President we have ever had."

The years when those remarkable, very different lives overlapped were exciting ones in our history, specifically the two decades on either side of the birth of a new century, from 1890 to 1910. So much of what we now know as America came into being during those twenty years. An agrarian union of states from before the Civil War had given way to a postbellum industrialized nation. In 1893, the frontier, which had been crucially formative in our history—part of what made the United States different from all other countries—was pronounced closed, the census three years earlier having found no uninhabited portions of the land left to penetrate, clear, and settle. In 1896, the Supreme Court decreed in effect, in *Plessy* v. *Ferguson*, that relations between the two races, black and white, were to be kept socially separate—"separate but equal"—a decision that stood until 1954; remnants of that iniquity litter our lives still. In 1898, America fought a war that transformed the nation abruptly into a world power, at the same time that one of its army officers, Colonel Theodore Roosevelt, became a national hero at age thirty-nine. In 1901, that hero was elevated to the presidency of the United States; and a year later he brought the force of his administration to bear upon trusts, huge corporate entities that had come together late in the preceding century, at a time of exploding growth and vast technological advances, as something entirely new in our economic life. Nothing like the trusts—the beef trust, the sugar, oil, steel, glass, tobacco trusts—had been seen in America until then; and it was during the years immediately after the turn of the century that the government refined the tools to trim their burgeoning excesses. It was, moreover, the patrician president Theodore Roosevelt who first wielded those tools; and during the same years it was Mark Twain, the Missouri democrat Samuel L. Clemens, who counted as his best friend—"the best friend that ever a man had"—an official presiding at the pinnacle of one such trust, and that the most intimidating of them all. H. H. Rogers of the Standard Oil Company, "Hell-Hound" Rogers, was far better known for his ruthlessness in business dealings (which Clemens, observing, admired) than for the very real generosity and considerateness he showed in private life.

Mark Twain and the Colonel tells the story of those rich decades in America through the fully engaged involvement of two of its most lively participants. The narrative unfolds in six sections, each focusing on a different aspect of the United States then that continues to matter after yet another century has opened, even this far along: America as an imperialist nation, America as a continental nation, America as a racial nation, America as a corporate nation, America in its domestic manifestations, and America striving for peace. Thus, while adhering roughly to chronology, the organization of what follows is thematic. As such, it lets us come to know the protagonists as we do our friends, not step-by-step from birth to death, but by entering lives at an all but arbitrary point, from which incrementally, through succeeding days, in succeeding pages, we gain insights and revelations as we watch Clemens and Roosevelt respond to concerns of their age. The scheme involves repetition (as with our friends in life), but it is a repetition that helps to orient and emphasize, recalling significant shapes and moments while, at each reminder, taking us more deeply into the subject at hand. That, after all, is how we ourselves live—do we not?—chronology informed by a past flowing constantly into the present hour.

The story starts in 1900, with a welcome on the New York piers extended to one of the nation's best-loved figures as he returns from nearly a decade of self-imposed exile. It nears its end ten years later, with that same figure returning once more to Manhattan, beshawled, seated in a deck-chair, bowler hat on his head, carried down the gangway while reporters wait on the pier yet again to welcome him home a final time. In the interval, *The Great Train Robbery* will have flickered its magical moving pictures over nickelodeon walls, the Wright brothers will have got their flying machine airborne at Kitty Hawk, and Henry Ford will have seen his Model T trundled along the assembly line, amid much else serving to move those far-off times at the start of the twentieth century substantially closer to this twenty-first century of ours.

Significant decades they were back then, and relevant decades; and no one was more responsive to their clamor than were Theodore Roosevelt, Colonel Roosevelt of San Juan Hill, and Samuel L. Clemens, the humorist Mark Twain.

A chronology of the principal events of the narrative, from the birth of Clemens in 1835 to the death of Roosevelt in 1919, appears on pages 429–38. Notes and works cited, on pages 439–76, acknowledge the many writers and scholars past and present who have helped me to tell the story. In addition to all those, I'm indebted, yet again, to the knowledgeable and ever-obliging staff of the Boston Athenaeum; and to Marcus Boggs, for responding supportively; to my editor, Carrie Broadwell-Tkach, for serving as a model of helpfulness and understanding; to Herman Gollob, longtime stalwart friend, for encouraging the project when it mattered most; to Jerome Loving, for reading the manuscript section by section with appreciation, insight, and ever stimulating suggestions; and, each for various kindnesses, to Wallace Dailey (in particular), curator of the Theodore Roosevelt Collection at the Houghton Library, Harvard University; to Patti Philippon, curator, and her assistant Mallory Howard, of the Mark Twain House in Hartford; to Neda Salem of the Mark Twain Project and Papers in Berkeley; and to Thomas Pilz, who explained to this nonengineer crystal-clearly, in a language not even his native one, why the World's Columbian Exposition could not have been lit as it was using the direct current that Edison favored. The dedication of *Mark Twain and the Colonel*, which repeats one gracing my first work of nonfiction, *Sojourners*, on Washington Irving and his times those several years back, allows me to acknowledge once more, with infinite gratitude, a love that for half a century and longer I've been blessed to receive and return.

PART One

WAR

CHAPTER One

Return to America

O pen to page 3 of the *New York Times* for October 16, 1900. Along the right-hand margin are advertisements for carpets, eyeglasses, whiskey, silvercraft, and Steinway pianos. The column at the far left, beginning at the top, furnishes a lengthy account of Governor Roosevelt's activities yesterday in Covington, Kentucky. Equally prominent on the page, four columns in, is a report on the arrival, at the downtown piers during that same lively long-vanished yesterday, of a newsworthy passenger aboard the Atlantic Transport Line's S.S. *Minnehaha*. "MARK TWAIN HOME AGAIN," the headline blares. "Writer Reaches America After His Prolonged Stay Abroad. GREETED BY MANY FRIENDS. Talks Freely of His Travels, His Experiences, and His Triumphs—In the Best of Health."

Yesterday, at ten in the evening and after nearly a decade away, America's favorite humorist had been kept busy at the Manhattan docks in the course of a jubilant homecoming: wife and daughters accompanying him; all those welcoming friends to greet; trunks and hampers to lay claim to. "Mr. Clemens"—the private name of a world-famous public pseudonym, the census-taker's name that signed Mark Twain's checks and booked his hotel rooms—"Mr. Clemens never looked better," readers of the article were assured, "was in a splendid humor, and greeted his friends with the most affectionate cordiality." Yet the *Times* makes clear it was not Samuel Langhorne Clemens whom the throng had gathered to welcome, but rather "the writer and lecturer, Mark Twain, who attracted to the pier so many friends and associates of former days."

He was sixty-four years old on that autumnal Tuesday, just weeks short of turning sixty-five. The bulk of his last nine years Samuel Clemens—Mark Twain—had spent in self-imposed exile, for the most part in Europe. Now here he was, home to stay, finally, joyfully, exchanging salutations with friends and well-wishers while some dozen newspaper-men hovered nearby. As soon as the traveler turned their way, the report-ers pressed him to tell them what he had been up to over so extended an absence from his native land.

"Now, that's a long story," the notable answered obligingly in his char-acteristic Missouri drawl, "but I suppose I must give you something, even if it is in a condensed form."

Of course he would give them something. Clemens had been a newspa-perman himself, had started out as a journeyman printer, years before had written for newspapers in various parts of the country and even—briefly—co-owned a newspaper, in Buffalo. To this day, besides contributing to magazines, he often as Mark Twain sent to the papers opinions that were widely quoted. Moreover, in a long, varied, and colorful career, he had granted hundreds of interviews like this one, always taking care to promote a distinctive, much-loved public image of the Mark Twain that Samuel L. Clemens had created thirty-seven years before.

He was promoting Mark Twain now, in 1900. The homecomer had left America, he reminded the pier-side reporters, in June of 1891 and gone to Aix-les-Bains, France. The reason—although he didn't tell them this—had been in large part because of health, so that he and Mrs. Clemens might benefit from France's therapeutic baths. The family had meant to remain overseas only a few months, while Mark Twain wrote six extended travel letters to pay for the excursion; but circumstances prolonged their stay. Soon they realized how much cheaper it was to live well in Europe than in America, and the Clemenses had need of economizing. Thus, nine years passed before their permanent return home, by which time this interviewee on the New York piers had accumulated a lengthy catalogue to recount to the clustering journalists, of places where the family had stayed during the long interval. After a fall and winter in Aix-les-Bains, for instance—their first stop abroad—they had moved to Berlin, so that Mark Twain could lecture and give readings, then on to the Riviera over three months, then to baths near Frankfurt, then—through most of 1892—in Florence, renting a villa while the author wrote his *Joan of Arc* and the novel *Pudd'nhead Wilson*. "For the next two years I was in France," he continued more or less accu-rately, taking care to reassure his listeners that "I can't speak French yet." Clemens could read the language, though, with ease, as he read Italian and read and spoke German, although his alter-ego, Mark Twain—thoroughly American; a folksy, down-home provincial, long on common sense if short on schooling—neglected to reveal those cosmopolitan skills to the report-ers gathered round. He did tell them that in the spring of 1895 (something the whole world knew already) he had started on a lecture tour from England that circled the globe, first across the northern United States, then to Australia and New Zealand, on to Ceylon and India, to South Africa, and finally back to England, where he lingered through another year abroad.

"At this time my family was with me. . . ." But the summary left much out. In London, "I was lecturing, reading, or working hard in other ways, writing magazine stories and doing other literary work." And after London came Vienna, "to which city we went in September 1898."

Actually, it had been in 1897, the family having spent a couple of summer months just before then in Switzerland. But let Vienna serve as a specimen of the traveler's life overseas. Clemens remained in the capital of the Austro-Hungarian Empire for nearly two years, arriving after those weeks in the village of Weggis, overlooking Lake Lucerne, and not leaving until twenty months later. Then—to conclude the itinerary—he and his wife and daughters spent additional time in England and in Sweden, again for reasons of health, before returning to England and at last, as of yesterday, in mid-October 1900, disembarking from the S.S. *Minnehaha* here in New York City.

But about the author's reception in Vienna. From Switzerland he had written ahead to the American Embassy there, an inquiry regarding available accommodations that let word of his intentions get out. Viennese newspapers, of which there were many—forty-five of them—seized on the news; and for a couple of weeks before the Clemenses arrived, the press of that city was writing in high excitement about *unser berühmter Gast*—our famous guest—coming to live among them. Why he was coming, he would tell reporters when he got there, was to observe and gather material for additional articles and stories—a motive flattering to his hosts, even if it fell wide of the real reason for his choice. Clemens was moving to Vienna so that his daughter Clara, approaching her mid-twenties, might pursue her study of music with the celebrated piano teacher Theodor Leschetizky, tutor of Paderewski, in hopes of becoming a professional pianist herself.

Thus, soon after arriving, father and daughter called at the maestro's home—her young heart pounding—at Karl Ludwig Strasse 42, and to Clara's amazement were greeted by "an utterly unimpressive, harmless-looking man of small stature," under whose gaze she was soon "stumbling" (her word) through a piece on the piano, while gray-haired eminences—famous pianist and famous author—hovered and listened. The audition disclosed a need for more technical preparation before such a teacher as this could take the young woman on. A disappointed father wondered whether they should even remain in the city, but Herr Leschetitzky assured his visitors that doing so would prove amply worth their while.

Already the Clemenses had found a place to live. Or it found them: the Metropole, an imposing hotel in the center of Vienna, on Franz-Josefs-Kai overlooking the busy Danube canal—fashionable enough that the sister of Germany's Kaiser Wilhelm II was lodging there. So eager had the proprietor of the Metropole been to include Mark Twain among his patrons that for the famous American he reduced his regular rate by 40 percent; and on such attractive terms the Clemens family moved into Suite 62, on the third floor: seven spacious, high-ceilinged rooms and a balcony, with attendants, heat, and meals for five persons as part of the bargain price—meals prepared by the premier chef in the city. All that allowed for pampering enough to keep this visiting celebrity at the Metropole eight months (until he removed to an even grander hotel, its rates also discounted); and at the Metropole very soon, as daughter Clara later remembered, it "came to be a daily habit in the family to receive callers from five o'clock on, and our list of acquaintances augmented so rapidly, representing all circles, that our drawing-room was often called the second U. S. Embassy."

Living so long overseas and being so welcomed, Mark Twain had come to see himself as sort of a spokesman for his country: "During 8 years, now, I have filled the post—with some credit, I trust—of self-appointed Ambassador at Large of the U. S. of America—without salary." The author of "The Celebrated Jumping Frog of Calaveras County," of *The Innocents Abroad*, of *The Adventures of Tom Sawyer*, of *The Prince and the Pauper*—to name the favorites among his works in Europe—the wonderfully amusing author whose writings had been translated into all the major European languages and many less major ones was by this time immensely popular around the globe, a household name on the Continent wherever he settled down. In Berlin, for instance—that other German-speaking metropolis—where the Clemenses had lived earlier in the decade, a "great fuss was made over Father," Clara bore witness, "and Susy and I felt proud to be his daughters. In fact, with satisfied vanity we enjoyed watching people point out our family when we entered a dining-room." At the moment the young women might feign indifference to the attention, but it did lead them to reflect on how odd it must feel to be part of a family in which nobody was famous. As for Mark Twain, he appeared, Clara tells us, "unconscious of the sensation he always created when entering a dining-room or restaurant." Germans actually rose and stood close by to watch the luminary eat, any among them who knew English hoping no doubt to overhear his table talk. "Look at those people, Father! They are getting a fine view of your appetite." The

leonine head—well-known shock of untamable gray hair, bushy gray eye-
brows, bright eyes, gray drooping mustache—would chuckle then, though
apparently unembarrassed at being so closely scrutinized. "And I often
wondered," wrote Clara, recollecting, "how the news of his identity could
possibly spread around so rapidly. It was also surprising that his popularity
should be international. With the exception of France, he seemed equally
famous in all countries."

As for France, Clemens cared less for Frenchmen than they for him—
his one admitted prejudice: their lax morals; what they did to Joan of
Arc; what they were doing to Zola and Captain Dreyfus. Here in Vienna
meanwhile, as another example of the goodwill the American humorist
inspired just about everywhere, he and his daughters on one occasion
couldn't return to their hotel even though guests were awaiting them up
there. Around an intervening public square spectators had gathered thick
to view the passing of the emperor's cortège. Police were everywhere. The
three Americans on foot did manage to press their way through the good-
natured crowd; but at its inside edge, just before starting across, they were
halted officiously. An armed guard commanded that they stay where they
were—*Halten Sie! Stehenbleiben!*—while at the same moment a policeman
on horseback came galloping forward, although "not with the purpose of
driving us back, but of reproving the guard: 'For God's sake, let him pass!
Don't you see it's Herr Mark Twain?'"

The humorist relished such prerogatives as this that his worldwide
fame entitled him to. "My! But that makes me feel d—d good!" he confessed to his daughters as they crossed the emptied square together. Meanwhile his guests at the hotel would likely have been people who mattered
in *fin-de-siècle* Vienna. Many such called on the Clemenses, in addition to an
unending stream of reporters, editors, and curious fans of Mark Twain. In
fact, the family came to know just about everybody of consequence in the
city, fourth largest in Europe and home to individuals whose names retain
meaning more than a century later: Gustav Mahler, Sigmund Freud, Ernst
Mach, Arthur Schnitzler, Gustav Klimt, Johann Strauss the Waltz King.
Clemens as Mark Twain was enjoying friendships among such company,
as well as among others comparably celebrated then, before the passing
decades dimmed their luster. The American family entertained many new
acquaintances; and Mark Twain faithfully attended the all but perpetual
round of soirées, balls, receptions, smokers, and dinners to which he
was invited. "Dinner at the Embassy"—a single example, from February
1898—"Present, the German Ambassador; Marquis Hoyos; Nigra, Italian
Minister; Paraty, Portuguese Minister; Löwenhaupt, Swedish Minister;

Ghika, Roumanian Minister, Secretaries &c from the various Embassies—& ladies. 30 guests." No less a personage than the emperor himself, Franz-Josef I, a half century on the Austro-Hungarian throne and desirous of his acquaintance, received the droll visitor from abroad at an imperial audience—Mark Twain bedecked in striped trousers, swallow-tailed coat, silk hat, and white gloves—as the American democrat had earlier been invited to dine with Kaiser Wilhelm and spent a congenial hour with the Prince of Wales.

Moreover, his months in this colorful city—a city famously rife with the pleasures of parks and music and architecture—were proving productive. Here the author wrote "The Man That Corrupted Hadleyburg," much of the Socratic dialogue *What Is Man?* and *The Mysterious Stranger*, as well as some of the more movingly vivid reminiscences of his early days that appear in his autobiography and a good bit besides at a level of excellence rarely reached elsewhere in the course of his family's trying, sometimes horrendous years during these same 1890s. In fact, the time in Vienna constituted a last great outpouring in Mark Twain's long career as an author. Through the first decade of a new century that lay ahead he would continue to write, often prolifically, but only a little of it would achieve the quality of what he set down during his months in the Austrian capital.

At the end of the family's stay there, when it came time to leave, the Clemens daughters were reduced to tears. By then, Clara had abandoned her ambition to be a pianist and would turn instead toward a career as a concert singer. Nevertheless, she had learned in twenty months to love Vienna and the Viennese, so that her heart was grieving on the midmorning in late May 1899 when a van arrived to take away trunks that were being sent directly to London. At two that same afternoon cabs bore the Clemenses, their traveling luggage, and their maid of nineteen years, Katy Leary, to Franz-Josefs-Bahnhof. "Was life," Clara wondered, "to be one long series of farewells?" At the train station a multitude had gathered: the many friends of the daughters, friends of the family, the many grateful friends and admirers of Mark Twain. Well-wishers had already filled the Clemenses' compartment with flowers. To the assembled group the humorist spoke briefly, seriously. In fluent if Missouri-accented German, he addressed the crowd that pressed adoringly close: *"Man kann nicht ein paar Jahre in Wien leben,"* he told them, *"ohne durch und durch dem Zauber der Stadt und der Leute zu verfallen. Mann gewöhnt sich bald ein in Wien, ist hier zufrieden und geht nie mehr ganz weg."* You can't live a couple of years in Vienna without thoroughly succumbing to the magic of the city and its people. One quickly grows comfortable in Vienna, feels contented here, and never entirely leaves it.

The train wheels began to turn. Handkerchiefs were waving from slow-moving windows as the cars gathered speed. The crowd on the platform receded, "our beloved friends," whose faces, at the commencement of yet another of so many journeys, the Clemenses blowing back kisses knew they were looking on for a last time.

They went to England, to Sweden, again to England, and, a year and a half after leaving Vienna, arrived finally in New York City. Thus ended Mark Twain's long absence from home. And "everybody's glad you're back," reporters greeting the *Minnehaha* on that mid-October evening in 1900 assured the traveler, "which you know of course," they added—for only the rare American newspaper had failed to take note of so signal and exultant a homecoming.

Figure 1.1.   Mark Twain in 1900.
Courtesy of the Mark Twain House & Museum, Hartford.

"They gave you the courtesy of the port, didn't they?" a bystander was calling out.

"Yes, I wrote to Secretary Gage"—Lyman Gage, President McKinley's secretary of the treasury—"telling him," Clemens answered, "that my baggage was on a 16,000-ton ship, which was quite large enough to accommodate all I had, which, while it consisted of a good many things, was not good enough to pay duty on, yet too good to throw away. I accordingly suggested that he write the customs people to let it in, as I thought they would be more likely to take his word than mine."

One more prerogative of fame: getting results when you appealed to a high official—let Herr Mark Twain through. But what about your plans? the reporters wanted to know. Tell us what comes next.

"I am absolutely unable to speak of my plans," was the reply, "inasmuch as I have none, and I do not expect to lecture."

The interviewers questioned the author on several additional matters, including his autobiography, parts reputedly so candid that they couldn't be published for a hundred years.

"It is true I am writing it," Mark Twain confirmed.

"That's not a joke, is it?"

"No; I said it seriously: that's why they take it as a joke. You know, I never told the truth in my life that someone didn't say I was lying, while, on the other hand, I never told a lie that somebody didn't take it as a fact."

Yet another voice called out: is there anything wrong with telling a lie sometimes?

"That's right," the celebrity agreed, "exactly right. If you can disseminate facts by telling the truth, why that's the way to do it, and if you can't, except by doing a little lying, well, that's all right, too, isn't it? I do it."

But the interview was winding down; the subject of all this curiosity had grown restless under the barrage of questions. Friends on the pier moved to intervene, extricating him from the reporters' clutches.

"I'll see you again," Mark Twain called genially to the newspapermen on turning away. "I'll be at the Earlington all Winter. I am not going to Hartford till next year."

And with that, the *Times* article closes on an image of the illustrious writer giving "a pleasant nod of the head," as he and his friends on the lighted pier set out to look for the Clemenses' trunks and hampers.

CHAPTER Two

Celebrity

The family remained only briefly at the Earlington Hotel. Soon they moved to a residence off Fifth Avenue at 14 West Tenth Street, lucky to find for rent a furnished home that was big enough for their needs. And hardly was Mark Twain settled at his new address than flattering attentions resumed on a scale even grander than in Europe. He was "overwhelmed," reports his daughter Clara, who witnessed it, "by an exhibition of the most sensational kind of cordiality from the public, press, and friends. One could never begin to describe in words the atmosphere of adulation that swept across his threshold. Every day was like some great festive occasion. One felt that a large party was going on and that by and by the guests would be leaving. But there was no leaving. More and more came. And the telephone rang so steadily that the butler got no time for other work, except when the faithful Katie offered to relieve him," the two servants hurrying back and forth with their phone messages to Mr. Clemens's study upstairs. Mail began arriving in bushel loads; and there were the public appearances, too, through that fall and into the winter: Mark Twain speaking at the Lotos Club, at the New York Press Club, at the Society of American Authors, at the Public Education Association, at the Aldine Association, at the St. Nicholas Association, at the City Club, at the Nineteenth Century Club. Everybody wanted to see and hear him, all those New Yorkers too long deprived of his presence. The sought-after writer and lecturer informed a friend in England that on one day in late December he had been obliged to decline invitations to as many as seven banquets, while during the same hectic hours penning no fewer than twenty-nine letters.

For years he had been popular—America's bestselling author of substance—his many titles contributing to the warm reception that greeted Mark Twain on his returning home at last. Those of his works loved in

Europe were adored here as well. The earliest, *The Innocents Abroad* (1869), describes a shrewd western provincial's initial voyage across the Atlantic and back again aboard America's first-ever overseas cruise ship: skeptic wandering clear-eyed through Europe and the Near East for nearly five months, encountering Old World monuments, high art, and squalor with unflagging humor and zest, in a travel account that remained, as late as 1900 and through the rest of the author's life, the book of his most purchased, read, and loved. In addition, young and old equally—here and abroad—were continuing at century's end to enjoy *The Adventures of Tom Sawyer* (1876), mature readers in an industrialized America relishing the novel's evocation of riverfront days during a simpler agrarian past. In *The Prince and the Pauper* (1880), Mark Twain muted his ironic, irreverent voice in order to impersonate the style and diction of early sixteenth-century England, a tour de force that through skillful mimicry told a story light on humor—a "serious" historical novel for young people—but, in its reassuring sentiment and morality, highly gratifying to the author's genteel, often female audiences on both sides of the Atlantic. Even his first great success remained popular, a newspaper sketch (1865) about a celebrated jumping frog surreptitiously filled with quail-shot—"pretty near up to his chin"—a burden that weighted down the competitive amphibian so that it lost a frog race: evocation of raucous mining-camp ways out West. And an additional title that brought pleasure overseas as well as at home was *A Tramp Abroad* ("tramp" in the sense of *hike* or *stroll*), which appeared in 1880—yet another lighthearted, digressive, mostly nonfictional narrative of the misadventures of Mark Twain and a friend wandering through Germany and Switzerland. *A Tramp Abroad* was the travel book that, at its appearance, young Theodore Roosevelt of New York City, twenty-one years old, a senior at Harvard and about to be married, read aloud to his intended and various chums while laughing so hard that he turned "literally purple," according to his sister, and could only just barely go on.

Others of Mark Twain's works, if somewhat less favored abroad, remained popular at home: *Roughing It* (1872), a report of the author's seven years in the Wild West—actually only a bit over five years, though facts didn't trouble Mark Twain unduly—during frontier days of the 1860s; and *Life on the Mississippi* (1883), a vivid, informative re-creation of a bygone era of steamboat travel between St. Louis and New Orleans—colorful traffic afloat on America's antebellum north-south Main Street, a traffic that the Civil War curtailed and the railroads ended forever.

Yet another book by Mark Twain adult readers of genteel views—and for a while the author himself—were inclined to esteem less highly: *Ad-*

ventures of Huckleberry Finn (1885), in conception and execution not quite in the spirit of the times. That novel relates a story of boyhood obstreperousness that a ragged young village scapegrace tells in his own words. "Bad" boys as a subject were popular enough—Tom Sawyer, for one—but a story told in the bad boy's voice, from his point of view, was novel; and was it even appropriate for children to be exposed to the narrator's coarse English?—not to speak of Huck's shenanigans and prevaricating. The well-read Mr. Roosevelt verged on heterodox in liking *Huckleberry Finn* just fine—thought it a classic—although he didn't care for Mark Twain's *A Connecticut Yankee in King Arthur's Court* (1889) any more than the English did. Neither the reading public in Britain nor the young patrician back here in New York found pleasure in satire involving a subject as hallowed as the Knights of the Round Table.

On balance, however, a succession of much-loved books published in the 1870s and 1880s contributed solidly to Mark Twain's abiding popularity as the new century began. Still, his books alone could hardly have awakened such an outpouring of affection as this that greeted the author on his return to New York City in 1900. During their lifetimes very few writers experience a clamor like that. Dickens perhaps? But like the late Charles Dickens, Mark Twain was also a performer, having appeared on stage off and on over the preceding thirty-four years, in the course of which time—when lecture halls in towns and villages across America provided about the only respectable public entertainment outside of churches—he stood among the most popular lecturers in the land. Thousands around the country felt they knew Mark Twain personally, having seen him up there on the platform: his bemused and drawling self, neighborly, down to earth, an appealing, canny observer of the life we share, genuinely funny, frequently and agreeably startling his audiences with the unexpected, eloquent when he needed to be—in evoking the sublimity of exotic landscapes, for instance—and uproarious in his deadpan way as he set about exposing cant, pomposity, and sham wherever he found them.

A superb self-publicist, this performer who had toured the land and gone all over Europe and around the globe kept his name in view not only through books, lectures, interviews, and after-dinner speeches, but in widely circulated magazine articles and by means of memorably witty observations on the passing scene that newspapers quoted gleefully. "It always puzzled me," his daughter Clara wrote later, "how Mark Twain could manage to have an opinion on every incident, accident, invention, or disease in the world. Merely to read the newspapers enough for a shadowy acquaintance with the bigger topics of the day would have been difficult, considering the many social engagements he had daily, but the questions asked him by the newspaper reporters were by no means limited to important affairs." He did seem to respond nevertheless, with humor and insight, to whatever they wanted to know, and in doing so brought pleasure to newspaper readers worldwide.

But more than his books and public demeanor accounted for the affection Mark Twain inspired, he of the avuncularly benign physiognomy, so often photographed over the years that it had come to seem as familiar as one of the family's. Did he ever in his life turn down a request to be photographed? People loved the man for such unpretentious accessibility, as well as for reasons that went beyond his appearing to be one of their own. Talent and luck had led him, after due struggle, to make a great deal of money—an American dream fulfilled—and his public loved him for knowing how to spend that money lavishly. With his earnings, and his heiress wife's inherited wealth, he had built a quirkily beautiful mansion in Hartford, Connecticut, where his family thrived in happiness: a glittering national success story that one man's wit, pluck, and persistence had lifted out of the humblest of small-town Missouri beginnings.

Until—early in the 1890s, in the midst of the financial panic of 1893—it all came tumbling down. Abruptly the following year Mark Twain's publishing firm declared bankruptcy. Although hardly unique, the humiliation was complete and very public, there for the entire world to gape at. But the world was next to learn that this suddenly beleaguered author had resolved to pay back every penny owed to the many creditors, 100 cents on the dollar, declining a legal remedy that would have let him off by discharging some fraction of the quite staggering debt, scorning any dodge that repaid what was owed only in part, even if to the law's satisfaction. No, he would pay it all back, dollar for dollar, by setting out on a lecture tour around the world, undertaking the ordeal while in less than hearty good health and (at a time when life expectancy in America hovered around fifty) at the then-advanced age of fifty-nine.

The world watched as Samuel L. Clemens—with his rheumatism, boils, bronchitis, and gout—and his daughter Clara and his hardly robust wife made their way, sometimes in shabby, cramped, roach-ridden discomfort afloat, over the far-flung Pacific and Indian and Atlantic oceans, in the course of the voyage offering once-in-a-lifetime opportunities to distant, vast crowds who flocked to hear Mark Twain lecture wherever he put in at English-speaking ports: in Canada and Australia, in Tasmania and New Zealand, in Ceylon, India, and South Africa. The money earned through that wearing year Clemens set aside for his creditors, sufficient finally—

when combined with royalties from *Following the Equator* (1897), the travel book he would write about his experiences—to pay off the entire debt, every penny of it. And not only his creditors were pleased when he did so. People all over the globe, having attended to Mark Twain's progress, ended by saluting the lecturer for a success that was also a remarkable display of character, grit, and a high sense of honor.

He had returned to England from the round-the-world tour in the summer of 1896, his financial goal within reach. Clemens would write his book about the voyage and in that way end by amassing the necessary funds to get out of debt once and for all. In a materialistic age, the world extolled him for his resolve; and having seen him discharge those fiscal burdens, his countrymen three years later felt a special admiration for Mark Twain as he arrived among them on the New York piers owing nobody in the world so much as a cent.

But one other circumstance helps explain the warmth of their greeting.

The Clemenses had three children, three daughters: Susy, Clara, and Jean. Clara, at twenty-one, had accompanied her mother and father on their voyage around the world. But when the family set out on that journey from Elmira, New York, in mid-July 1895, Susy and Jean remained behind with relatives there in their mother's hometown. Neither of those girls—neither Susy, twenty-three, nor Jean, sixteen—was as sturdy physically as was the middle, more adventuresome sister, Clara. All three looked forward, however, to a grand reunion in London at the end of the year-long separation. "My! When we meet in England won't it be nuts?!" Clara wrote excitedly from out West to the stay-at-home Susy near the start of the excursion; and for her part Susy responded from Elmira with warmest affection: "Your letters are a perfect delight." And "What great adventures you are having! I sometimes wish I were with you with all my heart." Again—the adventurers having sent back photographs: "My how natural you and Mamma do look in your veils and your travelling hats! I feel as if I must be with you and as if these were pictures of our wanderings in Europe." Yet again from Susy to Blackie, to Spider—her pet names for Clara: "We *are* such a congenial family. It seems to me no one ever understands us as we understand each other. We *do* belong together," not separated by thousands of miles as at present. And this, one more specimen: "England looms before me in the future," Susy wrote, "beautiful and golden and alluring. When the time comes to start toward her, I will throw *up up* my hat!"

"Do have a nice winter," Clara for her part was urging her older sister, her Pigg, her Pea, her Sweet Pea, "and get your health in perfect condition." Meanwhile, the voyagers sailed on and on until, the following summer, they finished their odyssey at last, landing at Southampton on August 5, 1896. In England, father, mother, and daughter rented a home south of London, in Surrey, in Guildford, and set about getting it ready for Susy and Jean's arrival from America.

But a cablegram came instead. The two girls journeying from Elmira toward the reunion had got as far as New York City, and now Susy was delayed with family friends at Hartford, indisposed. Nothing serious, yet she must remain there a few more days before sailing. The news alarmed Mrs. Clemens. She and Clara booked passage at once and set out for America; but while they were still on the high seas, with the unsuspecting father left behind in Guildford, another cable arrived that included four stark words. Susy "was peacefully released today." In Hartford on August 18, 1896, Olivia Susan Clemens had died at twenty-four of spinal meningitis, the family's eldest child attended in her frenzied, delirious final hours by the faithful maidservant Katy Leary.

The dead girl's father was devastated. Of course he was, but the abundant written record of his grief cries out in unrestrained heartbreak, inconsolable in its anguish. Remorse and self-blame added their burdens to an acute sense of love lost forever, the depth of that love for his daughter only plumbed fully at her death. To his wife, still innocently at sea, Clemens wrote in the immediate, shattering aftermath words she would read on landing: "I have spent the day alone, thinking; sometimes bitter thoughts, sometimes only sad ones. Reproaching myself for laying the foundation of all our troubles." If it were not for a father's imprudent business ventures, they might still be living happily together in Hartford. Instead: the bankruptcy, their wandering over the world, their leaving Susy behind in Elmira. He wrote that he charged himself with "a million things whereby I have brought misfortune and sorrow to this family."

A year would pass before the bereaved was able to reclaim a semblance of emotional balance in public. In private, he threw himself into work as soon as he could, laboring compulsively at the book about the lecture tour just finished, which his financial situation condemned him to write. All the while he felt guilty working at all. And to his amazement he found in solitude that he was composing a mostly unclouded, always observant, sometimes amusing account of a voyage he had come to regard as the indirect, hateful cause of Susy's death. If he had only managed his affairs more sensibly. As for Mrs. Clemens—for Olivia Langdon Clemens, for Livy—her husband would become convinced that in the time left to her she never recovered from the desolation of her eldest daughter's sudden, unforeseen, unprepared-for demise.

The world at large knew only as much as the papers told it about the Clemenses' ordeal, what the headlines and obituaries reported: that at their moment of successfully completing the lecture tour, with all the family about to be reunited and Mark Twain's financial obligations on the point of being met, a favorite daughter had been snatched from them forever. The author's huge public took sorrowful note and condoled with him in spirit, adding a good man's unmerited grief to all the other reasons they had for loving him.

Back home at last, he seemed, according to reporters greeting him on the New York piers, "in the Best of Health," "never looked better." But during his absence much had changed in Mark Twain's life. To be sure, over those same nine years much had changed here as well. The country that the humorist and his diminished family were returning to differed from the one they had left, bound for Aix-les-Bains, in June 1891. For one thing, the very shape of New York had changed, with the incorporation into its boundaries two years earlier, in 1898, of four outer boroughs: Brooklyn, Queens, the Bronx, and Staten Island. The population of this new Greater New York City now stood at something over 3 million people. True, Fifth Avenue, just east of the home on Tenth Street that the Clemenses were renting, would have appeared much the same, still and ever clogged with traffic: carriages, buggies, wagons, drays, horse-drawn cable cars, carts, hacks, glossy four-in-hands. Now, however, as of this very year, a vehicle known as an autostage had been introduced, an electric-driven bus that for five cents apiece would carry eight people inside, four outside, up and down the avenue, a horseless means of locomotion signaling other great changes on the way. Even now, occasionally, a steam or electric vehicle might be spotted in the midst of the other conveyances, a roofless rarity forbidden to proceed at more than nine miles an hour, even on open roads, and required to have on board a gong to warn of its presence. Meanwhile, here alongside busy Fifth Avenue, pedestrians strolled the sidewalks and crossed at intersections as they had done nine years earlier—as they do now, dressed differently—gentlemen then in vests and blue serge suits and derbies and ankle-high shoes, executive types with their frock coats and silk hats, women in long skirts down to the sidewalk, corseted, in wide-brimmed, feathered chapeaux crowned with fruit, birds, or artificial flowers, all those people going about their urgent lives while newsboys, matchgirls, and hawkers at stalls cried out for their business.

This was an era of stereopticons and hand-pushed carpet sweepers— these final years in the long reign of Queen Victoria—of bicycling and coal-fired kitchen ranges and cuspidors not yet entirely decorative, of ice-cream parlors and wooden Indians in front of tobacco shops, of parades and bunting that festooned a last great age of oratory, and of streets still most often gaslit at nighttime, the marvel of electric lights only just coming widely in.

A few statistics, for acclimatization to a world so different from ours, a world continuing to change in our direction from what it had been when Mark Twain set out for Europe nine years earlier. As of 1900, approximately 76 million Americans lived in forty-five states and the hardly populated territories (as compared with the 312 million of us living in fifty states now). During the Clemenses' absence, Utah had been admitted to the Union, in 1896; Oklahoma would become a state in 1907, in the course of Mark Twain's remaining years; and four other states—New Mexico and Arizona in 1912, Alaska and Hawaii in 1959—would join the Union after Samuel L. Clemens's corporeal form had been laid in Elmira earth. Through the one year 1900, with the humorist still very much alive, 450,000 immigrants had been arriving on these shores, swelling a decades-long stream that was doing much to alter the culture. Meanwhile, only a few skyscrapers had risen as yet, most in New York and Chicago, made possible by the wonders of structural steel, of water pumps, and of Elisha Otis's mid-nineteenth-century invention of safe, mechanical transport indoors up and down. As yet, the highest building in New York City, at 13–21 Park Row, rose 382 feet, to twenty-nine stories.

This same year, a contract was signed to build a first subway, which would move New Yorkers rapidly underground from place to place. The city and country provided other innovations: the Brownie dollar camera, introduced in 1900; the earliest automobile show, held this year in Madison Square Garden; the earliest organized automobile race ever, run on Long Island in April, which an electric vehicle won by covering the fifty miles in an impressive two hours and three minutes.

The American Baseball League was formed in 1900, to rival the National League organized twenty-four years earlier. And, disembarking from the S.S. *Minnehaha* on a mid-October Monday near the start of a new century, Samuel L. Clemens and family encountered as well a nation in the midst of a presidential campaign. Election day loomed, just three weeks off. In fact, reporters at pier-side were wondering: which of the candidates did Mark Twain favor? But when they asked him, the celebrity protested that he had been out of the country so long: "I don't know who I am going to vote for. I must look over the field."

CHAPTER **Three**

Vice Presidential Candidate

The field was a crowded one: Eugene Debs for the Socialist Labor Party, Wharton Baker for the Populists, Seth Ellis for the Union Reform Party, Jonah Leonard for the United Christian Party, along with candidates for the couple of factions into which the Prohibition Party had split. But those people hardly counted. Two other candidates dominated the race. The Republican in the field for president that year was the incumbent, seeking reelection: William McKinley, formerly chairman of the ways and means committee in the House of Representatives and two-term governor of Ohio. The President's only real opponent was the Democrat: the silver-tongued William Jennings Bryan, the Great Commoner, Boy Orator of the Platte, who had run against McKinley in 1896 and lost. Still only forty, the Nebraskan was back these four years later for another try. As for the parties those leading candidates represented, they differed most obviously (then as now) along economic lines. "There are two ideas of government," Mr. Bryan the Democrat had clarified in launching his earlier campaign. "There are those"—Republicans, like McKinley—"who believe that, if you will only legislate to make the well-to-do prosperous, their prosperity will leak through on those below. The Democratic idea, however, has been that if you legislate to make the masses prosperous, their prosperity will find its way up through every class which rests upon them."

As with masses of people throughout history, these that Bryan spoke for had been feeling pinched, specifically the debtors among them: miners and laborers, as well as small farmers during this infancy of agribusiness—of corporate agriculture—when many Americans still lived directly off their land. In the rural Midwest and West for sure, but in the agrarian South, too. Most voters in that region were Democratic anyway, despising Republicans, who had led the North to victory in the Civil War. And southern landowners, like farmers everywhere, owed money. Wintertime found those mortgage holders with broken equipment to replace, livestock to replenish, seed to buy; so whether down South or out West, farmers borrowed money that they planned to pay back in the fall, after their crop had been harvested and taken to market and sold.

But money was scarce in 1896. To pay for fighting the Civil War, the North those thirty-some years earlier had printed an abundance of paper currency, greenbacks. When the war was won, the victors gradually, year by year, withdrew the inflated greenbacks from circulation, restoring fiscal matters to the ways of peacetime. In 1873, gold was reestablished as the basis of exchange, pleasing the creditor class, the wealthy who held the political power and who, through banks, lent farmers and others dollars that would be worth more next year than they were right now. For the steady deflation all this while—reducing the amount of paper currency in circulation—had made dollars harder to come by and thus more valuable, a situation that weighed heavily on anybody in debt. The farmer found himself obliged to repay, say, fifty of last year's dollars in currency of this year's valuation, worth fifty of those older dollars and, by now, something more besides.

There was less gold around anyway, the wealth of the California Gold Rush having been pretty well extracted—a scarcity that ran up the value of the precious metal even higher. Silver, however, had been dug in abundance out of the Nevada mountains; so what the Democrats were agitating for was a return to bimetalism, making debts payable, at a set ratio, in either gold or the cheaper silver. Republicans dismissed that idea as inflationary and fiscally irresponsible; yet it was an electrifying speech on the floor of the Democratic convention in Chicago in July 1896, a speech decrying the gold standard—*"You shall not press down upon the brow of labor this crown of thorns! You shall not crucify mankind upon a cross of gold!"*—that had suddenly propelled the thirty-six-year-old orator and journalist William Jennings Bryan over more venerable heads to the leadership of his party and a race against Governor McKinley for the presidency.

Bimetalism and the tariff were the great issues of the tumultuous election campaign that followed. Neither issue matters in the same way now, the very terms likely to stir a yawn and glaze the eyes of the economically ill-at-ease. The issues mattered then, however, in 1896. Borrow fifty dollars and, without even figuring interest, you owe what amounts to maybe sixty of those earlier dollars when the debt comes due. Five hundred dollars borrowed becomes $600 to repay, plus interest. That matters. As for the other issue, the federal government got most of its operating revenue from the tariff—did so until 1913, when the Sixteenth Amendment (*"The Congress shall have power to lay and collect taxes on incomes, from whatever source"*) was finally ratified. Until that crucial date, tariffs were as important as taxes are now.

William McKinley, sturdy Republican, was a high-tariff man who as a legislator had shepherded through Congress a duty schedule that made him a popular favorite of his party. The McKinley Tariff of 1890 put up a steep barrier that kept out foreign goods. Inside the protective wall, here at home, factory owners might prosper unthreatened by competition from overseas. But—as with the gold standard—those same protective tariffs, adding cost to whatever foreign merchandise did make it in, placed an additional burden on debtors and the poor. Without, for instance, cheaper foreign sugar available duty-free in the sugar barrel at the grocery, Americans ended up paying more for the higher-priced sugar refined here at home.

Beyond all that, many (like the bankrupt Mark Twain) would suffer further in the wake of the horrific Panic of 1893. William Jennings Bryan, Democrat, campaigned to benefit not the creditor—not the American beet-sugar refiner with something to sell—but the debtor obliged to buy: help the little people get prosperous. Accordingly, through the summer and autumn of 1896, the young orator, just arrived on the national scene, traveled by rail thousands of miles around the country to deliver speech after fiery speech demanding relief for the hard-pressed farmer and working man. He pleaded for legislation favoring bimetalism and a lower tariff that might benefit average folks so that their new prosperity could, as he said, "find its way up through every class which rests upon them."

For his part, Candidate McKinley stayed home in Ohio. The Republican nominee was hardly flamboyant in any case: a little dull, in truth, a handsome, clean-shaven, square-jawed, cleft-chinned gentleman in his fifties, imposing enough, if shorter of stature than photographs generally allowed the public to see. He was an avid cigar smoker, too—though that was omitted from public photos as well—an effective speaker (if not in Bryan's spellbinding class), and a kindly, thoughtful individual who tended to keep his own counsel. Moreover, when first aspiring to the presidency, in 1896, the circumspect McKinley—like candidates before him—maintained his dignity by seeming not to grasp for the job. Campaigning, he stayed home in Canton, Ohio, content to greet any voters whom supporters might choose to transport to his front yard.

Well-heeled railroad owners (friendly to the Republicans) made available special low rates, or charged nothing at all, to let such travel happen.

So—to take a single example of many repeated that fall—during the morning of September 12, 1896, the so-called "Democratic McKinley Club of Chicago," nearly a thousand strong, was enabled to arrive at the Canton depot in two merry trainloads, to be met by the Canton Troop and the Canton Commercial Travelers' escort, who, with appropriate fanfare, ushered their visitors to nearby hotels for breakfast. Next, the club members marched festively past Mother McKinley's home, giving forth lusty cheers in the street while that twinkly lady on her porch—at a spry eighty-seven—beamed down on their progress. Along North Market Street the voters tramped, bedecked in their McKinley-Hobart buttons, waving their banners right up to the governor's house, arriving by the appointed hour of eleven and erupting enthusiastically as their candidate appeared on his doorstep. Chief Marshall Higbee introduced a Mr. Hoffstadt, the leader of this latest deputation, who explained that his group comprised "only men who have always voted the Democratic ticket"—men now backing the Republican, however—"and representing every branch of the mercantile interests" of Chicago. Hoffstadt went on to assure the candidate of his group's "most cordial greeting" and to pledge its "earnest support."

To all of which Governor McKinley responded with his customary graciousness, welcoming and thanking these recruits to his cause in words repeated many times that autumn. On this same Saturday, for instance, the Chicago contingent having been dealt with, a Pennsylvania delegation arrived to hear McKinley welcome and thank them, too: steel workers of the Carnegie Mills at Homestead brought to town in a special train of thirty-three coaches, their holiday merriment mingling with "the music of a dozen bands," so that "the noise all over the business section of Canton was simply deafening." Group photographs on the lawn before the candidate's modest frame house—McKinley at the center seated in a chair, upright supporters behind him—provided many such delegations with personalized souvenirs to display back home in Republican-minded households across the land.

By such almost sedentary campaign tactics—and despite an opponent scampering his thousands of miles around the nation—Governor McKinley triumphed in the election of 1896, winning 271 electoral votes to Bryan's 176. Even so, the Democrat in defeat had polled nearly 48 percent of the popular votes cast, a showing respectable enough to warrant another go at it. Here he was, then, four years later, back on the trail campaigning for the presidency in 1900, William Jennings Bryan and his vice presidential nominee, Adlai E. Stevenson (grandfather of a later governor of Illinois—

born this very year, in February 1900—who twice, in 1952 and 1956, was the unsuccessful Democratic candidate for president himself).

On the Republican ticket, meanwhile, McKinley this second time around was obliged to choose a new running mate, Vice President Hobart having died in office in 1899. Despite some qualms, the President took other people's advice and settled on young Theodore Roosevelt, then governor of New York. Roosevelt would turn forty-two in late October of this year, with the race in full progress. It was a race that the top of the ticket had chosen once more to run from the comfort of his own front porch, leaving his new vice presidential nominee to scurry around America in the way that Bryan the Democrat had set about doing yet again, through this second of his tries for the presidency.

Although at first reluctant to be shunted aside in the dead-end office of the vice presidency, Governor Roosevelt under urging had agreed to accept his party's nomination and, once enrolled in the campaign, determined with characteristic vigor to cover more ground than even Bryan could keep up with. During that summer and fall of 1900, the New York governor traveled by rail a remarkable 21,000 miles through twenty-four states, delivering just under 700 speeches—two words for every one that fell from his voluble opponent's mouth. Roosevelt's tactic was simple, as he later explained it: "I drowned him out." On a long looping tour out West, up into Michigan, down into Colorado, the vice presidential nominee spoke eight or ten times a day from the rear of his railroad car to citizens whom local newspapers had alerted beforehand to gather at their various depots. By the end of his tour, the *New York Times* estimated that Governor Roosevelt had addressed as many as 3 million people in all.

Back East, too, he campaigned at whistle-stops far and near, and with unflagging zest. In West Virginia. In Kentucky. The Republican had reached Kentucky, up across from Cincinnati, on the fall evening that Samuel L. Clemens and family returned from their long absence in Europe to disembark at the New York piers. "MARK TWAIN HOME AGAIN"—while on the same page of the *Times* for October 16, 1900, three columns over at the far left, appears the equally clamorous headline: "ROOSEVELT AT COVINGTON. Says Mr. Bryan Has Not Answered Questions. DEMANDS FAIR ELECTIONS. The Vice Presidential Candidate Discusses Size of the Army—His Kentucky Campaign Ended."

Questions that Roosevelt, on his whirlwind tour through the Bluegrass State, wanted President McKinley's opponent to respond to included whether the Democrat, if elected, meant to pay veterans' pensions

Figure 3.1.   Theodore Roosevelt on the campaign trail, autumn 1900.
Courtesy of the Theodore Roosevelt Collection, Harvard College Library.

in gold or in silver. It made a difference. And what about the size of the Army? Bryan had been arguing that our army was big enough. Roosevelt thought it should be bigger. And did the Democratic nominee mean to accept the results of the North Carolina canvass, where legitimate if darker-skinned voters had been denied their right to vote? Here in Kentucky, too, officials were depriving certain voters—ex-Confederate as well as ex-Union soldiers, gold Democrats, silver Democrats, and Republicans alike—of an opportunity to cast their ballots. "I regard the currency issue as an important issue," Roosevelt shouted that evening from the speaker's stand in Covington's courthouse square; "I regard our prosperity as an important issue; but more important than anything else is the right of every man"—rich or poor, white or black—"to cast his vote as he chooses and to have it counted as cast."

Republicans at the rally would have approved that sentiment; their party stood to benefit from any such swelling of the franchise. According to the *Times* man on the scene, reporting back to New York readers, Roosevelt was speaking to "one of the largest crowds that ever assembled in this city to listen to a candidate for public office"; and his reception resembled similar enthusiastic responses to nine earlier such speeches delivered since morning, the first at Lexington, Kentucky; then another at Winchester; others at Mount Sterling, at Morehead, at Ashland and Greenup and South Portsmouth, at Vanceburg and Maysville, and on through the state until arriving here at the Covington depot at 6:30 prompt. In the home of a local dignitary Roosevelt had been entertained at dinner just now, before commencing these well-received remarks in the center of town at eight in the evening.

Another speaker addressed the rally after the vice presidential nominee finished, but his own day was not yet over. The First Voters Club of Cincinnati came forward to usher Governor Roosevelt ten miles and across the Ohio River to their city and the Grand Hotel, where yet one more reception called forth additional cordial handshaking, with more voters to inspirit. Only then, its final duty discharged, was this typical campaign day completed, allowing the candidate to retire to his room to rest before entering tomorrow, as the *Times* reported, "upon his itinerary in Ohio."

The issues Roosevelt had been speaking of all this while—and would go on addressing—were not invariably those that determined the outcome of the election. Silver and gold, for instance, which had stirred such fierce emotions four years earlier, felt less urgent now. Silver was getting mined out and pricier, and more gold—and thus less expensive gold, gold priced closer to silver—had become available. New gold mines had been discovered in the Yukon, and in South Africa a new cyanide process was extracting more gold from ore, far more easily. Those developments brought down the price, helping debtors. Besides, from straitened economic times prevailing four years ago, in 1896, the nation by 1900 had risen into prosperity, for which the Republican Party was taking credit. In fact, "Prosperity and the Full Dinner Pail" adorned the banner under which the McKinley-Roosevelt ticket had been waging these electoral battles—a slogan designed precisely to appeal to laboring classes in the opposition party.

The vice presidential candidate would carry his dinner-pail banner on through Ohio and into New York, at the far side of which, on Manhattan Island, elaborate preparations were even then under way to greet the governor when he returned ten days hence. Roosevelt still had a formidable itinerary to pursue north from Cincinnati, beyond Pennsylvania and into the Empire State, the schedule for the latter already posted in the *Times* town by town, day by day, hour by hour. Thus, voters of Camden, New York, could make their plans to gather at 8:40 A.M., on Thursday, October 25 (more than a week off yet); those at Watertown that same morning at 10:30 A.M.; at Oswego at 1:15 P.M.; and so on. Armed with such assurances, citizens might in the meantime go about their lives with the certainty that at an hour not far away, at the depot in each stated place, Governor Roosevelt would appear on the observation platform of his train—right up there in his solid besuited flesh: mustache, big smile, big teeth, glinting eyeglasses, gesticulating arms—and, in that clipped, rasping voice of his speak to them personally of theirs and the nation's concerns.

Then, on Friday, October 26, he was to reach New York City, where one more jubilant demonstration would await him, the most elaborate of all. For even this late, near the very end of the nineteenth century, politics continued, circus-like, to bring spectacle into communities far and near: a break from the ordinary, an ongoing sport—and the principal sport—that it had proved to be since near the beginning, since 1800, when partisans of Messrs. Adams, Burr, and Jefferson had clashed indignantly, raucously, scurrilously, and reveled in the loud reverberations of their conflict. The campaigns of Old Hickory, the Harrison Log Cabin and Hard Cider campaign that touted Tippecanoe and Tyler too, Young Hickory, Young Hickory of the Granite Hills, Honest Abe the Railsplitter and his party's torchlit Wide-Awakes, the Plumed Knight James G. Blaine—"Rum, Romanism, and Rebellion"; "Ma, Ma, where's my Pa?"—all in their turn had offered equal portions of substance and diversion, with newspapers hurling invective at benighted opponents and rallying around their champions to gratify readers in an era possessed of far fewer spectator amusements than we have now, an era that only toward its end, in the final years of the century, was getting national baseball rivalries lined up, an era that only at its conclusion was beginning to see, flickering on curtains strung before far walls beyond darkened New York store fronts, the novel, barely respectable sight of large black and white images in motion. More than 500 such nickelodeons would have appeared in New York City by 1905, in those opening years of a new century that found its own distinctive ways to be entertained.

For now, though, in late October 1900, New Yorkers could look forward to a familiar rousing spectacle downtown—excitement for the whole family—that would welcome Governor Theodore Roosevelt back to the metropolis. On that Friday, October 26, Grand Marshall William Halperin of the Ninth Assembly district was to provide a suitable parade of fourteen large groups, not including 7,000 Italians under separate leadership: 40,000 men to be in line (all that stirring, living multitude scattered and fallen silent now), plus musicians in their various bands, with Richmond County alone—Staten Island—furnishing four such bands transported over on special ferryboats and marching from the Battery north to Madison Square Garden, filling the air along the way with music to lift the heart. Meanwhile, representatives from each assembly district will have left their different headquarters to converge on the square, "where Gov. Roosevelt will arrive about 6 o'clock, and where there will be a grand demonstration both inside and outside of the Garden."

Such bustle and cheer, all that hopeful stir to exalt spectators gathered along blaring urban streetscapes. And afterward, in the quiet after his Republican supporters had returned to their homes, the candidate even then would press forward with his campaign. Next morning, Saturday the 27th, Roosevelt was to be off once more to speak, in Jersey City, and from there by special train toward Binghamton, making thirteen speaking stops in his progress on Sunday and continuing through the five weekdays following: a mere three speeches on Monday from Cortland to Elmira; but twelve on Tuesday; seven on a Wednesday that was slated to end in Buffalo; eleven on Thursday; and another seven on Friday, November 2, his last speech to be delivered at Oswego. From Oswego, the *New York Times* of October 16 concludes, "Gov. Roosevelt will come to this city and remain until Monday, when he will go to various points on Long Island"—pausing to address neighborly crowds on the final day before election morning, at the end of a long journey that would leave this fighter exhilarated, zestful still, riding the last few miles of track toward his home at Oyster Bay.

CHAPTER Four

Warfare

Oyster Bay lies east of Manhattan, across the East River and some fifteen miles beyond Queens, on the north shore of Long Island. The railroad reached the village in the mid-1880s, about the time that builders were getting young Theodore Roosevelt's house there finished and ready for occupancy. It was (and is) situated on a rise that gave its name to the place, Sagamore Hill, from the Native-American *sagamore*, or chieftain, who signed over the rights to the land two and a half centuries earlier. A sprawling big residence, the Roosevelt home rose then in rural isolation—"We have no one looking into our pantry and there is no need to close a shutter"—woods and rolling meadow to the south and east, to the north Long Island Sound, over which glistening expanse on appropriate late afternoons Mr. and Mrs. Roosevelt, seated in rocking chairs at the western end of their broad veranda, took delight in watching the sun amid sky-filling splendors go down.

Theirs was a large family—of six active children after 1897—and a happy one. Inside Sagamore Hill, under various dormers and gables towering in the Queen Anne style, were twenty-two rooms for the children to romp through, with eight big fireplaces to help warm the interior in wintertime—the Bird Cage, the family called their drafty home with affection, perched as it was on its windswept exposure—while two wheezing furnaces struggled to contribute their bit of heat from the basement. Outside, the place looked heavy and solid and rather drab, but for all that a distinctive domicile, and one very much lived in. Inside were a broad front hall, bay windows, a spacious bright parlor that exuded comfort, a paneled, book-laden library, on the top floor a well-stocked gun room, signs everywhere of the wide-ranging interests of those within, pets everywhere and of all

Figure 4.1.   Sagamore Hill in 1904.
Courtesy of the Theodore Roosevelt Collection, Harvard College Library.

kinds, and an abundance of young people at play, at their chores, at their studies, often engaged with like-minded cousins visiting.

"At Sagamore Hill we love a great many things," the paterfamilias wrote justly in years ahead, "birds and trees and books, and all things beautiful, and horses and rifles and children and hard work and the joy of life." His own life Theodore Roosevelt had been leading intensely all this while, joyfully for the most part, thereby setting an example that inspired those around him in his great rural residence. And it was to this same populous, livable, loving Sagamore Hill that the candidate was returning on election eve, Monday, November 5, 1900, at the conclusion of yet another demanding job well done.

During the campaign, the governor had succeeded in drawing forth large numbers to hear his and President McKinley's Republican side of the national electoral argument—large numbers being the point of it all—crowds eager to gaze at and perhaps shake hands with not only the current Republican vice presidential nominee but with one, in the same person, who two years before had abruptly become the most famous man in America. At their various depots voters had assembled to lay eyes on and listen to a sudden celebrity, as well-known here at home as was that other, older American celebrity Mark Twain, then absent overseas. For this same New Yorker, in the summer of 1898, two years before running for vice president, had gone off to war and returned a national hero. The United States had fought a war with Spain that year, while the Clemenses were abroad, and had won the war, in part through such notable efforts as that of Lieutenant Colonel Theodore Roosevelt's, at age thirty-nine distinguishing himself by leading troops of the First United States Volunteer Cavalry as they charged on foot up a foreign hill to victory at the summit.

The Spanish-American War had been waged over Cuba. Late in the nineteenth century, that island and Puerto Rico were the last remnants in the Western Hemisphere of a once proud Spanish empire, which for some 300 years had spread across most of South America and northward to include what is now Central America through Mexico, on into much of western North America, along the Pacific coast up to Alaska, eastward beyond Louisiana down through the whole of Florida, and out into the islands of the Caribbean. Of all that, only two small possessions remained under Spanish sovereignty—the rest lost through rebellion and set up as independent countries, a northern part of the vast area absorbed in time by the United States. Moreover, one of the two remaining islands, this Cuba of the 1860s into the 1890s, had itself been troubled with repeated instances of insurrection: of native rebels—patriots, as they saw themselves—striving to throw off the Spanish yoke.

Cubans had long attracted America's notice. The South before the Civil War, ever in need of more land to support its slave-driven economy and of senators to uphold its interests in Congress, had hoped to turn the island into a state of the Union. President Polk, from Tennessee, quietly offered Spain the then colossal sum of $100 million to purchase Cuba in the 1840s, in vain. Spain wouldn't sell to Polk, or to President Pierce, or to anybody else. After the Civil War—and with the American South no longer interested—native agitation for independence from Spain intensified, taking the form of a ten-year insurrection on the island, harshly suppressed. Of course some Cubans—Spaniards and *Criollos*, of Spanish descent, at the top of the social ladder—liked things just as they were, wanting to retain close ties with the mother country. But natives with less to lose went on struggling to set up an island republic. To the north, Americans remained officially neutral, although many privately supported the republican aspirations of their Cuban neighbors both in spirit and in unofficial, concrete ways: early on with filibustering expeditions dispatched from Florida, later with money sent over in sympathetic response to pro-insurgency propaganda of a Cuban junta in exile.

By the final decade of the nineteenth century, Spain had installed over 100,000 troops on the island, charged with supporting a regime that had grown increasingly corrupt and arbitrary. Against so massive a force native resistance was reduced to guerilla warfare: burning crops, blowing up train tracks, striking hit-and-run at isolated detachments of soldiers. Madrid fought back. A new military governor arrived in Cuba in 1896, General Valeriano Weyler, who set about herding the rural population into "fortified towns," enforced concentrations that sought to separate the peasantry from their guerilla look-alikes. Soon those *reconcentrados*— distant foreshadowings of the twentieth century's horrendous concentration camps—grew overcrowded, unsanitary, and fever-ridden. Thousands of Cubans died in their confines. News of "Butcher" Weyler's harsh methods reached the United States, his inhumanities well-documented. President McKinley protested. Madrid moved to ameliorate conditions. The reconcentration policy would be suspended, political prisoners released. Negotiations between America and Spain went forward. As a gesture of friendship and to help stabilize relations, the two countries agreed that a U.S. warship would visit Havana.

Thus, toward the end of January 1898, the battleship *Maine* dropped anchor at Buoy 4 in Havana harbor. Officers in civilian clothes went ashore to a cordial welcome. Three weeks later, at 9:40 on the moonless evening of February 15, still riding peacefully at anchor, the *Maine* suddenly, spectacularly, horrifically exploded. The vessel blew up without warning, and within moments sank in flames, only its mast and a bit of the twisted superstructure protruding above the waterline. Two officers, 222 crew members, and twenty-eight marines perished at the site, eight among the wounded dying soon after.

What had caused such a catastrophe? Was it internal—a spontaneous fire in a coal bunker on board that may have ignited stored ammunition? Or external—a torpedo, a mine placed alongside? Spain condoled with Americans but insisted there were no mines in the harbor. An investigation of the calamity got under way. Meanwhile congressmen went to the island, among them the elderly, respected Senator Redfield Proctor of Vermont. In March, Senator Proctor reported back on what he had seen: "the entire native population of Cuba, struggling for freedom and deliverance from the worst misgovernment of which I ever had knowledge." The island was afflicted, Proctor told an attentive Senate, with "concentration and desolation." That bleak view of things confirmed an earlier report from an American traveling in Cuba by rail who had found the countryside empty of all life "except an occasional vulture or buzzard sailing through the air."

The inquiry into the source of the *Maine* explosion reached its conclusion: the rupture had been externally caused. That is, a force in the harbor, obviously hostile, had destroyed the ship and the lives of the crew on board. American newspapers waxed indignant. Could any self-respecting nation permit such an insult to go unpunished? And how could a country born in revolt against tyranny let conditions such as those in Cuba persist, within a hundred miles of our shores? Calls for war grew shrill: "Remember the *Maine*! To Hell with Spain!" In mid-April, finally, reluctantly, McKinley acceded to the mounting clamor, and Congress went along on the grounds that war had already begun.

If the numbers of volunteers who rushed to enlist are indicative, tens of thousands of Americans were jubilant, but none could have been more eager to join in the conflict than was Theodore Roosevelt. Serving at the time as assistant secretary of the navy, Roosevelt resigned his office on May 6, 1898—the day he secured a commission—and set about putting together a cavalry regiment to lead into battle.

This newly minted lieutenant colonel was well equipped to assemble such a force. He had a wide range of friendships and acquaintances east and west to draw upon, money to help outfit volunteers, and influence with national power to move his regiment briskly forward. A mustering area had been set up in San Antonio, not far from the Alamo. At the end of the coming adventure, Theodore Roosevelt back home would dictate an eyewitness account of the turmoil met with at that Texas campground— a nation's suddenly converting its much shrunken peacetime army into something vastly larger and made battle ready—plus the embroilments in Cuba that followed. The account was serialized in *Scribner*'s magazine between January and June 1899; and before the end of that year it appeared as a book entitled *The Rough Riders*, after the sobriquet applied to Roosevelt's colorful regiment, a term out of Buffalo Bill's Wild West Show that the troops adopted with pride.

And a choice assortment of troops they were. The voice dictating *The Rough Riders* is quintessentially Roosevelt's own, filled with his joy, his youthful excitement, his love of it all, with the scenes that his spectacled eyes beheld, and above all with his unflagging enthusiasm for people in action. For instance: applications to join his regiment were overwhelming; no more than one in twenty could be let in. The commanding officer admitted Harvard, Yale, and Princeton men—could have signed up many more of them—and four New York policemen, along with others from farther afield. "Cherokee Bill, Happy Jack of Arizona, Smoky Moore, the bronco-buster, so named because cow-boys often call vicious horses 'smoky' horses, and Rattlesnake Pete, who had lived among the Moquis and taken part in the snake-dances": all had rushed to volunteer, as did a gentle, courteous South Carolinian "on whom danger acted like wine. In action he was a perfect game-cock"; and a regular army major from Arizona, "whose men worshipped him and would follow him anywhere"; and yet another, one Allyn Capron, "tall and lithe, a remarkable boxer and walker, a first-class rider and shot, with yellow hair and piercing blue eyes," Roosevelt's ideal of a soldier, "the archetype of the fighting man." Many such rough riders joined up, all eager to fight, "tall and sinewy, with resolute, weather-beaten faces, and eyes that looked a man straight in the face without flinching," cowboys, hunters, miners, prospectors, even a handful of Indians among the lot, every one, whatever his origins or social position, possessed of "the traits of hardihood and a thirst for adventure."

Very few needed disciplining. Those who did got dealt with severely, for the good of the regiment—and they profited from it. The rest took to army ways. All were expert riders already, knew how to shoot, how to stand tall and do their duty; and the New York City patrician, this Harvard man who was leading them, came to relish each recruit, low-born and high alike. For two weeks he drilled them, trained them, watched over them, got to know and admire them, knew them all by name, while his own superior—and close personal friend—Colonel Leonard Wood, was much of the time tending to logistics, cutting through red tape, making sure that the regiment would be the first of the volunteers transferred to the staging area in Tampa, Florida.

Roosevelt had done his part that way, too, "hurrying up the different bureaus and telegraphing my various railroad friends, so as to insure our getting the carbines, saddles, and uniforms that we needed from the various armories and storehouses." The trains from Texas to Florida, supposed to take forty-eight hours, ended by taking four days. All was delay and confusion. At the frequent stops, people came out to the rails to cheer on the soldiers, bringing them flowers, watermelons, pails of milk. Once arrived at Tampa, the regiment met with more chaos on that pine-covered sand-flat, hardly surprising with 25,000 men crammed suddenly together, ill-equipped at the end of a single-track railway. It was very hot. No one knew where the newcomers were supposed to go. Finally the regiment found its allotted space and set up camp, then waited, and drilled, and waited, and drilled. And waited. No proper means had been provided for feeding and watering the Rough Riders' hundreds of horses. There were too few wagons and mules. Rations were insufficient, much of the canned meat inedible. Transports in the harbor were soon overloaded with troops, helter-skelter. Enlisted men's horses had to be left behind. "At last, on the evening of June 13th, we received the welcome order to start. Ship after ship weighed anchor and went slowly ahead under half-steam for the distant mouth of the harbor, the bands playing, the flags flying, the rigging black with the clustered soldiers, cheering and shouting to those left behind on the quay and to their fellows on the other ships." But even then the fleet met with delay, in the summer heat sweltering for another six days before the order was given to steam out into the Gulf. Astern finally, Tampa Light sank below the horizon.

None of them knew where they were going, or what kind of force they would encounter once they got there, or how long the war would last, or which ones among them would come back and who wouldn't. Along the way the men—westerners for the most part—whiled away time telling stories, of "the mining camps and the cattle ranges, of hunting bear and deer, of war-trails against the Indians, of lawless deeds of violence and the lawful violence by which they were avenged, of brawls in saloons, of shrewd deals in cattle and sheep." A band on a vessel ahead played music: "There'll be a Hot Time in the Old Town Tonight." The thirty-one transports, brightly lit in darkness, straggled over their reflections along a miles-long chain, bits of gold across the black velvet.

After six days, the fleet dropped anchor off Daiquiri, a drab village on the southeast coast of Cuba. The surf was high. The officers' underfed horses had to be shoved into the sea and made to swim toward shore. Many drowned. Small boats bobbed the troops to the ancient pier and the shingly landing area. Had the enemy been positioned in force on the hillsides, the operation might have ended in disaster. Once on solid earth, soldiers gaped at tall palm trees, a large pool of stagnant water, huge grotesque land crabs scuttling out of jungle underbrush. Vultures circled overhead. The troops started inland up hills thick with vegetation, pushing forward so as not to be late for the action. By the second day of marching through hundred-degree heat, they were footsore and weary. Most had thrown away their coats and blanket rolls.

Food was coffee, bacon, and hardtack—hard saltless biscuits—and not much of any of that. Most afternoons it poured rain, torrents of tropical storms that turned paths into quagmires. Tents leaked. Troopers rousted out in the mornings were drenched in dew. Within two days after landing, on a nondescript hillside at a place called Las Guásimas, Lieutenant Colonel Roosevelt's men first skirmished with the Spaniard, firing blindly into underbrush, unable to see enemy snipers wearing green and using smokeless powder. In the engagement eight Rough Riders died, thirty-four were wounded. But it was the Spaniard who fled.

The commander of the Second Brigade came down with fever. Colonel Wood in the field was promoted to brigadier general and put in charge. Within his brigade, his deputy Roosevelt was given command of the unhorsed volunteer cavalry regiment and elevated to the rank of full colonel. It was the most coveted title that Roosevelt would ever earn, the one he preferred to be called by from that day on. In a bright future the warrior became governor, then Mr. Vice President, then, during nearly two terms in the White House, Mr. President. But from this day in the Cuban jungles forward through the remainder of his time on earth, he was proudest to be Colonel Roosevelt, the Colonel.

On July 1, 1898—"the great day of my life"—on San Juan Heights, near Santiago de Cuba, Colonel Roosevelt and his band of somewhat fewer than 500 Rough Riders found themselves at the base of what came to be called Kettle Hill. At its crest were Spanish entrenchments. What happened that busy day, in the course of crowded hours, was obscured in smoke, noise, and confusion: his men crouching, rising, yelling, charging up Kettle Hill in the midst of battle. Two divisions of Americans were present, five brigades engaged, regulars and the one regiment of volunteer cavalry on foot. As a mere regimental commander, Roosevelt played less than the leading role in the overall conflict, but throughout he behaved with great courage. The war correspondent Edward Marshall of the *New York Journal* was moved to call him on site "the most magnificent soldier I have ever seen." Alone of his men the Colonel rode on horseback, an obvious target galloping the war pony Texas in full view of the enemy up the slope of the next hill over, to a barbed-wire fence that halted his advance not forty feet from the summit. He leapt down, turned the horse loose, and looked back across the slope, shouting for his men to come on. "What, are you cowards?" But in the din of battle they hadn't heard his order: "We're waiting for the command!" He screamed it at them. Across the open field all ran under fire upward against defenders in their ill-aligned trenches at the crest. In the minutes ahead many on both sides died. American losses proved to be three times those in the trenches. But the enemy was bested, leaving the attackers in possession of the hilltop, with Santiago de Cuba exposed below.

"Long before we got near them," Roosevelt would write in *The Rough Riders*, "the Spaniards ran, save a few here and there, who either surrendered or were shot down. When we reached the trenches we found them

Figure 4.2. Colonel Roosevelt and his Rough Riders victorious on San Juan Heights, Cuba, July 1898.

Courtesy of the Theodore Roosevelt Collection, Harvard College Library.

filled with dead bodies in the light blue and white uniform of the Spanish regular army. There were very few wounded. Most of the fallen had little holes in their heads from which their brains were oozing."

The world soon learned of all this. Traveling with Roosevelt's regiment was the journalist Richard Harding Davis, who regularly sent dispatches from the front to enthralled readers of the *New York Herald*. Davis informed America of Colonel Roosevelt's heroism on San Juan Hill that day, and of his inspiring leadership of the sharp-shooting Rough Riders. The news raced far and wide. A photographer had been on hand as well, to take pictures on the crest: Roosevelt prominent in his war hat, neckerchief, and suspenders, his men clustered around him. The Colonel was proving scarcely less able at self-promotion than was that other gifted publicist of the era, Mark Twain.

These San Juan veterans had seen death up close, their own dead as well as the enemy's. Captain Allyn Capron, Roosevelt's ideal of a soldier, "the archetype of the fighting man," was killed leading his advance guard at the start of the first engagement. On an early morning, survivors buried seven Rough Riders together, Chaplain Brown reading the Episcopal rites "while the men stood around with bared heads and joined in singing 'Rock of Ages.'" Their colonel would reflect that no burial could have been more honorable "than that of these men in a common grave—Indian and cow-boy, miner, packer, and college athlete—the man of unknown ancestry from the lonely Western plains, and the man"—Hamilton Fish, Columbia '98—"who carried on his watch the crests of the Stuyvesants and the Fishes, one in the way they had met death, just as during life they had been one in their daring and their loyalty."

For all that, those who survived were eager for more, and their colonel for more of the values that warfare instills: discipline, alertness, resourcefulness, physical prowess, teamwork, courage, pride. He longed for his men to take part in the forthcoming invasion of Puerto Rico, or to join the assault on Havana, or to attack Spain itself. But the war, so bravely begun, was already just about over. Santiago would surrender within ten days; and, soon after, Madrid sued for peace. It was just as well. By then, in the noxious tropic summer, the Rough Riders—and the American expeditionary force in general—had been overcome by fever. Malaria and dysentery so weakened the troops that before July was out they could scarcely muster strength to march as far as the transports that were waiting offshore to take them to a healthier climate. On wholesome Long Island far to the north, at Montauk, eighty miles east of Oyster Bay, a makeshift military camp was being set up; and there through August

Roosevelt's troops convalesced and grew strong again. Journalists appearing at Camp Wikoff reported on shameful insufficiencies that had greeted these returning heroes; but at least, at last, the cavalry could mount horses. Photographers documented the Rough Riders' equestrian skills, and President McKinley arrived to thank the boys, and Colonel Roosevelt's family paid them all a visit.

An armistice was declared in mid-August. The regiment disbanded, its veterans going home to take up their widely disparate places in civilian life. Their beloved commander, the now ultrapopular Colonel Theodore Roosevelt, was easily persuaded to run for governor of his home state. Within a couple of months, just turned forty, he won election to that high office. At Albany he went on to serve the two-year term and—relishing his new duties as he relished just about everything he undertook—was eager by the summer of 1900, when his time in office neared its end, to seek reelection as New York's chief executive.

But a different call summoned him. In Philadelphia that June, delegates at the Republican national convention nominated Theodore Roosevelt to be their candidate for vice president of the United States.

CHAPTER Five

Imperialist America

W hy did his men love him so? Roosevelt was hardly inspiring to look at—round-faced, of average height and less than rugged features, his ever-present spectacles the facial trait seen first. One of his sons recalled watching this warrior father at Sagamore Hill pack twelve pairs of glasses before setting off for battle in the spring of 1898. So crucial were the spectacles to the myopic's getting about that spare pairs were sewn into his war hat. For their part, cowpokes and rough-riding ranchhands arriving in San Antonio that May to enlist in the new volunteer cavalry regiment would have first noticed the spectacles—noticed their commander's four eyes even before his toothsome grin or mustache or hardly daunting if barrel-chested stature. Those same centaur-like riders, unused to working up respect for men wearing glasses, would next and promptly have seen that this new, politically appointed lieutenant colonel in his tailored Brooks Brothers uniform sat on his horse ungracefully. He admitted as much himself. But what the Colonel on horseback lacked in grace he made up for in competence. Long an experienced rider, Roosevelt had spent forty continuous hours in the saddle during one Dakota cattle roundup. The taking in stride of such a two-day stint meant that by this time he was entirely comfortable on and around horses, and had known and worked closely with ranchhands too, and with hardy Maine guides, and with all kinds of outdoor types, who would each have testified to how well he got along with them and how much he knew about their world.

Rough Riders were to find all that out in short order, and would soon be admiring their commander for his many skills that went beyond barn and corral. They were impressed, too, by his assurance, his air of authority. No one could miss that. And they liked him because he treated them fairly, making no distinctions between the eastern college dudes among their numbers and the hardbitten western types, favoring no one over the others, demanding the same of them all. Moreover, the Colonel did what he expected his men to do: rode as hard as they, ate what they ate, slept where they slept, drilled as long, marched where they marched—and just as far. Soon they discovered Roosevelt's mettle: that his endurance was phenomenal, and that his joy in the soldier's life was all-encompassing. During the monotony and boredom of army routine he thrived as well as he did in rare, high moments of glory.

And he looked after his men, took care of them. He and Colonel Wood got them out of San Antonio and onto the trains to Tampa ahead of the other volunteer regiments, and got them on a transport, too, while regulars stood cooling their heels on shore. Reaching Cuba, his men with their inadequate provisions having trudged through wet heat up into the interior, Roosevelt camped down with them, then after a while took a detail and went back to the coast to the commissary and pried beans out of the officers' mess ("But your officers cannot eat eleven hundred pounds of beans." "Give me the beans!"), agreed to pay for them himself, and brought them up to his hungry, grateful regiment.

Later, with their victories won and the men down with fever, it was Colonel Roosevelt who wrote to his commanding general—to the irritation of the secretary of war when the letter (a round-robin that the Colonel got other officers to sign) leaked to the press—all but demanding of General Shafter that the soldiers be transferred out of the miasma that was summertime Cuba, where they were no longer needed, to a healthier northern location. Later still, with the Rough Riders safely ensconced at Camp Wikoff on Long Island, it was the Colonel once more who found them horses to ride, during recuperative days as the warring powers were laying down their arms and arranging to deliberate on terms of the peace.

Roosevelt genuinely loved these men, and the Rough Riders felt that love and returned it. Part of their bond arose from the fact that, for all their differences, this East Coast sophisticate shared many of the values of the ill-lettered western soldiers who served under him: a love of adventure, of manly behavior, of home and motherhood, of country, of flag. At this same moment in American history, one soldier gave voice to some of those values from the far-off Philippines, unexpected prize falling into the nation's hands as the Spanish-American War progressed. "Just as soon as we could pull that Spanish flag down," Private Henry Skilman wrote home from Manila, "up went the Stars and Stripes, our beloved 'Old Glory' and, mother dear, I never felt before like I did at that moment. The tears filled my eyes and I choked up so that I could not shout for a moment, and I knew then what it was that you felt when you told me not to forget for one moment that the most glorious thing in all the world was that same flag, and that it was my first duty to protect it at all hazards. I have not forgotten your glorious words, for the happiest moment in all my life was when I saw that flag on high. You ought to have heard the sailors cheer when it went up—that beautiful banner," Private Skilman scribbled on, adding fervently: "the United States is God's country."

Theodore Roosevelt would have disputed none of what the private set down, or thought one word of it overdrawn. This child of wealth, this New York aristocrat, Harvard-educated, world-traveled, close friend of the elite on two continents, astonishingly well read and well informed, for all his spacious views would have felt his own heart throb, his eyes mist over, if in Manila he could have watched the Spanish flag come down and Old Glory ascend the staff in its stead. And assuredly the Colonel would have concurred with Private Skilman's sentiment that the United States is God's country. To Roosevelt, America was all but incapable of doing wrong. And this same nation, by means just now of a war expeditiously, triumphantly concluded, had not only removed the last remnant of the Spanish Empire from our Western Hemisphere. In doing so, the United States had taken its proper place among the great powers of the world.

As for the Philippines, a distant archipelago ruled for three centuries by now-vanquished Spain and about which Americans knew hardly anything at all: in Roosevelt's view we should of course take possession of the Philippines. If we didn't, some other power would. Germany would, or Japan. Those nations and their like were all expanding through the late years of the nineteenth century. You either expanded or you withered. Look at Africa. In late 1884, at Chancellor Bismarck's invitation, Europe's great powers had convened in Berlin and cavalierly parceled up just about the whole of Africa among themselves. Germany, England, France, Spain, Portugal, Belgium, and Italy had all appropriated chunks of the Dark Continent in the form of colonies and protectorates, even as imperial Russia was expanding beyond its own vast borders and imperial Japan was reaching into Manchuria while casting covetous glances at Korea. Empires expanded, and it was well that they did, in Roosevelt's view. It was good for the world and good for the people of the weaker countries "that France," as the Colonel said, "should be in Algiers, England in the Soudan and Russia in Turkestan." To backward peoples, civilized nations brought the benefits of progress, and thus the world advanced.

Or consider China: a colossal empire, true, and one about whose rich history and culture Colonel Roosevelt had informed himself. China had resources, great wealth, and an all but innumerable population. Yet it was weak. Unlike its neighbor Japan, astir with greatness, China under the Manchu dynasty huddled slothfully behind its paper walls, feeble and timid, vulnerable, inviting intrusion. As a consequence, the great powers had lately been dividing up the wealth of China, carving out spheres of influence and making off with profits from the rich Chinese mainland.

That was how the world worked, and it was naive or sentimental to think otherwise. Thus, regarding the Philippines—which some Americans felt we had no business acquiring, which President McKinley (who, Roosevelt believed in private moments, exhibited the backbone of a chocolate éclair) had doubts that we should meddle with beyond setting up a coaling station for our ships—the Colonel was certain that of course we must take possession of the Philippines. "Now what is our duty in the Philippines?" the campaigner for vice president demanded of voters in October 1900, and furnished them the answer. "It is a duty to govern those islands in the interest of the islanders, not less in accordance with our own honor and interest." If Americans behaved honorably toward Filipinos, what followed would benefit both sides. To a tribal people scattered over thousands of islands now suddenly unburdened of Spain's centuries-old rule, yet in their primitiveness left unable to govern themselves, the advantages of having Anglo-Saxon legal, social, civic, and cultural institutions set up among them were manifold. The transformation resulting from that overlay promised an end to Philippine disunity and backwardness, while bestowing on the archipelago the blessings of a modern, English-speaking civilization.

Filipinos would benefit, but America as a great power stood to benefit as well. In the Eurocentric bias of those times, the ancient world was seen to have grown up around the Mediterranean Sea, the modern world around the Atlantic Ocean; but the future, in Colonel Roosevelt's view, lay in the Pacific. In 1900 he was among the few who looked forward with such prescience, who peered that clearly into the coming decades. "I wish to see," he wrote privately in October 1900, "the United States the dominant power on the shores of the Pacific Ocean." And campaigning during that same year, in September, he had pleaded for the reelection of President McKinley, victor in war, "because now at the dawn of a new century we wish the giant of the West, the greatest republic upon which the sun has ever shone, to start fair in the race of national greatness." America must seize its opportunities. Three years later, Roosevelt would travel for the first time to California. Even before coming there he had been an expansionist, he told his San Francisco audience in May 1903, and now arrived on the

Pacific Slope, he failed to understand how anyone could be "anything but an expansionist." And he went on, emphatically: "In the century that is opening, the commerce and the command of the Pacific will be factors of incalculable moment in the world's history."

This was the global range over which the Colonel's many thoughts were roaming, he whose feelings had been in harmony with the simplest values of his Rough Riders. Love of country, love of home, love of adventure, getting things done without whining: the Colonel's feelings were much like those of his humble troopers, but his complex thoughts went far beyond theirs. His coveting of the Philippines and Cuba, for instance, was more than mere chauvinism. It arose, rather, from deeply considered motives. Others in America might urge our hanging on to the island possessions for their own reasons. American merchants, flourishing during these last two or three years of the nineteenth century, were looking for markets on which to dispose of inventory piled up through a long depression and added to in the new prosperity, a veritable glut of goods for sellers to find buyers for. Markets awaited in the Philippines as in Cuba. And Protestant churches in America welcomed new fields for missionary labor among such as the benighted Filipinos, misguided for centuries by Roman Catholic dogma, now mercifully ripe to be led from superstition. These were considerations that moved religion and commerce in the United States to push for acquiring the Philippines, and Cuba, and Puerto Rico—all of them spoils of the present victory over Spain.

By contrast, the Colonel's motives for gathering in those same spoils had to do with neither church nor marketplace. "During the year preceding the outbreak of the Spanish War," Theodore Roosevelt begins his *Rough Riders*, "I was Assistant Secretary of the Navy. While my party was in opposition"—from 1893 to 1897, during Grover Cleveland's Democratic administration—"I had preached, with all the fervor and zeal I possessed, our duty to intervene in Cuba, and to take the opportunity of driving the Spaniard from the Western World. Now that my party had come to power" under the Republican McKinley, "I felt it incumbent upon me, by word and deed, to do all I could to secure the carrying out of the policy in which I so heartily believed."

And why had this public servant urged his country to meddle in another nation's business? One of his motives was humanitarian, to relieve distress among the Cuban people. "We should decline longer to allow this hideous welter of misery at our doorsteps," Roosevelt wrote to a friend just days before the war began, voicing a sentiment he had earlier expressed time and again. As for his other motive, that was strategic.

Figure 5.1.   "Atlas": Roosevelt in imperialist mode. Cartoon
by Charles R. Macauley in the *New York World*, June 1910.
Courtesy of the Theodore Roosevelt Collection, Harvard College Library.

With the Spanish-American War under way, United States naval forces
in the Caribbean had called for reinforcements. Accordingly, the battleship
Oregon, far off in San Francisco, was dispatched on the long voyage south,
14,700 miles around Cape Horn and northward to bolster the squadron
off Cuba. Americans, apprised of the warship's progress, took note of the
sixty-seven days that the *Oregon* required to complete its voyage. By the
time it arrived, the war was just about over. But well before the war started,
Roosevelt had reminded one audience that we "cannot avoid, as a nation,
the fact that on the east and west we look across the waters at Europe
and Asia." America's continental expanse required a navy large enough to
serve simultaneously in two oceans. And we needed—the case of the *Oregon*
made all the more obvious what had been talked of for a long time—a canal
through Central America to connect the Atlantic and the Pacific, so that

any transit from one to the other would be cut more than by half, thus allowing for the safeguarding of both our shores.

As the Philippines commanded the gateway to the Far East, Cuba stood at the gateway to Central America, against any future day when an interoceanic canal might be built across Nicaragua or the Isthmus. That was the strategic motive for removing Spain from Cuba, those scant ninety miles off our shores, and for our acquiring the Philippines: in order to bring crucially situated territories under our influence. And we must build a bigger navy. For Colonel Roosevelt, heroic commander of the First Volunteer Cavalry in the Second Brigade of the Fifth Army Corps, was, paradoxically, first of all a navy man, who had written a highly regarded history of the naval war between England and the United States from 1812 to 1815, a history so well thought of that the volume was placed aboard every American naval vessel and remains a standard reference work on that rather recondite subject. Later, while hostilities with Spain loomed as an ever increasing threat—just ten days after the *Maine* exploded in Havana harbor and two full months before war broke out—then Assistant Secretary Roosevelt, in the temporary absence of the secretary of the navy himself, cabled orders to Hong Kong, to Commodore George Dewey (appointed earlier to the Pacific command at Roosevelt's behest):

KEEP FULL OF COAL. IN THE EVENT OF DECLARATION WAR SPAIN, YOUR DUTY WILL
BE TO SEE THAT THE SPANISH SQUADRON DOES NOT LEAVE THE ASIATIC COAST,
AND THEN OFFENSIVE OPERATIONS IN PHILIPPINE ISLANDS.

Accordingly, during the earliest week of hostilities, the commodore's seven warships and two transports steamed the three days to Manila and there, on May 1, 1898, in a stunning victory that cost not a single American life, caught unawares and sank or disabled Spain's entire Pacific fleet. That achievement demoralized the adversary at the very start, as it astonished and elated our own side; and two months later, on Sunday, July 3, our navy in the Caribbean dealt a finishing blow off Cuba's southeast coast, where Admiral Sampson's squadron, with the *Oregon* finally on station, met and demolished Spain's antiquated Atlantic fleet as it emerged from Santiago Bay. After that second seaborne pummeling, with 500 Spanish casualties and the loss of only one American, the enemy gave over all will to fight on.

It was the navy, then—modern, industrialized, efficient—that had most to do with bringing on victory. And the army, beset with sudden growth pains from enlarging the numbers of its personnel to wartime status, hampered by transportation tie-ups and inedible beef and time-honored profiteering, plagued by long delays and tardy arrivals, by malaria rampant through the camps, by a tendency to fight the last war and a hankering after such outdated tactics as cavalry charges—it was the army that received the well-earned brunt of citizens' ire and newspaper carping. Yet despite the ineptitude of the war department, one army specimen of untainted courage and gallantry stood forth: Colonel Theodore Roosevelt with his colorful Rough Riders on the spot in Cuba, challenging the Spaniard face to face for the San Juan Heights.

Already well-known before the Spanish-American War began, Roosevelt—partly through his own promotional gifts—emerged from it the most sympathetic of its heroes and the most admired. (By contrast, the hero Dewey, having returned home from Manila an admiral, bungled his political ambitions with maladroit comments and clumsy posturing.) And when, two years later, the still popular Governor Roosevelt of New York found himself running for vice president of the United States, he could speak the language of a people bursting with pride in their nation's newly acquired world stature. The candidate shared that pride, as he shared the values that many of his listeners lived by.

For instance: in China objections to merchant and missionary efforts to Westernize their country had led to the growth of a society of "Righteous and Harmonious Fists"—as one secretive group of young Chinese called themselves—who set about murdering intrusive foreigners in violent protest. During this same election year, this June of 1900, those Fists, or "Boxers," laid under siege the "foreign devils," who had sought refuge in the legations in Peking, until the great powers, including the United States, sent in an armed expedition to aid the terrified foreigners and lift the siege. Roosevelt that autumn cried out to voters crowding around his campaign train: "The Chinese Boxer, his hands red with the blood of the slaughtered women and children, has flinched as he heard the drumming guns" of a relief force marching across the rice fields under the American flag. Elsewhere, a Filipino here and there had been resisting our taking possession of his archipelago. Each "bandit" of that sort—as the candidate labeled any such wretched, misguided Malay—has also "had cause to fear the flag as he lurked in ambush to shoot our men." Spanish soldiers a couple of years back "had cause to dread the flag," too; for, as candidate Roosevelt went on to tell voters clustering around his train platform or in this or that courthouse square, the roar of Admiral Dewey's cannon across Manila Bay had been but one of the explosions of late that had waked the world "and bid the older nations know that the young giant of the West had come to his glorious prime."

CHAPTER **Six**

Anti-Imperialist

In the spring of 1898, at the outbreak of America's war with Spain, Samuel L. Clemens was in Vienna. From that far-off vantage point, delighted in the war's purposes and progress, the humorist was moved to describe Commodore Dewey's victory over Spain's Pacific fleet on May 1 as nothing less than glorious. To his friend Joe Twichell back in Hartford, he wrote a month later, in mid-June: "I have never enjoyed a war—even in written history—as I am enjoying this one. For this is the worthiest one that was ever fought, so far as my knowledge goes. It is a worthy thing to fight for one's freedom; it is another sight finer to fight for another man's. And I think this is the first time it has been done."

What was different, then, about the present conflict was America's selfless part in it. We were waging war only to liberate Cuba from the cruelties of an oppressive regime, with no interest in acquiring the island for ourselves. Even as hostilities erupted, Congress passed a joint resolution bearing an amendment filed by Senator Henry Teller of Colorado. Relating to Cuba, the Teller Amendment stated specifically that the United States "hereby disclaims any disposition of intention to exercise sovereignty, jurisdiction, or control over said island except for pacification thereof, and asserts its determination, when that is accomplished, to leave the government and control of the island to its people." What could be clearer? True, America—promulgator of the Monroe Doctrine—would benefit from the removal of the last vestiges of Spain from the Western Hemisphere, as well as by having an independent Cuban Republic, a *Cuba libre*, as a grateful neighbor at peace off our Florida shores. But first of all, the reason for the war was altruistic: to give a suffering island its freedom.

Off in the capital of the Austro-Hungarian Empire, Clemens followed newspaper reports of the war back home very closely. For that

47

matter, where else except in letters from knowledgeable friends could he keep abreast of current events? The birth of radio lay more than a decade in the future; not until January 13, 1910, at New York City's Metropolitan Opera Company, would the tenor voice of Enrico Caruso be "trapped," in the words of the *Times*, "and magnified by the dictograph directly from the stage and borne by wireless Hertzian waves over the turbulent waters of the sea to transcontinental and coastwise ships and over the mountainous peaks and undulating valleys of the country." Through such means news of the world would be spread in years that followed; but for now, on either side of 1898, one got one's news from newspapers. Accordingly, like so many others, Clemens was a tireless newspaper reader, and like many people he read more than one a day. For newspapers were Clemens's and Mark Twain's principal way of finding out what was going on in the larger world.

Incidentally, as there was no radio in this era, there were no microphones either, which would have to wait until the early 1920s for practical development. Thus, candidate William Jennings Bryan giving his rousing Cross of Gold speech to 18,000 people gathered at the Democratic National Convention in Chicago's Coliseum in 1896 had declaimed without electronic amplification; and each of his hundreds of speeches from the rails campaigning outdoors through the fall, and again in 1900, and Roosevelt's speeches by the hundreds through those same months—eight, ten, or more shouted out daily over the upraised faces of crowds—were projected bare-voiced, leaving us to wonder how any orator's vocal chords, however leathery, could survive the strain of addressing the multitudes that gathered together back then.

Through much of 1898, meanwhile, Clemens was reading the papers for news of America's war with Spain. He was still exulting in early July, when Admiral Sampson's squadron demolished the enemy's Atlantic fleet along the coast of Cuba. That late, the humorist remained convinced that our martial undertaking was filled with merit. Only in August, apparently, did he begin to have second thoughts. He had received another letter from home, this one from his close friend the editor and novelist William Dean Howells. Howells writing on August 2, with the conflict just about over, noted in passing that, at a time when navies ran on coal, "our war for humanity" appeared to have turned "into a war for coaling stations." So how disinterested were America's motives in the present conflict after all?

Ten days from the date of Howells's letter, an armistice was declared, and on October 1, 1898, five commissioners from the two warring sides met in Paris to draw up the terms by which peace would be restored.

The treaty having been agreed on, they signed it on December 10; and in February 1899, the United States Congress ratified the Treaty of Paris for President McKinley's signature.

Three months later, in May, the Clemenses left Vienna. Additional time passed—nearly a year and a half spent in England, in Sweden on account of their youngest daughter Jean's health, then back in England—before the family, now thoroughly homesick, boarded the S.S. *Minnehaha* bound for New York in October 1900. Reporters were waiting on the pier at their arrival, as reporters had been present at Mark Twain's hotel in London the night before the expatriates set out at last for home. By then, the war with Spain was two years behind them; and over those twenty-four months much of interest had happened on a globe that Samuel L. Clemens was seeing far more of than virtually any of its then billion and a half inhabitants ever would.

As an instance, in his round-the-world voyage to pay off debts four years earlier, in the summer of 1896, he had spent more than two months in South Africa. Since then much had been happening in South Africa, which was not one nation in the late nineteenth century but, rather, four separate entities. Two of them (the Orange Free State and the Transvaal) were republics of Boers, or Afrikaners, descended from the Dutch who had settled there in the mid-seventeenth century; that is, nearly 250 years earlier. The two other national entities (the Cape Colony and Natal) were English provinces, the English having seized a part of the Cape in 1806 to keep it out of Napoleon's hands and to monitor trade routes to and from the East. After 90 years the English were still there, alongside the Boers (the Dutch word means *farmers*), whose power through the century had been waning as British influence grew.

But in the second half of the nineteenth century gold and diamonds had been discovered in the Boer republics. In Cape Town, the English high commissioner coveted those newly rich regions; and for its part, Parliament back home was eager to establish an uninterrupted Cape-to-Cairo passage overland across all the vast African holdings that Great Britain had appropriated to itself during Chancellor Bismarck's Berlin Conference of 1884–1885. The Boers stood in the way of those ambitions. In 1899, war broke out between the two South African peoples. The Boers promptly invaded Natal and the Cape Colony and laid siege to three English towns, throwing Britain's imperial drive unexpectedly on the defensive. The sieges were lifted at last, and in June 1900 (month of the Boxer uprising in China), Britain—its army massively reinforced from home—captured the capitals of the two enemy republics and declared the war over.

Yet for all the destruction and the loss of life, the Boer War was far from over. Afrikaner forces withdrew into the brush and from there waged costly guerilla warfare for two more years. In the end, 22,000 British soldiers perished, while thousands of Afrikaner men, women, and children suffered in British concentration camps, many of them fatally.

Clemens read all the news he could on the Boer War. Like most Americans he favored the Boers, two small republics with morality on their side, invaded by a great imperial power and gamely defending themselves. But he was living in England as the war progressed, after leaving Vienna and before returning to America. During that English stay his hosts made much of Mark Twain, continually dining and fêting him and paying him the most flattering attentions. Thus, although his heart was with the defending descendants of the Dutch in South Africa, Clemens's mind supported the English, our Anglo-Saxon cousins, whom he had first visited—and where he was received with adulation—a full quarter century earlier. Even now, around hospitable English banquet tables he as Mark Twain was giving frequent speeches filled with gratitude for yet another warm reception of the visiting author and lecturer whom the British adored as much as ever his own countrymen did.

If Clemens's feelings about the Boer War were publicly ambiguous, torn between the claims of the combatants—heart with the Boers, head with the English—his feelings about another imperialist venture of the time were, surprisingly, crystal-clear. About the Boxer uprising in China, which came to a climax in this same summer of 1900, Mark Twain setting out for America two or three months later could speak with certainty. The day before leaving, he let a reporter from the *New York World* interview him at his hotel; so that under a headline in the *World* for October 6, 1900—"MARK TWAIN, THE GREATEST AMERICAN HUMORIST, RETURNING HOME"—appeared the departing traveler's opinions on current affairs. "You ask me," he had said, "about what is called imperialism. Well, I have formed views about that question. I am at the disadvantage of not knowing whether our people are for or against spreading themselves over the face of the globe. I should be sorry if they are"—in favor of, rather than opposed to, such outreach—"for I don't think that it is wise or a necessary development. As to China," he went on, "I quite approve of our Government's action in getting free of that complication. They are withdrawing, I understand, having done what they wanted. That is quite right. We have no more business in China than in any other country that is not ours."

Two or three months earlier, American forces had gone into China. The secret Society of Glorious and Harmonious Fists—those "Boxers," as the West called them, in reference to their curious martial arts—had been running riot over the Chinese countryside, roaming armed through the streets, setting houses on fire, attacking foreign devils of all kinds: missionaries, merchants, clerks, women, children—slicing some victims to death with their rusty swords. A German envoy was murdered. For fifty-five days terrified westerners cowered under siege in the legations in Peking. In Taiyuan, some 200 miles from there, more rioting Boxers, intent on driving intruders out and restoring China to its ancient ways, massacred 48 Catholic missionaries, nearly 200 Protestant missionaries, and several thousand Chinese Catholics as well.

In response, an eight-nation alliance of powers, which included Germany, Japan, Russia, Britain, France, Italy, and Austria-Hungary, assembled an army that eventually numbered 55,000 men. The United States Fourteenth Infantry Regiment was shipped over from the Philippines to join them. Together those forces crushed the Boxer uprising, and in their wrath some of the soldiers committed their own atrocities—plundering, raping, murdering—the Germans among them guided by their kaiser's explicit, infuriated directive to behave like Huns, so that the Chinese would never dare so much as squint at a German for the next 1,000 years. After the dust settled, the Western powers imposed heavy monetary penalties on China.

Mark Twain thought the United States had been right to get out of that imbroglio as soon as it could. He had more to say about the Boxers once he got home, and said it forthrightly while speaking that fall to the Public Education Association in New York City. "It is the foreigners who are making all the trouble in China," he drawled in his semicomical, deadpan, disarming way, "and if they would only get out how pleasant everything would be! The Boxer is a patriot; he is the only patriot China has, and I wish him success." Moreover, the speaker—still rendering with comical delivery his distinctly uncomical views—made bold to go on: "The Boxers on this side have won out. Why not give the Boxers on the other side a chance?"

The part about Boxers on this and the other side referred to Cuba and the Philippines. Upon landing in New York on October 15, Mark Twain had been questioned at the piers about his views on what was going on in the Philippines. The archipelago had been on nobody's mind when war over Cuba began in the spring of 1898. Right off, though, in the first days of the war, Commodore Dewey destroyed sovereign Spain's Pacific fleet in Manila Bay, leaving little else to impede our conquest of the islands. But native Filipinos, like their Cuban counterparts, had all this while been waging an insurrection against Spain's long domination, intent on throwing out the foreigner, Boxer-like; so that however prompt the commodore's triumph at sea, Filipinos on land had already conquered most of their archipelago and set up a republic. About all that remained on shore to be wrenched from Spanish hands was the capital, Manila.

Before the end of May in that same 1898, 20,000 American troops had arrived in the Philippines; and those forces, cooperating more or less with the native insurgents, soon drove the Spanish from their last foothold in the Pacific. What should follow? President McKinley frankly admitted that he couldn't have found the Philippines on a map within 2,000 miles; but now that the centuries-long sovereignty of Spain had been overthrown, what would become of the archipelago?

The insurgents had set up their republic, with their leader, Emilio Aguinaldo, as president. But as early as June 2, the Washington correspondent for the *New York Tribune* was reporting that "the United States has no idea of surrendering the newly acquired territory in the Far East." Our own president inclined to think we ought at least to retain a coaling station on one of the islands, to service our warships in the vast Pacific and our merchant vessels sailing to and from China. There were people in high places, however, who could envisage ways to put the Philippines to even better use. Those self-termed expansionists included Colonel Roosevelt, just then with his Rough Riders on their way to fight in Cuba, and Roosevelt's close friend and powerful ally back home, Senator Henry Cabot Lodge of Massachusetts. Senator Lodge, who had President McKinley's ear, saw to it that yet another expansionist and good friend, John Hay, was installed as secretary of state. Some called such people imperialists, intent on establishing an American empire; but by whatever name, they held enough key positions in government by now that they could persuade McKinley we had better take over the Philippines ourselves, all of it. Either that, or give the islands back to Spain. The expansionists insisted that Filipinos were incapable of governing themselves; and Germany, meanwhile, remained on the prowl with its ever-growing navy, having recently conducted heavy-handed gunboat diplomacy in Venezuela, Haiti, and Samoa. Japan, too, was restless. Abandoning the islands would leave them prey to one of those grasping powers; and neither Roosevelt nor Lodge nor Hay meant to let that happen. McKinley was urged to act.

On October 28, 1898, impelled, as he said, "by the single consideration of duty and humanity," the President instructed his commissioners negotiating the treaty in Paris to demand from Spain not just one island for a coaling station but rather all 7,000 islands and the 8 million inhabitants of the Philippines as spoils of war. The Spanish bargainers protested, yet they could do little on behalf of a nation so soundly thrashed as theirs. Accordingly, Article III of the Treaty of Paris reads, "Spain cedes to the United States the archipelago known as the Philippine Islands," with the face-saving addendum that the victor "will pay to Spain the sum of twenty million dollars ($20,000,000) within three months after the exchange of the ratifications of the present treaty." A later article, VIII, specified that the surrender did not affect "the peaceful possession of property of all kinds," including "ecclesiastical or civic bodies, or any other associations" that may legally possess such property in the ceded territories.

Nothing remained—as it appeared to Mark Twain, sardonically observing—except for the Americans, having helped drive the foreigner, the Spaniard, out of the Philippines, to move in themselves. And indeed, that very December, on the twenty-first, President McKinley issued instructions to General Otis on station in Manila to "proclaim in the most public manner that we come, not as invaders or conquerors, but as friends to protect the natives in their homes, in their employments, and in their personal and religious rights." In addition, the general was to make clear that "the mission of the United States is one of benevolent assimilation, substituting the mild sway of justice and right for arbitrary rule."

Benevolent assimilation: the term would live on. Congress ratified the Treaty of Paris the following February, of 1899, by chance two days after warfare had broken out between insurgent Filipinos and these new friends of theirs. The insurgents had demanded independence first, before any talk of setting up a temporary American protectorate could proceed. The new arrivals insisted on Filipinos' first acknowledging United States sovereignty; we would talk about independence later. On that point negotiations collapsed, and war began. Conflict in the islands was persisting, by then in the form of relentless guerilla warfare against the Americans, when Mark Twain returned from his self-imposed exile a year and a half later, in the fall of 1900.

Asked on the New York piers for his views on the Philippines, he obliged reporters with a detailed reply. "I left these shores, at Vancouver"—near the start of his debt-paying voyage around the world, in the summer of 1895—"a red-hot imperialist. I wanted the American eagle to go screaming into the Pacific. It seemed tiresome and tame for it to content itself with the Rockies. Why not spread its wings over the Philippines, I asked myself? And I thought it would be a real good thing to do." Why? Because "here are a people who have suffered for three centuries. We can make them as free as ourselves, give them a government and country of their own, put a miniature of the American constitution afloat in the Pacific, start a brand new republic to take its place among the free nations of the world."

Since then, however, Mark Twain had brought to bear on the issues his newspaper reading and considerable firsthand knowledge of Europe and the world, "and I have read carefully the treaty of Paris, and I have seen that we do not intend to free but to subjugate the people of the Philippines. We have gone there to conquer, not to redeem." For one thing, as per Article VIII of the treaty, America has "pledged the power of this country to maintain and protect the abominable system established in the Philippines by the friars." What Mark Twain knew of friars, and missionaries—and politicians, for that matter—led him to hold none of those practitioners in high esteem. In particular, friars in the Philippines just now: 2,600 of them, Europeans all, mostly Spanish, ruling over and exploiting the natives, having appropriated property by rights not theirs. "It should, it seems to me, be our pleasure and duty to make those people"—whom the same friars, like the departed Spaniards, had long trampled on—"free and let them deal with their own domestic questions in their own way. And so," the returning exile ended by pronouncing, "I am an anti-imperialist. I am opposed to having the eagle put its talons on any other land."

CHAPTER Seven

Election Results

While campaigning over this same fall of 1900, Governor Roosevelt had repeatedly dismissed the opposition's charges that the McKinley administration was bound on a course of imperialism. Such an imputation was a mere ghost, a specter without substance, conjured up to scare people. The same went for accusations of militarism, also heard at rallies supporting Bryan, the Democratic presidential candidate. Both terms were misapplied when used synonymously with expansionism. Ours was not a militaristic nation, never had been; nor were Republicans interested in setting up an American empire. *Expansion*, on the other hand, had been a feature of our history from the start. Even at the very beginning, while fighting for our freedom from George III, we were expanding across the Alleghenies westward. Not many decades later, President Jefferson effected a massive expansion with the Louisiana Purchase. Thereafter we expanded into Florida, into Texas, into Oregon, at midcentury into the acquisitions that were the spoils of the Mexican War, later into Alaska. Just the other month, while the Spanish War was waging, we had sheltered Hawaii from threats by Japan, whose emigrants had been descending in such numbers that Japanese were finally barred from entering the islands altogether. As one consequence, a warship of imperial Japan had steamed menacingly in the vicinity, until Sanford Dole and American sugar interests out there in the Pacific appealed for our help. At the time, in the summer of 1898, President McKinley told his private secretary that we needed Hawaii "just as much and a good deal more than we did California. It is manifest destiny." Now Hawaii was a territory of the United States. That was expansion, not empire; and those who professed to see no difference between the two were either guilty of disingenuousness or burdened with wanton ignorance.

One such, apparently, was Mark Twain, landing in New York in mid-October 1900 at ten in the evening. On the piers he had told reporters that he was an anti-imperialist, stoutly opposed to America's recent moves in the Pacific.

Then you're for Bryan? they queried.

"I guess not," was his answer. "I'm rather inclined toward McKinley, even if he is an imperialist. But don't ask political questions, for all I know about them is from the English papers."

Still, this newly returned exile was hardly alone in his views. Earlier, while Samuel Clemens and family were in Vienna and the terms of the treaty that would end the Spanish-American War were being argued about in Paris, in Boston a group of like-minded citizens had met in an office on Milk Street, in November 1898, to found the Anti-Imperialist League. By 1900, the League claimed a membership of 30,000; and the list of names of those who either had joined outright or held opinions in sympathy with the group's outlook was impressive. Present-day readers, even those only casually acquainted with American cultural life toward the end of the nineteenth century, will recognize many among the distinguished roster: the two living former presidents, Benjamin Harrison, Republican, and Grover Cleveland, Democrat, as well as various other politicians (Carl Schurz, George Frisbie Hoar, Bryan himself); journalists (Ambrose Bierce, Lincoln Steffens, Finley Peter Dunne); social workers and theorists (Jane Addams, Thorstein Veblen); editors (E. L. Godkin of the *Nation*, Thomas Bailey Aldrich, William Dean Howells); professors (Bliss Perry, William Graham Sumner); novelists (Henry James, Hamlin Garland); poets (William Vaughn Moody, Edwin Arlington Robinson, Edgar Lee Masters); historians (Charles Francis Adams, Henry Adams, James Ford Rhodes); and philosophers (William James, George Santayana); as well as many other notables of the era, including Andrew Carnegie, Thomas Wentworth Higginson, Charles Eliot Norton, Gamaliel Bradford, and Clarence Darrow. All were anti-imperialists; but no one enlisted in the cause was more highly valued for his influence than was this recently declared partisan, Mark Twain.

The objections of the anti-imperialists to our interfering in the Philippines and elsewhere overseas were based on several considerations. Many charter members of the group were New Englanders of an earlier era who held in memory a homogeneous America of Enlightenment values and an Anglo-Saxon heritage. Migrations westward had spread that heritage and those values across contiguous areas of the continent to the edge of what served as a natural western boundary, the Pacific coast. Now, as the

Detroit Journal put it: "The best thought of the country is opposed to holding the Philippines"—for one thing because to many Americans it didn't
seem right, according to our traditions, to rule 7,000 miles beyond our
west coast over noncontiguous lands that were populated by an oriental
people, Spanish-speaking, non-Protestant, unversed in Anglo-Saxon ways.
But even more important, as the venerable senator from Massachusetts,
George Frisbie Hoar, argued tellingly in the Senate chamber: America had
been founded on the bedrock principle that governments derive their just
powers from the consent of the governed. Yet all this while our military had
been increasing troop levels in the Philippines until finally they reached
60,000 men, sent there under arms to do battle with Filipino insurgents
who most emphatically were withholding *their* consent to be governed—
were fighting doggedly, in fact, against our far superior forces in order that
they might rule their own land under their impressive young leader Aguinaldo. "You have no right," Senator Hoar insisted, "at the cannon's mouth
to impose on an unwilling people your Declaration of Independence and
your Constitution and your notions of freedom and notions of what is
good." To which Henry Adams, knowledgeable historian of America's past,
agreed: "I fully share with Hoar," he wrote to a friend, "the alarm and horror of seeing poor weak McKinley, in gaiety . . . plunge into an inevitable
war to conquer the Philippines, contrary to every profession or so-called
principle of our lives and history. I turn green in bed at midnight if I think
of the horror of a year's warfare in the Philippines," warfare where "we
must slaughter a million or two of foolish Malays in order to give them the
comforts of flannel petticoats and electric railways."

Such a grotesque posture as this that we had assumed didn't seem to
differ much from that of the Spaniards whom we had replaced in the archipelago. Spaniards had battled against the natives just as we were doing.
William James, distinguished thinker and Theodore Roosevelt's professor of
anatomy during his years at Harvard, wrote publicly in March 1899: "We are
now openly engaged in crushing out the sacredest thing in this great human
world—the attempt of a people long enslaved to attain to the possession of
itself, to organize its laws and government, to be free to follow its internal
destinies according to its own ideals." And what was our army doing so far
from home anyway? Here in the United States we had troubles enough,
plenty of them. "Until our nation has settled the Negro and Indian problems," said Booker T. Washington, the foremost African-American of the
time, "I do not believe that we have a right to assume more social problems."
For his part, Mark Twain reminded his countrymen that Filipinos had never
in any way, to any degree in the slightest, threatened America's safety.

Then what were our soldiers doing over there? Others expressed a rather crasser reason for deploring our meddling. Benjamin Tillman, as one example—Democratic senator from South Carolina—protested the further mongrelization, as he put it, of America's ruling race by the proposed dilution of whites with eight or nine million Filipinos, not to mention one and a half million swarthy Cubans most likely, and just under a million Puerto Ricans. A while back, Tillman, a pugnacious gentleman farmer, had threatened to deal harshly with the then Democratic presidential candidate Grover Cleveland, with whom he differed over the silver-coinage issue. Cleveland was "an old bag of beef," Tillman cried, "and I am going to Washington with a pitchfork and prod him in his old fat ribs." From then on, the senator was "Pitchfork Ben" Tillman, a plainspoken joy to southern mill workers and upcountry farmers, whose biases he articulated with profane flair; but for the Democratic party at large, Tillman's swagger posed difficulties.

In this current presidential campaign of 1900, to be specific, William Jennings Bryan, Democrat, needed every vote he could get, north, south, east, and west. Senator Tillman, boss of South Carolina politics, was for such progressive causes as a graduated income tax, and so was Bryan. Pitchfork Ben advocated regulating railroad rates; so did Bryan. He was for the free coinage of silver; Bryan was too. And the senator favored limiting hours of labor in the mills, as did Bryan. But in addition, Tillman was an uncompromising, hot-blooded segregationist who had called a South Carolina constitutional convention as recently as 1895, the sole purpose of which, as he made abundantly clear—"the sole cause of our being here"— was to deny the vote to African-Americans. A poll tax would help with that, and establishing a certain educational level for voters, and imposing a property requirement, and instituting a test on the Constitution, one that officials at polling stations could administer in ways that made sure whites passed and blacks didn't.

Candidate Bryan needed South Carolina's votes in 1900, needed all the Democratic South to stay with him. His strength on his earlier run in 1896—outside of big urban centers—had been in the South and the West, in that latter region where his Nebraska home and his views that favored farmers and miners attracted western votes to the Democrats. On this second try for the presidency, he had to hold on to those votes and find more, because the times had turned prosperous over the last four years, and prosperity favored the incumbent. So the way William Jennings Bryan—grasping for southern votes—dealt with the issue of Senator Tillman's virulent racism was by ignoring race altogether, saying nothing in his campaigning down South either to or about African-Americans, who (where they could vote at all by now, mostly up North) would be voting Republican anyway, for the party of Lincoln.

The Democratic candidate had another problem to deal with. This foremost orator of his time was a man of vast and abiding popularity, decent, humane, deeply religious, magnetic, one who inspired loyalty in the hearts of millions. But he had stumbled in addressing the issue of imperialism. He and his party were vigorously opposed to any ventures toward an American empire; so why hadn't he spoken out against the Treaty of Paris, which appropriated the Philippines as, effectively, our new colony overseas? He hadn't spoken out. He gave his approval to the treaty, and in doing so offended many Democratic party regulars as well as those of whatever party who might sympathize with the goals of the Anti-Imperialist League. Bryan's thinking was that we had better accept the treaty (since Democrats alone couldn't defeat it in Congress and mustn't appear to be against peace anyway) and then work toward Philippine independence in the near future. But to many of the faithful, that seemed like temporizing, and it assuredly looked like that to the League. As a consequence, Bryan's stand on the treaty that Congress ratified in 1899 cost him votes in the election the following year.

The vigor of Theodore Roosevelt's vice presidential campaign cost Bryan votes, too, especially out West, where, despite his eastern roots, the rough-riding colonel was himself very popular. Roosevelt had owned ranches in Dakota Territory, had famously hunted big game in the West, and had led a bunch of doting western cowpunchers from their mustering camp in San Antonio to the heights of glory on San Juan Hill. The Colonel didn't like Bryan a bit—was sure the Democrat's program posed a threat to what America stood for. In the previous presidential campaign, Roosevelt, then police commissioner of New York City, had given a major political speech in Chicago's Coliseum before the American Republican College League on a Thursday evening, October 15, 1896. Robert Todd Lincoln, son of the martyred president, had chaired the proceedings, indulging the audience of 15,000 while it cheered Commissioner Roosevelt for two full minutes. "Bryan's dominant note is hysteria," the speaker called out to his many listeners when they quieted down. "Instead of a government of the people, for the people and by the people, which we now have, Mr. Bryan would substitute a government by a mob, by the demagogue for the shiftless, the disorderly and the semi-criminal." Bryan and his followers were "fit representatives," Roosevelt charged, "of those forces which simmer beneath the surface of every civilized community and which, if they could break out, would destroy property and civilization." Democrats teach "not merely class hatred, but sectional hatred"—South and West against Northeast. They advocate paying debts in silver instead of gold; but paying in silver would, according to the speaker, cut the wages of every worker in America in half. Meanwhile, Bryan attacks the trusts, those combinations of commercial enterprise that have helped make America strong; for a "good capitalist," cried Roosevelt, "who employs his money and his business aright is often the most useful man in the community." Yet Mr. Bryan "champions that system of dishonesty which would steal from the creditors of the nation half of what they have saved." And, given a chance, the Democrat would replace the government of Lincoln and Washington with "a red government of lawlessness and dishonesty as phantastic and as vicious as the Paris Commune itself."

The Commune stood as the current emblem of bloody revolution, that interlude when workers had seized the municipal government of Paris for a couple of months in the spring of 1871, in the wake of France's humiliating defeat by Bismarck and his Germans. Under the red flag of socialism the Communards had begun passing legislation that was anathema to the propertied classes. The takeover was brief. The armies of the National Assembly crushed the Commune mercilessly; and during *la semaine sanglante*—the bloody week—up to 30,000 Communards were executed. But the furor had sent a shiver through the status quo, in both Europe and America; and for years thereafter a mere mention of the Paris Commune here in the States was enough to get propertyowners to the polls to vote Republican.

In 1896, the Great Commoner William Jennings Bryan had been new on the political scene, with his huge clear voice, the freshness of his youth, his handsome features, his dazzling smile, and his advocacy for the downtrodden, the overlooked, the unrepresented. As such, in the midst of hard times, Bryan had posed a real threat to the Grand Old Party. But by 1900 things were different. Voters in their prosperity these four years later had grown apathetic. Even farmers, receiving good returns now for their staples, were feeling less hard-pressed. The silver issue was just about dead; Congress had even passed a gold-standard act in 1898 without much opposition. Republican coffers meanwhile were full, made so in part by the unwavering support of railroads and of the great trusts of the era. So in this present 1900 campaign, Republicans could count on ten times the financial resources of Democrats, and three times as many local speakers out there as could be found to speak for the opponent in pleading their different causes.

Bryan had been campaigning, he said, for democracy against plutocracy, for voiceless minorities, for free silver—and against the trusts and imperialism. But the candidate's lack of funds was no help, and hardly anybody cared about the silver issue any more. As for imperialism, why had he supported ratifying the Treaty of Paris? The Anti-Imperialist League, more divided than even the Democrats, wasn't able to do much for him. Many league members, like Mark Twain, leaned toward the amiable, unexciting McKinley despite his faults; and Republican anti-imperialist Senator Hoar couldn't abide Democrats in general. Although the League sent out pamphlets and other documents supporting its aims, it proved unable to launch rallies or put together audiences of any size and liveliness. Bryan meanwhile railed against the trusts to some effect, but the real issues were war and prosperity: the full dinner pail and our overseas conquests. Not the tariff. Not the size of the army. Not whether blacks could vote in Louisiana or North Carolina. What seemed to matter was that we, the voters—the 13.5 million who voted—were living better now than four years ago, and in that space of time the incumbent president had won a war against Spain, promptly and decisively, thereby raising America to the level of an international power.

Returned from his long stay overseas, Mark Twain had wondered whether our people were for or against spreading themselves over the face of the globe, but the answer coming together that autumn appeared to leave the question in no doubt. Prosperous America relished its new role as a power to be reckoned with on that larger stage. In vain did Bryan plead: "We cannot preach the doctrine that governments come up from the people and at the same time practice the doctrine that governments rest upon brute force. We cannot set a high and honorable example for the emulation of mankind while we roam the world like beasts of prey, seeking whom we may devour." Such talk was stirring feelings approaching contempt in Governor Roosevelt as he campaigned with unabated vigor nationwide—contempt for Mr. Bryan's sentimentality, for his blatant religiosity, but most of all for his "criminal" and "vicious" platform that seemed "fundamentally an attack on civilization."

Election day in 1900 fell on November 6. "The expected has happened," the *New York Times* reported next morning in its lead story, under the banner headline "M'KINLEY RE-ELECTED." "The Republican Presidential ticket has swept the country." The incumbent won by 292 electoral votes to Bryan's 155, and increased his share of the popular vote nearly a quarter of a million over the 1896 tally, while Bryan's fell 100,000 from his previous showing. "At the close of another presidential campaign it is again my lot to congratulate you as the successful candidate," the Democrat in defeat telegraphed his opponent, more grudgingly than might have been expected from so affable a politician. But Mr. Bryan was sorely disappointed. He had lost heavily in the western states—in Kansas, South Dakota, Utah, Washington, and Wyoming, all of which his party had won four years ago. Bryan even lost his home state of Nebraska, his hometown of Lincoln, even his home precinct.

As for Samuel L. Clemens, he had had nothing to do with all that. Clemens had skipped the voting altogether. Speaking some weeks later to the City Club in New York, Mark Twain admitted to a personal shortcoming. "I don't know much about finance," this erstwhile bankrupt confessed drily; yet some friends who did had told him "that Bryan was all wrong on the money question, so I didn't vote for him. I knew enough about the Philippines," however, he went on to explain in his disarming drawl, "to have a strong aversion to sending our bright boys out there to fight with a disgraced musket under a polluted flag, so I didn't vote for the other fellow" either. But America's muskets *disgraced*, its flag *polluted*? The following morning, the humorist admitted that he had let slip at the City Club more than he meant to say. "I've got this vote, and it's clean yet," he had gone on to tell yesterday's audience—and told them it was a vote he intended to use whenever he found a party that put up only the best men for public office.

CHAPTER Eight

The Strenuous Life

Had you been alive at the time, you would have known the new vice president of the United States already, as surely as you would have known Mark Twain. You would have known Colonel Roosevelt as the hero of San Juan Hill. But you would have been aware of him also as a prominent politician in New York—formerly a member of the New York Assembly in Albany and a police commissioner of New York City—and as a government official in Washington, where he had served as civil service commissioner and assistant secretary of the navy. Most recently, Theodore Roosevelt had been concluding a two-year term as governor of New York State. Beyond all that, you might well have known him as a writer, the author of numerous magazine articles—in *The Outlook*, in *McClure's*, in *The Century*—as well as of many books. He had written histories, biographies, and books about nature: about ranching and hunting, about life outdoors and under the stars. By 1900, in short, you would have already seen and heard the name of this particular American repeatedly, and in a number of different contexts.

Election night the celebrated Colonel Roosevelt had spent with his family at Oyster Bay. In the course of the evening, he had not once "seemed anxious about the result," the *Times* informed its readers the following morning. "He did not make any special arrangements to receive the news, and depended on messages to be brought from the telegraph office in the railroad station, nearly three miles away." At around ten, confirmation of the Republican victory was delivered by a knock at the front door of Sagamore Hill. Roosevelt was in the reception room with his wife and daughter. "When he appeared at the door to meet a newspaper correspondent he was in evening dress. He invited his visitor into the parlor and closely scrutinized the returns and briefly commented on the result. After reading the

Figure 8.1. Inauguration of President McKinley to his
second term, March 4, 1901. The new vice president stands
behind and to McKinley's right.
Courtesy of the Library of Congress.

message, he said: 'Isn't that fine. It shows what the American people are.
It shows that they want the good times to continue, and are in favor of
honest money and are for the flag.'" At once the new vice president–elect
dictated a message to President McKinley in Canton, Ohio: "I congratulate
you," he telegraphed, "and far more the Nation. You have my heartfelt
gratitude over the result. Theodore Roosevelt."

Not many days after the returns came in, during that same November
of 1900, Mark Twain, who at this stage of his life was nearly as inveterate a
diner-out as he was a newspaper reader, alluded in public to Roosevelt's elevation. The humorist was addressing the Lotos Club, at Fifth Avenue and

Twenty-First Street—"The Ace of Clubs," that longtime member called it, a club that thrives yet, farther uptown. Clemens's remarks allow a present-day reader to encounter the Twainian irony in full blossom, while all but hearing on the page those somewhat bemused pauses that so delighted contemporaries lucky enough to be seated in range of the living voice. The after-dinner speaker had got on the subject of New York's governor, "an illustrious Rough Rider, and we liked him so much in that great office that now we have made him Vice-President, not in order that that office shall give him distinction," doubtless with a pause here, before "but that he may confer distinction upon the office. And it's needed, too [*pause, amid appreciative chuckles around the banquet table*]—it's needed. And now, for a while anyway, we shall not be stammering and embarrassed when a stranger asks us, 'What is the name of the Vice-President?' [*general laughter*]. This one is known, this one is pretty well known [*pause*], pretty widely known [*longer pause*], and in some quarters [*pause*] favorably [*much laughter over that last*]. I am not accustomed," Mark Twain went on, "to dealing in these fulsome compliments [*laughter at the irony*], and I am probably overdoing it a little [*heartier laughter*]; but, well, my old affectionate admiration for Governor Roosevelt has probably betrayed me into this complimentary excess [*laughter mounting*]; but I know him [*pause*], and you know him [*another pause*]; and if you give him rope enough [*pausing in feigned confusion*]—I mean [*starting again*] if—[*and giving it up*] oh, yes [*suspenseful pause*—"he will hang himself"?—*and the release*], he will justify that compliment; leave it just as it is."

Newly returned from abroad, the anti-imperialist Mark Twain had been making it clear that he was out of sympathy with a number of Theodore Roosevelt's views here at home. The two had met in the mid-1880s, when the politician was in the midst of an unsuccessful run for mayor of New York City; and since then the paths of those gregarious, very public figures, both of them often in Manhattan, would have crossed more than once. Personally, they had no objection to each other. Over the years who could have felt anything but affection for the shrewd and entertaining Mark Twain, author of so much that was delightful, insightful, and funny? And the personality that Samuel L. Clemens had polished for his pen name was as well known by this time as the much-loved works themselves: the frequently photographed, commonsensical aphorist, puncturer of pretense, declaimer against hypocrisy and cruelty, but for all that a bit of the canny, good-humored old idler. As for Roosevelt—anything but idle—Clemens professed never to have shaken the man's hand without feeling an electric charge run through him, so ebullient, so filled with energy was the politician's greeting.

But Clemens didn't like politicians much in general, had first taken a dislike to them as a journalist covering the Nevada territorial legislature out in Carson City way back in the 1860s. A brief stint later in that same decade, in Washington, where he served as secretary to a Nevada senator, had confirmed his opinion: tip-top people don't let themselves get bogged down in legislative shadiness; they give it up promptly and choose some other line of work.

Yet regardless of how the one viewed the other's profession, there were enough similarities between Roosevelt and Clemens to cause friction anyway. Both were writers and public performers possessed of restless, perpetually youthful temperaments. Each grew a bit nettled when the spotlight wandered off him. And both had a wide circle of friends, the circles often overlapping: with Kipling, for instance, a warm admirer of each; and John Hay, littérateur and diplomat, the journalist Finley Peter Dunne, and many more keeping the one, if only inadvertently, aware of the other's views and doings.

And the two were moralists. Both Clemens and Roosevelt liked to preach, although in the guise of Mark Twain the former was by far the more artful preacher. His sermons came out more like entertainment, like genial enlightenment; he preached with humor—though he had never, he insisted, written anything in his life to be funny: only put the humor in if it arose naturally during the course of the point he was making. What Mark Twain said or wrote had a serious point, expressed in a colloquial style distinctly his own—so much so as to be instantly recognizable and, on the page, enormously influential, even to the extent of changing the direction of American letters. By contrast, Roosevelt's style in his hortatory mode was serviceable—it did the job, with clarity—but only now and then in a distinctive way, as something no one else could have written: only rarely, that is, rising to the level of literature.

Roosevelt preached with little artifice and no apology. "I wish to preach, not the doctrine of ignoble ease," he said in a well-known instance, "but the doctrine of the strenuous life." No reader could confuse such an earnest, irony-free utterance with any comparable sentence of Mark Twain's, Roosevelt's forthright prose as here exhibited displaying characteristics—the generalizing tendency, the resoluteness, the openness to moralizing—indistinguishable from thousands of specimens that might be adduced from the multitudinous exhortatory pages that the Colonel wrote over a prolific lifetime.

The statement quoted comes from a volume published this same year, when one might have thought that the governor of a major state, candidate for national office, tireless campaigner, and father of a large family already had enough on hand to fill his crowded hours. Yet this is but one of a couple of books the Colonel published in 1900; his biography *Oliver Cromwell* came out this same year. As for the former volume, a collection of speeches and magazine articles, it opens with an address, delivered in Chicago in April 1899, that furnishes the title of the book as a whole: *The Strenuous Life*. To repeat: "I wish to preach," Roosevelt says near the start of his address at the Hamilton Club, "not the doctrine of ignoble ease, but the doctrine of the strenuous life, the life of toil and effort, of labor and strife; to preach that highest form of success which comes, not to the man who desires mere easy peace, but to the man who does not shrink from danger, from hardship, or from bitter toil, and who out of these wins the splendid ultimate triumph."

Figure 8.2.   Mark Twain at his ease, 1906.
Courtesy of the Mark Twain House & Museum, Hartford.

Any such exemplar of the "highest form of success"—shirking neither bitter toil nor hardship nor danger—would seem at some remove from the image of Mark Twain that his creator Samuel L. Clemens had cultivated over a long career. Granted, the humorist had not always been his present age, in this November of 1900, when he was about to turn sixty-five and with the fires of ambition somewhat banked, any more than the Colonel would remain the youthful forty-two that he had achieved three or four weeks ago. Twenty-three years separated the two, so that Mark Twain would be photographed now, with his bushy white mustache and unruly white mane of hair, as an elderly gentleman most likely lounging here or there: at a ship's railing, or beside a billiard table, or in a rocking chair on somebody's veranda, or in late morning still in bed, propped up on pillows with cigar in hand and reporters gathered round. The postures smacked more of slothful ease than of hardship, toil, or danger; whereas during these same days young Roosevelt would more likely be shown on horseback leaping a rail fence; or leaning forward vigorously campaigning from some platform or other, mouth open, fist slamming emphatically into palm; or in the midst of one of those arduous treks he subjected his friends to, surmounting (over or under, but never around) whatever obstacles in Rock Creek Park got in his way.

The differences between the two men went beyond age to temperament. When the Civil War came, Clemens traveled west and sat it out. (Roosevelt would never willingly have sat out a war.) Out West, Clemens found a calling and a pen name, which would become the most famous in the world. Young Mark Twain, as he then was, emerged as a journalist with his own idiosyncratic voice, as well as a poker player, drinker, swearer, and restless wanderer on the edges, observing clear-eyed, whether in California mining camps or off in the Sandwich Islands or back East or overseas rambling amid the treasures and overrated absurdities of Europe. He had married since those wild bachelor days and settled down, at least somewhat, and sired a family. Now world-famous and eminently respectable, he remained nevertheless unique, a citizen of the globe, in his versatile imaginativeness unclassifiable—and in want of no such guidance as is to be found in the pages of Colonel Roosevelt's essay "The Strenuous Life."

The whole tendency of that essay is collective, generalized, addressed to Americans as a group. How should we lead our lives? The author will tell us, and his answer revolves around the word *strife*, a word that runs through the address insistently enough to grate on the ears of certain elderly gentlemen. "Above all," the author concludes his essay, "let us shrink from no strife, moral or physical, within or without the nation, provided we are certain that the strife is justified, for it is only through strife, through hard and dangerous endeavor, that we shall ultimately win the goal of true national greatness."

The path to such a conclusion encounters struggle all along the way, and the path is duty-ridden. Man's duty. Woman's duty. Our duty in the Philippines. Man's duty is first of all to his home. He must be glad "to do a man's work, to dare and endure and to labor; to keep himself, and to keep those dependent upon him." He and his wife and his children must "lead clean, vigorous, healthy lives," the children "so trained that they shall endeavor, not to shirk difficulties, but to overcome them; not to seek ease, but to know how to wrest triumph from toil and risk." Only then will the nation that such families inhabit be healthy. For the man of the house has duties beyond the family, duties to his nation. As for the woman, she must be "the housewife, the helpmeet of the homemaker"—that is, of her husband—as well as being "the wise and fearless mother of many healthy children." The well-read Roosevelt here alludes to "one of Daudet's powerful and melancholy books," the French novelist and man of letters having spoken (quite reasonably, one might have thought) of "the fear of maternity, the haunting terror of the young wife of the present day." Yet so cringing a sentiment stirs the Colonel's contempt. "When such words can be truthfully written of a nation," he avers, "that nation is rotten to the heart's core. When men fear work or fear righteous war, when women fear motherhood, they tremble on the brink of doom; and well it is that they should vanish from the earth, where they are fit subjects for the scorn of all men and women who are themselves strong and brave and high-minded."

Those truly fit will survive. The speaker goes on: man's first duty is to his home. But that doesn't excuse him from doing his duty to the state; for failing in that, he ceases to be a free man. "In the same way, while a nation's first duty is within its own borders, it is not thereby absolved from facing its duties in the world as a whole; and if it refuses to do so, it merely forfeits its right to struggle for a place among the peoples that shape the destiny of mankind."

Of course not every duty that the state exacts of us involves warfare. But whatever duty we undertake must be aggressively discharged. A man of wealth (such as Roosevelt himself) may be "freed from the necessity of work," but "only by the fact that he or his fathers before him have worked to good purpose. If the freedom thus purchased is used aright, and the man still does actual work, though of a different kind, whether as a writer or a general, whether in the field of politics or in the field of exploration and adventure, he shows he deserves his good fortune." Otherwise, if he should settle for "mere enjoyment," he will be no better than a "cumberer of the earth's surface," unfit to hold his own with his fellows. In brief, our aspirations should never be toward timid peace, but toward victorious effort, toward pursuits worthy of men of virile qualities, of manly men. "All honor must be paid," for instance, "to the architects of our material prosperity, to the great captains of industry who have built our factories and our railroads, to the strong men who toil for wealth with brain or hand; for great is the debt of the nation to these and their kind."

For each of us, meanwhile, there will be no dearth of challenges. Life is full of challenges. The question is not whether we will encounter them in the century immediately ahead, but *how* we will encounter them. In the time of our fathers, in 1861, many cried out for peace. And we might have had peace, and saved our blood and treasure, and spared the millions their heartache, saved hundreds of thousands of lives and hundreds of millions of dollars "simply by shrinking from strife. And if we had thus avoided it, we would have shown that we were weaklings, and that we were unfit to stand among the great nations of the earth." Thank God for the iron in the blood of Lincoln and Grant! Let us, "the children of the men who carried the great Civil War to a triumphant conclusion, praise the God of our fathers that the ignoble counsels of peace were rejected," for in the end the slave was freed and the Union saved.

Roosevelt makes clear that no such challenges as faced our fathers confront this generation, "but we have our own tasks, and woe to us if we fail to perform them! We cannot, if we would, play the part of China, and be content to rot by inches in ignoble ease within our borders, taking no interest in what goes on beyond them, sunk in a scrambling commercialism; heedless of the higher life, the life of aspiration, of toil and risk, busying ourselves only with the wants of our bodies for the day, until suddenly we should find, beyond a shadow of question, what China has already found, that in this world the nation that has trained itself to a career of unwarlike and isolated ease is bound, in the end, to go down before other nations which had not lost the manly and adventurous qualities." No, we must never content ourselves with becoming "an assemblage of well-to-do hucksters who care nothing for what happens" in distant places.

And so to the Philippines of the present hour: "no small share of the responsibility for the blood shed in the Philippines, the blood of our brothers, and the blood of their wild and ignorant foes"—insurgents even now waging guerilla war against our soldiers out there—lies at the threshold of those who "by their worse than foolish words deliberately invited a savage people to plunge into a war fraught with sure disaster for them—a war, too, in which our own brave men who follow the flag must pay with their blood for the silly, mock humanitarianism of the prattlers who sit at home in peace." The Colonel is referring to the Anti-Imperialist League and its sympathizers, whose prattling cannot obscure the fact that our nation's first duty in the archipelago is to put down armed resistance. There must be no faltering, no parleying, until peace is restored. "As for those in our own country who encourage the foe, we can afford contemptuously to disregard them; but it must be remembered that their utterances are not saved from being treasonable merely by the fact that they are despicable."

By implication, the anti-imperialists, including Mark Twain, are committing treason by speaking against our present policy in the Philippines. Meanwhile, Vice President Roosevelt looks forward eagerly to what lies ahead, but with this caution. "The twentieth century looms before us big with the fate of many nations. If we stand idly by, if we seek merely swollen, slothful ease and ignoble peace, if we shrink from the hard contests where men must win at hazard of their lives and at the risk of all they hold dear, then the bolder and stronger peoples will pass us by, and will win for themselves the domination of the world. Let us therefore boldly face the life of strife."

Mark Twain would be looking ahead too, but from a different vantage point. Those stronger and bolder people referred to—among the great world powers—had awakened Theodore Roosevelt's gratitude: "All civilization has been the gainer by the Russian advance" southward in Asia, he writes in a neighboring essay of *The Strenuous Life*, "as it was the gainer by the advance of France in North Africa; as it has been the gainer by the advance of England in both Asia and Africa, both Canada and Australia." Before the forces of civilization expanded thus, bloody violence raged through backward lands. "The same will be true of the Philippines. If the men who have counseled national degradation, national dishonor, by urging us to leave the Philippines and put the Aguinaldan oligarchy in control of those islands, could have their way, we should merely turn them over to rapine and bloodshed until some stronger, manlier power stepped in to do the task we had shown ourselves fearful of performing."

Those same expanding powers Mark Twain esteemed less highly: Russia bullying its way into Manchuria; the German Asian Squadron overpowering Kiaochow to set up a protectorate by brute force on Chinese soil; Great Britain and America imposing their sovereign will far off overseas, much of such nationalistic self-serving couched in the language of markets opened, souls saved, and civilization bestowed. At year's end, the humorist was moved to compose a bitter salutation from the nineteenth century to the twentieth, one that would be widely disseminated and commented on. It was dated December 31, 1900. "I bring you," he had the old century greet the new, "the stately matron called CHRISTENDOM—returning bedraggled, besmirched and dishonored from pirate raids in Kiaochow, Manchuria, South Africa and the Philippines; with her soul full of meanness, her pocket full of boodle and her mouth full of pious hypocrisies. Give her soap and a towel, but hide the looking glass."

PART Two

WEST

CHAPTER Nine

Rural Upbringing

Quite different environmental forces shaped Samuel Langhorne Clemens and Theodore Roosevelt into the contrasting figures they became. Clemens was born the sixth child in a southern family all crammed into a one-story, two-room, shake-roof, rented frame house in Florida, Missouri. Florida survives into our day as a hamlet of some eight inhabitants total. On November 30, 1835, at Sammy's birth, the place was four years old and had a population of about a hundred, lying close to what was then the American frontier. Less than a year earlier the Clemenses had migrated to the spot from Tennessee—worthy immigrants and proud, though hardly prosperous: yet another family of small slaveholders scraping by in an agrarian land. The family lingered four years in the hamlet of Florida before relocating once more, in November 1839, still in Missouri but thirty miles northeast, to Hannibal, then hardly more than a woodlot for replenishing steamboats on the Mississippi River.

Born two months prematurely, Sammy was just turning four at the time of the move. In Hannibal the boy's father, John Marshall Clemens, ran a general store, borrowed to buy town lots, and as a village lawyer pursued what ill-paid legal business came his way. None of it worked out well. America was in the throes of a severe economic depression after the Panic of 1837, an ordeal that stretched well into the 1840s. But part of the problem lay in the elder Clemens's temperament. As child and man, he rarely smiled and was never heard to laugh. Thus, "my father and I were always on the most distant terms when I was a boy," Sam recalled years afterward, "a sort of armed neutrality, so to speak," the boy's spirited ways displeasing to a parent austere and undemonstrative.

Sam's other parent was different. During a long life the mother, Jane Lampton Clemens, was "all animation and champagne and charm," according to her son after her death at eighty-seven. Life seemed a holiday to her, and she relished every innocent festival. Yet for all her liveliness, Jane Clemens was of a reverent disposition, as her husband—Sam's stern father—was not. Freethinking Judge Clemens went to church once and never again, but his wife attended regularly, in her easygoing way. Thus the minister Joshua Tucker of Hannibal recalled Sister Clemens as "a woman of the sunniest temperament, lively, affable, a general favorite," whereas Brother Clemens, her husband, appeared on briefer acquaintance to be "a grave, taciturn man," although recognized as the "foremost citizen in intelligence and wholesome influence" of that riverfront village out on America's edges.

In Hannibal young Sam Clemens developed from his fifth into his eighteenth year. Delicate early in childhood, given too much to thinking—a cousin remembered—he was nevertheless always full of fun, from the start funny. And Sam outgrew his feeble first years, so that by seven or eight he could romp as vigorously as any of his playmates. He came to have many such, this high-spirited, imaginative shunner of school and organizer of village pranks and escapades. Will Bowen, John Briggs, Norval ("Gull") Brady, Barney Farthing, Sam Honeyman, Arch Fuqua: all banded together and played at pirates and Robin Hood or waved green garter snakes at terrified girls or swam in Bear Creek and the Mississippi, in which waters Sam nearly drowned nine times, on each occasion fetched up by some villager or other, drained out, reinflated, and set on his way. There was a hill at the north end of Hannibal, wooded, rising nearly 300 feet above the river— Holliday's Hill—and a great limestone cave gaped three miles south of town; so that among such stimulating surroundings Sam and his friends found endless recreation to fill their summer hours.

In two wonderful novels, Mark Twain has done more than anyone else will ever be able to do to preserve the feel of childhood in the 1840s in one immortal place, on the west bank of the Mississippi a hundred miles upstream from St. Louis. The majestic, mile-wide river itself provided much to nourish a youngster's imagination; and from Hannibal's wharf it offered scope for aspiration by furnishing daily sightings of strangers aboard steamboats mooring, amid belchings of smoke and the stopping of paddle wheels and the gauge-cocks screaming. Exotics on deck gazed down through eyes that had seen or soon would rest upon far-off places: St. Jo, St. Looey, Memphis, New Orleans. This daily recurring evidence of elsewhere might in itself have sufficed to infect one young villager with wanderlust and a restlessness that lasted in perpetuity.

Sam Clemens's riverfront childhood wasn't all summertime pleasure, of course: "a boy's life is not all comedy; much of the tragic enters into it." And the horrifying contributed its part, too, in shaping so unique a temperament, one ever curious about the surrounding world, retentive, waking to the town's absurdities and cruelties, alert as well to all the different voices heard, to the furnishings of different rooms in houses, to the views from high bluffs and the glorious river sunsets and the scent of trees blooming and the graveyard silent on its hilltop in eerie, shadowy moonlight.

At different times the boy witnessed a murder in broad daylight on the town's main street, and at the water's edge a runaway slave's body, drowned, was freed from underbrush and shot straight upward waist-high. Again, there was a fire in the jail one night, the town derelict inside screaming, moaning, pleading to be saved; but the keys were on the far side of the village with the marshal, who didn't get there in time. And in 1847, Sam Clemens peered through a keyhole at the autopsy of his uncle, as he later recorded. He was eleven, and one observes the child in disbelief: bent over at the keyhole of a closed door, rapt in an upstairs hallway on Hill Street. Only it wasn't his uncle, as Clemens when grown wrote privately, because no uncle of Sam Clemens died in 1847. It was the father who died that year and lay lifeless under Dr. Meredith's knife on the bed in the room beyond the keyhole. The eleven-year-old was peering at the autopsy of his own dead father.

Pneumonia had taken John Marshall Clemens. He was forty-eight, dying in Hannibal on March 24, 1847. On his deathbed, with his family gathered round, the judge beckoned to his favorite child to come near. Pamela bent down, and her father kissed her. It was about the only time the man was seen to kiss anybody; and even then, with death looming, he offered to kiss no one else, not even his wife at the last, Sam's mother. She had married the grave young lawyer back in Kentucky twenty-four years earlier to spite another man; and for all her exuberance, no affection had ever been openly expressed between the two of them. Not much affection was manifest in Hannibal anyway—the frontier village wasn't a kissing town—so that "the absence of exterior demonstration of affection for my mother had no surprise for me," Sam, observing at the bedside, would later recollect. "By nature she was warm-hearted, but it seemed to me quite natural that her warm-heartedness should be held in reserve in an atmosphere like my father's," even during these final farewells.

Judge Clemens kissed his favorite child, and afterward he addressed all his family. "Cling to the land and wait," he told them; "let nothing beguile it away from you." With that, and without further goodbye to wife or children—nothing beyond three final words, "Let me die"—Judge Clemens passed from the earth and left his survivors deep in shameful, humiliating poverty.

But they did own the land that their sire had spoken of: 70,000 acres bought and paid for along the Obed River in northeast Tennessee. When the railroad reached there, the land would make every one of the Clemenses rich. For now, though, they were very poor, a widow in her mid-forties taking in boarders, with a family left to provide for. She had borne seven children. Three had died, two when old enough to count among Sam's early griefs. Now her husband was dead as well. Of the remaining children, Pamela at nineteen might earn a bit of money giving piano lessons. The eldest, Orion, at twenty-one had gone off to St. Louis to make his way and send back what earnings he could. And the two others, Sam not yet twelve and Henry a couple of years younger, before the end of the decade found their schooldays effectively over.

Sam was apprenticed to a newspaper office as a printer's devil. Years later a niece reported that this interval had been a hard, unhappy time for all the Clemenses. She said that her mother—the Pamela who had been kissed by a dying father—only spoke of the time "once or twice. Uncle Sam was very lonely at that printer's. They came home late one night and found him asleep on the floor," forsaking his pallet at the shop for more companionable surroundings.

Then his older brother returned from St. Louis a printer himself and acquired a Hannibal newspaper. Sam could come work at the paper for Orion, ten years his senior. This was early in 1851. The fifteen-year-old lasted a year and a half in his brother's printing shop. There he made a start at acquiring the directness and clarity of his literary style, learning to discriminate between good and bad writing while correcting copy and reading the newspapers from far and wide that exchanged issues with the *Western Union*. In time the apprentice was allowed to insert squibs of his own as filler for blank column space. Readers of Orion's Hannibal paper were regaled as well with "Our Assistant's Column," brother Sam's contribution, treating miscellaneous topics for a riverport grown to a population of some 2,500 people. On May 26, 1853, for instance, the column informed its readers of America's first world's fair, opening in New York City on Sixth Avenue between Fortieth and Forty-Second streets, where, according to reports, fifteen to twenty thousand people were congregating around the Crystal Palace, a great exhibition hall built for the occasion and before which "drunkenness and debauching are carried on to their fullest extent."

Sam wanted to have a look at the Crystal Palace up close. He was restless in Hannibal anyway, and longed to see the world. But he told nobody
of his plans, only letting his mother know that he was headed downriver
to St. Louis, to where his sister Pamela had moved, she two years married
by that time and the mother of a year-old daughter. By then, too, Sam
had learned a trade that he could ply just about anywhere; every town
supported a newspaper or two or three. So not long after his column with
the note on the fair appeared, Sam Clemens in early June 1853, halfway
through age seventeen, set off on the packet boat downriver ("WANTED!"
reads Orion's urgent advertisement in his paper, "AN APPRENTICE TO THE
PRINTING BUSINESS! APPLY SOON") and never lived in Hannibal again.

In St. Louis the seventeen-year-old spent a couple of months working
at typesetting jobs and putting aside money for the fare that would let him
launch forth on his travels. Then he made his way to New York, visited
the Crystal Palace, and wrote his sister Pamela about it. "From the gallery
(second floor) you have a glorious sight—the flags of the different countries
represented, the lofty dome, glittering jewelry, gaudy tapestry, &c., with the
busy crowd passing to and fro—tis a perfect fairy palace—beautiful beyond
description." He wrote to his family of other sights: of the Washington
Street market downtown; and of Edwin Forrest, viewed perishing at the
Broadway Theatre in *The Gladiator*; and of the travails of getting across
traffic-clogged Broadway, inserting yourself into the mob to be "borne, and
rubbed, and crowded along" so that your feet never touched the pavement,
he said, from one side of the wide boulevard to the other.

Sam wrote to his sister, and to his mother, and to his younger brother
Henry and his older brother Orion; and that last-named, the newspaper
editor who by then had relocated to Muscatine, Iowa, 120 miles upriver
from Hannibal, reprinted portions of those letters in his *Muscatine Journal*.
For at a time when pictures were rare and many people stayed put all their
lives, readers savored verbal descriptions of far-off places. Orion's reporter
back East was meanwhile moving on, after two months, to Philadelphia. "I
will try to write for the paper occasionally," Sam answered a brother's appeal, "but I fear my letters will be very uninteresting." Still, for subscribers
in Muscatine he wrote about the Liberty Bell and Franklin's gravesite and
the Fairmount Bridge spanning the Schuylkill in Philadelphia's outskirts—
America's earliest cable suspension bridge, and thus "the first bridge of the
kind I ever saw."

This nomad—he had gone on down to Washington briefly for a look,
before wandering back to Philadelphia and again to New York City—was

having a fine time all this while. Philadelphians had sought to encourage him lest he grow downhearted. "'Downhearted,' the devil! I have not had a particle of such a feeling since I left Hannibal, more than four months ago." He was relishing his freedom, so that not until April 1854 did Clemens return to his family, first to St. Louis, where sister Pamela and her husband, Will Moffett, and little Annie were living, then to Muscatine, with his mother, Orion, and Henry.

Late that same year, newly married, Orion Clemens moved to his bride's hometown of Keokuk, Iowa, as proprietor of the Ben Franklin Book and Job Office, on the third floor at 52 Main Street. There his two younger brothers joined him, helping to print posters, circulars, and bills of lading to customers' orders. Sam would remain in Keokuk a year and a half, mostly a happy interval, during which he labored alongside his brother Henry and grew close to that favorite of the family. But he tired of job work, underpaid at a not always reliable five dollars a week. Sam had been reading about the Amazon River, another frontier much in the news at the time. To brother Henry, he proposed journeying to South America and up the Amazon to harvest coca leaves. Sam meant "to start to Brazil, if possible, in *six weeks* from now, in order to look carefully into matters there" and with luck make his fortune selling coca leaves to pharmacies in the States. Meanwhile he had contracted with a Keokuk newspaper to write travel letters at five dollars apiece along the way.

He wrote only three of them, two from St. Louis and one from Cincinnati. In Cincinnati, waiting over winter till the ice melted and river traffic resumed, Sam got by setting type through a succession of lonely days. Those ended after five months, in mid-April 1857, when the young man, now twenty-one, boarded the packet steamer *Paul Jones* bound for New Orleans, on the first stage of a journey to the Southern Hemisphere to make his millions.

During that passage downriver another dream intruded on the first. The pilot of the *Paul Jones* let young Clemens steer the boat a ways, and for a consideration was talked into taking him on as a cub, to teach him the craft of steamboat piloting. It would cost $500 and start straight off with a trip back up from New Orleans to St. Louis, the cub standing watches in the pilot house alongside this veteran, Horace Bixby. Once arrived at St. Louis, Sam borrowed $100 from his brother-in-law, Pamela's husband and a prospering commission merchant; and with that down payment he entered yet another phase of his education, the Amazon put behind him.

He was about to become what youths along the river back then most wanted to be, watching from shore day after day while, amid black smoke and fanfare, steamboats touched in and departed: ornamented decks crowded with passengers; gorgeous paddle-boxes; flag snapping at the jackstaff; the captain sounding his bell; and, high in filigree splendor above all the commotion, the pilot in the glass pilot house forty feet above the water gazing down. Just about every boy in every riverside village longed to be that pilot, for his was the best job in the world. The pay, once you were licensed, was $250 *a month*, much more than a preacher made in a year. And having moved out into the stream, you answered to nobody; not even the captain told a pilot what to do, guiding the great laden craft through chutes or shaving in close or striking for the middle of the road along 1,300 miles of the Lower Mississippi, each shifting feature of which he knew by heart, in daylight and darkness, upriver or down.

Once licensed—as Sam Clemens was officially licensed in April 1859— he would have gone on being a pilot for the rest of his days if fate hadn't interfered. But meanwhile he had set his younger brother Henry on the way to a life on the river as well, getting him aboard the *Pennsylvania* as a mud clerk. Under a different pilot, William Brown, they steamed downriver, Henry at every stop leaping ashore to keep track of cargo, Sam up above the texas deck in the lofty pilot house as an apprentice steersman still.

But this other pilot, Brown, proved to be a scoundrel, "a middle-aged, long, slim, bony, smooth-shaven, horse-faced, ignorant, stingy, malicious, snarling, fault-hunting, mote-magnifying tyrant," as Clemens would later immortalize the man. During the voyage, Brown quarreled with his mud clerk, springing at young Henry and meaning to do him harm. Sam, steering, broke off and swung a stool a good solid blow that stretched Brown out on deck. Not stopping there, he leapt on the hated pilot and, avenging his innocent younger brother along with much else, pummeled the man in an act of insubordination that constituted a supreme offense aboard any vessel under way. Brown was so generally disliked, however, that the *Pennsylvania*'s captain merely transferred the offending cub to another boat at New Orleans, secretly in sympathy with what Sam had done and meaning to rehire him as soon as he found a pilot to replace this present one. Thus the *Pennsylvania*, with the captain, the pilot Brown, and the mud clerk Henry still aboard, started on the return trip northward toward St. Louis, Sam reassigned to the *A. T. Lacey* and due to follow a couple of days later.

It was the fate of the *Pennsylvania* to be blown up on that northbound trip. Sixty miles below Memphis at six in the morning, on a half-head of steam and a call from the pilot house to come ahead full, four of the vessel's boilers exploded, leaving good Captain Kleinfelter unscathed amid the shrieks and flames, but hurling Brown overboard to perish and sending Henry Clemens high aloft to fall into the river. Badly scalded, Henry swam back toward the boat to help others of the more than 400 aboard; but he himself was so seriously burned that with the rest of the grievously wounded he had to be taken to a public hall in Memphis for very tardy care. Sam, following behind, found his brother on a pallet in that grim scene of suffering; "as the newspapers had said in the beginning, his hurts were past help." Henry died, delirious, eight days after the accident, Sam at his side through much of the long ordeal.

A letter Sam Clemens composed from Memphis on June 18, 1858, as Henry lay dying, amounts to a prolonged wail of remorse and self-recrimination, bemoaning the injustice of his brother's impending death, wishing it could have been his own instead. "Men take me by the hand and *congratulate* me, and call me 'lucky' because I was not on the Pennsylvania when she blew up!" The loss of one whom he saw as blameless—"my poor sinless brother" Henry, the glory, pride, and light of his life, he said—this most painful loss was made the more so because of the feeling that Sam was not only responsible for it but had escaped his own death unfairly.

Four months later, on October 3, 1858, in Keokuk, Iowa, the eldest Clemens brother, Orion, sat down to write to a Miss Wood, answering her inquiry about that youngest in the family, deceased. Miss Wood had been on hand in Memphis through the eight days of Henry's mortal agony, "like a good angel," wrote Orion, "to aid and console, and I bless and thank you for it with my whole heart." He told her he wished he could have been the family member who was with Henry when he died, but fate had willed otherwise. Another Clemens brother had been there to grieve helplessly through those final, heart-wrenching nights and days. "Sam, whose organization is such as to feel the utmost extreme of every feeling, was there. Both his capacity of enjoyment," Orion wrote, "and his capacity of suffering are greater than mine; and knowing how it would have affected me to see so sad a scene, I can somewhat appreciate Sam's sufferings."

CHAPTER **Ten**

Urban Upbringing

I n the same month when Orion Clemens wrote to Miss Wood from his Iowa town (although it happened 900 miles east of Keokuk and, in many respects, whole worlds away from the Clemenses), Theodore Roosevelt was born, on October 27, 1858, amid comfort and affluence in New York City. The metropolitan location foreshadows an approaching end to agrarian America's dominance in national affairs, for the infant newly arrived at 28 East Twentieth Street would grow up to become the earliest of our city-born presidents. All twenty-four of the chief executives who preceded Roosevelt had first seen the light of day in country estates, on farms, or in small towns or villages. In addition, beyond the urban fact of his birth, it was Theodore Roosevelt's presidency early in the twentieth century that would first address the less agreeable consequences of an America transformed from its rural beginnings into a newly industrialized, centralized, and corporate nation.

Having arrived at his adulthood, this particular New Yorker of 1858 told Richard Watson Gilder that there was nothing to be said about his early days; "they were absolutely commonplace. It was not until I was sixteen"—as late as 1874—"that I began to show prowess, or even ordinary capacity." But that isn't true. He was a remarkable child born into anything but a commonplace family, and from the beginning Roosevelt's life was far removed from the ordinary. Moreover, his capacity for appreciating the world around him was both precocious and prodigious. So why did the adult dismiss those childhood years?

Matter was in them that he shied away from contemplating. Sam Clemens, born sickly, grew out of his frailty by age eight, whereas Roosevelt— or Teedie, as he was known in the family (all of them had pet names)—was born healthy and "brimming full of mischief," coming into a prolonged illness only when three years old. The illness was asthma, potentially life-threatening and even less well understood then than now. "One of my memories," Roosevelt writes in his *Autobiography* (1913), "is of my father walking up and down the room with me in his arms at night when I was a very small person, and of sitting up in bed gasping, with my father and mother trying to help me." Asthma is a terrifying malady, the afflicted struggling to draw breath, to take in air, terrifying for a tiny sufferer and for helpless witnesses alike. And Teedie's asthma persisted beyond adolescence: cruel, unpredictable visitations that led the child's father to hurry his bundled son on desperate midnight rides in an open carriage in quest of fresh moving air, led his mother to bring the boy with her for extended stays at health spas and cures, searching for relief. There were no inhalants, and no clear understanding of the causes of the ailment: coal dust, all that dust on the heavy furnishings and draperies, the ubiquitous cigars, those pets of all kinds that the Roosevelt children cherished.

To be sure, the attacks came only intermittently, though without warning and with great and prolonged severity. As a child Theodore was slight of build, spindly, understandably timid and fearful. His younger brother Elliott had to defend him against rougher kids when they teased or bullied; and there was one occasion as late as when Teedie was thirteen, traveling alone to Maine, during which rural youngsters his age taunted the well-bred city boy, who in setting about gamely to punish them discovered that those two, one at a time, could hold him off with ease, laughing all the while at his impotent fury.

Such humiliations were rare, however, in part because the four Roosevelt children grew up cosseted at home, in a circumscribed world. The three youngest had for playmates each other, and cousins, and a quite proper neighbor child, Edith Carow, her father their father's friend and Edith thus admitted to the group from a nearby residence. Because of his health, Teedie didn't go to school, was home-tutored instead; so his contacts with people outside his immediate family were limited for the most part to servants, to strangers met briefly in traveling, and to relatives and close friends of his father and mother.

Teedie's mother, Martha Bulloch Roosevelt—or Mittie—was, in her elder son's memory, "a sweet, gracious, beautiful Southern woman, a delightful companion and beloved by everybody. She was entirely 'unreconstructed' to the day of her death"; that is, Mrs. Roosevelt retained a devotion to her native Georgia and its antebellum ways all through the raging Civil War and as long as she lived thereafter. She *was* beautiful—everybody agreed on that—married at eighteen, late in 1853, and taken north for the first time as a bride, to live out her life in the Roosevelts' Yankee household. Mittie it was—devotée of art and music, exile from the graces of a plantation existence—who nourished young Theodore's strong romantic traits, regaling his childhood with stories of life in the slaveholding South, of feuds and duels, of disappearances at sea, of her many colorful relatives out of the pages of Sir Walter Scott, their adventures and valor, their honor and sacrifice. A sample of the boy's appreciation, one of a number from a diary kept when he was ten, was written in Bavaria: "I was verry sick last night"—again with asthma—"and Mama was so kind telling me storrys and rubing me with her delicate fingers."

Both parents were kind, and wise, and devoted to their children. Teedie's father was, flatly, "the best man I ever knew," the son would adjudge from the vantage point of his mid-fifties, after he had met hundreds, thousands of people far and wide and worked closely with many of them. The best man I ever knew: an opinion quite unlike the guarded one that a border-state son expressed of *his* father, the severe, ineffectual John Marshall Clemens of Hannibal, Missouri, who was never heard to laugh, and whose strained relations with son Sam were in the nature of an "armed neutrality." By contrast, the handsome, robust, genial Theodore Roosevelt Sr.—Thee, or Greatheart—"combined strength and courage with gentleness, tenderness, and great unselfishness. He would not tolerate in us children selfishness or cruelty, idleness, cowardice, or untruthfulness. As we grew older he made us understand that the same standard of clean living was demanded for the boys as for the girls; that what was wrong in a woman could not be right in a man. With great love and patience, and the most understanding sympathy and consideration, he combined insistence on discipline. He never physically punished me but once"—for biting sister Bamie—"but he was the only man of whom I was ever really afraid."

The mother, then, inspired in her son romance, imaginativeness, wonder; the father, values and discipline. And in the love-filled household that those two created, the doted-on Teedie grew up possessed of a strong sense of self-worth. It isn't quite true, however, that his father was the only man he ever feared—and that fear, in any case, was qualified: "I do not mean that it was a wrong fear, for he was entirely just, and we children adored him." But there were other people besides his father, and other things, that the younger Roosevelt feared while growing up and even as an adult. Elsewhere he tells us so, and tells us how he overcame those fears. Whether as a tenderfoot set down among jeering ranchhands or as a hunter confronting a grizzly, Roosevelt acted as though he weren't afraid and by doing so—*sounds easy*—was able to put fear behind him.

The values learned from his father, meanwhile, of kindness, selfless-ness, truthfulness, and bravery, included a shunning of idleness. "My fa-ther always excelled in improving every spare half-hour or three-quarters of an hour, whether for work or enjoyment." The son, too, would come to spurn idleness, to an extent that amazed those who knew him. As one means of filling spare time, young Teedie developed into a formidable and very rapid reader, able to concentrate just about anywhere, reading a couple of books an evening in adulthood. But although he read vora-ciously all his life and with a trap-like memory, Roosevelt did much more than read. He crammed his days with activity, with getting things done. Thought and action: both were crucial, and Teedie learned the impor-tance of both from his father.

The same source taught him to enjoy life and to do his duty. "I never knew any one," Roosevelt later wrote, "who got greater joy out of living than did my father, or any one who more whole-heartedly performed ev-ery duty; and no one whom I have ever met approached his combination of enjoyment of life and performance of duty." The elder Roosevelt was a merchant, as his forebears had been merchants on Manhattan Island back nearly to eight generations in the past: for the most part sturdy, generally successful merchants. The earliest of them, a farmer, had come over from Holland as long ago as 1649—Klaes Martenszen van Rosenvelt—when New York was Dutch Nieuw Amsterdam. More than 200 years later, still on Manhattan Island at the time of Theodore Roosevelt Jr.'s birth in the late 1850s, this present father was a partner in the plate-glass importing firm of Roosevelt & Son. The head of the firm was Cornelius Van Schaack Roosevelt, among New York's wealthiest citizens, not just from import-ing plate glass, much in demand in a burgeoning city, but from mining interests, from banking, from insurance, and from real estate holdings on Manhattan and upstate, all of which enterprises the youngest of his five sons, Theodore Sr., had a hand in helping to manage.

Teedie's father was involved in other matters as well. He was a very ac-tive public benefactor: a cofounder of the American Museum of Natural History, of the Metropolitan Museum of Art, of Roosevelt Hospital and the Bellevue Training School for Nurses, a sponsor of the Children's Aid Society and founder of the New York Orthopaedic Dispensary for the De-formed and Crippled. He was, in addition, a warm supporter of the News-boys' Lodging House, every Sunday evening visiting those near-destitute young people, providing them with meals and attending to their other needs: a train ticket here, a shipment of coal to warm a family's dwelling there. In that charitable spirit, Roosevelt & Son included no tenement buildings among its extensive real estate holdings, the family declining to profit from the cramped circumstances of the poor.

Not that the senior Roosevelt was a saintly ascetic. Not at all. For all his good works, Thee lived very well, loved fashionable clothes and furnishings, loved sleek horses and fast riding, loved entertaining lavishly and being entertained. During Teedie's childhood, the family spent their summers in attractive resort locations within range of the city: in New Jersey, in the Adirondacks, along the Hudson, in time on Long Island at Oyster Bay, where the grandfather, old C. V. S. Roosevelt, had acquired a home along with others of the clan. The youngest, Theodore Sr., set his own family up for several summers in a rented home nearby. "We were always wildly eager to get to the country when spring came," his son Teedie grown to adulthood remembered, "and very sad when in the late fall the family moved back to town." In the country the children could run barefoot and have all kinds of pets—"cats, dogs, rabbits, a coon, and a sorrel Shetland pony named General Grant." Out there they watched the seasons pass "in a round of uninterrupted and enthralling pleasures—supervising the haying and harvesting, picking apples, hunting frogs successfully and woodchucks unsuccessfully, gathering hickory-nuts and chestnuts for sale to patient parents, building wigwams in the woods." The children's play was enlivened (as was Tom Sawyer's) by their reading tastes, especially by Teedie's love of adventure tales: *The Last of the Mohicans*, Scott's novels, Marryat's *Midshipman Easy*.

That older of the two boys, eldest of the three who played together, became their natural leader, the most widely read, the most articulate, the most active. The younger ones—his brother Elliott (Ellie) and his sister Corinne (Coney)—looked up to Teedie from an early age. The remaining sister, Anna (Bamie), was four years older than Teedie and thus always more of an adult, more often grouped with her parents than with the younger siblings. Yet she, like the other children, like the father and mother, adored Theodore, when he was young and throughout his life. Elliott, too, as a child became more than a brother—was Teedie's principal competitor, his goal-setter, and his best friend.

Early on, young Theodore Roosevelt's ever-active mind, while steeping itself in history and literature, grew interested in natural science: in those frogs that the children hunted, in snakes, in mice, which the boy kept as pets, naming them ("Lordy," "Rosa"), sketching them with precision, carrying them in his pockets, allowing them to run over him as he lay in bed at night. The interest deepened into obsession; so that even in youth Teedie became a gifted amateur ornithologist, with the various birds in his region classified in notebooks by their Latin names. He graduated into mastering the smelly, messy business of taxidermy, receiving instruction in a shop nearby that was run by a friend of Audubon's. "My father and mother encouraged me warmly in this, as they always did in anything that could give me wholesome pleasure or help to develop me." Game to study was abundantly on the wing back then, when an essential tool for such a pursuit was the shotgun. Young Roosevelt was given a shotgun and took to hunting, emulating his uncles down South, about whose exploits in quest of bear and wildcat—the ritualistic going forth, the kill, the triumphant return—he had relished hearing of at his mother's knee.

Teedie's younger brother and cousins would go hunting with him. At one point the boys were firing at targets together, "and it puzzled me to find that my companions seemed to see things to shoot at which I could not see at all." They read aloud words in large print on a distant billboard, but Teedie could barely make out the billboard, let alone any words. He told his father about it and—this late in his development—was fitted with glasses. The glasses "literally opened an entirely new world to me. I had no idea how beautiful the world was until I got those spectacles. I had been a clumsy and awkward little boy, and while much of my clumsiness and awkwardness was doubtless due to general characteristics, a good deal of it was due to the fact that I could not see and yet was wholly ignorant that I was not seeing."

Until as late as age thirteen that crucial enlightenment had been withheld. The fact may help explain a dismissal, by the adult whom the boy grew into, of his childhood years as not worth consideration. His *Autobiography* implies that Roosevelt had more or less stumbled awkwardly through those early years, a nervous, shy youngster condemned by nearsightedness to learn no more than what was underfoot or close at hand, all the while hampered not only by impaired vision but frequently by headaches, diarrhea, and those crushing bouts of asthma.

One other shadow fell across what, for all that, were often supremely happy times in Theodore Roosevelt's childhood. He would have been too young to be bothered by it then; but, according to his sisters, it bothered him later, deeply. He was only six when the Civil War ended, in the spring of 1865. During that conflict his able-bodied father—twenty-nine at its commencement—had declined to serve his country in uniform. His wife, Mittie, as well as her sister and mother—who had come North and were living in the Roosevelt household—all three much-loved family members stayed loyal to the Confederate cause; and it would have killed Mittie, the delicate, beautiful Mittie, "for him to fight against her brothers." The two Bulloch brothers, among numerous other Georgia relatives, had enlisted down South, Teedie's Uncle Jimmie as a captain in the Confederate navy, the other brother, Irvine, as a midshipman in his early twenties who served at sea aboard the *Alabama*. Accordingly, Thee up North—rather than wage war against brothers-in-law—purchased substitutes to go in his stead, a common practice that wealthy gentlemen resorted to. The senior Roosevelt paid what would amount to over $10,000 now and kept out of the fighting. Instead, he chose to help Union soldiers' families, shorthanded and sometimes destitute in the absence of their men in uniform. Thee arranged for a portion of the soldiers' earnings to be sent to their loved ones. It was noble work, humanitarian work; but it was not directly answering the President's call for volunteers. It was not serving the Union on the battle lines; and in a sense, Thee's son, Theodore Roosevelt Jr., would spend his own life striving to atone for his father's dereliction.

With the Civil War ended and the Union blockade of the Confederacy lifted, Atlantic sea lanes were opened at last for the resumption of civilian travel; and among affluent inhabitants along the eastern seaboard a vogue set in to venture abroad to behold the wonders of the Old World that four years of civil conflict had put beyond reach. There was more money up north from the profits of war in any case; so that when, in the spring of 1869, the Roosevelt family departed on a yearlong excursion in Europe, they were doing nothing out of the ordinary for people of their class and circumstances.

Bamie—Anna—was fourteen; Teedie was ten; Elliott was nine; and the youngest child, Corinne, was seven. "I do not think I gained anything from this particular trip abroad," Roosevelt declared in later years. "I cordially hated it, as did my younger brother and sister." The family had sailed from New York aboard the *Scotia* bound for England, where Mrs. Roosevelt's brother and half-brother, James and Irvine, were living in exile, former Confederate naval officers as yet unpardoned. On May 22, 1869, Teedie writes in his journal: "Liverpool. We saw our cousins to day and ran round the hotel with them." Those were the children of Captain James D. Bulloch, who during the war had successfully smuggled weapons from England through the Union blockade and overseen the building of the *Alabama*, Confederate raider that in two years sank or captured some sixty Yankee vessels at sea. "We ran about and once when we jumped on a wall it nearly broke. They live at Waterloo about 5 miles from here." Next day, Sunday in Liverpool, May 23: "We went to church and had a walk. We went to church with the Sears one of whom will be married to Uncle Irving. We walked in the Princes and Botanist park"—ten-year-old Teedie conscientiously recording this start of his yearlong European tribulation, for the first time far from home and determined to make the best of it.

CHAPTER Eleven

Clemens Goes West

Within a year of the boiler explosion on the Mississippi that killed his brother Henry in 1858, Samuel L. Clemens earned his pilot's certificate. "Time drifted smoothly and prosperously on," he wrote later, looking back at twenty-four contented months as a well-paid, full-fledged steamboat pilot, "and I supposed—and hoped—that I was going to follow the river the rest of my days, and die at the wheel when my mission was ended."

Then the war came, in April 1861. Federals and Confederates both moved to control the Mississippi, shutting off peacetime traffic on the river. Clemens's piloting days were cut short by the Civil War, in which conflict he was to play a decidedly unheroic part. In New Orleans when Louisiana seceded, he returned to Missouri and in Hannibal, in June of that tempestuous year, joined a local group of Confederate militia. But two weeks of campaigning in Missouri woods were enough for Second Lieutenant Clemens, who therewith resigned, joking later that "I was 'incapacitated by fatigue' through persistent retreating." The rest of the war he spent far away from the fighting.

His brother Orion had been appointed secretary of the Nevada Territory. Sam offered to pay for the journey west if the elder Clemens, always in financial need, would let him come along as the secretary's secretary. Thus on a Saturday morning in July 1861, at St. Joseph, Missouri, the two boarded a stagecoach at the start of a 1,700-mile journey across unsettled America to the Nevada territorial capital of Carson City. Sam was jubilant. This perpetual adolescent loved the gypsy-like leaving behind of responsibilities, the confronting of new adventures, new people, with no remorse yet and so far no regrets. Moreover, ever since his youthful days in Hannibal, when as a thirteen-year-old he had watched eighty townsmen start for

California's newly discovered gold fields, Sam longed to know what lay out there toward the sunset. Now he would see the fabled West himself, the driver cracking his whip as the Clemenses settled back among mail sacks in the great swaying stagecoach. Soon they were bowling along the plains that stretched flat ahead for 700 miles, and Sam was feeling, he said, "a tranquil and contented ecstasy," puffing his pipe and watching the curtains flap, hearing the driver calling "Hi-yi! g'lang!"—in the midst of what he judged to be the "one complete and satisfying happiness in the world."

The brothers had stumbled on bliss just as an era was ending, although neither suspected as much, sitting up craning to look for the pony-express rider due to pass by any minute. All earthly romance would be riding on a lightweight saddle out there, horseman hunched over and speeding like the wind, fifty miles through daylight and darkness, bearing letters that traveled over 1,900 miles in only eight days! None but important messages on tissue-thin paper strapped to his thigh— But HERE HE COMES!

Black speck far off growing larger, horse and horseman "rising and falling, rising and falling," hoof sounds closer, until in a moment "a whoop and a hurrah from our upper deck, a wave of the rider's hand, but no reply, and man and horse burst past our excited faces and go winging away like a belated fragment of a storm!"—so abruptly come and gone that, "but for the flake of white foam left quivering and perishing on a mail-sack," the passengers might have doubted seeing the apparition at all.

These present days of romance will be almost as fleeting. A mere two months from now, in October 1861, the first transcontinental telegraph line will open, ending the need for the pony express after no more than a year and a half of its picturesque service. And just a few weeks ago, on June 28, with Second Lieutenant Clemens camped out in the Missouri woods, the Central Pacific Railroad had been incorporated in Sacramento, Leland Stanford president, Collis P. Huntington vice president; so that a brief eight years from now, at Promontory Summit in Utah Territory, tracks of that same Central Pacific will have edged eastward and met those of the Union Pacific pressing westward. Celebrants at the junction will tap in a Golden Spike on May 10, 1869 (two days before the Roosevelts sail on Teedie's first voyage to Europe), and almost everything in America will change, the pace of the frontier gone forever, leaving as memories images of a pony-express rider hunched at the point of a lengthening dust cloud and a stagecoach rumbling westward toward Nevada, two brothers inside, the younger contentedly puffing his pipe and scanning "the world-wide carpet about us for things new and strange to gaze at."

Figure 11.1.   Completion of the transcontinental railroad, Promontory Summit, Utah, May 10, 1869.
Courtesy of the Library of Congress.

In mid-August they reached Carson City. Sam had planned to spend three months out there—until the war was over—observing the Wild West as he had observed New York's Crystal Palace and Philadelphia's Liberty Bell, a spectator writing occasional travel letters for (in this case) the *Keokuk Gate City* back home. But by chance the Clemenses arrived in Nevada around the time that a silver strike had opened up the Comstock Lode, with silver mining soon in full swing. A few more years and big money would take over, providing the capital needed to get at deeper veins; then miners would work for mineowners or not at all. But just now, when lone prospectors could scrabble for shallow veins and placer ore, hordes with their pans and sieves had swarmed into the region. "Joy sat on every countenance," Clemens later recalled, "and there was a glad, almost fierce, intensity in every eye, that told of the money-getting schemes that were seething in every brain and the high hope that held sway in every heart." Everybody was either rich or soon going to be, "and a melancholy countenance was nowhere to be seen."

Sam shared the general frenzy. He had known poverty after his father's death, and from riverboat days he knew what it was to be well-off. Of course the Clemenses owned that Tennessee land, which would make them all rich at last; but for now, with his brother set up as secretary of the Nevada Territory, Sam ventured into the hills to gather a present fortune mining for silver.

He kept at it a year, working hard and getting his hands dirty. "Stint yourself as much as possible," he told his brother in Carson City, "and lay up $100 or $150, subject to my call. I go to work to-morrow with pick and shovel"—and wouldn't stop until he had silver in hand. "I shall never look upon Ma's face again," Sam vowed, "or Pamela's, or get married, or revisit the 'Banner State,' until I am a rich man." And on a couple of occasions it seemed it might happen. Deep into the night Sam lay awake musing on how to spend his wealth—go to Europe, buy a mansion on Nob Hill—only to have those fancies disappear in daylight. To Orion from Esmeralda, on May 11, 1862: "Two years' time will make us capitalists, in spite of everything." But more weeks passed and still no strike, and funds were about gone, with debts to pay. "The fact is," he wrote at the end of July, "I must have something to do, and that *shortly*, too."

What he found to do proved the professional making of Sam Clemens. Already, when holed up in mining cabins on rainy days, he had scribbled humorous letters and sent them around to newspapers. The *Territorial Enterprise* in Virginia City, Nevada's liveliest paper in a lively, rowdy silver town, had published a few. In September 1862 Clemens was invited to join the staff of the *Enterprise* as a reporter at six dollars a day. He did, and the experience turned him into a full-time journalist. He worked at the *Enterprise* twenty months, until May 1864, and took to it heartily. "Those were the days!—those old ones," he exclaimed many years later, looking over a list of names of fellow Nevada pioneers: Goodman, McCarthy, Gillis, and the others. Those days! "They were so full to the brim with the wine of life; there have been no others like them."

In part, Sam relished the wine that fate had poured out for him because of the town. Three years old, Virginia City already had 10,000 people in it, mostly a man's world at that lofty altitude, and a young one, full of high hopes and spirits raring for fun. So some of the appeal was the town itself, but part was the people inside and outside the *Enterprise* office. Clemens's coworkers at the newspaper were as young as or younger than he (about to turn twenty-seven), and everybody in this hardworking, hard-drinking, profane, poker-playing, and surprisingly talented community seemed to share his enthusiasm. Gifted at mingling, the new hire got along fine with most of those rowdy fellows, reporters on rival newspapers not excepted.

The town and the rambunctious people appealed to him, but the work did too. Sam knew the printing trade well enough to be at ease from the start. He could speak the print-shop lingo, as he had earlier mastered the lingo of the Mississippi riverboat world and more recently that of the Nevada silver mines. His forcible diction he took down to Carson City, thirty miles away, to cover sessions of the territorial legislature, and from there wrote back news copy and lampoons. From Carson City, for instance, early in the new year he filed a feature that described nothing more than a recent party in the capital, humorously portrayed. The piece was forgettable except for one line at the last: signed "Yours, dreamily, MARK TWAIN." In the *Enterprise* thus, on February 3, 1863, appears the earliest surviving use of a pen name—out of riverboat days, the cry to the pilot from a leadsman on the bow plumbing depth of water ahead: mark two fathoms deep, twelve feet, safe water—a pen name destined to become the most famous in American letters.

In Nevada and soon over the Sierras in California, amusing articles started appearing above the odd new spondee signature. People got to recognize it and look for it. "Everybody knows me," Sam wrote home to his family, "& I fare like a prince wherever I go, be it on this side of the mountains or the other." In time he would cross those mountains and leave Virginia City for good. "I began to get tired of staying in one place so long," was one explanation he gave for the departure. "I wanted to go somewhere. I wanted—I did not know *what* I wanted. I had the 'spring fever' and wanted a change, principally, no doubt."

Already well thought of in California, Clemens spent nearly two years there, from this May of 1864 to March 1866. For four months he did routine reporting in San Francisco and hated it: anonymous labor over long, late hours. Then he freelanced to earn money, during a dreary interlude in a life relearning how it felt to be hungry, as Clemens found himself slinking down San Francisco side streets to avoid a growing list of creditors.

Late in 1864 he left the city and took to the Tuolumne Hills, east in the direction of Yosemite, living with chums in a cabin up there for three months and poking around for gold. At some point, at nearby Angel's Camp, the idlers heard Ben Coon tell his jumping-frog story; and by February 1865, Clemens was back in San Francisco bearing that verbal treasure. He wrote the story up and mailed it east, where it was published in the New York *Saturday Press* in mid-November—although not before well into the new year did the author come across a notice in the San Francisco *Alta California* that his Jumping Frog sketch was setting "all New York in a roar."

Sam's luck appeared to be turning, as it had already taken a turn upward late in 1865, spectacularly. At last a buyer had come forward to purchase the Clemenses' Tennessee land. Herman Camp offered $200,000—millions in our terms—to buy a good chunk and clear it, plant grapes on it, bring European grape growers over, and out of the mild air and hilly southern soil make vineyards flourish. Sam signed the papers and sent them on to his brother. One more signature would make a newspaperman growing famous grow rich as well. For, precisely now, in late December 1865, the freelancing Sam was very poor—poor enough to have written bleakly to Orion's wife: "If I do not get out of debt in 3 months,—pistols or poisons for one—exit *me*."

But Mollie Clemens's husband refused to sign the contract. Thrown out of a job when Nevada became a state late in 1864, with no clients at his new bare law office, the hyperidealistic Orion, even worse off than was Sam, nevertheless wouldn't sign. "The temperance virtue was temporarily upon him in strong force," the younger Clemens later explained, and thus Orion wouldn't be a party to debauching a nation by abetting the planting of vineyards.

So the deal fell through. The land that for a moment was worth $200,000 returned to being worth nothing at all, with taxes to pay on it. As soon as he could, and in high dudgeon, Sam Clemens left California on the steamer *Ajax* bound even farther west, across an ocean 2,400 miles to the Sandwich Islands. He arrived at his destination in mid-March 1866, and there two months later was still brooding over his brother's not sign-ing the papers. Sam had come to these outskirts, these faraway Sandwich Islands—the largest one Hawaii—having persuaded the *Sacramento Daily Union* to pay him to write more of his informative travel letters. And he was working hard. Moreover, despite grumbling about Orion (about his brother's "slow, stupid" ways, his "eternal cant about law & religion," the prayers he insisted on sending along), despite saddle boils from the mule-back riding, despite the discomforts attendant on four months of rugged tracks and primitive accommodations, Sam was soon having a wonderful time. "It has been," he summarized, "a perfect jubilee to me in the way of pleasure." And from all that exotic experience he crafted twenty-five letters at $20 apiece on a region of great interest to Californians.

The letters were laced with Mark Twain's humor. For their author had come to terms with his fate, only this late discovering a profession. Sam Clemens was not to be a printer after all, or a riverboat pilot, or a silver miner, or a newspaperman. "But I *have* had a 'call' to literature," he had confided to Orion last fall: to literature "of a low order—*i.e.* humorous. It is nothing to be proud of, but it is my strongest suit." Long ago, he now realized, he should have stopped meddling "with things for which I was by nature unfitted & turned my attention to seriously scribbling to excite the *laughter* of God's creatures." That would have to furnish his livelihood; and exciting the laughter of God's people may have been purpose enough for now, as he discovered on returning to San Francisco toward summer's end.

Those letters from the Sandwich Islands, by the author of "Jim Smiley and His Jumping Frog," had proved popular, picked up from the *Sacramento Union* by newspapers elsewhere in California and throughout the mainland West. In his absence Mark Twain's fame had continued to rise. But however satisfying such fame might be, Sam hated coming ashore, jotting in his jour-nal on landing: "Aug 13—San Francisco—Home again. No—*not* home again—in prison again—and all the wild sense of freedom gone. The city seems so cramped, & so dreary with toil & care & business anxiety."

He would hurry back to St. Louis for an overdue visit with his family, then maybe set out on a voyage to China before pushing ever farther west, around the world, writing more travel letters to subsidize a grand, earth-encircling odyssey.

But a different opportunity offered, right there in San Francisco. Lectures were popular then, and interest in all things Hawaiian high. Sam had spoken informally before a few groups earlier; maybe he ought to take a stab at giving a humorous, instructive talk on the Sandwich Islands. He put himself in debt to rent a hall, run advertisements in the newspapers, and have handbills printed and posted. "The trouble begins at 8 o'clock," the handbills read; and soon after eight on Tuesday evening, October 2, 1866, Mark Twain emerged on stage at the Academy of Music, looking bewildered at the audience as though uncertain of why he was there. He lit a cigar.

Later he insisted that for the first full minute he was terrified, so much so that it cured him ever after of stage fright. But he need not have worried. The lecture was a smashing success. Before Mark Twain even opened his mouth—just standing on stage puffing the cigar and looking confused—his audience broke into laughter and wild applause; and when he did start speaking in that dry, drawling way of his, with never a hint that he knew he was funny, his listeners' enjoyment was uncontained. He gazed in puzzlement. Next day the San Francisco papers trumpeted his triumph: "one of the most interesting and amusing lectures ever given in this city"; "valuable information and eloquent description"; "side-splitting similes, grotesque imagery, and fearfully ludicrous stories"; in short, "a hit, a great hit." Suddenly Mark Twain the journalist was also Mark Twain the lecturer, setting off on a profitable five-week lecture tour to Marysville, Grass Valley, Red Dog, You Bet, Gold Hill. And everywhere he went he brought laughter with him.

But would such frontier humor play back east? Coming west meaning to stay three months, Sam Clemens had watched five and a half years slip by. In the nation's new peace he wondered whether audiences in New York and Boston could be persuaded to take to this Wild Humorist of the Pacific Slope. Thus, on December 15, 1866, Samuel L. Clemens, "Mark Twain," boarded the steamer *America* bound southward to Nicaragua, his name listed first on the manifest. The voyage before him would prove storm-tossed and cholera-ridden, with death on board on the Atlantic passage northward; but finally Clemens reached wintry Manhattan early on a January morning in 1867.

And despite shipboard terrors, he stepped ashore eager to sail forth again. Voyages to and from the Sandwich Islands had provided his first experience of ocean-going life, and he had loved it. At sea were leisure, freedom, a sense of adventure; whereas on shore were chores and a livelihood to grovel for. Now in New York, he did accept his current obligations, dutifully reporting to *Alta California* readers through seventeen additional letters and arranging for the publication of a first book: *The Celebrated Jumping Frog of Calaveras County and Other Sketches*. In March, still busy, he boarded a train for St. Louis to visit a month—the first such in six years—with his family. But Sam met with discontents going home, the city in the wake of war much altered and old friends changed or departed. In St. Louis he lectured twice, before taking the steamboat up the Mississippi to perform at earlier haunts in Hannibal and Keokuk.

Yet, as always, he was fidgety. In late February, before leaving New York for St. Louis, Clemens had told his California readers of the Reverend Henry Ward Beecher's plan to accompany flush members of his Brooklyn congregation on a leisurely excursion in June aboard a chartered steamer to the Holy Land. "Isn't it a most attractive scheme?" the *Alta* correspondent wrote in envy. "Five months of utter freedom from care and anxiety of every kind." Clemens longed to go with them. Suppose he agreed to write letters back; would his San Francisco employers indulge him? And indeed, on returning from the Midwest in April, Sam was greeted by the *Alta California*'s New York agent bearing a check that covered the hefty fare for the cruise on the *Quaker City*.

Meanwhile, much remained to do on land. On May 6 Mark Twain lectured before 2,000 New Yorkers at Peter Cooper's Institute at Astor Place, where Lincoln had delivered a pivotal speech to launch his national campaign for the presidency seven years before. As on the earlier occasion, the press approved this later talk ("seldom," according to the *New York Times*, "has so large an audience been so uniformly pleased as the one that listened to Mark Twain's quaint remarks last evening"). His cobbled-together book of sketches appeared that same May to disappointing sales, but its mere existence enhanced a western humorist's eastern reputation. In addition, he wrote the last of the onshore *Alta* letters for California readers.

All the while he was chafing to get under way. "All that I know or feel," he wrote as June 1867 arrived, "is, that I am wild with impatience to move—move—*Move*! Half a dozen times I have wished I had sailed long ago." He wanted, he said, never to stay *any*where longer than one month, because as soon as he stopped moving he did more mean things than he could be forgiven for. "I am so worthless," he wrote to his family back in St. Louis on June 7, just before setting out, "that it seems to me I never can do anything or accomplish anything that lingers in my mind as a pleasant memory. My mind is stored full of unworthy conduct toward Orion & toward you all, & an accusing conscience gives me peace only in excitement & restless moving from place to place." Only under way did this penitent feel absolved of guilt; "& so, with my parting love & benediction for Orion & all of you, I say good bye & God bless you all—& welcome the wind that wafts a weary soul to the sunny lands of the Mediterranean!"

CHAPTER Twelve

Grand Tours

The *Quaker City* steered out toward sea the following afternoon, June 8, 1867. For Clemens, the cruise and its immediate aftermath amounted to life-changing experiences: five months afloat and at ports in the Mediterranean, across the Holy Land to Jersualem, and back via Egypt, Spain, and Bermuda, before once more heaving in sight of the East River piers in mid-November. Through it all the journalist wrote travel letters, many published with the voyage still under way, letters providing not so much a guide to Europe as an account of how one American reacted afresh to Old World scenes that the guidebooks eulogized, recording his often contrarian views in candor, good humor, and high spirits.

In old age, in the last article he ever published, Mark Twain remembered arriving back in America aboard the *Quaker City* those forty-two years earlier to discover a professional opportunity "waiting on the pier—with the *last* link" in a chain that contained the turning points of his life. "I was asked to *write a book*, and I did it." The opportunity was not exactly waiting on the pier; but the Hartford publisher Elisha Bliss did approach this wanderer a couple of days after his return from overseas. Someone even more important than Bliss was about to enter Samuel Clemens's life, though. On New Year's Day of 1868, Sam set out to make a series of social calls, as was the New York custom, stopping first at the Berrys' on West Forty-Fourth Street. He got no farther. "Charlie Langdon's sister was there (beautiful girl,) & Miss Alice Hooker, another beautiful girl, a niece of Henry Ward Beecher's. We sent the old folks home early, with instructions not to send the carriage till midnight, & then I just staid there & deviled the life out of those girls. I am going to spend a few days with the Langdon's," he exulted shortly afterward to his family back home, "in Elmira, New York, as soon as I get time."

Seven and a half months passed before Clemens visited Elmira, in August 1868. What took so long? For one thing, Olivia Langdon was ill with diphtheria during a part of that time. And maybe Sam was awed, as he later told Livy. "I did have such a struggle, the first day I saw you at the St Nicholas," he confessed in January 1869, remembering those meetings in the city the year before, "to keep from loving you with *all* my heart! But you seemed to my bewildered vision, a visiting *Spirit* from the upper air—a something to *worship*, reverently & at a distance—& *not* a creature of common human clay, to be profaned by the *love* of such as I." While the *Quaker City* had been anchored last fall in far-off Smyrna Bay, in Ottoman Turkey, a fellow passenger, eighteen-year-old Charley Langdon, had shown a miniature of his sister to his shipboard friend; later Clemens professed to have fallen in love with the image on the spot. Fresh from the West Coast, not unimpressed by young Langdon's wealth and eastern aplomb, all the while eager to smooth off his own rough edges, Sam may well have felt a bit cowed at the end of the voyage when he met the beautiful sister at last, although not so much at the Berrys' on their second meeting as to keep him from deviling the life out of Miss Langdon and her friend Miss Hooker right up to midnight of New Year's Day.

More likely than diffidence in explaining the long delay was the fact that during this first half of 1868 Clemens was busy putting together a live-lihood. The *Quaker City* had returned to New York on November 19, 1867. Two days later, Elisha Bliss in Hartford, Connecticut, wrote to Samuel L. Clemens, Esq.: "We are desirous of obtaining from you a work of some kind, perhaps compiled from your letters from the East, &c., with such interesting additions as may be proper." Even more arresting information followed. Bliss's American Publishing Company flattered itself that "we can give an author as favorable terms and do as full justice to his produc-tions as any other house in the country." In fact, we "have never failed to give a book an immense circulation."

Clemens answered as soon as he could, describing how he might turn the fifty-two letters written aboard the *Quaker City* into an entertaining travel narrative. "If you think such a book would suit your purpose, please drop me a line," being sure to specify "what amount of money I might pos-sibly make out of it. The latter clause," admitted this ex-silver miner, still hoping for a strike, "has a degree of importance for me which is almost beyond my own comprehension."

About money, Bliss could speak reassuringly, for his American Pub-lishing Company was a subscription publisher. Conventional publishers sold books in bookstores, limiting their initial printings to maybe 5,000 copies. Subscription publishers sold to the many readers in nineteenth-century America out of range of bookstores. Canvassers bearing samples of a new title would call door to door in towns and villages and persuade readers one by one to sign up for the book described, to be delivered as soon as it was ready. That way the sales force might gather as many as 30,000 or 40,000 names of subscribers signed on to buy a title before the book had even been bound. Conventional publishers looked down their noses at that kind of aggressive marketing; but for Sam Clemens of Hannibal, Missouri, publishing by subscription offered, in addition to higher profits, a readership not of the urban few but the rural many—his kind of people, he insisted, who were without access to books otherwise.

To meet Mr. Bliss, Clemens hurried to Hartford and soon could tell the folks back home of having "made a splendid contract for a Quaker City book of 5 or 600 large pages, with illustrations, the manuscript to be placed in the publishers' hands by the middle of July," scarcely six months off. Yet writing such a book proved harder than putting together sketches or letters. The author wearied of his task long before it was over; yet he did get it done and did it very well—so well that *The Innocents Abroad; or, The Modern Pilgrims' Progress* would gain instant popularity when published and remains to this day the most read and loved travel book ever written by an American, still very funny and crammed with zestful life on page after page.

Clemens of course could know nothing of so bright a literary future when he delivered his manuscript to Bliss in Hartford. And the following month, on a late Friday evening, August 21, 1868, this budding author of a full-fledged book finally reached Elmira.

Within the Langdons' brownstone mansion in a mid–New York town just over the Pennsylvania border, Clemens was introduced to those of his shipmate Charley's wealthy family whom he had not met earlier in Manhattan; and in Elmira he spent a couple of weeks with them all—the happiest fortnight of his life till then—in the course of which he professed his love for Charley's twenty-two-year-old sister Olivia. She would come to love him too, although it took a while. On three occasions that fall he proposed marriage to Miss Langdon; each time she turned him down. But when, in November, Livy at last accepted Mr. Clemens's proposal, she did so ardently, from then on pampering her lover with "affections in kisses and caresses and in a vocabulary of endearments whose profusion was always an astonishment to me." Such unrestrained outpourings were something new; in Hannibal, that non-kissing village, the late, stern Judge Clemens had left behind a family ill-practiced in expressing affection. Livy taught

Figure 12.1.   Olivia Langdon Clemens. Photograph by H. L. Bundy of Hartford, Connecticut,
c. 1873.
Courtesy of the Mark Twain House & Museum, Hartford.

Sam how. Through the fall and winter season of 1868–1869, and again
the following year, he would be away earning his living delivering lectures;
but the absences provided occasions for developing fluency in matters of
the heart. From far-flung hotel rooms across the Northeast, Sam wrote his
beloved daily. As a sample, on March 6, 1869, from Hartford: "Livy dear,
I have already mailed to-day's letter, but I am so proud of my privilege of
writing the dearest girl in the world whenever I please, that I must add a few
lines if only to say I *love* you, Livy. For I *do* love you, Livy—as the dew loves
the flowers; as the birds love the sunshine; as the wavelets love the breeze
. . ." And on in that vein through several pages, Livy for her part treasuring
whatever her suitor chose to write and faithfully answering it all.

Her parents had come to love Sam too. Their precious daughter confessed her love for the newcomer in November 1868. In days ahead Jervis
Langdon as well—that self-made Pennsylvania coal and lumber baron—
grew to care deeply for "Youth," as he called Sam. Both parents cared for

him. For his part, Clemens had been working hard all this while to make himself worthy of such company. He stopped swearing and gave up spiritous liquors. He read his Bible. He even prayed, or for Livy's sake tried to. The East made him conscious of his rough, raw western ways; so that aboard the *Quaker City*, as far back as then, a lady passenger a few years older had been helping him bear himself more like a gentleman. Now, in 1869, with proofs of the new travel book arrived and Clemens—his seasonal lecture tour completed—returned to Elmira that spring, his betrothed was helping as well. Through a couple of weeks the lovers pored over galley pages together, Livy's suggestions making Sam's prose more acceptable to the eastern audience he coveted, to those genteel American families he could picture gathering around their firesides of an evening to read aloud the flavor and fun of the *Quaker City* pleasure cruise that his book memorialized.

The Innocents Abroad was well subscribed for before publication in July 1869, sold briskly afterward (in its first two years nearly 70,000 copies, with the author collecting nineteen cents a copy), and would go on to make Mark Twain the most popular writer in America. Jervis Langdon, meanwhile, had helped his future son-in-law purchase one-third ownership of a newspaper in Buffalo, where Sam upon marrying was to earn an easy, respectable living as editor and co-proprietor of the *Buffalo Express*. But beyond even that, most important of all, Livy loved him—an all but inexplicable fact that humbled the Missourian and filled him with gratitude.

The wedding took place on Wednesday evening, February 2, 1870, in Elmira, in the Langdons' parlor. The following day the wedding party proceeded by palace car to Buffalo, three hours away. A rooming house had been found for the newlyweds; so on reaching the depot, family and guests set off in one sleigh for that destination, the bride and groom following in a sleigh of their own.

But the driver of the bridal sleigh had trouble finding the house. To Clemens's annoyance he glided over Buffalo byways until at last pulling tardily up before a mansion on Delaware Avenue. This couldn't be right—gazing upon a home far too fashionable to be renting out rooms. Then the front door opened. There in the foyer stood the wedding party, beaming; and thus the secret came out, one kept from Sam off at his lecturing all these months. This beautiful mansion was a gift of the Langdons, decorated at Livy's direction, complete with cook and housemaid, a carriage, and a liveried coachman who would remain a devoted servant of the Clemenses for the next twenty years. Sam's father-in-law was handing over the deed to the place and a sum of money to cover initial operating expenses, the whole worth $48,000 (maybe $800,000 now), while the tearful groom, overwhelmed, managed a lighthearted response to such astounding largesse:

"Mr. Langdon, whenever you are in Buffalo, if it's twice a year, come right up here, and bring your bag with you. You may stay overnight if you want to. *It shan't cost you a cent.*"

Three months after that fairy-tale moment, the now eleven-year-old Teedie Roosevelt—on the other side of New York State—returned, in May 1870, from his own first excursion overseas. His family had been gone precisely one year, the year that Theodore in adulthood recalled having cordially hated. Yet a diary that the boy kept through those twelve months reveals a young person not only of quite impressive curiosity, observant and plucky, but one who strived to make the best of each experience. From Liverpool: "We went to Waterloo to day. We played on the beach and in the yard and had fine fun." Five days on, riding donkeys with the children's cousins nearby at Southport: "We had great fun for they galloped so funnily and it was so nice." At York two weeks further along: "We had a row down the river ouse for 2 miles. It was great fun. Ellie and I rowed." The three children romped in parks, gardens, and hotel corridors; visited museums and a dungeon and a couple of zoos; and had jolly fun extemporizing games and teasing chambermaids. And Teedie's pages record the occasional contented judgment concerning his family: "Bamie is such a kind sister and I have such kind parents"; or this, on October 1, 1869, in Vienna: "At an artificial fountain Mama climbed up on hands and knees to get a drink. We walked up to a temple (so called) and came down through the woods. In three places it was so steep that I could slide down it. Papa, Mama, and Bamie went to an opera and Father was more handsome than I ever saw him."

Still, Teedie remained a child through it all, far from home and not very sturdy. In November, illness had confined him to his hotel room for six days, "a verry dull time." Soon afterward, "I was expecting a sociable evening and Mama tried to make it so but Papa effectuly stoped it by telling me of a french friend which I must have when we come back to Paris and when I went to bed (in Dijon) I cried for homesickness and a wish to get out of the land where friends (or as I think them enemies) who can not speak my language are forced on me." His illnesses recurred: headaches, toothaches, upset stomach, severe asthma attacks. So by the end he was overjoyed to be home, as no doubt all of them were. They had gazed on numberless sights, stayed in more than eighty hotels, and traveled several thousand miles in every conceivable conveyance. Once more at sea, west-bound at last on May 23, 1870, the by then fretful children "had a real fight in the morning but made it up and had a game of tag and hide and go seek." Then, two days later: "This morning we saw land of America and swiftly coming on passed Sandey hook and went in to the bay. New York!!! Hip! Hurrah! What a bustle we had geting off."

In Manhattan finally, Teedie was once more set to his home schooling, in French and other subjects. Then, during the course of the following year, 1871, the family patriarch, old C. V. S. Roosevelt, died, leaving an estate of around $7 million to be divided among his several sons. Theodore Roosevelt Sr. would find an already sizable fortune increased substantially, so that the now very wealthy humanitarian was soon making plans to move his family farther uptown, from Twentieth Street to Fifty-Seventh, to a lot just southwest of Central Park, on which he would erect a mansion close by the hills that were being leveled in that new, upscale section of the city.

Meanwhile, during this present busy interval ashore, father took son aside. According to sister Corinne, writing later, Theodore Jr. was charged with building up his physique. The boy possessed the mind but not the body, his father told him, "and without the help of the body the mind cannot go as far as it should. You must make your body. It is hard drudgery to make one's body, but I know you will do it."

Teedie at thirteen took on the challenge with a will. He attended a gym, Mittie coming along, and back home started working with exercise equipment installed on a second-floor piazza. Corinne watched her brother out there hoisting himself on the horizontal bars hour after hour, day after day. The task required enormous discipline, but discipline was a quality that Roosevelt possessed in abundance all his life. He set out on horseback rides, rowed whenever he had the chance, hiked, took up wrestling and boxing, and returned relentlessly to the dumbbells in the upstairs gym, relentlessly to the bars and to the punching bag.

The exercise had other benefits, but it didn't cure his asthma. Maybe a second trip abroad would help, including extended visits to the dry air of Egypt and the Holy Land. Thus in October 1872, a couple of years after returning from their first European excursion, the Roosevelts, along with their horde of servants and battery of steamer trunks, boarded the *Russia* to spend another year and longer traveling overseas. For young Theodore, who was to celebrate his fourteenth birthday in Liverpool, this trip, in contrast to the first, formed, he said, "a really useful part of my education"—two months of it sheer joy spent on the Nile, ascending by luxurious houseboat as far as Aswan and back, a leisurely thousand miles in all. The whole family loved that protracted adventure, children and parents alike—loved the heartstirring land of antiquity from the beginning. "How I gazed on it!" Teedie recorded of his initial sight of Alexandria. "It was Egypt, the land of my dreams; Egypt, the most ancient of all countries! A land that was old when Rome was bright, was old when Babylon was in its glory, was old when Troy was taken!" In December 1872 the family boarded a commodious *dahabeah*, amply supplied and waited on, to ascend the Nile, going ashore on donkeyback to see wonders along the way.

For an aspiring naturalist, the country was paradise. Wildlife was everywhere, especially the birds: snipe, plover, quail, hawks, kingfishers, warblers, kites, herons, larks, wagtails, ibis, cranes, dunlins, ziczacs, sand chats, peeweets. "In the morning"—on December 31—"Father and I went out shooting and procured eighteen birds." Day after day they did that together, tirelessly, happily, bringing game bags back in the afternoon for the young ornithologist at his station under a canopy on deck to cut carefully open, applying his taxidermic skills to prepare the kill as specimens. "In a walk in the Afternoon"—by no means atypical—"I observed five small waders viz: Gotanus Hypoloucus and ochropus, Gallinago media & gallinula, and Charidrins minor. These and Rhyncca Lengalensis are the only small waders I know of that inhabit Egypt"—that entry of January 4, 1873, hardly unique, in a diary written solely for the writer's benefit. In all, young Roosevelt killed upward of 200 birds during the grand adventure, with never a hint in its unhurried course of satiation or remorse—or of asthma—to dissuade him. And emerging at Cairo, moving to Shepherd's Hotel in mid-February, the youth discovered that during the barge trip he had passed through a growth spurt. All his clothing for onshore wear had suddenly to be replaced with longer-sleeved, longer-legged garments. Now he stood eye to eye with other young men of his age.

This second overseas excursion was proving almost as transformative in Roosevelt's life at fourteen as the *Quaker City* cruise had been for Clemens in his early thirties. Yet during a number of nights that lay immediately ahead, Teedie's asthma returned, cruelly. At Port Said, at the far end of the nearby Suez Canal (opened four years earlier), the lad suffered a sharp nighttime attack, and again a "bad" one in the Holy Land, another that left him "very sick" in Constantinople, yet another while cruising up the Danube.

In Saxony, in Dresden, the younger three children were to be left for five months with a German family, Theodore Sr. returning to New York and Mrs. Roosevelt proceeding with Bamie to Paris and health spas nearby. For Teedie, the Dresden stay with the Minckwitzes proved a happy interlude, that kindly family including German children to befriend and be instructed by. The young scholar made good headway in mastering their language, while developing an admiration for all things German: for their joy of living, "the capacity for hard work, the sense of duty, the delight in studying literature and science, the pride in the new Germany . . ."

Then, in early November 1873, the voyagers returned to New York City, to a mansion far grander than the relatively modest brownstone on Twentieth Street. The new address, 6 West Fifty-Seventh Street, marked a home of high luxury: inlaid wood floors, a massive hand-carved staircase, crystal chandeliers, huge mirrors, imported furniture, a gymnasium, room in the attic for Teedie's natural-history museum, room enough overall to entertain up to 500 guests, with servants in livery and—among various carriages—a claret-colored, gilt-trimmed landau. These were Knickerbockers, after all, descendants of the earliest Dutch inhabitants of Nieuw Amsterdam. Some Manhattan families might be wealthier, but few stood higher on the social scale than the Roosevelts. Young Theodore, like his siblings, was being reared to exhibit the graces of that elevated station. In this same year as the devastating Panic of 1873 (which seems to have fazed the free-spending Roosevelts not at all), the siblings were soon partaking of dancing lessons at Dodsworth's ballroom, and Bamie would be honored with a great housewarming dinner ball, even as Teedie and his father made time for resuming their humanitarian visits to the city's unfortunates in hospitals, prisons, asylums, and slums.

The lad set his sights on Harvard, with its superior science program. An irregular education had left young Roosevelt strong in some fields (science, history, literature, geography, modern languages) but weak in others, especially in mathematics and the classical languages; so a tutor, Arthur Cutler, was hired to help prepare him to take the entrance examinations. For two years Theodore kept at his studies until, in late July 1876, he was able to write to his sister Bamie with grateful relief: "Is it not splendid about my examinations? I passed well on all the eight subjects I tried."

CHAPTER Thirteen

Western Writings

Roosevelt entered Harvard in September 1876, a month before turning eighteen. During his college years, his life underwent three changes of great consequence to this member of the class of 1880. For one, he began directing his intellectual interests toward political science. After the family's return from Europe, his father had become involved in civil-service reform, the choosing of public officials on merit rather than through the rancid old patronage system that had polluted Tammany Hall and the corrupt Grant administration. Once again the elder son felt stirrings to follow in his father's footsteps: rather than professing zoology (although he never lost his interest in science), Roosevelt Jr. began to think about going into public life.

A second great change during Theodore's college years concerned, sadly, that same father, whose sense of duty and joy in living had been a young man's inspiration. Always in the past Theodore Sr. had appeared in splendid health: broad-shouldered, virile, indefatigable. Yet in Theodore Jr.'s sophomore year, on February 9, 1878, that estimable father died in New York City, in great pain, at age forty-six, of a tumor in the bowel. At his death he could have had no idea of the high destiny awaiting his elder son, any more than the son did himself. "I often feel badly," young Theodore recorded in the throes of deep grief soon afterward, "that such a wonderful man as Father should have had a son of so little worth as I am"; and "How I wish I could ever do something to keep up his name!" As it happened, in the entire course of his presidency, which began twenty-three years later, Roosevelt never made a serious decision, he said, that he didn't first think of what his father would have done in his place.

A third vast change during young Theodore's time at Harvard occurred in his junior year, after a period of grieving that he kept hidden from others. In the fall of 1878, the young man fell in love. Alice Hathaway Lee was seventeen years old, well-connected, uniformly admired, the neighbor and cousin of a Harvard classmate. Roosevelt courted as ardently as he did everything else; and his diary makes clear how thoroughly he was smitten: "I cannot take my eyes off her; she is so pure and holy that it seems almost a profanation to touch her, no matter how gently and tenderly; and yet when we are alone I cannot bear her to be a minute out of my arms."

The courtship prospered. Graduating from Harvard in 1880, Theodore set off in mid-August with his brother Elliott to hunt for six weeks, as far west as Minnesota—last fling of bachelor days. Then in late September, with another 200 kills behind him, Theodore hurried to Boston, where he and Alice Lee were married on the groom's twenty-second birthday, October 27, 1880. They set up residence in the family mansion on West Fifty-Seventh Street, New York City; and in May 1881 the happy couple sailed for Europe for a tour of six months through nine countries, in the course of which the exuberant Theodore brandished his physical fitness by scaling the Matterhorn. The two returned home in early October, and before the month was out young Roosevelt had got himself nominated the Republican candidate for the New York State Assembly.

Years later he summarized his career in the legislature: "I was the youngest man there, and I rose like a rocket. I was re-elected next year by an enormous majority in a time"—1882—"when the republican party as a whole met with great disaster; and the republican minority in the house, although I was the youngest member, nominated me for speaker, that is, made me the leader of the minority." But his head swelled; he lost perspective, "and the result was that I came an awful cropper and had to pick myself up after learning by bitter experience the lesson that I was not all-important and that I had to take account of many different elements in life. It took me fully a year before I got back the position I had lost, but I hung steadily at it and achieved my purpose."

Three terms he served, highly creditable ones. Roosevelt found he loved the give and take of politics, the mingling with all sorts of people, the sense of consequence, the dealing with crises. Politics furnished so many ways to be useful. At twenty-five, he was engaged in Assembly business in Albany on Tuesday, February 12, 1884, when a telegram arrived announcing the birth of his and Alice's first child, a girl. Within an hour came another message that told of complications. Roosevelt boarded the earliest train for New York City. At the door of the mansion he found his brother Elliott, ashen, crying that the family's home was cursed. Inside, upstairs, their mother, Mittie, lay mortally ill with typhoid fever. She died in the small hours of Valentine's Day morning, forty-eight years old. Twelve hours later, at two that afternoon, occurred another death. Elsewhere in the house Alice Lee Roosevelt had died of Bright's disease—kidney failure—her husband at her bedside. She was twenty-two.

With those deaths, "the light has gone out of my life," the doubly bereft husband and son set down in anguish; and even now, these many years later, we can scarcely fathom the grief of simultaneous losses on such a scale. Sam Clemens, who felt agonies with full effect—"whose organization is such," his brother wrote, "as to feel the utmost extreme of every feeling"—would have expressed those emotions in full. Roosevelt was different. That the younger man experienced all the weight of the catastrophe is certain, but he didn't talk about it. In the blackness of the hours afterward, he wrote in his diary the one stark sentence quoted above, then composed a memorial of Alice that recorded the chronology of their brief, happy years together. From that time on, with one or two rare, early exceptions, he never was heard to utter his deceased wife's name. For a long while Roosevelt would not even speak the name of his daughter, another Alice. He turned the child—"Baby Lee," he called her—over to his competent older sister, Bamie, went back to Albany as soon as he properly could, and never spoke of his losses again. Alice Lee Roosevelt is not so much as mentioned in his *Autobiography*, and through its ample length his mother is allotted no more than a sentence or two.

When his third one-year term was up in May, Roosevelt declined to stand for reelection to the Assembly. That spring of 1884 he led the New York delegation to the Republican presidential convention in Chicago, then took the train farther west, to the Dakota Badlands north of the settlement of Medora, close to the Little Missouri River in what is now the western part of North Dakota. There, on a hunting trip the previous summer, he had bought a cattle ranch and hired hands to run it. Now he built a low frame house with a veranda that faced the river and the buttes beyond. Staving off morbidity, he hunted, roamed the bleak terrain, and got to know the rough frontier types of the region, hands whose laconic competence he much admired, as those same cowboys soon came to admire this energetic, decisive, uncomplaining, hard-riding dude from the East.

Roosevelt liked the saying, "Black care rarely sits behind a rider whose pace is fast enough." He kept busy, the following year writing a book that was published in July of 1885. *Hunting Trips of a Ranchman* was not the first book he had written, and by no means the last; but none of the author's other works is more appealing. Like those others, this one is filled with information: the hunter-naturalist's knowledge of what he is seeing out West combined with the ornithologist's keen awareness of earth, pond, and sky. But there is more to *Hunting Trips of a Ranchman* than observation. Granted, those not attuned to the quest may wonder, as Sam Clemens would have wondered, about the distinction insisted on between killing and slaughtering. In late fall the ranch is out of fresh meat, so Roosevelt sallies forth at dawn and slaughters five grouse, on another occasion four prairie fowl. "Now, of course I would not have dreamed of taking either of these shots had I been out purely for sport, and neither needed any more skill than would be shown in killing hens in a barn-yard." Was it more like sport, then, when you had no pressing use for the meat? Nor would Clemens likely have comprehended such an emotion as this: "No sportsman can ever feel much keener pleasure and self-satisfaction than when, after a successful stalk and good shot, he walks up to a grand elk lying dead in the cool shade of the great evergreens, and looks at the massive and yet finely moulded form, and at the mighty antlers which are to serve in the future as the trophy and proof of his successful skill." Still, while maybe skimming through details of the specific hunts for grouse, deer, mountain sheep, elk, and the lordly buffalo, the reader does find much along the way of interest and attractiveness.

There will be, Roosevelt tells us, "days and days of sunny weather, not cold enough to bring discomfort, but yet so cool that the blood leaps briskly through a man's veins and makes him feel that to be out and walking over the hills is a pleasure in itself, even were he not in hopes of any moment seeing the sun glint on the horns and hide of some mighty buck, as it rises to face the intruder." One night this hunter and his companions camp at the foot of a butte and build a huge fire near its face, pitching their beds off under the pines. The flames "leaped up the side of the cliff, the red light bringing out into lurid and ghastly relief the bold corners and strange-looking escarpments of the rock." It was a magical spot and moment. A full moon's flood of light silvered the cliffs, so that "the place seemed almost as unreal as if we had been in fairy-land."

But some nights on the trail were less agreeable. On one occasion, with both men and horses exhausted, Roosevelt and his companion were obliged to bed down by a mud-pool, with nothing to drink but that slimy, near gelatinous water, nothing but a biscuit apiece for supper. During the night the horses took fright and ran off, their vexed riders wearily retrieving them from a distance. Back in makeshift beds the men were rained on, drenched by morning and glad, after one more biscuit for breakfast, to leave the mud-pool far behind.

Of a similar night and day: "fortunately we had all learned that no matter how bad things are, grumbling and bad temper can always be depended

Figure 13.1.   Roosevelt in western garb, a studio portrait that appeared as the frontispiece of *Hunting Trips of a Ranchman,* 1885.

Courtesy of the Theodore Roosevelt Collection, Harvard College Library.

upon to make them worse, and so bore our ill-fortune, if not with stoical indifference, at least in perfect quiet." That was part of what Roosevelt admired about these western types, these cowpokes and ranchhands of few words, "the bronzed and sinewy cow-boy, as picturesque and self-reliant, as dashing and resolute as the saturnine Indian fighters whose place he has taken; and," the author goes on, "alas that it should be written! he in his turn must at no distant time share the fate of the men he has displaced." In his stead will come the plodding farmer; and "I suppose it is right and best" that these great fenceless expanses "should be in the end broken up into small patches of fenced farm land and grazing land." But meanwhile, as of 1885, nowhere else but on the plains does one feel as far off from mankind; and upon living awhile surrounded by such solitudes, "their very vastness and loneliness and their melancholy monotony have a strong fascination for him," for such a rider as Roosevelt, coping with losses, fleeing his eastern demons, often quite by himself traversing mile after mile over the limitless spreads of scorched brown earth, under the multitudinous stars of nighttime, in daylight amid objects shimmering in the hot distance in ways that made even the familiar look strange.

On February 18 of this same year, 1885—the year that Roosevelt's *Hunting Trips of a Ranchman* appeared—Charles L. Webster & Company issued a new novel by Mark Twain, *Adventures of Huckleberry Finn*. The author of that work had long been a family man by then. Much had changed for Sam Clemens since the fairy-tale beginnings of his marriage in Buffalo fifteen years earlier, in February 1870. Back then, within their nuptial mansion on Delaware Avenue, gift of the bride's father, he and Livy had felt overjoyed at the start. "She is the very most perfect gem of womankind that ever I saw in my life," the groom reported to a childhood friend, speaking of one who even then was "lying asleep upstairs in a bed that I sleep in every night, & for four whole days she has been *Mrs. Samuel L. Clemens!*" Livy for her part assured her mother: "We are as happy as two mortals can well be"; and to her sister she wrote in mid-April: "nothing seems able to mar our joy."

Yet that early joy was to be short-lived, for the months that followed the Clemenses' wedding filled up with grief. In August 1870, after a painful illness, Livy's father died at age sixty-one; and his younger daughter, like all his devoted family, was devastated. Jervis Langdon's son-in-law, Livy's husband, felt the loss deeply as well, because Sam had loved the man as the father he never had, amiable where the late Judge Clemens had been cold and stern, self-made like that other but with glittering worldly success to set alongside Judge Clemens's string of professional failures.

Livy, grieving, was pregnant by then. In September, a childhood schoolmate came from Elmira to Buffalo to help; but Miss Nye had scarcely settled in at Delaware Avenue before she fell ill. "Livy & a hired nurse watch her without ceasing,—night & day," Sam wrote on September 7, 1870. Never robust, the new Mrs. Clemens spent much of her remaining strength tending her now delirious friend, to no avail. "Miss Emma Nye lingered a month with typhoid fever & died here in our own bedroom in the 29th Sept."

The Clemenses' baby was born in early November, prematurely, a boy so sickly that his father felt sure he couldn't survive infancy. They named him Langdon. Livy was ill too, careworn, bedridden, her child turned over to a wet nurse. Not far into 1871, the new mother contracted typhoid in her turn. Clemens despaired, sure that his wife was doomed to the fate that Miss Nye had met with in this same house of death. He had come to hate Buffalo anyhow, including the boring routine of editing at the *Express*. In March he offered the Delaware Avenue house and his shares in the newspaper for sale, ending by letting both go at a loss. Meanwhile Livy's condition was, finally, slightly improving. On Saturday, March 18, after fifteen months in the city, the Clemens family—infant son, mother lying on a mattress, burdened father, and servants—left Buffalo for good, bound by train the hundred miles to Elmira.

Since last August the author had been trying to write a new book, 600 more lighthearted pages to be spun out from within a shrine of mourning. In Elmira he set out to finish it, an account of his time in the West. To be sure, the subject was trite. Ever since the Gold Rush twenty years earlier, reports of Forty-Niner and post-Forty-Niner life out West had flowed east in a steady stream. Yet there could be advantages to Mark Twain's trying his hand at western subject matter. The result might provide a satisfying companion to his earlier volume. *The Innocents Abroad* was of the European present, far to the east; this new western book—innocents at home—would be of an American past, and a past no longer visitable. Already the romantic Old West that Clemens had traveled through was gone; railroads and the telegraph had seen to that. Back when Sam rode overland with his brother, in 1861, crossing the 2,000 miles from St. Joseph, Missouri, to Sacramento, California, took fifteen days by stagecoach. On the railroad this decade later, it took four days and a half. "I can scarcely comprehend the new state of things," Mark Twain would marvel of the changes. In 1861, "perhaps not more than ten men in America, all told, expected to live to see a railroad follow that route to the Pacific" over which a stagecoach had carried the Clemens brothers part way. Now you glide in Pullman hotels on wheels, stepping one car forward from your sleeping palace to dine at tables with snowy linen and silver service, waiters in spotless white magically bringing forth repasts that would do credit to the finest New York restaurants: antelope steak, mountain brook trout, choice fruits and berries, all served in the "sweet-scented, appetite-compelling air of the prairies" and "washed down with bumpers of sparkling Krug," as one anonymous traveler through the early 1870s bore witness, having himself been sped along thus at thirty miles an hour.

By 1871, the postwar North and West seemed in motion at speeds ever faster. Railroads and the telegraph were binding those parts of the continent together, wilderness made accessible so that the entire West would soon be opened to settlement. Railroads were transporting culture coast to coast as well, bestowing knowledge continentally by means of books and such lectures as Mark Twain himself delivered, traveling like others from town to town in the cars, with books and magazines distributed nationwide now, cheaply, rapidly, selling at a popular price and over a geographic range undreamed of before. Get his own book out describing the era displaced, and Clemens stood to benefit from commercial opportunities unavailable to authors of any previous generation.

He had begun to write the new book—and ended by creating a priceless eyewitness account of a time gone for good: of stagecoach travel and mining for silver and a boom-town newspaper enterprise high in the western Sierras. Yet through much of the writing of *Roughing It*, the foundations of Clemens's personal life had been heaving and shifting, leaving him all but overwhelmed in distractions. Did his publisher Bliss understand, he queried at the end of the Buffalo sojourn, "that for *seven weeks* I have not had my natural rest but have been a night-and-day sick-nurse to my wife?" After all that, you might think "that the vials of hellfire bottled up for my benefit *must* be about emptied.—By the living God I don't believe they ever *will* be emptied." In the months before *Roughing It* was finally delivered to Hartford, Sam, or Mark Twain—"my hated nom de plume (for I do loathe the very sight of it)"—had moved his family back to Elmira, where he had gone on struggling to put this second account together. Finally he did amass the bulky 600 pages that subscription publishing demanded, but only by tacking on three barely relevant appendices, as well as sixteen late chapters devoted to his Sandwich Islands excursion of 1866. Present-day readers may wonder—after so much lively historical material describing the mainland Old West—why those are there. What has Hawaii to do with all that? But Clemens wasn't shaping a polished literary work, its length determined by the urgings of unity and coherence. Instead, he was improvising, putting in to fill out until he had enough to pare down. Nor was his literary judgment of the result always sound. "I admire the book more & more the more I cut & slash & lick & trim & revamp it," he wrote to Livy from Hartford in the final stages of revising. To get that last step taken care of, *The Innocents Abroad* had needed two months. "But this," he told her, "is another sight easier job, because it is so much better literary work—so much more acceptably written." He even thought for a time that he had manuscript enough to "leave off all the Overland trip—what a pity I can't."

The overland trip, which occupies chapters 2 through 21 of *Roughing It*, includes pages among the most exhilarating in the story, wonderfully evocative pages—and what a pity it would have been to lose them! True, much of what appears there and elsewhere in *Roughing It* didn't happen just as described. Truth was often embellished, truth literary rather than historical (yet hardly less true for that; no other surviving source gives so accurate a picture of how it would feel to have been traveling west just there and at that time). What kind of literature is this, then? The author wouldn't have worried about it. He was a performer, edging his way forward by means of his distinctive voice, starting with what he had seen on his travels and putting together a kind of fictionalized memoir or autobiography, what he called a "personal narrative." Or maybe what results is more of an incipient novel, a quasi-*bildungsroman*, with a greenhorn setting blithely forth into a wilderness to encounter marvels at every turn, in time becoming initiated into the great world of experience that lies westward across the plains and beyond the mountains toward the setting sun.

You write a book, the humorist felt, the way you write a lecture. Think of a plank stretching the necessary distance: a book's 600 pages or a lecture's hour or two. The plank gets you from here to there, and in the plank are holes opened up all along. You plug those holes with anecdotes or yarns or other more or less relevant intrusions, some funny, some serious; and the trick is to make sure the yarn plugging the very first hole is a good one, drawing your reader or listener in. Then another, and another, keeping the audience a little off balance with the unexpected, until your narrative—that plank laid out—gets you as far as you need to go. It was not how, say, Henry James would craft narratives beginning two or three years hence; but Mark Twain's method got the job done. *Roughing It* ends up being full of life, humor, variety, and historical significance; and if some of the material used to fill holes in the plank—illustrative clippings from newspapers, excerpts from other people's books—can be skimmed without much loss, other such intrusions remain fresh and funny. Yet throughout the narrative, it is Mark Twain's mastery of style, his varied, inimitable voice, that accounts—more than the yarns themselves—for the laughter reverberating into our own times.

By midsummer 1871, Sam had finished a first draft of this new work, just as Livy was beginning to grow stronger. Accordingly, in early August, leaving his wife and their infant son with her sister's family, the author boarded a train out of Elmira to deliver his manuscript to Elisha Bliss of the American Publishing Company in Hartford, Connecticut. While there he looked around for a place to live, because this was the town that he and his wife had decided to move to. He did find a house to rent for the winter, and would find a new life there as well. The Clemenses made Hartford their home for the next twenty years.

In retrospect, most of those years appear to have been happy ones. Sadness came only at the beginning and toward the end. At the beginning the Clemenses lost their son Langdon, never hardy, of diphtheria, on June 2, 1872; the child had lived no more than a year and a half. But in the spring before that loss, in March was born a first daughter, Susy; another, Clara, would be born two years later; and a third daughter, Jean, was born in 1880. In Hartford the Clemenses could indulge themselves, flush with money from Livy's inheritance and Sam's royalties from *The Innocents Abroad*, now augmented by the success of his second book, *Roughing It*, which came out in 1872. The husband from humble background insisted that his wife of means have the best. They bought a lot in a fashionable section on the western edge of Hartford and there built a gorgeous home among congenial neighbors. Socially active winters were spent with their many friends in Hartford. Summers in Elmira provided time for the author Mark Twain, less distracted, to continue his productive writing. A novel—the first by this author—was cowritten with a Hartford neighbor, Charles Dudley Warner: *The Gilded Age*, published in 1873. In 1875, in the august pages of the *Atlantic Monthly* over a period of eight months appeared Mark Twain's "Old Times on the Mississippi." In 1876 (as young Theodore Roosevelt was entering Harvard) came *The Adventures of Tom Sawyer*. The very popular *A Tramp Abroad*, Mark Twain's account of a return to mainland Europe, was published in 1880. The following year saw *The Prince and the Pauper*, and two years later *Life on the Mississippi*, a book-length enlargement of the author's career as a steamboat pilot, worked up from the *Atlantic* articles earlier.

All this while, Clemens's restless mind was teeming with ideas, literary and otherwise, some of them worth good money. He wrote plays that he saw successfully produced. He patented inventions. In the early 1880s he was introduced to an inventor at the Pratt & Whitney plant in Hartford, a man named Paige, who was perfecting an ingenious machine that would set type far faster and better than any human hands. Clemens as a former typesetter knew the value of such an invention, which stood to make shrewd investors in it richer than books ever could. In love with gadgets, he began putting money into Paige's evolving machine, and meanwhile bought himself a newfangled typewriter and used it earlier than any other author, and had a telephone installed in his house before anyone else in Hartford did.

And he founded his own publishing firm, placed a nephew by marriage in charge, and called it by the nephew's name, Charles L. Webster & Company. In 1885, in November, Samuel L. Clemens reached fifty. Earlier that year (the same year that Theodore Roosevelt's *Hunting Trips of a Ranchman* appeared), Charles L. Webster & Company published *Adventures of Huckleberry Finn*, which sold a gratifying 39,000 copies in its first month off the press. All this—this prosperity, this vast, varied, and continuing good fortune—almost frightened the lucky author; for it had come to seem that whatever Mark Twain touched turned to gold.

CHAPTER **Fourteen**

Continental America

At the end of his narrative of the 1840s, Huckleberry Finn tells us that he's about to light out for the Territory—for the unfettered West, that safety valve that let a fellow start over, let him escape from Aunt Sally's efforts at sivilizin' by leaving civilization's shackling rules behind. Out West four decades later, in the Dakota Territory, Theodore Roosevelt found his own relief from eastern burdens and losses. For many other Americans of the era the spacious West beckoned beyond the Mississippi as a golden promise, a pledge of new beginnings whenever the ways back East grew clogged and impassable.

But the West changed you. It changed the very animals out there, the cougar, for instance. Roosevelt instructs us in *Hunting Trips of a Ranchman* that when "the continent was first settled, and for long afterward, the cougar was quite as dangerous an antagonist as the African or Indian leopard, and would even attack men unprovoked," but that "the nature of the animal has been so changed by constant contact with rifle-bearing hunters, that timidity toward them has become a hereditary trait deeply engrained in its nature." Grizzlies, too, are less fierce now than formerly, when they would not hesitate to attack early explorers and trappers. Now no grizzly will charge a man unless cornered; for "constant contact with rifle-carrying hunters, for a period extending over many generations of bear-life, has taught the grizzly by bitter experience that man is his undoubted overlord, as far as fighting goes; and this knowledge has become an hereditary characteristic."

Like others of the times, Roosevelt, hunter and scientist, student of (among much else) the French naturalist Jean-Baptiste Lamarck (1744–1829), subscribed to the Lamarckian theory that traits instilled by the environment become hereditary, the demands of a creature's surroundings developing in it attributes that are passed on to its progeny. And as with animals, so with people. Pioneers from the East who journeyed westward were called upon to develop certain attributes in order to survive on the frontier. Thus those adventurers grew into something different from what they had been setting out; and they passed the differences—of initiative, adaptability, inventiveness, independence, toughness, resilience, even patriotism—on to their descendants. In doing so, frontiersmen over time created a new race unlike any of their ancestors—created, in a word, Americans.

It seemed providential: the gift to a young nation of near-empty lands stretching clear to the farther ocean, lands unburdened by the tyranny of tradition or the prerogatives of class or by a grasping, priest-ridden church or the dying remnants of feudal ways. Out there, one person stood as good a chance as another if he possessed the grit and stamina to go ahead. Moreover, there was wealth to be had: grazing land, farmland, hills full of timber, silver, and gold. And just when such bounty as the California gold fields was discovered, more of Providence's blessings on America emerged in the means for getting at that wealth: the steamboat, the railroad, the telegraph that joined parts of the whole together to their mutual advantage. Nowhere else on earth did opportunities appear so manifest, people who seized them so exuberantly free and democratic, or achievements of those people so evident as in this continental nation of the New World.

World's fairs extolled such achievements. The fairs were recurring phenomena during the second half of the nineteenth century, some nineteen of them worldwide by century's end. The first such was held in London, in 1851, the so-called Crystal Palace in Hyde Park, a celebration of far-flung benefits from England's Industrial Revolution. In New York City two years later arose another Crystal Palace, like the first all glass and framing iron that enclosed a vast, breathtaking machine- and banner-filled interior. That was the spectacle ("a perfect fairy palace—beautiful beyond description") that the seventeen-year-old typesetter Sam Clemens had left his Hannibal home by way of St. Louis to see. Later, the same Clemens, forty by then with *Tom Sawyer* about to be published, attended the second great fair in America, the Centennial Exposition, which commemorated the hundredth anniversary of the Republic, in the very city where the birth of these United States had been proclaimed on July 4, 1776. At the later time, with the population of the entire nation still numbering only 46 million, Clemens was among a remarkable 9 million people, including President Ulysses S. Grant, who made their way to Philadelphia to help celebrate America's century-long industrial and cultural progress at the so-called

International Exhibition of Arts, Manufactures and Products of the Soil and Mine, which opened its gates from May into November 1876.

World's fairs followed, notably overseas in Paris in 1889, an *Exposition Universelle* on the hundredth anniversary of the start of the French Revolution. But here at home, soon after that triumph (with its Eiffel Tower, built to serve as an entrance arch to the fair), the American West aspired to host a world's fair of its own. Easterners scoffed at the presumption. Chicago, all but destroyed by fire as recently as 1871, lacked the resources, the culture, or the business acumen to pull off so grand an event. The worthy occasion for any such effort was to be the 400th anniversary of Christopher Columbus's landing on these shores, a World's Columbian Exposition scheduled for 1892 to display America's mighty achievements over the intervening centuries. Included would be evidences of future national greatness, along with distinctive houses on the grounds to accommodate and show off individual states of the Union, as well as pavilions from countries around the globe, all to enlarge patrons' horizons in an era less mobile than ours.

Plans out west grew so expansive that the anniversary year came and went, and what skeptical easterners had been belittling as no more than a Cook County Fair (where Chicago is) still wasn't ready. Not until May 1893 did President Grover Cleveland at last get to press the gold telegraph key that unveiled the exposition and set the fountains flowing. When he did, what those earliest visitors beheld on the shores of Lake Michigan was a vision materialized: a magnificent White City—an alabaster city!—of glittering buildings around a court of honor, with blooming gardens and lagoons and pillared monuments and statuary and welcoming benches, the spaciousness made easy to move about in, all of it spotless, cleaner and brighter than any earthly city that the 27 million visitors who ended up coming to see it had ever laid eyes upon.

Chicago was a rail hub, and it was the railroad that made such massive attendance possible. Foresighted school teachers, farmers' families, clerks, and telephone operators saved their dimes and quarters through a year or two beforehand so that they could make the trip, many gazing out of train windows at a part of the country never seen before. And what they saw at their destination they didn't forget. When they reached home they regaled their neighbors with it, displayed their souvenirs, told their grandchildren about it for years afterward: about the visionary city they had basked in back in the 1890s. At the fair was so much that went beyond one's wildest expectations, much that was educational and much that was pure entertainment.

Figure 14.1.   The World's Columbian Exposition, Chicago, 1893.

The entertainment lay astride the celebrated mile-long Midway Plaisance, with its Moorish Palace, its Natatorium, its tethered balloon ride, its Cairo and Vienna street scenes, its Wild West Show adjacent, and—the exposition's most popular exhibit—its Ferris Wheel, the world's first such, Chicago's answer to the Eiffel Tower, each car on the giant structure holding up to sixty passengers, a ride comprising two scenic, nine-minute revolutions 250 feet up into the sky and down. One of the thirty-six cars contained a live band that played music while the huge wheel turned.

Back on earth there was much to enjoy in the formal exhibition halls, and so much to learn about and be amazed by: the Machinery Building with its dynamos and world's longest conveyor belt; the Agricultural Building and its monster 22,000-pound cheese from Canada, its replica Liberty Bell made out of wheat and oats; the Fisheries Building with its floor-to-ceiling aquaria containing hundreds of species of fresh- and salt-water fish; the United States Government Building; the dazzling Transportation Building; the Palace of Fine Arts. Each evening electric lights illumined those gorgeous structures, the effects of Edison's still novel invention never seen on such a scale before. And there were serious (if less well-attended) educational opportunities in and around the fair. The American Historical Association, for one, offered attendees a chance to hear papers read by distinguished professors, among whom—rather less well-known than eminences from the East—was Frederick Jackson Turner, thirty-one years old, from the University of Wisconsin, here in the West. Toward the end of Wednesday evening, July 12, 1893, Professor Turner read his contribution to the fair's cultural aspirations, on "The Significance of the Frontier in American History," tenacious listeners in the new Art Institute at the foot of Adams Street following as well as they could at so late an hour.

Over that hot summer night, four lengthy, erudite papers had preceded Professor Turner's; so the audience of scholars and passersby had dwindled from the couple of hundred gathered at the beginning. Nor, in days immediately afterward, was much made of this perhaps single most significant essay in all of American historiography. Accordingly, in the next few weeks the shrewd young professor, back home in Madison, sent copies of his paper to influential readers around the country who might be interested. One such was Theodore Roosevelt, author by that time of two volumes of a projected multivolume historical work entitled *The Winning of the West.*

Earlier, in the *Dial* for August 1889, Turner at twenty-seven had reviewed his fellow historian Roosevelt's volumes on their appearance; and the professor would later say that in preparing the review he had first realized "the need of a history of the continuous progress of civilization across the continent." For Roosevelt's pair of volumes had told only fourteen years of the epic story, from 1769 to 1783. (Two additional volumes would appear by 1896, but they carried the narrative no farther than 1807; and by then Roosevelt was too busy with other matters ever to find leisure to return to his ambitious undertaking.) Turner, meanwhile, reviewing even the few years that the first two volumes covered, had been inspired to assert that the West, with the frontier retreating across it through successive generations, was the true center of gravity in American history. Starting in the early seventeenth century at the piedmont behind the shoreline settlements of the East Coast, the West had pressed successively through the Mohawk Valley and the Cumberland Gap of the Alleghenies into what would become the Old Northwest and Kentucky, on past the Mississippi along the Platte over the plains into Oregon and California, doubling back at last to make the plains themselves prosper as ranchland. It was those nearly three centuries of westering that had molded the crucible in which was shaped the American character. Hardly intellectual, a bit coarse perhaps, but that distinctive national character had proven strong, inventive, practical, freedom-loving, uniquely filled with optimism, and restlessly energetic.

This was the insight that Frederick Jackson Turner gave voice to at the World's Columbian Exposition. The frontier—more than Puritanism, more than slavery—had made America exceptional, and now the frontier was gone. In 1890, for the first time, the decennial census had been unable to discover a clear line between wilderness and habitation; "at present the unsettled area has been so broken into by isolated bodies of settlement that there can hardly be said to be a frontier line." The dynamic westward movement, which throughout our history had caused Americans to adapt to an expanding society by altering their institutions into unique expressions of democracy, appeared at an end. "American social development has been continually beginning over again on the frontier," and that has meant "a steady movement away from the influence of Europe, a steady growth of independence on American lines." It has meant, too, that our past is unlike that of any other nation's. "The United States lies like a huge page in the history of society. Line by line as we read this continental page from West to East"—from primitivism to civilization; from Indians to hunters, traders, ranchers, farmers, and lastly manufacturers encroaching from the East—"we find the record of social evolution."

Now all that would appear to have ended with the end of the frontier. And what comes next? "He would be a rash prophet," Turner cautions as he nears his conclusion, "who should assert that the expansive character of American life has now entirely ceased. Movement has been its dominant fact," so that "the American energy will continually demand a wider field for its exercise." For now, however, "four centuries from the discovery of America, at the end of a hundred years of life under the Constitution, the frontier has gone, and with its going has closed the first period of American history."

Back east, Theodore Roosevelt, soon in receipt of Turner's thesis, wrote to the author on February 10, 1894, thanking him for what had arrived just at the "right time," while the Oyster Bay historian was working on his own third volume of *The Winning of the West*. He would make grateful use of the professor's paper, of course with full attribution. "I think," Roosevelt went on, "you have struck some first class ideas," putting into shape "a good deal of thought that has been floating around rather loosely."

A decade earlier to the month—almost to the day—of this reply from Sagamore Hill (and did he think of it in dating the letter?), Roosevelt had lived through the appalling ordeal of losing both his wife and his mother from different causes, in the same home, within a span of twelve hours. Since then, an orphaned widower had declined to run again for the New York State Assembly, had led the New York delegation to the Republican nominating convention in Chicago in the spring of 1884, had returned to his ranch alongside the Dakota Badlands, and on a trip back east in the fall of 1885 to visit his sister Bamie—caring for his and the late Alice Lee Roosevelt's daughter—had encountered a dear friend of his childhood and youth, Edith Carow. The rigidly moral Roosevelt did not believe in second marriages; and yet (condemning himself in private for his faithlessness to Alice's memory) he became secretly engaged to Edith that December. In the fall of the following year, he ran for mayor of New York City and lost; but "anyway, I had a bully time." And in London that December of 1886, Theodore and Edith were married.

Back home, the winter of 1886–1887 was proving horrendous in the upper midwestern states and territories. When, in March of the new year, the Roosevelts returned to New York from a three-months' European honeymoon, it was to learn that more than half of the Roosevelt cattle herds at the Elkhorn and Chimney Butte ranches had frozen or starved to death in the blizzards and deep snows of so fierce a season. The owner ventured west to assess the damage in April. From then on, though visiting Medora several times in the course of hunting trips and campaign tours to follow, Roosevelt took an ever diminishing part in active ranching as a livelihood.

He had lost heavily in his western venture. Nor did he see any clear opportunities ahead in politics. Yet the man must provide for his new wife,

who was pregnant, and his daughter, now living with them. Theodore Jr.,
"Ted," was born that September of 1887. By then in his late twenties, Roosevelt took to writing, prolifically, books and magazine articles, in order
to augment his shrunken income. *Ranch Life and the Hunting Trail*, a second
evocation of Dakota days after *Hunting Trips of a Ranchman*, was published
in 1888; and in 1893, the year of the Chicago Exposition, appeared *The Wilderness Hunter*. Meanwhile, this self-styled "literary feller" had been working
on what he hoped would be a project of lasting merit, his multivolume
Winning of the West, worthy of sitting on the shelf alongside the great Francis
Parkman's seven-volume masterpiece, *France and England in North America*.
Roosevelt's volumes 1 and 2 (dedicated to Parkman) were published in
mid-1889, volume 3 in 1894, and volume 4 two years later.

In total days, the New Yorker had spent hardly more than a year out
West, but his name henceforth would be closely linked with that region,
partly because of all his western-centered writing, those three vivid personal accounts and the four volumes he completed of his formal history.
Nor in years to come would he do anything to discourage the linkage,
which was of great value in his political life ahead. An urban, intellectual
New York aristocrat, whose maternal roots lay in the plantation South,
stood only to benefit from yet another regional connection, to the rawhide,
adventurous, democratic West of fact and myth.

But Roosevelt's professed attachment to the West was in no way cyni-
cal or insincere. His love for the region was genuine, and his knowledge of
it formidable, all the more so after vigorously digging into archives, securing copies from far and wide of letters, diaries, and official documents of
the westward movement in the nation's early years. From those resources
the author unfolded his saga with a Parkmaneque narrative drive, filled
with fact but full of color as well, of romance, drama, and vividness, history
less as science than as literature. *The Winning of the West*, which had been
more than eight years off and on in the writing, was in consequence both
a critical and a financial success, easing the cares of Edith Roosevelt as she
kept track of a growing family's expenses at Sagamore Hill.

But it is the three personal accounts, even more than his impressive
history of the West, that reveal Roosevelt's love for the region most clearly.
In their pages non-hunters (of whom Samuel L. Clemens was decidedly
one) might even come nearer to understanding their author's compulsion to fire bullets into living four-legged creatures. In the preface to *The
Wilderness Hunter*, Roosevelt writes of "the keen delight of hunting in
lonely lands." Only for him who has done so "is the joy of the horse well
ridden and the rifle well held; for him the long days of toil and hardship,

resolutely endured, and crowned at the end with triumph. In after years there shall come forever to his mind"—and we picture the author, far off in New York City, or Washington, or in his lofty gun room at Sagamore Hill recalling—"the memory of endless prairies shimmering in the bright sun; of vast snow-clad wastes lying desolate under gray skies; of the melancholy marshes; of the rush of mighty rivers; of the breath of the evergreen forest in summer; of the crooning of ice-armored pines at the touch of the winds of winter; of cataracts roaring between hoary mountain masses; of all the innumerable sights and sounds of the wilderness; of its immensity and mystery; and of the silences that brook in its still depths." Yet even more: "The free, self-reliant, adventurous life, with its rugged and stalwart democracy, the wild surroundings, the grand beauty of the scenery, the chance to study the ways and habits of the woodland creatures—all these unite to give to the career of the wilderness hunter its peculiar charm." And beyond charm, the value of the hunt may be summed up in a word: it cultivates *manliness*, "for the lack of which in a nation, as in an individual, the possession of no other qualities can possibly atone."

CHAPTER **Fifteen**

The Philippines

66"He would be a rash prophet," Frederick Jackson Turner wrote regarding the end of the frontier, "who should assert that the expansive character of American life has now entirely ceased. Movement has been its dominant fact," so that "the American energy will continually demand a wider field for its exercise." Yet for now, having reached the Pacific Ocean, the nation could go no farther geographically.

Roosevelt, meanwhile, that literary feller of the late 1880s, had been called back into public service on his party's return to power at the end of the decade. Republican President Benjamin Harrison was persuaded to appoint the author-historian to the civil service commission in Washington. Thus, from May 1889 through the next six years, Roosevelt the writer would be pursuing as well the political aims of his father some fifteen years earlier, seeking to replace the crony-infested patronage system with a system that appointed government officials on merit alone. The tenure of the Republican commissioner proved effective enough that he was asked to stay on even after the Democrat Grover Cleveland returned to the White House in 1893. Thus it was Civil Service Commissioner Roosevelt who visited the World's Columbian Exposition that year in May, at the opening of the fair. And for another two years, the New Yorker discharged his duties in Washington.

Then in April 1895, a reform-minded mayor of New York persuaded Roosevelt to come back to his native city to be police commissioner. Here was a job that the manly politician particularly relished—and did much good in—although he held the position only a couple of years; for in April 1897, under yet another Republican president, William McKinley, he was to reenter federal service in the nation's capital, as assistant secretary of the navy.

All this while, Cuba was seething in misery and revolt. Precisely a year after Roosevelt returned to Washington, war between Spain and the United States erupted. Whereupon the assistant secretary resigned his post and assumed command of the Rough Riders, leading them to triumph on the San Juan Heights. Victory over Spain soon followed; and the fruits of victory included not only a Cuba freed from Spanish tyranny but also Puerto Rico and, in the Pacific, the Philippines (along with tiny Guam), all liberated from Spain's 300 years of domination. On a personal level Colonel Roosevelt rode his new fame into the governorship of New York.

But what was to be done with the sprawling Philippines? For Governor Roosevelt, only one course was open: take over the archipelago. Filipinos hated Spaniards, so returning the islands to Spain meant reinstating grief, revolt, and inhuman mistreatment. It was our duty to rule the Philippines ourselves in the islands' interest, to apply our Anglo-Saxon sagacity to the task of administering them for their own good while keeping them out of the covetous hands of such prowling world powers as Germany and Japan. The United States at large shared Roosevelt's view. American energy, as Professor Turner had noted, "will continually demand a wider field for its exercise," and for many the Philippines provided that field.

Earlier, President McKinley had not wanted to fight Spain. As Major McKinley during the Civil War, he had been at Antietam and seen the dead piled high and wanted no more of it. Nor did he much want the burden of possessing the Philippines now. But in earshot of the President were those who did: among them John Hay, secretary of state; Henry Cabot Lodge, chairman of the Senate foreign relations committee; and the loquacious Governor Roosevelt of New York, fated soon to become vice president. And the American people—filled with pride in their recent, breathtaking Chicago world's fair and all the technological achievements on display there; flush with victory over a European power (such as it was); strong in their exceptionalism and their faith in progress; and assured that America's coming commercial prosperity lay in markets of the Far East—wanted the Philippines too, as their foothold in the Pacific, their gateway to the fabled Orient. What could McKinley do? Denying any imperial designs, he nevertheless reinforced American troops in the archipelago, even while making clear that they came not as conquerors but as friends, to perform an act of benevolent assimilation. Congress approved the treaty with Spain that surrendered the Philippines in February 1899; the United States agreed to pay Spain $20 million, apparently for islands that Spaniards no longer owned; and before February was out, American soldiers 7,000 miles from home found themselves in brutal combat with insurgent Filipinos.

The struggle that followed through months stretching into years came to involve racism, deception, concentration camps, torture, massacre, scorched earth, and—relic of the Inquisition—a treatment of the recalcitrant that American troops adopted from the Spaniards they displaced. Called the watercure, it involved blindfolding and gagging a prone prisoner, then ladling water over his face and into his mouth for an hour or longer to make him cooperative. Sometimes the prisoner drowned.

But what other course could the President follow? Mark Twain had an answer, if McKinley would listen. Returned to America from his nine years of self-imposed European exile, the humorist felt far removed from golden Hartford in the mid-1880s. Back then, Samuel L. Clemens had been almost frightened by the sense that everything he undertook would prosper: his own publishing firm; *Huckleberry Finn*; the *Memoirs* of Ulysses S. Grant, a publishing coup so phenomenal that the impoverished family of the general, who had died—in July 1885—just days after completing his book, could be presented with a single royalty check for $200,000 (perhaps $4.5 million now) in partial payment of earnings. That same year Mark Twain had completed a very profitable lecture tour; and in days to follow, Clemens would begin what he thought would be the final book by Mark Twain, *A Connecticut Yankee in King Arthur's Court*. That appeared in 1889. Thereafter the author meant to lay down his pen and become a capitalist. His publishing firm looked to be thriving, and largely at Clemens's expense James W. Paige was perfecting his typesetting machine, the elaborate compositor that must become a vital part of every printing establishment of substance in the entire world, with a value beyond calculation. Admiring and approving, the public in the meantime watched while Mark Twain mounted success on success as lecturer, commentator, novelist, playwright, inventor, and investor, to all appearances making not so much as one misstep along the way.

Yet it had all turned sour. In June 1891 the Clemenses closed up their magnificent Hartford home and sailed for Europe. The family remained abroad for most of nine years, although Clemens himself returned to America repeatedly on brief forays in the interest of business. In the fall of 1893, for instance, he was in Chicago conferring with Paige about his invention, in which the author was very heavily invested by then. In demonstration trials the typesetter did fine, but it must stand up to a harsher test, in the clamor of a newspaper pressroom. The times, meanwhile, had turned dismal, during the sudden economic Panic of 1893; yet even so—especially so—an anxious visitor back briefly from Europe took a day out of business, like millions of others, for the pleasure and escape of visiting the World's Columbian Exposition, as he had visited the Centennial in Philadelphia seventeen years earlier, as the youth Sam Clemens had visited New York's Crystal Palace in 1853.

The panic intensified. Paige's ingenious, fragile typesetter wasn't managing well under hard daily use; it kept breaking down. More modifications were called for. In addition, early in 1894 Mark Twain's publishing firm was forced into bankruptcy. Humbled, the author embarked on a round-the-world lecture tour to pay off his huge debts of honor. Then, returned to England at the end of that year-long circuit of the globe, Clemens had his newly earned peace shattered in August 1896 by the sudden death of his beloved daughter Susy. From that loss the bereaved father only slowly (if ever) recovered, partly through work, by writing *Following the Equator*. The proceeds of the book when combined with fees from the lecture tour did finally pay off all debts, to the last penny. And in October 1900, Samuel L. Clemens—the beloved Mark Twain—returned with his surviving family, debt free, to the warmest of welcomes on the New York piers.

Just before leaving England, in speaking with a reporter on that side of the Atlantic, Clemens had expressed his approval of President McKinley's decision to remove all troops from China with the Boxer uprising quelled. "We have no more business in China," Mark Twain had told the man from the *World*, "than in any other country that is not ours. That is the case of the Philippines. I have tried hard, and yet I cannot for the life of me comprehend how we got into that mess." Maybe it couldn't have been helped; "perhaps it was inevitable that we should come to be fighting the natives of those islands—but I cannot understand it, and have never been able to get at the bottom of the origin of our antagonism to the natives." What seemed most troubling was this: "I thought we should act as their protector—not try to get them under our heel. We were to relieve them from Spanish tyranny to enable them to set up a government of their own, and we were to stand by and see that it got a fair trial. It was not to be a government according to our ideas, but a government that represented the feeling of the majority of the Filipinos, a government according to Filipino ideas. That would have been a worthy mission for the United States. But now—why, we have got into a mess, a quagmire from which each fresh step renders the difficulty of extrication immensely greater. I'm sure I wish I could see what we were getting out of it, and all it means to us as a nation."

On such thoughts Mark Twain continued to brood after landing in New York and setting up residence on Tenth Street off Fifth Avenue. Three weeks after the Clemenses' return, voters took part in a presidential election that the humorist sat out, unwilling to cast his ballot for either candidate, for Mr. McKinley or Mr. Bryan either one. No matter. Votes cast, when counted, registered a decisive victory for the Republicans. For the first time in many years the Grand Old Party controlled the White House and both chambers of Congress as well, McKinley's policies having been roundly endorsed. Prosperity. Victory in war. America ascendant on the world stage. And, despite whatever bother it was causing, the Philippines to all intents an American colony.

A month after the election, through five days in December, Mark Twain worked on an essay, which he saw published in February 1901 in the *North American Review*. He called it "To the Person Sitting in Darkness," as in Matthew 4:16: "The people which sat in darkness saw great light." Such people in Mark Twain's current musings were the formerly benighted of the earth—among them the Chinese, the Boers, and the Filipinos—on whom the great powers were currently bestowing the Blessings of Civilization. Nine years in Europe and travels around the globe had given this particular American unusual opportunities for studying both sides closely: on the one hand the colonizing European nations, as well as Russia and Japan; and, on the other, the "lesser breeds without the law," in Kipling's phrase of 1897, the backward people in their dark places. Mark Twain's essay undertakes to clarify the enlightenment of those latter—the great light that the people which sat in darkness were now being bathed in. The essay raises the question: "shall we go on conferring our Civilization upon the peoples that sit in darkness, or shall we give those poor things a rest?" Granted, what we've been doing has resulted in "a good trade and has paid well." And there's money in it yet; "The Blessings-of-Civilization Trust, wisely and cautiously administered, is a Daisy." Yet we've been playing it badly, the humorist contends. We've been promising Love, and Justice, and Gentleness, and Christianity, and Protection of the Weak, and Temperance, and so on—Law and Order, Liberty, Equality, Honorable Dealing, Mercy, and Education. "There. Is it good?" he asks of the list. "Sir, it is pie. It will bring into camp any idiot that sits in darkness anywhere."

Yet what we've been delivering in fact is ruining the game, and the people in darkness are starting to notice. What we've delivered in China, in South Africa, and in the Philippines is something quite different from Love and Justice and Gentleness. In China, for example, "the Kaiser went to playing the game without first mastering it." Having lost a couple of missionaries in a riot over there, he overcharged for them, demanding $100,000 apiece for the two, plus twelve miles of Chinese territory, including several million Chinese living thereon, plus—as a monument memorializing the missionaries—a Christian church that the Chinese were to build themselves. Bad play: it helped lead to the Boxer uprising. "Civilization is gracious and beautiful, for such is its reputation," those in darkness had likely reflected, "but can we afford it? There are rich Chinamen, perhaps they could afford it; but this tax is not laid upon them, it is laid upon the peasants of Shantung; it is they that must pay this mighty sum, and their wages are but four cents a day. Is this a better civilization than ours, and holier and higher and nobler? Is not this rapacity? Is not this extortion?"

Great Britain, for its part, manufactures a war in South Africa "out of materials so inadequate and so fanciful that they make the boxes grieve and the gallery laugh," all the while trying to convince its people "that it isn't purely a private raid for cash, but has a sort of dim, vague respect-ability about it somewhere," and that the Union Jack can be scoured clean again after having been dragged through the mud fighting Boers. Another bad play. "For it exposes the Actual Thing to Them that Sit in Darkness, and they say: 'What! Christian against Christian? And only for money? Is this a case of magnanimity, forbearance, love, gentleness, mercy, protection of the weak—this strange and over-showy onslaught of an elephant upon a nest of field mice, on the pretext that the mice had squeaked an insolence at him—conduct which 'no self-respecting government could allow to pass unavenged?' as Mr. Chamberlain said"—Britain's colonial secretary Joseph Chamberlain. Well might the backward wonder: "Is this Civilization and Progress? Is it something better than we already possess? These harryings and burnings and desert-makings in the Transvaal—is this an improve-ment on our darkness?"

Then comes America, "and our Master of the Game," President McKin-ley, "plays it badly—plays it as Mr. Chamberlain was playing it in South Africa. It was a mistake to do that," Mark Twain submits; "also, it was one which was quite unlooked for in a Master who was playing it so well in Cuba. In Cuba, he was playing the usual and regular *American* game, and it was winning, for there is no way to beat it." In Cuba we got in and got out, making clear at the start that we had no territorial ambitions there, merely helping a spunky people fight to be free, while announcing in so many words that forcible annexation would be "criminal aggression." Help Cuba rid itself of the curse of Spanish tyranny, then leave it to make its own future.

But what we've done in the Philippines is succumb to the temptation to play the European game, be a great power at the very place and time when we should have played the American game once more. And we would have played it "at no cost. Rich winnings to be gathered in, too; rich and permanent; indestructible; a fortune transmissible forever to the children of the flag. Not land, not money, not dominion—no, something worth many times more than that dross: our share, the spectacle of a nation of long harassed and persecuted slaves set free through our influence; our posterity's share, the golden memory of that fair deed." Play by American rules, and "Dewey would have sailed away from Manila as soon as he had destroyed the Spanish fleet—after putting up a sign on shore guaranteeing foreign property and life against damage by the Filipinos, and warning the Powers that interference with the emancipated patriots would be regarded as an act unfriendly to the United States. The Powers cannot combine, in even a bad cause, and the sign would not have been molested."

What would have happened next? The competent Filipino army of 30,000, veterans of successes that had already freed all the Philippines except Manila, would have defeated the last Spanish garrison on its own, then set up a government according to ideas, the essayist says, as legitimate "as any that prevail in Europe or America." But we didn't do in the Philippines what we did in Cuba. And what we did do left the Person Sitting in Darkness wondering. "There must be two Americas: one that sets the captive free, and one that takes a once-captive's new freedom away from him, and picks a quarrel with him with nothing to found it on; then kills him to get his land." For what we were seen to do was enter "into a military alliance with the trusting Filipinos" so that they could hem in Manila on the land side, thinking they were fighting against the Spaniard for freedom— "and we allowed them to go on thinking so. *Until Manila was ours and we could get along without them.* Then we showed our hand." We had seemed so friendly, affectionate even, restoring their leader Aguinaldo from exile, bringing him in honor on a warship from Hong Kong to lead his people, then fought alongside those people against "'the Common enemy' (our own phrase)," praised their courage, then took over their positions on land, "fooled them, used them until we needed them no longer; then derided the sucked orange and threw it away." Filipino "patriots" became "rebels," and we paid Spain—her sovereignty over the Philippines at an end—$20 million for islands she no longer possessed. With that, "we had no further use for Aguinaldo and the owners of the archipelago. We forced a war, and we have been hunting America's guest and ally"—that same General Emilio Aguinaldo—"through the woods and swamps ever since."

It is a sorry tale as Mark Twain tells it, although no doubt all for the good: "True, we have crushed a deceived and confiding people; we have turned against the weak and the friendless who trusted us; we have stamped out a just and intelligent and well-ordered republic; we have stabbed an ally in the back and slapped the face of a guest; we have bought a Shadow from an enemy that hadn't it to sell; we have robbed a trusting friend of his land and his liberty; we have invited our clean young men to shoulder a discredited musket and do bandit's work under a flag which bandits have been accustomed to fear, not to follow; we have debauched America's honor and blackened her face before the world; but each detail was for the best." All was in the name of the lucrative Blessings-of-Civilization Trust. And all was supported by every state and legislature here at home, for it will bring additional prosperity while lifting the Master of the Game up among the Trinity of our national gods: Washington, bearing the Sword of the Liberator; Lincoln, the Slaves' broken Chains; and now McKinley—"the lousy McKinley," as Clemens in private referred to the President—holding the Chains Repaired.

CHAPTER Sixteen

Pan-American Exposition

M uch of Mark Twain's writing after his return to America in 1900 went unpublished during his lifetime. His wife Livy, whose opinion he valued above all others, pleaded with him to show his more genial side; and anyway, he was wary of alienating readers. Should he die, in those years before pensions and social security, sales of his books constituted the bulk of the provision he would leave behind to his family. Yet the author did publish in all its candor "To the Person Sitting in Darkness," and the New York Anti-Imperialist League disseminated the essay far and wide as a pamphlet. In coming months, because he had strong opinions on current matters, Mark Twain wrote a number of other vigorously argued articles and reviews on controversial issues and put some of them prominently into print. Reaction followed on the instant, invariably, indignantly, and with great noise from the many opposed to his views, more quietly from those who shared those views and were willing to say so. To an Edmund B. Kirby of Rossland, British Columbia, who had written early in 1901 to express the "enthusiastic gratitude of that crowd of silent men who welcome the clear voice when it speaks for them," Mark Twain responded with gratitude of his own: "you do me a helpful office; we can always speak with more courage when we know that we have backers." Again, not long after "To the Person Sitting in Darkness" appeared, William Dean Howells, novelist, editor, longtime friend of the humorist—from Boston and Hartford days—now living in New York, wrote to his sister: "I see a great deal of Mark Twain, and we have high good times denouncing everything. We agree perfectly about the Boer war and the Filipino war, and war generally. Then, we are old fellows, and it is pleasant to find the world so much worse than it was when we were young. Clemens is, as I have always known him, a most right-minded man, and of course he has an intellect that I enjoy.

He is getting some hard knocks now from the blackguards and hypocrites for his righteous fun with McKinley's attempt to colonize the Philippines, but he is making hosts of friends, too."

About "war generally," which editor and humorist mulled over together, the well-mannered Howells had things to say publicly himself, and places to say them in as a regular columnist for *Harper's Weekly* and contributor to the *North American Review*. Howells would soon be writing, in contradistinction to Vice President Roosevelt, that men learn no virtues in war, nor is war the only cradle of heroes. Peace has its heroes too; "it is not rough-riding up San Juan hills alone," Howells wrote, "that is the event of heroism." As for *patriotism* and *treason*, this particular anti-imperialist, like Mark Twain and the others, was being buffeted lately by such terms hurled in his direction, charged with lacking the one and being guilty of the other. Howells was not much of a public speaker, but Mark Twain was about the best going, and could rebut, and did. Although suppressing a great deal of what he wrote on current issues, he did speak out candidly regarding those same issues over many a ceremonial function to which he was invited, the bite of his outrage only somewhat blunted by the ever-present humor in his delivery.

"Mark Twain is not to be taken seriously," a certain Dr. Frank Van Fleet of the New York Medical Society pronounced dismissively in February 1901. "When he came back from his trip abroad he talked of a dishonored flag; we did not take him seriously. If we had, some of us might have mobbed him, and rightly, too." And Roosevelt in 1899, delivering his speech on "The Strenuous Life," had already branded (and would go on branding) the efforts of all such anti-imperialists as no less than treasonable, giving aid and comfort to an enemy among whom were Filipinos even then firing on American soldiers in their archipelago. "As for those in our own country who encourage the foe," the then governor of New York had pronounced in Chicago, "we can afford contemptuously to disregard them; but it must be remembered that their utterances are not saved from being treasonable merely by the fact that they are despicable."

But that "Mark Twain is not to be taken seriously": it was a belittlement that the Wild Humorist of the Pacific Slope had been dogged with all his professional life, despite his many nonhumorous efforts such as *The Prince and the Pauper, Joan of Arc,* and "The Man That Corrupted Hadleyburg." Now his countrymen, some of them, were accusing him of being unpatriotic. "Where's the evidence?" he drawled to members of the Lotos Club, whom he was entertaining after a banquet in March 1901. "There are seventy-five millions of us"—the population of the United States then—"working our patriotism." Those crying treason were working theirs in making the charge. And who's to say who is patriotic? "It would be an entirely different question if the country's life was in danger, its existence at stake, then—that is one kind of patriotism—we would all come forward and stand by the flag, and stop thinking about whether the nation was right or wrong; but when there is no question that the nation is in any way in danger, but only some little war away off, then it may be that on the question of politics the nation is divided, half patriots and half traitors, and no man can tell which from which."

Vice President Roosevelt could tell. Roosevelt was clear in his mind about many things—about Aguinaldo for one, leader of the Philippine resistance. General Wesley Merritt, commander of our forces over there early on, had reported back in August 1898 that Filipinos "are superior as a people than is generally represented; their leaders are mostly men of education and ability." Roosevelt knew otherwise. A fierce nationalist, he had no patience when nationalism stirred in what appeared to him to be backward lands—among Boxers, for instance, or Filipinos. Only natives sensible enough to collaborate with American forces on their soil were displaying loyalty and virtue, so it became mere justice to deal harshly with those who weren't. Whoever didn't cooperate was a rebel, a bandit, a traitor, as was (in Roosevelt's eyes) the corrupt Emilio Aguinaldo, president of the Philippine Republic that had been proclaimed in January 1899. In leading the resistance against a vastly superior American force, Aguinaldo in turn dealt harshly with Filipinos who betrayed his imperiled republic, thereby displaying what Roosevelt took to be not justice but savage cruelty, even though such conduct mirrored what Americans were regularly meting out to disloyalty on their own side.

Roosevelt's blind spot about other people's nationalism is curious. As for warfare, the new vice president stood ready to go to war any time it seemed warranted. Unlike William Dean Howells, who maintained that men learn no virtues in war, Roosevelt thought that combat—like hunting—taught the most important of all virtues, manliness, lacking which, in individuals as in a nation, no others sufficed. Out in Dakota in 1886, the New York ranchman had been raring to exercise his own manliness by gathering a regiment of cowboys and putting it at the service of his government to ride against Mexico and avenge a border incident, grieved when diplomacy prevented his leading into battle what he called "as utterly reckless a set of desperadoes as ever sat in the saddle." Again, in 1891, when America was embroiled in a dispute with Chile over a mob's slaying of two American sailors in Valparaiso, Roosevelt was disgusted to learn that President Harrison had accepted an apology, "hissing through clenched teeth," according to John Hay, "that we are dishonest. For two nickels he would declare war himself, shut up the Civil Service Commission, and wage it sole." In 1896, with the United States again at odds with a foreign power, this time with Britain over a border dispute between Venezuela and British Guiana, Roosevelt wrote to his friend Henry Cabot Lodge, "I do hope there will not be any back down among our people. Let the fight come if it must; I don't care whether our sea coast cities are bombarded or not; we would take Canada." As for McKinley's hesitating two years later about going to war against Spain, Roosevelt felt only contempt for a presidential backbone made, as he said, from a chocolate éclair.

America *needs* war now and then, all the more so in such a materialistic age as the present one. What John Hay called that "splendid little war" against Spain, recently and satisfactorily concluded, had strengthened the nation's moral fiber and toughened up a people at risk of going slack and self-indulgent. Whoever opposed so righteous a conflict had been either naive, sentimental, cowardly, or lacking in virility; and the same applied to those protesting our efforts in the Philippines. They should understand that the time was overdue for America to assume its rightful place as a world power here at the entrance to a new century.

For the twentieth century was beginning in 1901 (as centuries properly do), 1900 having been the final, hundredth year of the nineteenth. Thus Mark Twain had issued his salutation to this new century on December 31, 1900; and now, in the spring of 1901, with the end of the preceding century finally come and gone, it appeared fitting that America should be welcoming so momentous an epoch as this just arrived with yet another world's fair.

It was held in Buffalo. Called the Pan-American Exposition, the fair honored unity in the Western Hemisphere, with much on the grounds foretelling glories that lay ahead. The extravaganza signaled its purposes through a distinctive architecture: great domed Beaux-Arts structures around courts and fountains and esplanades as at Chicago eight years earlier, but not a White City like that one, rather a rainbow city, the many buildings—at least those without domes—roofed in simulated red tiles to evoke the Spanish heritage of our southern neighbors and of our own Southwest. The walls of the buildings were tinted in hues of rose, pale yellow, warm orange, or tawny brown, their details accented with gold trim or in brilliant greens and blues. There were as well mirror lakes, two brightly colored bandstands, and a stadium that seated 12,000, in addition to pergolas, colonnades, a triumphal bridge, a grand court of fountains, and horticultural delights abloom on all sides. There were miniature railways to carry visitors about the grounds, and in the Midway whole worlds awaited: an African village, streets of Mexico, a journey Around the Beautiful Orient, even a spectacular Trip to the Moon. There was an Electric Tower that rose high above its reflecting pool, a gorgeous ivory-colored central edifice, from the summit of which spread glorious views of Buffalo and beyond to the distant mists over Niagara Falls. A newfangled automobile was displayed in the Machinery and Transportation Building; an infant incubator that would save lives was to be marveled at on the Midway; and in the Electricity Building an amazing X-ray machine that let you look inside people and see what you never had seen before.

Indeed, even more than at the earlier White City, electricity was the soul of this present fair, electricity from Niagara Falls twenty miles off that promised safety on streets in the nighttime and productive work indoors long after the sun went down. Accordingly, near sunset each evening visitors gathered along the Pan-American Exposition's imposing triumphal bridge and its esplanade to watch darkness descend and myriad lights come on, tiny orange orbs that grew stronger in wattage in the course of nine seconds until they outlined all the marvelous buildings and artifacts, while the Seventy-Fourth Regiment band played and the thousands and thousands of lights cast bright duplicates in the lakes and pools strategically placed about the grounds. It was breathtaking; it was scarcely credible in its loveliness. And that we all, of whatever age, might be lucky enough to live long into this new century, to witness the progress: those incubators; the X-ray machines; the wondrous improvements in food preservation already on display here; the automobiles that will whisk us from place to place; but above all the light, the light, everywhere the magic of gorgeous light defying and enhancing darkness.

In addition, this fair like its predecessors offered manifold opportunities for self-indulgence and the satisfying of material desires: right from the start, at the two entrances to the Pan-American Exposition, the just-invented Kodak Brownie camera was on sale for a dollar, allowing you to record your visit and take it home with you. And though, in Theodore Roosevelt's view, materialism and self-indulgence loomed as threats to America's moral fiber, the vice president came to see the exposition anyway, an early visitor and doubtless one of its most enthusiastic. President McKinley was to come to Buffalo as well, on President's Day, scheduled for June 13—as presidents Grant and Cleveland had respectively attended the Philadelphia Centennial and the Chicago World's Columbian Exposition earlier. First, however, the current chief executive would depart with Mrs. McKinley and a team of forty-three on a grand cross-country, post-election, springtime railroad tour to San Francisco and back, out by the southern route and home across the spacious Northwest. The presidential party left Washington aboard a special train on Monday morning, April 29, 1901.

By that date William McKinley was popular across the country, both West and East. Level-headed, amiable, reassuring, he was the friend of business who had brought prosperity back to the land. He had won the war against Spain. He had pacified the Philippines, where his program was lately taking a turn for the better. In March, the rebel Aguinaldo had been captured in his mountain lair. On July 4, General Arthur MacArthur, military governor, would turn over control of the Philippines to his civilian successor, the jovial Judge William Howard Taft. And lest the benefits from all this national effort be doubted, Senator Chauncey Depew of New York had recently reminded America of what else was at stake: "the pacification of the Philippines gives a market of ten millions of people. It will grow every year as they come into more civilized conditions and their wants increase." Depew's insight only confirmed what Mark Twain had been saying all along: whatever else it might accomplish, the bestowal of Civilization's Blessings had the potential of turning into a highly profitable enterprise.

Mrs. McKinley, meanwhile, was ailing in San Francisco. She had developed a painful infection of the finger; so the presidential party was obliged to cut short its progress and set out early for home, on July 5, in hopes of spending a restful summer in Canton. President's Day at the fair was rescheduled for September. Thus the chief executive and his wife, both well rested, found themselves at last in Buffalo on Wednesday evening, September 5, 1901, in good time for McKinley to deliver a speech at the fairgrounds the following noon. He spoke before some 50,000 enthusiastic fairgoers, crowded around the bandstand and onto the broad esplanade. The President's theme, which accorded well with the Exposition's, concerned the need for trade between nations of the hemispheres. In this new century, "God and man"—the latter with his steamships and railroads and telegraphs and cables—"have linked the nations together." Such fairs as this are "the timekeepers of progress," in McKinley's happy phrase; and progress, as we can see all around us, has made the globe grow small. America meanwhile, in its "almost appalling" prosperity, produces far more, the speaker declaimed, than it can ever consume within its borders; yet "we can not forever sell everything and buy little or nothing." The world has changed. "Isolation is no longer possible or desirable." We must trade reciprocally. We must sign reciprocity treaties with other nations.

The crowd in its merry mood welcomed the President's remarks with applause and ovation. Afterward, amid much further waving and cheering, the honored guest strolled through the grounds, entered buildings, viewed exhibits, and that evening returned from the mansion on Delaware Avenue where he and Mrs. McKinley were staying, in order to watch the ceremony of illumination and witness a spectacular fireworks display, including one final pyrotechnic radiance that spread the presidential image on the skies and spelled forth: "Welcome to McKinley, Chief of our Nation." Gratified, he and his beloved Ida rose next morning and set out with a party to visit Niagara Falls. They returned in mid-afternoon. Bidding goodbye to Mrs. McKinley, on her way back to rest at the Milburn mansion, the President mounted a waiting victoria and proceeded to a scheduled reception on the fairgrounds at the Hall of Music.

Thousands had already gathered there in hopes of shaking the President's hand. Among them was a nondescript steelworker who, upon reaching the head of the line, extended a left arm toward McKinley, a bandage-like handkerchief wrapped around his right. The President reached forward obligingly, and in that instant two shots tore through the handkerchief at point-blank range. McKinley staggered backward. Amid screams and chaos the assailant was hurled to the floor, held there and severely beaten. Chairs overturned, the crowd pressing, surging, some panicky. Seated, dazed, the President urged his tardy protectors to go easy on the misguided fellow.

Figure 16.1.   Assassination of President McKinley, September 6, 1901.

Courtesy of the Library of Congress.

An ambulance arrived to rush the wounded statesman to the emergency clinic on the fairgrounds.

From Saranac Lake in the Adirondacks, where he and his family had been spending their summer, Samuel Clemens wrote to a friend next day: "There was a report last night that the President has been shot. But there are no newspapers, and no one knows whether it is true or not. It may be only talk; I will hope so." Vice President Roosevelt was attending a luncheon of the Vermont Fish and Game League at Isle La Motte in Lake Champlain when he received word of the attempted assassination; at once he set out for Buffalo and remained anxiously on the scene until doctors assured him that the President was out of danger.

Such assurances were overhasty. The physician who performed the operation was a gynecologist, not a surgeon. For all the electricity about, the light in the clinic had been poor; an attending physician had held a mirror at the window to direct late afternoon sunbeams onto the operating table. There was an X-ray machine nearby, but no one knew how to use it. One of the two bullets could not be got at and remained in the body; the instruments probing for it had been inadequately sterilized, the wound left undrained.

On September 13, a week after the fanatical anarchist Leon Czolgosz, twenty-eight years old, had made his attempt on McKinley's life, the President's recovery took a sharp turn for the worse. The assassin would be tried in the New York courts and promptly executed, sulfuric acid poured over his corpse to disfigure and destroy it. But well before then, President McKinley on Delaware Avenue in Buffalo (not far from where Samuel L. Clemens had begun his married life three decades earlier, inside the Langdons' joyous gift of a mansion on the same boulevard) had lost consciousness, his heart and stomach failing. "I'm so sorry that this should have happened here," he murmured at one point, thinking of the hard work and high hopes that had gone into creating such a wonderful effort as this Pan-American Exposition, now forever to be blighted as the setting for a national tragedy.

On the fourteenth, at two in the morning, William McKinley died. The Vice President, who had traveled on with his family to a remote part of the Adirondacks by then, was just returning from a hike to the crest of Mount Marcy when the summons reached him to hurry again to Buffalo. A wagon took Roosevelt at breakneck speed to the nearest rail line, where a train was waiting. That sped him across New York State, although delivering him to his destination twelve hours after the President had ceased to breathe. Even so, Mr. Roosevelt declined to take the oath of office until he had extended his condolences to Mrs. McKinley. All agreed that the New York patrician conducted himself with exemplary sensitivity and considerateness throughout the ordeal. But on the funeral train that carried the corpse of a martyred statesman to Washington, a grieving Mark Hanna—Cleveland industrialist and McKinley's closest friend, his campaign manager, the kingmaker who had put the Ohio governor in the White House—fumed "in an intensely bitter state of mind." A seatmate on the sad trip, the publisher H. H. Kohlsaat, listened and recorded Hanna's opinion of Roosevelt: "I told William McKinley it was a mistake to nominate that wild man at Philadelphia. I asked him if he realized what would happen if he should die. Now look, that damned cowboy is President of the United States!"

PART Three

RACE

CHAPTER **Seventeen**

Yale Bicentennial

The General Court of Connecticut, on October 9, 1701, authorized the establishment of a school that would prepare young men, as its charter says, "for public employment both in church and civil state," in order to advance the welfare of the colony. Within a couple of decades, having in the interim moved from town to town, the new institution came to rest at New Haven, where it received the benefactions of a merchant named Yale, who had made a fortune in the India trade. In gratitude, the Collegiate School changed its name to Yale College. Years passed. The college grew into Yale University and, within two centuries of its founding, had engendered an imposing progeny whose surviving members were eager to celebrate the bicentennial of their alma mater. Many months beforehand, preparations had been set in motion—programs devised, invitations extended—to honor the grand occasion. Festivities would be held on the New Haven campus over four days in October 1901.

Yale suspended classes for the jubilee. Sunday morning, October 20, in oak-paneled Battell Chapel, the Reverend Joseph Hopkins Twichell of Hartford, an alumnus and one of Samuel L. Clemens's three closest friends, helped to inaugurate the anniversary with a sermon and prayer, thanking the Almighty for having in the former time led our fathers forth into a wealthy place and set their feet in a large room. "What protections, what guidances, what deliverances hast Thou vouchsafed unto the nation they founded, from the beginning even until now!" Blessings were sought of our Heavenly Father on "Thy servant the President of the United States" and "on the University within whose precincts we are assembled," and may Thy benediction "rest also upon the honored guests and friends who, in Thy kind providence, are gathering here at this time to share the gladness and the gratitude with which we call to remembrance the multiplied

147

mercies and bounties Thou hast in Thy loving favor bestowed upon us in all the years gone by."

Honored guests were many, from far and wide, including those to be awarded degrees as well as delegates from European institutions of learning (among others, the universities of Paris, Oxford, Cambridge, Padua, Leipzig, Uppsala, and Aberdeen), from Asian institutions (Tokyo, Kyoto, Peking), from Australian (Sydney, Adelaide), from South American and from universities, colleges, and learned societies all over North America, those last numbering in the dozens. There would be an organ recital for guests and friends on Sunday evening and a dedication of the Cheney-Ives Gateway tomorrow morning at 9:30, to be followed in the afternoon by President Hadley's welcome, with responses from the mayor of Hartford and Connecticut's governor and senior senator, as well as from various university presidents, including President Eliot of Harvard. A reception in the art school at 5 P.M. would precede a torchlight procession of some thousands of students and graduates starting at nine.

Tuesday morning, the twenty-second, was filled with addresses around campus expounding on Yale's various roles in the world of the present. The afternoon offered football games, with a student dramatic performance later that included the singing of college songs, and an evening illumination of the campus to highlight scenes from Yale's long history. Commemoration exercises were held in the Hyperion Theater Wednesday morning at 10:30 A.M. David Josiah Brewer, Justice of the United States Supreme Court, addressed the assembly, after which honorary degrees were bestowed. Candidates on stage rose as their names were called and stood before the president of the university while he read each citation and conferred the appropriate honor. Marshals would then invest the gentleman with the academic hood and usher him back to his seat. Later in the afternoon, guests were welcomed at a concert on campus by the Boston Symphony Orchestra; and a farewell reception at University Hall at 5 P.M. concluded the festivities.

The list of degree honorees was impressive. The roll call rumbles solemnly down the page: professors, university presidents, the current secretary of state, a Shakespeare scholar, an artist, a bishop, an archbishop, each saluted with a single-sentence tribute encapsulating the reason for the bestowal. Authors and editors hear their names called alphabetically. One by one they rise: Thomas Bailey Aldrich, George Washington Cable—until only at the third name do the proceedings suddenly leap from the page in noisy jubilation as a familiar figure stands (his trim build, his abundant white hair, his droopy mustache), the audience uniquely greeting the seven syllables of the name with loud cheers and sustained applause. "For whom . . ." Arthur Twining Hadley begins; is Yale's president ad-libbing, responding to the sudden happy clamor all around him in the theater, or has the written tribute anticipated what would happen when that particular name was sounded? The dry account of the proceedings records SAMUEL LANGHORNE CLEMENS, and President Hadley pronounces when he can: "For whom the universal acclaim which has just now been heard renders any assignment of reasons a work of supererogation, we confer upon you the degree of Doctor of Letters and admit you to all its rights and privileges."

A behooded Mark Twain is led back to his seat in a hall suddenly alive with good feeling as the names roll on: Richard Watson Gilder, William Dean Howells, Brander Matthews, Thomas Nelson Page. But what a day this must have turned into for a Missouri native born nearly sixty-six years before in a two-room, one-story rented frame frontier dwelling, now here in New Haven having just heard, yet again, an audience's tumultuous love called forth at the mere utterance of his name, as Clemens had heard the same response over his remarkable career many times, had heard it overseas as early as the fall of 1872—nearly three decades ago—when, on a first visit to England in his mid-thirties, the author of *The Innocents Abroad* found himself dressed in full formality among an entitled crowd at London's Guildhall, attending the lord mayor's inaugural ceremonies. Unrecognized, the American had reached his assigned place and modestly taken his seat. Liveried servants were everywhere. Agreeable to ancient custom, the name of each guest was being called out, "a horde of great names," he would write soon after, "one after another, which were received in respectful silence." Until one name was reached, at which "there was such a storm of applause as you never heard," the recipient reported promptly, proudly, on September 28, 1872, to his wife Livy back home in Hartford. "The applause continued, & they could not go on with the list. I was never so taken aback in my life," utterly unprepared for the outpouring. "I thought I was the humblest in that great titled assemblage—& behold, mine was the *only* name in the long list that called forth this splendid compliment."

Now he had heard the happy welcoming roar once again, the westerner here in this bastion of eastern culture; and all his many friends attending at Yale's bicentennial ceremony had heard it, too, grinning and joining in gladly: Twichell, Howells, Aldrich, Gilder, Cable, Norton, Matthews, Hay. All good friends of his: by now Clemens knew them all. Whom didn't he know by this time? Who wouldn't have welcomed the acquaintance, the friendship of such a beloved celebrity, creator of characters—Dan'l Webster the jumping frog and Colonel Sellers and Tom Sawyer and Huck and Jim and Hank Morgan and the rest—who lived ineradicably in the American mind, utterer of folk wisdom and witty, quotable common sense that by now were universal currency? Beforehand, Twichell—the Reverend Joseph Hopkins Twichell, M.A., Senior Fellow of the Yale Corporation; Joe Twichell, dear, dear friend of more than thirty years, he who had officiated at Olivia Langdon and Samuel Clemens's wedding, who had officiated at Susy Clemens's funeral, who would officiate at Livy's funeral, and at Clara Clemens's wedding, and at Jean Clemens's funeral, and at last would utter a prayer at Samuel L. Clemens's lying in repose at the Brick Church in New York City—Joe Twichell had written his onetime Hartford neighbor some weeks before: "I want you to understand, old fellow, that it will be in its intention"—this conferring of the most exalted rank that an American institution of learning had at its bestowal—"the highest public compliment, and emphatically so in your case, for it will be tendered you by a corporation of gentlemen, the majority of whom do not at all agree with the views on important questions which you have lately promulgated in speech and in writing, and with which you are identified in the public mind." Of course the Yale Corporation acknowledged Mark Twain's right to express his opinions, on the Philippines as on all else; but it was Mark Twain as man of letters, Samuel Langhorne Clemens as man of letters that Yale was saluting, not the social activist, the anti-imperialist gadfly.

Salute him Yale did, this much loved figure seated on stage in the Hyperion Theater as the names rumbled solemnly on through an October morning: Woodrow Wilson, Professor of Jurisprudence and Politics in Princeton University; the president of Union Theological Seminary; the president of Amherst College; the ambassador of the United States at the Court of St. James; the chief justice of the United States; the principal of McGill University; the editor of the *New York Tribune*; Admiral Sampson of the United States Navy, victor at Santiago.

When the roll was called in its entirety, one name remained at the very last. President Hadley read that name out himself. "To THEODORE ROOSEVELT, while he was yet a private citizen, we offered the degree of Doctor of Laws, merited by his eminent achievements in letters, in history, and in public service. Since in his providence it has pleased God to raise him to the position of Chief Magistrate of the Nation, we now owe him a double homage as citizen and as President." Although a Harvard man, this last-named honoree was possessed of qualities (a democratic spirit, a breadth of national feeling, an earnest pursuit of what is true and right) "that represent the distinctive ideals of Yale and make us more than ever proud to enroll him among our Alumni." Thus—to Colonel Roosevelt directly—"at this crowning moment of our commemoration, we offer the degree of Doctor of Laws and admit you to all its rights and privileges."

This, too, along with the earlier clamorous award to Samuel L. Clemens was a high point, for which the new president of the United States expressed his appreciation gracefully. He told the assembly that he had never worked at a task worth doing without finding himself shoulder to shoulder with some son of Yale, had never struggled for righteousness and decency without finding Yale men to aid and give him courage and strength. "I thank you from my heart," the President concluded his brief remarks, "for the honor you do me, and I thank you doubly because you planned to do me that honor while I was yet a private citizen."

By this time (today was Wednesday, October 23, 1901), the public servant had been at work in his new quarters in Washington precisely one day beyond a full month. Having attended his predecessor's funeral at Canton, Ohio, Roosevelt spent a first full day at the White House on September 22, reading documents and signing papers. It was his father's birthday—Roosevelt Sr. would have been seventy years old that day had he lived—and throughout those initial hours the father's spirit had seemed to stand at the son's shoulder, Teedie suddenly elevated to the highest office in the land at an age (forty-two) younger than any of his forerunners or successors. The elevation had come about through means that its beneficiary of course deplored: the third presidential assassination, after Lincoln's and Garfield's, in less than forty years. Like the grieving nation, Roosevelt abhorred what had happened at Buffalo; yet it would be morbid to dwell on the catastrophe, morbid and weak. The Colonel would not let himself do that. Don't brood on the past, which can't be changed: on a president recently murdered; on an adored father's untimely, excruciating death two decades earlier; on the death of Roosevelt's mother and his young first wife all in a single horrible night and day. Keep busy and try not to think of it; that was his manner of coping—precisely the advice Roosevelt once urged his sister to offer a friend who had suffered tragically. "She should try not to think of it; this she cannot wholly avoid, but she *can* avoid speaking of it. She should show a brave and cheerful front to the world, whatever she feels; and henceforth she should never speak one word of the matter to anyone."

Too much needed doing to allow oneself the indulgence of morbidity. In Roosevelt's case, first off, the new president had had to reassure a nation reeling from the Buffalo murder. At the hastily rigged swearing-in ceremony in the library of the Wilcox mansion on Delaware Avenue on September 14, the day of McKinley's death, his successor had vowed: "It shall be my aim to continue, absolutely, unbroken, the policy of President McKinley for the peace, the prosperity, and the honor of our beloved country." And so far Roosevelt had made good on that vow. He had retained in office McKinley's cabinet, including his secretary of state, John Hay—just honored here at Yale—and Elihu Root as secretary of war; and the new president had assigned McKinley's confidential secretary to organize the new administration's procedures at the White House and deal with the press on a daily basis. Thus faces of continuity went about their tasks, soothing public anxieties through hectic transitional days.

Yet in the White House itself—it was Roosevelt who made official the use of the colloquial designation, removing the pompous "Executive Mansion" from office stationery—that fall in the White House change came rushing in. How could it not? In place of the childless McKinleys (both their daughters had died very early), in place of a sedate president in his late fifties and his invalid wife, came suddenly to Washington the irrepressible young Roosevelt with his large, energetic family: his very capable wife Edith and their six children. The beautiful, willful Alice was seventeen; Theodore Jr., "Ted," was thirteen; Kermit was eleven; Ethel nine; Archie six; and Quentin three. The nation relished what was happening: toys scattered about; those noisy, happy games on the White House lawn; all the pets the children had; the hide-and-seek inside historic hallways; the stilts; the sliding down stairs on trays from the White House kitchen. And President Roosevelt himself, accessible, outspoken, impulsive, appeared at all times to be in a whirl of motion.

"One of the most astonishing things in the President's life," read an early introduction to "MR. THEODORE ROOSEVELT" in the *New York Times* on September 14 ("Varied Career of the Next President of the United States. His Achievements in Politics, War, and Literary Pursuits Have Been Notable.")—after alluding to the new president's urban upbringing, his Knickerbocker heritage, his family's wealth, his self-discipline in transforming a puny childhood frame into the solid athletic body of the wrestler and the ranchhand, his service in the New York Assembly, his unsuccessful race for mayor of New York, his six years as civil service commissioner, his achievements as New York City police commissioner, his role as assistant secretary of the navy, his war service commanding Rough Riders in Cuba (from which he returned to the United States "the idol of the country"), his two years as governor of New York, and his election to the vice presidency—"One of the most astonishing things in the President's life is the great amount of literary work he has accomplished despite his manifold other concerns." The *Times* lists titles: *The Naval War of 1812*; lives of Thomas Hart Benton, of Gouverneur Morris, of

Oliver Cromwell; accounts of ranch days and hunting out West; a history of New York City; collections of addresses and essays such as *The Strenuous Life* and *American Political Ideals*; and—Mr. Roosevelt's masterpiece—*The Winning of the West*. All of those writings the newspaper adjudges to be "remarkable for their vigor of style and clearness of expression."

But President Roosevelt's days were too full now to contemplate adding to the list. In the early weeks of the new administration he was conferring, gaining familiarity with issues, dealing with federal appointments, and seeking advice over working breakfasts, lunches, and dinners. He invited to dinner, for instance, on October 16—in the week before Yale's bicentennial festivities—a distinguished educator to advise him about appointments down South. "Dear Mr. President," came the dutiful reply, "I shall be very glad to accept your invitation for dinner this evening at 7:30." Few others would have been better informed on such matters than was that night's dinner guest, who conferred "at considerable length" with the President concerning political matters in a South only beginning to recover from the devastations of civil war.

However, a week later, President Roosevelt, now in the Hyperion Theater in New Haven, felt troubled about whether he had been wise to consult with the head of Tuskegee Institute as he had done last Wednesday evening. The President ran into Mark Twain at the Yale festivities and asked him about it. Some years after the fact, Clemens recalled the encounter privately, remembering "the freshet of honorary degrees at Yale, and the President was there to get part of the ducking and I was there on the same errand, and there were sixty more gowned and hooded for baptism. The President asked me if I thought he was right in inviting Booker Washington to lunch at the White House. I judged by his tone that he was worried and troubled and sorry about that showy adventure, and wanted a little word of comfort and approval."

Dictating confidential reminiscences those seven years later, in the summer of 1908—words that he meant to leave unpublished while anyone then alive still breathed—Clemens represents himself as answering Colonel Roosevelt in a way that may rather surprise and disappoint us who are here to read more than a century afterward, after all those others have gone. "I said it was a private citizen's privilege to invite whom he pleased to his table," the humorist reports having answered, "but that perhaps a president's liberties were more limited; that if a president's duty required it there was no alternative but that in a case where it was not required by duty it might be best to let it alone, since the act would give offense to so many people when no profit to the country was to be gained by offending them."

The people offended would have been white southerners, white supremacists. There is something about Clemens's reply that sounds uncharacteristically prim in any case, stylistically feebler than we've come to expect from that punchy source, and condescending. We of a later age would have wished him to answer directly: "Of course you were right, Mr. President, to invite Dr. Washington to dine at the White House," even as, in wishing so, we make use of historical insights that only the intervening hundred years and more have broadcast widely. Those earlier people were not so enlightened. To gauge Clemens, Roosevelt, and their contemporaries justly, we of this twenty-first century must—to the extent that we can—betake ourselves to where they were standing at the start of the twentieth.

CHAPTER **Eighteen**

Racial America

The terms *racism* and *racist* (coined in the 1930s) were not in use in 1900, although the idea was flourishing at the earlier date, no matter the name it went by. Race was much in evidence and taken for granted: that there were five (or six, or seven) races into which God or Darwin's evolution had divided humanity, self-evident to all through visible physical traits. The five races most commonly settled on were the white or Caucasian, the yellow or Mongolian, the red or American Indian, the Tartar and Esquimaux (presumed to share a common ancestor), and the black or African race. Beyond physical differences, each race possessed distinctive attributes of temperament, disposition, and character, the identification of which allowed for a hierarchical taxonomy, a classifying from highest to lowest. In the science-engrossed nineteenth century—geologists, anthropologists, archeologists, ethnologists, biologists amateur and otherwise: Teedie Roosevelt for one, as a young ornithologist affixing Latin labels to his various birds (to say nothing of all the engineers and inventors of the time)—in such a climate, the classifying and analyzing of racial types seemed to point the way toward understanding. A Eurocentric result of the effort, thought to be empirically arrived at, placed the Caucasian race at the highest level of civilization and the African race at the lowest.

Booker T. Washington was a member of the African race. He had been born in 1856, to a black mother living in the humblest of circumstances and an absent white father whose identity Washington never discovered or troubled himself much about. The birthplace was an earth-floor, single-room slave cabin, fourteen by sixteen feet, "in the midst of the most miserable, desolate, and discouraging surroundings" of a plantation in Franklin County, Virginia. One of three children, the boy spent his first nine years in bondage. Then the Civil War brought slavery to an end. With freedom,

Booker's stepfather, a black man living on a plantation nearby, made his way into the mountainous new state of West Virginia, to the Kanawha Valley, where he summoned his emancipated wife, their two children, and the stepchild Booker to join him, more than 100 miles off at a town called Malden, close to the city of Charleston.

Malden existed because of its salt industry, in the grim packing houses in which Booker and his stepbrother—after the family's arduous, three-weeks' trek had brought them there—were promptly set to work. By age twelve Booker was working in coal mines nearby, under appalling conditions. His circumstances in Malden were worse than during slavery: blacks and degraded whites laboring side by side in the mines, their clothes rags, their cabins and shacks crammed together in filth. There was no sanitation. "Drinking, gambling, quarrels, fights, and shockingly immoral practices were frequent." Yet somehow, through all that, young Booker got his hands on reading matter. His illiterate mother, whom he adored, had found him a spelling book, and he struggled at figuring out letters and slowly, with help from others black and white, at making out words.

Newly freed blacks of whatever age hungered for education, and high-minded northerners aspired to provide them with it. One such was a white missionary's son born in Hawaii who at nineteen, during the war, had joined the Union army and rose to command a regiment of African-Americans. Afterward, this young officer remained down South in charge of a branch of the Freedmen's Bureau, a recent creation of Congress to ease the transition of former slaves to freedom. The officer, Brigadier General Samuel Chapman Armstrong, at age twenty-nine started a school for blacks in Hampton, in southeast Virginia, where he had been managing his branch of the bureau. Three or four years later, merely by chance, Booker Washington overheard a couple of miners talking about a new school for colored people and determined to find it. Young Washington did so, in 1872—made his way the 400 miles from Malden to the Hampton Normal and Agricultural Institute, much of the journey on foot. He arrived with fifty cents, gained admission to the institute, and through aptitude and diligence ingratiated himself with General Armstrong. "It has been my fortune," this unlikely future luminary would write thirty years after these events in his life, "to meet personally many of what are called great characters, both in Europe and America, but I do not hesitate to say that I never met any man who, in my estimation, was the equal of General Armstrong."

Armstrong had taught at missionary schools in Hawaii, set up to instill Christian values in the native population while imparting useful, practical work skills. That same regimen the general brought to his Hampton

Institute, where white teachers instructed former slaves through school days that were shaped to allow time for study, religious observance, and the acquiring of such crafts as carpentry, masonry, and brickmaking. "The whole machinery of slavery," according to Washington himself, "was so constructed as to cause labour, as a rule, to be looked upon as a badge of degradation, of inferiority. Hence labour was something that both races on the slave plantation sought to escape." After emancipation, many freedmen retained that cultural aversion: slaves worked, not men who were free. So it became a principal part of Booker T. Washington's mission to teach members of his race the dignity of labor.

He himself had taken to the practical regimen at Hampton and flourished, graduating as the institute's commencement speaker in 1875. Thereafter for a few years Washington tried his hand at such different endeavors as teaching, studying law, and attending a Baptist seminary. None of it suited him. Then General Armstrong invited his prize pupil back to Hampton in 1879 to head the night school. Two years later, in the spring of 1881, the general received a request from the state of Alabama to recommend a principal to lead a school for colored people down there, a school for which the legislature had agreed to appropriate $2,000 annually. Instead of the white candidate asked for, Armstrong recommended his young African-American assistant. Thus at age twenty-five, Booker T. Washington ventured into the Deep South to take on duties as head of the newly founded Tuskegee Institute.

Arriving at Tuskegee, a town in southeastern Alabama half white and half black, the new head discovered that nothing at all had been done in preparation. There were no students, no faculty, no buildings, no campus, not even any land. Undaunted, Washington set about persuading well-wishers in the area to support the educational project; recruited a small, all-black faculty; enlisted thirty students of different ages longing to be educated; and borrowed money to buy a derelict plantation outside of town. Classes met in a broken-down henhouse. Faculty and students together filled their afternoons crafting rude furniture, clearing a campus out of the unkempt acreage, and erecting the classroom buildings and dormitories of this new coeducational enterprise.

From such humble beginnings, Tuskegee Institute grew within two decades, by 1901, to encompass 2,300 acres of land on which had arisen a campus assessed at more than a million dollars. It contained some forty buildings, all but four of them erected entirely by student labor. Eleven hundred students were enrolled by that time, and they had arrived from twenty-seven states as well as from Africa and the Caribbean. In addition to providing its students with academic and religious training, the institute boasted twenty-eight industrial departments that taught them farming, gardening, fruit-growing, dairying, and such artisan skills as tinsmithing, wheelwrighting, mattress-making, wagon-building, and metalworking. The institute's benefactors included John D. Rockefeller, Andrew Carnegie, Collis P. Huntington, and the head of Sears-Roebuck, Julius Rosenwald. By then Washington was famous nationwide and in Europe, entertained in the homes of the wealthy and much sought after as a public speaker. Harvard awarded him an honorary degree in 1896. Two years later, President McKinley paid a visit to Tuskegee Institute, in a speech on campus saluting its founder as "an accomplished educator, a great orator, and a true philanthropist."

This, then, was Booker T. Washington, Wizard of Tuskegee—dedicated, eloquent, the nationally celebrated leader of his race—whose knowledgeable opinions Theodore Roosevelt, soon after his elevation to the presidency, solicited over dinner at the White House in October 1901.

The occasion provoked the South to screams of outrage. "White men of the South, how do you like it?" the *New Orleans Times-Democrat* demanded to know. "White *women* of the South, how do you like it? When Mr. Roosevelt sits down to dinner with a negro, he declares that the negro is the social equal of the white man." Ex-Governor Gates in Montgomery pronounced categorically that no "respectable white man in Alabama would ask Washington to dinner or go to dinner with him." The *Memphis Scimitar* erupted that it was the most damnable outrage ever when the President "invited a nigger to dine with him at the White House." Governor Candler of Georgia assured the nation that "no self-respecting Southern man can ally himself with the President after what has occurred." Augusta's Mayor Phinisey added that the move "will hurt his"—Roosevelt's—"influence, not only in the South, but will be condemned in the North." The editor of the *Richmond Times* presumed that Colonel Roosevelt was urging white women to entertain Negroes and receive their attentions, thereby implying that the two races should intermarry. The *New Orleans Daily States* saw the act as "a studied insult," undertaken early in the President's administration with the intention of showing "his contempt for the sentiments and prejudices of this section, and of forcing upon the country social customs which are utterly repugnant to the entire South. In addition to all this, he is revivifying a most dangerous problem, one that has brought untold evil upon the whole country in the past, but which it was hoped, and believed, had been removed by the firmness and wisdom of the South."

The South, in the form of such terrorist persuaders as the Ku Klux Klan, had been exercising its firmness over these recent three decades in order to deny African-Americans social and political rights guaranteed them in the Fourteenth and Fifteenth amendments of the Constitution. The former, ratified in 1868, asserts that no state "shall make or enforce any law which shall abridge the privileges or immunities of citizens of the United States," among whose numbers slaves now emancipated were included. The other amendment, ratified in 1870, gives all adult male citizens the right to vote. During the decade immediately after the Civil War, the North made real efforts to enforce those amendments, the Freedmen's Bureau being one such instrument for doing so. Accordingly, black people under the protection of federal troops ventured to the polls in those early postbellum years and voted for lawmakers, some of them African-American, as their representatives in state legislatures and in Washington.

What the *New Orleans Daily States* refers to as "a most dangerous problem" that President Roosevelt has revivified, "one that has brought untold evil upon the whole country in the past," lay in black people's striving to assert their political rights. Grant the idea that black lawmakers can legislate for white constituents, and next will come blacks grasping beyond political to social equality. That last will lead inevitably to miscegenation, to the amalgamation of the races; and even white southerners of moderate views found such a prospect distressing.

For the many moderates in the South, segregation of the races was a part of God's inscrutable plan, not to be tampered with. The Almighty had designed that the races live apart from each other, one race in Africa, another in Asia, another in Europe, and so on. Only mankind's far-ranging restlessness had muddled the providential scheme. Yet even so, even when two races live side by side, they may treat each other with courtesy and consideration without doing violence to the integrity of either. For mankind is made in God's image, and all races exhibit distinctive virtues, attuned to the different needs of their ancestral homes. The African race, for instance, displays (so went the common belief) the gifts of patience, of a cheerful and forgiving nature, and of a sensitivity to religious experience, as well as traits that adapted them well to service: docility, physical strength, gratitude for kindness and fair treatment, and a tendency not to dwell on cruelties or griefs. But blacks (it was thought) lack discipline, lack initiative and imaginativeness, lack the ability to sustain mental effort—traits that Caucasians by contrast have clearly exhibited, along with organizational skills that have spread the dominance of white people over the globe. There was no reason even so, in the view of moderate white southerners, why Caucasians and Africans couldn't live side by side in mutual comity and to each other's benefit, provided the inferior race accepted its God-given status without aspiring to become the political or social equal of its white neighbors.

Booker T. Washington came into his adulthood just as race relations in America were entering the most shameful decades of their long, shameful history. He turned twenty-one in 1877, the year that the North abandoned its efforts at post–Civil War Reconstruction, withdrawing federal troops from the South and turning the fate of black freedmen over to the murderous terrorizings of white supremacists. Thus Washington had to build his life's work in a period of the most violent racial intolerance—election frauds, night-rider murders, the bloodlust of rioting white mobs, seemingly endless lynchings. The help the young educator received all that while depended in large part on white philanthropy, as he worked with black people of the humblest means, without literacy or craft skills, without even habits of cleanliness, often unfamiliar with such matters as bedsheets and toothbrushes. Tuskegee Institute saw its role as providing hygiene, morals, book learning, and occupational skills. Students by the end were to have made themselves valuable to the community where they lived, to have mastered a craft that the community needed. "The wisest among my race understand," Tuskegee's leader proclaimed in 1895, in a speech before a predominantly white audience in Atlanta (the first such that a black man had been permitted to make to a white audience in the South), "that the agitation of questions of social equality is the extremest folly, and that progress in the enjoyment of all the privileges that will come to us must be the result of severe and constant struggle rather than of artificial forcing." Of course his white listeners roundly applauded the sentiment, as they applauded another of the speaker's assertions: "In all things that are purely social we can be as separate as the fingers, yet one as the hand in all things essential to mutual progress."

That was precisely how moderate white southerners saw the two races living together: socially separate, with politics managed by the far more able whites, and for the rest mutual cordiality and kindness. Meanwhile, under such guidance as Booker Washington provided, blacks would develop self-reliance. Maybe in time, over hundreds of years in the slow unfolding of evolutionary time, their race will have raised itself to a position of political equality with the white man. Along the way, white moderates in the South felt that blacks should be paternalistically encouraged in their efforts and the earnest and industrious among them treated with every reasonable regard.

Extremist southerners felt otherwise. None spoke for such people more resoundingly than did the senator and South Carolina political boss Benjamin Tillman, who had once vowed to take his pitchfork to Washington, D.C., and prod presidential candidate Grover Cleveland—that "old bag of beef"—in his "old fat ribs." Pitchfork Ben, a violent man from a large and violent family, spoke ostensibly for poor whites: mill workers and up-country farmers whose livelihood black aspirations appeared to threaten. But Tillman spoke for many other white people as well, in the South and in the North. He spoke often and widely, on the Senate floor, at Chautauqua meetings, in churches, town halls, lyceums, and village squares, and he professed to have been as warmly received up North as down South. What he told his listeners—in invective-filled, profanity-laced language that the respectable deprecated—was that the Negro had progressed not at all since the War Between the States. On the contrary, blacks behaved far worse now than before the war. There were exceptions, of course. Joe Gibson, in service to the Tillmans for forty years, was one. "A more loyal friend no man ever had. Every child that I have would share his last crust with that negro tomorrow." Indeed, the senator didn't know whether Joe belonged to him or he belonged to Joe: "we have agreed to live together until one or both of us die, and when I go away, if I go first, I know he will shed as sincere tears as anybody." But as for the generality of black people down South these days, they had been spoiled by the Civil War and the Reconstruction that followed, right up to when that disastrous social experiment was terminated by settling the disputed presidential election of 1876.

Tillman, like most other white Americans of his time, was convinced that blacks were biologically inferior. All of his racial thinking rested on that certainty. Look at Africans in their native environment, exhibiting "barbarism, savagery, cannibalism and everything which is low and degrading." Left on its own, the race could rise no higher toward civilized life than that. By contrast, blacks brought to America had for the most part behaved well under slavery; there were "more good Christian men and women and ladies and gentlemen" among blacks in the slave states than in the whole of Africa. Then came the war, and emancipation, and afterward northern interference to reconstruct the South by educating the Negro, encouraging him to vote, and letting him sit in legislatures and help make laws. Those efforts have been the ruin of the race. Blacks, according to Tillman, were not educable in the first place; whatever smattering of learning they picked up only made them discontented with their lot by causing them to aspire to what their natural limitations kept them from attaining. The consequence, he said, was "enervating and destructive of the original virtues of the negro race." We in the South had seen that already. And we were seeing blacks presume to fill roles beyond their capacity that led them to further, more ominous presumptions.

For the Negro—and this was another core conviction of Senator Tillman's, as it was of many white people of his time, South and North—the Negro male lusted after white women. Slavery had kept the appetite in check, but emancipation unleashed it, and Reconstruction had so elevated the black man's ambitions as to place white women's safety in jeopardy. In lurid terms before large, responsive white audiences around the country, Tillman preached this message of black men's lust, of the threat to virtuous white womanhood posed by the unchecked savage nature of blacks aspiring to social equality. "I have three daughters, but, so help me God, I had rather find either one of them killed by a tiger or a bear and gather up her bones and bury them, conscious that she had died in the purity of her maidenhood, than to have her crawl to me and tell me the horrid story that she had been robbed of the jewel of her womanhood by a black fiend."

South Carolina had dealt with African-American presumptions some years earlier, and Tillman had been a part of it. He had not been able to fight with Confederates during the war; a brain operation in his late teens, which had cost him his left eye, kept him out of the conflict. But he had been in the postwar battle of 1876, when whites in South Carolina took back their government from blacks. "We took the government away. We stuffed ballot boxes. We shot them"—African-Americans trying to vote. "We are not ashamed of it." For in that way the South had been redeemed. "We will not submit to negro domination under any conditions that you may prescribe," Tillman cried out in defiance of the North. "Now you have got it. The sooner you understand it fully and thoroughly, the better off this country will be."

White people heard, and the more refined members of the population murmured their disapproval of the senator's blunt expressiveness, while some of them wondered privately whether the content of what he said didn't make a good deal of sense. But all that was a southern problem. White people up North were coming to feel the South should be left alone to deal with it. Many of Senator Tillman's humbler listeners, meanwhile, were vocal in supporting his views, farmers and mill workers and poor whites who gathered around as large and enthusiastic crowds to hear him out. He said he couldn't tell them what to do about the Negro Problem. He didn't know. As much as he could propose was repealing the two constitutional amendments, not likely to happen anytime soon.

But over and over he told his listeners that the black man must be kept in line. As for Booker T. Washington's dinner at the White House, South Carolina's one-eyed, race-baiting former governor and current senator predicted bleakly that the President's action "in entertaining that nigger will necessitate our killing a thousand niggers in the South before they will learn their place again."

CHAPTER Nineteen

Back to Hannibal

arlier, in years just after the Civil War, southern states had responded to former slaves set free in their midst by passing so-called Black Codes, regulations to control the movement and employment of freed black people. Varying from state to state, the codes generally restricted such people from roaming about at will. Freedmen had to sign annual contracts for labor and work from sunup to sundown. Vagrancy— that is, not being thus employed—was severely punished. Employers, white farmers mostly, could discipline workers as a father would his children. There were other such ordinances, the effect of which was to move African-Americans back toward the doleful condition of enslavement that had existed before the war.

For northerners, Black Codes appeared to negate a high purpose of all the war's bloodletting. The federal government intervened. Troops were sent south to enforce the Fourteenth and Fifteenth amendments. Congress instituted the Freedmen's Bureau to help blacks vote and acquire property and get an education. But the white South resisted, keeping up its violent, extralegal intimidation of black people; and thus a decade passed, until the contested presidential election of 1876, between the Republican Hayes of Ohio and the Democrat Tilden of New York. Samuel Tilden won the popular vote, but the electoral vote went to Rutherford B. Hayes, although the count in Florida, Louisiana, and South Carolina remained in doubt. A deal was struck. Democrats would break the deadlock by conceding the presidency if the new Republican administration agreed to remove federal troops from southern soil.

By then the North was about ready to abandon its crusade on behalf of blacks anyway. White northerners in general had scarcely more use for the African-American than did white southerners. "They love him," Pitch-

fork Ben Tillman said, "according to the square of the distance" between the two races. If a black man was down South, fine. But up North he was hardly made welcome. Ordinances forbade his living where he chose, or patronizing white restaurants and hotels, or traveling alongside whites, or marrying a white woman, or working except at such designated employments as waiter, stevedore, or coachman. Free blacks were forbidden by law from even entering Illinois. By 1877, the North, encumbered with antipathies of its own, had grown weary of championing black rights south of the Mason-Dixon Line. Meanwhile the South had begun recasting the Civil War, waged ultimately over slavery, as a gallant contest fought not about slavery at all but about states' rights, a War Between the States to determine whether individual states were sovereign, or whether sovereignty rested in the union of the United States. The Union had won that fight between white men (as thus represented) fair and square; and as the climactic struggle receded and dimmed in time, as white friend and foe, once again donning the blue and gray, met together at anniversary reunions on peaceful green fields of earlier battles, as former enemies shook hands and fondly reminisced and returned each other's captured battle flags, the North—feeling a residual guilt about war's reckless slaughter—lost any lingering bitterness toward these southern white cousins of theirs.

Well before the mid-nineties, every state of the former Confederacy had passed Jim Crow laws, which strictly segregated the two races, and the North offered no effective resistance. In 1896, a conservative Supreme Court, in *Plessy* v. *Ferguson*, determined that such segregationist ordinances were constitutional, that whites could provide facilities "separate but equal" for coloreds; so that thereafter, for just short of sixty years, the South exhibited separate and, for blacks, far from equal schools, hotels, restaurants, waiting rooms, restrooms, and drinking places. Science all this while, including the new science of eugenics, appeared to endorse the appropriateness of racial discrimination. In addition, in 1898, during the Spanish-American War, erstwhile Confederates found themselves fighting side by side with former Union troops against the Spaniard; in Cuba the Confederacy's "Fighting Joe" Wheeler was second in command of the Fifth Cavalry Corps, in which Colonel Roosevelt served. At war's end, in December 1898, President McKinley toured the South and, in Atlanta, told the Georgia legislature, "Sectional feeling no longer holds back the love we bear each other." That would be white people's love. The band played "Dixie," the President rose for it, and his white audience applauded the gesture. American soldiers in the Philippines soon after, shouldering "the white man's burden," encountered what looked a lot like the Negro

Problem back home. A member of the First Nebraska, during the uneasy truce with Aguinaldo's Filipinos early in 1899, assured his homefolks: "If they would turn the boys loose, there wouldn't be a nigger left in Manila twelve hours after." Thus, within four decades of the Civil War, whites South and North were finally reuniting in their pride as a new world power. And thus in effect did the New South repeal the Fourteenth and Fifteenth amendments, which had guaranteed blacks full citizenship and (for African-American males at least) the right to vote.

Early in the twentieth century, Samuel L. Clemens set out on his own trip west and southward into the border-state, Jim-Crow world of Missouri. The president of the state university there had written in April 1902 inviting him to come. "My Dear Mr. Clemens,—Although you received the degree of doctor of literature last fall from Yale, and have had other honors conferred upon you by other great universities, we want to adopt you here as a son of the University of Missouri." Would he do them the kindness of returning to his native state, to the campus at Columbia, on June 4, to receive at President Jesse's hands the degree of Doctor of Laws?

Mark Twain was happy to oblige. Thus, at the end of May 1902, the humorist arrived by rail in St. Louis, met there by Horace Bixby, who had taught Sam Clemens riverboat piloting forty-five years earlier. This final trip back home was filled with occasions for reminiscence such as Bixby's spry presence awakened. Clemens spent five days in Hannibal, 100 miles upriver amid scenes of his childhood, meeting old friends, among whom was Laura Hawkins, now elderly Mrs. Frazer, she the model for blue-eyed Becky Thatcher in *Tom Sawyer*. The author attended a high school commencement, viewed stones of family and former playmates in the graveyard, and had his picture taken in front of the Clemens home on Hill Street ("It all seems so small to me; a boy's home is a big place to him") as he stood beneath upstairs windows that he had gazed out of as a ten- or twelve-year-old more than fifty-five years before.

Back then Sam at seventeen, in June of 1853, had left Hannibal for good. He told his mother that he was headed downriver to St. Louis, where sister Pamela and her husband and baby daughter lived. Next thing Jane Clemens knew, her son was in New York City. Typesetting work had run out in St. Louis, and he hadn't wanted to be idle; so here the youth was, after six days of travel by steamboat, railroad, and stagecoach to Chicago, east across Michigan, across Lake Erie the 250 miles by boat to Buffalo, on to Albany by rail—such were the interrupted modes of long-distance travel back then—and by steamer down the Hudson: "an awful trip," which

Figure 19.1.   Mark Twain standing before his childhood home in Hannibal, May 31, 1902. Photograph by Herbert Tomlinson.
Courtesy of the Mark Twain House & Museum, Hartford.

would require him to take a day to let his jostled insides settle before setting forth to look for a job.

The young southerner venturing for the first time out of a slave state had already observed much in his travels up North: "when I saw the Court House in Syracuse," he wrote to his mother, "it called to mind the time when it was surrounded with chains and companies of soldiers, to prevent the rescue of McReynolds' nigger, by the infernal abolitionists. I reckon," Sam went on, "I had better black my face, for in these Eastern States niggers are considerably better than white people."

Not really; not treated better by a long shot, or nearly so well. Northern customs that enforced the status of free blacks as inferiors had been long and firmly established by 1853, and were appalling in their discriminatory severity. The McReynolds referred to was a landowner near Hannibal whose slave, Jerry McHenry, had escaped several years earlier and fled to Syracuse, where he lived unmolested as a cooper until the fall of 1851, after Congress had passed the infamous Fugitive Slave Act. Under the terms of that new federal law, slave catchers arrived in Syracuse and—meaning to return McHenry to bondage—hauled him off to jail. An indignant anti-slavery crowd broke in, rescued the runaway, and got him safely to Canada toward the end of a highly publicized episode that added its tinder to the smoldering tensions of the decade just before the Civil War.

But what could a Hannibal seventeen-year-old understand of such matters? "In my schoolboy days," Clemens would write years later, "I had no aversion to slavery. I was not aware that there was anything wrong about it. No one arraigned it in my hearing; the local papers said nothing against it; the local pulpit taught us that God approved it, that it was a holy thing and that the doubter need only look in the Bible if he wished to settle his mind." The views of Sam's mother would have been similarly untroubled. Jane Lampton Clemens's entire life thus far had been spent among slaves; yet, her son reflected in after days, "kind-hearted and compassionate as she was, I think she was not conscious that slavery was a bald, grotesque and unwarrantable usurpation. She had never heard it assailed in any pul-pit but had heard it defended and sanctified in a thousand; her ears were familiar with Bible texts that approved it but if there were any that disap-proved it they had not been quoted by her pastors."

As for his own childhood, at play through six or seven summers on an uncle's farm three miles north of Florida, Missouri, Sammy Clemens had made friends of several black slave children, and in particular had taken to an older Negro, Uncle Dan'l, who would entertain those playmates white and black with wonderful stories. "It was on the farm that I got my strong liking for his race and my appreciation of certain of its fine quali-ties," Clemens noted of that family retainer, a model for Jim in *Huckleberry Finn*. "This feeling and this estimate have stood the test of sixty years and more"—into the early 1900s—"and have suffered no impairment. The black face is as welcome to me now as it was then."

But in New York at this earlier moment in 1853, for the first time on an extended stay in a free state, young Sam Clemens, seventeen years old, em-bodies the conventional attitude of white southern adolescents then—and of most of their elders. A boardinghouse roommate who knew him during that period wrote to Clemens later, after he became famous; and Mark Twain at forty responded: "You think I have grown some; upon my word there was room for it." Considering such growth from Hartford, where he then lived, caused the transplanted southerner to gaze back at his youth with a regret that was characteristic. "Ignorance, intolerance, egotism, self-assertion, opaque perception, dense and pitiful chuckle-headedness—and an almost pathetic unconsciousness of it all. That is what I was at 19 and 20"—and at seventeen as well.

We can chart the young man's enlightenment on racial matters. At seventeen, on his way to a first visit to New York City to see the Crystal Palace, Clemens carried with him all the racial prejudices of the typical provincial southerner. When the war came, he joined a makeshift Confederate militia unit in Hannibal and lasted two soggy weeks in the Missouri woods before retiring from the conflict. A month later, in July 1861, Sam seized an opportunity to travel west to the Nevada Territory with his high-minded brother Orion (an avowed abolitionist by then) and remained out there five years. From Nevada early in 1862, late in the first year of the war, Sam was writing to a friend about "our Missourians," that is, those in the border state who remained loyal to the South, noting of Union forces that "they have taken Fort Henry"—the *our* and *they* registering his continuing allegiance to the Confederacy. But some months later, in the fall of that same 1862, Clemens was writing to another friend that "we"—and here the context makes clear he means Federals—"have been playing the brag," his allegiance switched from the one side to the other. He would remain on the Union's side from that time forward.

The Langdons of Elmira, New York, strengthened the young Missourian's conversion to more liberal views. Clemens arrived in the East from San Francisco early in 1867, and later that year sailed from New York City aboard the *Quaker City* bound for Europe and the Holy Land. On board he befriended a fellow passenger, Charley Langdon; and after the vessel returned to Manhattan five months later, Clemens met young Langdon's family. In August 1868, he spent a fortnight at their home in Elmira, till then the only two weeks of his life, he said, without a single regret. The Langdons proved to be "the pleasantest family I ever knew. I only have one trouble," their guest wrote home while there, "& that is that they give too much thought & too much time & invention to the object of making my visit pass delightfully." The family's Elmira mansion at Main and Church streets displayed grounds that attested to the prosperous lives led within: flower beds and greenhouses in back and a lawn stretching to gates and a wrought-iron fence out front, rare native trees, palms in green tubs, a vine-covered stable, garden-seats, a fountain playing over tiers near the main entrance, a porte cochère, side porches, balconies, columned porticoes, bays, and a windowed cupola rising above the rooftop.

Inside were a richly furnished parlor, a conservatory, a grand mahogany staircase, and seemingly limitless bedrooms upstairs. Jervis Langdon's wealth had come relatively late in life. He had started as a storekeeper, and after a number of years of upward movement among villages in central New York brought his family to Elmira in 1845, the year of his younger daughter Olivia's birth. By then he was in the lumber business. Profits from lumber he invested in coal mining, and in time acquired a lucrative interest in railroads as well. Earnings grew substantial for J. Langdon, Miner & Dealer in Anthracite & Bituminous Coal, and his philanthropies spread ever wider. The coal baron furthered all kinds of public benefactions. He was a founding member of Elmira's Park Church and a supporter of the Gleasons' hydropathic sanitarium, the nationally famous watercure there in town. He helped to underwrite the impressive Elmira Female Academy, which his two daughters attended. He gave funds to the new industrial school and to the model prison, and—with his wife and daughters—to Elmira's antitobacco league and the town's very active temperance movement. Moreover, before the war he had been a fervent abolitionist, his home a station on the Underground Railroad. In 1838, while living in Millport, Langdon entertained Frederick Douglass soon after his escape from slavery, later welcoming that spokesman for his race as a guest in Elmira. So the family's social attitudes lay at a far remove from those of the Missouri household where Sam Clemens had been reared, modest southern slaveholders of village views with their black bondservants in the Hannibal of the 1840s.

Clemens admired Jervis Langdon: "You are the splendidest man in the *world!*" And he had fallen in love with the Langdons' younger daughter, with Olivia, ten years his junior. Sam had met her in New York City at the end of 1867, visited over those two happy weeks in August 1868 with her and her family, and through that fall pursued his courtship with all the ardor that young Theodore Roosevelt, Harvard undergraduate, would pour into his own pursuit of Alice Lee in Cambridge ten autumns later. As with Roosevelt, so with Clemens. Each had made a vow that he would marry the girl though she was unwilling, and both succeeded. Clemens and Miss Langdon were engaged in 1869 and married in the family parlor in February of the following year.

By then the western journalist and lecturer had established himself in the East—by chance, following a publisher's chance suggestion—as the author of a book. The book contained a lively description of the cruise he had taken two years before with Olivia's brother and some seventy other pilgrims aboard the *Quaker City. The Innocents Abroad* turned into a great success, even as the newly wed Mr. and Mrs. Clemens were setting up housekeeping in Buffalo. Not only did Mark Twain's account of his travels manage to sell in quantity, making real money for its author, but it was attracting favorable critical notice, unusual for a volume peddled from door to door. The genteel literary trade rarely deigned to notice such subscription efforts, which weren't advertised in newspapers or made available in bookstores. Yet here was the prestigious *Atlantic Monthly*, arbiter of taste, in December 1869, two months before the Clemenses' wedding, running a substantial, laudatory review of *The Innocents Abroad*, praising its "always good-humored humor," which "even in its impudence" is charming, a humor never "indulged at the cost of the weak or helpless," never insolent, even "with all its sauciness and irreverence." Moreover, at the base of Mark Twain's humor lies "excellent sense and good feeling. There is an amount of pure human nature in the book that rarely gets into literature."

Lecturing in Boston late that fall, Clemens in those final weeks of his bachelorhood stepped around to call gratefully at the *Atlantic* offices on Tremont Street, where he met and thanked the young writer of the review, one William Dean Howells. Thus was inaugurated a lifelong and most productive friendship. In years ahead, after the Clemenses had moved to Hartford and were rearing their children in a grand home there, Mr. Howells, by then a novelist as well as an editor and critic, was a frequent and welcome visitor. For, as daughter Clara later remembered, he "always brought sunshine and cheer into the house as no one else could. Everyone loved him and wanted him to stay a long time. His sense of humor and capacity to show it refreshed the hearts of all. To see him and Father enjoy a funny story or joke together was a complete show in itself. Both of them red in the face from laughing, with abundant gray hair straggling over their foreheads and restless feet that carried them away from their chairs and back again! I am sure no children ever laughed with more abandon."

The two men spoke of grave matters as well. About slavery, for instance, Howells testified many years later that his border-state friend was "entirely satisfied with the result of the Civil War." Indeed, he had proved to be the most desouthernized southerner Howells had ever met. And Mark Twain, late in his Hartford years, in 1888, confirmed as much by speaking publicly of the monstrous disfigurement in America's past: "we used to own our brother human beings, and used to buy them and sell them, lash them, thrash them, break their piteous hearts—and we ought to be ashamed of ourselves." That same Mark Twain, thoroughly reconstructed, wrote for publication in 1899: "It would not be possible for a humane and intelligent person to invent a rational excuse for slavery." Over so far a distance had he traveled from his youthful, provincial opinions about bondage, upon leaving Hannibal at seventeen, in 1853.

CHAPTER Twenty

Roosevelt and Race

The distance that Theodore Roosevelt traversed from youth to what in his maturity passed back then for racial enlightenment was shorter than Sam Clemens's, over ground sooner covered. Clemens had been born in humble, rural circumstances in a slaveholding state. Roosevelt was born into a wealthy, urban family up North. The New Yorker's mother was southern, to be sure, and the stories she told of life in antebellum Georgia were of a time and place in which superior white Anglo-Saxons dealt with what they took to be innately inferior blacks as though they were children. But young Teedie's father was a northerner and an abolitionist. True, he was of Dutch descent rather than of the then favored English stock, but it was a descent from a family that had settled in Nieuw Amsterdam as far back as the 1640s, a solid-gold pedigree that just about anyone living on that later, much changed island of Manhattan would have been proud to lay claim to. Besides, the Dutch, like the Anglo-Saxons, were Teutonic. In the race-saturated ethos of the nineteenth century, such a heritage mattered. As an adult, moreover, Roosevelt would make much of what he called "the race of English-speaking peoples," which together could rule the world, to the world's benefit—and into which ranks a far-back Dutch ancestry in no way barred his own admission.

Unlike the provincial Sam Clemens, confined to Hannibal until he broke loose at seventeen, young Teedie Roosevelt by early adolescence had already experienced two year-long, informative sojourns overseas, studying foreign languages over there and turning into a well-mannered young cosmopolite. In Cairo, for instance, the budding scientist recorded in his diary at fourteen, in 1873, the "various races of men" he saw, including "the white, black, Egyptian and Eastern whites, Arab or Syrian," during what he professed at that early time to have been the most interesting hour of his life. And through it all, the asthmatic Teedie, like others burdened with illness in childhood, had become a prodigious reader, establishing a lifelong habit that further broadened his horizons.

But the values instilled in the lad stressed action as much as thought, doing as well as reading. Early on, his father had exposed young Roosevelt to charitable visits in poverty-stricken areas of New York City: in tenement slums, Italian soup kitchens, and newsboys' lodging houses. Beyond that, as a fervent outdoorsman Teedie camped in the Adirondacks and went off to Maine to climb Katahdin with a local guide, Bill Sewall, who would later join him in managing one of Roosevelt's Dakota ranches. Thus, though privately tutored through a privileged boyhood, by the early years of his adolescence the youth had found occasions to mingle with people in humbler stations of life, with the result that the adult Roosevelt's comfort at all social levels remained (like Clemens's, but for different reasons) easy and assured.

And he had that undergraduate education to widen his views. Sam Clemens was denied any such formal opportunities, getting his learning—hardly deficient, as it turned out—in the printing shop, on the river, in the silver mines, in the newspaper office, and traveling to Hawaii and Europe. Theodore Roosevelt traveled and went to college both, at Harvard studying under eminent professors in such Teutonic courses as "German Historical Prose" and "Richter, Goethe, and German Lyrics." A major influence on this particular undergraduate's intellectual growth at Harvard was Professor Nathaniel Shaler, paleontologist and historian, who wrote and lectured extensively on racial characteristics that scientific studies had appeared to confirm. Shaler expressed views widely held in any case, but he endowed them with the luster of academic endorsement. The professor taught as current science the natural superiority of the Caucasian race above all others, the inferiority of the African race, and black people's lecherousness, which slavery had kept under control. He taught, as well, the doctrines of the French naturalist Lamarck, concerning the inheritability of traits shaped by one's environment, by such a rugged environment as was met with, for instance, on the American frontier.

Much of Shaler's teaching permeates Theodore Roosevelt's own historical writings, starting with his earliest volume, *The Naval War of 1812*, which the author began while still a student at Harvard, and which extols, in its account of that salt- and fresh-water Anglo-American conflict, the high merits of both combatants, fighting to a standoff. Both sides demonstrated martial gifts that the narrative sets out to relate objectively. Thus nautical skills on display on the Great Lakes and in the

Atlantic near the start of the nineteenth century would have seemed to confirm Roosevelt's judgment conveyed to a British friend at the century's end: together "the two branches of the Anglo-Saxon race"—English and American—"can whip the world."

By that time, at the end of the century, the American branch had soundly whipped an enfeebled Spain, driving it out of Cuba, Puerto Rico, and the Philippines. The Spanish-American War, by the way, was awash in racial bigotry. From the beginning, as white troops mustered with black in San Antonio, Texas, tensions seethed. White southerners took offense at the sight of blacks in uniform, who seemed to have forgotten their place and were slow to step off sidewalks to let their betters pass. The same tensions roiled the staging area at Tampa. There, in fact, white contempt for blacks led to an ugly racial incident soon after colonels Wood and Roosevelt detrained their Rough Riders, in preparation for launching forth to fight the Spaniard in Cuba.

Soldiers assembled in that makeshift encampment on the Tampa sandflats were hot, bored, restless, and looking for mischief. On a Monday evening, June 6, 1898, four days after the arrival of the Rough Rider volunteers, a white regular infantryman from Ohio set about amusing himself by snatching an African-American two-year-old from his mother's grasp and holding the child at arm's length upside down so that roistering mates might use him for some playful target practice. One drunken lout, winner of the ensuing contest, exhibited marksmanship so skilled that he put a bullet through the child's sleeve. With the contest won, the soldiers gave the dazed youngster back to his mother, in hysterics by then, and went on their rambunctious way.

Retaliating, blacks of the Twenty-Fourth and Twenty-Fifth Infantry regiments set out on a rampage. They trashed a white cafe, raged through white brothels, and charged into white taverns that had earlier refused to serve them. Tampa police and the provost guard couldn't deal with the riot, so the Second Georgia Volunteer Infantry, white, was called in to restore order. It did, with gusto. Twenty-seven blacks were carted off to the hospital, along with several white soldiers and civilians. The army strove to hush the matter up, but accounts leaked into local papers and spread farther afield, late in a decade during which white southern animosity toward blacks had entered its long-term period of greatest intensity.

American troops, Roosevelt's Rough-Rider volunteers among them, steamed off to Cuba soon after, on transports crowded but rigidly segregated. Once at their destination, the expeditionary force found that native insurgents, whose courageous resistance to Spanish tyranny had inspired admiration back home, were for the most part dark-skinned. The Spanish tyrants were the ones who looked white to these liberating Americans; local allies turned out to be black in the view of white soldiers over from Florida. Before long the new arrivals—most of them from the South and West—had convinced themselves that the insurgents were a pack of untrustworthy, cowardly thieves and liars, good only for consuming provisions and making trouble. Thus ill-supported by dubious Cubans, the expeditionary force marched into battle.

Charging San Juan Heights, the hard-pressed Rough Riders welcomed aid from an American regiment of black infantry regulars. The hills were taken, the victory won. But in peacetime a year later, Colonel Roosevelt, writing of his adventure for *Scribner's* magazine, alluded to the behavior of certain of those black troops when under fire. They had started for the rear, the Colonel recalled, and he had had to draw his weapon and threaten to shoot any soldier who didn't return and hold position in line. A year after the fact, black people reading of the accusation were indignant, and made their feelings known; and white officers who had been on the scene in Cuba disputed Roosevelt's recollection as well. The Colonel had conceded that for the most part black regulars made fine soldiers, although privately he went on to insist that under fire in Cuba they had shown "extraordinary panic," which was hardly surprising, he explained, for a race laden with superstition, a mere generation out of slavery "and but a few generations removed from the wildest savagery." No wonder soldiers with such blood in their veins were overly dependent on direction from white officers and fled to the rear when combat erupted.

That Theodore Roosevelt made the accusation fell particularly hard on the African-American community, which had regarded the New York politician as a friend. Veterans both black and white spoke up, contradicting the Colonel's account. Nobody had fled. Black soldiers had been working with whites to transport the wounded to the rear, nothing more sinister than that. In fact, a white regular officer at the time had been seen reproaching Colonel Roosevelt for his impulsiveness in threatening the black soldiers, who were simply following orders. Governor Roosevelt should apologize, and retract what he had written.

But it was a policy of this author—this very prolific author, of more than 150,000 letters and works that would finally fill twenty volumes—never to retract a word of what he set down. Still, soon after, as a vice presidential nominee with no wish to alienate black voters in the upcoming election of 1900, Roosevelt revised his account to the extent of faulting a white captain for having ordered black troops to the rear in the first place.

And during the 1900 canvass, those gathered around the observation platform of his campaign train heard the candidate insist emphatically that he would be the "last man in the world to say anything against the colored soldiers."

The truth is that Roosevelt, for all his enlightenment, didn't think much of black people in the aggregate. He didn't think much of American Indians, or Chinese, or Mexicans, or South Americans, or Slavs, or Filipinos in the aggregate either. To hold such views seemed to this intellectual elitist from one of New York City's first families to be no more than clear-eyed logic. He had been trained in science, was widely and deeply read in history, and kept himself informed on the latest racial thinking. Inferior races—using the term more casually perhaps ("the French race," "the race of English-speaking peoples") than might be expected from a scientist and from one whose expository prose is generally quite precise—inferior races through a distant future may evolve into peoples as elevated in intellect and accomplishment as the present-day heirs of the white Anglo-Saxons, Caucasians whose skills of organization, initiative, and leadership were allowing them to dominate the globe. But for now, here at the start of the twentieth century, facts couldn't be gainsaid. That races had markedly different capabilities was everywhere apparent.

True—like so much else, including fauna, religions, and social cultures—races did evolve. Roosevelt's broad reading and phenomenal memory could furnish myriad instances from science and history, ancient and modern, in confirmation. Steeped in Darwin's biological perceptions and in anthropologists' transposing of those insights into the realms of social theory—into Social Darwinism—Roosevelt was convinced that human cultures evolve through stages: out of chaotic savagery into aggressive barbarism, on into civilization, stage by stage, and—if not guarded against—from there finally into decadence, civilized man amid his comforts growing contemplative and effete, losing the barbarian's fighting spirit. Thus, in a westward-moving process across history's vast expanse over the earth's surface, civilization after civilization had risen and been supplanted: Mesopotamia, Egypt, Greece, Rome, Spain, on currently to Great Britain, and now America. And all this while, had the process been tending ever westward toward the formation of one great continental civilization, greatest of all, fated, with the English, to spread its values of democracy and freedom throughout the earth, as it advanced to the continent's far edges and gazed finally over the wide Pacific? Or perhaps even now a materialistic America had lost the virile virtues, leaving other peoples on far-off shores, ever farther westward, to shake off their savagery and barbarism and evolve into civilizations destined to flourish in this nation's stead.

Roosevelt relished pondering such grand arcs of history and culture; and at the heart of his thinking lay race. As for our own history, he felt that certain races here on our soil were doomed to extinction. When a more civilized people comes into contact with one less civilized, that is what happens: either that, or the lesser race is assimilated. Thus the American Indian's fate was to dwindle and disappear. The Chinese posed a different case entirely, having entered the American West in droves through the second half of the nineteenth century, first drawn by the Gold Rush, then flocking to help build the transcontinental railroads. Left unstaunched, the Chinese inundation—"The Yellow Peril," as it was called—had threatened to drown what was best of America. Therefore, the Chinese Exclusion Act of 1882 (the first law that treated immigration as a problem) forbade the admission of Chinese for ten years, a prohibition renewed thereafter and made perpetual, until repealed at last no earlier than 1943, when China was our ally in the war against Japan. That earliest federal exclusionary act had been a wise and necessary measure in Roosevelt's view: "the Chinaman is kept out," he wrote, "because the democracy, with much clearness of vision, has seen that his presence is ruinous to the white race." America was a white man's country; and the world was blessed that descendants of Anglo-Saxons, having wrested this temperate land from savages—who knew no more how to use it than as a vast, mostly empty hunting ground—were securing it against races beyond the Pacific too different from ours ever to be assimilated.

On our soil, meanwhile, what was being formed, Roosevelt felt certain, was a better race entirely, for the whole world's benefit. "We are making a new race, a new type, in this country." The frontier's harsh conditions had instilled in settlers manly virtues of self-reliance, resourcefulness, and stoic perseverance. These environmentally engendered traits were then handed from mother down to daughter, from father to son, to create a new people best exemplified in the Kentucky frontiersman's family or the western ranchman and cowboy: a sinewy people, lithe, bronzed, taciturn, who looked men straight in the eye and got things done.

Immigrants to this new world should take note. On arriving here, they must become Americanized. They must change their names, because to have an American name was "to bear the most honorable of titles." They must adopt our ways and learn our language. Speak English. And forsake Old World customs, which, if retained, would turn newcomers and their progeny into mere obstructions in the current of American life, a current destined to spread the high values of freedom and democracy worldwide. Thus, whatever perpetuates diversity is to be renounced. Rather, study our principles of government. Learn our speech and our habits. Be patriotic; be proud to be Americans. And remember above all, Roosevelt instructed readers of his "True Americanism" in 1894, "that the one being abhorrent to the powers above the earth and under them is the hyphenated American—the 'German-American,' the 'Irish-American,' or the 'native-American.' Be Americans, pure and simple."

To our ears the admonition sounds oddly amiss, as does so much of the incessant racial talk of the era, all of it based (as was thought) on hard science: measuring cranial capacities, weighing brains, calculating slopes of foreheads, detecting signs of apishness in body types, analyzing other anthropological data—and all of it self-serving for Anglo-Saxon researchers. The dismal results of their efforts leave us wondering which of our own certainties the future lies in wait for, to hurl as nonsense onto history's towering rubbish heap.

Yet for all its breadth and scope, Roosevelt's description of a new, American race leaves out what we hyphenate (or not) as African-Americans. He confesses—this informed commentator on his times—that he has no answer to what was known then as the Negro Problem. It was, Roosevelt reminds us, a problem that nineteenth-century democrats were not responsible for, "a legacy from the time when we were ruled by a trans-oceanic aristocracy." Yet it abided. Pitchfork Ben Tillman (that extremist, that white supremacist) could not solve the problem beyond advocating the repeal of the Fourteenth and Fifteenth constitutional amendments. And Roosevelt likewise—a more moderate voice, a far more penetrating mind—had only a single suggestion to put forward.

He had been astonished when the South screamed in protest at their chief magistrate's inviting Booker T. Washington to the White House to dine, in October 1901. There was a moment beforehand, the host confessed privately, when he had felt a qualm about extending the invitation, but he had rejected the feeling as unworthy. Thereafter, even though those from below the Mason-Dixon Line voiced their outrage at length, shrilly, the President refused to be bullied. He would invite to dine with him whomever he chose. Yet, although on various later occasions Roosevelt did consult with Dr. Washington, he never again received the educator, or any other black, as his guest at a White House dinner.

Feelings of white southerners had to be taken into account. Their Negro Problem differed from problems out West posed by either the Indians or the Chinese. Black Africans in America were no more assimilable than were the yellow-skinned Chinese or the red Indians; but Congress could hardly pass an act to exclude them, nor would blacks wither away. Indeed, they were multiplying, from something over four million at the beginning of the Civil War to just under nine million by 1900. Booker T. Washington was one such Negro, and he a doer, a leader, a visionary, possessed of capabilities every bit as impressive as any white man's. Roosevelt readily acknowledged that, and acknowledged as well that many a white man was a brute and an idler. So in the end, his solution to the Negro Problem came down to this. The "wise and honorable and Christian thing to do," the President urged, "is to treat each black man and each white man on his merits as a man, giving him no more and no less than he shows himself worthy to have." Throughout his adult life, Theodore Roosevelt tried to do that—and succeeded as well as his temperament and the times permitted—thereby adhering to a course that appeared enlightened, even progressive, in a racially explosive, racially benighted age.

CHAPTER **Twenty-One**

Livy

In June 1902, Mark Twain returned East with an honorary degree from the University of Missouri, after a trip that included a visit to his modest childhood home in Hannibal on the Mississippi River. Now (so well had the author prospered since childhood—and since the days of his bankruptcy in the 1890s), he was living in a mansion overlooking a different river, the Hudson, twenty-five minutes by rail north of New York City. The Appleton homestead had been leased to the Clemenses for $3,000 a year (maybe $77,000 in current money); and the family had been able to move in last October, just before the bicentennial festivities at Yale. The place was called Riverdale. Today it survives much altered, as Wave Hill, near the western end of 252nd Street, still commanding its glorious views of the river below and the Palisades beyond.

Back in 1870, before Teedie Roosevelt entered his teens, the Roosevelt family had rented the same home as a country retreat, returning the following summer to spend another season in its bucolic surroundings. Now the Clemenses lived there, amid furnished comforts and a dining room measuring an imposing thirty by sixty feet. "The girls and Mr. Clemens wanted to be *near* but not *in* New York this winter," his wife explained, "so we came here." And they were thoroughly enjoying their stay, entertaining on a scale unlike any since decades before, in their prime, in Hartford, in the 1870s and '80s. During numerous weeks, we're told, guests were on hand at Riverdale for three nights of the seven, with other guests up from the city joining their hosts in the spacious dining room for as many as seventeen meals out of any week's twenty-one.

We wonder how Olivia Clemens managed it all. She had help, of course—a staff of servants—and her health since returning from Europe, the year before moving up here, had been relatively good. Yet from the start

she had been delicate. At fourteen, as a much admired young lady in Elmira, New York, Miss Langdon was already subsisting more on nerves than
on muscle, a sympathetic elder noted sadly. In that year, 1860, the young
woman was taken ill and lay bedridden with a crippling Victorian ailment
for long months at a time. Often she couldn't lift her head from the pillow. Maybe it was tuberculosis of the spine, Pott's disease; but whatever it
was, her loving family sought remedies through four anxious years that
followed. Livy spent time at the hydropathic sanitarium in Elmira (where
she roomed with a sister of Harriet Beecher Stowe, over from Hartford on
a health quest of her own), and at sanitariums in Washington, D.C., and
in New York City, treated at the Swedish Movement Cure in that last location for over twenty months. By the middle of 1864 the patient was back in
Elmira, still bedridden in a darkened room; and before the year was out, the
desperate family had summoned a faith healer, Dr. James Rogers Newton,
who entered Livy's sick chamber, raised the shades, and bade her sit up. She
did, miraculously; yet as late as April 1867, her mother noted that Olivia
"knelt at family worship for the first time in 6 yrs." She was still not well
five months before meeting her brother's shipmate off the *Quaker City* in
Manhattan. Perhaps fate had kept the beautiful heiress fragile in order that
she might be available in 1870, at the then advanced age of twenty-four, to
marry a Missouri wanderer tardily arrived at Elmira eighteen months earlier (and two years after their Manhattan meeting) from such far-off places
as New Orleans, San Francisco, Hawaii, Europe, Africa, and the Holy Land.

With the demands of the lecture circuit separating him and his betrothed on her twenty-fourth birthday, Sam Clemens pondered the miracle
of their love during a late autumn evening in 1869. "I have kept this day
and honored this anniversary alone, in solitary state," he wrote to Livy, "the
anniversary of an event which was happening when I was a giddy schoolboy a thousand miles away, playing heedlessly all that day"—a child just
shy of ten years old in Hannibal on Thursday, November 27, 1845—"and
sleeping heedlessly all that night unconscious that it was the mightiest day
that had ever winged its viewless hours over my head—unconscious that
on that day two journeys were begun, wide as the poles apart, two paths
marked out, which, wandering and wandering, now far and now near,
were still narrowing, always narrowing toward one point and one blessed
consummation, and these the goal of twenty-four years' marching!—unconscious as I was, on that day of my heedless boyhood, that an event had
just transpired so tremendous that without it all my future life had been a
sullen pilgrimage, but with it that same future was saved!—a sun had just
peered above the horizon which should rise and shine out of the zenith

upon those coming years and fill them with light and warmth, with peace and blessedness, for all time."

Equally enraptured, Livy had assured her Samuel in the same month: "I am so happy, so perfectly at rest in you, so proud of the true nobility of your nature—it makes the whole world look so bright to me."

Samuel Clemens and Olivia Langdon were married three months later, in February 1870, and spent their first year as husband and wife in a fairy-tale home in Buffalo. But the bliss of that beginning was soon intruded upon by a succession of griefs connected with health. Livy's beloved father died; a visiting schoolmate died of typhoid in the newlyweds' very bedroom; the Clemenses's first child was born so sickly as to make doubtful his chances of living to maturity; and Livy fell ill with typhoid as well. In little over a year, the Clemenses left Buffalo for good, returning to Elmira briefly before settling in Hartford, Connecticut, where they would live for the next two decades, from 1871 to 1891.

Earlier, Clemens had visited the place a number of times, and this lecturer who had been in communities all over the country adjudged it the prettiest town he had ever seen. Halfway between New York and Boston, it was—with its banks, insurance companies, and publishing houses (including Mark Twain's publisher)—the richest city per capita in the nation. Moreover, Livy had friends in Hartford, one in particular: Alice Hooker, daughter of the Isabella Beecher Hooker who had spent five months at the watercure in Elmira, rooming with Livy and befriending the Langdons. It was the beautiful young Alice Hooker, in fact, and the equally beautiful Olivia Langdon whom Samuel Clemens, not long back from his *Quaker City* cruise, had encountered at a New York City reception on New Year's Day in 1868, lingering until midnight to bedevil the life out of those two girls and gain an invitation to visit Elmira, as he wrote home to St. Louis ecstatically soon after.

Now one of the girls had become his wife, and Mr. and Mrs. Clemens were living at the moment in the other girl's family home in Hartford, having rented it from its absent owners for what turned into a couple of years. The Hooker home was located in Nook Farm, an area of well-kept lawns and affluent, companionable neighbors on the western edge of the city, fifteen minutes from downtown by carriage. In time, the Clemenses bought a lot for themselves at Nook Farm, on Farmington Avenue, three and a half acres at the crest of a rise sloping down to the Park River, with meadows and woods stretching off to the west. There in 1874 they built a steep-gabled, high-turreted, vermillion-brick residence in which to entertain friends and raise their family in comfort.

The little boy, Langdon, did die, in June 1872, within a year of the Clemenses's moving to Hartford; but before then, Susy had been born, and Clara would come along two years later, and Jean six years after that. By then, Mark Twain was internationally famous, the family made wealthy not only through Mrs. Clemens's substantial inheritance but also because of the success that came to her husband from his lecturing and writing. Well before 1880, Mark Twain had become the most prosperous author in America on the basis of such popular titles as *The Innocents Abroad, Roughing It, The Gilded Age* (in collaboration with a Nook Farm neighbor, C. D. Warner), and *The Adventures of Tom Sawyer*.

William Dean Howells, editor and budding novelist down from Boston, was among those whom the Clemenses urged to visit them early on, while their new mansion was rising, in the spring of 1874. "It seems to me quite an ideal life," Howells reported after his March visit. At Nook Farm the Clemenses and Warners, cohosts, "live very near each other, in a sort of suburban grove, and their neighbors are the Stowes and Hookers, and a great many delightful people. They go in and out of each other's houses without ringing, and nobody gets more than the first syllable of his first name—they call their minister *Joe* Twichell. I staid with Warner, but of course I saw a good deal of Twain, and he's a thoroughly great fellow. His wife is a delicate little beauty, the very flower and perfume of *ladylikeness*, who simply adores him—but this leaves no word to describe his love for her."

Howells enlarged on his sketch of Livy many years later, noting that "she merited all the worship he"—her doting husband—"could give her, all the devotion, all the implicit obedience, by her surpassing force and beauty of character. She was in a way," their friend of forty years goes on, in his fine tribute to *My Mark Twain* that was published in 1910, "the loveliest person I have ever seen, the gentlest, the kindest, without a touch of weakness; she united wonderful tact with wonderful truth; and Clemens not only accepted her rule implicitly, but he rejoiced, he gloried in it."

The chorus of praise from those who knew Olivia Langdon Clemens is so universal as finally to stir wonder. Not a single dissent appears in the surviving record. The great Boston editor James T. Fields and his wife came for a visit in 1876, the perceptive Annie Fields (herself a celebrated hostess) resorting to floral imagery, as did Howells, to convey her delight. Mr. Clemens, she observed, had "such a sincere admiration for his wife's sweetness and beauty of character, that the most prejudiced and hardest heart could not fail to fall in love with him. She looked like an exquisite lily as we left her. So white and delicate and tender! Such sensitiveness and self-control

Figure 21.1. The Clemens family—Clara, Samuel, Jean, Olivia, and Susy—on the porch of their Hartford home in 1884.

Courtesy of the Mark Twain Project, The Bancroft Library, University of California, Berkeley.

as she possesses are very rare." Laudatory superlatives adorn judgment after judgment of Livy, and all appear unqualified. Much later in life, in 1895, when Clemens set off to lecture around the globe, he, Mrs. Clemens, and their daughter Clara left Elmira headed westward, stopping at cities and towns on an overland railroad tour involving twenty-two lectures, all managed by the impresario James B. Pond, who accompanied the Clemenses as far as Vancouver. "To travel with people is to know them," Major Pond wrote of that adventure. From experience he had learned that someone in a party will invariably prove annoying; but in this case, "*this* party seems to have been just right all round." Pond gave the credit to Livy, for, he makes clear, "it was not I, nor Mr. Clemens, nor Mrs. Pond" who possessed "so much gentleness, amiability, sweetness and good sense" as to assure that all went smoothly. It was Mrs. Clemens, he was certain, "the most noble example of woman I have ever had the honor to know."

Olivia Langdon had been reared amid wealth, culture, and leisure, in a hospitable Elmira household filled with humor and good feeling. Houseguests had been a part of her life from the beginning, as they were now at Nook Farm. Yet, although suffering a formidable array of illnesses, somehow she was able to carry on through the heavy demands made on her. "I told Mr. Clemens the other day," she wrote to her widowed mother from inside her grand Hartford home in 1879, "that in this day women must be everything: they must keep up with all the current literature, they must know all about art, they must help in one or two benevolent societies—they must be perfect mothers—they must be perfect housekeepers & graceful gracious hostesses, they must know how to give perfect dinners they must go and visit all the people in the town where they live, they must always be ready to receive their acquaintances—they must dress themselves & their children becomingly and above all they must make their houses 'charming' & so on without end—then if they are not studying something their case is a hopeless one." All of that Livy managed, and managed well, though it was not easy. Living with the restless, mercurial Sam Clemens was not always easy. Rearing her children, entertaining, attending to the logistics of travel all made their unceasing demands on her; so that early on, Livy had admitted to self-doubts, writing as a twenty-six-year-old Nook Farm hostess to her mother in Elmira, in 1872, of wanting to lay her head in the maternal lap "and cry just a little bit. I want to be somebody's baby—I have two babies, have four servants to manage, I have a glorious husband to try and be a woman for, but sometimes I would like to lie down and give it all up—I feel so incompetent for everything, I come so very far short, yet I think I do try earnestly every day."

No one else so much as whispered of Mrs. Clemens's falling short. She reared their three daughters, her husband—by his own account—allowed merely to enjoy them, while he deferred to Livy's direction entirely. He did enjoy the children, enormously, got down on the floor and romped with them, improvised stories for them that featured objects on the mantle in the library as characters, each in its proper order. "Father also taught us to skate on the little river that flowed through the meadow behind the house, and often we glided back and forth on the white ice until the sun had set and the trees looked like giant specters. Then the stars came out and the lights of our 'castle' beckoned us home, a home that was filled with cheer." And filled very often with Nook Farm neighbors: the Warner children, the numerous Twichell children. They came and played charades, and staged elaborate theatricals, and went on hayrides in the fall and sleigh rides in winter. "We had Susy, Julia and Harmony Twichell, Daisy Warner, Fanny Freese, Susy Corey and Miss Foote here for supper," Livy wrote of a by no means untypical occasion, when the eldest Clemens daughter was thirteen, her sister eleven. "A jolly time playing games, dancing, and so on. It is a great pleasure to see the children together they do have such a good time. There is much satisfaction in doing anything for Susy and Clara they are so grateful for every thing that is done for them, and express it so earnestly. It seems almost strange when they have always had so much done for them. When I came up to bed tonight they were both wide awake waiting to tell me what a good day they had had and how much they thanked me for it. They are blessed children and tremendous comforts."

Guests from all over continued to come: from Boston and New York, from out West and overseas. There were billiards on the top floor, and up there Clemens strove when he could to get on with his work. He was often working on more than one book at a time, and on articles for the magazines, when he wasn't inventing household gadgets or applying for patents. And he wrote plays. In fact, his dramatization of his part of the co-written novel *The Gilded Age* proved a great success. *Colonel Sellers* it was called, with John T. Raymond touring for twelve years in the title role; that effort earned the playwright serious money. And always there were the guests to welcome, and neighbors to dine with happily and treat to stories and to Mark Twain's wonderful readings aloud.

So much was going on at Nook Farm. "I can write ten chapters in Elmira where I can write one here," the author came to realize. "I work at work here, but I don't accomplish anything worth speaking of." So the family took to spending long, relaxing summers in Elmira. There they lived three miles east of downtown and the Langdon mansion, at Quarry Farm, the summer house on the cooler hillside that Jervis Langdon had willed to his older daughter Susan Crane. Saint Susan, Sam Clemens called her, for her kindness and generosity. She had built at the top of the hill an octagonal study for her brother-in-law to work in. He could go up there in the morning, high over the town and the Chemung River in the valley and the blue hills beyond, and work all day undistracted, then come down and rejoin his contented family, the children with their pony and dogs and kittens and games, Livy on the front porch, the Cranes up from the Langdon home, each ready to listen to his reading of the day's handiwork. It was the audience he valued above all others.

Tom Sawyer was written in his hilltop study in Elmira, amid the Spartan comforts of a table, wicker chair, cot, fireplace, cat door, and windows on six sides. A couple of years earlier, in 1874, Mark Twain had composed something else in Elmira, something different: "A True Story" based on an exchange on the Quarry Farm porch with Susan Crane's black cook one summer evening after the day's work was done. It was twilight. The white folks rocked in chairs on the porch, the cook—Mary Ann Cord, "Aunt Rachel" as represented—sat on the steps below, laughing at some foolery or other. In the presence of such good humor Mr. C— (the account calls him) was moved to ask: "Aunt Rachel, how is it that you've lived sixty years and never had any trouble?"

What follows was her answer, "Repeated Word for Word as I Heard It," as the true story's title goes on to clarify. What the questioner meant, he hurries to explain when Aunt Rachel asks if he's in earnest, is that she *can't* have known trouble. "I've never heard you sigh, and never seen your eye when there wasn't a laugh in it."

The woman turns to face him. "Has I had any trouble?" She will leave it to Mr. C— to decide. Before the war she had lived all her life as a slave in Virginia, married to another slave "lovin' an' kind to me, jist as kind as you is to yo' own wife." They had seven children. But the plantation ran into debt and the slaves had to be auctioned off. Aunt Rachel tells of the inhumanity of the slave auction, where people were sold precisely like chattel, all of them prodded about: her husband torn from her, and her children torn from her one by one, twenty-two years ago last Easter. As cook at the plantation house, Rachel was spared. Then the war came, and the white family fled, and Union officers set up headquarters in the abandoned mansion, keeping Rachel on to cook for them. Unfolding in the woman's dialect, the account next tells of her chance discovery of her lost son Henry among the black Union soldiers encamped on the grounds. Her other six children and her husband she never sees or hears of again, but the end of her story has her clasping Henry, her grown Union soldier, in her arms. "Oh, no, Misto C—," she finishes. "I hain't had no trouble. An' no *joy!*"

Howells had been after Mark Twain to give him something for the *Atlantic Monthly*. In early September 1874, from Elmira, Clemens sent the editor "A True Story," which, as its author explained, "has no humor in it. You can pay as lightly as you choose for that, if you want it, for it is rather out of my line. I have not altered the old colored woman's story except to begin it at the beginning, instead of the middle, as she did—& worked both ways."

The editor did want the story, thought it capital, and published it in the November 1874 issue, Mark Twain's first appearance in that highbrow American magazine. Though at first puzzled, looking for the joke, the *Atlantic*'s 50,000 subscribers were soon moved by the story, by a pathos that invariably appealed to sensitive Victorian readers. Thereafter Mark Twain's work began appearing regularly in this most influential of the nation's magazines. In January 1875, for instance, were initiated reminiscences that continued through August, of the author's days as a steamboat pilot between St. Louis and New Orleans before the war. In time, all of this became almost frightening, the extent of Mark Twain's success through these years in the 1870s and on into the decade that followed. He said so himself. "I am frightened at the proportions of my prosperity," he was heard to remark one evening in Hartford in the mid-eighties. "It seems that whatever I touch turns to gold."

Such grand fortune could hardly last. Soon storm clouds were gathering, and in the torrent's dark aftermath Sam and Livy Clemens were obliged to live with their memories and regrets: leaving Hartford in 1891, wandering abroad, plunging into bankruptcy, losing their beloved Susy, trying to cope with a new, chronic, appalling illness that befell their youngest child, Jean. Moreover, just now, back from fetching his honorary degree at the University of Missouri, Clemens had discovered his wife's health deteriorated, in this June of 1902, from what it had been even as recently as when he left Riverdale to go west two weeks before.

"One day at Riverdale-on-Hudson," he recalled some years later, in 1908, "Mrs. Clemens and I were mourning for our lost little ones. Not that they were dead"—Clara and Jean were alive—"but lost to us all the same. Gone out of our lives forever—as little children. They were still with us, but they were become women, and they walked with us upon our own level. There was a wide gulf, a gulf as wide as the horizons, between these children and those. We were always having vague dream-glimpses of them—" O Death in Life, the days that are no more! "—of them as they had used to be in the long-vanished years—glimpses of them playing and romping, with short frocks on, and spindle legs, and hair-tails down their backs—and always they were far and dim, and we could not hear their shouts and their laughter."

CHAPTER **Twenty-Two**

Huckleberry Finn

K aty Leary had worked for the Clemenses since 1880. She was from
Elmira, twenty-four years old when they hired her and brought her
back to Hartford as a maid, seamstress, and nanny, after their regular summertime stay at Quarry Farm. She would remain in the family's
employ until 1910. Long afterward a friend of Clara Clemens interviewed
the servant over a couple of weeks, taking down her recollections—more or
less in Katy's own words—of thirty years in a household full of joys and its
share of sorrows. During the Hartford period all had seemed joyful as Katy
recalled it, living in a home "that you would like more than anything else in
the world. A happy, happy home—happiness budding all over—everybody
always happy. Our life—it just rolled on like a smooth sea—wasn't a thing
for eleven years—not a bit of sadness of any kind. There was always fun and
excitement, especially when Mr. Clemens was around." And of Mrs. Clemens, Katy couldn't say enough. "Oh! She was a lovely woman and there
never was a happier couple lived in this world than they was. They never
had a cross word—I don't think they ever spoke a cross word to each other,
and she was so kind, and so sweet and true."

Yet this loyal servant, who would accompany the Clemenses on their
extensive travels, who would be with Susy at her death, who would hold
Mrs. Clemens in her arms as she was dying—this kindly, tender, faithful
servant gives blunt voice to the era's racial bigotry. She is remembering
George Griffin, another loyal and much loved servant of the family in
Hartford. George was black, and according to Katy, "really very nice for a
colored boy." And she grants that he was "a nice-looking nigger," too, "but
he was a nigger just the same. We used to have great arguments about the
niggers. We was always arguing—just like Mr. Clemens. He"—George—
"used to say:

189

"'Well, Katy, they never could have plays or anything else that was funny, if it wasn't for the Niggers and the Irish.' And I'd say to him:

"'Uh! Don't talk to me that way about the niggers and the Irish. Don't you *dare* put the nigger *ahead* of the Irishman!' I says.

"That used to make me mad when he did that. George was always very grand," she rambles on, "and he just adored Mrs. Clemens. He thought there wasn't anybody in this world like Mrs. Clemens; but even so, she couldn't stop him," while serving as the family butler, "from laughing out loud at the dinner parties when they was telling stories and having them good jokes. Mrs. Clemens used to take George to task very often about this."

In *Adventures of Huckleberry Finn*, which Mark Twain began soon after finishing *The Adventures of Tom Sawyer*, in 1876, the word *nigger* appears over 200 times. Huck of the riverfront village in the 1840s uses the term as freely as does Katy Leary in her interview in the 1920s, she confident, that far along, that her white northern listener won't take exception any more than white southerners had eighty years before. It is the term by which Huckleberry refers to people of dark skin, and once the author had made his decision to tell the story in the boy's own voice, no other word would have been authentic. Huck didn't know any way of speaking differently.

With his wonderful ear, Mark Twain worked hard on authenticity in this matter of people's speech. Capturing how the Cranes' cook Mary Ann Cord expressed herself in "A True Story" had called for an effort. "I amend dialect stuff by talking & talking & *talking* it till it sounds right," he wrote Howells in explanation, "& I had difficulty with this negro talk because a negro sometimes (rarely) says 'goin'' & sometimes 'gwyne', & they make just such discrepancies in other words—& when you come to reproduce them on paper they look as if the variation resulted from the writer's carelessness. But I want to work at the proofs & get the dialect as nearly right as possible."

He took the same care with *Huckleberry Finn*. A note at the start of the novel explains. "In this book a number of dialects are used, to wit: the Missouri negro dialect; the extremest form of the backwoods South-Western dialect; the ordinary 'Pike-County' dialect; and four modified varieties of this last." Without the clarification, the author goes on, "many readers would suppose that all these characters were trying to talk alike and not succeeding."

As for *Tom Sawyer*: after he had finished that manuscript, Mark Twain wondered whether he should have written it all in the first person, Tom speaking, from the boy's point of view. He hadn't; he wrote his novel in the third person, thinking all along that he was writing for adults. Livy and Howells convinced him otherwise. They both said that *Tom Sawyer* was for young people, and Howells knew at once that young people would adore it. So the novel was published for that audience; and right after finishing it, the author began a sequel, also for young people, although now in the first person:

"You don't know about me, without you have read a book by the name of 'The Adventures of Tom Sawyer,' but that ain't no matter. That book was made by Mr. Mark Twain, and he told the truth, mainly. There was things which he stretched, but mainly he told the truth. That is nothing. I never seen anybody but lied, one time or another, without it was Aunt Polly, or the widow, . . ."

Having found a distinctive narrative voice, the author was on his way. When he was done, Clemens's sister, Pamela, right off recognized the boy who was telling the story in her brother's new novel. "Why, that is Tom Blankenship!" and she was right. "In *Huckleberry Finn* I have drawn Tom Blankenship exactly as he was," Mark Twain explained much later. "He was ignorant, unwashed, insufficiently fed; but he had as good a heart as ever any boy had. His liberties were totally unrestricted. He was the only really independent person—boy or man—in the community, and by consequence he was tranquilly and continuously happy and was envied by all the rest of us. We liked him; we enjoyed his society. And as his society was forbidden us by our parents the prohibition trebled and quadrupled its value." A few years before thus identifying his model, Clemens had heard, in 1902, that Blankenship ended up as justice of the peace in a Montana village, "a good citizen and greatly respected," having lit out for the Territory in truth, just as Huck at the end of his story threatens to light out in order to escape Aunt Sally's sivilizin'.

Huck's story had been a long while in the writing, seven years before the boy gets to the part where "there ain't nothing more to write about, and I am rotten glad of it, because if I'd a knowed what a trouble it was to make a book I wouldn't a tackled it and ain't agoing to no more." Mark Twain began *Huckleberry Finn* in the summer of 1876 and wrote the first fifteen chapters rapidly, much of it in the vein of *Tom Sawyer*, with Huck at the start called forth by Tom to sneak out and join in a midnight escapade. But some time later Huck's father, the town's brute of a drunk who has been out of sight for a year, returns, drags his son off to a cabin upriver on the Illinois shore, and ends by keeping the boy locked up up there. Using pig's blood to fake his own murder, Huck escapes and hides on Jackson's Island nearby. There he runs into Miss Watson's slave Jim, hiding too, to avoid being sold and sent downriver. The two resolve to flee together on a raft that they've recovered from floating debris. Their plan is to go as far as Cairo, Illinois, then make their way up the Ohio to Jim's freedom. Thus they set out to drift downstream by night, lazily, happily, at the speed the current carries them, three or four miles an hour.

With the two well launched on that progress, Mark Twain breaks off. He put the book aside and turned to other matters, not sure that this present effort would work out. It did work out, gloriously, when the author picked up the manuscript again in 1883, after a lapse of several years during which he had revisited the world of his childhood in hard fact. That had been in the spring of the year before. The articles Mark Twain published in the *Atlantic* back in 1875—"Old Times on the Mississippi," about his life as a steamboat pilot—he had decided to work up into a book of the requisite length for subscription publishing. Before doing so, Clemens in 1882 took the train to St. Louis, descended to New Orleans as a steamboat passenger, then retraced the 1,200 miles upriver by boat past St. Louis as far as Hannibal, then on to St. Paul, Minnesota. The river travel not only helped him put together *Life on the Mississippi* (1883), but provided him with inspiration to return to *Adventures of Huckleberry Finn*, images of the river and the town of his boyhood fresh in his mind.

Thus down the great Mississippi Huck and Jim resume their voyage. By day the humblest of transients—a runaway slave and an "ignorant, unwashed" thirteen-year-old white boy—hide their raft and the trailing canoe, then travel at night, lying on their backs gazing at the stars, talking, fishing, taking a swim now and then, each night passing towns, "some of them away up on black hillsides, nothing but just a shiny bed of lights, not a house could you see." Evenings Huck slips ashore to buy a few pennies worth of meal or bacon and maybe, if he's able, to appropriate a chicken "that warn't roosting comfortable." Before dawn he might go ashore again and borrow some new corn from a corn field, or a watermelon or pumpkin "or things of that kind." And thus in warm starlit weather, the two aboard their magical raft prosper on a river that bears them ever southward between banks, a half mile off on either side, beyond which civilization hovers, mindless of these fugitives.

But the two miss the juncture with the Ohio River at Cairo, the path to freedom obscured in a night of heavy fog. Later, descending deeper into slave country, they encounter stormy weather at last. Worse than the weather, though, are the specimens of humanity met with along the way. Contrasts are striking, between the child Huck and the childlike Jim, on their raft afloat, and the adult world that impinges with ever increasing insistence from shore: a world of blood feuds and cowardice, of fraud, hypocrisy, deception and betrayal, of random cruelty and murder and attempted lynching, all revealed through a succession of adventures that impose themselves on good-hearted innocents escaping their evils back home. Given the darkness of Mark Twain's satire, not the least wonderful aspect of this wonderful novel is the exhilaration it furnishes the reader amid so much squalor and ugliness. To be sure, the author adheres to the taste of his times by tamping down the ugliness, by only implying the full nastiness, for instance, of the Dauphin, that fraud of a "King" who intrudes on the raft and ends by deceiving Huck and his friend so utterly as to sell Jim back into slavery, in Arkansas, and pocket the forty dirty dollars.

What makes all this rascality palatable—aside from the perverse allure of fictional wickedness—is the variety of characters met with, Huck's spirited resourcefulness in dealing with them, Jim's loyalty and humanity throughout, the peace and lyrical beauty when the two in flight are alone on their raft, and over all the irony, sound sense, and humor, the humor as fresh as when it was written a hundred and thirty-some years ago. Thus, despite bleak prospects ashore and afloat, Huck's and Jim's adventures remain a joy to be part of.

And all the while, the developing relationship between the two adds to the novel's profundity. At the start Huck imposes on the runaway, teasing him, playing practical jokes on him on the island and the raft. He props a dead rattlesnake on Jim's blanket in camp, "thinking there'd be some fun" in it when Jim goes to bed. But Huck forgets about the snake, and its live mate is there when Jim climbs under the blanket. The snake bites, and Jim pulls through only after four days of swelling and pain. Again, when the two are separated in fog, Huck in his canoe finally catches up with the raft, on which Jim sprawls asleep, exhausted. When his friend wakes up, Huck pretends to have been there all along, that all the ordeal of their separating and calling each other through the fog and battling the current and crashing into banks of the river was only in Jim's dream. "Well, den, I reck'n I did dream it, Huck," Jim is persuaded finally, and at Huck's urging he describes his dream in full, superstitiously interpreting what it all must have meant. But then—that done—how does Jim interpret the leaves and rubbish on the raft, and the broken oar?

Jim looks at the trash, and at Huck, and back at the trash. "What do dey stan' for?" he says at last. "I's gwyne to tell you." Jim had felt heartsick in the storm, sure that Huck was lost for good. And when he woke and found his friend on the raft, "all safe en soun'," tears had welled up in his joy. "En all you wuz thinkin 'bout wuz how you could make a fool uv ole

Jim wid a lie. Dat truck dah is *trash*; en trash is what people is dat puts dirt on de head er dey fren's en makes 'em ashamed."

With that, Jim withdraws silently to another part of the raft.

"It was fifteen minutes," Huck tells us, "before I could work myself up to go and humble myself to a nigger—but I done it, and I warn't ever sorry for it afterwards, neither. I didn't do him no more mean tricks, and I wouldn't done that one if I'd a knowed it would make him feel that way."

Well into the novel, in chapter 31 of the forty-three chapters, after the King ashore has sold Jim back into slavery, Huck left alone starts thinking about the bad turn he has inflicted on Miss Watson, "stealing a poor old woman's nigger that hadn't ever done me no harm." He will write and tell her where Jim is. "Miss Watson your runaway nigger Jim is down here two mile below Pikesville and Mr. Phelps has got him and he will give him up for the reward if you send. HUCK FINN."

Having done the right thing, the boy feels fine, sinless, light as a feather, "thinking how good it was all this happened so, and how near I come to being lost and going to hell," stealing some nice old lady's property that way. But then his thoughts turn to the long voyage downriver, and the singing on the raft, the talking low and lazy in the night, the laughing, and Jim's standing Huck's watch sometimes so the boy could get more sleep. Huck remembers how glad Jim was "when I come back out of the fog," and how he would do "everything he could think of for me, and at last I struck the time I saved him by telling the men we had small-pox aboard, and he was so grateful, and said I was the best friend old Jim ever had in the world, and the *only* one he's got now; and then," Huck tells us, "I happened to look around, and see that paper."

He takes up his note to Miss Watson. Would he do the right thing: make sure that she got her lawful property back? Or the wrong thing, as he had been doing all along?

"I studied a minute, sort of holding my breath, and then says to myself: 'All right, then, I'll *go* to hell'—and tore it up."

It is one of the supreme moments in all of American fiction, a boy discovering that the social conscience—that patchwork of hypocrisy, cruelty, and threadbare Calvinism—is a fraud, that his own native instincts offer sounder guidance.

Trust thyself. The present writer has been privileged to teach *Huckleberry Finn* to able high-school sophomores on three or four occasions. Each time, our consideration elicited enthusiasm for a novel that the teacher loved. Students, multiracial, multiethnic, followed along attentively. Afterward, at the end of the course, they were asked in one instance to write down for the instructor's guidance which of the readings over the semester had been their favorite and which they enjoyed least. *Brave New World* was at the top of the list, and *Their Eyes Were Watching God*. High up was *The Odyssey*, with *Macbeth* not far behind. There were others; but to my surprise and dismay, the book least enjoyed—despite classes alive with participation, with their instructor enthusiastically teaching a book that he wholeheartedly admired—the work reported as least enjoyed was *Adventures of Huckleberry Finn*. This despite preparatory explanations of its historical and linguistic contexts, and despite the pleasure students had appeared to take at the time of our reading the novel.

Perhaps they were using those later means to urge me tactfully to exclude *Huckleberry Finn* from future syllabuses. For it may no longer be a novel for young Americans to consider in classrooms of the twenty-first century. Not so much because of difficulties posed by the dialect, a consequence of Mark Twain's brilliant decision to tell the story in Huck's own voice. Each passing decade does push the orthography of that child of the 1840s farther from the English in which twenty-first-century high-school students are fluent. But those latter can manage dialect, as they manage it in *Wuthering Heights* and Shakespeare. On the other hand, the novel's irony does pose a challenge, one that many adults appear to have trouble with as well. Appreciating verbal irony is, after all, a late-developed reading skill: being able to hear the ironical tone emanating from a silent white page on which mute black marks have been shaped into letters, words, sentences, and paragraphs. Those marks convey meaning; but when is the meaning to be taken literally, and when is it to be heard as something different from what is literally stated? Huck will "go to hell," then; and readers must understand that at that moment he saves his soul.

Yet the principal problem with *Huckleberry Finn* in the classroom is neither dialect nor irony. Rather, it lies in the uneasiness that stirs with each recurrence of the word *nigger*. That uneasiness arises less from any overactive political correctness than from white classmates' empathy for the discomfort of their black classmates and friends. Will the day arrive—with American society serenely accepting people for who they are rather than for what their creed or skin color or sexual orientation might be—that *nigger* has been rendered as inoffensive as *Brit* seems now, or *Yank*, or *Mick* (this Mick avers)? Until such unlikely time, high school students may of course read *Huckleberry Finn* on their own, one by one, whenever they choose to. In class, though, at present, the group experience feels too fraught with unspoken malaise, at least until the blissful hour when we get our increasingly heterogeneous racial house in order. Here's irony for you.

With *Tom Sawyer*, Mark Twain thought he was writing a book for adults, although it turned out to be for young people. With *Huckleberry Finn*, for a nineteenth-century readership far more homogeneous than our own, he was writing a novel for young people that—despite its many merits, its literary significance, and its vast influence—the current historical moment may have rendered suitable only for adults of whatever age among us.

Even in Mark Twain's day, and although it sold very well, some readers didn't like the book, not because they thought it racist, but because those genteel readers thought it was vulgar, "cheap and pernicious stuff." In Concord, Massachusetts—citadel of culture, erstwhile home of Thoreau, Emerson, and Hawthorne—the Free Public Library banned the novel for its coarseness and inelegance, as "the veriest trash." Nor was *Huckleberry Finn* Mrs. Clemens's favorite among her husband's works. She much preferred *The Prince and the Pauper*, published three years earlier and set in England in 1547, where clowning is held to a minimum, where the moral emerges free of irony, and where the wealth of history recovered in the novel's pages demonstrates that the author is far more than merely a phunny phellow.

So, finally, is *Huckleberry Finn* with its recurring "nigger" a racist text? A few educators today make careers out of denouncing the book in its entirety, and school boards ban it—this novel that Hemingway in *Green Hills of Africa* (1935) saluted as the source of all modern American literature, "the best book we've had. All American writing comes from that. There was nothing before. There has been nothing as good since." And for all the uproar over its diction, such distinguished African-American authors as Langston Hughes, Richard Wright, and Ralph Ellison have acknowledged their love for and indebtedness to the novel's author, Ellison keeping a photograph of Mark Twain above his writing desk. Irony does pose challenges. But for those who respond to *Huckleberry Finn* sensitively, who can see beneath its accurate descriptive surfaces into the depths of its sympathy and truth, what comes clear is the author's salutary loathing of sham, injustice, and cruelty, exposed here in a quintessentially American setting through which two innocents—both of them objects of Mark Twain's love—forge their friendship afloat on a raft: one white, the derelict son of a village drunk, the other black, a runaway slave who, once on the river, develops beyond his role as the stereotypical, shuffling, superstitious, semi-civilized black buffoon to become, for the first time in our literature, a white boy's peer.

CHAPTER Twenty-Three

Roosevelt and the Philippines

No obvious way of ending *Huckleberry Finn* would have suggested itself. The novel is set before the Civil War, in the 1840s, with slavery still legal and unassailable all over the South. Once the fugitives on their raft slip beyond the fogbound mouth of the Ohio River—Jim's route to freedom—each passing night on the Mississippi carries them more deeply into slave country, until finally, inexorably, they will have drifted the thousand miles all the way to southern Arkansas. In those grim times, a runaway slave that far from free soil would have had no hope of escaping such hostile surroundings.

The final eleven chapters of *Huckleberry Finn*—a quarter of the novel—strive to rescue Jim from his dilemma. Structurally the author's solution to the slave's predicament makes sense. Tom Sawyer, present in the opening chapters, reappears (however implausibly) in the concluding ones, so that the spirit of the ending resembles that of the beginning—and of *The Adventures of Tom Sawyer* that preceded the beginning. After the marvelous weeks afloat, we are back in the more conventional juvenile world ashore, of boyish pranks and escapades. But *Huckleberry Finn* is not *Tom Sawyer*. It is that literary rarity, a sequel far greater than the novel that inspired it. Thus very few readers, dazzled by the power of the long central rafting portion of *Huckleberry Finn*, will encounter the concluding pages without a sense of sharp falling-off.

The despicable fraud of a "King" (it turns out) has betrayed Huck by selling Jim to a farm family near the squalid Arkansas village of Pikesville. For the moment Jim's new owners, the Phelpses, have confined their acquisition in a shed on their property. Huck hunts down his friend, but on arriving at the farm is mistaken for Tom Sawyer, a nephew of the Phelpses who by chance is expected any hour on a visit. Tom does show up, assumes the identity of his brother Sid so that Huck may go on passing for Tom, then sets about "liberating" Jim from what in fact is a bondage relatively benign and easily cast off.

To effect Jim's "escape," Tom resorts to methods of deliverance he's read about in notable dungeon narratives. For this child of romance is a great reader of books, in that respect resembling not only Sammy Clemens but also Teedie Roosevelt. Moreover, as were both of those real-life children, Tom Sawyer is the leader among his chums, guiding their activities by the lights of what he has read. Hence, in order to "rescue" Jim, he now sets about directing the digging of an unneeded tunnel, the tearing up of a bed sheet for an unneeded escape rope, the smuggling into Jim's shed of an unnecessary grindstone, and the importing inside of spiders and snakes to create the proper dungeon atmosphere. Through all the ensuing torment, Jim—the noble, compassionate, sympathetic Jim whom we watched emerge as a rounded character on the raft—reverts to the bumbling, superstitious stereotype of the comical black man current in white writings throughout the nineteenth century and far into the twentieth: "Mars Tom, I's willin' to tackle mos' anything 'at ain't onreasonable, but ef you en Huck fetches a rattlesnake in heah for me to tame, I's gwyne to *leave*, dat's *shore*." And all the while, Tom Sawyer knows—and has kept to himself—that Jim is actually a free man now, Miss Watson having died in the interval since Huck's flight and left a will that manumitted her servant.

The author's outline and surviving manuscript of *Huckleberry Finn* reveal that he worked particularly hard on this portion of the novel, however strained the results may seem to us. A case has been made that Mark Twain, writing in the early 1880s, was by these means satirizing the post-Reconstruction plight of the African-American down South, technically granted his freedom but returned to darkness and effectively in bondage, to be frustrated, tormented, and deprived of his rights and his dignity. That rings true. Yet in years ahead this same author took up his three profitable characters—Tom Sawyer, Huck Finn, and Jim—and set them loose on further adventures: "Huck Finn and Tom Sawyer among the Indians," *Tom Sawyer Abroad*, and "Tom Sawyer's Conspiracy," one manuscript finished and published, two of them not, those inferior sequels all three featuring a Jim along on the adventures as a free black possessed of the hapless, minstrel-show characteristics that Mark Twain's white readership found so delightfully comical: "Whoosh! Dem's de ticket for Jim! Bust ef it doan' beat all, how rotten ignorant a body kin be." Only in *Adventures of Huckleberry Finn*, and only on the river—the substantial heart of that great novel—does Jim achieve the reality and nobility of character that place him among the preeminent creations of American fiction.

As noted earlier, white denizens of the late nineteenth far into the twentieth centuries, including Samuel L. Clemens, predicated their attitudes toward race on certainties since refuted—at least to the satisfaction of people of good will—during the course of the many decades that have elapsed between then and now. Now, in America, each passing week exposes a fundamental tenet of racial faith back then as false. If for one day Roosevelt and Clemens could reappear among us, both would be astounded to behold the numbers of black people high in success in American life: businessmen, corporate officers, military officers, physicians, musicians, athletes, newscasters, television and movie stars, judges, professors, authors, stockbrokers, scientists, politicians, a black president in the White House—and to witness the increasingly casual acceptance by white Americans of that enriched state of affairs.

For their part, just about everybody in the earlier period was convinced that the darker races—black, red, yellow, or brown; Negro, Indian, Oriental, or, say, Mexican—were unassimilable within a white society. True, most among those whites acknowledged and, in their paternalism, relished black people's merits as they perceived them: that they were patient, loyal, cheerful, quick to laugh, and that they were funny. We've heard Clemens's black servant George make the last-named point, teasing his coworker Katy Leary: what would white people have to laugh at in their plays without the niggers and the Irish? And invariably his observation provoked Irish Katy's outraged response: "Don't you *dare* put the nigger *ahead* of the Irishman!"

The exchange illustrates that other, related dogma of the times, all but universally subscribed to among whites, one that our present is categorically disproving. Blacks, it was known as a truth, were *by nature, biologically* inferior. Whites clung to that conviction despite any evidence that might be adduced to the contrary. Thus, however humble the white person, he or she had the consolation of being superior to any black: "Don't you *dare* put the nigger *ahead* of the Irishman!" If the example of such an able, accomplished black man as Booker T. Washington was cited, that could be accounted for by his white blood, from his absent father. Yet those same explicators, so sure of what they knew, were equally certain that miscegenation led to degeneracy.

"Mongrelization" was one word for it; mixing the races mongrelized them, as in mating donkeys with horses. Pitchfork Ben Tillman feared the mongrelization of the "highest and noblest of the five races," the

Caucasian, if aspirations of the black race to social equality weren't put a stop to. In prehistoric times—so went the mythical history, taken for truth—one group of Aryans had migrated from the western slopes of the Himalayas into Europe, exterminating natives along the way, maintaining their blond, blue-eyed racial purity into Germany at last, in time on into England, driving the non-Aryan Celts, those not killed, into the corners of the British Isles. This was the strain, pure Anglo-Saxon, that developed democratic institutions and exhibited the initiative and the organizational skills to spread its influence finally far and wide. One little island off Europe achieved all that. Similarly, another Aryan group had moved eastward those ages ago, from the eastern slopes of the Himalayas, but mated with the natives it encountered. The results, as understood and promulgated by thinkers in the nineteenth century, were the oriental races—Chinese, Indians, Mongolians—the consequence of racial mixture and therefore of mongrelization. Hence a few thousand Anglo-Saxons were able now to rule over millions of Indians, degraded inhabitants of the Asian subcontinent. Hence the imperative that descendants of Anglo-Saxons here in America— unique masters of the complex arts of democracy—be left to manage our political affairs, amid the equally constraining imperative that whites remain pure and blacks stay socially separate.

"Nineteenth-century democracy needs no more complete vindication for its existence," wrote Theodore Roosevelt, "than the fact that it has kept for the white race the best portions of the new world's surface." His was thinking representative of the time. America was for white people, "a nation of pioneers" who had brought their initiative, their hardihood, their skills, and their love of democracy to settle a temperate land. "Our history has been one of expansion," the then vice president pronounced in a speech on September 2, 1901, days before McKinley's assassination (after which doleful event that same speaker would ascend abruptly to the White House). From the eastern seaboard Anglo-Saxons had expanded ever farther westward, and that is "not a matter of regret, but of pride," Roosevelt went on. "We were right in wresting from barbarism and adding to civilization the territory out of which we have made these beautiful states"; for barbarism has "no place in a civilized world. It is our duty toward the people living in barbarism to see that they are freed from their chains, and we can free them only by destroying barbarism itself."

He was referring to Indians, of course, to Native Americans living in barbarism who were to be freed from their chains. Or destroyed? Many attributes account for the popularity that accrued to Theodore Roosevelt after he moved into the White House those few days later: his colossal energy, his youth, his incorruptibility, his heroism in war, his appealing family, the joy he so obviously took in living. But not the least of Roosevelt's attractions lay in his articulating views shared by so many of his fellow citizens both low and high. Here, for example, is a view from on high, from William John McGee, president of the National Geographic Society, president of the American Anthropological Association, chief of the Department of Anthropology at the great St. Louis World's Fair of 1904 (twice the size of the gigantic World's Columbian Exposition of 1893). The affable, much admired McGee, whom President Roosevelt would appoint to the Bureau of Soils in the Department of Agriculture and to the Inland Waterways Commission in 1907, was on record with this opinion: that "white" and "strong" are synonymous, and that it is "the duty of the strong man to subjugate lower nature, to extirpate the bad and cultivate the good among living things" and "in all ways to enslave the world for the support of humanity and the increase of human intelligence."

Perhaps the strong man's duty to *subjugate, extirpate,* and *enslave* sounds different now from how it sounded back then, before an Austrian in his mid-teens at the time, pursuing bohemian dreams of becoming a painter or an architect in the fiercely anti-Semitic city of Vienna, had unleashed the consequences of his diseased mind to alter all Europe and cast a massive, horrific shadow over human life thereafter. After Hitler, we speak less glibly of extirpations, as we may also have learned to be wary when duty summons us to "subjugate lower nature" for humanity's sake.

In those years before two world wars, President Roosevelt could sometimes utter opinions as disquieting as are the ones just quoted, of W J McGee, geologist and anthropologist. When the new president of the United States came into office abruptly in the fall of 1901, he faced unfinished business that his martyred predecessor had left behind. One such matter concerned the Philippines. Late in McKinley's administration, on July 4, 1901, two months before the President was murdered in Buffalo, America's military governor in Manila, General Arthur MacArthur, had yielded his authority to a civilian, Judge William Howard Taft of Ohio. The transfer implied that the insurrection of Filipinos against American troops occupying their archipelago—a resistance that had been going on for two and a half years—had finally wound down. But on September 28, two weeks exactly after President Roosevelt was hastily sworn into office, guerillas on the island of Samar, some 500 miles southeast of Manila, massacred forty American soldiers of the Ninth United States Infantry Regiment, stationed there to prevent supplies from reaching rebels holding out in the interior.

The reaction back home was predictable, newspapers drawing comparisons to the massacre twenty-five years earlier of Custer's troops at Little Big Horn. People in 1901 were still thinking in terms of those not-distant Indian Wars, and some people thought of Filipinos as Indians. Roosevelt in private referred to America's adversaries in the archipelago not only as savages and barbarians, but as Apaches and Sioux. As commander in chief, he now ordered that the Philippines be pacified once and for all. A veteran Indian fighter, Brigadier General Jacob Smith, was accordingly sent to the island of Samar to mete out reprisals.

Much of what went on in the archipelago, in McKinley's time as later, was kept from the public back home. It was not immediately known, for instance, that General Smith, arriving at Samar, ordered his troops to make of the island a "howling wilderness." Those were his words. "I want no prisoners," he told his subordinates. "I wish you to kill and burn, the more you kill and burn the better it will please me. I want all persons killed who are capable of bearing arms in actual hostilities against the United States."

Major Littleton Waller sought clarification. "I would like to know the limit of age to respect, sir?"

"Ten years," the general told him.

"Persons of ten years and older are those designated as being capable of bearing arms?"

"Yes," Smith confirmed.

Vengeance against all who slew the forty American soldiers, as well as against those Filipinos who had the misfortune of being on the island and born at least a decade earlier, proceeded apace, in thorough fashion. All the while, American soldiers were writing letters home that began finding their way into newspapers. "I am probably growing hard-hearted," one soldier wrote, "for I am in my glory when I can sight my gun on some dark skin and pull the trigger." Another cleared his conscience thus: "No cruelty is too severe for these brainless monkeys, who can appreciate no sense of honor, kindness or justice." A third soldier told of having been ordered to administer the watercure to captured Filipino insurgents as many as 160 times; 134 of his interventions led to death.

To readers back then the term *watercure* would have denoted the popular hydropathic sanitariums that had flourished in America through fifty years, from 1843 until near the end of the century. Elmira, New York, was the site of a famous one, to which Beechers, Stowes, Hookers, and many others came from as far away as Hartford on extended visits in agreeable surroundings to improve their health. In the Philippines, watercures were something else: means adopted from Spanish predecessors on the archipelago whereby a prisoner was encouraged to divulge information. Gagged, forced to the ground, held down, his mouth pried open by a pole or rifle barrel, the victim had water ladled over his face until his stomach swelled like a pregnant woman's. A soldier might then step on the stomach to vomit the water forth so that the process could be repeated. Private Evan Wyatt of the Eighth Infantry Volunteers reported that "the spectacle was so horrible I walked away."

Official communiqués sought to reassure the American public of progress toward democracy in the Philippines, omitting such disagreeable facts as watercures, and the setting up of concentration camps, and Governor Taft's forbidding of political parties over there, and the governor's limiting of the vote to the richest Filipinos on the islands, to the top 3 percent, whose ballots were to be cast only for low-level officials. Americans retained the major posts. All the while, privately, the President in Washington and his governor in Manila shared the conviction that Filipinos would not be ready for self-rule in twenty, in fifty, maybe not in a hundred years.

Yet reassurances continued from official sources, while soldiers' letters home and increasingly skeptical newspaper accounts led finally, in the early months of 1902, to congressional hearings. Senator Hoar, anti-imperialist senior senator from Massachusetts, had doubted the reliability of governmental reports. A senate committee (chaired by Massachusetts's junior senator, Henry Cabot Lodge, the President's closest friend) called witnesses; and it was the witnesses' testimony that uncovered General Smith's ambition to make of Samar a howling wilderness. "Howling Jake" Smith, as he was known thereafter, was court-martialed for his conduct, and not for the first time in his career; but being near retirement, the general was permitted to resign from the service, his commander in chief judging retirement to be punishment enough.

President Roosevelt, himself a veteran, was well aware that bad things happen in war, and that wars waged between the civilized and the savage were of all conflicts the cruelest. He had learned as much from his reading of Parkman and his studies in preparation for writing *The Winning of the West*. As in the West those couple of decades earlier, our soldiers in the Philippines were up against a wild and ignorant people, so there were bound to be cruelties on both sides. Of course Americans didn't condone torture as policy. If there were instances of the watercure's being resorted to, if there were mutilations and dismemberments and lynchings and burnings and castrations and burials alive, those were the acts of individual soldiers against a savage enemy—and any perpetrators would be tracked down and punished. But we must extinguish the insurrection for the benefit of right-thinking Filipinos, for the sake of those loyalists who had the true welfare of their homeland at heart. With their help Americans were setting the archipelago along the path to attaining the finest of all civilizations, one blessed with the English language and the democratic institutions of Anglo-American culture.

Indeed, the insurrection was already all but put down. Roosevelt as vice president had declared as much back in April 1901, although his announcement proved premature. Resistance dragged on. Still, as of July 4, 1902—America's Day of Independence and one year exactly after the military governor in Manila had yielded power to Big Bill Taft, his civilian counterpart from Ohio—President Roosevelt felt confident in proclaiming that the "insurrection against the authority and sovereignty of the United States is now at an end, and peace has been established in all parts of the archipelago except in the country inhabited by the Moro tribes."

On islands predominantly Roman Catholic, the Moros—Spanish for *Moors*—were Muslims, an exception of some significance.

CHAPTER Twenty-Four

Placating the South

The Muslims fought on, are fighting the central Philippine authority to this day. But notably in 1906, nearly four years after President Roosevelt had declared resistance at an end—just three months, in fact, after he had reassured Congress, in December 1905, that peace reigned at last, not only in the north but throughout most of the southern, Muslim islands as well—that is, as late as March 10, 1906, would occur a troubling incident on the volcanic island of Jolo in the southwest Philippines, down near Borneo. American army reconnaissance had discovered a group of Moros holed up in a village in an extinct mountain crater, as many as 600 of them apparently in defensive posture, some armed, 2,200 feet above sea level. General Leonard Wood, formerly Colonel Roosevelt's superior in Cuba, later governor-general of that island, now commanding in the Philippines, ordered his men to kill or capture the enemy. Whereupon our troops succeeded in ascending over difficult terrain, stealthily, using tackle to hoist artillery in place. Five hundred and forty American soldiers took position up there on the rim. Down in the crater were the 600 Moros, unsuspecting. A battle ensued that lasted a day and a half. When the firing ceased, Americans counted fifteen of their own dead, thirty-two wounded, some only slightly. Of the Moros, not one had been left alive.

Mark Twain read about it in the papers that spring of 1906. At the time he acknowledged that the Moros, "as they were hostiles, and bitter against us because we have been trying for eight years to take their liberties away from them," must have appeared to our troops as a menace. Thus the battle was joined. This civilian back home felt no affinity for Muslims ever since finding himself among them way back in 1867, in his early thirties, as an innocent abroad in the squalor of the Holy Land. Still, he deplored the army's actions on this occasion, "firing down into the crater with their

artillery and their deadly small arms of precision; the savages furiously returning the fire, probably with brickbats—though this is merely a surmise
of mine, as the weapons used by the savages are not nominated in the
cablegram. Heretofore the Moros have used knives and clubs mainly; also
ineffectual trade-muskets when they had any." Whatever, the battle was
one-sided, with General Wood present and looking on. "Kill or capture
those savages," had been his order, and the soldiers presumably took the
"or" to mean that the choice was left to their taste, and "their taste had remained what it has been for eight years, in our army out there—the taste,"
wrote Mark Twain bitterly, "of Christian butchers."

And how had America responded to such a signal victory as this over
the enemy? Surprisingly: in days just after the cablegram announcing the
Battle of the Crater triumph, newspapers fell silent about it. Editors kept
quiet; and readers—usually ready to damn or praise whatever big or little
transpires—also had nothing to say. "So far as I can find out," this observer
reports, "there was only one person among our eighty millions who allowed himself the privilege of a public remark on this great occasion—that
was the President of the United States. All day Friday he was as studiously
silent as the rest. But on Saturday he recognized that his duty required him
to say something, and he took his pen and performed that duty. If I know
President Roosevelt—and I am sure I do—this utterance cost him more pain
and shame than any other that ever issued from his pen or his mouth." For
here is what the President cabled: "Washington, March 10. Wood, Manila:
I congratulate you and the officers and men of your command upon the
brilliant feat of arms wherein you and they so well upheld the honor of the
American flag. (signed) Theodore Roosevelt."

But that was just convention, Mark Twain assures us; that was his
duty. The humorist would have done the same had he been president. One
was obliged to do no less, even though Colonel Roosevelt "knew perfectly
well that to pen six hundred helpless and weaponless savages in a hole like
rats in a trap and massacre them in detail during a stretch of a day and
a half, from a safe position on the heights above, was no brilliant feat of
arms." Nor, in this citizen's opinion, had "our uniformed assassins" upheld
"the honor of the American flag." Rather, they had done "as they have been
doing continuously for eight years in the Philippines—that is to say, they
had dishonored it."

The next day, "Sunday—which was yesterday," brought more news,
that the number of Moros slain was not 600 but actually 900, and that
women had been slaughtered in the massacre, and children. "They were
mere naked savages," Mark Twain writes in dismay at this latest informa-

Figure 24.1.   Aftermath of the Moro massacre, March 9, 1906. A woman and infant lie dead near the center of the picture.

From Oswald Garrison Villard, *Fighting Years*, opposite page 156.

tion, "and yet there is a sort of pathos about it when that word children
falls under your eye, for it always brings before us our perfectest symbol of
innocence and helplessness; and by help of its deathless eloquence color,
creed and nationality vanish away and we see only that they are children—
merely children. And if they are frightened and crying and in trouble, our
pity goes out to them by natural impulse. We see a picture. We see the small
forms. We see the terrified faces. We see the tears. We see the small hands
clinging in supplication to the mother; but we do not see those children
that we are speaking about. We see in their places the little creatures whom
we know and love."

It came down to empathy. Of course soldiers in combat had better put
empathy aside, and perhaps General Wood had as well. But the governor
of the Philippines? The President in Washington? President Roosevelt's
spiritual vision was afflicted with a blind spot already alluded to. An ardent
nationalist, he was incapable of recognizing nationalism as a legitimate
aspiration among peoples whom he considered backward. The list of such
peoples was long, and it included Filipinos. Well-educated Filipinos, well-
educated Chinese, well-educated Negroes, well-educated Mexicans and
Slavs and Colombians the President could deal with as equals, courteously,

graciously, without condescension. He was speaking the truth when he said that he had no prejudice based on a man's skin color, any more than he had on his creed or place of birth. Treat individuals on their merits. But people in the aggregate were a different matter. In the loose sense that the late nineteenth century often used the term *race*, to delineate any large group joined by language, or religion, or nationality, or culture, or level of development, Filipinos were a race of savages; and the very fact of their savage insurgency, far from being an expression of nascent nationalism—of their wanting to rule their own country in their own way—gave evidence of an inability to rule themselves at all. Boxers in China, in another backward nation, provided similar evidence, coolies slaughtering foreigners in order to drive the intruder from their land. Roosevelt's friend General Wood had his views on that. The Chinese have developed "no national spirit," Wood wrote to the President in late 1905, imperceptively. "They have neither patriotism nor morals." As for Filipinos, whom the general, as governor of the Moro Province, was observing at the time, "We have enough national weakness and humiliation from the negro," he submitted, "to avoid further trouble by the introduction of races with which we can never mingle."

At least we wouldn't have to mingle with more Chinese back home. Our West Coast was fed up with them. During the Gold Rush, immigrants from the region of the Pearl River Delta had descended on California in mass, their pigtails and slant eyes making them funny-looking miners, miners who kept to themselves, didn't drink, didn't fight, worked hard, and mined gold with superior efficiency. Other prospectors loathed them and drove them off the mountainside. More Chinese came to build the railroads. Leland Stanford, in a position to know, wrote President Andrew Johnson that without the Chinese, "it would have been impossible to complete the western portion of this great National highway." Yet the new California Constitution of 1879 proceeded to discriminate against Chinese in ways so ugly as to anticipate decrees supplementing Germany's Nuremberg Laws of fifty-six years later. Soon after, in 1882, our federal government passed the Chinese Exclusion Act, which came up for reconsideration during President Roosevelt's first term in office. Thus Congress in April 1902 renewed the act and made it perpetual, with added prohibitions to bar Chinese laborers from Hawaii and the Philippines as well. The President signed the bill without demur.

Regarding African-Americans, this same ever-active Roosevelt (so active that he kept a book in the front hall at Oyster Bay in order not to waste time waiting for his wife to come downstairs to attend social engagements) considered blacks as a group to be lazy and shiftless, one of the "most utterly underdeveloped of the races." Reasons for the underdevelopment were left unexplored for now, as he wrote of Negroes to Owen Wister, novelist and friend since Harvard days: "I entirely agree with you that as a race and in the mass they are altogether inferior to the whites." Booker Washington was an exception, one of the "occasionally good, well-educated, intelligent and honest colored men" who should be allowed to vote. Maybe one percent of the black population appeared thus qualified. (And on these matters Mark Twain entertained his own opinion, privately, that Booker Washington was "worth a hundred Roosevelts, a man whose shoe-latchets Mr. Roosevelt is not worthy to untie.")

Yet the President's view of blacks wasn't rank prejudice. He saw it as arising from science, the application of evolutionary biology to social organisms in a way that disclosed traits and achievements of races as they appeared in the early 1900s. At that evolutionary moment some particular races were weak, some obviously strong; some inferior, some superior; some backward, some in the vanguard. Evolution might change the present disposition and no doubt would. But for now, the African race in America must be patient. It "cannot expect to get everything at once. It must learn to wait and bide its time; to prove itself worthy by showing its possession of perseverance, of thrift, of self-control. The destiny of the race," Roosevelt counseled in *American Problems* (1910), "is chiefly in its own hands, and must be worked out patiently and persistently along those lines." For now, "the prime requisite of the Negro race is moral and industrial uplifting." Develop better values and learn a trade.

Meanwhile, this president meant to reward merit wherever he found it. Thus, in his first months in office and on Booker Washington's recommendation, Roosevelt appointed a black man to be justice of the peace in the District of Columbia, as well as a Democrat—Thomas Goode Jones, former Reconstruction governor of Alabama and a white moderate who had fought under Lee—to a United States district judgeship in Montgomery. Blacks were elated; southern Democrats were gratified to get any applicant from their party chosen; and Republicans were not unhappy. But a year later, in late 1902, when the President sent up the name of William D. Crum, a black physician, to be collector of the Port of Charleston—that Cradle of the Confederacy, site of historic Fort Sumter—white southerners cried out against a Negro placed so high in office, and their senators in Washington managed to delay confirmation for two full years. Meanwhile, around the same time as the Crum nomination, toward the end of 1902, little Indianola in Mississippi had fired its postmistress, Minnie Cox, appointed back in Benjamin Harrison's administration—fired her for no better reason than that she was black. Roosevelt demanded that Mrs. Cox be reinstated. The town refused, raucously; so the President shut down their post office and let them go the thirty miles to Greenville to get their mail.

Still, it had become evident that a policy favoring blacks was diminishing Roosevelt's popularity; so that after the spring of 1903, he refrained from provoking southern whites that way. This accidental, unelected President, elevated to fill what assassination had made vacant, very much wanted to win election by vote of all the people in 1904. As that date neared, he regretted any continued disaffection from south of the Mason-Dixon Line. "Not a law has been passed or threatened," he protested, "affecting the negro or affecting the southern white in his relation to the negro during the three years that the South has been indulging in hysterics over me." He pointed out that the number of black officeholders, "which was insignificant even under McKinley, has been still further reduced" during these years of the current administration. Anyway, for now the Negro's best hope lay in a white man's party that was honest and responsible. Henceforth, Roosevelt's appointments would be white, candidates of quality who would gratify southern delegations and help shape the vote count on election day. By signing into law the bill excluding Chinese, the President had pleased voters out West. In this new century of brotherhood among all regions of the country, he felt equally disinclined to antagonize voters down South, the overwhelming majority of whom were white.

It was the course that Mark Twain at the Yale bicentennial had hinted the President should have followed when inviting Booker T. Washington to dine at the White House: why give offense to that many people when the country gained no profit by your doing so? To be sure, Clemens had his own reasons for placating the South. Not that he was in sympathy with postbellum southern culture. He wasn't. He had taken his trip out to Missouri back in 1882 and gone down and up the Mississippi River and been appalled by the backwardness of what he saw: southern ignorance, southern violence, southern bigotry, all that rancid southern faux-romanticism and its glorifying of feudal ways. The white South that he encountered had not pleased him; what pleasure he found down there was most often in the company of lively, good-humored black people. Back home, some of the traveler's distaste seeped into pages of *Life on the Mississippi* (1883). A vicious cockfight in New Orleans, for instance—both pitiful fowls bloody, exhausted, eyes pecked out but fighting blindly on to the crowd's loud delight—he hadn't been able to stay to watch clear through.

Since 1883, the author's aversions had only grown stronger. Thus, in 1901, not long returned from his European exile, he wrote a scalding indictment entitled "The United States of Lyncherdom." In the 1890s, during the Clemenses' absence abroad, lynching had become a national scandal, lynchings North and South, of white and black both. But after the turn of the century it became increasingly a southern phenomenon, aimed at black people. Alabama, Georgia, Louisiana, and Mississippi were the worst offenders. The occasion for resorting to such "democratic" measures—the "people" taking justice into their own hands—was usually given forth as rape, a black man's rape of a white woman (that fixation of the time), notwithstanding research in 1942 disclosing that no more than 17 percent of lynchings between 1889 and 1941 involved even so much as an accusation of rape, let alone proof. Roosevelt, a man of the strictest uprightness, deplored lynching, not out of any sympathy for the lynch victim, who (he said) had forfeited all claims to sympathy by the nature of his deed, but from "a very lively sense of the train of dreadful consequences which follows the course taken by the mob in exacting an inhuman vengeance for his inhuman crime." And in 1901, the lynchers' vengeance had come at last to Missouri, near Pierce City, in the southwestern corner of the state. A young white woman was murdered on a Sunday after church. Three Negroes, "two of them very aged ones," were lynched for it, and five Negro homes burned down, and thirty-five black families driven into the woods.

In "The United States of Lyncherdom" Mark Twain, Missouri native, seeks to understand why lynching has become the means of regulating such "cases of 'the usual crime' in several parts of the country." He insists that whatever may be the provocation to lynch, provocation has nothing to do with the matter. The issue is the assassin's taking the law into his own hands. But why so often? Some of it is the tendency of dreadful deeds to awaken imitation, some of it is people's fear of differing from their neighbors. A horde awash in self-righteousness charges forth in full cry, and people join it, unwilling to be "unpleasantly conspicuous, pointed at, shunned, as being on the unpopular side." Yet contrary to the general impression, the lynch mob doesn't enjoy what it is doing. Farmers hitch up and come miles with their wives and children "only because they are afraid to stay at home, lest it be noticed and offensively commented upon."

Such moral cowardice is no less reprehensible because we all, when under enough pressure, share in it. And Mark Twain draws out the full despicableness by citing details of a recent lynching in Texas, where a black man was taken to a tree and swung in the air, and a hot fire was made under him. *"Then it was suggested that the man ought not to die too quickly and he was let down to the ground while a party went to Dexter, about two miles distant, to procure coal oil."*

They got the coal oil and lit it on him and let it burn. Missionaries should come back from China and help Americans in their need. Forget about China; there was so much wrong with us here. Yet when it came to that, humanity at large—what an elderly Mark Twain took to thinking of as the damned human race—appeared afflicted with greed and cruelty and indifference to suffering. Europe's rapacious incursions into the Far East. The trumped-up war against the Boers. Our land-grab in the Philippines. This of the South and lynching.

"The United States of Lyncherdom" wasn't published in its author's lifetime. A great deal in these late years that Mark Twain wrote out of seething indignation was left unpublished. He didn't publish his comments on the massacre of Moros in their crater on Jolo Island. He didn't publish his views on Theodore Roosevelt, leaving them for posterity to read, as he thought, a hundred years after his death. For with the South as with the nation at large, Mark Twain alive felt he had to protect his genial image. He couldn't afford to offend his readership because when he died, the continued financial welfare of his wife and children would depend on keeping that readership well disposed.

Yet even so, so strong were his feelings that he felt obliged to publish some of what he set down. In the *New York Herald* on December 30, 1900, appeared Mark Twain's caustic Salutation from the Nineteenth Century to the Twentieth, offering its introduction by the one to the other of "the stately matron called CHRISTENDOM—returning bedraggled, besmirched and dishonored from pirate-raids" overseas. Early in 1901, "To the Person Sitting in Darkness" appeared in the *North American Review* and made a great stir, anti-imperialists warmly welcoming the polemic against the Blessings-of-Civilization Trust while the far more numerous imperialists in America coolly dismissed such natterings of an aging humorist who was not to be taken seriously. To Annie Fields, Mrs. Clemens admitted that in the wake of her husband's article a couple of letters had arrived from dear friends "hotly reproaching" the author. "Other friends are silent, so we feel their disapproval." Nevertheless, about current public exploitations and outrages—and there were many others: in the Congo, where hands of natives who gathered insufficient rubber were chopped off to appease the greed of the King of the Belgians; in Russia, where the Czar's despotism went on grinding down a long-oppressed people; right here at home, where the municipal government of New York City was shamelessly, fetidly corrupt—this observer felt too deeply to remain silent and unheard.

So he published some of his thoughts, wrote other indignant pages to file away, and made wry reference to current affairs in numerous after-dinner speeches. His wife for the most part shared his views; but at some point around this time, perhaps in early 1902, Olivia Clemens left an undated, anguished note on her husband's desk. "Youth darling," she wrote—*Youth* being her pet name for Samuel during their years together—"have you forgotten your promise to me? You said that I was constantly in your mind and that you knew what I would like & you *would not* publish what I would disapprove." Did he think she would approve of the captious letter he had just composed taking a popular female novelist to task? When he wrote as he did in that letter, "people forget the cause for it & remember only the hateful manner in which it was said." Why, she asked, didn't he let his better side work? "I am absolutely wretched today on account of your state of mind—your state of intellect." He went too far, much too far. "Where is the mind that wrote the Prince & P. Jeanne d'Arc. The Yankee &c &c &c. Bring it back! You can if you will—if you wish to. Think of the side I know, the sweet dear, tender side—that I love so. Why not show this more to the world? Does it help the world to always rail at it? There is great & noble work being done, why not sometimes recognize that? Why always dwell on the evil until those who live beside you are crushed to the earth & you seem almost like a monomaniac. Oh! I love you so & wish you would listen & take heed. Yours

"LIVY"

PART Four

OIL

CHAPTER **Twenty-Five**

The *Kanawha*

In the new, twentieth century, darker shadows fell over Mark Twain's writing, shadows that his wife regretted even when wit and irony brightened the pages. Specifically, Livy deplored his abandoning such kinds of work as she mentions in the note left on her husband's desk in 1902. "Where is the mind that wrote the Prince & P. Jeanne d'Arc. The Yankee &c &c &c. Bring it back!" Yet for all her entreating, her husband's view of these present times kept falling on evils. The lynchings. America's betrayal of its ideals in order to emulate European powers by grabbing at colonies. The hypocrisy of our new international swagger, as we sought out markets to plunder while veiling those crass aims behind evangelizing pieties and claims of bestowing the blessings of civilization. Our current, showy jingoism. The branding of native Filipinos as rebels because they resisted a sovereignty to which they hadn't sworn allegiance. To a wanderer not long returned from nearly ten years abroad, such national offenses appeared unignorable.

Humor, a tearful clown, rises out of dark places in any case. Of those earlier works that Mrs. Clemens cites, *The Prince and the Pauper* and *Personal Recollections of Joan of Arc* (neither one humorous) are today considered among the author's weaker efforts; and the third book that she speaks of, *A Connecticut Yankee in King Arthur's Court*, ends in holocaust. For the rest, *Huckleberry Finn* is replete with shadows, some of them of the darkest hue; and *Tom Sawyer*, for all its mischievous whitewashing of fences and showing off for the new little girl in the village, contains much of the bleak and the sinister: midnight grave-robbing; murder; a half-breed's vengeful vow to mutilate the face of an innocent woman; boys presumed drowned and grieved for; two children lost in a cave's deep bowels; that same half-breed found dead, bat bones around him, starved at the cave's sealed mouth.

Many of Mark Twain's works, and almost from the beginning, evince a strong sense of the cruel, the unjust, and the horrifying. He said himself that "a boy's life is not all comedy; much of the tragic enters into it"—and into the life of Youth grown old as well. For Clemens was getting older, and watching others grow older and die—others he loved—and there was no cheer in that. Nor was his health unaffected by age, despite his protests to the contrary. "Jean is getting along fairly well," he had reported from England in early 1900; "her mother's heart & gout bad; Clara in pretty good shape; I healthy as granite." But the gout had visited him too, and would return and put him in bed for weeks. And bronchitis afflicted this longtime, immoderate smoker; and Livy in all that secondhand smoke had to deal with bronchitis herself, and asthma. In addition, Clemens suffered attacks of rheumatism, while a rich diet—dinners and multicourse banquets galore—brought on boils that bedeviled his ease.

Somewhere Dr. Johnson says that the difference between an optimist and a pessimist is a sound digestion. The wonder is that there were any affluent optimists back then, given what surviving menus tell us the well-off ate. Moreover, the singing daughter, Clara, had her own throat problems, and nerves that made her withdraw to seek rest; while Jean was struggling through these late years with what was then the shameful, hushed-up disease of epilepsy, a ceaseless worry for parents bent on hiding the girl's frightening, unpredictable seizures from public view. And all the while, Susy's death—that favorite and most promising daughter's death, now five or six years behind them—remained a haunting grief, sometimes scarcely bearable.

Still, despite all the reasons, public and private, that Samuel Clemens might have adduced to explain his change of mood in the direction of the somber, these same years saw him just as often capable of the old joy and high spirits and fun. Much in his present life brought satisfaction. After bankruptcy, he was again, by 1901, well-to-do. He was famous, perhaps the single most famous person on the planet as the century opened. He was loved and sought after, more now than ever. Would he speak at the New York Press Club, at the City Club dinner, with Booker Washington in Carnegie Hall to commemorate the twenty-fifth anniversary of Tuskegee Institute? He would and did; and accordingly he was admired, not only for his writings but for his stimulating, obliging presence, as well as for the character and integrity shown in his paying off debts of staggering proportions not strictly his own. All those merits elevated this singular American to the status of international celebrity, the first on the scale that our later media-enabling age of megawattage entertainers and politicians has made so familiar. When Mark Twain walked along Fifth Avenue (which he loved

Figure 25.1.   Booker T. Washington speaks at Carnegie Hall, January 22, 1906. Mark Twain is seated directly behind him.

Courtesy of the Mark Twain Project, The Bancroft Library, University of California, Berkeley.

to do), heads swiveled; photographs of New York street scenes from back then capture the gazes of evanescent pedestrians fixed for a lasting moment upon that famous, instantly recognizable face and figure.

One resident of Manhattan, William Dean Howells, wrote their mutual friend Aldrich of walking yesterday, December 7, 1902, with Clemens to his train at sunset. "He has no time table, but all the gatemen and train starters are proud to know him, and lay hold of him, and put him aboard *something* that leaves for Riverdale. He always has to go to the W.C., me dancing in the corridor, and holding his train for him. But they would not let it go without him, if it was the Chicago limited! What a fame and a force he is"—and, Howells adds, how astonishing was the unique, hearty survival of that fame.

Such friends as Howells and Thomas Bailey Aldrich brought joy into Clemens's life, and he had dozens, scores, seemingly hundreds of friends. "Goodness, who is there I haven't known?" Yet of them all, William Dean Howells was someone special, one of the three closest to him. Now Howells was living in Manhattan only twenty-five minutes away by train from Riverdale, so he would come visit from time to time. A visit on the night of February 11, 1903, provoked a letter next morning up to Riverdale from West Fifty-Ninth Street. "My dear Clemens," Howells wrote, "I know you are harassed by a great many things, and I hate to add to your worries, but I must really complain to you of the behavior of your man Sam. I called last night at your place with our old friend Stoddard, and found that to reach the house, I had to climb a plowed field, at the top of which Sam was planting potatoes." But wait: no plowed field marred the elegant lawns of Riverdale, no potatoes were being planted, and the Clemenses had no servant named Sam. Nevertheless, Sam last night had "called very rudely to us," Howells goes on, "and asked us what we wanted. I said we wanted to see you, and he said, 'Well, you can't do it,' and no persuasion that I could use had the least effect with him." Nobody could see Mr. Clemens, the gardener decreed, and though Howells pressed his card on the man, "he sneered and said he would not give you the card." Expecting all the while to be called back, Howells and Stoddard left reluctantly; "we made our way home the best we could. This happened, as nearly as I can make out, at about three o'clock in the morning," the letter-writer takes pains to specify. "I have only too much reason to believe that Sam really withheld my card, and I wish you would ask him for it, and make him account in some way for our extraordinary treatment. I cannot remember that Stoddard said anything, but I felt he was as much annoyed as myself. Yours ever, W. D. Howells."

What fun this old friend must have had putting that together and sending it off. He had his answer in short order. Riverdale, February 13, 1903. "Dear Howells—I am infinitely sorry. I was lying awake at the time, & felt sure I heard voices; so sure, that I put on a dressing-gown & went down to inquire into the matter, but you were already gone. I encountered Sam coming up as I turned the lower corner of the house, & he said it was a stranger, who insisted on seeing me—'a stumpy little gray man with furtive ways & an evil face.'"

How Howells would have grinned at that. So what was the stranger's name? "He didn't say. He offered his card, but I didn't take it."

Clemens told the fellow he should have. Why hadn't he?

"I didn't like his manners" was the excuse; for the visitor had called Sam "a quadrilateral astronomical incandescent son of a bitch."

"Oh," said Clemens, enlightened, "that was Howells. Is *that* what annoyed you! It was meant as a compliment."

"I don't think so," the gardener countered; "it only just sounds so. I am not finding any fault with the main phrase, which is hallowed to me by memories of childhood's happy days, now vanished never to return, on account of its being my sainted mother's diminutive for me, but I did not like those adverbs. I have an aversion for adverbs. I will not take adverbs from a stranger."

Clemens found that unacceptable. "'Very well,' I said, coldly, 'such being your theology, you can get your money after breakfast, & seek another place. I know you are honest, I know you are competent, & I am sorry to part with you; you are the best gardener I have ever had, but in matters of grammar I think you are morbid, & this makes you over-sensitive & altogether too God dam particular.'"

And he concludes his part of the fun with his friend: "I am sorry & ashamed, Howells, & so is Clara, who is helping write this letter, with expressions she got of her mother, but the like will not happen again on this place, I can assure you. Ys Ever Mark."

The humorist retained high spirits enough to hold up his end in such an exchange as this, about Howells's recent dream at three in the morning. Howells was, after all, Clemens's most cherished literary friend, of more than thirty-three years' standing. Joe Twichell, minister of the Asylum Hill Congregational Church in Hartford, remained another close friend, of thirty-four years, who patiently endured Clemens's heterodox thrusts about God's outrages as revealed in the daily newspapers. And by now a third was numbered among this select group of intimates, an oil magnate whom the author had met no longer than a decade ago, in 1893. His name was Henry Huttleston Rogers.

Three close friendships (for "It is friends that make life," Clemens had said): one literary, one with spiritual concerns, the third in business. Like so many others, H. H. Rogers had been a fan of Mark Twain's books before meeting their author, briefly earlier, but effectively in the fall of 1893, when a mutual acquaintance brought the two together in New York City. Rogers was vice president of the Standard Oil Company as well as president and director of the Amalgamated Copper Company; trustee of the Mutual Life Insurance Company; director of the Atchison, Topeka, and Santa Fe Railroad Company; director of the Staten Island Ferry Company; director of the Atlas Tack Company; director of the Guaranty Trust Company; etc., etc.—in fact, one of the wealthiest men in America at the time, very widely known back then and by some admired, by many feared, by just about everybody envied.

Rich as he was—Rogers's fortune was reputed to amount to $100 million, maybe $2.5 billion in our currency—he had not started out that way. *The Adventures of Tom Sawyer* appealed to the tycoon partly because the novel reminded him of his own modest, antebellum childhood in the agrarian 1840s, growing up in Fairhaven, Massachusetts. Fairhaven is on Buzzards Bay opposite New Bedford, both then thriving ports at the height of the whaling industry. Rogers had been born at the very beginning of that decade, on January 9, 1840. (Toward the end of the same year Herman Melville, age twenty-one, crossed to Fairhaven from New Bedford to look over the *Acushnet*, a whaling vessel that the young man shipped out on the following month at the start of its maiden voyage to the Pacific, the genesis of *Moby-Dick*.)

An accountant's son, young Rogers attended schools in Fairhaven and, after high school, did menial jobs in town for five years, delivering groceries and handling baggage for the local railroad. Then, in 1861, he left Fairhaven for the newly discovered oil fields of western Pennsylvania. There, in a frontier world, he and a partner prospered, both of them in at the rough-and-tumble start of an industry that would put whaling back home out of business. Till then, whale oil had furnished the best source of light available—brighter, cleaner-burning lamps—until oil was pumped from under the fields of Pennsylvania, refined into kerosene, and put to use as equally good and cheaper illumination. Rogers & Ellis, oil refiners, gave way in 1867 to a larger refinery on Long Island that Rogers managed, which in turn merged with the Standard Oil Company in 1874. Unimaginable profits followed.

Twenty-five years later, nearing the century's end, in midsummer 1899, Samuel Clemens in London got word that his friend Rogers, the Standard Oil magnate, was thinking of acquiring a yacht. The two men had become close earlier in the decade of the 1890s, during the humorist's numerous trips from Europe back to America to attend to his faltering publishing company and check on progress of the Paige typesetter, in which he was heavily invested. Rogers's knowledge of business had been enormously helpful to the exile, indispensably helpful in guiding him through financial mazes that creditors were erecting. However, in London by 1899, skies were clear, with smooth sailing ahead and bankruptcy's storms well astern. Now it was that Clemens learned from Rogers's daughter, visiting England, that her father proposed to get himself a yacht, to travel between New York and Fairhaven, where the oil baron had built an eighty-five-room bayside mansion. "Don't discard that idea," Mark Twain wrote his friend on July 3, 1899, "and put in a berth for me."

For he loved the sea, this son of Missouri. Looking back on his round-the-world lecture tour three and four years earlier, Clemens professed to have detested the grind of it all, every minute of the entire experience, except for India and the numerous days spent at sea. In the event, Rogers did get his yacht, in April 1901, purchased a vessel two years old, the *Kanawha* (stressed on the second syllable)—that being the name, incidentally, of the river and valley in West Virginia to which Booker Washington's black step-father had followed the Union army during the Civil War, summoning his freed family to join him at the settlement of Malden, where young Booker, age nine, was put to work in the dismal salt-packing houses.

Kanawha would have connoted one thing to Booker T. Washington, quite another to Henry Huttleston Rogers. Rogers's new yacht proved to be a beauty, fastest on the East Coast, at twenty-two knots faster even than J. P. Morgan's *Corsair*. And Mark Twain, back in America, was welcomed aboard. It was of steel construction, a spacious 227 feet overall with a lovely sheer, a fine, sharp clipper bow, and two powerful steam engines below. In the forward deck house was a plush dining saloon, stewards standing by to serve one's every need. By July of that same year Clemens had suggested guests for a forthcoming summer cruise. Maybe ex-President Cleveland, or retired Speaker Tom Reed? Both of them, if they're friendly. Do the two get along? If so, "they would make a grand team," he assured Rogers. "Shall I write and invite them?" No use having Cleveland without Reed, though; "*we* couldn't bait him and make him roar; we couldn't draw him out and make him do music, but Reid [*sic*] could." And should Judge Howland be invited as well?

As it happened, the *Kanawha* got under way with a somewhat different but equally compatible complement on August 3 and was gone two weeks, stopping at Fairhaven, then proceeding along the coast of Maine (picking up Czar Reed at Portland) past New Brunswick to Nova Scotia, putting in at various ports for excursions ashore on the way out and back. At sea the boys played poker, drank Scotch, ate well, fired their gibes at each other, and had a glorious time. It was like bachelor days in the high air of Virginia City, but with no work to do. And when the cruise ended, the "chief steward delivered me in good order and well conditioned on board the train," Clemens wrote to "Admiral" Rogers, his host, "and thus put the finishing and perfecting touch upon the most contenting and comfortable and satisfactory pleasure-excursion I have ever made."

There would be more of them. There was a cruise the following spring, in March 1902, out of Miami, sailing over the Caribbean. From Riverdale in early March, now possessed of his doctorate of letters from Yale University, Clemens telegraphed Rogers in Fairhaven: "Can't get away this week I have company here from tonight till middle of next week will Kanawha be sailing after that and can I go as Sundayschool Supt at half rate Answer and prepay. Dr. Clemens." He did go and enjoyed another grand vacation afloat, for six weeks this time, with veterans of the earlier cruise along and new faces besides, stopping at Nassau, Santiago (Colonel Roosevelt's San Juan Heights in view), Kingston, and Havana (the ruins of the *Maine* still in the harbor), before returning to New York via Charleston and Norfolk. Once back at Riverdale, Clemens was off again in late spring to visit Hannibal a last time and to receive that other honorary degree, from the University of Missouri. To Rogers from Riverdale, May 26, 1902: "I leave to-morrow night for the West, to return by June 12th. Take care of the business the best you can, and telegraph me if you get stuck."

By now H. H. Rogers would have known Mark Twain's erratic business traits full well, all the more striking in contrast to the shrewd, wily, invariably successful dealings around the conference table of this titan of Standard Oil. Mr. Rogers managed affairs just fine left alone. But when Clemens did return from his emotional journey to childhood haunts out West, it was to discover at Riverdale, to his dismay, that Mrs. Clemens's health had sadly deteriorated, even in a couple of weeks. A change of scene might help, a more restful setting for the summer months. They would go to Maine, to Kittery. Banners flying, the *Kanawha* steamed up the Hudson to Riverdale that June, and the Clemens family went aboard—all but Clara, off in Paris with her music. The humorist and his wife, with daughter Jean, traveled thus in private luxury to The Pines, a cottage they had rented overlooking York Harbor. William Dean Howells was at his own summer retreat only a forty-minute trolley ride away, and the two friends looked forward to frequent visits together.

But in August—on August 12, 1902, at seven in the morning—Livy was stricken with a violent, terrifying fit. Physicians were hastily called while nurses struggled to give relief. Everyone felt sure the patient was dying. She feared so too: heart palpitations, muscle pains, horrible gaspings for breath. The doctors resorted to "heroic measures," but even so, it wasn't until noon of that dreadful day that the crisis eased. Had it been a prolonged panic attack? Hypertension? Congestive heart failure? The diagnosis was, vaguely, "nervous prostration." Absolute rest would be required. Mrs. Clemens must be spared all excitement. Distressing news was to be kept from her, and visits from her excitable husband held to a minimum. Even so, it was not until October, two months later, that the patient (about to turn fifty-seven) recovered enough to be moved back to Riverdale.

This time she traveled not on Rogers's yacht, which awaited the family's orders, but by the more stable railroad, a special, invalid train hired to bear the Clemenses directly home to familiar surroundings. As he had at York Harbor, the husband stayed out of the sick room in Riverdale for the sake of his wife's health, though he wrote Livy loving notes twice a day. At year's end, on December 30, 1902, he recorded: "saw Livy 5 minutes by the watch—the first time in more than 3 months."

Howells came calling at Riverdale on a sunny afternoon in the spring. He and Clemens sat out on the grass in front of the mansion, far enough away that their talk wouldn't disturb the patient, although they kept an eye on the balcony before Livy's window upstairs, "where by-and-by that lovely presence made itself visible, as if it had stooped there from a cloud. A hand frailly waved a handkerchief," Howells remembered; "Clemens ran over the lawn toward it, calling tenderly: 'What? What?' as if it might be an asking for him instead of the greeting it really was for me. It was the last time I saw her," this loyal friend reports, "if indeed I can be said to have seen her then, and long afterward when I said how beautiful we all thought her, how good, how wise, how wonderfully perfect in every relation of life, he"—Clemens—"cried out in a breaking voice: 'Oh, why didn't you ever tell her? She thought you didn't like her.' What a pang it was then not to have told her, but how could we have told her?" How could a gentleman have spoken thus intimately to another man's wife? Still, Howells finishes with the thought that his friend's irrationality in wishing for such a sentiment to be uttered "endeared him to me more than all his wisdom."

CHAPTER Twenty-Six

Corporate America

When civil war broke out in April 1861, not everybody up North rallied round the flag to save the Union. Joseph Twichell, twenty-two years old, did step forth to do his part. Having graduated from Yale two years earlier, young Twichell was studying at Union Theological Seminary as rebels fired on Fort Sumter in Charleston harbor. Promptly he enlisted and served with honor in the field through most of the hostilities—at Fredericksburg, at Gettysburg, in the Wilderness—chaplain of the Seventy-First New York State Volunteers. Some others, though, were less committed. The father of Teedie Roosevelt for one—the child only two that April, when his father was an able-bodied twenty-nine—bought his way out of serving, paying for substitutes in order not to fight against his Georgia wife's Confederate brothers. It was an evasion that Roosevelt Sr. soon regretted and that his adoring son later strived hard to make up for. William Dean Howells of Ohio, age twenty-four when Sumter fell, spent the war years abroad as American consul in Venice, rewarded for having the year before written a campaign biography of the winning presidential candidate, Abraham Lincoln. On the southern side of the conflict, Samuel Clemens, twenty-five years old and a riverboat pilot when fighting erupted, briefly joined Hannibal pals in a makeshift Confederate militia unit before venturing west and waiting out the war with other shirkers, from South and North, in Nevada and California. And—up North once more—young Henry Huttleston Rogers of Fairhaven, Massachusetts, finessed the war by traveling that fall, at age twenty-one, to the oil fields of Pennsylvania, where he launched a career while the Union tore itself asunder.

The oil business was scarcely two years old at the beginning of the Civil War—a war that would change just about everything in America. But even earlier, the move from an agrarian union of sovereign states to an industrialized, centralized nation had got under way. Railroads east of the Mississippi had already begun altering nearly everybody's life in the North; and on a Sunday afternoon in August 1859, a year and a half before the first rebel cannons roared, Edwin L. Drake succeeded in drilling down sixty-nine and a half feet in the Oil Creek region of northwestern Pennsylvania and bringing up dirty green grease that was destined to spread across the nation and over the globe.

Railroads and oil led the way to a different world. Oil had been observed since ancient days, mostly as a nuisance, seeping from rocks and polluting farmers' fields in floodtime. Rock oil it was called, petroleum. Unlike the increasingly scarce illuminant sperm oil, which whaling ships set forth from ports such as Fairhaven to hunt for, petroleum was apparently useless except to grease axles, soften leather, and furnish putative medicinal remedies. Only in the 1850s were means devised to refine crude oil into kerosene and thus make it valuable, and only later in that decade did Edwin L. Drake figure out how to drill deep underground for the crude, inside a pipe that kept the drill hole from collapsing as it passed through soil, clay, and water. Drake drilled to bedrock and farther until at last, under a fold in the rock, his team struck oil. And—if not to him (who would die all but destitute)—to many, great fortunes accrued, as the oil was refined into various uses: into kerosene for illumination, into candles, into paraffin wax, and (following upon inventions in the latter half of the nineteenth century by the Europeans Gottlieb Daimler, Rudolf Diesel, and Karl Benz) into lubricant for the internal combustion engine, rapidly developing in the wake of this sudden vast supply from underground. In time, crude oil would be refined into gasoline as well, and asphalt, and plastics. But that was for later. For now, in the 1860s, in the oil fields around Titusville, Pennsylvania, black gold was gushing from under the ground of a new frontier—chaotic like the gold-rush settlements inland from Sacramento and the raucous silver towns near Virginia City—this new site in the Oil Creek Valley that held forth a promise of enormous wealth when petroleum was refined into kerosene to light lamps for just about every shelter on earth.

Henry Huttleston Rogers got in at the start of it, he and his Fairhaven friend and partner Charles H. Ellis setting up their oil refinery in Rouseville toward the end of 1861. Rouseville, Pennsylvania, survives these days with a population of 500 people—the site where, there and at nearby Titusville through the war years of the 1860s, Rogers and Ellis learned the oil business amid squalor, sleaze, mud, and the exhilaration of upstart, ramshackle frontier settlements. On hearing news of an oil strike two years earlier, multitudes had rushed to the region; so that makeshift derricks, shacks, saloons, and brothels had sprung up, with plenty of hardy young men on hand ready to do whatever it took to get money. Phony oil stocks were peddled, crooked deals offered, and promises sworn to and broken. H. H. Rogers attended at this roughhewn business school in the sixties, and from then on he remembered what he had learned in his six years in Pennsylvania. Hold your cards close to your vest. Give nothing away. Don't let your feelings enter into it. Yield no quarter when the stakes are high. And play to win.

When war began in the spring of 1861, John Rockefeller, twenty-one years old, was a wholesale produce commission merchant living in Cleveland, Ohio. Rockefeller threw in his lot with those who avoided the fight. Instead of enlisting, this sober, pious Baptist paid for substitutes and went on putting aside money, until he had enough by 1863 to enter the oil-refining business. Within two years Rockefeller and a partner owned the largest refinery in Cleveland. Another year passed, and they had established a second refinery in town and opened an office in New York City—brother William in charge—to handle eastern sales and export kerosene overseas. Thereafter the firm of Rockefeller & Andrews grew rapidly, dealing in enough volume by the late sixties to arrange special low rates for shipments with the railroads. In 1870 the thriving business was reorganized as the Standard Oil Company.

Rockefeller hated competition. Competition was wasteful; it led to unpredictable pricing and overproduction. Yet the oil business was fiercely competitive: all those independent refineries competing with one another across the Northeast. What Rockefeller intended was to combine with them, pull each one into his own joint stock company. He extended the invitation. "We will take your burdens, we will utilize your ability, we will give you representation; we will all unite together and build a substantial structure on the basis of cooperation." Those who did join him prospered on a grand scale. The refineries that didn't Rockefeller crushed and never felt a qualm about it. They had had their chance and made their choice. So he crushed them by every means available. His agents bullied the reluctant ones, bribed them, lied to and about them, set spies among them, sabotaged them. Alongside lingering holdouts Standard Oil built competing refineries, dropped its prices, and took its losses until the competition crumbled. And it further undercut adversaries by negotiating—with the promise of a volume of business that nobody else could match—rebates from the railroads that allowed for secret freight charges up to fifty percent lower than what those rivals were paying.

In the single year 1872, twenty-one of the twenty-six refineries in Cleveland joined Rockefeller's Standard Oil. There was nothing illegal about any of this. Your business was your property, just as sure as your house and your furniture and your wagon were, to do with as you liked. If you chose to keep secret the terms of rebates and drawbacks that the railroads granted you exclusively, that was simply so that shippers not thus advantaged would remain in the dark, uncomplaining. No laws prohibited rebates. The Erie, or the Pennsylvania, or the New York Central would ostensibly be charging all shippers the same, while under the table returning up to half of the charges levied on its most valued customer, returning that money as rebates to Standard Oil.

H. H. Rogers had moved from Pennsylvania to Brooklyn in 1867 to take a job with a larger oil refinery. There he continued organizing independent refiners to hold out against the Standard, fighting the way contestants over oil always fought, giving no quarter. Yet Rockefeller's company had grown too big, with too many resources, too many ways to fight back. Now what Standard Oil was bent on was controlling every phase of the operation, from the wells to the pipelines to the refineries to the brokering and selling and shipping of the product. Rogers came to understand the futility of resisting. In 1874 his Long Island refinery joined the larger company, and the able Rogers was named a director. It proved to be a profitable capitulation. Within six years Standard Oil controlled 90 percent of the nation's oil business, and Henry Huttleston Rogers sat high in the company's councils. He was forty years old.

It was but one of several such spectacular rises, from modest beginnings to the heights of worldly success, that the Standard Oil Company enabled. John D. Rockefeller himself was born in modest circumstances, his father a trader in patent medicines, horses, and herbal remedies who was often away from home wandering from town to town. The son went to work at eighteen as a clerk and bookkeeper. John Archbold, another figure at the summit of Standard Oil, lost his own father before he reached his teens, started working when he was eleven in a country store in Salem, Ohio, got wind of an oil strike over the border in Pennsylvania, made his way to Titusville, and was partner in an oil refinery by nineteen. Like Rogers, Archbold sought to bring independent refineries together to fight Standard Oil, and fought hard, but had to give it up and join the larger company, ending as president of the Standard after its founder retired.

But opportunities abounded beyond the oil industry. Booming post-war America appeared suddenly full of opportunities. Even while the Civil War was in progress, Congress had passed two acts that moved far toward opening up opportunities in the bustling peacetime years ahead. One was the Homestead Act, which President Lincoln signed into law on May 20, 1862. Land was abundant in the West, and you could have your share of it. Anybody could. By the terms of the act, all you had to do was apply for 160 acres of federal land to settle on, move out there and improve the land by putting up a shelter and working your claim, then file for a deed of title; it was yours. The second legislative act set up a way to get you there: the Pacific Railroad Act, which President Lincoln signed a couple of months later, in July 1862. What grew out of that second act was the engineering feat of the transcontinental railroad, the Union Pacific proceeding from Council Bluffs and Omaha westward—land graded, ties laid down, rails joined athwart them mile after mile—while, from Alameda opposite San Francisco, the Central Pacific pushed eastward into tunnels, through cuts, and on fills over the high Sierras toward where the two lines would meet, in northern Utah Territory, in the spring of 1869.

Building that great Overland Route established a pattern that the new Corporate America followed in shaping the future. Never before had capital been amassed and managed on such a scale as this involved in laying rails across a continent. And often, as with oil, the fortunes made in railroad building fell to men from modest backgrounds. Collis Huntington was a Connecticut farmer's son. James J. Hill, born on a farm in Ontario, worked in his teens in dry goods and grocery stores. E. H. Harriman grew up in an Episcopal rectory on Long Island and at the start of the Civil War went to work as a messenger and office boy on Wall Street. They, along with others, acquired prodigious wealth from the railroads. Sometimes, in fact, during the years after the war ended, wealth seemed to be what America was all about. Through those same postbellum decades Horatio Alger Jr.'s popular dime novels for boys told the rags-to-riches story over and over again: *Struggling Upward, Rough and Ready, Sink or Swim, Strong and Steady, Slow and Sure, Bound to Rise: or Up the Ladder, Do and Dare.* Such novels made clear that a lad held his fate in his own hands. The wealth of the country was out there for any enterprising youngster with the luck and pluck to earn his share of it.

Examples of the success that attended such pluck were easy to come by. Take Edison. Thomas Edison was born in February 1847 the son of a shingle-maker in Milan, Ohio. The boy had only a limited education. By twelve he was boarding local railroad cars to sell passengers newspapers and candy. At the depot he got interested in the telegraph and mastered the skill of taking down high-speed messages. During the Civil War he saw some service as a telegrapher for the Union Army, continuing in that line of work after the war while taking mechanisms apart for fun, reading technical manuals, and at twenty-one applying for the first of what would grow into 1,093 patents in his name over a long, productive lifetime. By the fall of 1882, in his mid-thirties, Thomas Edison was in J. P. Morgan's office throwing a switch that activated power in a station near Wall Street to bring his recently invented electric light to New York City's newspaper district. Seven years later Edison's various profitable enterprises merged, and in 1892 that aggregation of ingenuity, imagination, and wealth adopted the corporate name General Electric.

Or consider Westinghouse. A half-year older than Edison, George Westinghouse was the son of a farmer with a knack for tinkering. In his father's farm-implements shop in Schenectady, the boy indulged his own mechanical aptitude and managed when he was twenty-two to perfect the railroad air brake. The brake allowed trains to run safely at much higher speeds, a modification at once widely and gratefully adopted. That same year the young man formed the Westinghouse Air Brake Company, progenitor of a corporation that thrives to this day. The Westinghouse Company got into providing electricity using Tesla's alternating current, which Thomas Edison opposed on the grounds that the high-tension wires it required were a public hazard. Edison's own direct current laid claims to being safer. Yet at the World's Columbian Exposition of 1893, Westinghouse's alternating current powered the unprecedented display of 92,000 incandescent lamps all simultaneously and safely alight, along with an electric sidewalk in motion and the first modern electric kitchen. Edison's direct current would have needed massive and impractically expensive power lines to do all that. Accordingly, it was the Westinghouse Company that built a hydroelectric power plant at Niagara Falls; and it is alternating current that powers America now.

President McKinley would call such fairs as the World's Columbian Exposition in Chicago, and the earlier Centennial Exposition in Philadelphia in 1876, and the forthcoming Pan-American Exposition adjacent to Niagara Falls in 1901 "timekeepers of progress." For it was America's progress that those popular, informative spectacles appeared to be celebrating. So much at the fairs filled visitors with awe and wonder. So much was new. At the Centennial Exposition 100 years after America's birth, nothing on the scale of the gigantic Corliss Steam Engine in Machinery Hall, which powered most of the other machines on the grounds, had ever been seen before. It loomed as a symbol of America's genius, of its rising industrial might. And the telephone! Alexander Graham Bell demonstrated his telephone publicly for the first time at the fair, and Heinz Ketchup was first offered at the Centennial Exposition, and Hires Root Beer. So much new; and what a fine time it was to be alive! At the World's Columbian Exposition, nearer century's end, were introduced neon, and Cracker Jacks, and the hoochee-koochee, and Quaker Oats and Shredded Wheat and the hamburger and Juicy Fruit gum and picture postcards, along with even grander wonders. Henry Adams visited the Chicago Exposition and was all but overcome with the changes on view. The fair left that fascinated visitor feeling adrift before the huge dynamos in the Electricity Building. Amid such novel surroundings Adams saw himself suddenly left behind, one of many "who knew nothing whatever—who had never run a steam-engine, the simplest of forces—who had never put their hands on a lever—had never touched an electric battery—never talked through a telephone, and had not the shadow of a notion what amount of force was meant by a *watt* or an *ampere* or an *erg*." Yet this world of batteries and telephones was here to stay. Adams—that grandson of one president and great-grandson of another—felt abandoned by the pace of change, helpless, the horse-drawn world of his aristocratic childhood slipping away. "Some millions of other people felt the same helplessness, but few of them were seeking education," as Adams invariably did, "and to them helplessness seemed natural and normal," he wrote, "for they had grown up in the habit of thinking a steam-engine or dynamo as natural as the sun, and expected to understand one as little as the other."

To such people, the newness all around them as a century turned was progress: the transition from an agricultural to an industrial society, from a producer to a consumer population, from a merchant to a corporate economy, from rural to urban ways of life. Charles Darwin had published his *On the Origin of Species* in London in the same year, 1859, that Edwin L. Drake's drill was descending sixty-nine and a half feet through Pennsylvania clay and rock to strike oil; and hardly less consequential than the changes that oil, and railroads, and the new postbellum wealth were bringing to the physical world were the changes in intellectual attitudes that Darwin's insights wrought. *On the Origin of Species* teaches that the natural world has evolved, and fairgoers observed that the physical world was evolving too. You could see it all around you. All the inventions: for the home, for the farm, for the factory. Religion had evolved, from the fearsome Calvinism of our forefathers to a more benevolent, muscular Christianity blessed by a God of Love. Humanity, even if in fits and starts, was evolving upward. That was progress. As a new century opened, thoughtful people looked back, for instance, on a long period of no major world wars. Not since 1815, with Napoleon in defeat, had the great powers unleashed their might against each other in all-out, years-long warfare. Many on this cusp of time felt sure that nations had evolved beyond such wars, had left that barbarity behind them forever.

And in the present peace, during one joyous span of six weeks in March and April 1902, yet another self-made American risen from humble beginnings—in a rented two-room farmhouse in Florida, Missouri—was lounging on board the luxurious yacht *Kanawha* at sea, the tropic sky blue overhead, green waters limpid deep, deep down. On board besides Samuel Clemens were "Admiral" H. H. Rogers, the so-called brains of Standard Oil—Hell Hound Rogers to his many adversaries, to his intimates a man of wit and warmth and generosity—as well as the very clever ex-Speaker of the House Tom Reed, the genial Dr. Clarence Rice, George Harvey the editor and publisher (all Mark Twain's good friends), and John Archbold, effectively Standard Oil's acting president. Yet for all his prosperity and present contentment amid such company, Clemens had reached a stage in life when accumulated griefs and a critical attitude toward current affairs made his writing as Mark Twain sometimes less buoyant, more mordant (to his wife's dismay) than when he was younger. Even so, he still knew how to enjoy himself, as here with the boys far from land, cosseted and waited on, among friends partaking of the bounty that a new century offered. On one occasion, the *Kanawha* having dropped anchor in Caribbean waters, Clemens and Archbold together, friends too by then, "swam far out into the enchanted solitudes," according to a journal the humorist kept of the cruise, "& rode the rich seas for half an hour."

CHAPTER Twenty-Seven

Roosevelt as Reformer

D arwin's *On the Origin of Species* postulates a world evolving over eons of time through natural selection. Multitudes of species in incalculable numbers have been born on our planet, including within each species individuals slightly different from the norm. Occasionally a variation—sharper vision, or a somewhat longer snout or bill for getting at food, or coloration more appropriate for avoiding predators in desert or forest—has proved useful in allowing the individual possessing it to adapt better to its environment. Such an individual is more likely to survive and propagate. Some of its offspring carry the beneficial trait on into the next generation, and the modification endures. Individuals without the trait are put at a disadvantage; and eventually the disadvantaged population dies off, survived by those with the more camouflaged coloration, the better eyesight, the longer bill or snout.

In that way, through slow evolution, species have gradually grown more complex and heterogeneous. The result over time has been the astoundingly varied world in which we, like our ancestors of the nineteenth and early twentieth centuries, have found ourselves. The meditative among those forebears—at least the ones persuaded by Darwin's thesis—pondered what the great biologist's explanation for all that variety implied. Geologists with their strata and fossils and anthropologists with their shards and bones appeared to confirm that Earth was not created in six days some few thousand years ago. All its present variety evolved from simpler organisms over millions of years through the process of natural selection.

In that earlier, inquiring age of Victorians and Edwardians, a new science—sociology—applied Darwin's biological insights to our man-made world, as Social Darwinism. One who did so notably, the English theorist Herbert Spencer (1820–1903), contributed a phrase in explanation that

Darwin never used: "survival of the fittest." In the effort to live and thrive, mankind has competed in an unending struggle for the planet's resources. The fittest survive; the unfit perish. From that struggle Spencer reached conclusions about how we should behave for the betterment of humanity. While rejoicing that the fit endure, we should do nothing to keep the unfit from disappearing. Logic led Spencer to denounce, for instance, public education, public libraries, and all such institutions that tend to thwart the playing out of nature's rigorous scheme in favor of the fit. Who are the fit? They are those who survive and prosper. They are Edison, Archbold, Rockefeller, and Mark Twain, people like that, who, wherever they started from, rose to the top. Such people rise no matter what. Meanwhile, public education and its like, although well-intentioned, interfere with the natural working-out of social progress by shielding the less able.

Spencer was no crank. He was a highly respected thinker whose books sold in great quantities, whose ideas exerted a worldwide influence, who was welcomed and honored in America as well as in England, a polymath who was a nominee for the Nobel Prize for literature in 1902 and a favorite both of the corporate class and—with his emphasis on individual self-improvement—of the skilled working class as well. Hardly less honored was Yale's professor of sociology William Graham Sumner (1840–1910). Professor Sumner differed from Spencer in advocating public education, but he was nevertheless convinced that society did wrong to support charities or to pass poor laws (the poor must be left to make their own way) or to regulate factory hours or to prevent convicts at hard labor from being abused. All such softheartedness was simply tampering with an evolutionary movement toward higher levels not only of biology, but of ethics, religion, racial development, and human culture. Don't aid the unfit. Let nature deal with the unfit, leaving the fit to reproduce. *Laissez faire.* David Starr Jordan, the much-admired first chancellor of Stanford University, put the matter succinctly. We do wrong, Jordan wrote, to pity the failures in society. Such pity is not only misplaced; it's dangerous. Poverty, squalor, and crime are the products of inferior men and women. "It is not," said this educator, "the strength of the strong but the weakness of the weak which engenders exploitation and tyranny." Save your pity, then, and let natural selection extinguish the unfit, in order that superior forms of life may prosper.

Attitudes such as those of Jordan, Sumner, and Spencer skirted close to eugenics—another new science of the time: breeding to improve the race—which in the early decades of the twentieth century would set out in a sinister direction toward the Nazi nightmare. Yet Jordan's and the others' were views widely shared: that the able-bodied poor should not ask for or expect handouts, and that progress demanded our leaving the poor, like the rich, to fend for themselves.

Mark Twain gave voice to a similar conviction, only slightly modified. Wealthy, world-famous, his public image one of kindliness and understanding, he was approached again and again by people wanting something from him. Would you send me your autograph? Would you read my manuscript? Would you answer a question about *Tom Sawyer*? Would you tell me what you think of x or y? Would you come speak at my high school graduation? Would you ask your editor to publish my poems? He did what he could to oblige his many admirers. He helped Helen Keller, blind and deaf since infancy, achieve the remarkable feat of graduating from Radcliffe College by seeing to it that his friend H. H. Rogers financed her education. But that was different. Miss Keller could hardly help herself unaided. As for those who could, "I do not believe," the humorist had occasion to tell one correspondent, "I would very cheerfully help a white student who would ask a benevolence of a stranger." At the height of his powers, age fifty, on Christmas Eve 1885, from his beautiful home in Hartford in the year that *Huckleberry Finn* was published, Clemens was writing about an appeal from one Warner T. McGuinn for financial aid in getting through Yale Law School. "Do you know him?" he wrote to inquire of the dean of the school, Francis Wayland. "And is he worthy?" McGuinn was African-American. Mark Twain would be uneasy about helping a white student he didn't know, "but I do not feel so about the other color. We have ground the manhood out of them, & the shame is ours, not theirs, & we should pay for it. If this young man lives as economically as it is & should be the pride of one to do who is straitened, I would like to know what the cost is, so that I may send 6, 12, or 24 months' board, as the size of the bill may determine. You see he refers to you, or I would not venture to intrude. Truly yours, S. L. Clemens."

Mark Twain did provide for Warner McGuinn's finishing law school, at the threshold of a distinguished career that would take the young attorney to Baltimore, where Thurgood Marshall got to know him well. "He was one of the greatest lawyers who ever lived" was Justice Marshall's informed, unqualified opinion; but the point here is that Samuel Clemens, like many, many others in the nineteenth century and earlier, was less than promiscuous in his charitable giving. If a person could help himself, then he should, and not ask others to do it for him. It was Clemens's responsibility, for instance—nobody else's—to provide for his own family; hence his despair in the nineties over his publishing company's bankruptcy, his concern through later years about his copyrights, and his determination to add to his autobiography so as to leave his wife and daughters income from those fresh pages, to be used in updating copyrights after his death.

That each man was responsible for taking care of himself and his loved ones held true despite—or perhaps all the more because of—the merciless-ness of the economic cycles that continued to beset the later nineteenth century, in the grip of great social and technological forces imperfectly understood. Severe panics erupted in 1873 and again two decades later, when banks failed, businesses shut down, shops closed their doors, and hunger mounted. Factories that stayed open cut back. Employers fired blameless workers, slashed wages of those not fired, and extended the workday, during hard times stretching well beyond the years—1873, 1893—when the panics commenced. In the wake of the second crisis, in 1894, Mark Twain himself felt the anguish of bankruptcy; and thereafter his sympathy for the working man grew livelier than in the heyday of his innocent prosperity in Hartford two decades earlier.

Many others, however, felt no such sympathy for labor, which was seeking through these same late years to gain strength against capital's raw power by organizing. Rarely has it been easy to organize workers. The American labor movement in its infancy and youth was cautious anyway, uncertain as to how best to advance its interests, and its membership was divided. Skilled workers had little in common with the unskilled, those latter being in large part immigrants, and no longer blue-eyed, blond-haired immigrants from Sweden, say, or freckle-faced redheaded Scotsmen who spoke their variant of English. Nor were they even, as often before, foreign-ers (derided in their turn) who had fled the Irish potato famine and the political upheavals in the German states of the 1840s. This current crop, arriving in huge numbers—ten million here as the 1800s neared their end—were still sometimes German and Irish but more frequently now from Italy and eastern Europe, the latter swarthy types bearing unpronounceable names and speaking consonant-laden, impenetrable tongues.

Theodore Roosevelt—his roots thrusting eight generations deep into American soil—was one of the many who had little use for all those East-ern Europeans, those Slavs, those itinerant Russians. "No human beings, black, yellow, or white," in Roosevelt's private view, "could be quite as untruthful, as insincere, as arrogant—in short, as untrustworthy in every way—as the Russians." The question became whether, in our Anglo-Saxon nation, such people were even assimilable. The Colonel doubted it. Blacks were not, and as a race could not become full-fledged Americans for an evolutionarily long time, if then. Like blacks, Japanese and Chinese by the very looks of them were not assimilable. Nor were Latin Americans, in Roosevelt's opinion, any more than were these recent, swarming Slavs.

This was white man's country. He expressed such thoughts often and forcefully enough, although mostly in private, among friends and acquaintances. But the views reflected Roosevelt's basically conservative bent. To New York's Senator Chauncey Depew the Colonel wrote early in his presidency, "How I wish I wasn't a reformer, oh, Senator! But I suppose I must live up to my part, like the Negro minstrel"—that white impersonator of blackness—"who blacked himself all over!" For despite his reputation as the people's friend against the powerful, Roosevelt at heart was at home in a conservative age. So where did his renown as a progressive come from?

Perhaps the man would have been at home in any era, he reaped such joy from living. And Roosevelt did despise the very rich when they were idle or corrupt. Not riches, then, but riches ill-gotten or ill-used were what repelled him. As for the new captains of industry and finance, the Rockefellers and Carnegies and Morgans, he felt and expressed a high regard for those contributors to America's growing power. He knew wealth firsthand, was comfortable with it, had grown up with it (if not on the scale of the titans). And he knew something of the very poor, too. Roosevelt's father had seen to that, taking the boy with him on philanthropic excursions into the slums of New York City. So when young Roosevelt, recently out of Harvard, began serving the first of his three terms in the New York State Assembly, from 1881 to 1884, he was not long in making a name for himself espousing enlightened causes. He railed against corruption in City Hall and on the state judicial bench. He supported bills that limited the hours that women and children could be forced to labor in factories, and he fought for safer conditions at their workplaces. No doubt some of his impulse was Lamarckian, on the assumption that environmental traits are inheritable: improve the environment and you improve the quality of progeny bred there. Thus he sat on a committee to investigate sweat shops in Manhattan and ended by advancing a law, which many deemed socialistic, that abolished cigar-manufacturing in slum dwellings, the assemblyman having seen up close children in their hovels making cigars through long hours for virtually no pay.

But labor had reason to be wary of this young legislator nevertheless. Because of the strain it would put on municipal budgets, Assemblyman Roosevelt blocked a bill to force Buffalo, Brooklyn, and New York to pay their employees a minimum wage of twenty-five cents an hour, two dollars a day. He voted against a bill that would abolish the contracting-out of convict labor, against another that would raise the salaries of New York's firemen and policemen, against a third that would more rigorously enforce the state's eight-hour law, and against yet a fourth that would prevent horse-car drivers from transporting their public fares for more than twelve hours in a single workday.

The assemblyman's taking of such positions revealed at the least a nonchalance toward labor's causes. Yet even this early in his career, at twenty-four, in 1883, Roosevelt spoke out against "the wealthy criminal class," as he called it, by whom he meant such notoriously corrupt pluto-crats as Jubilee Jim Fisk and Jay Gould and Uncle Dan Drew, "the most dangerous of all dangerous classes" in its flouting of the public good, prospering in league with the many purchasable politicians on the order of Boss Tweed of New York City's Tammany Hall. With so much money about in postwar America, both private and public corruption flourished through the seventies and eighties, outside government and in. So an ever more pressing political issue of the time became civil-service reform. Root out relatives and cronies of those in high places, hacks holding office only to pick the public's pocket. Instead, from career candidates appoint hon-est, capable people chosen by examination, on merit alone.

Early in 1883, in the wake of an embittered (and unqualified) office seeker's assassination of President Garfield, Congress finally passed an act to reform the civil service. The Pendleton Act created a civil service com-mission; and six years later Theodore Roosevelt, former New York state assemblyman, afterward an unsuccessful candidate for mayor of New York City, since then a rancher and literary feller, returned to public life, this time in Washington to serve as one of the three civil-service commis-sioners. In that visible capacity, his work through the next six years further associated the young man's name with reform, of a cause—the integrity of government—that his own father ("the best man I ever knew") had advo-cated in the months before his early death in 1878. The younger Roosevelt, like the older, was personally incorruptible, a gentleman of the highest morals devoted to attracting the very best people into public service. But all his present efforts as commissioner, weeding out incompetence in federal administrations both Republican and Democratic, had little directly to do with the cause of labor. If anything, the interval shortly before Roosevelt's unsuccessful run for mayor of New York City in 1886 and his return to of-fice as civil service commissioner in 1889 saw his support for labor waning.

Many people turned against labor during those three years. The im-mediate cause was the Haymarket Riot, so-called, in Chicago in early May 1886. The issue fought over was the eight-hour day. Labor was agitating that workers be paid a living wage while allowed enough leisure to improve

Figure 27.1.   The Haymarket Riot, May 4, 1886. Pictured across the top are the slain policemen.
Courtesy of the Library of Congress.

their lives. But factory owners would not be dictated to. Factories were the owners' property, and people who didn't like working there twelve or fourteen hours a day six days a week for whatever the owners chose to pay them were free to quit. Others stood ready to take their places.

To protest such terms, a general walkout was called for May 1. Tens of thousands of laborers participated nationwide. Two days later, workers in Chicago coming together clashed with scabs—nonunion workers—filling the jobs of strikers locked out since February at the nearby McCormick reaper factory. In the melee two workers were killed. Broadsides went up announcing a subsequent meeting tomorrow evening, Tuesday, May 4, to protest such treatment as McCormick doled out. During the course of that second meeting some 175 policemen moved to disperse the crowd. Out of the darkness somebody—no one ever found out who—threw a bomb into the policemen's midst. In the confusion, patrolmen fired weapons and clubbed heads. It was all over in minutes; but seven policemen died from their wounds, some of them victims of the wild shots of other officers. And when the guns fell silent, at least four workers lay dead.

In the hysteria of the public reaction, nine agitators were hauled to court and convicted of the death of the one policeman inarguably killed by the bomb. All of the accused were anarchists—authorities had rounded up anarchists—most of them German immigrants. Some of those charged were not even on the premises when the bomb was thrown, and none of the accused could be linked to the act itself. Still, four defendants were hanged, on November 11, 1887, after a trial that has since then been widely condemned as a travesty of justice. Not at the time, however. At the time, Theodore Roosevelt expressed the popular sentiment when he wrote that America would benefit if all nine "Chicago dynamiters" were put to death, adding that if, instead of being out West at his ranch, he had been on hand at Haymarket Square that fatal night, he would have shot the rioters on the spot, never mind that some of those hanged hadn't even been at the site, and others who were had left before the bomb was thrown.

Dynamite—that new, terrifying weapon—struck fear in the hearts of law-abiding citizens anyway, because of its explosive power, the ease with which an agitator could get a stick of the stuff to toss, and his relative safety from harm while handling it; so that all through these years, with this Haymarket affair of 1886, with the wildcat Pullman strike of 1894, with all the other instances of unrest and protest through these not only turbulent but, for labor, often grindingly hard two decades at century's end, newspapers went on reinforcing the perception in an anxious middle class that unions were foreign imports, socialistic, under the thumb of bomb-throwing anarchists, and un-American.

An anarchist bearing the unpronounceable name of Czolgosz would murder William McKinley in 1901. Roosevelt, meanwhile, felt his inherent distrust of extremes strengthened by all this that appeared to threaten social order: mobs gathering, agitators exhorting in their broken English from atop wagons or barrels, stirring up workers to walk out, strike, boycott. He liked none of it. In 1895 he left his federal post as civil service commissioner in order to serve as police commissioner for the newly elected reform mayor of New York City. For two well-publicized years Commissioner Roosevelt discharged those duties by scrupulously enforcing city ordinances—shutting down saloons and beer halls on Sunday, for instance, despite the outcry from working folk long accustomed to refreshing their rare leisure hours with liquid comfort. The Rooseveltian rigor hardly catered to labor's taste; but a Sabbath-closing law was on the books, and violations would no longer be winked at. More popularly, the commissioner took to walking city streets late at night, fearlessly on the prowl for patrolmen found idling or asleep at their posts. Serving his party, meanwhile, he campaigned against the Democratic rabble-rouser Bryan, who was inflaming the masses in a run for the presidency in 1896. Within three years—now a war hero—Colonel Roosevelt had returned to public life himself, as New York's governor, where he would defend the people's interest against all extremes: governing not for labor, or for corporations, or for farmers either, but for all the citizens of the Empire State, for the public good. Thus he came to support what he had opposed as an assemblyman seventeen years earlier: the eight-hour day for workers on government contracts. And he toured the city sweat shops—something no other governor had done—and pushed hard to have the legislature outlaw those caves of human misery that till then had been hidden from sight.

Later, in the fall of 1901, Roosevelt entered the White House and brought all his rich experiences with him. The youngest of our presidents was as well prepared as any of the others—and better qualified than most—to meet the challenges of the office. But only reluctantly would he confront his challenges in the role of reformer, and not as a reformer in the vanguard. Rather, the President meant to steer a middle course, eschewing what he called the "lunatic fringe" on the left and the robber barons at their crassest on the right. Thus "on the other hand" became a favorite transition, as in 1904, when he wrote of capital and labor: "The friends of property, of order, of law, must never show weakness in the face of violence or wrong or injustice, but on the other hand they must realize that the surest way to provoke an explosion of wrong and injustice is to be shortsighted, narrow-minded, greedy and arrogant." In brief, "it is peculiarly incumbent upon the man with whom things have prospered to be in a certain sense the keeper of the brother with whom life has gone hard."

CHAPTER **Twenty-Eight**

The Gilded Age

Things had prospered for the Bradley Martins. At sixteen, their daughter married an English earl; and now these rising, affluent Americans from Albany, New York, currently of New York and London, were planning to brighten the drab winter of 1897 by putting on another of their parties, this one "the greatest party in the history of the city." It was to be a costume ball to which 1,200 of the socially elect would be invited. But the Martins—he a prominent banker—were by no means indifferent to those for whom life had gone hard. In fact, Mrs. Bradley-Martin (she preferred the hyphenation) held off issuing her invitations until three weeks before the event itself, precisely to keep guests from traveling to Paris for their costumes. Costumes must be fashioned here in America, to benefit local milliners, seamstresses, bootmakers, jewelers, florists, and hairdressers, many still suffering from a depression that had followed upon economic panic four years earlier, in 1893.

Meanwhile, the rich did right to enjoy their money. That was better than giving it to charity, which robbed recipients among the poor of self-respect. Far better (the argument ran) that those with means spend lavishly and thus let craftsmen servicing their extravagances earn an honorable living. Some in the press and the clergy objected, one pastor complaining that "you rich people put next to nothing in the collection plate, and yet you'll spend thousands of dollars on Mrs. Bradley-Martin's ball." But spend they did, the social set of many an eastern city buzzing excitedly in the course of preparations through the three weeks early in 1897 that preceded a historic New York evening.

That began at 10:15 P.M. on Wednesday, February 10, when the Bradley-Martins' carriage arrived at 15 West Thirty-Third Street, at the entrance to the Waldorf Hotel (where the Empire State Building rises now),

243

and Mr. Martin, his costume cloaked, alighted to help his wife step down. They went inside, and fifteen minutes later the first of a steady stream of carriages began discharging guests at the three openings over the canvas-covered sidewalk. Liveried servants drew back the canvas, allowing gawkers in the street no more than a glimpse of the brilliance within; but those privileged to enter ascended a staircase to eight rose-bedecked dressing rooms for the ladies (ladies'-maids and makers-up standing by to repair a smeared blush or retrain an unruly lock), while gentlemen retired to the Astor suite, to be attended by valets and perruquiers. From there, guests crossed to the small ballroom, inside which Mrs. Bradley-Martin as Mary Stuart, in a gold-embroidered gown trimmed with pearls and precious stones worth more than $60,000, waited in front of magnificent tapestries under a velvet canopy on a velvet-covered dais to receive them. Rose petals were underfoot, fresh vines and flowers everywhere. Mr. Martin had come as Louis XV—*Après moi le déluge*—the cost of even the buttons on his costume amounting to a princely sum. Chairs in the ballroom were of the Louis XV period, white and gold, and on them guests lounged while the receiving line took its leisurely ninety minutes to pass, couples when done proceeding through a simulated woodland walk to the main ballroom, to a fantasy in there brought dazzlingly, fragrantly to life.

Roses garlanded the chandeliers, within the brilliance of which mingled all the magical people, reflected in eighteen huge mirrors against one wall, as at Versailles, each mirror decorated with mauve orchids, 3,000 of them streaming "carelessly to the floor, like the untied bonnet strings of a thoughtless child." Out of sight behind a vine-screen in the gallery, a fifty-piece orchestra played Mozart, Beethoven, and Chopin. Stanford White was among the guests, and Miss Pierpont Morgan as Queen Louise of Prussia, and Mrs. Hamilton Fish Webster as Maria Theresa. One gentleman came as the Duc de Guise, in white corded silk embroidered with pearls and silver lace. Mr. Belmont moved stiffly about in his gold-inlaid armor. Mrs. James Beekman was Lady Teazle; Mrs. John Jacob Astor Marie Antoinette. Caroline Astor—*the* Mrs. Astor—wearing $200,000 worth of jewelry, led the *quadrille d'honneur*, followed by an exhibition minuet and the debutantes' dance, before the general dancing began. George Washington was on hand, and Pocahontas, and Henry IV, amid powdered coiffeurs, plumed three-cornered hats, antique lace, heirloom jewelry, and swords with gold hilts protruding.

It was magnificent. It was without precedent, unduplicatable. Soon after midnight the doors were thrown open for supper: among much else consommé de volaille, homard á la Newburg, huitres á la Viennoise, terrapene desossée á la Baltimore, canard Canvasback, terrine de foie gras, gateaux Madeleine, sorbet Fin de Siècle, tutti-frutti, petits fours, and bonbons, all served at 125 tables for six, 100 waiters attending. At three in the morning the cotillion began, and when the ball wound down at daybreak, guests—despite Police Commissioner Roosevelt's fears that he would need as many patrolmen to maintain order as were called for at a labor strike—dispersed unmolested: fatigued, but in rare satisfaction and good humor. Only afterward did the Bradley-Martins learn that their tax assessment was to be raised sharply upon news of their having spent for the festivities $369,000 (nearly $10 million now). In some dudgeon, the couple departed New York for good, to a London home and their leased Scottish estate of 65,000 acres, leaving behind memories of the most talked-about fête in that age of excess, which stretched from just after the Civil War into a new century.

Some mark the Bradley-Martin ball as the culmination of an era. In the 1920s, Van Wyck Brooks and Lewis Mumford labeled the three decades that preceded it in America "the Gilded Age," a name that stuck. Specifically, the term denotes years between, say, 1870 and 1900, when Vanderbilt's chateau and Mrs. Astor's huge home were erected along Millionaires Row on New York's Fifth Avenue, when Mrs. Astor's Beechwood, and William K. Vanderbilt's Marble House, and the seventy-room Breakers of Cornelius Vanderbilt II were rising as splendid seaside "cottages" of the very rich at Newport. Those later cultural historians derived their phrase for all that showy surfeit from the title of a novel written near the start of the postbellum material glut, during the corruption scandals of the Grant administration and in the year of an earlier sharp economic downturn, in 1873 (the same year that Theodore Roosevelt Sr., undeterred in the midst of general financial panic, was building his own New York mansion near the southwest corner of Central Park). Romantics may lament a Golden Age far in the past from which humanity has fallen, while enlightened Classicists envisage the same Golden Age as lying ahead, the perfectibility toward which progress is leading us. But in the late nineteenth century their own lavishly bright postwar era looked to some, for all its exorbitance, like a golden age right then, even if others thought it less gold than gilt, shiny but meretricious, as satirized in *The Gilded Age*, a novel written by two neighbors in Hartford, Connecticut, and published in December 1873.

The year before, Mark Twain and his Nook Farm friend Charles Dudley Warner had been visiting together, the gentlemen at dinner that Christmas of 1872 good-naturedly berating contemporary fiction. Their wives challenged them: why didn't they write something better then? So they set out to—Warner a popular essayist and editor of the *Hartford Courant*, Clemens already the author of *The Innocents Abroad* and *Roughing It*—and got their novel jointly written in a little over three months. *The Gilded Age: A Tale of To-day* was published at the end of that same year, a satire on the era's worldly scheming: former war profiteers with funds on hand to multiply, promoters full of inflated get-rich promises, land speculators ever hopeful of turning a profit wherever the railroad ran, politicians as ready to take the bribe as to deliver the pious Sunday-School lecture. Mark Twain was responsible for most of the satire in the novel, in particular for the creation of the memorable Colonel Sellers, ever alive with the next big opportunity, which somehow never pays off. Melodrama as well as satire entered *The Gilded Age*: orphans, bigamy, blackmail, unrequited love, and a beautiful young woman betrayed by a cad, whom she follows to his hotel and murders, of which deed she is declared, at the end of a sensational jury trial, not guilty by reason of insanity. Later the now notorious Laura Hawkins joins the lecture circuit, speaks before jeering auditors in a half-filled hall, then withdraws in shame to die, still beautiful, of a broken heart. Warner wrote much of that burlesque melodrama, which sits uneasily beside the other, crisper, angrier satirical plot of this long book, of subscription length—Mark Twain's first effort in the novel form.

Curiosity about the famous, funny travel writer's venture into a new literary genre—into fiction, and fiction satirizing the present—caused *The Gilded Age* to sell briskly at first, although, partly because of hard times, sales fell off after a year or two and never recovered. Nor has this very early specimen of the American novel of realism aged well: lacking in unity, with longueurs and a timeliness that pleased then but has dated, its specific satirical targets of the 1870s long forgotten. Anyway, how could *The Gilded Age* achieve the status of art when written like that, as a lark, Clemens composing the first eleven chapters, then turning it over to his less able friend Warner to write the next twelve, before Mark Twain got the manuscript back to take up the story again, back and forth until, in some haste, all sixty-three chapters were finished?

For the Clemens family was off to England as soon as the novel was done. It would be the author's second trip there, in the glory years of his sudden fame when everything was possible. At the time, Mark Twain seemed to accomplish whatever he wanted to, even to writing a first novel on a dare. During the earlier trip to England the preceding fall, in September 1872, away from his family to explore the writing of a book about the British Isles, the humorist in his mid-thirties had been astounded, while attending ceremonies in London's Guildhall, to hear his name when announced greeted with a lengthy storm of applause, the only one of the many guests to be thus honored. Now in the following spring he was bringing his family along to share in the homage, on a sojourn that lasted from May 1873 to January 1874. The Clemenses were received rapturously in England, Scotland, and Ireland, made many notable friends, reveled as the English flocked to hear Mark Twain lecture, saw the sights there and on the Continent, and—assuredly in Clemens's case—felt a long love of British history gratified and strengthened. "God knows I wish we had some of England's reverence for the old & great," the author in the midst of his family's overseas adventure wrote wistfully to a friend back home. One long-term outcome professionally was *The Prince and the Pauper*, set in the England of 1547; another was *A Connecticut Yankee in King Arthur's Court*, set in Britain in the sixth century; and yet a third was a game the author worked hard at perfecting that would allow children at home to commit to memory the beginning and ending dates of all the English monarchs.

For this restless, enormously imaginative mind could not be satisfied with merely writing books. And this satirist of a postbellum nation, who pined for the antebellum simplicities of its lost agrarian past ("When I was a boy" became a dreamy Mark Twain mantra: "When I was a boy on the Mississippi . . ."), could—even as he ladled scorn on the low corruptions of the Gilded Age—conspire with all the zest of Colonel Sellers himself for his portion of America's wealth, now tantalizingly in reach. The hankering had started with the Tennessee land that his father bequeathed to the impoverished Clemens heirs to make them all rich; and though nothing ever came of that, a twenty-one-year-old Sam Clemens on his way down the Mississippi in 1857 was nurturing plans to ascend the Amazon and build a fortune out of coca leaves; even as Clemens the Nevada miner would later swing an ax in vain quest of the silver strike that he hoped might buy him a fancy home on Nob Hill; even as later still Clemens the travel reporter, returning from a five-months' European voyage, would leap at the offer to write a book on the subject, provided the publisher would tell him "what amount of money I might possibly make out of it." The money, Mark Twain wrote Elisha Bliss late in 1867, "has a degree of importance for me which is almost beyond my own comprehension."

That initial exchange between publisher and potential author occurred soon after the *Quaker City* reached New York at the end of its precedent-setting cruise to the Holy Land. Now, six years later, by early 1874, with the Clemens family back in triumph from eight months of British and Continental travels, Mark Twain was in the money in truth. He had married his heiress, written three lucrative books, and lectured to great applause on two continents. From the proceeds of such industry a beautiful home was even then rising on one of the choicest lots in Hartford, at the time fairest of America's cities. "I *am* the gladdest man," the new homeowner exclaimed in surveying what is now 351 Farmington Avenue. The stables out back were finished, and "exceedingly handsome. The house and grounds are not to be described, they are so beautiful. Patrick"—the coachman, Patrick McAleer—"and family occupy large handsome rooms in the stable. I don't think I ever saw such a bewitching place as ours is."

During the next seventeen years the Clemenses lived in that bewitching place, from October 1874 to June 1891. For the most part the years were supremely happy ones. Clemens proved to be a good neighbor, joining in the spirit of Nook Farm, a green Connecticut compound that clung to the best of the past—to stability, civility, community—which the brash present appeared to jeopardize. Neighbors took care to know each other as family, their children growing up together, playing together, skating, sleighing together, attending ice-cream parties, putting on theatricals, fathers meeting on Monday nights to share papers they had written and exchange talk about matters civic or literary, mothers gathering in supportive cohesiveness on Saturday mornings, with buggy rides, whist parties, musical recitals, and neighborly suppers filling their pleasant evenings.

Figure 28.1.   The Clemenses' Hartford home around 1875.
Courtesy of the Mark Twain House & Museum, Hartford.

Yet even with all that activity, and even with the visitors from near and far who availed themselves of the Clemenses' ample hospitality, and even despite the books that somehow got written, the articles, stories, and lectures delivered, despite all that and a rich involvement with his family, the irrepressible Mark Twain made time for additional occupations. For travel: he appeared constantly on the move, to Europe, to Boston and Cambridge, to New York, to Elmira each summer (where much of the writing was done), on a return to the Mississippi, lecturing widely and profitably in the Northeast and Midwest. Moreover, Clemens had a nineteenth-century knack for tinkering, for inventing remedies to alleviate life's vexations. Such handiwork he patented and put money into: a vest that attached to trousers and did away with suspenders, a notebook that opened to where you left off, a shirt that needed no buttons or studs, a fire extinguisher in the form of a hand grenade, a perpetual calendar, a clamp to keep babies from kicking off their blankets, that history game that taught children the reigns of the English monarchs. The last, on which much time was spent, proved in the end too complicated to market; and all the other devices, however ingenious, failed to make the inventor rich or even return him a profit. Except for one: Mark Twain's Scrap Book, which required no paste. People in an age of newspapers kept clippings, and with this new scrapbook they needed only to moisten the appropriate lengths of strips on the page and press their clipping down. Mark Twain's Scrap Book appeared for sale in 1875 and went on to earn its inventor ("An inventor is a poet," he wrote, "a true poet—and nothing in any degree less than a high order of poet") $50,000 over his lifetime, in the neighborhood of a million dollars now.

But the humorist would invest far more than that tidy sum in enterprises that failed again and again to live up to their promise. He put money into a steam generator that couldn't ultimately be made to work, $32,000 into a steam pulley that after all didn't hoist, $25,000 into a marine telegraph that never delivered a message. An engraving process caught the investor's fancy; it would revolutionize the publishing business. He put $50,000 into that, only to see his chalk-plate process beaten out by a rival, photoengraving. The public, meanwhile, knew little or nothing about such missteps. It saw the inventive Mark Twain's Memory Builder and Mark Twain's Scrap Book for sale. It followed news of a grand, successful lecture tour in the mid-1880s that Mark Twain made with the celebrated New Orleans author George Washington Cable. The public went on reading Mark Twain's entertaining books as they appeared—*Tom Sawyer* (1876), *A Tramp Abroad* (1880), *The Prince and the Pauper* (1881), *Life on the Mississippi*

(1883)—read his articles in the magazines, delighted in his witty maxims that the newspapers quoted, and basked in the very presence among them of so engaging a personage surrounded by his attractive family and his many bright, multifaceted achievements.

Elisha Bliss, publisher of the author's works (if rarely to Clemens's satisfaction) from *The Innocents Abroad* of 1869 on, died in 1880. Thus any obligations to Bliss ended, and Samuel L. Clemens entered into arrangements for setting his writings before the public himself. He had returned to a long-standing project, a novel finished finally in 1884; and in order to bring that out he established his own publishing house, putting his sister's daughter's husband in charge. The sole purpose of the new Charles L. Webster & Company (named after that young civil engineer) was to publish Mark Twain's writings, beginning with the novel just completed: *Adventures of Huckleberry Finn.*

But while the book was in production, the ever restless, ever alert Samuel Clemens stumbled upon the chance to publish the emerging memoirs of a hero of his ever since Nevada days. General Ulysses S. Grant, after two terms in the presidency and subsequent business indiscretions that had left his family penniless, was struggling to write his memoirs for the money in the thing, even while suffering the agony of terminal throat cancer. Clemens persuaded the general to let his own new firm publish the memoirs as subscription volumes. To do so, Webster & Company put sixteen agents to work supervising 10,000 canvassers who peddled subscriptions around the country. Within a little over two months after the signing of the contract on February 27, 1885, those canvassers had gathered in orders for a remarkable 60,000 sets assured of being purchased as soon as the volumes were ready.

General Grant all this while, in pain and writing against time, finished his manuscript a brief five days before his death, in early July of that year. His *Personal Memoirs of U. S. Grant* (which remains a classic) was at once a phenomenal publishing triumph. The late general's family grew prosperous once more, with royalties totaling 450,000 of 1885 dollars; and Charles L. Webster & Company could thereafter take its pick of the 500 and more projects that came pouring in: Sherman's memoirs, Sheridan's memoirs, the autobiography of Henry Ward Beecher (which Protestants would devour), an authorized biography of the present Pope Leo XIII (which surely every Catholic in the English-speaking world would want to read).

Besides all that, there was James W. Paige's typesetter, bound to make an investor rich beyond any author's dreams, even if he had nothing else to fall back on. As early as October 1881 Clemens was writing

Charley Webster about scraping up money to buy more stock in Paige's miraculous invention. "I reckon it will take about a hundred thousand machines to supply the world," this former printer wrote knowledgeably, "& I judge the world has got to buy them—it can't well be helped." Just as the world, including candlelit hovels, had got to buy kerosene. Every sizable printing establishment on earth would need that typesetter; so Mark Twain was to be rich like Rockefeller. Four years later, in November 1885, Clemens was writing Dear Charley again, in high spirits: "Please send a check for $3,500 to Wm. Hamersley, payable to his order—send it to him here, Hartford, right away. Charge to me, & make a particular entry of it to remember the circumstance by, for it finishes the type-setter business in a very satisfactory fashion."

CHAPTER Twenty-Nine

Bankruptcy

The typesetter business was not to be finished so easily, and even then hardly to anybody's satisfaction. From the height of his success in 1885, Mark Twain watched good fortune forsake him through the years ahead. It was not a sudden abandonment. His daughter Susy, thirteen, wrote on February 12, 1886: "Mamma and I have both been very much troubled of late because papa, since he has been publishing Gen. Grant's book, has seemed to forget his own books and work entirely, and the other evening as papa and I were promonading up and down the library he told me that he didn't expect to write but one more book, and then he was ready to give up work altogether, die or do anything, he said that he had written more than he had ever expected to, and the only book that he had been pertickularly anxious to write was one locked up in the safe down stairs, not yet published." The story referred to was "Captain Stormfield's Visit to Heaven," which the author revised and published finally as late as 1909. Meanwhile he did complete, in 1889, after four years' labor—and benefited Charles L. Webster & Company by publishing under its imprint—*A Connecticut Yankee in King Arthur's Court*, which Mark Twain envisaged as his swan song. Henceforth he meant to be a capitalist, raking in money from the publishing business (by then Webster & Company was one of the major publishers in America) and from the typesetter, whose 20,000 parts Paige was meshing in ways that would provide it with near-human capabilities. And that amazing machine, the inventor kept reassuring his several investors, was about ready to market: just a few more months, a few weeks more now.

Instead, in June 1891—with the typesetter still not perfected those two years later—the Clemenses felt obliged to move to Europe. There they could live more cheaply in the manner to which the humorist had accustomed

his family: servants, comfortable travel arrangements, roomy accommodations, boarding schools, the girls' music lessons, stays at spas, doctors
attending their various ailments. Behind them they left the high cost of
running the Hartford home, daughter Clara remembering forty years later
the day of their departure: "a sorrowful episode," she recalled. "We adored
our home and friends. We had to leave so much treasured beauty behind
that we could not look forward with any pleasure to life abroad." Two
days before turning seventeen, she gazed a last time into "the library; the
conservatory sweet with the perfume of flowers; the bright bedrooms; and,
outside, the trees, the tender eyebrights, the river reflecting clouds and
sky. These were our friends. They belonged to us; and we to them. How
could we part?" The schoolroom upstairs was filled with loved ghosts of
"snowstorms raging about the many windows, against which a fire on the
hearth cozily defended us. And our Shakespeare club! Oh, the wonderful
plays we produced with a larger cast of actors than auditors! Memory tests
of books we had read and hated. Recitations of poetry we adored. Concerts
performed on our baby upright." Could Europe offer anything so pleasurable? "Instinctively, we felt that life would never be more vivid or bright
than it had been during these years of childhood." With heavy hearts the
girls moved from room to room, an inner voice whispering that they would
never return. Then they said their goodbyes to servants, to friends, to pets,
"and, tear-blinded, passed, for the last time, through the front door and
away to unknown lands."

The family never did come back to Hartford to live. They kept the
house, thinking they would some day, but finally had to rent it out, at
last—as late as 1902—putting it up for sale, only to learn that there were no
takers. The place was too idiosyncratic, too expensive to run. They lowered
the price. The land, his agent instructed its anguished owner, was worth
more than the mansion itself. Maybe turn it into a school? Tear it down?
Which called forth Mark Twain's wail, in the spring of 1903, from Riverdale-on-Hudson to F. G. Whitmore, acting in Hartford on his behalf: "For
the Lord Jesus H. Christ's sake *sell or rent that God damned house.*" Whitmore
did finally somehow sell it, at a drastic reduction in price, and brought that
sad story to its end.

What had gone wrong, meanwhile, with Mark Twain's flourishing
publishing firm and the miraculous typesetter? Self-exiled in Europe after
June 1891, Clemens crossed the Atlantic fourteen times over the next four
years trying to cope with business matters in America. The sudden success of *Huckleberry Finn* and Grant's *Memoirs* had led Charles L. Webster
& Company to take on too much. Irresistible projects had been proposed,

and the publisher jumped at too many of them. Henry Ward Beecher offered his autobiography, and who in America wouldn't want to read that? But Beecher died, in 1887, the advance paid for his book left with his family out of compassion, his manuscript not yet begun. Sherman's memoirs, and Sheridan's, and McClellan's all came to hand, but Grant had pretty well sated the taste for memoirs by Union generals, even as Mrs. Custer was writing about her late husband for Webster & Company, and Mrs. Hitchcock about hers. Meanwhile, the authorized biography of Pope Leo XIII when it appeared barely broke even, hordes of English-speaking Catholics quite able to pass it by.

Under the strain of his responsibilities, magnified through the company's sudden growth, young Webster collapsed. He was forced to retire, dying in the spring of 1891 at age thirty-nine. His successor as manager was Fred Hall, an underling hardly up to the job. Soon the company was embroiled in trying to assemble an eleven-volume *Library of American Literature*—devastating for a subscription publisher, inasmuch as subscribers in their villages had only to put down a deposit to establish a claim for whenever the books might be ready, whereas the overextended publishing house was obliged to borrow capital to print, bind, and distribute the costly sets complete before it could collect a penny of the subscriber's balance far down the road. In any case, subscription books were less in demand now than earlier. Postbellum America, increasingly urbanized, had moved more readers closer to bookstores, with fewer awaiting the knock on rural doors that announced canvassers offering titles for sale. All the while, Mark Twain, mesmerized by the possibilities of the typesetter, watching it set type in trials at speeds far faster than young Sam Clemens in his print shops along the Mississippi had ever been able to do by hand, had been dipping into the apparently solid profits of Charles L. Webster & Company to help Paige realize his lofty ambitions. By 1889 the besmitten Mark Twain had purchased a half interest in the typesetter and become James Paige's partner.

"He is a poet, a most great and genuine poet, whose sublime creations are written in steel," the humorist reported, falling back on a trope he had first used twenty years earlier to describe inventors in general. Paige, Clemens felt sure, could charm fish out of the water and get them to come take a walk with him. For thirteen years he dealt with that magician, remaining spellbound all the while: "When he is present I always believe him; I can't help it."

A bit of the skeptic was called for; but to the very end of their working together, the author failed to muster much in the way of skepticism toward James W. Paige. Way back in 1885—that *annus mirabilis*—in July he wrote to Charley Webster, whose publishing firm was doing so well: "Three years from now I calculate to have about 1000 of those machines"—the typesetters—"hired out in this country at $2,500,000." Already Clemens was thinking on a grand scale, full of an excitement that persisted even as the three years passed with not a one of the two and a half million dollars to show for it. Instead of pouring in from Paige, money kept flowing out—from royalties on Mark Twain's writings, from Mrs. Clemens's inheritance, from the coffers of Webster & Company—to help the inventor and his crew perfect their complicated marvel.

Early in 1889 Clemens, ever optimistic, informed his brother Orion that in two or three weeks "we shall work the stiffness out of her joints and have her performing as smoothly and softly as human muscles, and then we shall speak out the big secret and let the world come and gaze." Paige had telegraphed: "Machine O.K. Come and see it work." Which Clemens did, up from New York three days later, ecstatic: "I have seen"—at 12:20 P.M., Saturday, January 5, 1889—"a line of movable type, *spaced and*

Figure 29.1.   Paige's typesetter.
Courtesy of the Mark Twain House & Museum, Hartford.

justified by machinery! This is the first time in the history of the world that this amazing thing has ever been done." Margins on the page both left and right could be evenly aligned without the touch of a human hand! Yet for Paige the perfectionist, things were still not quite right. Again the typesetter was dismantled for further adjustments. Meanwhile, Clemens had removed the ailing Webster from his publishing company, where matters were going less well. Debts had begun piling up, but the typesetter would save them all. "All the other wonderful inventions of the human brain sink pretty nearly into commonplaces contrasted with this awful mechanical miracle," Clemens assured his brother. "Telephones, telegraphs, locomotives, cotton-gins, sewing-machines, Babbage calculators, Jacquard looms, perfecting presses, all mere toys, simplicities! The Paige Compositor marches alone and far in the lead of human inventions." The burnished-steel wonder would last a century and, the former Missouri printer confidently predicted, "do the work of six men, and do it better"—wouldn't get tired, or drunk, or go on strike, or fail to show up in the morning—"than any six men that ever stood at a case."

Paige moved his operations from the Pratt & Whitney plant in Hartford to Chicago, where the typesetter was to be tested in the hurly-burly of a newspaper pressroom, after which units would be manufactured for sale. In the late summer of 1893 Clemens sailed to New York on business yet again, on the sixth of those many voyages across the Atlantic. He disembarked on September 7 with a cold that put him in bed nursing a bottle of whiskey. Most of the bottle he drank, then woke next morning cured. But in an economy suddenly turned dreadful—the previous month the Erie and Northern Pacific railroads had declared insolvency—banks under siege were calling in loans. In this developing Panic of 1893, Fred Hall at Webster & Company cried out for funds to pay off debts. Clemens set about rounding up capital. He had begun writing again; and "I've sold the Esquimaux Girl's Romance to the Cosmopolitan, for eight hundred dollars," he let Livy know—money he would use to live on here—"& Pudd'nhead Wilson to the Century for six thousand five hundred, which will go to you by & by—first payment after Nov. 1—for it is even hard for the Century to get money." Hard for everybody in those grim times; so must Mark Twain return to the loathed lecture platform? For now, the "billows of hell have been rolling over me," he wrote to his wife ten days later. "I have never lived any such days as those beginning last Monday & ending at 4 Friday afternoon." The publishing house was about to go under "for lack of $8,000 to meet notes coming due to morrow, Monday. I raced up to Hartford & back again—couldn't get it." None of his friends up there could lend him anything.

"At Hartford I wrote Sue"—Livy's sister in Elmira—"telling her I had no shame, for the boat was sinking—send me $5,000 if she possibly could. Mr. Halsey, Mr. Hall & I raced around Wall Street Thursday, assailing banks & brokers—couldn't get anything." That night "ruin seemed inevitable," but next morning Clemens was up early to venture out once more. Sue's answer arrived: she hadn't any money but would send negotiable bonds if that would help. Hall said it wouldn't. What Webster & Company needed was $8,000, not Susan Crane's five—and needed it Monday. By noon that Friday "all schemes of Hall & Halsey (who worked for us like a beaver) had failed." There was nowhere else to turn.

Yet how oddly, sometimes, matters are resolved. Clemens in New York had been visiting with his physician friend Dr. Clarence Rice, whose patients included Enrico Caruso, Edwin Booth, and Lillian Russell. A fellow member of the Players Club, the nose-and-throat specialist took an interest in his clubmate's financial troubles. Thus, at this darkest moment, "a messenger came from Dr. Rice," Clemens was able to write to his wife overseas, "to call me back there"—to East Nineteenth Street—"& he told me he had ventured to speak to a rich friend of his who was an admirer of mine about our straits. I was very glad. Mr. Hall was to be at this gentleman's office away down Broadway at 4 yesterday afternoon, with his statements." Hall and Clemens went down together, "& in six minutes we had the check"—for $8,000, the full amount—"and our worries were over till the 28th."

The office at 26 Broadway was on the eleventh floor of the Standard Oil building (which still stands), and the gentleman to whom Dr. Rice had spoken was Henry Huttleston Rogers. "We were strangers when we met," Clemens recalled years later, "and friends when we parted, half an hour afterward. The meeting was accidental and unforeseen but it had memorable and fortunate consequences for me." For the busy Rogers agreed to take in hand Webster & Company's muddled financial affairs.

First off, Standard Oil's titan found a purchaser to lift the multivolume *Library of American Literature* from Webster & Company's burdened shoulders. Even so, some hundred of the publisher's creditors, including banks, binders, printers, and paper suppliers, remained unrelenting, one in particular: the Mount Morris Bank of Montclair, New Jersey. Accordingly, as the only possible way ever to repay the debts, Rogers advised Webster & Company to declare bankruptcy. On April 18, 1894, it did. Mark Twain's vast public was stunned at the news, having long thought of the humorist as a superbly gifted businessman. Surely the fault lay with his employees? Instead of going abroad, if he had remained in New York to manage and supervise? But in those sad times many a bank and private company were going under, and many good people had lost everything. The newspapers for their part set about reporting the fall of Webster & Company in full, if sympathetically, and in doing so subjected Clemens's interesting plight to widespread public scrutiny.

Behind the scenes, however, out of reach of the press, Rogers was continuing to serve his new friend. Some $60,000 of Mrs. Clemens's inheritance had been lent to Webster & Company, making her the preferred creditor for the $160,000 of debt that was owed. Her claims must be paid off first. She owned the Hartford house already; that was not to be touched. More important, Rogers decreed that the copyrights—Mark Twain's most valuable assets—were to be turned over to Mrs. Clemens, out of reach of any of the other creditors. For the rest, Clemens in his distress had been considering paying a fraction on the dollar to get out from under such a weight, but both his wife and his new friend insisted that he commit to repaying the debt in full. To Mrs. Clemens, it was a moral obligation, whatever the law might say, and Mr. Rogers maintained that the author's exalted reputation was so precious as to outweigh any monetary advantages he might gain by resorting to legal technicalities.

Their combined advice prevailed. In Vancouver in 1895, near the start of his round-the-world tour, Mark Twain told the press what he meant to do with his lecture proceeds; and in the years just ahead, his public watched him do it—from his earnings watched him pay off the debts entire—and when the last dime had been handed over, that same huge public bestowed on him an all but universal admiration and love. They would be his for the rest of his life.

Rogers had done all that for his friend, and would do more. Early in their friendship the Standard Oil executive had agreed to look into the typesetter affair. Clemens's enthusiasm for that expensive project (in all he contributed around $300,000 to Paige's enterprise) remained undaunted. "When the machine is in proper working order," he felt certain even at the last, "it cannot make a mistake. When the operator is a good operator, he will not make any mistakes worth speaking of—say 2 in 1000 ems, 16 in an hour. These 16 should be corrected in 4 minutes. Half an hour is enough to devote to correcting an entire 8-hour output." In every printing office two or three printers stand out for speed. "Those men set 1,500 ems an hour," he told Rogers authoritatively. "I have seen them do it." Yet even that pace would increase tenfold with Paige's remarkable invention. Rogers had his experts look into the matter, and to Clemens's joy, the hard-nosed businessman reported that the typesetter—and Paige himself—were all that their investors thought they were. So the factory could set about building a hundred of the machines, or fifty at least; and the *Chicago Times-Herald* was ready to install one and put it to work in its pressroom. The evasive Paige must be persuaded to sign a new contract; would the inventor do that? And could details be worked out to the satisfaction of all interested parties? In Manhattan, Clemens held his breath, awaiting the outcome of the Chicago negotiations.

In mid-January 1894, Rogers sent word that left the recipient unmoved at first, he had waited for it so long. Calmly he cabled Livy overseas: "Look out for good news." And with that, "I came up to my room & began to undress, & then, suddenly & without warning the realization burst upon me & overwhelmed me: I and mine, who were paupers an hour ago, are rich now & our troubles are over!" Pacing the floor alone for half an hour, he once or twice felt like sitting down and crying, the strain of three and a half exacting, exhausting months removed, the fear all gone. Alone in his room, far from his wife and family, he could find no way to express his joy.

The bankruptcy of Charles L. Webster & Company followed three months later, but there was the typesetter, the wonderful typesetter. All would be well. At last, in May, after seven months in America—the longest since their marriage that he had ever been away from Livy, or ever would be again in her lifetime—Clemens sailed for France. Behind him, Paige's typesetter had proved itself the marvel he had always thought it was. Only, for now they would manufacture ten of them instead of fifty. Maybe only one for now. For in extended trials at the *Times-Herald* in months ahead the machine was behaving altogether too much like a human being. It kept getting sick on the job. The type broke. Stoppages for additional repairs increased in number. "Great guns, what is the matter with it?" Clemens from Europe wrote in alarm in November. Rogers and his son-in-law had gone out to Chicago to have a look. Rogers held watch in hand as he counted the mistakes. He stayed by the machine a long while, "for it was most interesting, most fascinating, but," the businessman was forced reluctantly to conclude, "it was not practical." It cost too much, was too elaborate, too delicate, got out of sorts too easily. Morgenthaler's new Linotype, by contrast, although far less sophisticated, much bulkier, clunkier, set type more reliably—and indeed would end up in pressrooms large and small around the world, whereas Paige's typesetter survives as a museum piece in only one specimen, one of only two ever built, its inventor dying forgotten in 1917, buried anonymously in Chicago in the poverty of a potter's field.

Rogers had to write and tell his friend the sad news of the typesetter's breakdown. "It hit me like a thunder-clap," Clemens responded from Paris, December 22, 1894. "It knocked every rag of sense out of my head, and I went flying here and there and yonder, not knowing what I was doing, and only one clearly defined thought standing up visible and substantial out of the crazy storm-drift—that my dream of ten years was in desperate peril and out of the 60,000 or 70,000 projects for its rescue that came flocking through my skull not one would hold still long enough for me to examine and size it up."

What he finally did—what he had to do—was accept the fact that the Paige dream was over (all that money lost!) while Webster & Company's creditors abided. In the summer of 1895, Clemens and his wife and daughter Clara sailed forth on their round-the-world cruise to pay off the publishing debts, Mr. Rogers shrewdly investing funds the lecturer sent back for that purpose. In January 1898, living by then in Vienna, Clemens learned that the last payment on the debt had been made, with something like $13,000 to spare. "Mrs. Clemens has been reading the creditors' letters over and over again," he wrote Rogers in early March, gratefully (this only the latest of so many things to be grateful to H. H. Rogers for), "and thanks you deeply for sending them, and says it is the only really happy day she has had since Susy died." Thereafter, the titan would continue to be of service, as a kind of New York literary agent placing Mark Twain's writings from overseas and as a broker investing his friend's money with all the advantages arising from (what was then not illegal) insider trading. At the start of 1899, still in Vienna: "Federated Steel does certainly brisken up these holidays with handsome surprises!" A week before, Rogers had bought for Clemens shares that were already showing a profit of $10,000. "By grace of you, we have had a Christmas and a New Year this time which knocked the gloom out of a season which we have grown acccustomed"— ever since their daughter's death—"to anticipate with dread." At century's end, when he and his family came back from exile, in October 1900, Mark Twain was affluent once more. A year later the Clemenses moved into the elegant Appleton mansion at Riverdale-on-Hudson, bringing with them all those benefits that Henry Huttleston Rogers had bestowed "at no cost to my self-love," their recipient marveled, "no hurt to my pride," for the magnate had never betrayed the slightest awareness that Clemens owed him a single thing in return.

CHAPTER Thirty

In the White House

When the Clemenses moved into Riverdale, in early October 1901, Theodore Roosevelt had been president of the United States for less than a month. New York's erstwhile governor had come to his new duties with (as he said) "certain strong convictions," but of course with no plan of action, not having expected to be called to the office at all. Only McKinley's murder had propelled the vice president into such high responsibilities; so that at his swearing-in in Buffalo, President Roosevelt made clear, in the interest of stability during a national crisis, that he meant to carry out his predecessor's program unchanged.

But the month that followed that hasty ceremony on Delaware Avenue revealed differences between the slain statesman and the public servant who succeeded him. As a child, Teedie Roosevelt had learned from his father to improve every half-hour he lived with work or vigorous play; don't waste a minute. That may sound overwrought, but it appears to be pretty much the way Theodore Roosevelt lived his life. People gaped in amazement. William Dean Howells, in the company of Roosevelt several years further along, staggered off from a breakfast with the former president during which he had witnessed "the wonder of his zest for everything. He is so strenuous that I am faint thinking of him. No man over forty has the force to meet him without nervous prostration." The Colonel seemed never to tire, at breakfast or any other time. Gifford Pinchot, who knew him well, remarked on Roosevelt's long, busy, zestful days, at the end of which, at ten or eleven in the evening, he would summon a secretary and begin dictating letters. Physically, he appeared inexhaustible. Those forty hours in the saddle at his ranch. Camping in the most dismal conditions of rain or sleet or hunger, and "Isn't this bully!" he would cry out with unfeigned joy amid the discomfort of it all. The wrestling, the boxing, the dueling, the singlestick, the jiu-jitsu—even in middle age while tenanting the White House—the woodchopping and rowboating and horseback riding with Edith at Sagamore Hill. The romping with his children during ball games on the lawn or at hide-and-seek. At White House receptions Roosevelt shook hundreds of hands, a pump of the extended arm while looking his guest straight in the eye with that flashing grin—"Dee-*lighted!*" "Dee-*lighted!*"—before pushing on. His high, frequent laughter, and the intense way he listened, the intense talk from that articulate source covering every conceivable subject. For, as Howells said, Roosevelt was interested in everything, and read—widely in science; in literature in three languages; in history modern, medieval, and ancient—at phenomenal speeds, with utter concentration, thus putting spare half hours to profitable use. Moreover, he who relished being among people wrote also, in private, extensively, devoting time to that solitary endeavor.

The religious term *charismatic* was not then in use in its present secular sense, but diction appropriate to the age expressed the force of Roosevelt's personality. When he entered a room, the effect as reported again and again was *magnetic*; it was *electric*; it was *explosive*. And it was far removed from the sedate, calm manner of William McKinley.

With all that, this new president was an intellectual, recognized as such by the intellectuals of his era, almost as brilliant as Jefferson, yet a practical politician soon called upon to make explicit his own program for governing. Article 2, Section 3, of the Constitution decrees that the chief executive "shall from time to time give to the Congress Information of the State of the Union, and recommend to their Consideration such Measures as he shall judge necessary and expedient." Presidents Washington and Adams provided that information in person; but Jefferson, thinking the pomp monarchical and regretting the time required, sent aides to deliver his annual messages for him. Subsequent presidents followed Jefferson's lead, up to and beyond Theodore Roosevelt. Woodrow Wilson, two presidents forward, revived the original custom, appearing before Congress in person to deliver his yearly State of the Union address. But Roosevelt's earliest annual message, like his subsequent ones and those of his immediate successor and nearly all of his predecessors, arrived as a printed volume—this first one of some eighty leather-bound pages—copies of which a secretary delivered and clerks read to the federal legislature.

Thus near year's end, not three months into the new president's term of office, the House and the Senate were separately attending through two and a half hours to the words of an absent Theodore Roosevelt, dated from the White House on December 3, 1901. Unlike many before him, who had delegated portions of their messages to relevant cabinet members to compose, Roosevelt had written his himself. Over preceding weeks he had dictated it, revised it, put it in his desk, and brought it forth so that his many visitors from various fields of expertise might comment on portions as appropriate. Thus the final, long document exhibits the coherence, unity, and tone of single authorship, in addition to a comprehensiveness and accuracy gained from responses by specialists both inside and outside of government.

"I have never seen an annual Message followed with so much interest and attention in the Senate," Cabot Lodge, on hand as senator from Massachusetts to hear it, assured his longtime friend Theodore afterward, "and I am told it was even more marked in the House." Roosevelt's message considers, at varying lengths, some forty different topics. It begins with a tribute to the fallen McKinley, a statesman "wholly free from the bitter animosities incident to public life," the kindliness of whose nature even his political opponents acknowledged, a man of exemplary conduct "in the most sacred and intimate of home relations" (alluding to the late husband's devotion to his invalid wife), a gallant soldier, himself from humble background and indifferent to wealth, the farmer's and the laborer's friend—bringing them prosperity and a "full dinner pail"—whose sole interest lay in doing the people's will, and whose murder has left a nation mourning, even as "we are lifted up by the splendid achievements of his life and the grand heroism with which he met his death."

It is true that at his assassination McKinley's popularity stood very high, and his reputation continued so for some years afterward, until the horrors of two world wars recalibrated the yardstick by which his era was measured. Monsters and giants of the later period overshadowed the more moderate Clevelands, Bryans, and McKinleys; but in its own time, in 1901, Roosevelt's eulogy for the slain predecessor appeared to describe that subject better than have many tributes to the recently dead before and since. And this was the stellar chief executive whom an anarchist struck down even as he was extending his hand in innocent brotherly greeting!

Moreover, Czolgosz had fired his weapon not at one president but at all presidents, "at every symbol of government." Anarchy as a political blight Roosevelt's message goes on to excoriate: a "crime against the whole human race; and all mankind should band against the anarchist." Meanwhile, Congress must take steps to keep such refuse out of the country and deport any anarchists already here. The President's message addresses as well the broader issue of immigration, because our "present immigration laws are unsatisfactory." This nation welcomes anyone "who brings here a strong body, a stout heart, a good head, and a resolute purpose to do his duty." But legislators must move to exclude, first of all, anarchists; second, the ignorant, who lack the ability "to appreciate American institutions and act sanely as American citizens"; and, third, the penniless, whose cheap labor undersells our own work force. "I regard it as necessary, with this end in view"—of upholding American wages—"to re-enact immediately the law excluding Chinese laborers and to strengthen it wherever necessary in order to make its enforcement entirely effective."

The exclusionary law against Chinese was duly reenacted, in 1902. Meanwhile, the President's message had gone on to consider among other matters the tariff, the gold standard, Hawaii, Puerto Rico, Cuba, the Philippines, the army, veterans, the civil service, the consular service, Indians, the census office, the postal service, China, Mexico, and, finally, international goodwill. Some of that follows the lines that President McKinley laid down. On Cuba, for instance: during this coming year, Cuba is to gain its independence as promised, its native government on a sound footing at last, with the island-nation's new constitution affirming what the United States had asked for (that is, demanded): "that she should stand, in international matters, in closer and more friendly relations with us than with any other power." To foster the intimacy, Congress should reduce tariff duties on imports from Cuba. Reciprocity (which would open markets for American industry) had been the subject of President McKinley's final speech, at the Pan-American Exposition on the very eve of his assassination. Tariff reciprocity—favored-nation trading—was precisely what the martyred statesman would have advocated, and what Roosevelt was urging now.

On the Philippines as well, the new president appeared to follow the course that his predecessor laid out. Two months before McKinley's murder General MacArthur had formally relinquished his military rule in favor of Judge Taft's civilian governance in Manila. Now, President Roosevelt could assure Congress that insurrection had dwindled to "an affair of local banditti and marauders," merely that, like highwaymen plaguing travelers along the roads of old. Consequently, any encouragement of such banditry from anti-imperialists here at home stands on the footing of support for highwaymen, "or on the same footing as encouragement to hostile Indians in the days when we still had Indian wars." If such behavior was disloyal and even treasonous then, it remains emphatically so now.

Much of this in Roosevelt's message sounds like what McKinley might have said had he lived, although doubtless with less fire. But on three matters the current president departed from his predecessor. For Roosevelt, full of assurance despite his youth, not at all diffident, already joyful in exercising the power of his office, was very much his own man. This wartime hero had served in municipal government, in state government, and in the federal government. All that while he had been thinking, conversing, writing, and speaking on many aspects of national life. Thus, when custom and the Constitution obliged him to set down, even during his earliest months in the White House, what his own program as president was to be, he took to the task with a will.

Roosevelt asserted (what McKinley had urged less forcefully) that in the wake of the Spanish-American War the United States stood as a world power on a rapidly changing planet. New technology, faster transportation, and improved communications had shrunk distances. Accordingly, "Whether we desire it or not, we must henceforth recognize," clerks read from his current message, "that we have international duties no less than international rights." Some of what Congress was now told addressed how the nation might best discharge its new duties, and those portions of the message bear Roosevelt's distinctive stamp, not only in their forthright expression but also in the nature of the doctrines advanced.

About the navy, for example. As assistant secretary of the navy under the peaceable McKinley, Roosevelt had fought hard for increasing the size of the fleet. As president, he pushed even harder. "The work of upbuilding the navy must be steadily continued," his message insisted. "No one point of our policy, foreign or domestic, is more important than this to the honor and material welfare, and above all to the peace, of our nation in the future." For, far from provoking war, a larger navy will be "the cheapest and most effective peace insurance." Only a substantial navy can protect the lengthening sea lanes of American commerce around the world. Moreover, a stronger navy will provide "the only means of making our insistence upon the Monroe Doctrine anything but a subject of derision to whatever nation chooses to disregard it."

The Monroe Doctrine—in Roosevelt's view "the cardinal feature" of our foreign policy—states that the "American continents are henceforth not to be considered as subjects for future colonization by any European power." For nearly eighty years that doctrine had furnished "a step, and a long step," the President emphasizes, "toward assuring the universal peace of the world by securing the possibility of permanent peace on this hemisphere." In part to defend the doctrine, the United States Navy would grow during Roosevelt's presidency from fifth largest in the world to a size—with twenty battleships at sea—second only to the Royal Navy itself. If European powers sought to interfere in the unstable affairs of Latin America, our naval vessels were there to convince them to think better of it. Of late, for instance, the Kaiser had been enlarging his German navy and prowling about in search of *Lebensraum*. Should Wilhelm II try to establish a German foothold off Venezuela, say, in defiance of the Monroe Doctrine, it would be the United States Navy that his warships in the Caribbean would have to contend with. Precisely that encounter did seem likely late in 1902, as Germany set out to recover by force debts owed to its nationals; but the mere presence of Admiral Dewey's fleet at Culebra persuaded the Kaiser to submit his dispute with Venezuela to disinterested arbitration. The German squadron withdrew, and an international crisis was averted.

Our navy did actual duty in the Caribbean a year later. At the time, Panama was a province of Colombia, although hardly an accessible one, with land passage over the Isthmus thick with scarcely penetrable jungle growth. And distant Panama—like Cuba earlier and like the Philippines— was beset with insurgencies, a number of which the United States (protecting our railroad across the Isthmus) had helped Colombia put down. But American interests shifted. At the start of 1903, Secretary of State John Hay negotiated a treaty that provided for a zone from sea to sea across the province of Panama, a zone that would remain under Colombian sovereignty but would be administered throughout its length and its six-mile width according to American laws and regulations. For this privilege the United States agreed to pay Colombia $10 million outright, and $250,000 annually for a lease that would extend through ninety-nine years.

By August, however, a less obliging régime had come to power down there. Refusing to ratify the Hay treaty as written, Colombia's senate demanded more money. President Roosevelt read the revised terms as blackmail. Soon, yet another revolt broke out in Panama, one engineered by non-Latins who stood to profit from a canal; and this time an American warship intervened at Colón and sent ashore forces that prevented Colombians from crossing the Isthmus to suppress the insurgency. It was all over in a day or two, with the blood of only one luckless Chinaman spilled. The United States recognized the independent Republic of Panama at once, on November 14, 1903, and the new sovereign nation promptly approved the treaty that Colombia had rejected and accepted the payment that Colombia had declined. Some in our Congress back home protested what they saw as executive highhandedness, interfering in the affairs of a neighbor; yet Roosevelt would come to regard his acquiring the Panama Canal zone, which allowed for beginning the decade-long task of cutting a fifty-mile channel from the Atlantic to the Pacific, as the single most important achievement of his presidency.

In that first annual message he had spoken of an isthmian canal, an engineering feat that "only a great nation can undertake with prospects of success," an interoceanic waterway of the highest value to the American people in terms both of prosperity and of national security. One does not easily picture the cautious McKinley thrusting a U.S. gunboat between a South American nation's army and the rebellion it had steamed forth to put down. Nor, for that matter, would a living McKinley, ever the friend of business, have pursued with anything like his successor's fervor yet another program—Roosevelt's second sharp departure from the past—which sought to protect America's natural resources from corporate greed.

The new president's interest in conservation was evident in his earliest message to Congress, under such headings as "Forest Conservation," "Game Protection," "Water Conservation," and "Reclamation and Irrigation." It was an interest that grew out of his childhood, his summertimes outdoors at Oyster Bay, his camping as a boy in the Adirondacks and in Maine, his study of birds and veneration of the trees they live in, his wild-game hunting later—all of it leading at last to the fruits of his ranching days. Out West the rancher was grieved by the despoliation of natural resources and the indiscriminate, exploitative destruction of animal life, whole populations of wolves, elk, bear, and buffalo driven out of the region, or in decline, or casually exterminated. Later, as governor of New York, Roosevelt took steps to arrest that decline statewide, and as president he found ways to do it nationally.

But Congress and the property interests that Congress by and large spoke for—lumbermen, ranch owners, mineowners, commercial hunters, the beef and other trusts—fought him along the way. The Constitution had charged the House of Representatives with spending the people's money; and Joe Cannon, speaker of the House, wouldn't spend one cent of it, he said, on scenery. Others protested the government's interference in what belongs to all of us. Why was the President meddling with that? Those were our lands out there, our forests, property to purchase and use as we chose. They were, yes, the young president agreed, except that "we" and "our" included Americans yet unborn, who far outnumbered the nation's current inhabitants. In their covetousness, people alive now were diverting rivers, polluting lakes, and destroying posterity's forests; and that wanton destruction would bring on erosion, and dust bowls—he predicted—and the incalculable loss of birds and wildlife, whose homes had been in those same trees and woods. Humbug, his adversaries flung back. America's forests are limitless and inexhaustible; and anyway, under McKinley and his predecessors forty-three million acres of forest had already been set aside. That was enough. Let commerce exploit the remaining resources for the people's use: lumber, meat, sport, feathers for the ladies' hats. As for Yellowstone Park, established in 1872 to lure tourists west on the new railroads, let those with initiative profit from that God-given resource. And from the Grand Canyon. And from Yosemite. Let government get out of the way and leave it to private enterprise to develop our natural treasures.

Roosevelt thought otherwise, and in support of his views pointed to man's tawdry intrusions in the Grand Canyon and at Yellowstone. So strong were the President's feelings that, during his time in the White House, he succeeded in setting aside 230 million acres of land for the public—*230 million acres!* roughly the size of California, Montana, and Michigan combined—in the form of 150 national forests, fifty-one federal game preserves and bird sanctuaries, five national parks, eighteen national monuments, and twenty-four reclamation projects that affected fourteen states, those last designed to control scarce water out West and redistribute a vital resource fairly, as well as to provide irrigation for arid lands and to erect dams to manage flooding. It was an astounding record, unprecedented and against all odds; for much of what the President did he had to do despite Congress. By executive order he brought many of those changes about, while his opponents—as he said—were doing cartwheels in protest, conducting "government by inaction" on the sidelines. They, for their part, accused the chief executive of being a usurper of power, a dictator, slippery, impulsive, unpresidential, erratic, a demagogue, a trampler on forms and precedents, and, for good measure, a hypocrite. But when, in the spring of 1903, Roosevelt set out on a two-month, 14,000-mile railroad trip across the West, crowds of villagers, ranchhands, Rough Riders, and ordinary folk—in their buggies come from afar—gathered to see and cheer on Teddy wherever and whenever his train came to a stop. Never mind that he disliked the nickname, and that no one who knew him called him that to his face—always "Theodore" from those on a first-name basis. Yet "Teddy" it was from the clamoring multitudes, and the Colonel let them shout it. For the crowds on that long, gratifying journey were unexpectedly large, cheering and grinning and reaching up to shake their hero's hand, waving and trotting after his train as it pulled out, in doing so bearing witness that, whatever the powerful might have thought of this cowboy in the White House, huge numbers of his fellow citizens adored him.

CHAPTER **Thirty-One**

Trustbusting

They loved it when their young president took on the trusts. In his first annual message to Congress, Roosevelt spoke of "the great industrial combinations which are popularly, although with technical inaccuracy, known as 'trusts.'" A *trust* (to be technically accurate) is, in law, "a fiduciary relationship [that is, one involving trust or confidence] in which an individual [the trustee] holds and manages the title to property [the estate] for the benefit of another [the beneficiary]." Think of orphans, grieving widows, or minors bequeathed a legacy. They may be unable to manage their money, so a court-appointed trustee manages it for their benefit, in trust, assuming a solemn obligation as legal guardian.

But trusts in the business world in the second half of the nineteenth century came to mean something else. The difference grew out of John D. Rockefeller's aversion to competition, which leads to unstable prices and wasteful overproduction. Rockefeller squelched competition by combination—by persuading competing oil refineries that it was in their interest to join with Standard Oil. And it was Standard Oil's success at combining with and thus removing competition that set the pattern for other huge aggregations of capital—the trusts—that the late nineteenth century, in an America bursting with new industrial power, demanded.

In a simpler past, in a domestic economy, an artisan would open his shop in the front of his house as sole *proprietor*—as a tailor or a weaver, say—and thrive. A more complicated commercial economy encouraged merchants to go into *partnership*, pooling their resources to buy a ship perhaps, to carry cargoes for trade with the mother country. But in order to amass capital for even costlier ventures, the King in Parliament chartered *corporations*, wherein shareholders risked money to sponsor exploring expeditions, or to trade for profitable spices in the Orient, or to establish colonies in the New World.

The Industrial Revolution, which began in Britain in the eighteenth century and spread to America in the early nineteenth, required ever larger amounts of capital to build factories, erect factory towns, and dig canals at an expense that sometimes lay beyond the means of proprietors and partners. Corporations—earlier a royal prerogative—now became government's public or the businessman's private way of assembling needed funds from shareholders. Form a corporation to amass, from many sources, the wherewithal to get things done: lay down rail lines, mine coal, drill for and refine oil, produce steel or whiskey in bulk, slaughter cattle from the western plains and send the meat to market. All of which costs money. In his first message to Congress, in December 1901, President Roosevelt alluded to the "highly complex industrial development which went on with ever-accelerated rapidity during the latter half of the nineteenth century" and which led to "the upbuilding of the great industrial centres" that have provided "a startling increase, not merely in the aggregate of wealth, but in the number of very large individual, and especially of very large corporate, fortunes." The patriarch C. V. S. Roosevelt of New York City—the President's grandfather—had been an individual possessed of a mercantile fortune, but the oil fortune of John D. Rockefeller was something else, and Carnegie's steel fortune something else again, both far larger. As for corporate fortunes, those amounted to truly staggering sums that the Standard Oil Company, Armour and Swift, General Electric and Westinghouse, and the newly formed United States Steel Corporation, among other industrial associations, had been enabled to accumulate through this booming postbellum era.

Corporate wealth flowing into the hands of individuals built mansions along Fifth Avenue in New York City and marble "cottages" at Newport, gleaming evidence of a gilded age that Mark Twain's pen had earlier satirized. "The process," a young president was acknowledging to Congress here at the start of the new century, "has aroused much antagonism, a great part of which is wholly without warrant. It is not true," Roosevelt instructed legislators, "that as the rich have grown richer the poor have grown poorer. On the contrary, never before has the average man, the wage worker, the farmer, the small trader, been so well off as in this country and at the present time." Of course there have been abuses of wealth; but it remains a fact, the President insisted, that large fortunes inevitably confer "immense incidental benefits upon others," and that such enterprises as those from which fortunes grow "can only exist if the conditions are such as to offer great prizes as the rewards of success."

In other words, the captains of industry *should* make huge amounts of money, because they wouldn't undertake the risks otherwise; and those risks taken have led to America's present prosperity. Yet industrialists in their success owe something back to the nation. Our laws, after all, have allowed corporations to exist, with all the benefits such structures provide management, shareholders, workers, and the general public.

The corporation is a strange creature anyway, an "artificial person" capable, just like a "natural person," of exercising rights (citizenship, equal protection, due process) conferred by the Fourteenth Amendment: buying property, making contracts, paying taxes, lobbying the government, and suing and being sued. Yet it is incorporeal, an abstraction endowed with immortality and possessed of a crucial legal right denied us real people, that of "limited liability." Limited liability protects all those whose money is invested in a corporate endeavor; for if a corporation goes bankrupt, investors' losses are limited only to what they've put in. Creditors seeking to recover the amount they're owed can't seize other assets of individual shareholders in the now bankrupt enterprise. And to be sure, without that limiting of personal liability, who with money to invest would ever enter into a bargain, whatever profits were promised beforehand, in which the investor was obliged to surrender everything—home, savings, family's economic well-being—if the enterprise went under?

In this matter of corporations lies Roosevelt's third early departure from the path pursued by presidents before him. We will conserve our natural resources. We will enlarge our navy—speak softly but carry a stick of a size proportioned to the world power that America has become. And, the President declares in this first of his annual messages, we will also regulate corporations. "Artificial bodies"—those same corporations and joint-stock companies that depend on statutory law for their existence and privileges—"should be subject to proper governmental supervision, and full and accurate information as to their operations should be made public regularly at reasonable intervals."

That had not been done before. A situation where a few men, some from the humblest of backgrounds, were able legally to gather together enormous wealth entirely untrammeled was something new under the sun, arising from the huge outlay of funds needed to fight a civil war and build the transcontinental railroads. It is true that an antitrust law was on the books already, the Sherman Anti-Trust Law of 1890, which aspired to mitigate free-market excesses by prohibiting combinations in restraint of interstate trade. You couldn't, for your own advantage, collude with others to keep trade from flowing openly and fairly across state lines. But in the administrations of McKinley and his immediate forerunners, all partial to business interests, that law had been used not to rein in corporations but

THE INFANT HERCULES AND THE STANDARD OIL SERPENTS.

Figure 31.1.   Infant Hercules and the Standard Oil Serpents. Zeus had fathered Hercules on a mortal woman. The god's jealous queen, the goddess Hera, sent serpents to kill Zeus's child in its cradle. Instead, the baby strangled the serpents. Standard Oil's H. H. Rogers is on the left, John D. Rockefeller is on the right, with Roosevelt playing the role of formidable infant. Cartoon by F. A. Nankivell in *Puck*, May 23, 1906.

to prosecute labor unions, workers conspiring to interfere with trade by walking off the job. As for employers, they owned their companies, they and the shareholders. The company—oil, coal, sugar, tobacco, beef, whatever—was property, to be managed as management saw fit. Yet here was a new man in the White House declaring: "It is no limitation upon property rights or freedom of contract to require that when men receive from government the privilege of doing business under corporate form, which frees them from individual responsibility, and enables them to call into their enterprises the capital of the public, they shall do so upon absolutely truthful representations as to the value of the property in which the capital is to be invested." No more falsifying of accounts. No more watering the stock, overvaluing its worth. No more accepting secret rebates from the railroads. No more sweetheart deals under the table or clandestine gifts of shares as bribes to legislators. Every transaction is to be transparent. "Great corporations exist only because they are created and safeguarded by our institutions, and it is therefore our right and our duty to see that they work in harmony with these institutions."

In his message to Congress, the President had maintained that "the wage worker, the farmer, the small trader" were all better off, here more than anywhere else, now more than ever before, having benefited collaterally from what our captains of industry had achieved. But not every wage worker felt that way. On May 12, 1902, only a few months after Roosevelt sent over his wintertime message to the Senate and the House, fifty thousand miners in the anthracite coal regions of Pennsylvania went out on strike for what may seem to us good reasons. The miners made four demands. They wanted their day's output of coal weighed fairly. They wanted to have their workday shortened from ten to eight hours. They wanted their very modest wages—ten dollars a week—increased by ten percent. And they wanted the mineowners to recognize their union as legitimate, management having refused to deal with the United Mine Workers at all. It was springtime when the miners struck, and they were still out in midsummer—management holding firm—and in early fall still away from the mines. They could stay out six months or six years, it didn't matter, George F. Baer, president of the Philadelphia & Reading Railway, taunted them through the press. Each year those miners brought up from underground ten million tons of anthracite coal as heating fuel for about every home, school, hospital, and factory in the Northeast; but as of October 1902—and winter in the air—they were still off the job. Baer, the owners' spokesman, defied them all. "Cripple industry, stagnate business or tie up the commerce of the world, and we will not surrender."

Although the President lacked authority to intervene, he persuaded management to meet with labor in the same room. They met on October 5, five months into the strike, at 22 Jackson Place, not far from a White House that was being thoroughly (and handsomely) renovated after years of neglect. George Baer, representing management, brought with him the rigid attitude he had shared with a correspondent sometime earlier: "The rights and interests of the laboring man will be protected and cared for—not by the labor agitators, but by the Christian men to whom God in His infinite wisdom has given the control of the property interests of the country." Those Christians whom a wise God favored included, of course, Baer himself. Let the miners dig coal and leave it to us at the top to look after their welfare. John Mitchell, thirty-two years old, revered head of their union, represented the miners. And, with winter closing in and no coal for sale, President Roosevelt was on hand to speak for the third interested party, the public.

The issues were complex. Management proved arrogantly unyielding, whereas Mitchell conducted himself on behalf of the miners with reasonableness and dignity, winning Roosevelt's admiration. Finally a panel acceptable to both sides was set up to arbitrate points at conflict. The strikers went back to work and, in the end, got all they had asked for except recognition of their union. Thus, that late fall and into the winter, amid coal-fired warmth in many a home in the frigid Northeast, the President was hailed for his mediation—his boldness in having brought the warring sides together, his patience hearing the mineowners (for all their stubbornness) out, his ingenuity in assembling a group of arbitrators whom both owners and workers would accept: in short, for his generally skillful diplomacy, which had succeeded in concluding the long strike just in time to avert a region-wide calamity.

Hardly a wonder then that, when the spring of 1903 arrived and President Roosevelt set out on his cross-country trip through the West, he was greeted enthusiastically by the ordinary folk whose interests appeared to have found their champion. All the more so because of the Northern Securities business. Although the term *trust* was applied at the time to just about any large commercial enterprise, it more precisely denoted holding companies such as United States Steel and Northern Securities. Both were recent creations of J. P. Morgan, the powerful Wall Street financier whose vast wealth had bailed out the federal government back in 1894 during a run on the gold supply of the United States Treasury. In the case of Northern Securities, Morgan, with Rockefeller's help, underwrote a merger of two warring railroad barons, both cutthroat, both fabulously wealthy: James J. Hill of the Great Northern Railroad and E. H. Harriman of the Union Pacific. Each had been striving to control access from the West to mid-America, each one determined to take over the Burlington & Quincy Railroad that would make such monopolistic dominance possible. Morgan had persuaded the rivals to settle the matter by sharing control through a holding company, this new Northern Securities, formed in November 1901, a trust in the sense that, through stock transfers, the former adversaries were entrusting their interests to a single association that would let the two of them monopolize rail traffic from San Francisco and Seattle clear to Chicago and back.

But all this had happened so fast, this new world forming of industrial colossi. Not long before, the West had been the frontier, a testing ground of individualism that Huck Finn might light out for, where the pioneer in his sod hut scrabbled a lonely living out of semiarid soil. Not an easy life, yet a man was his own boss out there, a proprietor on his homestead. Now, increasingly, such a livelihood looked like a relic. Speculators had bought up much of the land anyway; and people nowadays were more likely employees, gone to work for the corporations: workers for wages, managers for a salary, with the owner somewhere far off beyond appeal, his directors and company lawyers making decisions behind closed doors in a distant city. And the rich were so much richer now, and there was more hard feeling among strangers, too—between management and labor, white collar and blue collar, skilled and unskilled, native and immigrant—and more lawlessness, and long hours away from the family doing somebody else's bidding at mines, factories, stockyards, or slaughterhouses. Or working on the railroad, with more shops run out of business and shuttered, more physical ugliness amid the new industrial grime.

In late February 1902, President Roosevelt instructed his attorney general, Philander Knox, to bring suit to break up this latest holding company, this Northern Securities merger. It was the first such action by government against a trust, and it left the capitalists bewildered and angry. Why was he doing it? J. P. Morgan hurried with his entourage to Washington to find out. Morgan's banker father had been a friend of Roosevelt's father, cofounders of New York's Museum of Natural History. The powerful financier now challenged the President: "If we have done something wrong, send your man to my man, and they can fix it up"—presumably Attorney General Knox to, say, Robert Bacon, high in the councils of the Morgan empire and a Harvard classmate and friend of Roosevelt's. The attorney general himself was on hand for the meeting. "We don't want to fix it up," Knox told Mr. Morgan; "we want to stop it." The financier frowned. "Are you going to attack my other interests? The steel trust and the others?" Certainly not, the President reassured him, unless, Roosevelt added, "they have done something that we regard as wrong."

But of the many trusts, why pick on Northern Securities? By engaging in interstate commerce, the far-flung railroad merger had made itself subject to the Sherman Anti-Trust Act; and the ranchers and cattlemen who were among the monopoly's principal customers were of the sort whom the ex-rancher Roosevelt knew firsthand. Moreover, Northern Securities had been set up recently enough to fall within this president's tenure. Now, through controlling all rail traffic across northwestern America, its directors would be able to set rates as the trust saw fit, favor this shipper over that, crush any competition that might be bold enough to mount a challenge, and profit in every other way that vast size encouraged. The justice department filed its suit on March 10; and almost exactly two years later, on March 14, 1904, the Supreme Court finally ruled, in a five-to-four decision, for the government. The huge rail network was broken down into smaller railroads, in what was hailed as a signal victory for the public.

It was the first of forty-three suits that the justice department brought against trusts in President Roosevelt's years in the White House. So the crowds of ordinary folk out West would be cheering Teddy on his tour in the spring of 1903 for his trustbusting, as for his conservation measures and for his settling of the coal strike just before the start of the winter now ending. But it was more than that, more than that people seemed to be getting the Square Deal the President promised them. The man was exuberant, exciting, not afraid of a scrap. And he departed from the expected: the first president to go down in a submarine, the first (albeit after he left office) to go up in an airplane, the first president while in the White House to leave the country, photographed in the cabin of a great steam shovel digging at the canal in Panama. He was the first to call the press in, meeting daily with a group of reporters who were not allowed to quote him directly but were answered with a candor that kept his doings in the papers. Cartoonists loved him: you drew merely the upswept brim of a Rough Riders hat above spectacles and a bushy mustache and a great toothy grin and set the result in perpetual motion. For the man seemed always in motion. He was invited on a hunting trip to Mississippi late in 1902, others of the party out of respect declining to shoot until the President had fired. Only, Roosevelt could find nothing to shoot at. Some in the party rustled around and finally came up with a scrawny bear, put a rope around its neck, then summoned the Colonel. At the scene, the President flatly refused to harm such a creature. A cartoonist back East got wind of it and drew a cartoon that delighted the homefolks: the woods, the big-eared bear, a flunky holding the rope, and Roosevelt with back turned, rifle down, arm outstretched, palm raised to shun the kill: "Drawing the line in Mississippi." A shrewd New Jersey toymaker promptly turned the bear into a cuddly stuffed animal, marketed it, and thus launched the Teddy Bear on a lucrative voyage that is still in progress, no end in sight.

Always now there seemed to be things going on and so much getting done in the White House, its tireless tenant unlike any of the mansion's earlier, stuffier occupants. In the spring of 1902 alone: the antitrust suit filed against Northern Securities, Cuba's independence proclaimed, Crater Lake designated a national park, the National Reclamation Act signed, which set up the first of twenty-four irrigation projects out West. That summer: negotiations with Colombia entered into over the Panama Canal. In the fall: a way devised out of the anthracite coal strike, followed by a hunting trip to Mississippi that returned with the trophy of an imperishable plush bear. In early 1903: the Kaiser backing down before Roosevelt's big naval stick that ended Germany's blockade of Venezuela. A border dispute between Alaska and Canada in the gold-bearing regions of the Yukon amicably and favorably settled. A new department of commerce and labor authorized, as the President had urged Congress to do in his first State-of-the-Union message. The army made more efficient, with the office of chief of staff established—another of the message's recommendations. The Elkins Act signed, at long last prohibiting railroads from secretly granting favored customers lower fares in the form of rebates. And, by executive order on March 14, 1903, the first national wildlife refuge created, on Florida's Pelican Island. So much the administration appeared to have achieved already, Roosevelt meeting with the press daily to keep his public informed of it all. And more than any president before him, he was reveling in his new job, in an office already greatly strengthened (to Congress's annoyance). Thus with a light heart, on the first of April 1903, this young chief executive had set forth to spend the next couple of months out West, camping with John Burroughs at Yellowstone and John Muir at Yosemite, stopping in Evanston and Osceola and Los Angeles and Santa Fe and dozens of other western cities, towns, and sites—in the Badlands, under the Sequoias, alongside the Grand Canyon—seeing much of it for the first time and heartened throughout by the plaudits of fellow citizens gathered at train stops to cheer him along his way.

CHAPTER Thirty-Two

Our Life Is Wrecked

Mark Twain was as susceptible as anybody to the twenty-sixth president's charm. "Mr. Roosevelt is one of the most likable men that I am acquainted with," Clemens recorded in his *Autobiography* in January 1906, for people a century later to come upon and read. Moreover, because of his "joyous ebullitions of excited sincerity," as the humorist chose to put it, this current holder of the office was "the most popular human being that has ever existed in the United States." So said a contemporary who himself may be the most popular human being who has ever existed in the United States. Yet whatever Samuel L. Clemens thought of Theodore Roosevelt as a person—and there were reasons to think very highly of him: the man's incorruptibility, his intellect, his boundless curiosity, his sense of fairness, his sense of humor, his integrity, his love of life, his energy, his devotion to making himself useful—what Clemens thought of Roosevelt the politician was more qualified. In fact, Theodore Roosevelt in Mark Twain's private opinion was "far and away the worst President we have ever had."

What led him to think so? We note this observer's penchant for hyperbole, but he expressed a like sentiment more than once. Thus (circuitously): "it would grieve me deeply to be obliged to believe that any very large number of sane and thinking and intelligent Republicans privately admire Mr. Roosevelt and do not despise him." Years before, Roosevelt had championed the cause of civil service reform, "and in this character," Clemens writes, "he won the strong and outspoken praises of a public sick unto death of the spoils system. This was before he was President." At that earlier time Mr. Roosevelt behaved like a man of principle. Since then he had turned into a politician, and Clemens never cared for politicians. In their effort to please everybody, politicians replace principle with pragmatism and expediency; so that in this specific instance, "each act of his, and each opinion expressed, is like to abolish or controvert some previous act or expressed opinion." It was that habit of Roosevelt's—"on the one hand," "on the other"—his contradictory way of coming down noisily on both sides of an issue, that Finley Peter Dunne's Mr. Dooley, the savvy bartender of a popular *Chicago Journal* column of the time, wonderfully captured in his thick Irish brogue, regarding the President's attitude toward trusts: "Th' thrusts are heejous monsthers built up be th' enlightened intherprize iv th' men that have done so much to advance progress in our beloved country. On wan hand I wud stamp thim unther fut; on th' other hand, not so fast."

Clemens would likely relish that, from the pen of his (and Roosevelt's) good friend Dunne. There was an excess of rhetoric out of the White House politician anyway, along with all that bustle—"He flies from one thing to another with incredible dispatch"—as compared to any action taken. And sometimes the bustle appeared unpresidential, lowering the dignity of the office. Mark Twain had known presidents from Grant onward, and none had been like the current occupant, whom one citizen twenty-three years his senior was having trouble getting used to in the Executive Mansion. Indeed, for Clemens, this present tenant was the Tom Sawyer of American politics: "still only fourteen years old after living half a century; he takes a boy's delight in showing off; he is always hugging something or somebody—when there is a crowd around to see the hugging and envy the hugged." But so much of Roosevelt's talk sounded overblown. The Colonel, for instance, was still bragging about San Juan Hill, whereas Napoleon would have contented himself with jotting the skirmish down on his shirt cuff so as not to forget it. And that Mighty Hunter pose, the trophies on display. "Joe," Twichell's old friend exploded at one exasperated moment in 1905, "even the jelly McKinley was a man, compared with this kitten that masquerades in a lion's skin."

"I took Panama," the President later boasted, "and let Congress debate that while I went ahead and built the canal." His bellicose gunboat diplomacy did take the Isthmus, and Roosevelt saw to it that American interests remained firmly ensconced in the Philippines, too, in Puerto Rico, in Cuba, in Hawaii, and in Guam—and he was collecting the customs in Santo Domingo to boot. In fact, America's new colonialism lay at the heart of the anti-imperialist Clemens's antipathy toward his president, because of what appeared to be a thorough betrayal of the nation's earlier ideal of non-entanglement in foreign lands and quarrels. That, and the ridiculous hunting, and Roosevelt's incessant war talk. "I think the President is clearly insane in several ways," was the private opinion of this (briefly)

Confederate militia lieutenant of 1860, "and insanest upon war and its supreme glories." Yet the very pugnacity that, to Clemens's mind, helped make Roosevelt so bad a president made him "also the most admired and most satisfactory" leader for a nation filled with blustering pride in its new empire and bent on endowing the chief advocate of that empire with a popularity all the more galling for being misdirected.

Another, more personal reason strengthened Mark Twain's dislike of Roosevelt as chief executive. In all of Clemens's time with Henry Huttleston Rogers, and after all that Rogers had done for him, the Standard Oil magnate asked finally no more than two small favors of his friend. One came early, back in 1894, when he wondered whether Mark Twain might say a few words at the dedication of a town hall that the philanthropist had presented as a gift to Fairhaven. "Mr. Rogers, do you think there is anything I could do for you that I wouldn't do" was Clemens's reply; and of course he was on hand in Rogers's hometown to deliver fitting remarks that February when the new hall opened.

The second favor came in the form of a letter from Rogers dated more than seven years later, on December 26, 1901. A staff writer at *McClure's* magazine, Ida M. Tarbell, had been preparing a history of the Standard Oil Company. "It would naturally be supposed," Standard's vice president observed, "that any person desiring to write a veritable history, would seek for information as near original sources as possible. Miss Tarbell has not applied to the Standard Oil Company, nor to anyone connected with it, for information on any subject." On the contrary, Rogers had reason to think that the reporter was talking exclusively with Standard's many enemies. Would Clemens call this to Mr. McClure's attention? His friend did speak promptly to an official at the magazine, and the upshot was that Ida Tarbell conducted a number of candid interviews with Hell-Hound Rogers himself, who emerges from her classic two-volume *The History of the Standard Oil Company* (1904) all but unscathed. Her treatment of the company that Rogers was serving, however, is unsparing in its depiction of Standard's utterly ruthless cannibalizing of every phase of oil production and sale. By means of rebates, spies, sabotage, price-cutting, and offshoot companies posing as Standard's enemies and as friends of the competitors they were out to destroy, Rockefeller's agents demolished whoever refused to join them, until at last a single oil trust monopolized 90 percent of the industry. Tarbell's meticulous exposure of the company's thuggish methods added to a prevailing sense that of all the trusts, Standard Oil was the most malevolent, and of all the tycoons, none was more loathsome than John D. Rockefeller.

Yet, as Mark Twain noted, there had never been a strike at Standard, because (he said) the pious Rockefeller treated his workers decently; and if the company paid shareholders what sounded like astronomical dividends, those appeared more reasonable in proportion to the company's total worth. In truth, the Missouri democrat entertained a certain sympathy for the capitalist point of view. He had founded a company himself—the Charles L. Webster Publishing Company, which had thrived mightily for a while. And he had made his calculations concerning the fortune to be earned from the Paige typesetter, a fortune big enough to turn Mark Twain himself into a tycoon. Moreover, an admiring Clemens had spent hours in the nineties in Mr. Rogers's office at 26 Broadway, lounging on a sofa behind a screen, smoking his cigars and marveling within earshot as Standard's vice president dealt coolly and brilliantly with the host of complex business matters that reached his desk, including Mark Twain's own tangled financial affairs. Now here was President Roosevelt railing on the one hand against the trusts—according to Clemens, "The hostility to the corporations was brought to its height by President Roosevelt's attitude toward them"—and on the other hand labeling those (by implication Miss Tarbell, and Lincoln Steffens on municipal crime, and Upton Sinclair with his exposé of the horrors of the meatpacking industry) whose writings, by uncovering current political, social, and industrial abuses, were stirring up class resentment along with hatred of the productive rich. Such writers were muckrakers: "you may recall the description of the Man with the Muck-rake, the man who could look no way but downward with the muck-rake in his hands; who was offered a celestial crown for his muck-rake, but who would neither look up nor regard the crown he was offered, but continued to rake to himself the filth of the floor." The words are from a speech that Roosevelt delivered in April 1906, and the allusion is to one of his favorite books, John Bunyan's *The Pilgrim's Progress* (1678). As for muckraking, yes indeed, those investigative reporters agreed, there was muck aplenty to be raked in the America of the early twentieth century if our political and industrial stables were to be cleansed of rampant corruption. The writers doing the raking were proud to appropriate the name that Bunyan's allegory had meant as disparagement. Tarbell and the others gloried in being muckrakers; and even the President would go on in his speech to acknowledge the many evils of the time that needed exposure. "I hail as a benefactor every writer or speaker, every man who, on the platform, or in book, magazine, or newspaper, with merciless severity makes such attack"—on economic and political wrongdoing—"provided always that he in his turn remembers that the attack is of use only if it is absolutely truthful."

That would have grated on Mark Twain's ears as more of Roosevelt's blather, his elaboration of the obvious while articulating cautionary points that pretty much had it both ways. Anyhow, by 1903, much of Clemens's time was taken up with matters other than politics. Ever since his wife's nearly fatal attack the previous summer at York Harbor, Maine, Livy's health had been the author's first concern. For three months that fall of 1902 he had been kept out of the patient's bedroom—in Maine and back at Riverdale—Livy's heart adjudged so delicate that her husband's intense presence might jeopardize her very life. So he wrote her loving notes instead; and only in the new year, toward winter's end, did her health recover sufficiently that he was allowed visits of five minutes on days when she felt better. By the spring (President Roosevelt's great western trip in progress), the visits together of husband and wife were increased to twenty minutes a couple of times a day; and when summer came, Livy's health had improved enough that Mr. and Mrs. Clemens could set off for Elmira. They would be leaving Riverdale-on-Hudson for good, the doctors having cautioned against submitting the patient to another New York winter. In the fall they meant to return to what they remembered as Italy's milder, sunnier climate; but first, Mr. Rogers's yacht steamed up the Hudson once more, and the Clemenses from the foot of their garden got aboard July 1, to sail on the *Kanawha* down to Hoboken. From there they traveled by rail to Elmira and Quarry Farm and Livy's sister's family.

It happened that two weeks before they left Riverdale, America, all unknowing, had taken a great lurch forward toward the future that we in our turn live in, when a mechanic, machinist, and builder of racing cars, on June 16, 1903, got his assembly plant operating in a warehouse on Mack Avenue, Detroit. This new Ford Motor Company employed twelve workers hired to fulfill the owner's goal of assembling automobiles that were both strong and cheap. The Model N would come along soon, and five years later, in 1908—"O brave new world"!—the Model T. (A curious coincidence arrived as well: even as the market for oil-based kerosene was shrinking, replaced by Edison's ever more popular electric lights, simultaneously a new market developed for oil, and a big one, with those Model Ts and their rivals demanding ever more gasoline.) Meanwhile, Livy visiting Elmira in the summer of 1903 for what would be a last time had been eating well, Clemens wrote to his friend Twichell, sleeping some, "is mostly very gay, not very often depressed; spends all day on the porch, sleeps there a part of the night, makes excursions in carriage and in wheel-chair; and, in the matter of superintending everything and everybody, has resumed business at the old stand."

August arrived; and the monkeys in Colombia (as an angry President Roosevelt referred to Colombians privately) rejected the treaty agreed on earlier with the United States, which would have allowed a canal to be dug in Panama. And in Elmira, in his octagonal hilltop study above Quarry Farm, high above the Chemung Valley, Clemens smoked, wrote, read his newspapers, and brooded. When October came, the family proceeded by rail to New York City.

Henry Huttleston Rogers had done them another service by the time they got there. Rogers negotiated with Harper & Brothers, and the outcome was to assure Mark Twain a fortune for the rest of his days. Clemens signed the contract on October 22, 1903. Its terms *"guarantee* me," the signatory may be pardoned for gloating, "$25,000 a year for 5 years, but they will yield twice as much [as] that for many a year, if intelligently handled." Computing on the basis of the consumer price index, $25,000 in 1903 came to $629,000 in 2010. "Four months ago I could not have believed that I could ever get rid of my 30 years' slavery to the pauper American Publishing Co—a worthless concern which always kept a blight upon the books." But Harper's had acquired all rights to the humorist's titles held by that other company, so from this time forward it could issue sets of uniform editions complete, along with any new works that came from Mark Twain's pen.

That October, his now exclusive publisher gave its star author a farewell dinner. Among other notables, William Dean Howells attended. Howells presumed his dear friend was leaving New York for good. "Clemens, I suppose, will always live at Florence, hereafter," he wrote to his sister. "He goes first for his wife's health, and then because he can't stand the nervous storm and stress here. He takes things intensely hard, and America is too much for him." Indeed, two days after signing the contract with Harper's, Mark Twain sailed for Europe: Clemens, his wife, his daughters, Katy Leary, and a trained nurse, a party of six aboard the elegant new *Irene*, their staterooms sunlit on what turned out to be a noisy promenade deck. Arrived at Florence, the location that Livy had chosen from fond remembrances, the family was soon set up in a villa on a hillside four miles out of town. Clemens's secretary from Riverdale, Miss Lyon, and her mother joined them a couple of weeks later.

November came, and revolution on the Isthmus in Central America, and on the fourteenth, the United States recognized the new Republic of Panama, which promptly signed a treaty that cleared the way for a canal to be dug at last. December arrived—the Clemenses' Italian winter proving unseasonably wet and cold, the villa disagreeable, its landlady obnoxiously on the premises. And back home the United States, again without knowing it, took another lurch forward into a future that has become the world's present. On isolated sands amid strong steady winds over the Kill Devil Hills near Kitty Hawk, North Carolina, on December 17, 1903, two bicycle builders from Dayton, Ohio, managed at last to get their powered aircraft twenty feet aloft for twelve seconds, flying it a distance of forty yards. Orville Wright had been at the controls; and soon after, on a fourth flight that day, his brother, Wilbur, stayed in the air over 265 yards for just under a full minute. Five witnesses gazed in awe, scarcely believing.

Six months later, on June 5, 1904, at the Villa Reale di Quarto near Florence, Olivia Clemens died. "And now she is at rest, poor worn heart! Joe," the baffled, distraught widower wrote three days later to his dear friend back in Hartford, "she was so lovely, so patient—never a murmur at her hard fate; yet—but I *can't* put her sufferings on paper, it breaks any heart to think of them. She sat up in bed 6 months, night & day, & was always in bodily misery, & could get but little sleep, & then only by resting her forehead against a support—think of those lonely nights in the gloom of a taper, with Katy sleeping, & with no company but her fearsome thought & her pathetic longings; it makes my heart bleed, it makes me blaspheme, to think of the gratuitous devilishness of it."

For nearly two years, since the awful attack at York Harbor in August 1902, the patient had suffered more or less continually, dreading the likely way—by strangulation—that death would come. "Five times in 4 months she went through that choking horror for an hour & more, & came out of it white, haggard, exhausted, & quivering with fright." In the immediate aftermath of his wife's death, which in the end arrived quietly—she "chatting cheerfully only a moment before," her heart suddenly failing, Katy at her side—Clemens had written to his friend Rogers, on the sixth: "Our life is wrecked; we have no plans for the future; she always made the plans, none of us was capable. We shall carry her home and bury her with her dead, at Elmira. Beyond that, we have no plans. The children must decide." Livy in life had done everything for the family: attended to the daughters, to the servants, to the entertaining, to travel arrangements, supervised the packing, made all the domestic decisions, approved all her husband's writing before publication. He was utterly adrift without her.

To Howells Clemens confided, "It was too pitiful, these late weeks, to see the haunting fear in her eyes, fixed wistfully upon mine, & hear her say, as pleading for denial & heartening, 'You don't think I am going to die, do you? Oh, I don't want to die.' For she loved her life, & so wanted to keep it."

In late June 1904, the surviving Clemenses sailed with their heavy burden, dead at fifty-eight, out of Naples bound for home. During the voyage the grieving husband wrote in his notebook: "In these 34 years we have made many voyages together, Livy dear, and now we are making our last. You down below & lonely. I above with the crowd and lonely." Many were grieving with him, messages pouring in "from shop-girl, postman, & all ranks in life, down to the humblest." President Roosevelt sent his condolences, instructing officials to pass Mark Twain's formidable luggage (including sixteen large trunks, as it turned out) through customs untouched, undelayed. At the New York piers Joe Twichell waited, and Charles Langdon—he who had been an eighteen-year-old aboard the *Quaker City* with a miniature of his sister that had captivated Mark Twain: Charley, Clara and Jean's Uncle Cholly. The sad procession boarded a private railroad car bound for Elmira. There, in her father's house, the Reverend Joseph Twichell had married Livy and Sam thirty-four years earlier, "& on the spot where she stood as a happy young bride then, she lay in her coffin seven days ago," the widower recorded, "& over it Twichell spread his hands in benediction & farewell, & in a breaking voice commended her spirit to the peace of God."

A month after the funeral Clemens wrote to his sister-in-law, Livy's sainted sister, to Dear Susy, whom he could address intimately: "Never a day passed that she did not say, with emphasis & enthusiasm, 'I love you so. I just worship you.' They were always undeserved"—those heartfelt affections—"they were always a rebuke, but she stopped my mouth whenever I said it, though she knew I said it honestly." And he goes on: "I know something, & I get some poor small comfort out of it: that what little good was in me I gave to her to the utmost—full measure, the last grain & the last ounce—& poor as it was, it was my very best, & far beyond anything I could have given to any other person that ever lived. It was poverty, but it was all I had, & so it stood for wealth, & she so accounted it."

A husband's anguish writhes on the page, and the remorse that never rested. Years before, way back in 1858, Orion had written that his brother's "capacity of enjoyment and his capacity of suffering are greater than mine"—far greater than most of ours are; and just the other month Howells had told his sister that Clemens took things "intensely hard." Indeed he did. "I try not to think of the hurts I gave her," the widower wrote to Susan Crane now, "but oh, there were so many, so many!"

PART Five

CHILDREN

CHAPTER Thirty-Three

A Seventieth Birthday

O ne reason that Mrs. Clemens's husband had been denied entry into her sickroom over so many days at York Harbor, at Riverdale, and later at the Villa Reale di Quarto in Italy arose from his compulsion to dwell on remorse for injuries he had done the family. Her doctors insisted that nothing be uttered that might agitate their patient's fragile heart; yet throughout his life Clemens was assailed by irrepressible feelings such as the following, about which he wrote to Livy earlier, during one of his absences dealing with business in America back in the 1890s. "Late last night I was smitten suddenly with shame & remorse in remembering how I forced you to drive through the thunder & lightning & rain"—in Elmira, passing the Gleasons's hydropathic sanitarium on their way up to Quarry Farm, and Livy in terror of storms—"that night that you were so frightened & wanted to stop at the Water Cure. I have remembered that brutality many a time since, & cursed myself for it. It is at times like these that I also visit with deep & honest curses the memory of those various people who plucked me from the water when I was a lad & drowning"—in Hannibal, nine different times as he remembered it, a child floundering in Bear Creek and the Mississippi. Better to have died right then. Such a one, seeing his beloved wife piteously bedridden in Florence in 1904—pallid sufferer propped up day, night, day, night, in order to keep from strangling—couldn't have stayed mute about his shame for the part he played in causing it. Thus for much of the time during the patient's last months he was barred from the sickroom. Until finally, on the night Mrs. Clemens died, her husband did return to linger at the bedside where lay her remains, keeping vigil in the small hours that ended only after he "looked for the last time upon that dear face—and was full of remorse for things done and said in the 34 years of married life that hurt Livy's heart."

Figure 33.1.   Clemens and Clara returning to America aboard the *Prince Oscar*, July 1904.

Courtesy of the Mark Twain Project, The Bancroft Library, University of California, Berkeley.

His older daughter had her own reasons for feeling guilty. Earlier at the villa there had been a scene, about which Clara wrote to a friend back home. "I don't know why I was so suddenly seized but at any rate I was seized by something & began to scream . . ." This was in February, four months before her mother's death, the nurse who had accompanied the family to Italy having returned to America by then, so that the task of caring for the patient fell entirely on Katy Leary and on Clara herself. Under the strain the daughter lost control and "began to scream & curse & knocked down the furniture Etc. Etc. 'till everyone of course came running & in my father's presence I said I hated him hated my mother hoped they would all die & if they didn't succeed soon I would kill them, well on and on for more than an hour, I don't know all I said but mother hearing the noise & being told that I was overwrought got a heart attack and as you can imagine today I can hardly meet anyone's eyes." The young woman at twenty-nine was highstrung in any case, as was the whole family. Earlier Sam went so far as to wonder whether he and Livy, both hypersensitive, had been right to have children at all. Now, at her mother's death, Clara collapsed utterly. As soon as the body was removed, she fell into Livy's empty bed and lay there a long while before taking to her own room in the villa and remaining for four days all but motionless, without speaking, without eating, unable to cry. Her father feared for her sanity. A photograph of the two of them survives, homeward bound on board the *Prince Oscar* out of Naples. Clara on the deck chair with her cat in her lap sits enshrouded in black: abundant black clothing, large black hat, thick black veil entirely covering her face and falling down over her shoulders. Clemens sits beyond her, staring bemused at Miss Lyon's intrusive camera. Once back in Elmira at the private obsequies (the father doubtful that his older daughter should have attended the funeral at all), Clara had to be held back at Woodlawn Cemetery so that she wouldn't leap into her mother's open grave.

The Gilder children were friends of the Clemenses' daughters; it was to Dorothea Gilder that Clara had written of her hour-long tantrum at the villa last February. Richard Watson Gilder, Dorothea's father, was editor-in-chief of the *Century* magazine, in the pages of which had appeared articles by both Mark Twain and Theodore Roosevelt. From Italy Clemens in his desolation had written to his friend Gilder asking whether, after their return, he and his daughters might make use of a cottage at Four Brooks Farm, the Gilders' property in the Berkshires in western Massachusetts. Thus with the burial service behind them, the bereaved took up residence at Tyringham, near Lee, at the start of their year of formal mourning.

Miss Lyon, the secretary, came along, she who had proved useful in grievous times: at the villa hurrying to Clemens with news of his wife's sudden death, at the New York piers rounding up trunks and getting them off to Elmira, throughout their ordeal sorting the correspondence pouring in. She had joined the family, in the fall of 1902, originally as Mrs. Clemens's secretary; but with the lady of the house ill, Miss Lyon's skills were redirected toward meeting the clerical needs of the husband. A woman of culture, impoverished when her father died, the attractive Isabel Lyon, forty years old, had proved to be a presentable substitute hostess for guests in the household, competent in dealing with reporters, skilled when called on to organize Mark Twain's schedule, and indefatigable playing cards through the many hours that helped Mr. Clemens pass long days in the Berkshires while his months of widowerhood dragged on. Gilder looking in recorded that "Mark, in our cottage next door, is most grim and unhappy, but full of life and abounding in scorn of a mismanaged universe."

That summer the widower did make his escape from Tyringham on several occasions by visiting in Manhattan or at Fairhaven with the

Rogerses. Clara for her part hated Four Brooks Farm and the porous walls of the cottage's tiny rooms. Within a couple of weeks she had fled to New York City herself, where she entered a sanitarium on the Upper East Side and remained—there and at another rest cure in Norfolk, Connecticut—for more than a year, declining to see her father or, for a good part of the time, read his letters or take his phone calls. Jean, who loved the country, and outdoors, and animals of all sorts, stayed in the Berkshires through the summer with Miss Lyon. The weeks proved difficult for both of them, this unfortunate younger daughter periodically afflicted with epileptic seizures. Moreover, at the end of July during a moonlit ride with young Rodman Gilder and others, Jean on her startled horse collided with a trolley (in those days when trolleys ran between towns) so forcefully that it killed the horse and hurled the rider to the ground unconscious. She suffered a torn ankle tendon as well as cuts and bruises all over her face and body, the latter alarming though mercifully superficial.

By the autumn of 1904 the young woman was well enough to accompany her father on a brief return visit to Elmira. Clemens had meanwhile leased a home for three years in New York City, at Fifth Avenue and Ninth Street, near where the family had lived earlier. With the maid Katy Leary on site, the gothic three-story structure was renovated and furnished with possessions brought down from the Hartford house, belongings out of storage for the first time in thirteen years. Katy's eyes welled up at the sight of them. Alterations moved forward over the autumn months, Clemens, Jean, and Miss Lyon residing at the Grosvenor Hotel a block away, in days that to the widower appeared unreal. He grieved that he wasn't able to recall Livy's face at will and that sometimes she slipped from his mind entirely. This close friend of Twichell's confessed to the minister that "a part of each day Livy is a dream & has never existed. The rest of it she is real, & is gone. Then comes the ache, & continues. Then comes the long procession of remorses, & goes filing by—uncountable."

All his life Sam Clemens had inflicted such scourgings on himself. As a child he managed, for reasons unclear, to assume part of the guilt for the death of an older sibling, Benjamin, gone before Sam turned seven. Later, in 1858, he blamed himself for his brother Henry's death in the steamboat explosion on the Mississippi; later still, for churlishness toward his mother, sister, and surviving brother. "My mind," he wrote those three after a visit to St. Louis in 1867, "is stored full of unworthy conduct toward Orion & toward you all," sufficient, Sam thought, to render him undeserving of their love. Still later, he felt that his negligence in 1872 had been responsible for the death of his and Livy's firstborn in Hartford, a victim before age two of diphtheria—the child's death quite unrelated to any fancied cause that the father berated himself for in having allowed little Langdon to take chill on a buggy ride two months earlier.

Friends and family remarked on Clemens's overactive conscience, Clara writing of her father's tendency to accuse himself of all sorts of "imaginary shortcomings and selfishness." Livy had agonized over it: "My dear darling child you *must not* blame yourself as you do. I love you to death, and I would rather have you for mine than all the other husbands in the world and you take as good care of me as any one could do." But as late as 1906, two years after Livy's death, Clemens in retrospective mood—and honored by then as few other Americans have been—was still able to conjure up "fifteen hundred or two thousand incidents in my life which I am ashamed of."

Meanwhile, through the dreary, guilt-ridden months of his bereavement, Mark Twain was receiving the support of a popularity grown to unprecedented size both here and abroad—and this despite his earlier anti-imperialist polemics that had ruffled then-current American political opinion. To be sure, many people continued to regard him as the nation's jester, and allowed him the jester's latitude of speech, up to and including references to our flag's being polluted in the course of the Philippine adventure. Increasingly, however, readers were taking note of Mark Twain's serious literary side. William Dean Howells had led the way in the revaluation, in a brilliant article published in the *Century* as far back as 1882. That long ago—with twenty-nine books yet to appear under Mark Twain's name in his lifetime—Howells was extolling the fact that the Missourian's writings contained "not an ungenerous line, but always, on the contrary, a burning resentment of all manner of cruelty and wrong." Nor had the humorist ever asked his readers "to join him in laughing at any good or really fine thing." Nothing he wrote could occasion a response so unfeeling. Indeed, an ethical intelligence underlay all of this author's humor; on that point Howells was insistent. "I warn the reader that if he leaves out of the account an indignant sense of right and wrong, a scorn of all affectation and pretence, an ardent hate of meanness and injustice, he will come indefinitely short of knowing Mark Twain." Mere humor endures no longer than the conditions that make it intelligible: Howells suggests that his readers look back "to what amused people in the last generation; that stuff is terrible." Thus Mark Twain as phunny phellow wouldn't survive thirty years "if he were not an artist of uncommon power as well as a humorist."

Howells's early, penetrating judgment was that of a sophisticated literary sensibility, whereas the general public loved Mark for its own reasons. To the multitude he was not only the quintessential American.

He wrote wonderfully readable novels and stories. He was lively and inexhaustibly amusing. He articulated folk wisdom in brisk, fresh, memorable ways. He paid his debts fully, at whatever cost. And he made the nation proud through being honored, one newspaper put it, "by so many countries, and under so many flags, the man who eased the world's pain with laughter, and who never penned a line to bring the sting or blush of shame to any reader's cheek."

People wrote to tell him how much he meant to them, and sometimes among the effusions arrived a letter of deep perception. Thus from Plainfield, New Jersey, to Riverdale in the year before Livy's death, had come an expression of appreciation dated August 4, 1903, from a Samuel Merwin. These past couple of years Mr. Merwin had been reading the great writers, "the best we have"—among them Malory, Spenser, Shakespeare, Boswell, Carlyle—in order to account for their greatness. Each, he concluded, "brought to his time some new blood, new ideas,—turned a new current into the stream." The painstaking writer is always with us and is always taken seriously by his fellow authors. It is the unconventional writer who is rare—"I mean," Mr. Merwin clarified, "the honestly unconventional man, who has to express himself in his own big way because the conventional way isn't big enough, because he needs room and freedom." The present era offers its share of more or less conventional authors, figures of dignity and reputation; but not one can be admired unreservedly, "not one whose ideas seem based on the deep foundation of all true philosophy,—except Mark Twain."

Merwin hopes his letter isn't an impertinence. Yet nowhere except in *Life on the Mississippi, Huckleberry Finn,* and *A Connecticut Yankee* has he found, among books written in his lifetime, claims on his unreserved interest, on his admiration, and above all on his *feelings*; and so he has been compelled to write to the author of those books. "I like to think," this reader concludes presciently, "that 'Tom Sawyer' and 'Huckleberry Finn' will be looked upon, fifty or a hundred years from now, as the picture of buoyant, dramatic, *human* American life. I feel, deep in my own heart, pretty sure that they will be. They won't be looked on then as the work of a 'humorist' any more than we think of Shakespeare as a humorist now." Not to make comparisons; but "Shakespeare was a humorist and so, thank Heaven! is Mark Twain. And Shakespeare plunged deep into the deep, sad things of life; and so, in a different way (but in a way that more than once has brought tears to my eyes) has Mark Twain." Still, it isn't a resemblance to other writers that matters here. Mark Twain's books strike so deep "because they've brought something really new into our literature—new, yet old as Adam and Eve and the Apple." That is what distinguishes the little group of great writers from the vast herd of medium and small ones. And of this Mr. Merwin (an aspiring novelist himself, in his late twenties) feels certain: "to the young man who hopes, however feebly, to accomplish a little something, some day, as a writer, the one inspiring example of our time is Mark Twain."

Moved, Clemens answered in a single sentence, on August 16, 1903.

> Dear Mr. Merwin,—What you have said has given me deep pleasure— indeed I think no words could be said that could give me more. Very sincerely yours,
>
> S. L. Clemens.

Public tributes joined the private ones as the widower's formal mourning ended. Late in November 1905, a year and a half after Livy's death, Samuel Clemens turned seventy. Colonel George Harvey, editor of the *North American Review* and president of Harper & Brothers, honored his premier author with a birthday party. It occurred not on the birthdate, the thirtieth, which fell on Thanksgiving Day that year, but rather on the following

Figure 33.2.   At Mark Twain's seventieth birthday celebration, December 5, 1905. Twichell is third from the left; H. H. Rogers is seated farthest right.
Courtesy of the Mark Twain House & Museum, Hartford.

Tuesday, the fifth of December, at eight in the evening at Delmonico's, the oldest and even that late the best and most fashionable restaurant in New York City. On Twenty-Sixth Street, in the parlor beside the great Red Room, 170 guests gathered in timely fashion, many of them distinguished authors themselves. A forty-piece orchestra struck up a march, and Clemens, accompanying Mary E. Wilkins Freemen, led the diners to their places. At his own table were seated, among others, Henry Huttleston Rogers and the Reverend Joseph Twichell, as well as the Canadian poet Bliss Carman and the esteemed editor Henry Mills Alden. Elsewhere around the twenty tables, the dignitaries included George Ade, Andrew Carnegie, John Burroughs the naturalist, Frances Hodgson Burnett (all luminaries, all well known then), Gelett Burgess, the African-American fiction writer Charles Chesnutt, the young poet and short-story writer Willa Cather, Finley Peter Dunne, Richard Watson Gilder, Rupert Hughes, Julian Hawthorne, Edwin Markham, Owen Wister, and William Dean Howells. The menu was typically elaborate and expansive, allowing time for guests at each table to be led in turn to an anteroom to be photographed for a memorial album, each invitee presented with a plaster-of-Paris bust twelve inches high of the guest of honor. Toasts and tributes abounded. Speakers read messages received from a distance, from Mark Twain's admirers in England, for instance: James M. Barrie, Gilbert Chesterton, Sir Arthur Conan Doyle, W. S. Gilbert, Thomas Hardy, Rudyard Kipling, and George Meredith among them. The President of the United States sent a letter, which the gathering received with enthusiasm. "I wish," it said in part, "it were in my power to be at the dinner held to celebrate the seventieth birthday of Mark Twain," a citizen "whom all Americans should delight to honor," for writings that none but an American could have composed, yet of "that small list which are written for no particular country, but for all countries, and which are not merely written for the time being, but have an abiding and permanent value. May he live long, and year by year may he add to the sum of admirable work that he has done. Sincerely yours, Theodore Roosevelt."

Much that memorable evening met with approval and prolonged applause, but nothing was received more warmly than Mark Twain's speech itself. For in time Colonel Harvey had stood as host to introduce William Dean Howells, whose pleasant duty it was at last to present the guest of honor. The hour was late, but the diners kept their places. Miss Clemens was there, and Clemens's nephew Samuel Moffett, and Livy's niece Mrs. Loomis—Charley Langdon's daughter—and Albert Bigelow Paine, author of a recent biography of Mark Twain's friend the late cartoonist Thomas Nast. With appropriate wit and grace Howells presented his dear friend

Clemens to the assembly; and amid a near riot of well-oiled cheering—enough (as the *Times* next morning reported) to satisfy anyone's vanity—Mark Twain rose, unabashed.

His words were received with rapture, with laughter where the audience should be laughing and with tears at the moving end. In truth, the speech would have been a joy to hear. More than a century later our eyes pass over its phrases hardly registering the drawl within them, the speaker's sly straightfaced delivery, the twinkle in the voice, the telling pauses, as he described for those discriminating, affectionate listeners his very first birthday dinner, so primitive by contrast to this one, the cradle not even whitewashed and neighbors in the little frontier village where nothing ever happened gawking at the curiosity of this rare naked newcomer in their midst. Those grim provincials offered the infant not a single compliment. "Well, I stood that as long as—," the speaker feigned indignation; "well, you know I was born courteous and I stood it to the limit. I stood it an hour," he said, "and then the worm turned. I was the worm; it was my turn to turn, and I turned. I knew very well the strength of my position; I knew that I was the only spotlessly pure and innocent person in that whole town, and I came out and said so. And they could not say a word. It was so true. They blushed; they were embarrassed. Well that was the first after-dinner speech I ever made. I think it was after dinner."

We busy readers of a later time hurry over the sentences; but if we had been there, in high comfort in the warm, select atmosphere, well-fed, well-wined, relaxed and responsive, we would have relished every drawled word and every pause—before "and I came out and said so," for instance, pause held just long enough; and, letting the laughter die down, before "I *think* it was after dinner"—and would have been laughing heartily along with the others. Without notes, Mark Twain went on to unfurl the eloquent remainder of his speech, memorized as speeches often were back then, his invariably delivered in a conversational manner, as here while instructing his listeners how they too might live to the advanced age of seventy. Essentially they must do what he hadn't done, who had smoked since he was nine or ten. All his life he had avoided exercise. He had had coffee and bread for breakfast, skipped lunch, and settled for the one meal a day at suppertime. He had gone to bed when there was nobody left to sit up with, and got up next day no sooner than he had to. But his listeners mustn't try those methods. They worked for him, but what works for one would be the death of others.

Seventy years, though! He pauses, nearing his conclusion, to repeat the phrase in wonder: "It is the Scriptural statute of limitations. After that, you owe no active duties; for you the strenuous life is over"—alluding to President Roosevelt's recipe for a meaningful existence. For you at seventy, you've served your term, are mustered out, emancipated, an honorary member of the republic. Compulsions aren't for you any longer, or "any bugle-call but 'lights out.' You pay the time-worn duty bills if you choose, or decline if you prefer—and without prejudice—for they are not legally collectable."

For instance, there's no more need to plead a previous engagement, that plea that "in forty years has cost you so many twinges." You can put that aside forever; "on this side of the grave you will never need it again. If you shrink at the thought of night and winter,"—and here surely the room would have grown quiet, detecting behind the good humor the encroaching strain of melancholy—"and the late home-coming from the banquet and the lights and the laughter through the deserted streets—a desolation which would not remind you now, as for a generation it did, that your friends are sleeping, and you must creep in a-tiptoe and not disturb them, but would only remind you that you need not tiptoe, you can never disturb them more—if you shrink at thought of these things, you need only reply, 'Your invitation honors me, and pleases me because you still keep me in your remembrance,' but I am seventy; seventy, and would nestle in the chimney-corner, and smoke my pipe, and read my book, and take my rest, wishing you well in all affection, and that when"—these final words, tomorrow's newspapers tell us, spoken in a voice quivering with emotion—"when you in your turn shall arrive at pier No. 70 you may step aboard your waiting ship with a reconciled spirit, and lay your course toward the sinking sun with a contented heart."

CHAPTER **Thirty-Four**

Susy

Publicly, Mark Twain spoke of contented hearts and reconciled spirits, although in private, Samuel Clemens's own spirit arriving at Pier 70 was anything but reconciled to a mismanaged universe; nor was his heart contented. Honors piled up, and they brought him satisfaction. Indeed, he loved compliments, could hardly get enough of them. Yet even in their abundance they proved only temporary assuagements: the numerous adulatory letters, sold-out lectures that he delivered rarely now and not for pay—merely as public benefactions—dinners where hosts exulted in his company, banquets without number. And birthdays: three years before, as another example, his publisher Colonel Harvey had sponsored a celebration at New York's Metropolitan Club on Mark Twain's sixty-seventh birthday. Newspapers dwelt on details of the fête, with some fifty guests (including the honoree's dear friends Twichell and Howells and Rogers) attending yet another set of birthday tributes.

But such evenings could go only so far in mitigating the widower's loneliness. And anyway, little was new in all that praise. As far back as twenty years ago, the pages of the magazine *The Critic* carried public salutes from notables (Oliver Wendell Holmes, Joel Chandler Harris, Frank Stockton, Charles Dudley Warner) at the fiftieth of Mark Twain's birthdays, in 1885: the semi-centennial of a public figure, *The Critic* said, who "had done more than any other man to lengthen the lives of his contemporaries by making them merrier." At that half-century signpost, the Clemenses had been thriving in their Nook Farm mansion in Hartford, with the author-publisher-inventor-investor almost frightened at the extent of his success. His youngest daughter, Jean, had turned five that summer; Clara was eleven; and Susy was thirteen. It was that eldest, in this same marvelous 1885, who had been writing, on her own and in secret, a biography of her celebrated father. Livy, finding out about it, showed what was written to her husband, then told Susy she had done so, and told her, as Clemens reminisced, "how pleased I was, and how proud. I remember that time with a deep pleasure," he remarked years afterward. "I had had compliments before, but none that touched me like this; none that could approach it for value in my eyes. It has kept that place always since. I have had no compliment, no praise, no tribute from any source"—as of this present date, February 7, 1906—"that was so precious to me as this one was and still is."

Susy Clemens's biography of Mark Twain, which commences in early 1885 and breaks off in mid-sentence in the summer of 1886, runs to some 20,000 words, no mean achievement for a child of thirteen and fourteen. It begins: "We are a very happy family! we consist of papa, mamma, Jean Clara and me. It is papa I am writing about, and I shall have no trouble in not knowing what to say about him, as he is a very striking character. Papa's appearance has been discribed many times, but very incorectly; he has beautiful curly grey hair, not any too thick, or any too long, just right"—a fine-looking man, in fact, and "a very good man, and a very funny one; he *has* got a temper but we all of us have in this family. He is the loveliest man I ever saw, or ever hope to see, and oh *so* absent minded!"

That last may suggest a kind of addled vacancy; but Clemens's mind, like those of some others thus charged, was less vacant than preoccupied from being overfilled. Nook Farm furnished unrelentingly agreeable social pleasures: neighbor friends and their children coming and going, and houseguests, and the frequent dinners, Mark between courses pacing beside the table to relate his entertaining stories until Livy would signal him by agreed-on gesture to sit down. There were inventions to distract him, investments, letters to ponder answers to, his publishing firm to oversee, and a brain all the while bristling with new projects. Howells said that Clemens's mind was the most imaginative he had ever encountered, and Mark Twain's range of interests and writing topics would appear to confirm as much. Even idle, he had multifarious matters to think about, so that Susy's father might well and often have appeared inattentive to the here and now.

She reveals much else about Mr. Clemens: that he loves kittens and billiards and cigars, that he is a Mugwump in politics and dislikes going to church ("he told me the other day, that he couldn't bear to hear any one talk but himself, but that he could listen to himself talk for hours without getting tired, of course he said this in joke, but I've no dought it was founded on truth"). She sketches her father's early years in Missouri, tells of young Sammy's playing hooky from school "all the time and how readily would papa have pretended to be dying so as not to have to go to school!" We read of his apprenticeship as a printer, of his going on the Mississippi as a pilot when he was "about 20 years old," of his promise to his mother before leaving home not to swear or drink intoxicating liquors, a promise he kept for seven years, "when Grandma released him from it." We are told of his trip out West with Uncle Orion, of his trying his hand at mining, of his reporting for a newspaper out there, of his return from the Sandwich Islands and his lecturing in San Francisco, of his voyage from New York on the *Quaker City*, aboard which vessel "he became equainted with Uncle Charlie, Mr. C. J. Langdon of New York." After the voyage, Grandpa Langdon had Uncle Charley invite Mr. Clemens to join the family for dinner "at the St. Nicolas hotel N.Y.," and there "he met mama, Olivia Louise Langdon, first. But they did not meet again until the next August, because papa went away to California, and there wrote the 'Inocense Abroad.'"

All that was family lore, and Susy shares with us what she has been told of her mother's early years as well: of Mamma's bedridden invalidism in adolescence, of hers and Papa's courtship and his love letters even more beautiful than Nathaniel Hawthorne's, of their wedding and her grandfather's gift of the bridal home in Buffalo ("Mamma has told me the story many times"), and of the death of Grandpa Langdon, who was Mamma's idol. And we read of the family's present happiness—endearing letters to Susy from her father on his travels, the donkey he surprised them with as a gift at Quarry Farm, visits to General Grant in New York City and to Vassar College in Poughkeepsie, where Mark Twain brought his eldest daughter along and lectured as a favor to a family friend.

The Clemenses in 1885 do appear to have been about as happy as their daughter of thirteen said they were. We've heard the servant Katy Leary pronounce the Hartford residence a home "you would like more than anything else in the world. A happy, happy home—happiness budding all over—everybody always happy." No doubt that overstates the case; yet Susy's biography furnishes abundant specimens of joy. Among them were the plays the children put on: Shakespeare in the schoolroom upstairs, family servants for their audience; and, far more elaborately, the theatricals downstairs in the library, eighty-four chairs in place to accommodate family and neighbors. Livy had written a dramatization of her husband's *The Prince and the Pauper*, in one of the several performances of which Susy's father stood in for a sick neighbor playing Miles Hendon: "'The Prithee pour the Water!' scene. I was the Prince," Susy tells us, "and Papa and I rehearsed together 2 or 3 times a day for the three days before the appointed evening." It went off beautifully, "great great funn with our Prince and

Pauper and I think we none of us shall forget how imensely funny papa was in it. He certainly could have been an actor as well as an author."

Clemens the widower returned in memory to those same happy days: the busy week of preparations, "home-traffic obstructed, interrupted, disordered, and sometimes even paralyzed for a while, for the play was the one important interest for the time being." Actors studied lines and rehearsed all day, with those not acting making costumes, props, and scenery. On the last morning the dining room and library were cleaned and dusted, the stage brought from the stable and set up before the conservatory, curtains hung, the green room—the downstairs guest room—filled with costumes, the drawing-room piano tuned and ready to play its marches, and in the afternoon the dress rehearsal. "Susy and her troupe were in a happy heaven of excitement all the day, and all the busy household moved and toiled in an atmosphere that was electric with their enthusiasm." Shortly before eight, with the hall fire lit and the house "in a drench of gas-light from the ground floor up," guests began arriving, bringing "a babel of hearty greetings, with not a voice in it that was not old and familiar and affectionate; and when the curtain went up we looked out from the stage upon none but faces that were dear to us, none but faces that were lit up with welcome for us." Katy remembered the same grand evening. "Oh, it looked brilliant and lovely!" she said, recalling Mr. Clemens's taking a part, "and he was so funny, just his walk was funny—the *way* he walked!" He called for water, and when it came, "he poured it out the wrong way—by the handle and not by the nose—and of course that took down the house."

Yet part of why Susy was writing her biography was to correct a misperception about her father. Recently, a reader had written to Mark Twain, as transcribed by the young biographer: "I enjoyed 'Huckelberry Finn' immensely and am glad to see that you have returned to your old style"; that is, to rendering vernacular voices along the Mississippi, after the same author's The Prince and the Pauper, with its refinements of English diction and setting. Susy, put off by Huck's comical crudeness, grumbles about the fan letter: "That enoyed me that enoyed me greatly, because it trobles me to have so few people know papa, I mean realy know him, they think of Mark Twain as a humorist joking at every thing." But in Susy's view The Prince and the Pauper "is unquestionably the best book he has ever written." All along she had "wanted papa to write a book that would reveal something of his kind sympathetic nature, and the 'Prince and Pauper' partly does it. The book is full is full," she stumbles, "of lovely charming ideas, and oh the language! it is perfect, I think."

Readers of our era may demur from so exalted an opinion of that specific achievement; but Katy Leary at the time felt pretty much as Susy did, especially concerning its author as humorist. "The public always thought he joked about everything," the Clemenses' servant remarked, "but that warn't so, he was really very serious about lots of things, but it took people a long while to find this out. Susy used to say, though, very often, that her father was what you might call a philosopher (which means a deep thinker), as well as a humorist. Susy always realized and saw things very clear—even when she was quite a little girl—and she was very proud of her father and said there warn't anything he couldn't do or be."

For their part, both father and mother adored their eldest daughter. Perhaps the timing of the girl's birth, in March 1872, figured in their adoration; for frail little Langdon, the family's firstborn, had less than three months to live then, his loss in June leaving Livy and Sam only their newborn infant to prize. In any case, they both showered love on the baby and rejoiced while watching her grow into the very special daughter she became.

The father loved all three daughters; and, according to Katy, "they loved him and used to abuse him, too (that is, Susy and Clara did). They used to sit on his lap and pull his hair and pull him all over the house, you know, and he was always ready to crawl on his hands and knees or lie on his back or do anything to make them laugh." He did love all three children, but (in a more innocent time, when such open partiality was commonplace) Susy was his and Livy's favorite. All the family knew it. "To us she was a prodigy," her father affirmed years later. "I mean, in speech she was that." Surely Susy would become a writer; for "she had no equal among girls of her own age in this regard"—of distinctive articulateness. "Even the friends thought highly of her gift, though they could never see her at her best, which was in the unembarrassing limits of the family circle." At seventeen, two years after her triumphs in *The Prince and the Pauper*, Susy wrote a play of her own, *A Love-Chase*, along Greek lines (muses, a cupid, and a shepherd lad for characters) in order that she, her sisters, and neighbor friends might act in it. Performed on the drawing-room's makeshift stage at Thanksgiving of 1889 ("I can see her yet," her father noted in late years, "as she parted the curtains & stood there, young, fresh, aglow with excitement, & clothed in a tumbling cataract of pink roses"), *A Love-Chase* proved to be another triumph for this budding talent, Nook Farm friends gathered becharmed on what, Clemens pronounced years later, was the happiest evening of Susy's life. The following day George Warner, brother of Charles Dudley Warner (coauthor of *The Gilded Age*), came over and talked with the young playwright for a long while and told her father afterward, "She is the most interesting person I have ever known, of either sex." Another neighbor appeared to corroborate that remarkable judgment. "I made this note after one of my talks with Susy," the erudite Mrs. Cheney said: "'She knows all there is of life and its meanings. She could not know it better if she had lived it out to its limit. Her intuitions and ponderings and analyzings seem to have taught her all that my sixty years have taught me.'"

The parents sent their prodigy off to Bryn Mawr College the following year, in the fall of 1890. She was leaving home for the first time—and such a home, such a family, such a neighborhood! Bryn Mawr, located ten miles west of Philadelphia, had been founded five years earlier (in that same 1885 that was the Clemenses' wonder year), as a means of giving young women the academic opportunities that men took for granted. In March before her matriculation, on the eve of her birthday, Susy had written: "Tomorrow I am eighteen! Eighteen! I dread to have to say I am so old! And nothing done and such unsettled notions of things. Why, I should be a well-poised woman instead of a rattle-brained girl. I should have been entirely settled and in mechanical running order for two years! I am ashamed I am not a more reliable, serene character, one to be depended upon. I know so well what a girl of eighteen should be." Still, ready or not for the adventure ahead, this unfinished woman (as she saw herself) was obliged six months later to launch forth into the world on her own.

True, her parents came along to help enroll Susy and get her set up at Bryn Mawr, and both returned from time to time in the fall and winter on visits. For they missed her, and for her part, Susy was homesick. Years later, one classmate remembered the new student as "frail, attractive, charming," and another, Evangeline Walker, described Olivia—she had chosen to go by her first name at college, no longer Susan, which was her middle name—as "emotional, high-strung, temperamental," and very close to her father, much attached to home.

The same might be said, of course, of many a freshman, now as then. That early in the college's history, during this academic year 1890–1891, the Bryn Mawr community was entertained in February by students performing Gilbert and Sullivan's *Iolanthe*, with Susy—Olivia—in the crucial role of the beautiful Phyllis. She sang her songs ("Good-morrow, good lover," "Nay, tempt me not," "Though p'r'aps I may incur thy blame," and the others) with a soprano voice that her classmates found to be clear and fine. Yet even after such public success, the young woman was unable to finish her freshman year. Early on she had written: "now that I am here there is a great deal that I enjoy most thoroughly. The work is delightful

Figure 34.1.   Olivia Susan Clemens, "Susy," in
1890.
Courtesy of the Mark Twain House & Museum, Hartford.

and the people are lovely and altogether Bryn Mawr is an ideal place, but
oh! it *does* not, *can* not compare with home!" Now, in April, for whatever
reason, Miss Clemens withdrew from the college. Was it homesickness?
Health? The cost? That last seems unlikely, even if two months later, the
entire Clemens family did leave America mainly for cost-cutting purposes—closed down their Hartford home as too extravagant at present and
set off at the start of an indeterminate stay in Europe.

They were gone a year when Grace King, the New Orleans writer, visited
the family in Italy. Afterward Miss King recalled that Susy, then twenty,
had appeared "exquisitely pretty, but frail-looking." Later still, in Paris in
the summer of 1894, a visitor from Hartford, the daughter of Alice Hooker
Day (Alice being one of the two—Livy Langdon the other—beautiful young
women whom Sam Clemens had encountered years before, in New York
City on New Year's Day of 1868, and lingered with for hours, bedeviling the
life out of both of them to their amusement and pleasure): Alice's daughter
in Paris had looked up the Clemenses in Paris and found Susy "especially

charming, a beautiful slender girl, fair, with light golden-brown hair and dark eyes full of intelligence and an alert eager manner. She was devoted to music and was cultivating her voice, already considered exceptional." Her father had thought Susy should be a writer; but, like Clara later, she was choosing to pursue a musical career. The young woman's health was not good, however: that frailness so often remarked on. Was it the onset of anorexia nervosa? In Paris, meanwhile, Susy consulted with the distinguished voice instructor Blanche Marchesi, who cautioned her that she must build herself up and strengthen her lungs if she hoped to sing professionally.

By then, Paige's typesetter back home had exposed itself as impractical for everyday use in a pressroom, with Samuel Clemens's massive investment in the overdelicate contrivance lost thereby, all $300,000 vanished. Webster & Co., Publishers, had fallen into bankruptcy that spring of 1894; so nothing was left for Mark Twain but to return to the lecture platform. Accordingly, he and his family set out for New York in mid-May 1895, bent on undertaking the rigors of a round-the-world voyage to raise money to pay off creditors.

They traveled west to the Pacific from Elmira, leaving Susy and Jean behind with Livy's sister, with Aunt Sue. The eldest daughter was to grow strong in the year ahead, at the end of which time—and the tour behind them—the family would be reunited in England. Thus at the Elmira depot Clemens said his goodbyes to Susy, watching as she waved from a platform ablaze in electric lights while the train bearing Mamma, Papa, and Clara pulled out. The hour was half past ten on the night of July 14, 1895. "One year, one month, and one week later," an unappeasably grieving Clemens would have occasion to set down, "Clara and her mother having exactly completed the circuit of the globe, drew up at that platform at the same hour of the night, in the same train *and the same car*—and again Susy had come a journey and was near at hand to meet them. She was waiting in the house she was born in, in her coffin."

The young woman had died of spinal meningitis at twenty-four. Her father off in England was desolated by the news, shattered, totally unprepared for it. "I did not know," he wrote to Twichell a full six months after Susy's death, "that she could go away, and take our lives with her, yet leave our dull bodies behind. And I did not know what she was. To me she was but treasure in the bank; the amount known, the need to look at it daily, handle it, weigh it, count it, *realize* it, not necessary; and now that I would do it, it is too late; they tell me it is not there, has vanished away in a night, the bank is broken, my fortune is gone, I am a pauper. How am I to comprehend this?"

He did have his writing, and he labored at that feverishly, of necessity. But Mrs. Clemens was left with nothing, with only some housework to distract her. "She does not see people, and cannot; books have lost their interest for her. She sits solitary; and all the day, and all the days, wonders how it all happened, and why." For Susy was her mother's comrade, her close companion, her treasure, her friend and favorite.

"But it is ended now," Clemens wrote. And he took the blame. If he had not squandered the family fortune on the typesetting machine and driven them all from their joyful Hartford home. If he had seen to the publishing company's being managed with competence. If he had been spared that hateful cruise around the world that left Susy behind. If he had been less the distracted husband, less the neglectful father. The consequences of his failures had broken a mother's heart. Although there would be easeful interludes, Livy never really was the same again after Susy's death; and that was much of what Clemens could brood about in late years up to the summer of 1904, at York Harbor, at Riverdale, and at the Villa Reale di Quarto outside Florence, denied access to the sickroom through most of the months—those twenty-two long months—of Olivia Langdon Clemens's final illness and agony.

CHAPTER Thirty-Five

America at Home

Census figures early in the twenty-first century reveal American families diverging sharply from the pattern that their forebears followed. We of the present age encounter divorce as a commonplace and divorcés in third or fourth marriages; women renouncing marriage for the sake of careers; middle-class households that single mothers head by choice, fathers nowhere in the picture; unmarried couples cohabiting; long-delayed marriages and mixed-race marriages and children with same-sex parents. In our era, half the population of the United States doesn't marry at all during prime marriageable age.

Things were different a hundred years ago. For millions of their fellow countrymen the Clemens and the Roosevelt families embodied the ideal of the late Victorian household. The Roosevelts' commodious home at Oyster Bay in the 1890s, like the Clemenses' steamboat gothic mansion in Hartford in the 1870s and '80s, resounded with the laughter of children; with friends, relatives, and neighbors gathered in affluent comfort; with parties setting out happily on picnics and boatrides and hayrides, playing charades after supper, romping wholesomely at tag or hide-and-seek outdoors and in, within homes presided over by fathers of force and character, successful at what they did, and mothers wise, gentle, accomplished, and loving.

Theodore Roosevelt's marriage to Edith Carow and Samuel Clemens's to Olivia Langdon were exceptionally close, the wives remarkable people and widely extolled in their lifetimes. At the end of Edmund Morris's massive, magnificent three-volume biography of Roosevelt (1979–2010)—just under 2,000 narrative pages, more than thirty-one years off and on in the writing—its author shares his considered judgment that Theodore and Edith's was "one of the great marriages in American history"; and nobody can read the love letters of Sam and Livy Clemens, in Dixon Wecter's hand-somely edited *Love Letters of Mark Twain* (1949), without feeling how deep was their love from first to last, from 1868 to as late as the fall of 1903, letters and notes to each other in the final years as devoted as the ones of their eager young courtship.

During the two decades between 1890 and 1910—a time of tumultuous changes, as noted: in attitudes toward religion and race, in invention and technology, in the impact of science on long-held moral certainties, in new concentrations of wealth, in the waves of immigrants pouring into cities ever more crowded, in strife between owners and workers, in the abruptly enlarged bulk of the nation on the world stage—during those two decades, late Victorians and their children moving into the Edwardian period clung for stability to familiar domestic ways. Beyond front stoops lay the road to the marketplace, the factory, the bourse, to stores and offices that offered crassly competitive means of getting ahead. Out there men might be less than diligently rectitudinous, in a world swollen with wealth and increas-ingly dog-eat-dog. But home was different. In the refuge of home, in that old-fashioned sanctuary of values that mothers strove to bequeath to their children, virtue abided. Men might dominate the world beyond the front lawn, but women ruled at home, and properly so; for a certainty of the times—as certain as the existence of five races (or six, or seven) exhibiting discrete capabilities—was the conviction that men and women were inher-ently different and put on earth to play different roles. The differences were everywhere apparent, from the nursery into the school grades and on up through all walks of life thereafter. Men were active, intellectual, com-petitive, striving for power, and beset by sexual needs; women were more passive, intuitive, collaborative, obedient, more religiously sensitive, pure of heart, and gifted at fostering domestic peace. Of course such distinc-tions oversimplify; and, at the time, they were understood to be subject to exceptions. But in general, men laid down law, women used persuasion; men embodied justice, women mercy; men were intellect, women were understanding; the one was history, the other poetry. Men, in short, were of the mind, women of the soul; men were of the head (and, although not talked about, the loins), whereas women were of the heart.

Home nourished virtues crucial to every community: kindness, gen-erosity, sympathy, cooperation. Religion the family buttressed by Sun-day attendance at church and sometimes still (if not in the Clemenses' household) by a gathering together of parents, children, and servants each weekday morning for a Bible reading; Mr. Roosevelt's father had observed that ritual, and his son followed the father's example. As children grew,

boys becoming men and setting out to help build the nation might neglect going to church; but proper young women were unwavering in their
piety. And they were pure. We recall how the rough-edged westerner Sam
Clemens felt late in 1867 at first sight of Miss Langdon, at dinner at the
St. Nicholas Hotel, as though beholding "a visiting *Spirit* from the upper
air—a something to *worship*, reverently & at a distance." During his courtship Clemens took pains to censor *Don Quixote*, a book he loved, to make
it suitable for his angel to read; and, soon after their wedding in 1870, he
was exulting to a childhood friend about the new Mrs. Clemens, who was
"the *best* girl, & the sweetest, & the gentlest, & the daintiest, & the most
modest & unpretentious, & the wisest in all things she should be wise in &
the most ignorant in all matters it would not grace her to know."

Knowledge was for men; women had wisdom. And women were naturally gifted as homemakers. Men might perform with skill at the office,
but trying to help around the house they got in the way as often as not.
Susy remarks on how absentminded her father was. Moreover, although
he loved gadgets, he couldn't figure out the burglar alarm, and an early
typewriter proved too much for him, as did the bicycle. Livy was left in
charge of managing family affairs. "Youth" she called him through their
lifetime together; and for his part, Roosevelt, equally young in spirit—the
Tom Sawyer of American politics—deferred to his wife at Sagamore Hill
almost as much as Clemens had to his at Hartford. Don't tell Theodore,
Edith would plead; he'll want to come along, and I already have my hands
full with the other children.

Daughters growing into womanhood prepared themselves for marriage: developed their taste and domestic graces, their skills as hostesses,
their ability to deal with servants. Of course the passages through childhood into adolescence and on into adult responsibilities were not always
effected smoothly, with bright young women more likely to meet trouble
along the way, as witness Susy Clemens on the eve of her eighteenth birthday lamenting her still being a rattle-brained girl instead of the well-poised
woman she should have become by then, and "nothing done and such
unsettled notions of things."

Some women, even young women, *were* getting things done meanwhile;
and that would have been part of Susy's frustration. Values in middle-class
homes prescribed the demeanor that an accomplished young lady should
adopt—of modesty, demureness, deference—to attract an appropriate
suitor; and all the while beyond the bounds of her narrow world our brash
democracy was expanding. From out there the nation looked limitless.
There were no bounds, for instance, to how much money you could amass.

And why, one wondered, should that cowboy in the White House have roped off vast chunks of America's inexhaustible forests, minerals, and wildlife from individual enterprise? Why, come to that, should limits be set on what women might reach for? Out West the women were hardy, active, and adventuresome. Not that Susy Clemens of Hartford's gentry aspired to raise barns in frontier settlements or open a village store; but she would have been aware of the New Woman elsewhere in America, marching, campaigning for equal rights, addressing legislatures, and speaking from platforms to demand the suffrage for her sex. That same New Woman was winning the vote, too—in Wyoming as early as 1869—and demonstrating that modern life offered her opportunities beyond the snagging of a husband. Susy was by no means alone, then, in longing to distinguish herself. She would become a writer. She would become a concert singer.

But it wasn't easy for bright young females to express their natures within the constrained expectations of American middle-class life in the 1890s. Miss Clemens had withdrawn from Bryn Mawr and, with her family, had gone to Europe. On occasion she did find happiness overseas. In Italy the Clemenses devoted some evenings to pure fun. A visitor reported on one such: "Susy, an inimical mimic"—a slip for *inimitable*—"would parody scenes from Wagner's operas and Mr. Clemens would give an imitation of a ballet dancer, posturing, throwing kisses, and making grimaces, while Susy played a waltz on the piano." Yet often the daughter was bored, with few friends her age and those few at a distance. Her parents let Clara go off to Berlin to take music lessons, but Susy remained with the family for now. "I am interested in reading and writing," she wrote, "but I *am* blue a good deal, I must confess, and lonely and anxious for a taste of 'the rage of *living*.' Reading all day *can* get tiresome. As for writing I never think of it nowadays. I should love to, but I can't now anyway, and I don't ever expect to be able to."

Thus she read and read. And sewed. And drank tea with her parents and their elderly friends. When Susy did go out, it was as Mark Twain's daughter. "How I hate that name!" she wrote in exasperation. "I should like never to hear it again! My father should not be satisfied with it! He should not be known by it! He should show himself the great writer that he is, not merely a funny man. Funny! That's all the people see in him—a maker of funny speeches!" Funny in public perhaps, but at home the father who was Mark Twain could turn short-tempered, abruptly so. Clemens had always been volatile, "creating day or night for those about him," Clara remembered, "by his twinkling eyes or clouded brows." "I have to go down to breakfast now," Susy wrote from Italy, "and I don't enjoy this one bit altho

Papa hasn't *stormed* yet. Still I feel constrained and he pierces me thru with his eyes as if he were determined to see whether I am embarrassed or not."

She was, in fact, often miserable, this delicate, ethereal, unworldly young woman who ate poorly, slept poorly, and pined for a friendship left behind at Bryn Mawr. We know of it because around forty of Susy's letters to Louise Brownell survive at the Hamilton College Library in Clinton, New York: passionate letters that profess longing and love. In the early autumn not many months after the family left Hartford, "I think of you these days, the first of college," she wrote to Louise. "If I could only look in on you! We would sleep together tonight—and I would allow you opportunities for those refreshing little naps you always indulged in when we passed a night together." Again: "My darling I do love you so and I feel so separated from you. If you were here I would kiss you *hard* on that little place that tastes so good just on the right side of your nose." And: "I throw my arms around you and kiss you over and over again. I hope you are happy and not depressed. I love you with all my heart and more every day. How sweet you are, how lovely you are my dearest!" And yet again: "now goodby darling, *my* darling and please write me very soon. I feel so near you today precious beautiful Louise! I take you in my arms. I kiss your lips, your eyes, your throat. I am, Your own own, *Olivia*."

Louise Brownell's letters responding to Susy's ardor have not survived, although they must have been comparably intense. After Susy left Bryn Mawr, Louise finished the school year there and returned in the fall to continue her studies. She did brilliantly, graduating in 1893, the year before Susy would have had she remained. Louise was awarded the highest postgraduate honor that Bryn Mawr offered, a fellowship allowing her to study at Oxford. Thus she was on the European side of the Atlantic in the summer of 1894. Susy had been able to visit with her friend in London, although nothing is known about the length or tenor of the visit. Now, from Fontainebleau in late July 1894, she is writing to "Louise, my *darling*" in Dresden, the last of the letters extant: "Your dear letter has come, met me in Paris the other night, saying you are likely to go to America this year." Devastating news! "I was all unforewarned and it made my heart stand still." But they *must* see each other before Louise sails. "I am so miserably helpless. I love you so. I wish you were here to comfort me. I think I wrote you that we cannot now afford to live in Hartford and are likely to stay over here until we can." That meant "another interminable unsatisfied longing to see you. This being apart breaks my heart," Susy cried out. Her letter swells with grief, grows abject. "It was so dreadful to see you go that morning in London that I feel now almost that I must have had a kind of premonition of this misfortune before us. I love you so much so infinitely, and you are so near and I cannot *reach* you." She grasps at a scrap of hope. "Is there a possibility that you and your sister could shorten your Italian trip a little and come to us in Etretat"—in Normandy—"late in September or early in October perhaps before you sail if you do?" She knows it is much to ask, and that her letter is laden with "propositions requests and lamentations." But there's no help for it. "Oh dear I cannot be brave at all. I am miserably unhappy and full of fear cold terror that I have *lost* you and that you will *go* after all go away"—syntax muddled in her grief—"across the ocean for an endless weary time and I shall not see you before, that you will go without saying goodby. What shall I do if you do?"

Louise did leave before they could meet again. The following spring the Clemenses sailed for home and Elmira, Susy, and her youngest sister, Jean, to spend the year at Quarry Farm with Aunt Sue while the parents and Clara circled the globe. Susy wrote to her family of how she missed them: "Ah me, was I not a fool to stay here instead of going with you?" To Clara she added: "*If* I ever can be with you again, I shall stick like a burr indeed!" But the voyagers ("We *are* such a congenial family," the eldest daughter wrote in that last year of her life; and "We *do* belong together") would never be reunited with their living Susy; for, after thirteen months apart, just before embarking to rejoin them in England, she took ill while visiting Hartford and, in two weeks, was dead.

Olivia Susan Clemens died at twenty-four, in August 1896, when another eldest child and daughter in a prominent American family was half that age and poised on the cusp of a tumultuous adolescence. In 1896, that other child's father, Theodore Roosevelt, had been serving as New York City police commissioner, writing the fourth volume of his *The Winning of the West*, and preparing to campaign for the Republican presidential nominee, Governor William McKinley of Ohio. The twelve-year-old, Alice Lee Roosevelt, was Mr. Roosevelt's firstborn, on February 12, 1884, two days before a hideous ordeal during which a new parent watched both his mother and his wife die within twelve hours of each other. Roosevelt bore that overwhelming grief silently, as was his way, going west to his ranch in the Dakotas and leaving the motherless infant in the care of his older, maiden sister, Bamie. He would refer to the child only as Baby Lee, unable to say the name Alice, which was both that of the child and of the young wife he had loved and lost. When, in December 1886, he married his childhood playmate Edith Carow, it was with the expectation, after their months-long honeymoon in Europe, of starting a new family, leaving Alice in the capable hands of Bamie, who had come to love her dearly. But Edith would not hear of that; so Theodore removed the child from Auntie Bye's Manhattan home and, after Alice's semiannual visit to her late mother's family in Boston—to Grandmother and Grandfather Lee—settled her into yet another home, at Sagamore Hill.

Although she welcomed the three-year-old, Alice's stepmother was preoccupied that summer of 1887 with her own first pregnancy. Ted Jr. arrived in September; and during the decade ahead, from 1889 to 1897, Edith would bear four more children—in all, four lively boys and a tomboy girl, little Ethel—while Alice, the eldest and by a different mother, was not always blending smoothly into the boisterous Roosevelt household.

Alice was twelve when the papers carried news of the death of Mark Twain's daughter. Less than two years later, in February 1898, three days after Alice Roosevelt's fourteenth birthday, the U.S.S. *Maine* blew up in Havana harbor; and the girl's father, by then assistant secretary of the navy, resigned his office and went off to war. He returned from Cuba the hero of San Juan Hill, a distinction that propelled Colonel Roosevelt into the New York governor's mansion. "We have never been happier in our lives than we are now," Edith declared from Albany; and at first that was true even for Alice, who had joined in and relished the excitement of her father's political campaign. But as a lively sixteen-year-old she soon grew bored. "She cares neither for athletics nor good works, the two resources of youth in this town!" her stepmother fretted. In the event, Governor Roosevelt's rapid political rise cut short the family's stay in Albany; for in June 1900 he was nominated as the Republican vice presidential candidate, elected to that position in November—occasioning a move to Washington—and before another November arrived had been elevated, through the assassination of his predecessor, to the presidency of the United States.

In the White House, the Roosevelt family's wholesome vigor captivated the country's imagination. Three months into the new president's tenure, newspapers were extolling Alice Roosevelt's debut—her introduction to society—shortly before her eighteenth birthday, at a celebration that brought youth, joy, and beauty into the Executive Mansion. Some 600 guests attended that unofficial White House function, which began at ten on Friday evening, January 3, 1902. More than 2,000 flowers adorned the dazzling Blue and East rooms. Dancing to music of the Marine Band commenced at eleven, with a sumptuous buffet supper served soon after midnight. And if the honoree (partly because of the punch that—perhaps for political reasons—stood in for champagne) had what she remembered as only a moderately good time, most everybody else enjoyed the occasion thoroughly. "A more charming debutante has rarely been introduced in Washington," the *New York Tribune* reported next morning. "She was as attractive in her dignified simplicity and natural grace as she was beautiful. Tall, with a striking figure, blue eyes, and a fine fair complexion, she is certainly one of the prettiest girls in Washington."

Alice was all that, and intelligent, and willfully high-spirited, which led to differences with her stepmother, and not just over punch for champagne at her debutante ball. Future entries in the young woman's diary referred with some regularity to "rows" and "temper fits" at home. This first teenager in the White House in a quarter century was experiencing familiar adolescent troubles, and not only with her stepmother. "Father doesn't care for me," she wrote in her diary a year later, "that is to say one eighth as much as he does for the other children. It is perfectly true that he doesn't, and, Lord, why *should* he. We are not in the least congenial, and if I don't care overmuch for him and don't take an interest in things he likes, why *should* he pay any attention to me or the things that I live for, except to look on them with disapproval."

CHAPTER **Thirty-Six**

Bully Father

What her father disapproved of was Alice Roosevelt's living for
sensation, admiration, men, and the company of her several
socialite girl friends. Bright as she was—and Alice may have
been the brightest of the Roosevelt children—she reveled in society's ap-
probations, a need that arose perhaps from her singular childhood: from
never having known her birth mother, never hearing her father so much
as mention the mother's name, being wrenched in the earliest years from
this home to that to find herself at last settled at Oyster Bay with a re-
served, preoccupied, and rigorously moral stepmother in a house filling
up with other, clamorous children dominated by a father outspoken in his
opinions and very moral as well. Colonel Roosevelt did disapprove of the
friends his older daughter had chosen: the rich at their play in Newport—
young Vanderbilts and their like—rather than more earnest Brahmins (her
Lee family being Boston Brahmins in good standing) or, say, ambitious
youths among the oldtime, well-bred New York Knickerbockers, the Roosevelts themselves of that long lineage.

Alice felt concerns of her own about her friends, doubtless inevitable
given the position she occupied. Did they like the beautiful young woman
for herself, truly, or was it because her father was currently president of
the United States? Her diary expresses doubts: about her friends, about
her beauty (which was in fact indubitable), about whether the men she was
drawn to cared for her or, more, for her new fame. For Alice in her arresting way had all at once become famous, the press's darling ever since her
debut. From the Lees, her mother's wealthy family, she enjoyed her own
quite generous allowance, which let her do pretty much what she liked; and
what she liked made for good copy. She was observed shockingly smoking a cigarette, drove a car unchaperoned from Newport to Boston at the

foolhardy speed of twenty-five miles an hour, carried a pet snake about, played poker, gambled, and danced on the Vanderbilts' roof at midnight. When His Imperial Majesty the Kaiser dispatched his brother to take possession of a royal yacht in a shipyard off Jersey City, Alice was chosen to break the champagne bottle over the prow and christen the vessel the *Meteor*. The press, as ever enraptured by her fresh and very photogenic face and figure, covered that February christening step by step, noting with approval Miss Roosevelt's composure and grace in the performance of her duty and commenting on the attention that gallant Prince Heinrich paid America's uncrowned princess. Journalists wondered whether she might be wearing a crown herself soon, a German one. Meanwhile, the nation's new sweetheart, still only eighteen, was ecstatic when her savvy father told her she might attend the coronation in Westminster Abbey of the new king Edward VII over this summer of 1902. The British, however, proceeded to take the princess business too seriously, talking of putting Miss Roosevelt up in royal style. With that, the President determined to keep Alice at home so as not to offend voters in our democracy. The young woman must content herself with a trip to Cuba instead.

Even so, Princess Alice became the toast of the land. Alice-blue, as in Miss Roosevelt's eyes, was the new fashionable color. Songs were written about her: "The Alice Roosevelt March" and, somewhat later, the vastly popular "Alice-Blue Gown," while other songs were dedicated to her or promoted as ones she favored. Through it all, the unconventional First Daughter, like her other female friends, proved conventional enough to be boy-crazy, focused on marriage as soon as the right suitor came along. It was what young ladies did when they could: marry someone handsome and rich. The press loved it. Not that Alice as a matron planned on breeding scads of children. A couple of years on, she and three girlfriends borrowed a favorite theme of her father's and formed the Race Suicide Club, meeting discreetly to amuse each other with the daring of their maidenly talk—not at all what Colonel Roosevelt had in mind when he used the term.

The President did speak often of race suicide, in his opinion the greatest evil the nation faced. As far back as the census of 1890, the one that led the historian Frederick Jackson Turner to discourse on the recently vanished frontier as a molder of American life, Roosevelt examining the same census figures noted the decline of the Anglo-Saxon birthrate, along with the swelling of immigrant ranks in our population. Side by side, the two trends alarmed him. Now as president, in March 1905, he addressed the National Congress of Mothers in Washington, in a speech that alluded yet again to race suicide and, by implication, to what he found distasteful

Figure 36.1.   Alice Roosevelt in her late teens, 1902.

Courtesy of the Theodore Roosevelt Collection, Harvard College Library.

about young lives led self-indulgently, such as those among Alice's snobbish Newport friends.

Before the mothers of the nation in congress assembled, the President scoffed at such easy lives. In their place he preached of duty, of "the first and greatest duty of womanhood," which was the bearing and bringing up of children "sound in body, mind, and character, and numerous enough so that the race shall increase and not decrease." A truth that would endure, he said, as long as the world did, a truth that no progress could alter, decreed that the husband be the breadwinner for his family and the wife the helpmate and mother. "This does not mean inequality of function," the speaker made clear, "but it does mean that normally there must be dissimilarity of function." That said, President Roosevelt regarded the woman's duty as "the more important, the more difficult, and the more honorable of the two; on the whole I respect the woman who does her duty even more than I respect the man who does his." For a mother's duty is hard, her responsibility great—bearing children, guiding their growth, tending to them day and night through their illnesses—"but greatest of all is your reward. I do not pity you in the least. On the contrary, I feel respect and admiration for you." For to the mothers of America is committed the destiny of the generations to come. Accordingly, they should instruct their children "that they are not to look forward to lives spent in avoiding difficulties, but to lives spent in overcoming difficulties. Teach them that work, for themselves and also for others, is not a curse but a blessing; seek to make them happy, to make them enjoy life, but seek also to make them face life with the steadfast resolution to wrest success from labor and adversity, and to do their whole duty before God and to man."

The President summed up for his listeners: "If either a race or an individual prefers the pleasure of mere effortless ease, of self-indulgence, to the infinitely deeper, the infinitely higher pleasures that come to those who know the toil and the weariness, but also the joy, of hard duty well done, why, that race or that individual must inevitably in the end pay the penalty of leading a life both vapid and ignoble"; for "the prizes worth having in life must be paid for, and the life worth living must be a life of work for a worthy end, and ordinarily of work more for others than for one's self."

President Roosevelt spoke with conviction, having struggled in recent years to right a life of one he loved that had proved both ignoble and vapid. An unfit life, in short, in this Darwinian universe. His only brother, Elliott, fourteen months younger, had been the dear companion of Teedie's youth, his defender in the enfeebled days of an asthmatic childhood, his admired competitor, and his bosom friend. Everyone had loved Elliott, the handsome and able Roosevelt, charming, outgoing, convivial. He was best man at Theodore and Alice Lee's wedding. The two brothers had traveled together, hunted together, and Theodore's *Hunting Trips of a Ranchman* (1885) is dedicated "to that keenest of sportsmen and truest of friends, my brother, Elliott Roosevelt."

In 1883, at twenty-three, Elliott had married a New York socialite, the rich, beautiful Anna Hall. The couple had three children: Anna Eleanor in 1884; Elliott Jr., who died at four; and Hall, born in 1891 and doomed to an early death as well, his at fifty, of alcoholism, in 1941—an apple fallen close to the tree. For the father of Hall Roosevelt that half-century before, back in the late 1880s and into the early '90s, although ostensibly a banker, had turned mostly into a *bon vivant*, a partygoer and singer of comic songs. From casual drinking among congenial friends, Elliott Roosevelt had developed a thirst that swelled into something ominous. Helplessly, Theodore watched as his brother's life began coming undone, until it grew so self-destructive that sister Bamie, along with Theodore and with Elliott's wife Anna, petitioned in the summer of 1891 to have the alcoholic's fortune put into trust for his family and Elliott declared legally insane. Newspapers covered the scandal in full; but Theodore, civil service commissioner in Washington at the time, was undeterred, intent on securing at whatever cost the welfare of his brother's wife and children.

Elliott had been enjoined to undertake a cure in France. Early in 1892 Theodore crossed the Atlantic to convince his brother that he should sign away his assets to his family. Contrite, "utterly broken, submissive and repentant," he agreed to do so—two-thirds of them—and return and continue treatment for his alcoholism in America. He enrolled for the five weeks of care in Dr. Keely's Bi-Chloride of Gold Cure in Illinois, to be followed by a year's proof of sobriety before moving back with his family. A managerial position was arranged for Elliott in Virginia, and from there he wrote letters, including tender ones to his first child, to Eleanor, eight years old. Eleanor had lived for her father's infrequent visits and (without ever condoning the drinking) would speak well of him all her life, a life that she led at maturity as a social activist and reformer—"more for others than for one's self"—and as wife of a future president. This same Mrs. Franklin D. Roosevelt, ugly-duckling child whom a socialite mother had never much cared for, was to grow into the most famous American woman of the twentieth century.

Back in 1892, meanwhile, near the end of that year, Elliott's wife Anna—little Eleanor's stylish, beautiful mother—had moved into a new town house on Manhattan's Upper East Side, getting her life in order for when her husband rejoined it sober. But within weeks Anna Hall Roosevelt took ill with diphtheria and, in early December, died at age twenty-nine. Elliott attended her funeral grief-stricken, although to his older brother's dismay the widower was reported within a fortnight "as gay as a butterfly." Theodore gave up. Asked, he declined to talk to his brother further: "I explained to them it was absolutely useless." Through 1893 Elliott's physical and moral disintegration advanced apace. He took mistresses, fathered a child by a housemaid, was drinking ever more ruinously, grew splotched and bloated, and finally drove drunk into a lamppost and was thrown from his carriage out onto his head. "Poor fellow," his brother commented; "if only he could have died instead of Anna." A fortnight later, in the grip of delirium tremens, Elliott tried to leap from his apartment window, somehow failed at that, then ran up and down stairs until seized by convulsions.

Those killed him, on August 14, 1894. He was thirty-four. Viewing the body, "Theodore was more overcome than I have ever seen him—cried like a child for a long time," Corinne wrote to her older sister Bamie. Comfort did come, "one great comfort I already feel," the surviving brother reported soon after; "I only need to have pleasant thoughts of Elliott now. He is just the gallant, generous, manly boy and young man whom everyone loved."

That same older brother, the successful one, died himself early in 1919, a quarter century after Elliott and a decade after leaving the presidency. Further into the year of his death was published *Theodore Roosevelt's Letters to His Children*, a bestseller that for the first time, posthumously, allowed admirers intimate glimpses into the private life of this extraordinary human being: author, soldier, historian, politician, rancher, hunter, naturalist, ornithologist, biographer, boxer, wrestler, polymath, and statesman—now revealed to have been as well a devoted husband and father. Where had Roosevelt found time for it all? For however busy he was in life, whether on his way to war in Cuba or managing the affairs of the nation, he had written to each of his absent children at least once a week. A bully father indeed—"bully" a favorite Rooseveltian Briticism having nothing to do with harassing or tormenting. Rather, it signifies excellence, as in the "bully pulpit" that, as this president said, the White House provides its occupant: when you preach from there, people listen.

To read the letters that a doting Roosevelt wrote to his half-dozen children is to feel the richness, joy, and love that invested the man's private life. With impartial affection he told them of whatever interested him or would hold his Blessed Bunnies' interest, mostly to "Blessed old Ted," "Darling Kermit," "Darling Little Ethel," "Blessed Archikins," and "Dearest Quenty-Quee." As they matured, the salutations did too, usually, but at all times Roosevelt shared with his children an engaging exuberance concerning theirs and their siblings' lives and his own. The 125 letters in the volume—Roosevelt himself helped make the selection during the last year of his life—extend from mid-1898 to the end of 1910. They are excerpts, some quite brief, a few to other adults proudly about the children's doings. At their start Quentin is not yet a year old, Archie four, Ethel just shy of seven, Kermit eight, and Ted ten. Ted will be at Groton School in Massachusetts a part of the ensuing decade, then at Harvard. The younger three boys follow along the identical academic path—except for Archie, expelled from Groton for disrespect to the school, who gets to Harvard by way of Andover.

Writing to them, their father never condescends, although he does of course adjust his diction to the ages of his different readers. And occasionally he illustrates his pages with childlike sketches of random scenes encountered at the time of writing: of little Ethel disciplining the two youngest boys by grabbing their hair, or of a rabbit and a tortoise discovered resting incongruously side by side along a local road, or of a hunting party's hounds contemplating the evening campfire. He writes to his children about his hunting excursions, as from Glenwood Springs, Colorado, to Ted: "I do wish you could have been along on this trip. It has been great fun. In Oklahoma our party got all told seventeen coyotes with the greyhounds. I was in at the death of eleven." To Ethel on the same adventure: "Of course you remember the story of the little prairie girl. I always associate it with you. Well, again and again on this trip we would pass through prairie villages—bleak and lonely—with all the people in from miles about to see me. Among them were often dozens of young girls, often pretty, and as far as I could see much more happy than the heroine of the story." And to Kermit: "I was delighted to get your letter. I am sorry you are having such a hard time in mathematics, but hope a couple of weeks will set you all right. We have had a very successful hunt. All told we have obtained ten bear and three bobcats." He writes to Kermit of a first trip on the Mississippi: "After speaking at Keokuk this morning we got aboard this brand new stern-wheel steamer of the regular Mississippi type and started down-stream. I went up on the *Texas* and of course felt an almost irresistible desire to ask the pilot about Mark Twain. It is a broad, shallow, muddy river, at places the channel being barely wide enough for the boat to go through." And down to Panama with Edith in the fall of 1906, four days at sea heading south: "So far this trip has been a great success, and I think Mother has really enjoyed it. As for me, I of course feel a little bored, as I always do on shipboard, but I have brought on a great variety of books, and am at this moment reading Milton's prose works, 'Tacitus,' and a German novel called 'Jorn Uhl.' Mother and I walk briskly up and down the deck together or else sit aft under the awning, or in the after cabin, with the gun ports open."

Back at Sagamore Hill Roosevelt writes to his absent children details of the country life they know and love. He reports on family horseback rides, "long and delightful" ones with Mother, "she on Yagenka and I on Bleistein, while Ethel and Kermit have begun to ride Wyoming. Kermit was with us this morning and got along beautifully till we galloped, whereupon Wyoming made up his mind that it was a race, and Kermit, for a moment or two, found him a handful." The family played hard and often. "Mother went up-stairs first and was met by Archie and Quentin, each loaded with pillows and whispering not to let me know that they were in ambush; then as I marched up to the top they assailed me with shrieks and chuckles of delight and then the pillow fight raged up and down the hall. After my bath I read them from Uncle Remus." Again, this to Ethel, recalling games of hide-and-seek: "Your letter delighted me. I read it over twice, and chuckled over it. By George, how entirely I sympathize with your feelings in the attic! I know just what it is to get up into such a place and find the delightful, winding passages where one lay hidden with thrills of criminal delight, when the grownups were vainly demanding one's appearance at some legitimate and abhorred function." There are letters from the White House, of yesterday taking Archie, Quentin, and Ethel, "together with the three elder Garfield boys, for a long scramble down Rock Creek. We really had fun." He tells of his wrestling matches, and boxing, and jiu-jitsu, and who won, and what fun those were. And of the pathos of a pet's burial: "his funeral was held with proper state. Archie, in his overalls, dragged the wagon with the little black coffin in which poor Peter Rabbit lay. Mother walked behind as chief mourner; she and Archie solemnly exchanging tributes to the worth and good qualities of the departed." And, in the children's absence from the White House, the emptiness: "I miss you all dreadfully, and the house feels big and lonely and full of echoes with nobody but me in it; and I do not hear any small scamps running up and down the hall just as hard as they can; or hear their voices while I am dressing; or suddenly look out through the windows of the office at the tennis ground and see them racing over it or playing in the sand-box. I love you very much."

This father of six took their travails seriously enough to offer paternal advice. "Don't worry about the lessons, old boy. I know you are studying hard. Don't get cast down. Sometimes in life, both at school and afterwards, fortune will go against any one, but if he just keeps pegging away and doesn't lose his courage things always take a turn for the better in the end."

That was written to Kermit on December 3, 1904, from Washington. Precisely a month earlier, Roosevelt had been uneasily anticipating the forthcoming presidential election, due in five days' time. Whenever his name appeared on a ballot, this candidate fretted about his chances, but especially now, at the national level, wary of the Democrats spreading late falsehoods and resorting to other shabby means of bringing about his defeat. Roosevelt wanted very much to win his own term in the White House—these four years from 1905 to 1909—as the choice of the people expressing their will freely at the polls. In the event, he need not have worried. Yet through the waiting, the victor wrote to Kermit afterward, it had been "a great comfort to feel, all during the last days when affairs looked doubtful, that no matter how things came out the really important thing was the lovely life I have with mother and with you children and that compared to this home life everything else was of very small importance from the standpoint of happiness."

CHAPTER Thirty-Seven

President in His Own Right

T heodore Roosevelt won the presidential election of 1904 with the largest popular vote ever recorded up to that time, by far, and by the crushing electoral tally of 336 to 140, against a Democratic opponent, the lackluster Judge Alton Parker of New York, whose candidacy as a thing to be feared seemed ludicrous in retrospect. On election night at Sagamore Hill, in the ebullience of his triumph and goaded by campaign charges of personal ambition—of his "intention to use the office of President to perpetuate myself in power"—the victor impulsively and gratuitously issued a statement to the press: "The wise custom which limits the President to two terms regards the substance and not the form, and under no circumstances will I be a candidate for or accept another nomination." The Colonel wouldn't quibble about having completed the martyred McKinley's aborted second term. Technically, because Vice President Roosevelt wasn't elected to serve out those forty-three months, he might now run for president four years hence, in 1908, without violating the two-term limit. But as a man of honor he meant to abide by the spirit rather than the letter of a custom observed since Washington's voluntary retirement from the presidency at the end of his second term in 1797. Colonel Roosevelt's election-night announcement was meant to allay any fears that he nurtured ambitions to become an autocrat.

His great popularity, which the polls had corroborated that very day, led a minority to entertain such misgivings about this president. Their concerns grew out of his behavior during the three and a half years just ending. In Roosevelt's insistence on serving what he, like Lincoln, called "the plain people," he had refused to limit himself to tasks that the Constitution specified as the executive branch's to perform. That is, he would not adhere to any doctrine that barred him, "unless he could find some specific authorization to do it," from undertaking what would be to the nation's benefit. Thus, as he later explained, "I did and caused to be done many things not previously done by the President and the heads of the departments. I did not usurp power, but I did greatly broaden the use of executive power"—although never for self-aggrandizement. "I did not care a rap for the mere form and show of power; I cared immensely for the use that could be made of the substance."

Accordingly, in the fall of 1902, Roosevelt had brought coal miners and mineowners together to settle a strike that threatened to plunge the Northeast into frigid misery, even though the Constitution nowhere authorized such intervention as part of the President's duties. Again, while Congress was in recess, Roosevelt had appointed and later reappointed—by executive order—the physician William Crum to serve (and ably serve) as collector of the port of Charleston, in defiance of southern legislators who objected to the well-qualified Dr. Crum simply because he was black. Yet again, on his own the President had instructed his justice department to move to break up the vast railroad monopoly out West formed in the Northern Securities merger. By executive order he created fifty-four wildlife refuges. And in the fall of 1903, while Congress dithered over Colombia's reneging on a treaty, Roosevelt, in his words later, took Panama: "I took Panama."

More such unilateral exercises of authority would follow in the years now opened to him. For the moment, on March 4, 1905, Theodore Roosevelt was being inaugurated president of the United States at the start of his own full term. Two weeks later he paid what he called "a scuttling visit to New York on Friday to give away Eleanor"—his favorite niece, his late brother's daughter, in marriage to her distant relative, the twenty-three-year-old Columbia law student Franklin Roosevelt—and to make two speeches on that same March 17 weekend, to the Friendly Sons of St. Patrick and the Sons of the American Revolution. Soon after, the Colonel was off on a five-week hunting trip to Oklahoma and Colorado, in pursuit of wolves in the one and bears in the other.

All this, and what had preceded it in the White House and more that was to follow, served merely to confirm prejudices long held by a current peevish New Yorker, Samuel Clemens, against "our windy and flamboyant President." About the hunting, for instance. Colonel Roosevelt, Tom Sawyer-like, did enjoy tallying up scores: of wrestling matches won, of how many coyote kills he was in on, of the bears he shot, one of which Clemens pretended to suspect was a cow. "Some say it was a bear—a real bear. These were eyewitnesses," the humorist conceded, "but they were all White House domestics; they are all under wages to the great hunter, and when a witness is in that condition it makes his testimony doubtful." Clemens is speaking to posterity a century on, not Mark Twain to contemporaries. "The fact," he dictates into his *Autobiography*, "that the President himself thinks it was a bear does not diminish the doubt but enlarges it. He," Roosevelt, "was once a reasonably modest man, but his judgment has been out of focus so long now that he imagines that everything he does, little or big, is colossal." Whichever it was, though—bear or cow— the creature was by general agreement exhausted, unable to go on, "in a frenzy of fright, with a President of the United States and a squadron of bellowing dogs" in three-hour hot pursuit, the cow-bear turning at last, according to the daily papers, "in an open spot, fifty feet wide," where it faced the President and mutely, humbly sought mercy. Clemens provides the script: "Have pity, sir, and spare me. I am alone, you are many; I have no weapon but my helplessness, you are a walking arsenal; I am in awful peril, you are as safe as you would be in a Sunday school."

Undeterred, the hunter had dispatched the bear or cow cleanly; that is, in sportsmanlike manner, his fellow countrymen were assured—none of which details in the news story made sense to Clemens back in New York. As for autocracy, according to this same follower of the press, America had already turned into an autocracy—Clemens's word was "monarchy," what we would call dictatorship—the very thing the White House's current occupant professed to be protecting us against by forswearing another run for the presidency. "Ours is not only a monarchy," Clemens averred, "but a hereditary monarchy—in the one political family." He is referring to the Republican Party, which by 1909 will have been in power (except for a couple of interruptions under the Democrat Cleveland) for just about the last half-century. The throne here at home "passes from heir to heir as regularly and as surely and as unpreventably as does any throne in Europe. Our monarch," moreover, "is more powerful, more arbitrary, more autocratic," Clemens insists, "than any in Europe, its White House commands are not under restraint of law or custom or the Constitution, it can ride down the Congress as the Czar cannot ride down the Duma."

So, in one observer's view at least, the United States had already turned into a hereditary monarchy all but absolute, as Princess Alice's grand wedding—soon much in the news—appeared to affirm. The beautiful Alice Roosevelt had settled on a suitor, one fifteen years her senior and bald, but in other respects entirely appropriate. Nicholas Longworth, Harvard '91, was scion of a wealthy, pure-blooded Cincinnati family with roots that went deep, four generations back, to the very founding of Ohio's Queen City. A gifted violinist and a witty, good-humored bachelor much sought after in Washington society, Longworth had been elected to the House of Representatives from Ohio's First District, launching a career in public service that Nick's soon-to-be father-in-law could take some pride in. Moreover, like Roosevelt, Mr. Longworth was not only politically inclined and hardworking. At Harvard he had been made a Porcellian, of which very exclusive social club Colonel Roosevelt was also a member; so that, among the hundreds of other guests attending the elaborate noontime wedding of Representative Longworth, thirty-six, and the President's daughter—just turned twenty-two—in the White House on a mild February morning in 1906, serenading Porcs were on hand, at what turned out to be the outstanding social event of the Roosevelt years. Of course the press covered the occasion breathlessly, as it had fully and tirelessly described all the many preparations leading up to so climactic an affair. But then, the metropolitan press covered everything. "These great dailies," according to Clemens, "keep us informed of Mr. Carnegie's movements and sayings; they tell us what President Roosevelt said yesterday and what he is going to do to-day. They tell us what the children of his family have been saying, just as the princelings of Europe are daily quoted—and we notice that the remarks of the Roosevelt children are distinctly princely in that the things they say are rather notably inane and not worth while. The great dailies kept us overwhelmed for a matter of two months," he grumbles, "with a daily and hourly and most minute and faithful account of everything Miss Alice and her fiancé were saying and doing and what they were going to say and what they were going to do, until at last through God's mercy they got married and went under cover and got quiet."

But Mr. Roosevelt never gets quiet, and that was part of what grated on Clemens's nerves. This same spring of 1906, busy as he was, the President had found time to read *The Jungle*, Upton Sinclair's just-published, sensational novel that exposed the horrors of Chicago's meatpacking industry; and although (in his exuberantly hyperbolic way) Roosevelt professed in private to feel "utter contempt" for the muckraking author as "hysterical, unbalanced, and untruthful," he responded to the public uproar by coming down on the other, popular side of the issue, sending inspectors to the stockyards and, in June, signing the Pure Food and Drug Act and a federal meat inspection act into law. In that same busy month Roosevelt signed the Antiquities Act, to protect ancient Indian ruins and artifacts in the West from destruction; and before the year was out he had used the law to set aside as national monuments not only the Petrified Forest but also the cliff dwellings of Montezuma Castle in Arizona, the Devil's Tower in Wyoming, and the ancient water hole at El Morro, New Mexico, with its 2,000 pictographs, signatures, and messages carved over the course of a centuries-long history. In June, too, President Roosevelt signed the Hepburn Act, which authorized the Interstate Commerce Commission to set maximum rates that railroads could charge, effectively doing away with free passes that were being granted to favored shippers.

All those matters the President was dealing with during the early busy months of his new term, those and much else both domestic and foreign, much of it simultaneously. Yet nothing caused more stir in the papers than the Brownsville incident, which broke upon the public awareness in mid-August of that same summer of 1906.

Some unimaginable ass in the War Department—in Clemens's phrase—had moved the Twenty-Fifth Colored Infantry from Nebraska to a posting on the Mexican border, at Brownsville, Texas, this at a time when Pitchfork Ben Tillman was reminding the Senate that "race hatred grows day by day" down South, with "constant friction, race riot, butchery, murder of whites by blacks and blacks by whites"—although far more of the latter (the senator neglects to add) than of the former. As for Brownsville, the army's commanding general in Texas acknowledged that citizens of that town of 6,000 "entertain race hatred to an extreme degree"; and those same overwrought Caucasians, getting wind of the color of troops assigned to replace the white soldiers on duty among them, pleaded with the secretary of war, in Clemens's words, "not to fling this firebrand into their midst." The black soldiers arrived, however, on July 25, 1906, and bunked down in barracks of a fort that nestled alongside the scruffy, highly charged border community.

Within three weeks, just before midnight on August 13, a crowd gathering in darkness at a back alley beside this Fort Brown went on a rampage. The ruckus was explosive and terrifying, shattering the night, although it lasted no longer than ten minutes. Next day townspeople, shaken, assembled a citizens committee that called before it twenty-two witnesses, all white. Only eight of them identified last night's rioters as black, and three of those hadn't seen faces, merely heard what they took to be black voices. Nevertheless, within two days the committee telegraphed to President Roosevelt at Oyster Bay that between twenty and thirty soldiers out of the fort, "carrying their rifles and abundant supply of ammunition," had randomly fired about 200 rounds into town shops and houses before returning to quarters. Behind them the rioters left two people wounded, one bartender dead, and a horse dead that a policeman had been riding away from the melee. There was talk that the outrage would be repeated; nor did white officers at the fort appear able to restrain their men. "Our condition, Mr. President, is this," the message concluded. "Our women and children are terrorized and our men are practically under constant alarm and watchfulness. No community can stand this strain for more than a few days. We look to you for relief; we ask you to have the troops at once removed from Fort Brown and replaced by white soldiers."

Twelve blacks suspected of taking part in the riot were in the Fort Brown guardhouse; but when the grand jury for Cameron County (with Brownsville as its county seat) considered the case, it could find no evidence on which to return an indictment. Meanwhile, the remainder of the three companies of blacks had been transferred to Fort Reno, in Oklahoma Territory; and to that site President Roosevelt ordered Inspector General Ernest A. Garlington to proceed on October 4, to carry out his own examination.

Garlington talked to the suspects one at a time. Whenever Brownsville was mentioned, each soldier in turn "assumed a wooden, stolid look, and each man positively denied any knowledge in the affair." They were given until five that afternoon to think it over. By then, no suspect had confessed to wrongdoing or implicated anybody else. Such unanimous denial might have hinted at innocence, but to Garlington it "indicated a possible general understanding among the enlisted men of this battalion as to the position they would take," even though he found "no such evidence of such understanding. The secretive nature of the race," however, "where crimes charged to members of their color are made, is well known." That led the official to conclude that the raid "was done by enlisted men of the Twenty-fifth Infantry." Therefore, because they were all standing together "in a determination to resist the detection of the guilty"—and even if innocent people had to suffer—they should all be made to "stand together when the penalty falls."

President Roosevelt concurred with Garlington's report. In early November he instructed Secretary of War Taft to carry out the inspector general's recommendation. One hundred sixty-seven soldiers were to be affected, and before the end of the month the last of them had been discharged from the army "without honor," forbidden ever to enlist again in any branch of the military or the civil service. Years later, in 1972—sixty-six years after the fact—the army revisited the case and reversed President Roosevelt's order of 1906. By then the newly exonerated were all dead except for one Dorsie Willis, to whom the Nixon administration granted a $25,000 pension for his pains.

What had led the Colonel to act as he did? Clemens wasn't alone in presuming it was all impulsively political. "Mr. Roosevelt had been anxious to convict some of those soldiers and thus get back into Southern favor," having early in his tenure offended the South by dining with Booker T. Washington at the White House, by appointing Dr. Crum to serve as collector at Charleston, and by shutting down a Mississippi post office rather than accede to the bigotry of white townspeople who had ousted their longtime postmistress solely for being black. Now the evenhanded president wanted some black soldiers to convict, but none came forward and confessed. Thus, "as he was not able to do it," Clemens concluded, "he did the next best thing; he convicted the entire command himself, without evidence and without excuse, and dismissed them from the army, adding those malignant and cowardly words, 'without honor.'"

Roosevelt, of course, saw the matter differently. His views on race were the scientifically informed ones of the era; and although he recognized the many exceptions to descriptions of each race's characteristics then current, and although he insisted on treating individuals as individuals whatever their race, nationality, creed, or social standing, he nevertheless did regard African-Americans as a group inferior in the evolutionary scale. Moreover, they exhibited a deplorable tendency to remain silent when others of their race committed atrocities, a trait well established in connection with the alleged incidences of black rapes of white women. "The white people of the South," the President elaborated in his annual message to Congress at this very time, "indict the whole colored race on the ground that even the better elements lend no assistance whatever to ferreting out criminals of their own color. The respectable colored people must learn not to harbor their criminals, but to assist the officers in bringing them to justice."

Let black soldiers learn that lesson as well. Yet in the end Roosevelt insisted that his decision had nothing to do with race. He would have acted exactly the same if the defendants had been white. It did have to do—had everything to do—with the honor of the army. African-American editors in unison protested the President's summary dismissals—which were (and remain) the largest in the army's history—deploring it all the more out of a sense of betrayal. This white man, they had thought, was their friend. Booker Washington appealed to Roosevelt to change his mind. Might the two at least discuss the matter? "You cannot have any information to give me privately to which I could pay heed, my dear Mr. Washington, because the information on which I act is that which came out of the investigation itself."

And maybe some black soldiers—rough and rootless in the peacetime army, bored and restless, bitter about extreme Jim Crow humiliations they hadn't met with up North or out West—were guilty. But over months of testimony in a Senate investigation that followed, their white officers all bore witness to the high character and discipline of the black soldiers involved. Moreover, the soldiers' pistols had been in their shipping cases on the night of the incident. If, as charged, pistols had been fired, soldiers couldn't have fired them. Other testimony spoke of seven white civilians seen loitering in the alleyway before the riot, and even on a bright night—which August 13 was not—neither the skin color nor the clothing of the rioters, whether uniformed or otherwise, could have been made out from where eyewitnesses said they were standing.

"I feel the most profound indifference to any possible attack which can be made on me in this matter," Colonel Roosevelt answered a critic at the time. "When the discipline and honor of the American army are at stake I shall never under any circumstances consider the political bearing of upholding that discipline and that honor, and no graver misfortune could happen to that American army than failure to punish in the most signal way such conduct as that which I have punished in the manner of which you complain."

He clarified his attitude thus, privately, to Governor Guild of Massachusetts on November 7, 1906. The following day President Roosevelt put cares aside and left the country, the first president to leave the United States while in office. In high spirits, he and Mrs. Roosevelt were on their way to Panama to inspect progress being made in carving out the isthmian canal.

CHAPTER **Thirty-Eight**

Global Visions

ounded in 1885, the Gridiron Club has flourished from the nineteenth century into the present day, notably through the annual dinner that its journalist members host in the nation's capital, a white-
tie affair where politicians including the President of the United States,
along with other public figures of distinction, are invited to dine with the
Washington press corps. Fellowship abounds amid speeches of wit, good
spirits, and self-deprecation. The club was entertained, for instance, by
Mark Twain speaking "in his happiest vein" for twenty minutes on a January evening in 1906. President Roosevelt was in attendance.

A year later, on Saturday, January 26, 1907, at the New Willard Hotel,
the President, back from Panama, was again a guest of the Gridiron Club,
as the featured speaker, among other such distinguished diners as Vice
President Fairbanks, Supreme Court Justice Harlan, Speaker of the House
Cannon, and—from the world outside politics—the financier J. P. Morgan
and the Standard Oil executive Henry Huttleston Rogers.

Proceedings at those annual banquets were meant to be kept in confidence, in order that politicians and journalists might trade jibes in good
fun, without fear of reading their sallies in newspapers next morning for
the public to misinterpret. But from this particular occasion emerged rumors that the President last night had spoken warmly for nearly an hour—
not at all what had been expected—defending his administration and chas-
tising not only big business but, more specifically, Senator Joseph Foraker
of Ohio, big business's good friend seated there at the banquet. Instead of
displaying the traditional conviviality, the young chief executive, still two
years short of fifty, had shaken his fist at venerable J. P. Morgan, sixty-nine,
and at H. H. Rogers of Standard Oil, about to turn sixty-seven, instructing
them both that Wall Street should thank its stars that its excesses were

being addressed by a Republican administration and the conservative leader standing before them. Far better these than the Democrats and Mr. Bryan, whose radical program would impose on the magnates a drastic set of reforms favored by "the mob, the mob, the mob." Rogers and Morgan were said to have turned fiery red at the scolding. As for Senator Foraker, who nurtured his own presidential ambitions and who a month earlier had called for the Senate to investigate the Brownsville matter, President Roosevelt let the senator know that any such investigation was already moot, inasmuch as the legislative branch lacked constitutional authority to review actions taken by the executive branch. Moreover, this particular chief executive would permit no one to interfere with his discharging his duty as he saw fit.

President Roosevelt's rambling speech was applauded only tepidly. Senator Foraker rose next to respond for twenty minutes, while the Colonel clenched his fists, gritted his teeth, and shook his head in negation. "I did not come to the Senate to take orders from anybody," Foraker exclaimed in the course of a reply that the audience applauded warmly. Roosevelt was reported to have spoken for ten additional minutes before leaving the room.

Senator Foraker offered nothing more that night, but he wasn't done. Many months later, on April 14, 1908, as the Senate's lengthy investigation of the Brownsville affair finally drew to an end, the legislator eloquently defended the 167 black soldiers whom President Roosevelt two Novembers earlier had discharged without honor from the army. "The vilest horse thief," said Foraker, "the most dangerous burglar, or the bloodiest murderer would not be required either to prove his innocence or to submit to a trial before a judge who had in even the most casual way expressed the opinion that the defendant was guilty." Yet that was how the battalion at Brownsville had been dealt with. "Who are these men that it should be even suggested that they should be treated worse than common criminals? They are," Foraker asserted, "at once both citizens and soldiers of the Republic. Aside from these charges, which they deny, their behavior, both in the Army and out of it, has justly excited the highest commendation. Their record is without spot or blemish." For that matter, the race that the men represent "has ever been loyal to America and American institutions; a race that has never raised a hostile hand against our country's flag; a race that has contributed to the nation tens of thousands of brave defenders, not one of whom has ever turned traitor or faltered in his fidelity." In every war in which they have been permitted to fight, blacks have distinguished themselves. "They have shed their blood and laid down their lives in the fierce shock of battle, side by side with their white comrades." And now, the senator concluded, they ask for "no favors because they are Negroes, but only for justice because they are men."

The commotion on the Senate floor that greeted those stirring words was loud and prolonged, even though the majority report that the military affairs committee submitted upheld the President's actions, with only four Republican senators dissenting on grounds that the evidence against the soldiers was inconclusive. In a separate dissent, Foraker and one other committee member went further, declaring outright that the soldiers were innocent.

Mark Twain agreed with the minority view; but it was not Brownsville and Roosevelt's brash, impulsive behavior in that wretched affair that constituted the humorist's principal quarrel with the sitting president. Nor the hunting. Nor the public rudeness and disrespect shown to Clemens's dear friend and benefactor H. H. Rogers at the Gridiron dinner. Nor was it that before the dinner Roosevelt, around the time he was setting off for Panama in November 1906, had instructed his overactive justice department to file suit to dissolve Standard Oil of New Jersey (a suit that would drag on into the administration of the Colonel's successor, when the Supreme Court finally settled the matter, in 1911—after Mark Twain's death—by finding in the government's favor: the monopoly had to be broken up). Nor were Clemens's objections based primarily on the 1904 Republican presidential campaign's accepting money from that same Standard Oil. (Actually, when Roosevelt found out about the contribution, he had it sent back.) Nor, finally, did the humorist base his dislike on the fact that the President, a politician like all those other politicians in Washington, had been buying votes through such means as the notorious Pension Order No. 78, an executive addition to a pension bill passed in Congress in April 1904.

To our ears pensions back then sound niggardly enough, this most recent one that Congress had authorized providing a maximum of $100 a month for Union veterans who had lost both hands or both feet or the sight of both eyes; $72 a month when a veteran's degree of helplessness required full-time aid; $55 a month for loss of an arm at the shoulder joint; $40 for loss of one hand or one foot; and so on. The President—with the election still seven months ahead of him—had chosen to supplement that congressional act by recognizing old age itself as a disability that required no further proof, so that veterans who had served honorably ninety days or more in the Civil War were now to receive an extra $6 a month at age sixty-two, $8 at sixty-five, $12 at seventy. In those pre–New Deal days before social security, the order would seem to do Roosevelt's humanity credit;

but for Clemens such a giveaway of public funds bore the stench of bribery, those "many and amazing additions to the pension list" from a motive that "dishonors the uniform and the Congresses which have voted the additions—the sole purpose back of the additions being the purchase of votes." So it had been in Roman times: "liberties were not auctioned off in a day," Clemens noted, "but were bought slowly, gradually, furtively, little by little; first with a little corn and oil for the exceedingly poor and wretched, later with corn and oil for voters who were not quite so poor, later still with corn and oil for pretty much every man that had a vote to sell—exactly our own history over again."

But to the humorist's way of thinking, none of all that, including Roosevelt's malodorous Pension Order No. 78, was as offensive as was what the Colonel's recent Panama trip bespoke: his striding over distant soil in his role as America's beneficent emperor, ruler of our new American empire. For it was the President's actions in foreign affairs that particularly galled Samuel Clemens. Back in 1898, in Major McKinley's reign, we had made a show of liberating the Philippines from the Spaniard—gratefully accepting Filipino aid while doing so—then turned around and replaced the former occupier with our own troops in encampment. Those American troops went on to make war on the natives with all the vigor of the forces they had driven out. Since 1901, homefolks had been repeatedly assured that the archipelago was pacified, that the Filipino "rebels"—who might as easily be called patriots fighting for their republic—had laid down their arms and accepted the "benevolent assimilation" that these present foreigners were imposing upon them. Yet just the other day, as late as March 9, 1906 (and the decorations hardly down from Princess Alice's wedding in the White House), we learned of Governor-General Leonard Wood's "victory" over a passel of some 900 natives—men, women, and children—Moros, Muslims whom American troops on the rim of an extinct volcano in the southwest Philippines had fired down upon in their crater and massacred. "I congratulate you and the officers and men of your command," their president had cabled the leader of such warriors, all but unscathed on their heights, "upon the brilliant feat of arms wherein you and they so well upheld the honor of the American flag."

In Clemens's view, Roosevelt was insane about war anyway, and feats of arms, and the honor of the American flag no matter in what sordid way the "honor" was upheld. On the penultimate day of his life President McKinley had spoken, to a crowd of 50,000 at the Pan-American Exhibition in Buffalo, about America's new prosperity and the need for reciprocal trade with other nations so that we might sell the amassing inventory of that prosperity in markets overseas. Prosperity is well and good, his successor in the White House agreed, "yet a really great people, proud and high-spirited, would face all the disaster of war rather than purchase that base prosperity which is bought at the price of national honor." While assistant secretary of the navy, Theodore Roosevelt had spoken thus at the Naval War College at Newport in the late spring of 1897, and Clemens might have wondered what he was talking about. Then as at other times, war was much on Roosevelt's mind, specifically war against Spaniards clinging to Cuba. Some American businessmen, profiting from trade with the island, deplored any bellicose posturing; but "the great masterful races," the secretary had told his naval officers, all "have been fighting races, and the minute that a race loses the hard fighting virtues, then, no matter what else it may retain, no matter how skilled in commerce and finance, in science or art, it has lost its proud right to stand as the equal of the best." Roosevelt had gone on to assure his listeners that cowardice in a race, as in an individual, is "the unpardonable sin, and a willful failure to prepare for any danger may in its effects be as bad as cowardice." The man afraid to fight, he said, is scarcely worse than "the selfish, short-sighted, or foolish man" who will not prepare himself to fight if he has to.

A year after those sentiments were uttered, we fought in Cuba and won, and won in the Philippines, and drove the Spaniard out of our hemisphere and out of the Pacific archipelago, we whom none could accuse of being a violent nation. "We are a great peaceful nation," Secretary Roosevelt had reminded Newport naval officers before the war; "a nation of merchants and manufacturers, of farmers and mechanics; a nation of workingmen, who labor incessantly with head or hand. It is idle," he had said, "to talk of such a nation ever being led into a course of wanton aggression or conflict with military powers by the possession of a sufficient navy." For this same assistant secretary had all the while been bent on building up America's armed forces afloat, in order to protect sea lanes for our trade with other countries and to defend ourselves from the menaces of rivals. In those days before air power, the navy possessed our principal weaponry; so that when, not five years later, that same young secretary had been transformed into a hero of the war in Cuba and become president of the United States, he pursued the strengthening of our armaments at sea with unabated vigor. He got Congress to add two battleships to the fleet each year (he wanted four) and, partly through naval means, was able to wrest from Colombia the Isthmus that became the Republic of Panama.

It was our navy that had vanquished the Spaniard in 1898, at Manila and at Santiago; our navy, in late 1902 and early 1903, that had dissuaded

Germany from imposing its imperial will on debt-ridden Venezuela, an imposition that appeared prelude to establishing a German colony in South America under our very noses; and our navy that secured Panama's autonomy in 1903 and allowed for a treaty that opened the way to digging the canal connecting the Atlantic with the Pacific.

The Venezuelan crisis had ended peacefully, the Kaiser retreating precisely because Admiral Dewey in the Caribbean stood ready to do battle. As one outgrowth of the German withdrawal, President Roosevelt's annual message to Congress in December 1904 contained what came to be known as his corollary to the Monroe Doctrine. The original doctrine, dating from 1823, had declared that the Western Hemisphere, including nations recently carved out of a moribund Spanish empire in South and Central America, was no longer open to colonization, however feebly any such newly formed nations might be defending their independence. Roosevelt's corollary eighty-one years later enlarged on the doctrine by stating that henceforth the United States alone would intervene, preemptively when necessary, in order to stabilize any country in our hemisphere in such disorder that it was incapable of meeting its international obligations. Europe must leave America alone to police our half of the globe. And as promptly as two months after the corollary had been promulgated, we signed a protocol with the Dominican Republic (deep in debt like many of those fragile sovereignties) to collect and distribute its customs duties until its foreign creditors were paid, a span stretching over the next two and a half years. Similarly, in the early fall of 1906 Roosevelt intervened in Cuba. "I am so angry with that infernal little Cuban republic that I would like to wipe its people off the face of the earth," the President blustered privately; for the island government had collapsed in chaos. Whereupon, our forces arrived and remained through the couple of years it took to empower a new regime, one incidentally that proved more accommodating to America's commercial interests.

None of this big-stick meddling in the internal affairs of sovereign countries would have sat well with the anti-imperialist newspaper-reader Samuel Clemens. Clemens would have scowled when Judge Taft, now secretary of war, returned to the Philippines in the summer of 1905, the former civilian governor of that archipelago back on a far-eastern inspection trip along with the President's as-yet-unmarried eldest daughter and a congressional delegation that included Representative Nicholas Longworth of Ohio. "I am not come to give you your Independence," Big Bill Taft informed his hosts on arriving. "You will have your Independence when you are ready for it, which will not be in this generation—no, nor in the next, nor perhaps for a hundred years or more." Meanwhile, the American press, following the grand tour's progress—garden parties, native dancers, colorful visits with heads of state from there to Japan to Korea to China and back to Japan—was preoccupied less with what Secretary Taft said to his hosts in the Philippines than with what Representative Longworth and Miss Roosevelt, at sea together, were saying to each other. Had the couple become engaged? The two kept quiet about that, even though Judge Taft himself would have liked to know.

For all his frontier Missouri upbringing, Samuel Clemens was meanwhile interpreting such global news as this of the Philippines from no provincial viewpoint. By now Mark Twain was a citizen of the world, having seen more of it than just about anybody else alive: a cosmopolite and intellectual (with a low regard for Mr. Roosevelt's intellect, by the way). Yet despite his own globe-girdling experiences, perhaps the humorist was naive. He thought, for instance, that the victorious Commodore Dewey, having destroyed the Spanish fleet in Manila Bay in May 1898, would have needed only to put up a sign on shore that the United States guaranteed the integrity of the Philippine Republic, then sailed away, and all the great powers of Europe and Asia would have left the islands alone. But naive or not, Clemens did have a sharp sense these few years later that, under the glory-craving Roosevelt, the nation had taken a wrong turn. After the Boxer uprising was quelled, McKinley had quite properly withdrawn our soldiers from China. What business did they have in China? And why were our troops holding the Philippines under their heel this late, having gone there only to give an oppressed people its freedom? What were our soldiers doing in the Dominican Republic? What were they doing in Cuba?

The humorist could never have foreseen—though he seems sometimes to have intuited—the America of our own day. Back then nobody could have: the more than 800 permanent United States military bases set up in foreign countries on every continent but Antarctica, not counting bases at present (2012) in Afghanistan and (still) in Iraq; the more than 300,000 troops on permanent deployment in Europe, the Far East, and elsewhere around the globe (again not counting those at war in the Near East); a military budget of some $671 billion annually (yet again discounting the wars, budgeted separately, that the nation has been engaged in for so many years); over 180 American interventions in foreign countries between 1900 and 2000 that have ranged from before Abyssinia in 1903 to long after Zaire in 1978; a Central Intelligence Agency that functions without oversight, essentially as the President's private army; and the chief executive himself invested with swelling imperial powers assumed on the all but unchallengeable grounds of national security. Throughout, our United States remains in what amounts to a perpetual state of war, fighting against an emotion, against terror. A $3 trillion war on terror. It would have been too much for Sam Clemens, who (as his friend Howells tells us) took America hard. Even his own times, at the outset of our progress toward policing the globe, was proving too much for the humorist. "The 20th century is a stranger to me," he wrote in his notebook. "I wish it well but my heart is all for my own century. I took 65 years of it," of that earlier century, "just on a risk, but if I had known as much about it as I know now I would have taken the whole of it."

CHAPTER **Thirty-Nine**

Bereft and Adrift

From the beginning Samuel Clemens as Mark Twain reacted to the world he lived in. His famous pen name first appeared out in Nevada in the *Territorial Enterprise* under a humorous report describing a party the journalist had just attended, in 1863, in Carson City. And even this late, into a new century, Clemens by means of that pseudonym was regularly setting down thoughts on current events, some of it to be printed, although much was left unpublished in his lifetime. He did publish his views, for instance, on Belgium's execrable King Leopold II, whose lackeys in the Congo were burning villages and chopping off hands—baskets filled with them—from the arms of African natives remiss in delivering their quotas of rubber to sate the royal greed. By means of his satirical "To the Person Sitting in Darkness," which appeared in 1901, Mark Twain exposed Europe's gross hypocrisy in pursuing colonial plunder in general. He published a scathing soliloquy as if spoken by Nicholas II, vain, dimwitted Czar of all the Russias. He put into print his thoughts on America's imperialist ambitions, muting the scorn he actually felt in order to avoid utterly alienating the many readers here at home who didn't share his views. But he wrote more bitterly, for his own sake, about such matters in pages left in manuscript, concerning his low opinion, for example, of a national hero and Roosevelt favorite, General Leonard Wood, and his hatred of a social outrage thriving at the time, through the searing essay "The United States of Lyncherdom," written in 1901 but left unpublished until 1923, long after its author's death.

From 1891, in fact, on into the twentieth century, Samuel Clemens as Mark Twain wrote all but constantly, even feverishly, with few intermissions, the same author who had presumed late in the 1880s that he was about done with writing, the same who had told his daughter Susy that he had written enough by then, and that his present project—which would appear in 1889 as *A Connecticut Yankee in King Arthur's Court*—would be his final book. How differently things had worked out! Hartford's Samuel Clemens was to have set aside his pen by the early 1890s and become a full-fledged capitalist, already one of America's most prosperous publishers, to be made infinitely wealthier, Rockefeller wealthy, through the success of Paige's amazing typesetter. Instead, in June 1891, the Clemenses moved to Europe to economize. From overseas Mark Twain returned to his writing through the next few years in order to make money, awakened from dreams of easy, uncountable wealth by the delicacy of the typesetter's 20,000 parts—that and by the bankruptcy the same year of Clemens's formerly resplendent Charles L. Webster & Company, Publishers.

In Europe and during frequent business trips back to America in the early nineties, the author went on writing, and in mid-decade he lectured around the world to support his family and pay off creditors of the failed publishing house. Then—those creditors soon to be satisfied—Clemens was forced to write out of the depths of grief, to preserve his sanity. For his daughter Susy had died, suddenly, unexpectedly, at the end of two dreadful weeks through hot summer days of August 1896, with her father far off in England unaware, unable to help her, to see her, to kiss her a final time.

Twice during that year in America away from her parents, Susy had spent time with Louise Brownell, her Bryn Mawr friend, once among relatives at Quarry Farm, later with other friends in New Jersey. Restless, this eldest daughter stayed for several weeks back East with the Howellses and the Rices, her father's intimates. During the summer she went up to Hartford and visited the Charles Dudley Warners, writing, practicing her singing, awaiting the day for boarding ship and sailing with younger sister Jean to England to rejoin the rest of her family after their worldwide travels. In August, Katy Leary, the Clemenses' maid of many years, arrived in Hartford to fetch her.

Katy found her charge ill. "'Oh, have I got to leave now?' She was really in an awful state and I said: 'Yes, Susy. We are sailing to-morrow, you know.'" But the young woman begged to wait until it turned cooler that evening. By then, though, she was "in a pitiful state," according to Katy, recalling details that Susy's mother and father would have her repeat again and again: "so sick and full of fever." Dr. Porter was sent for. Uncle Charley and Aunt Sue, Mrs. Clemens's brother and sister who had come east to Manhattan to see the young people off, hurried to Hartford. Joe Twichell—Uncle Joe—came from an Adirondacks vacation to be with Susy. The patient grew worse. They took her across the way to the Clemenses' home, unoccupied just then, where she might feel more comfortable in familiar surroundings. Dr. Porter identified the young woman's malady as spinal meningitis. "She was very sick," Katy recalled, "and she wouldn't take a bit of medicine from anybody but me."

Her father brooded on all such details that Katy relayed to him later. "In our house," he described Susy's last days, "after they took her there she was up and dressed and writing all the time—poor troubled head!" Delirium led Susy to scribble page after incoherent page: "to me darkness must remain from everlasting to everlasting forever sometimes less painful darkness but darkness is the complement of light yes tell her to say she trusts you child of great darkness and light to me who can keep the darkness universal and free from sensual taint and lead her on to strength and power and peace . . ."

Such ramblings held about all that was left of a sufferer's dying. "In the burning heat of those final days in Hartford," her father wrote afterward, treasuring whatever Katy, Susan Crane, Charley Langdon, or Joe Twichell could tell him, "she would walk to the window or lie on the couch in her fever and delirium, and when the cars went by would say: 'Up go the trolley cars for Mark Twain's daughter. Down go the trolley cars for Mark Twain's daughter.'" By Saturday, Susy's condition had deteriorated drastically; she took a bite of food for the last time that evening. The next day her affliction reached the eyes: "I am blind, Uncle Charlie"; and finally she put out her hand and touched Katy's face and said "Mama"—her last word—then, a father steeped in heartbreaking images from far off recorded, "composed herself as if for sleep, and never moved again. She fell into unconsciousness and so remained two days and five hours, until Tuesday evening"—the 18th of August, 1896—"at seven minutes past seven, when the release came."

Clemens was overwhelmed with self-reproach. "If I could call up a single instance," he wrote to Livy away in America, "where I laid aside my own projects and desires and put myself to real inconvenience to procure a pleasure for her, I would forget all things else to remember that." He raged: if only he and Livy could have been with Susy in her illness. If only Livy and Clara, sailing from England at the earliest news, had got to Hartford in time, instead of reaching the New York piers three days too late. "Yes, God would not give us that little solace, not even to you. I should not mention myself—I deserve all I get. But you! What has He done to you? Punished you on the rack for living the life of a ministering angel, a faultless mother. I hate Him for that."

After the funeral in Elmira, the abandoned mother was left with nothing to turn to for balm, too grief stricken back in England to venture out or see guests or so much as read. Poor Jean in this same horrible year, 1896, was gripped with seizures that for the first time revealed her disorder to be epilepsy. As for the father, his salvation lay in work. The family took up quarters in London, at 23 Tedworth Square, and shut themselves off from society. Holidays, which had such meaning earlier—birthdays, the elaborate Christmas festivities over joyful winter weeks in Hartford—were ignored, passed by without a word. Clara recalled that it was a long time "before anyone laughed in our house." Clemens had thrown himself into his writing, from after breakfast until seven in the evening without a break, as always dabbling in several projects at once, although primarily struggling with what would emerge as *Following the Equator: A Journey Around the World*. That volume, which appeared late in 1897, sold well enough to pay off the last of the creditors, with—under H. H. Rogers's skillful management—money left over to invest in whatever might remain of the Clemenses' diminished future.

His fans welcomed this newest of Mark Twain's travel books. The author had started out as a travel writer, with *The Innocents Abroad* (1869) and *A Tramp Abroad* (1880) remaining popular even now, in 1897; in all three—those two and this new one—a traveler responds to the present that he and his readers share. But unlike those three books, much of Mark Twain's writing—including much of the best of it—is located far from any present, at a distance well into the past: in the vanished stagecoach West described in *Roughing It* (1872), composed while the railroad was transforming that region; or in the antebellum Mississippi River valley that *Tom Sawyer* (1876), *Huckleberry Finn* (1885), and *Pudd'nhead Wilson* (1894) evoked three or four decades later; or in England of the sixteenth century as depicted in *The Prince and the Pauper* (1881); or in the fifteenth-century France of *Joan of Arc* (1896); or again in England as far back as King Arthur's time in the sixth century, where *A Connecticut Yankee* is set. And although in the dark wake of Susy's death, Mark Twain was obliged again to write of a present he had come to detest—or, rather, of the hateful recent past encountered on his lecture tour—he did somehow finish *Following the Equator*, reproaching himself all the while for being able to suspend his grief to do so, even finding the means to fill what he was writing with sunlight and some humor, with much information and the vivid color that readers of Mark Twain's various excursions had learned to expect.

But gloom threatened to creep in. Earlier the author had talked about how to write narratives like this one: lay down a plank to get the reader from here to there—around the world, say, to the 600-page length of a subscription book—then fill holes in the plank with anecdotes, as digressive as you want as long as they're interesting. One such devised for *Following the Equator* turned into "The Enchanted Sea-Wilderness," supposedly told by a crewman on board the ship that had borne the Clemenses across the Indian Ocean. The author claims to have heard an old salt on the forecastle one midnight those couple of years back recall a horrific adventure he had been part of decades earlier, in 1853, in that same limitless sea. The mate had been on the *Mabel Thorpe*, which had a dog aboard, a beautiful St. Bernard that had wandered up the gangway just before the vessel set sail. The crew loved that pet: "full of play, and fun, and affection and good nature, the dearest and sweetest disposition that ever was." Not a man but would share his grub with the dog. And smart: would turn out at eight bells with the larboard watch and tug at lines to help take sail in.

Then came a night on the *Thorpe* becalmed at sea, all hands asleep except for the lookout and the drowsy deckwatch, when suddenly "a tremendous scratching and barking at the captain's door," the dog alerting the ship to a fire on board. Just in time: powder kegs jettisoned, boat launched, the dog dancing around, cavorting, happy in the excitement. With all hands in the boat, old Captain Cable—"a rough man and hardhearted"—delayed on the ship's deck long enough to tie the dog to the mainmast, then leapt in himself, flames rising behind him. "All ready," he cried. "Give *way*!"

Appalled, the crew fell to pleading. You can't leave the dog. But they did: too big for the boat, the captain yelled; would be underfoot, eat more than a family. Now give way!—and the boat pushed off, the dog barking in the ship's red glare, prancing on deck at the length of the rope until abruptly it sat down, puzzled as the boat grew smaller. All at once the creature rose on its hind legs and strained with all its might, moaning and shrieking as the crew, receding, watched the flames advance. Within minutes it was all over.

Old Captain Cable fancied he was lucky—always had been—and for a while it appeared so, for the men in their boat weren't long in sighting a ship on the horizon. They rowed for it and scampered aboard, aware that the dog could have been brought along after all. On board, sickness had robbed the *Adelaide* of its captain and some of its crew, so the new hands were welcomed, old Cable taking charge and setting a course toward safety. But judgment followed promptly for what that captain had done back there with the dog. Just ahead lay eighteen nights and days of violent tempest, through which the *Adelaide* was tossed hundreds of miles without a sighting to fix its location, utterly lost by the end of the storm, at which time the vessel was enveloped in nine days of impenetrable fog. Noon turned to night and the compass spun wildly, the captain white with fear, the crew in terror. They had entered the dense gray Devil's Race-Track, a miles-thick circle of gloom not on any chart but known to every sailor. At last the fog gave way to the deadly calm of the eye within. Everlasting Sunday: sky blue overhead and frost in the rigging. "The stillness was horrible, and the absence of life. There was not a bird or a creature of any kind in sight, the slick surface of the water was never broken by a fin, never a breath of wind fanned the dead air, and there was not a sound of any kind, even the faintest—the silence of death was everywhere."

Throughout, Mark Twain evokes the crew's world with the vividness of one who has spent months at sea himself. Images create the misery and hopelessness of the sailors' plight. They've rowed to and boarded one of the nearby ships trapped for decades in the calm, in this same motionless Everlasting Sunday, corpses sprawled about and turned to leather. The horror is palpable.

But how rescue the doomed men from their colossal prison? Having got them aboard the derelict vessel, the ten pages of narrative break off in mid-sentence. Completed, it would doubtless have been too bleak a digression to include in *Following the Equator* anyway: this account written in the fall of 1896, Susy's death only weeks in the past, the beautiful, beloved creature having perished feverishly in the flames of Hartford's summer, and punishment afterward levied on a father who had left her behind and sailed off into what would prove to be storms, thick fog, and finally a sense of perpetual absence in a void without meaning.

Disaster informed much of what Mark Twain wrote through the months and years that followed Susy's death; and much of it—although often worked out at length and with care—he couldn't finish. In "Which Was the Dream?" (1897) he describes a brilliant graduate of West Point who has served with distinction in the Mexican War, recently elected to the United States Senate, now talked of for president. The gentleman's adoring wife inherits a fortune, which the two use in part to build a Washington mansion. In his new home one evening he falls asleep at his desk, only briefly—a matter of moments—and the remainder of the forty pages that the unfinished story comprises recounts his dream: all his worldly success betrayed by a trusted associate, so that the gentleman, hopelessly in debt, deep in disgrace, is forced to move his wife and daughters into dire poverty, in the rudest of shacks in the California woods. Again, Mark Twain breaks off (the dreamer was to have waked with a start back in his mansion), but the applicability of the fragment to the author's own situation is clear, right down to the betrayal by a trusted associate, Clemens convinced that the bankruptcy of Charles L. Webster & Company, Publishers, had come about through his employees' incompetence and defalcations.

Much of what the author struggled to create after Susy's death, in the midst of his exile overseas, involved such disasters and dreams as this. Clemens's own dreams appear to have been singularly vivid, letting him perceive the very texture of clothing, for instance: "its dull white color, and the pale brown tint of a stain on the shoulder." The girl dreamed as dressed thus he had never seen before; "I was not acquainted with her—but dead or alive she is a reality; she exists and she was there." Perceptions in such sharp focus had led him to conclude that "my other self, my dream self, is merely my ordinary body and mind freed from clogging flesh and become a spiritualized body and mind and with the ordinary powers of both enlarged in all particulars a little, and in some particulars prodigiously." His dreams, then, were simply "immense excursions in my spiritualized person. I go into awful dangers; I am in battles and trying to hide from the bullets; I fall over cliffs (and my unspiritualized body starts). I get lost in caves and in the corridors of monstrous hotels; I appear before company in my shirt; I come on the platform with no subject to talk about, and not a note; I go to unnamable places, I do unprincipled things; and every vision is vivid, every sensation—physical as well as moral—is real."

Thus in the 1890s a dreamer such as this one self-exiled in Europe was led to wonder: were earlier times—those far-off glory years, all that bliss beyond an ocean in Hartford—real? Did they really happen? Is this present—bankrupt, bereft, adrift—no more than a nightmare to wake from? In 1897, having left England, Clemens and his family lived in Switzerland for a couple of months, at Weggis, before moving on to Vienna for a stay of nearly two years. Among other projects Mark Twain was working then on an untitled novel, posthumously known as "The Great Dark," which reached some 25,000 words. Again a family is enjoying an idyllic life, father and two daughters peering through a toy microscope (gift for one child's eighth birthday) at the infinitesimal creatures in a drop of water, while the mother looks contentedly on. Abruptly a dream by the nodding father intrudes, the family aboard a ship under sail in perpetual darkness. No one on board knows where they are now or where the ship is bound. Which world is real: these dire surroundings afloat or that other life on land, in a happy home peering through a microscope that is a child's eighth birthday present? As before, the dream lasts no longer than a minute, but the time on shipboard stretches through the nearly fifty pages that the story occupies, and the longer the voyage to nowhere continues, the more real it becomes and the fainter becomes the life left behind on shore. The family, miniaturized, is revealed to be sailing on that very drop of water studied earlier, along the dark edges beyond the microscope's lighted circle. The drop had been full of minuscule creatures that now resemble giant squids, threatening, indeed at one point devouring one of the children—those same harmless creatures that in a different life had been viewed complacently under the lens.

At one point William Dean Howells remarked to his friend: "Clemens"—this was in the 1890s, in New York, the delighted recipient promptly passing the compliment on to his family overseas. "Clemens, you have got the most magnificent imagination of anyone in literature today, and the freshest and newest, and most striking. You have already written the longed-for Great American Romance, though nobody seems to know it"—that would be *Huckleberry Finn*—"and you will do it again. What stupendous fame you would have if you were only a foreigner!" To which the author thus singled out adds: "How is that for praise?"

He did write voluminously in the nineties and on into the early years of the new century, some of it only for money and not very good: *The American Claimant* (1892), *Tom Sawyer Abroad* (1894). Some of what he wrote was set in the present, some of it topical, some published, some not; but there was other writing that he worked on hard and long and was never able to complete, projects that stretched his wonderful imagination to the limit. In one amazing effort that, printed after his death, runs to 120 pages even unfinished, the protagonist has been transformed through a medical mishap into a cholera germ. His new surroundings are worked out in detail, revealed to be the insalubrious intestines of a tramp named Blitzowski, riddled with disease and thus a paradise for a germ colony. In this "3,000 Years Among the Microbes," earth time is converted into microbe time, traces of the Microbic language appear in the occasional untranslatable term, and the tramp's body is revealed as a spacious and varied cosmos within which bacteria live out their dutiful, faith-filled lives corrupting Blitzowski's interior, piously oblivious of their murderous occupation. Which suggests "that man is himself a microbe, and his globe a blood corpuscle drifting with its shining brethren of the Milky Way down a vein of the Master and Maker of all things." Maybe, in other words, some creature of a dimension that fills the universe contains us all, the way Blitzowski's gut encompasses its billions of ignorant germs.

In writing thus—here as elsewhere in these late years—Mark Twain responds not only to the present world he lives in. He evokes as well the past that his present grew out of, its microscopic constituents, and the infinity of space, the eternity of time through which earth in its galaxy hurtles.

CHAPTER **Forty**

Young People

The Clemens and Roosevelt families were both steeped in the values of their Victorian age. But the one family was feminine, the other predominantly masculine. To be sure, the Roosevelts of Sagamore Hill—the masculine one—numbered two girls among their half-dozen children. Alice, however, stood off from the rest, something of a rebel in her youth, although a sensible one, her sins always venial—smoking, dancing, playing poker, driving fast in automobiles—causing her proper parents more exasperation than grief. And in her young adulthood Alice, by then married to a congressman from Ohio, became devoted to the political world in which husband and father both thrived, as excited as they about maneuverings of political parties, the drama of nominating conventions, and tensions on election night. Even in her late teens and early twenties Alice as the President's representative had shown a gift for spreading goodwill in Cuba and Puerto Rico; and in the summer of 1905 she had gone on that four-month cruise to Hawaii and the Far East with Secretary Taft and a congressional delegation. Celebrated by then as Princess Alice, the handsome, poised, and gracious young woman made a fine impression wherever she appeared: in the Philippines, in Japan, in Korea, and in China. She was married the following year; and from her elaborate wedding day on, she and her father grew increasingly close.

Alice Roosevelt was a being apart, however. The other Roosevelt daughter, Ethel, by the same mother as the boys in the family, was more conventional, a tomboy when young—thus at ease in her brothers' rambunctious world—but at an appropriate age, twenty-one, marrying an old friend, a surgeon with whom she lived out her long and useful adulthood as Mrs. Derby, mother of four and so-called Queen of Oyster Bay.

Figure 40.1.   The Roosevelt family at Sagamore Hill, 1907. From left: Kermit, Archie, Theodore, Ethel, Edith, Quentin, and Ted. Alice, recently married, is absent from the picture.

Ethel's four brothers—Ted, Kermit, Archie, and Quentin—were the ones who by sheer numbers set the decidedly masculine tone at Sagamore Hill. It could hardly have been otherwise, given a father so committed to manliness. Theodore Roosevelt strove to be for his children all that his own father had been for him, passing along the values he had learned as a child. Enjoy life. Don't waste time. Do your duty. Play hard; play fair; and when you work, don't play at all. The boys, like their father, strove toward the same clean living that was expected of the girls, father and sons alike eschewing profanity and raunchiness. All six of the children were readers; and the boys were intensely competitive, some better than others in the struggle, but all of them fearless through life, independent-minded, and determined to win.

They didn't lack for advice. Ted, the eldest, was off at Groton in the fall of 1903. His father took time from presidential duties to worry the question of whether the boy should play football on the school's second squad. "I am proud of your pluck, and I greatly admire football," he wrote, "though it was not a game I was ever able to play myself, my qualities resembling Kermit's rather than yours. But the very things that make it a good game," he went on, "make it a rough game, and there is always the chance of your being laid up." Which would be all right; this boy's father "should not in the least object to your being laid up for a season if you were striving for something worth while." Ted was too slight of build, however, to make the varsity, or even his class team next year at Harvard; so "I do not know," Roosevelt responded to his son's request for guidance, "that the risk is balanced by the reward."

From there, a paragraph reinforces paternal counsel that conveys the masculine faith the family lived by. "I am delighted to have you play football. I believe in rough, manly sports. But I do not believe in them if they degenerate into the sole end of any one's existence. I don't want you to sacrifice standing well in your studies to any overathleticism; and I need not tell you that character counts for a great deal more than either intellect or body in winning success in life. Athletic proficiency is a mighty good servant, and like so many other good servants, a mighty bad master."

Character, intellectual development, athletic prowess, winning success—those were handed down among other values often repeated. One such was democratic: treat every man as his merits warrant. Another was patriotic: serve your country in time of war, for war to the Roosevelts was a testing and a glory. The sons took that last lesson to heart, all four fighting on battle fronts in the First World War, one of them killed there, two badly wounded, the three remaining sons reenlisting when the Second World War began and conducting themselves once more with exemplary courage.

That was the Roosevelt family. The Clemens family was equally Victorian in its values, although different: smaller for one thing, predominantly feminine, and a bit earlier in time. At the height of the Clemenses' thriving, in the wonder year of 1885, with *Huckleberry Finn* just published and Grant's *Memoirs* in press and Susy young, bright, and in health writing a biography of her father, Clemens at Nook Farm told his readers: "I am a fortunate person, who has been for thirteen years accustomed, daily and hourly, to the charming companionship of thoroughly well-behaved, well-trained, well-governed children. Never mind about taking my word; ask Mrs. Harriet Beecher Stowe, or Charles Dudley Warner, or any other neighbor of mine, if this is not the exact and unexaggerated truth." This particular father's three children were all girls, from ages thirteen to four, about to turn five. But soon enough the children he spoke of vanished: dreamlike in another place, in another century, as the widower Clemens, home at 21 Fifth Avenue, New York City, gazed about him on the morning after 171 guests had helped Mark Twain celebrate his seventieth birthday at Delmonico's. By then, by December 6, 1905, while the Roosevelts were thriving as the enormously popular national family in the White House in Washington early in the President's own full term that had been won in a landslide, the Clemens family in and about Manhattan was in disarray. Livy, the wife and mother, had died. Susy, the eldest daughter, was dead. Clara, now thirty-one, high-strung and emotionally fragile, was in and out of sanitariums while fitfully pursuing a singing career, with throat problems that sometimes obliged her to cancel concerts. Her sister Jean, Clemens's youngest daughter, at twenty-five faced a lifetime of battling the unpredictable, incurable disease of epilepsy.

Those had been among Samuel Clemens's private travails as he turned seventy. Publicly, on the other hand, he appeared at the time in fine fettle, leading a social life through the winter months of 1905–1906 that would have worn down a far younger man. In the fall he had gone up to Boston to visit old friends and speak at the Cambridge Authors Club, then had traveled to Washington, where he lobbied to reform the copyright laws. While at the capital he dined at the White House with Mr. and Mrs. Roosevelt (once again succumbing to the President's personal magnetism over a cordial chat about copyrights), before returning home to sing Mrs. Roosevelt's praises: "charming—simple—& without any shred of self consciousness—a lovely woman." Back at Fifth Avenue, Clemens had his own guests in to dine: Twichell, the Rogerses, the Colliers, the Hapgoods, Susan Crane, Witter Bynner. And he attended banquets at the Society of Illustrators, at the Players Club, with the Astronomical and Astrophysical Society, with the American Congo Reform Association, at the Press Club. As Mark Twain he spoke publicly to benefit the YMCA; and at Barnard College; and, on January 22, 1906, at Carnegie Hall to help Booker T. Washington commemorate the twenty-fifth anniversary of the founding of Tuskegee Institute. These busy months of his life Clemens would refer to later as his "washing about on a forlorn sea of banquets and speechmaking in high and holy causes—industries which furnished me intellectual cheer and entertainment, but got at my heart for an evening only, then left it dry and dusty."

For despite all the bustling about he was lonely—and lonely despite distractions at home. Back home Miss Lyon had turned into something more than a secretary: she was the author's companion, who all but worshiped the King, as she called him: attending to his correspondence, playing euchre with him, operating the elaborate orchestrelle that provided him with music, toweling dry Clemens's hair after it was washed

Figure 40.2. Miss Lyon and her "King." Ralph Ashcroft stands behind Clemens.

Courtesy of the Mark Twain Project, The Bancroft Library, University of California, Berkeley.

each morning, listening raptly in the evening as he read aloud what he had written that day, on occasion smoking her little Meerschaum pipe in his company. Her journals are filled with homage. "Never, never on sea or shore of spiritual or terrestrial being could there be a man to equal Mr. Clemens," she wrote as early as March 1905; "all my days are hallowed by Mr. Clemens's wonderful presence. 'All my days I go the softlier' because of his influence." Ten months later: "Oh, the richness of his nature, and his brain and his soul. He sounds the awfulest depths of the tragedies of earth and heaven and hell—he bubbles over with gaity—he melts with grief into silent sobs—he slays with satire your beliefs—he boils over into profanities that make you feel the terrors of the thunderbolts that must come—and he is the gentlest, most considerate, most lovable creature in all the earth." In that same year, 1906, among many such paeans scattered through her journals, this by no means untypical one: "These pages are full of repetitious adoration of the King, but that's how they should be, for each day brings its wave of recognition of his greatness and my spirit sings and claps its silent hands over the wonder and the beauty of him. He is the saint and the shrine before the saint—the God behind it all." And this in early 1907: "There is nothing I love so much in all the world as I love to wait upon him, to order his cigars, to clean his pipes, his dear old cracked Peterson pipes; to fill his pen, to tie his necktie; to order his clothes & to brush him off when he is ready to start for somewhere."

Not the least of Miss Lyon's duties involved helping attend to Clemens's grown daughter Jean, who lived at the Fifth Avenue home and who in the early weeks of 1906 appears to have exhibited alarming tendencies toward violence. On January 22, a Monday, Miss Lyon records that she returned from shopping and went to Jean's room to have tea with her, when "she told me that a terrible thing had happened. In a burst of unreasoning rage she struck Katie a terrible blow to the face." Epileptics were deemed prone to such violence, and Jean now described, according to Miss Lyon, "the wave of passion that swept over her as being that of an insane person." The entry includes the epileptic's stark confession that "she had wanted to kill Katy," kind Katy Leary, near-constant attendant in the Clemens household for a quarter century. In early February, after Jean had suffered three more seizures, Clemens learned of the crisis. Thereafter his daughter was watched more closely, until in the fall she was sent to Dr. Frederick Peterson's sanitarium in Katonah, New York, remaining under the specialist's supervision, away from her father, for more than two years.

Clara was away, too, much of the time. But the Clemens household did have a new distraction in the presence of forty-four-year-old Albert Bigelow

Paine, a literary gentleman who had attended the humorist's seventieth birthday party. Learning that Clemens admired his biography of Mark Twain's friend the cartoonist Thomas Nast, Paine now, on the morning of January 7, 1906, came calling at 21 Fifth Avenue to propose that he be allowed to write another biography, this one of the great author into whose bedroom he was being admitted. Propped up in bed answering letters—Clemens seldom rose before noon these days—the subject of Paine's proposal thought for a moment, then, to his visitor's astonishment and delight, responded: "When would you like to begin?"

Three days later Mark Twain's new biographer was set up in a neighboring bedroom that would serve as an office, with a trunkful of Clemens's personal papers to sort through. Of course there were gaps in the story. Soon Paine was urging that his subject fill those gaps by resuming his autobiography, portions of which the humorist had written and dictated earlier, from as far back as 1870. The researcher would furnish questions to prompt Clemens's memory. They hired a secretary, and on weekday mornings this Miss Hobby, attended by Paine and Miss Lyon for audience, took shorthand notes while Clemens recovered recollections of his childhood, youth, and manhood in no particular order, according to whatever the day's whim or Paine's queries suggested. The group made great progress. Before the project was finally abandoned, in April 1909, Clemens had dictated half a million words of memories, portraiture, grudges, and topical commentary.

Colonel Harvey of the *North American Review* got wind of the project and came to have a look. He left impressed, agreeing to publish generous portions from Mark Twain's work in progress, his "Autobiography as from the Grave," to run through twenty-five installments in the *Review*, beginning in early September 1906 and extending into the spring of the following year. In that publication, therefore, readers of the third installment, of October 5, 1906, would encounter recollections of the remarkable Nook Farm childhood led by Clemens's eldest daughter, of the character of the mother who reared her, and of the anguish of Susy's early death on returning to Hartford at age twenty-four.

On October 16 of that same year, Clemens wrote a note to a Mrs. Saunders of Clinton, New York:

> Dear Mrs. Saunders:
>   Your moving letter has reached me—and my heart—and finds a grateful welcome. It is a deep pleasure to me to know that you think I am writing worthily of Susy and her mother—that beautiful and

inspiring and pathetic theme. So rare they were! I think they left not many of their lofty rank in the world when they quitted it. I wish, with you, that Livy could have known that your child was to bear Susy's name and keep her dear memory green in your heart.

I thank you, thank you, for your letter.

With my love—S. L. Clemens

Mrs. Saunders was Louise Brownell, Susy's intimate friend of Bryn Mawr days, now the wife of a professor of chemistry at Hamilton College in upstate New York. The daughter she refers to, named Olivia for Olivia Susan Clemens, would grow up—one of four siblings—as Via and marry the author and film critic James Agee in 1933. Louise herself would live to be ninety-one. Nothing in Clemens's note, meanwhile, suggests that he knew of the intensity of Louise and Susy's relationship at and immediately after Bryn Mawr; but that he refers to his wife as "Livy" rather than "Mrs. Clemens" and that he closes his message with his love would appear to imply a warm, personal regard for this college friend of Susy's who was continuing to honor her memory. Further, the note expresses the abiding sense of loss its author feels for two of such "lofty rank," a daughter now dead a decade, and a beloved wife two years and more in her grave.

Their survivor was left with his two living daughters, and fame, and wealth, and honors, and friends without number. Yet Clemens was lonely. Miss Lyon noted that the King "of all people must have companionship," and she recorded an occasion when he had sat for a half hour in his empty living room waiting in vain for company, "and then a blast of cold and bedeviled loneliness swept over him and made him hate his life."

One new friend did briefly warm the widower's hours. The two met by chance in a crowd coming out of Carnegie Hall on a day in December 1905, soon after the seventieth birthday dinner. Clemens introduced himself, and learned that the fifteen-year-old's name was Gertrude Natkin. In the weeks just ahead he provided this "dream grandchild" with a nickname— Marjorie—invited her to attend lectures he had consented to give for charity, and wrote her more than a dozen affectionate messages. As one sample, this, on March 18, 1906: "*Aren't* you dear! Aren't you the dearest child there is? To think to send me those lovely flowers, you sweet little Marjorie." Miss Lyon had come up and arranged them, "& they certainly do look like you. Consequently they are very acceptable company." His secretary had brought him the girl's telephone messages as well, "& I was very glad to have them, Marjorie dear. To-morrow or next day I can leave this bed, then I can talk to you myself. No, to your shadows—for that is all a telephone can furnish of you. It makes you vague & unreal; & the voice is somebody else's & unfamiliar." He ended by bidding his young friend goodnight and sleep well; then "blotting" his page with a decorous kiss, he signed it "SLC."

All such missives his young correspondent answered with delight, even ones that appeared to be scolding gently, as when the great man commanded: "Marjorie! don't get any older. I can't have it. Stay always just as you are—youth is the golden time."

In his friend's innocence the widower had found something that alleviated his losses, something that stirred memories of a Hartford home once filled with the laughter of girls much like Marjorie. Then came a day in early April 1906. "So you are 16 today, you dear little rascal!" he wrote to her. And added: "you mustn't move along so fast, at this rate you will soon be a young lady and next you will be getting married." Clearly the prospect was troubling, enough so that the new friendship—so intense and important over its brief duration—would hardly survive the change. "*Sixteen*! Ah what has become of my little girl? I am almost afraid to send a blot, but I venture it. Bless your heart, it comes within an ace of being improper! Now, back you go to 14!—then there's no impropriety."

But "Your little Marjorie," as the girl signed her notes, couldn't go back. In May she entreated him: "Dear Grandpa, please dont love me any the less because I am sixteen. No matter how old I am in years, I shall always be your young little Marjorie as long as you wish it." Still, it wouldn't do. She was Gertrude Natkin now, sixteen years old going on seventeen, and whatever dream his Marjorie embodied had vanished, leaving an old man to look elsewhere for the joy that her ephemeral innocence had furnished him during that little while.

PART **Six**

PEACE

CHAPTER **Forty-One**

Carnegie

amuel Clemens and Andrew Carnegie were born within a week of each other, in November 1835. Clemens's birthplace was in the raw, newly founded settlement of Florida, Missouri, at the edge of what was then the American frontier. Five days before, on November 25, Carnegie had been born across an ocean in Scotland, a few miles north of Edinburgh in the town of Dunfermline, which earlier, for four centuries, had served as the home of Scotland's kings, as in the medieval ballad "Sir Patrick Spens":

> The king sits in Dumferling toune,
> Drinking the blude-reid wine. . . .

When Sammy was four, the Clemenses moved from his birthplace to settle thirty miles northeast in Hannibal, on the Mississippi River, where the boy grew up through the same years that Andy's childhood was unfolding near the Firth of Forth in Scotland, in his own modest circumstances. Andrew Carnegie's father, Will, was a handloom weaver of fine linens, a genial man and skilled, though not one who cared overmuch for work. It was the mother who held the Carnegies together, selling sweets and binding shoes for money when hard times came, in the international aftermath of America's Panic of 1837. Mrs. Carnegie's sisters had moved meanwhile to Pennsylvania and were writing back about opportunities in their new home. Come join them—which in time the Will Carnegies did, on borrowed money, in 1848, when Andy was twelve.

In Pittsburgh the lad started work as a bobbin boy in a cotton factory, twelve hours a day six days a week, for a weekly wage of $1.20. Soon he was tending a boiler, then working as a messenger boy, then as a clerk, then—like Edison later—as a telegraph operator. But what an amazing career this turned out to be, this rags-to-riches story of the little Scottish lad—full grown, Carnegie stood only five feet tall—unschooled, coming to America with nothing but a sunny disposition, a head for numbers, and an ingratiating eagerness to be useful. In later years, Carnegie seldom remarked on his worldly success, causing Samuel Clemens, who got to know him well, to marvel at how modest the industrialist was about things he should have been proud of, and how proud he was of things he should have been modest about. For Carnegie was inclined to dismiss his amazing wealth as little more than being in the right place at the right time: in Pittsburgh because his aunts were living there, and in the 1850s, when Thomas A. Scott became Pittsburgh station agent, then superintendent for the western division of the Pennsylvania Railroad.

Tom Scott was twenty-nine years old when, in 1853, he took on an industrious telegraph operator as his assistant near the start of his own career that was headed upward. From agent, Scott rose to general superintendent and, by 1860, to first vice president of this largest American railroad—largest American company at the time—bringing Carnegie along with him. On the way he taught the young man the wonders of compound interest, urging him to borrow $500 to buy ten shares in the Adams Express Company. Carnegie did so, his mother mortgaging their tiny home so he could; and in due course he held in his hand a dividend check for $5, money that the wage earner hadn't had to work for, payable not just in Pittsburgh but wherever he might happen to be. It was a revelation: how "money could make money, how, without any attention from me, this mysterious golden visitor should come."

At twenty-six, when he returned at his leisure to Dunfermline, the Scottish town that his family had slunk away from on borrowed money fourteen years earlier, Andrew Carnegie was a rich man. Now it was 1862, our Civil War raging and Sam Clemens blistering his hands swinging a pickax out West in vain quest of Nevada silver. By that time Carnegie had invested in a sleeping-car company, taken profits and invested them in Titusville oil, and from those two enterprises along with a number of others had amassed dividends that were paying him over $20,000 annually, that in addition to his $2,400 salary as western superintendent of the Pennsylvania Railroad, a position he had ascended to when Tom Scott moved on to the vice presidency. Twenty thousand dollars in the 1860s would amount to, say, $500,000 now, more than enough coming in each year to allow for purchasing, in a bucolic suburb away from Pittsburgh's soot, a mansion furnished with servants attending to an adored mother's every need. No longer was Mag Carnegie to bind shoes and sell sweets to provide for the family; her older son had long since taken charge of all that and paid off her tiny mortgage besides. Andrew's father died in 1855. Now, these seven years later, the younger Carnegie was back with his mother ("holy name!" he wrote—"nurse, teacher, guardian angel, saint, all in one") for a leisurely visit to Dunfermline, leaving brother Tom in Pittsburgh to look after affairs at home. For three months Carnegie was away on this extended, most gratifying vacation, an arrangement that he would follow virtually every year thereafter, delegating responsibilities to trusted associates and—although keeping in touch—taking long summers off for recreation and travel.

All the while, money kept pouring in, some that he earned, much of it in dividends. The Civil War provided boom years for certain civilians up North (Carnegie, like Theodore Roosevelt Sr. and John D. Rockefeller, paid for a substitute to do his fighting for him); and after the war there was money aplenty to be made in railroads. More money lay in building than in operating them, and Carnegie as a friend of Scott and others high in the Pennsylvania management was positioned to know in advance where a lot of the money would flow. Fortunes preceded and followed wherever the tracks were headed; so if you knew beforehand of a projected railroad route, you could buy up land cheap and hold it till after the railroad ran through. And you could buy shares—their value sure to go up—in the construction company that was to build the line. Do it legally, too: taking advantage of privileged information was legal up to 1934, when the New Deal finally established a securities and exchange commission that forbade such insider trading and profiting.

It was an era, meanwhile—those speculative years awash in vast sums just after the Civil War—when corruption flourished under city bosses and far into the halls of federal power in Washington, D.C. Samuel Clemens, married and moved to Hartford, and his Nook Farm neighbor Charles Dudley Warner satirized those same years in *The Gilded Age* (1873), a novel that featured the irrepressible, dizzily optimistic speculator Colonel Beriah Sellers (Mark Twain's creation entirely), who, transferred to the stage, was to become almost as much of a nineteenth-century cultural fixture as Washington Irving's Rip Van Winkle and Mrs. Stowe's Uncle Tom. "There's millions in it!" Sellers would cry out ebulliently of this or that harebrained scheme, his materialistic times full of fraud, bribery, and shady deals, where hopes soared high and many an investor crashed in ruins. But in the same years a few prospered, Andrew Carnegie among them, his name untarnished by scandal, his holdings (unlike Clemens's wild speculations) invariably profitable, and his industry amply rewarded.

Retaining the friendship of its directors, Carnegie moved on from working for the Pennsylvania Railroad to manufacturing iron and steel. His Pittsburgh mills made cast iron to replace worn-out wooden railroad trestles and to lay rails to the Pacific. As head of the enterprise Mr. Carnegie left management to associates on-site, spending most of his time in New York City, in a suite at the St. Nicholas Hotel that he shared with his mother, venturing by private railroad car out to the Pennsylvania iron and steel mills no more than two or three times a year. Just then the St. Nicholas, at Broadway and Twenty-Fourth Street, was New York's finest hotel, where the Langdons of Elmira stayed when visiting the city, and where Sam Clemens, back from his tour to the Holy Land, met a shipmate's sister, Olivia Langdon, at dinner with her family late in 1867. Mr. Carnegie resided in the same hotel, although the capitalist and his mother as often as not were away on their travels.

For the diminutive Scotsman felt as attached to his childhood home as was Clemens to his; and like Clemens, Carnegie was a restless and eager tourist, ever happy revisiting scenes and friends of his youth. Moreover, both men, early regretting their lack of formal education, had taken steps to amend the deficiency. Like Clemens, Carnegie read abundantly in books, magazines, and newspapers; and he traveled almost as widely as Clemens did, in Carnegie's case with the purpose at first of acquiring culture, visiting the great cities of Europe and studying their art and architecture, attending plays, concerts, and social gatherings, enlarging his knowledge and swelling his circle of friends. Money attracts; so that in time the little man, his coffers full, his burr refined, could—and did—boast of distinguished friendships, with Matthew Arnold, with Prime Minister Gladstone, with Gilder the *Century* editor, with Herbert Spencer.

That last, the philosopher Spencer, was the prophet of Social Darwinism, a doctrine to which Carnegie subscribed wholeheartedly—and to its assurances that humanity was evolving upward, so that all was for the best, whatever might happen in the short run and however doleful for the trampled-on weakest of the species. Race, manners, culture, literacy, technology, creature comforts, health: all were progressing according to evolutionary laws that made life on the whole better and better, never mind incidental appearances to the contrary. Such faith confirmed Carnegie's optimism, and his optimism made him pleasant to be around. All the more so because he liked people, and was generous with his wealth, and bright, and told good stories, and knew how to be amusing.

Such a one would relish counting Mark Twain among his friends (as who would not?); and an opportunity was bound to arise for the two to meet. Both Clemens and Carnegie traveled in comfort, first class on the newest of Cunard ships, and stayed at fine hotels. Some years back Mr. Carnegie had shrewdly declined a chance to invest with Clemens in the Paige Automatic Typesetting Machine, but a way of furthering into friendship his acquaintance with Mark Twain arose when the two happened to take the same steamer bound for Europe in the spring of 1895. Carnegie's mother had died nine years earlier, and in 1887 the orphan at age fifty-one had married Miss Louise Whitfield, a New York merchant's daughter thirty years old, whom Carnegie had known for several years previous (and whom his mother had objected to sharing him with). At their marriage, in the year after the mother's death, the bride and groom moved into the former mansion of the railroad magnate Hollis P. Huntington, at Fifty-First Street and Fifth Avenue.

Mr. and Mrs. Carnegie lived there for something over a decade, were living there when they sailed for Europe on the same liner with Mark Twain in late March of 1895. But by the end of the century the Carnegies had bought themselves a spacious, salubrious lot farther up on Fifth Avenue, at Ninety-First Street, at the highest point on the island, and had begun building there a "palace," as Clemens called what is now the Cooper-Hewitt Design Museum, a sixty-four-room estate in the style of a Georgian country house, brick faced and elegant, with an interior full of innovations and light pouring in from its abundance of windows. This was the first private home in America built with a structural steel frame, and among the first to have effective central heating and the nearest approach that the times allowed to air conditioning. The mansion was finished in 1901, for their daughter to grow up in—Margaret, their doted-on Baba, who had been born four years earlier, when her mother was forty, the only child the couple would have. The Carnegies moved north from Fifty-First Street in 1902, the husband and father retired from business by then, having sold his various iron and steel enterprises to J. P. Morgan for $480 million the year before. Morgan's purchase allowed the financier to create US Steel, the earliest billion-dollar American corporation, and the Scotsman's sale of the same made Andrew Carnegie one of the two or three richest capitalists in the world.

Samuel Clemens and family had returned from exile in the fall of 1900 and set up residence on Fifth Avenue far down at Tenth Street. During years ahead they would move to Riverdale-on-Hudson, then to Italy, then—after Livy's death—the widower would live from late 1904 to mid-1908 in yet another home on Fifth Avenue, at No. 21, on the southwest corner of Ninth Street. Sometimes Carnegie came calling at that address, so friendly had the two become by then, and for his part, Clemens as Mark Twain spoke during these same years at more than one public banquet honoring the retired industrialist and philanthropist.

For in retirement, Carnegie was keeping busy bestowing his money on worthy causes. One of the Scotsman's maxims—and newspapers quoted Andrew Carnegie's maxims only somewhat less frequently than those of Mark Twain—was to the effect that (inasmuch as we're merely stewards of our wealth) the man who dies rich dies disgraced. So Carnegie was working hard to get rid of his money. There was so much of it, though! Even bestowing it with an open hand and even spending lavishly to indulge his family's taste for comfort, with this magnificent mansion just completed on Ninety-First Street and with the derelict twelfth-century castle, Skibo, overlooking Dornoch Firth far to the north in the Scottish Highlands, which Carnegie had bought in 1897 for £85,000 and made opulent with the staggering sum of £2,000,000 applied for renovations—even with all those expenses, dividends kept piling up. Skibo meanwhile was (and is) utterly gorgeous—its towers, turrets, and ancient stones, its magnificent view, its stained glass and breathtaking entry hall, its 200 rooms and all modern amenities, its man-made, trout-filled lake, its nine-hole golf course, its imported natural waterfall, and the 40,000 acres surrounding. Carnegie made no apology for such outlays: leisure, which wealth in good taste provides for, nourishes the fine arts and culture.

But although he spent sumptuously on his family, the philanthropist balked at giving out money for alms. Giving to beggars encourages begging (another maxim), and Social Darwinism deplored any such perpetuation of the unfit that retarded evolutionary progress. Rather, give your money to help people help themselves. Thus, Carnegie's civic benefactions went toward building libraries. At a time when libraries in towns were uncommon, he built what came to be 3,500 of them. For social enrichment he built public halls, as with Carnegie Hall in New York; and he donated 7,000 organs to churches, and endowed schools and universities. Among much else, he founded the Carnegie Institute of Technology in Pittsburgh, gave generously to Tuskegee Institute, supported the ill-paid teaching profession with a retirement fund that academics now know as TIAA-CREF, and invested in simplifying English spelling to encourage Anglo-American brotherhood.

Help others to help themselves. Dealing, meanwhile, with the hundreds of appeals for money that his staff sifted through each day kept the retired steel magnate busy, and assuredly all that philanthropic work was something to be proud of. Carnegie could be proud as well of having

Figure 41.1. Andrew Carnegie in the mid-1890s.
Courtesy of the Library of Congress.

raised himself from humble beginnings to so exalted a height of prosperity. Yet he had little to say about any of that. On the first of December, 1907, Clemens paid him a visit uptown—one of a number—and, according to this caller, what Carnegie talked about then was what he always talked about. "He never has any but one theme, himself." Himself, however, not as autobiography; for Carnegie rarely reminisces about a poor friendless boy struggling bravely for a livelihood in a strange land, or about the many obstacles he met with on his way upward. Nor does he tell you how he became the employer of 22,000 men, "and possessor of one of the three giant fortunes of his day; no, as regards these achievements he is as modest a man as you could meet anywhere, and seldom makes even a fleeting reference to them." What he does talk about, Clemens tells us, "forever and ever and ever and untiringly," are the compliments paid him and the attentions shown.

He will take you into his study and get out his signed photographs, and autographs, and presentation books, and keys he's been given to cities far and near, "buzzing over each like a happy hummingbird," and read you a workingman's poem in Scottish dialect that sings Andrew Carnegie's praises, read it well, too—"so well that no one born out of Scotland could understand it." Some of these compliments manifest honest admiration for the man's many public contributions, but others are "merely sorrowfully transparent tokens of reverence for his moneybags." The latter, however, bring their recipient just as much joy as the former.

Carnegie will tell, not once but often, of King Edward VII's visit to Skibo Castle and of a meeting with the Kaiser on board the *Hohenzollern*. Here Clemens exhibits his wonderful gift for mimicry, taking on the voice of his plainspoken host: "There is an American here, your majesty, whom you have more than once expressed a desire to see." Who is that? "Andrew Carnegie." Ha! Bring him to me, and Kaiser Wilhelm "advanced halfway himself and shook me cordially by the hand and said, laughing, 'Ah, Mr. Carnegie, I know you for a confirmed and incurable Independent, who thinks no more of kings and emperors than of other people, but I like it in you; I like a man that does his own thinking and speaks out what he thinks, whether the world approve or not; it's the right spirit, the brave spirit, and there's little enough of it on this planet.'" To which he of the independent mind professes humbly to have replied: "I am glad your majesty is willing to take me for what I am. It would not become me to disclaim or disown, or even to modify, what your majesty has said of me, since it is only the truth. I could not be otherwise than independent if I wanted to." Yet although unalterably constituted thus, Carnegie does admit to having reverences. He reveres and respects a *man*!—"a whole man, a fearless man, a manly and masculine and right-feeling and right-acting man; let him be born in a garret or palace, it is the same to me." And it is for that alone, he assures the Kaiser, "that I revere you, not for your mighty place in the world."

The impersonation is wickedly revealing. About this visit yesterday at Carnegie's mansion, which Clemens was recalling on Monday morning, December 2, 1907, one of the first things his host had said had been doubly characteristic. Right off, Carnegie had mentioned a new attention received. And he had dragged the subject in by the ears, not bothering with a pretext for announcing: "I have been down to Washington to see the President."

Then he added, as his listener was sure he would: "He sent for me."

"I knew he was going to say that," says Clemens, for Andrew never seeks the great; the great always seek him.

Let this present witness not be misunderstood. He likes Andrew Carnegie, admires him, enjoys his company—even though "I don't believe I can stand the King Edward visit again." It is curious, though: never a word of brag from so astonishing an achiever about his many impressive accomplishments. Only this intense, this unflagging interest in the flatteries large and small, from high and low, that have come his way, vanities that others might value but would go to some lengths to conceal.

CHAPTER **Forty-Two**

America at Peace

W hy had Carnegie been summoned to the White House just
now? Clemens reports that President Roosevelt "had desired
his advice regarding the calamitous conditions existing today, commercially, in America and Mr. Carnegie furnished that advice."
In October a run on New York's Knickerbocker Trust had intensified the
Panic of 1907, alleviated only when J. P. Morgan intervened and, in those
days before the Federal Reserve, came up with funds enough to steady the
market by the end of November. Calling at Ninety-First Street on December 1, Clemens learned that Carnegie had been conferring at the White
House about the fiscal crisis. "He knew," his visitor tells us, "and I knew,
and he knew that I knew, that he was thoroughly competent to advise the
President and that the advice furnished would be of the highest value and
importance; yet he had no glorification to waste upon that." It was enough
that Mark Twain hear of President Roosevelt's sending for the philanthropist for guidance.

For as Clemens aspired to be more than a mere humorist, Carnegie
aimed at being more than a mere moneymaker. The Scotsman had fashioned himself into a writer, a thinker, a sage. And a public awed by his
achievements was eager to read the man's views and opinions: on the uses
of wealth ("Neither the individual nor the race is improved by almsgiving."), on capital and labor, on imperialism. When Carnegie introduced
a volume of his essays with an account of his apprenticeship in industry—how he had found a pathway leading from humble beginnings to
astounding success—people read that avidly. And when he published an
essay on the labor question, as he did in the spring of 1886, shortly before
Chicago's bloody Haymarket Riot, this titan of industry could be sure of an
audience, all the more so because his opinions on the subject were different

from what might have been expected. "The right of the working-men to combine and to form trades-unions," he wrote, "is no less sacred than the right of the manufacturer to enter into associations and conferences with his fellows, and it must sooner or later be conceded." Other capitalists and much of the American public weren't so sure about labor's right to unionize, all the less sure a short while later when somebody threw a bomb into a crowd of policemen charging striking workers as they rallied peacefully at Haymarket Square. Strikes themselves are ridiculous, Carnegie declares in this same essay, in that their outcome determines not where justice lies but simply which side has more strength and endurance. In his "An Employer's View of the Labor Question," this employer of thousands proposed to make strikes unnecessary by basing wages on a sliding scale, keyed month by month to what owners must charge as prices vary through boom times and bust. Adjusted thus, if iron sells high one month, wages go up; if next month the price of iron drops, so do wages. That way management and labor work shoulder to shoulder, sharing prosperity and adversity, with any lingering differences left to binding arbitration to settle.

That had been Carnegie's suggestion in 1886, just before the Haymarket Riot erupted in Chicago, and his liberal views earned him the thanks of American workers. But six years later, their regard for him perished with the other victims that fell during eighteen hours of riot and bloodshed at Carnegie's own steel mills in Homestead, near Pittsburgh. As usual, the industrialist had gone off to Scotland over the fateful summer of 1892; later he insisted that if he had been on hand, things would have worked out differently. Back in Pennsylvania, Henry Clay Frick was left in charge, and Frick had no use for unions. Frick (who eventually would build his own great mansion on Fifth Avenue) wasn't much for coddling workers in any case, the less so because their skills were becoming redundant at the Carnegie mills. For it was a characteristic of a Carnegie enterprise to be up-to-date—to have installed in it the very latest technology, in this instance for producing steel more efficiently than any competitor could. Rockefeller, who hated competition as wasteful, sought to force rivals in the oil business to join his company. But the steel magnate Carnegie relished competition as a mechanism by means of which evolution leads on to progress, in the same way that he relished the latest technology as fruits of that evolution, to be installed at the earliest moment in his homes and his factories. And in those factories, technological advances (which Carnegie traveling overseas was always on the lookout for) had proved able to do what only skilled workmen did earlier. Increasingly, laborers without skills were operating the new machines; and those mostly immigrants would work for less and could be replaced with ease. Nor was the Carnegie organization averse to working its laborers, skilled and unskilled, as hard as competition warranted, and to working them longer hours, often eighty-four hours a week, and to paying them less in order to trim costs and make the product (steel rails, structural steel, steel armor plate) more competitive.

At Carnegie's Homestead plant in the summer of 1892, Henry C. Frick in charge defied the workingmen's union by increasing hours and cutting wages. Millworkers walked off the job and massed around the plant to keep scabs from taking their places. Frick had called in the Pinkerton Agency, 300 agents brought upriver overnight to be on hand next morning to guard the factory and protect any nonunion laborers willing to work the longer hours for the lower pay. But the boats bringing up Pinkerton's agents arrived late, in early daylight with an armed mob gathered on shore to meet them. A battle ensued between the threatened union strikers along with their supporters and the hired guards still crowded on their couple of barges offshore. The all-day violence ended with a dozen men dead—both guards and strikers—up to sixty wounded, and at least a hundred Pinkertons mauled and beaten as they stepped on firm ground to surrender. The nation's press was filled with the fracas through days ahead.

It looked like a victory for the workingman, but in the end capital won out, on the grounds widely shared that owners could do what they liked with their property—in this case, the steel mill—and could hire whoever was willing to work on their terms. Even so, it took Andrew Carnegie years of building libraries across America before he restored even a part of his good name with labor.

More than his concerns about labor, however, and more than all his benefactions in brick, glass, and stone, the philanthropy nearest Carnegie's heart in these late years centered on world peace. Nicholas II, Czar of all the Russias, appeared to share the Scotsman's longing, to the extent of issuing a summons in 1898 (year of the Spanish-American War) for nations to send delegates to The Hague, in the Netherlands, to a conference seeking "the most effective means of ensuring to all peoples the benefits of a real and lasting peace, and, above all, of limiting the progressive development of existing armaments." Twenty-six countries responded to the Czar's appeal, their representatives meeting from mid-May 1899 until the end of July. They didn't get as much done as they had hoped for—nothing to speak of on disarmament—but they did set up a Hague Tribunal, a court of arbitration to mediate future disputes among nations; and they agreed to meet in The Hague at a later date to continue their efforts.

For Carnegie, world peace was of overriding importance. In the months immediately before this 1899 Hague Conference convened, he had published in the *North American Review*, in the issues of January and March, an essay on "Americanism and Imperialism," which alluded to expansionist America's new colony, the Philippines. According to the anti-imperialist Carnegie, our acquisition of that Pacific archipelago put us squarely in the midst of "dangers of war and the almost constant rumors and threats of war to which all nations interested in the far East are subject. There is seldom a week which does not bring alarming reports of threatened hostilities, or of new alliances, or of changes of alliances, between the powers arming for the coming struggle. It is chiefly this far Eastern question which keeps every ship-yard, gun-yard, and armor-yard in the world busy night and day, Sunday and Saturday, forging engines of destruction."

Carnegie, owner of steel shares, profited hugely from the day-and-night forging of those same guns and armor-plated battleships, so his quest for peace was hardly self-serving. Nor was the rising use of weaponry that he deplored restricted to the Far East. War fever had spread more widely than that, armed conflict in the two decades from 1890 through 1910 erupting in Cuba, in South Africa between Boers and English, in China with the Boxers fighting foreign devils, and in far Siberia between Russians and Japanese—while it threatened to break out in South America as German, Italian, and English creditors menaced Venezuelan debtors and in Europe between the colonial powers of Germany and France over Morocco. In Carnegie's opinion, what the world needed to settle all that strife was far fewer arms in everybody's hands and a means of arbitrating differences instead of fighting over them. The Hague Peace Conference had provided a start toward the latter reform by establishing a court of arbitration; and before long Carnegie would give $1.5 million—some $40 million now—to build the new court a permanent home, the Peace Palace. That structure towers in grandeur at The Hague to this day, where it houses not only the Court of Arbitration but the Academy of International Law and the International Court of Justice—agencies deriving from meetings after the second Hague conference, when delegates from the various nations assembled once more to strive for arms limitations (and to lay the cornerstone of the palace) in 1907.

Disarmament and arbitration: Carnegie's recipe for world peace. Yet disarmament proved even harder for the delegates of 1907 to deal with effectively than arbitration was back in 1899. In truth, European powers—and assuredly the United States during the administration of Theodore

Roosevelt—didn't believe in discarding their arms in hopes that peace would follow. At the very start of these two decades, in 1890, Alfred T. Mahan, a captain in the U.S. Navy and instructor at the Naval War College in Newport, had published a book with a dry title that belied its enormous significance: *The Influence of Sea Power Upon History, 1660–1783*. Reviewing Captain Mahan's volume in the *Atlantic*, young Roosevelt, then civil service commissioner and himself a naval historian of the War of 1812, called it "distinctively the best and most important, also by far the most interesting, book on naval history" in a very long time. Many of Mahan's recommendations Roosevelt sought to put into practice as soon as he came by the means of doing so, as assistant secretary of the navy and president of the United States. Captain Mahan had stressed the importance of a navy in establishing the primacy of Britain—that small island—among the world's empires, Great Britain's the vastest empire of all, and all because of her warships at sea. Thus the lesson for other nations was not to disarm but, rather, to build up their navies, equip them with firepower, man them with crews highly trained, and send them forth to protect commercial routes in peace and destroy the enemy in time of war. To support such a fleet, a nation must actively acquire coaling stations. When, for instance, in this same decade America had a chance to gain possession of Hawaii, in 1898, it was right to seize that opportunity. And any country aspiring to be a world power must be able to move its fleet of battleships, cruisers, and torpedo boats about with speed, by means, for example, of canals strategically placed, as at the Isthmus of Panama.

The British admiralty read Mahan. So did the Japanese: considered Captain Mahan's *Influence of Sea Power* along with two more volumes in which the strategist developed his thinking further, and ended by studying all three volumes closely, with profit. Meanwhile, the apostle of peace who had initiated the Hague conference in 1899—Czar Nicholas II—was aggressively expanding Russian territory across Siberia, absorbing and "Russifying" ethnic groups as his own transcontinental railroad crept ever farther eastward along the 5,800 miles from Moscow to Vladivostok. But that seaport on the Pacific lay far enough north to be icebound in winter; so the Czar, with Germany's help, persuaded China to lease to imperial Russia the ice-free harbor of Port Arthur, on the Liaodong peninsula in southern Manchuria, across the bay from Korea. The Russians took possession in 1897 and proceeded to fortify their ice-free port while the railroad edged closer. Those developments alarmed the Japanese, with their own designs on the feeble Korean empire—this Slavic incursion into what they regarded as their particular sphere of influence; so that the ultimate result of Nicholas's Russification eastward, as one civilization nudged up against another, was the Russo-Japanese War. After months of fruitless negotiations, that conflict erupted with a surprise attack that the Japanese navy launched against the Russian fleet at Port Arthur on the night of February 8, 1904.

A European power and an Asiatic power were at war, and the outcome seemed foreordained. Certainly the complacent Nicholas thought it was; but to the astonishment of Western observers the Japanese, after great loss of life on both sides, emerged triumphant at sea and on land. For almost a year Port Arthur lay under siege before surrendering to the investing Japanese in January 1905. The colored race—as they were regarded in the West—went on to win the Battle of Mukden on shore after three weeks of bloody fighting, in February 1905; and in May they dealt a crushing blow at sea to a second Russian fleet, which had sailed 18,000 nautical miles around the Cape of Good Hope only to be destroyed in the Tshushima Straits that lie between Japan and Korea: eight Russian battleships sunk and over 5,000 Russian lives lost, while Japanese losses were limited to 116 crewmen and three torpedo boats.

The war stretched through a year and a half, its battles including the largest military engagements the world had yet seen. By the spring of 1905 both sides appeared spent and ready for peace. Nicholas was beset with revolutionary outbreaks at home, while the war's cost threatened to wreck Japan's economy. At that juncture, the Japanese asked the President of the United States to mediate. He agreed to; so the combatants sent delegates to Portsmouth, New Hampshire, to work out terms, Roosevelt entertaining them en route aboard the presidential yacht at Oyster Bay. The two sides signed the Treaty of Portsmouth in September 1905; and for his efforts in bringing that resolution about—his substantial efforts, his crucial efforts that required great patience and tact and diplomatic finesse—the often combative Theodore Roosevelt was awarded the Nobel Peace Prize, the first American so honored.

Soon the President was intervening to settle another quarrel, at Russia's request, between France and Germany over conflicting colonial claims in Morocco, in northwest Africa. The disputants agreed to meet with various European powers at the Spanish port of Algeciras in January 1906. The story grows complicated because of the intricate, wary maneuverings of those same powers late in the nineteenth century and into the twentieth, each mistrusting the others and all seeking alliances for strength in their competitive race toward colonies and markets. France wanted a protectorate over Morocco. Germany objected. France and England, enemies for centuries, came to an understanding: France could have Morocco and

England would take Egypt. Such cavalier disposals sound high-handed, greed-soaked, and sordid, but at the time much of national prestige appeared at stake. Apparently Russia, formerly an ally of Germany, was now allied by secret treaty with France. Germany, a nation created as late as 1871 through the unification of various duchies and principalities (Prussia, Saxony, Hanover, and others), had for its allies only bloated Austria-Hungary and fragmented Italy, hardly a match for the triple alliance that threatened to encircle that weaker trio of nations.

Having read Mahan himself, Kaiser Wilhelm II was bent on building up the German fleet until it rivaled Britain's. In the 1890s and on into the new century German shipyards launched battleship after battleship, and English shipyards responded with battleships and dreadnoughts of their own, in an arms race that the rest of the world watched with apprehension. "The Kaiser sincerely believes," President Roosevelt wrote privately in April 1905, "that the English are planning to attack him and smash his fleet, and perhaps join with France in a war to the death against him. As a matter of fact the English harbor no such intentions, but are themselves in a condition of panic terror lest the Kaiser secretly intend to form an alliance against them with France or Russia, or both, to destroy their fleet and blot out the British Empire from the map!" The American president was in touch with both Edward VII and the Kaiser, so his words bore weight. "It is as funny a case as I have ever seen," Roosevelt added, "of mutual distrust and fear bringing two peoples to the verge of war."

The Algeciras Conference in the winter of 1906 appeared to settle the Moroccan question for the time being, giving the sultan certain powers over customs and tax collection and limiting France's involvement in that small nation's internal affairs. Roosevelt off in Washington played his part in resolving the dispute, as he had played a key role in defusing that other German crisis four years earlier, when the presence of Admiral Dewey's squadron building up steam in the Caribbean persuaded the Kaiser to take his quarrel over Venezuela's debts to the Hague Tribunal—an early case brought (at Roosevelt's urging) to the new international court of arbitration for settlement.

In truth, as president the Colonel was behaving more temperately than might have been expected, given his saber-rattling words and acts in earlier years. The responsibilities of high office appeared to have modified Roosevelt's views, so that he could write to a friend at the end of the Russo-Japanese War, midway through his presidency: "I have grown to feel an increasing horror for pointless, and of course still more for unjust, war"; specifically, for the exhaustion and waste, for the slaughter of "gallant men to no purpose," that a continuation of the present conflict in the Far East would have entailed. On the other hand, just wars, righteous wars, were different. For peace-at-any-price types the President still felt nothing but scorn: for those who, "whether from folly, from selfishness, from short-sightedness, or from sheer cowardice, rail at the manly virtues and fail to understand that righteousness is to be put before peace even when, as sometimes happens, righteousness means war."

To which Andrew Carnegie, pacifist manufacturer of armor-plate, furnished a response that in most instances would appear unanswerable. Think of our Revolution, or of our Civil War—or of World War I, even then brewing in 1906, as armed rivals met grimly at Algeciras. "Disputants are both seeking righteousness," Carnegie reminded President Roosevelt; "both feel themselves struggling for what is just. Who is to decide? No one. According to you they must then go to war to decide not what is right but who is strong."

CHAPTER **Forty-Three**

Late Pleasures

How all these topics converge, though! How each interacts with the others, coalescing to form the present narrative. The theme of WAR, at the start of the story, derives in part from the geographical expansiveness of the age, with civilizations at varying levels of development clashing to the detriment of the less advanced. In the United States such expansion took the form of a steady migration WEST, so preoccupying in post–Civil War America—cavalry, Indians, miners, lumbermen, cowboys, ranchers, and homesteaders having seized the public's imagination—that it was all Roosevelt and the other disciples of Captain Mahan could do to direct the attention of fellow citizens back to the central importance of sea power, of the navy rather than the army, of the sea rather than the land as determining a great nation's future. Meanwhile, expansion spread people not only across the American continent but just about everywhere else: into Africa, into Siberia, into the Far East, into China. Under a kaiser who was represented as having greeted Mr. Carnegie warmly on the *Hohenzollern*, Germany was striving to expand into wherever would furnish his newly formed country at the center of Europe with *Lebensraum* (a word coined in 1901), room for a burgeoning population to live in: maybe in South America, or Africa, or the Far East, or maybe in Slavic lands in Europe proper. Doctrines about RACE that Caucasians subscribed to encouraged such expansion, European powers venturing forth to encounter what they judged to be inferior peoples, subsisting in darkness on the African continent or as aborigines in Australia or south from Siberia as nomadic Mongols in Manchuria. In the Philippines lived, in their governor Taft's phrase, "our little brown brothers"; and for all those peoples the great powers were taking up the white man's burden to bring to the benighted the blessings of civilization.

Only, as Mark Twain scathingly noted, there was more to expansion than that. OIL was emblematic of the wealth that the postbellum technology was creating, and wealth bulged boundaries outward. While their new prosperity was amassing inventory, what the United States and European powers sought beyond their borders in addition to any bestowal of blessings overseas were natural resources for their factories as well as markets for the merchandise that those factories produced. Technology had provided gunboats and Maxim guns, and science was furnishing cures for malaria and other tropical diseases, all of which allowed the powers to penetrate where they hadn't been able to go before, armed up rivers into the heart of Africa, for instance, to impose their will and get what they wanted. And if war resulted, against Native Americans or Boers or Chinese or in Cuba or the Philippines, all that provided a testing ground for the CHILDREN of a materialistic age, shaping them into strong women tempered by duty and virile men possessed of the martial virtues.

Those virtues, instilled, would bring PEACE, as America's righteous, disciplined youth furnished the big stick of military strength while the United States spoke softly. For his part, President Roosevelt had long been convinced that nobody listens "to the weakling or the coward who babbles of peace; but due heed is given to the strong man with sword girt on thigh" when he preaches of an end to war, not from any weakness but from strength and from "a deep sense of moral obligation." Thus, our delegates to the first Hague Peace Conference, in 1899, played a leading role "chiefly because we had just emerged victorious from our most righteous war with Spain."

Samuel Clemens had his own doubts about people who babble of peace, specifically about Czar Nicholas II, that pious young hypocrite, who had issued the summons for nations to attend the 1899 conference on arbitration and disarmament. Between the issuance of his call in the fall of 1898 and the convocation of delegates at The Hague the following spring, the ostensibly peace-loving czar had condoned the slaughter by his troops of unarmed civilians gathering in Helsinki to protest the Russification of their nearly century-old Duchy of Finland; and within a very few years this same anti-Semitic, pogrom-indulging czar was entangled in an unprecedentedly bloody war with the Japanese. That protracted bloodbath ended only through the good offices of the President of the United States, who won great credit for his efforts: "the world's first citizen," Roosevelt was called, who "has sheathed the swords of a million men." Yet even that grand achievement was not enough to lead Mark Twain to think well of the Colonel as politician. Revolution had been erupting in Russia in 1905 and, according to the humorist, appeared about to overthrow an appalling despotism, when our flamboyant president "conceived the idea, a year ago, of advertising himself to the world as the new Angel of Peace, and set himself the task of bringing about the peace between Russia and Japan and had the misfortune to accomplish his misbegotten purpose." Few others judged what Roosevelt had done so sourly, but for Mark Twain "that fatal peace had postponed Russia's imminent liberation from its age-long chains indefinitely—probably for centuries," the President's interference having "given the Russian revolution its death-blow."

It was on March 30, 1906, that Clemens privately dictated so glum an assessment of Roosevelt's efforts for peace, by that late date about done with his public pronouncements. Having arrived at Pier 70 some four months earlier, Mark Twain was resigning from his role as social critic. "I have worked pretty steadily for 65 years," he said, "and don't care what I do with the 2 or 3 that remain to me so that I get pleasure out of them." Anyway, Colonel Roosevelt was hardly to blame for his shortcomings. None of us is. As soon blame the tiger for being fierce, or the hare for being timid. We're all mere machines, Clemens had come to think, constructed by our genes and our environment—what he called heredity and training, in a brief book that he limited to 250 copies and published anonymously this same summer of 1906. Begun back in Vienna in 1898, *What Is Man?* was a piece of writing that Livy had thoroughly disliked, and one that Clemens's daughter Jean, having learned to type, refused to type up for him. The Socratic dialogue between an Old Man and a Young Man develops a grimly deterministic philosophy. Neither altruism nor heroism motivates human behavior, ever. We do what we have to—the assertive Roosevelt, the mercurial Clemens—to placate selfish needs that nature and nurture have instilled in us. God, if you will, made us what we are, and as surely as a coffee mill grinds coffee, we enact only what our temperaments allow us to. We may have choices, but we have no more free will than the tiger or the hare does. And invariably we choose not what is selfless but what least bruises our self-approval. Thus, leaving the family unprovided for, we march off to war not out of patriotism or heroism but simply to avoid the scorn of the neighbors if we had stayed home. And if such deterministic convictions rob humanity of its credit and glory, at least they assuaged one aging widower's incessant remorse for the wounding of those he loved: wife, children, friends. He convinced himself that, as heredity and training bound him in traits as surely as the tiger and the hare are bound, Samuel Clemens could not have done otherwise.

So he would put remorse behind him, or try to, determined to enjoy whatever years he had left. These days Mark Twain worked in the morning an hour or so—although it was hardly work, propped up in bed dictating opinions and recollections for readers unborn, while household admirers relished his every word—then would play billiards with his biographer Paine in the afternoon and far into some evenings, or on other evenings read aloud to Miss Lyon or listen while she played the orchestrelle, or attend one of countless banquets, or have friends in. Over two summers he joined a colony of writers in the cooler rusticities of Dublin, New Hampshire, he and Jean and Miss Lyon in a cottage away from hot, dusty, noisy New York, from which rural retreat Mark Twain found time now and then to go cruising with Rogers and the boys on the *Kanawha*. In late August 1906, for instance, he returned to Dublin after ten days away, "gay and jolly and darling," Miss Lyon recorded, "and full of his yachting trip to Bar Harbor, and Mrs. Harry"—H. H. Rogers's lively, lovely daughter-in-law Mary—"and the joy of living. Sly, he was; and like a boy fresh from his wild oats." No longer would he worry about wasting time, Clemens said, before wasting three more happy weeks on another cruise that fall.

In December he journeyed with Howells to Washington to lobby for extending the copyright law. In the hearing room on that winter day of 1906, his friend was astonished to see Mark Twain abruptly uncover a new style of men's dress. "Nothing could have been more dramatic than the gesture with which he flung off his long loose overcoat, and stood forth in white from his feet to the crown of his silvery head. It was a magnificent *coup*; and he dearly loved a *coup*"—dressed all in white serge before the darkly clad congressional committee. Henceforth, Clemens wore white in winter and summer both. He said he had grown tired of funereal black; and to an inquiring public Mark Twain explained that his clothes signified purity, he being the one pure man in the land. As for the speech urging copyright extension that he treated the congressmen to, Howells thought that even more magnificent than the clothing the petitioner wore. It was, after all, Mark Twain's copyrights that would provide for his loved ones when he died. Although death had already reduced the size of the family by three, two daughters still lived, both unmarried. For their sake the author wanted his intellectual property protected, having pursued his autobiography in part to stretch out the value of the bequest. The plan was to apportion sections of the newly dictated work among his various titles before their copyrights expired, in order that the works might be reissued with enough changes to warrant new copyrights, thus prolonging the royalties they paid.

The daughters were grown, of course, and often away, Jean this fall of 1906 at the sanitarium in Katonah for protracted treatment of her epilepsy. Clara was at her own rest cure, preparing for a forthcoming concert tour in Europe. But their father's money supported them both. Meanwhile, in their absence, the Fifth Avenue home felt lonely as often as not, a dark old gothic pile that Clemens had come to dislike. He spent many days away from it, at Fairhaven with the Rogerses, or in Dublin, or through one of these summers at affluent Tuxedo Park by the Hudson, or some of the time in Bermuda.

Early in 1907 he took his old friend Joe Twichell to those happy isles, not their first stay there together. Clemens had seen Bermuda in his early thirties, ashore from the *Quaker City* during a brief layover back in 1867, near the end of his five-month cruise to the Holy Land. After a decade he went back, this time for four days on an impulse with his Hartford minister and good friend—"to get the world and the devil out of my head." And again, thirty years after that, in January 1907, he was back with Twichell for a week in that glorious subtropical paradise, two elderly gentlemen returned to midlife scenes. How Livy would have loved the place, though! How he wished he had thought to bring her here in her final year, instead of to damp, cold Florence! The pellucid waters: from the deck coming in you looked right down to the clear sunlit bottom of the bay, marveling that the ship's hull could pass over boulders that appeared so close to the surface. And the white, white houses of Hamilton, brilliant in sunlight, with the oleander and jasmine and lilies and blue morning glories, the fragrant orange trees, the fig trees, the cocoa palms. A voyage of two nights and a bit over a day delivered you to those islands some 775 miles southeast of New York, basking in their sublime weather that the Gulf Stream warmed year round. Tourists had scarcely discovered them yet, remote as Easter Island, as Juan Fernandez; Mark Twain's writing about Bermuda would help change all that during the forty years of his visiting the place. Eight separate times he returned, for a total of six months on the islands (actually more than a hundred outcroppings out there on twenty square miles in the middle of nowhere), each time relishing the serenity, the absence of telephones and newspapers, of motorized traffic on the coral roads that led to glittering ocean vistas. He loved the weather, the bathing, the donkey-cart rides, the congenial company, the salubrious easing of his bronchitis, his gout, and his rheumatism.

Not long back from this present excursion with Twichell, he was off again with Henry Rogers aboard the *Kanawha* in the spring of 1907, on his way to a world's fair at Norfolk, Virginia, that commemorated the tercentenary of the landing, at nearby Jamestown on April 26, 1607, of settlers establishing the first English colony in the Western Hemisphere. President Roosevelt came down to open the exhibition, one with decidedly militaristic overtones—sign of a new era. In place of the Midway, as at the Chicago world's fair of 1893 and its imitators, this Jamestown Exposition featured a Warpath as the site for its amusements. An adjacent campground held tents to accommodate 5,000 soldiers, who entertained spectators with their drill maneuvers. The most popular attraction, however, recreated history's earliest engagement of iron warships, at nearby Hampton Roads in 1862, between the *Monitor* and the *Merrimac*. And out in the harbor rode—in addition to the *Kanawha*—an international fleet of over fifty vessels, including sixteen American battleships for President Roosevelt to review on opening day. Before sailing from New York, Clemens had informed pier-side reporters that he and Mr. Rogers were going down to Norfolk "to see the naval review. There's something inspiring about seeing a lot of big warships that seem to say: 'Now, be good and there won't be any trouble, but if you aren't good and peaceful, then look out.'" Not that we're any nearer universal peace this year than last, he said. "But peace conventions are a good thing for the world. They set a shining example of what people think they will do before the occasion arises that might precipitate the unleashing of the martial canines." Anyway, "I guess it's a mighty good thing to have a whacking big navy. In times of peace prepare to have peace continued." Colonel Roosevelt could hardly have said it better.

Back from that springtime voyage in pursuit of pleasure, Mark Twain was overjoyed in May to receive word that he was about to be awarded an honorary degree from Oxford University. To claim such a prize he would go to Mars if he had to, he said—this formerly barefoot truant from Hannibal schooldays, self-educated, about to receive what he judged to be the world's most prestigious intellectual distinction. Never mind that his friend Howells had been awarded precisely the same honor three years earlier, and Roosevelt would be similarly recognized at Oxford three years hence. For the moment, Samuel L. Clemens, soon to be Hon. D.Litt. Oxon., was boarding the S.S. *Minneapolis*, on June 8, 1907, bound for Tilbury on the Thames, on his way to taking possession of what he regarded as the supreme honor of his life.

He was accompanied overseas by Ralph Ashcroft, an Englishman in his early thirties whom the author had come to know as a business associate. For despite an Oxford-grade intelligence, Clemens appeared to have learned very little from the Paige typesetter debacle. As soon after the bankruptcy as H. H. Rogers could restore his fortune to him, the author had set about looking for more schemes to invest in. Rogers dissuaded him from putting money into a carpet-patterning contraption, but the coffers of an English dried-milk preparation called Plasmon benefited substantially from Clemens's openhanded enthusiasm, the humorist's health much strengthened, he felt sure, by mixing the stuff with liquids and drinking it down. Ashcroft was involved with the American branch of the Plasmon enterprise, and from that office he moved into Clemens's confidence, became a trusted part of the household, and helped with the author's finances. Now they were traveling together, Ashcroft as secretary and Mark Twain as bearer of instructions from his daughter Clara, seeing him off, as to how to behave abroad—bearer as well of numberless invitations cabled to him the moment word got out that the humorist might be on his way over.

The very dockworkers on the pier cheered Mark Twain's arrival: "a hundred men of my own class," he called them gratefully, "grimy sons of labor, the real builders of empires and civilizations, the stevedores! They stood in a body on the dock and charged their masculine lungs, and gave me a welcome which went to the marrow of me." Once ashore in England, from that point on for a month the cheering hardly stopped. George Bernard Shaw happened to be on the platform when the boat train reached London. Did he know Mark Twain was inside? No, but Shaw did know that Mark Twain "is by far the greatest American writer. America has two great literary assets—Edgar Allan Poe and Mark Twain," the Irishman making clear that he was speaking of Mark Twain not as humorist but as social critic and as the finest writer of English in the world today. Later Shaw and Clemens had lunch together, but that was only one of so many occasions that celebrated this unexpected and—everyone sensed—final return of a frequent and much loved visitor to these shores.

Clemens had first come among them, already greatly honored, in 1872, thirty-five years earlier. Now reporters were dogging him everywhere, English newspapers full of his doings; and quiet, sedate Brown's Hotel was turned into a post office and a congested public gathering place. Ashcroft and another secretary, hurriedly hired, kept busy through long hours each day winnowing invitations. The welcome proved overwhelming. For one used to being warmly received, this present extraordinary reception went beyond any that Clemens had ever experienced. Breakfasts with new friends. Luncheons at the Ritz, at Dorchester House, at the king's garden party at Windsor Castle. Speeches before members of the Athenaeum, of the Garrick Club, of the Savage, of the Pilgrims. And old friends galore to see: Bram Stoker, Conan Doyle, Lady Stanley, Archdeacon Wilberforce, Mr. and Mrs. Henry Rogers come over from America and staying at Claridge's.

The ovations were endless, and endless the greetings of friends new and old—or, alas, of their widows. And when finally, on June 26, candidates clothed in brilliant academic robes (Kipling, Rodin, Saint-Saëns, General Booth, Prime Minister Campbell-Bannerman, Mark Twain) assembled at Magdalen College and followed the chancellor, Lord Curzon, over the stones of Oxford to the Sheldonian Theatre to receive their degrees, the tumult of approval from the joyful crowd rose loudest as Mark Twain, Sam Clemens of Hannibal, Missouri, stepped forward to hear the chancellor address him in Latin: "Most amiable and charming sir, you shake the sides of the whole world with your merriment. . . ."

If only Livy could have been in the audience. If only Susy could have seen this. "I have led a violently gay and energetic life here for four weeks," Mark Twain assured an interviewer in Liverpool on the eve of his departure, "but I have felt no fatigue, and I have had but little desire to quiet down. I am younger now by seven years than I was, and if I could stay here another month I could make it fourteen." It was, he said, the most enjoyable holiday he had ever spent, "and I am sorry the end of it has come. I have met a hundred old friends and made a hundred new ones. It's a good kind of riches—there's none better, I think." Cheered by the renewal of such connections, he went on to confess that for the last couple of years he had been planning his funeral, "but I have changed my mind and have postponed it."

CHAPTER Forty-Four

TR Steps Down

Roosevelt didn't care for the nickname "Teddy," although crowds at his open-air appearances shouted it out with enthusiasm, and close friends (John Hay, Henry Adams, Cecil Spring Rice) used *Teddy* in correspondence, behind Theodore's back, in affectionate irony. But to the shorthand "TR" the Colonel made no objection; and by the summer of 1907, as Mark Twain was bringing his scarlet robe home from Oxford, TR had grown to be a familiar abbreviation, with Theodore Roosevelt's career already (so soon!) approaching the Republican convention, less than a year away, that would seek to choose his successor. In fact, the President had been busy with that very matter of succession during these same spring and summer months, determined that the policies he had furthered should end up in sympathetic hands when he left the White House.

For leave it he must, although most reluctantly. On election night in November 1904 Roosevelt had pledged to do so—that he would observe the spirit rather than the letter of a custom limiting a president to two terms in office. Elevated from the vice presidency to complete the slain McKinley's unfinished three years and more, Roosevelt at the end of his own term would have served a bit over seven and a half years, not far short of the eight-year limit. But now, as the time for departing approached, he sorely regretted the impulse that had led him to vow not to seek reelection in 1908, as technically he might have done for only his second run at the highest office. To a friend he admitted in candor that he would give *that* up—pointing down toward his other hand—if he could take back his election-night pledge of 1904.

The vow that he now regretted and that many were urging him to renege on had turned Roosevelt into a lame duck, whom opponents deferred to rather less often than they might have if he had been in a position to win reelection and remain in office until 1913. As for winning, TR's popularity had mounted so high that there seemed little doubt he could have prevailed over any Democrat in November 1908. And just a couple of weeks before that election day he would turn fifty, at the start of the decade in a man's life from which many presidents before and since have been chosen.

Even so—still young, vigorous, and broadly admired—Roosevelt had enemies, lots of them. Legislators through these late years of his administration were proving increasingly obstructive, resenting the appropriation of powers and prerogatives to the executive branch that, they thought, belonged in Congress—or that weren't constitutional powers at all. The President granted that the Constitution was the greatest document ever devised by man, but he also insisted that it wasn't "a straitjacket cunningly fashioned to strangle growth." Thus Roosevelt interpreted constitutional provisions loosely, in whatever way helped him help Americans help themselves. Meanwhile, many of those same disgruntled senators and representatives were beholden to interests that roundly despised President Roosevelt. Timber interests resented his seizing of millions of acres of forest for posterity's benefit—what had posterity done for *them*?—and mining interests wanted at the copper, silver, and coal in those same forested hills. Wall Street investors deplored what they took to be Roosevelt's antagonistic attitude toward business, hobbling it by pushing such measures as the Pure Food and Drug Act, by sending inspectors to snoop around stockyards, and by setting rates for railroads to charge, all the while speaking out against "malefactors of great wealth," as he memorably called the unprincipled rich—not all rich people, but those who behaved like criminals, behaved in fact, in his own blunt phrase, as "the most dangerous of all classes." As for the trusts that Roosevelt's department of justice prosecuted for monopolistic practices—the sugar trust, the tobacco trust, above all Standard Oil with its ruthless means of destroying competition—the tycoons in those great conglomerates were generally aligned against the President, as were some anti-imperialists, as were Democrats in a body, and as was the Republican Old Guard, so called, which scorned Roosevelt's progressivism, all that talk of a Square Deal for the "plain people": his trustbusting, the eight-hour work days, the safety protections for factory workers, the easing of working conditions for women and children. To his foes, this president's way of governing seemed a constant meddling where government didn't belong.

Not that Roosevelt had turned into some sort of radical. Consistently he saw himself as a moderate, even a conservative, conserving the party of Lincoln, taking it back from the unscrupulous rich who had seized control of the levers. "On the one hand; on the other hand": that was the place where our twenty-sixth president felt most comfortable: in the middle, representing all the people against the extremes on either side, "as much against anarchic violence and crimes of brutality," he insisted, "as against corruption and crimes of greed; as much against demagogic assaults on the well off, as against crimes by the well off." He would save the Republican Party from itself; for if the Old Guard—offspring of the Gilded Age, when robber barons plundered unchecked—persisted in using the party to rule for the benefit of the few, Democratic rabble-rousers might yet succeed in ushering in a mobocracy, as poisonous to the general welfare as were the greedy rich whom demagogues were ever stirring up the mobs to supersede.

Looking for someone to carry on his work of governing for all Americans, Roosevelt by the summer of 1907 had settled on William Howard Taft. "I do not believe there can be found in the whole country a man so well fitted to be President," he wrote. Judge Taft "is not only absolutely fearless, absolutely disinterested and upright, but he has the widest acquaintance with the nation's needs without and within and the broadest sympathies with all our citizens. He would be as emphatically a President of the plain people as Lincoln"—regarding whom Roosevelt rated no other public figure so highly—"yet not Lincoln himself would be freer from the least taint of demagogy, the least tendency to arouse or appeal to any class hatred of any kind."

In these late months the people were growing reconciled to the portly Taft as the Republican candidate (a reluctant one, who would rather have been named chief justice), although their first choice for 1908 was Roosevelt, TR, their Teddy—"a practically unanimous demand from my own party that I accept another nomination, and the reasonable certainty that the nomination would be ratified at the polls." But Roosevelt stood by his pledge to the end and won credit for doing so. An editorial in Collier's, for instance, saluted the Colonel for the "dexterity and sincerity with which he avoided a renomination for himself, and secured it for a believer in his policies," highly honorable behavior that has "solidified the affection and the confidence of mankind."

Collier's rather overdid the praise, in the view of Samuel L. Clemens, absorbing the news in June 1908 that Taft had won the Republican nomination in Chicago decisively, on the first ballot. Still, whatever his feelings, Clemens would refrain from saying a word against Theodore Roosevelt in public—had sealed his mouth for the rest of his life against any such utterance, following upon an unspecified courtesy that the President had extended to his family in a time of sorrow. (Presumably the allusion was to

Roosevelt's order in 1904, after Mrs. Clemens's death, that the distraught husband and daughters be passed through New York customs without delay, their abundant luggage from ten months abroad unopened.) Henceforth Mark Twain would keep quiet in public, although privately these four years later he had a great deal to say against Roosevelt, all the while marveling at a politician's garnering praise simply for not running again. "In what way has the President set a high example?" he wondered. "Is it a high example for a president of the United States to keep his word?" If a burglar kept his word, we might say that he "has thereby set a high example for the other burglars." But the President? Surely this about keeping his word by not seeking reelection was the feeblest compliment ever fired in any president's direction. And anyway, Mr. Roosevelt hasn't given up power; "he has merely," according to Clemens, "gone through the form of transferring it to his serf, Mr. Taft, who runs to him daily with the docility of a spaniel to get his permission to do things."

Verily—if it were ever in doubt—we have a monarchy here in America, as witness this passing of the scepter to the ruler's designated heir, the Republican Party furnishing as certain a means of assuring the succession as does the House of Saxe-Coburg-Gotha guarantee the royal descent at Westminster. In July, Democrats in convention assembled at Denver would turn to their tired old warhorse William Jennings Bryan—for the third time!—to carry their banner; and under those circumstances what could any reasonable citizen do in November but vote for Taft, which Clemens did, despite his dissatisfactions with the outgoing president who controlled Taft's puppet strings.

Mark Twain recounted those dissatisfactions for the benefit of readers a hundred years hence, after the present players would all be dead and gone. Some of his hostility arose from Roosevelt's constant showing off, like a fourteen-year-old going on fifty. The great-hunter pose, and the jiu-jitsu, and "Hasn't he kept up such a continual thundering from our Olympus about football and baseball and mollycoddles and all sorts of little nursery matters" that there'll be no thunder left when something important comes along? But the things this president does that were "hitherto deemed impossible, wholly impossible, measurelessly impossible for a president of the United States to do, is much too long for invoicing here."

Clemens would mention, nevertheless, the Colonel's inveterate self-advertising: off to Panama, or last spring reviewing the fleet he had sent to the Jamestown Exposition. After the fair closed in November 1907, His Excellency dispatched those sixteen battleships from Hampton Roads on a cruise around the world. "He is sending the United States Navy to San

Francisco by way of the Strait of Magellan," Clemens complained at the time, "all for show, all for advertisement—although he is aware that if it gets disabled on its adventurous trip it cannot be repaired in the Pacific, for lack of docks; but the excursion will make a great noise and this will satisfy Mr. Roosevelt."

All the more noise when the Great White Fleet (as it came to be called) sails across the Pacific and blusters into the ports of Japan, before proceeding to circumnavigate the rest of the globe. Japan was in warlike mood anyway, the recent victor over Imperial Russia incensed with California's decision to spare its Caucasians by forbidding immigrant Japanese children from attending "white" schools. Why flaunt our battleships in Tokyo Bay just now? But that was Roosevelt: a greater calamity (Clemens opined) than the San Francisco earthquake of 1906, which at least had been limited in scope, whereas the consequences of the President's earthshaking extended worldwide: "the most formidable disaster," Clemens charged, "that has befallen the country since the Civil War."

There was the engagement in the Philippines in 1906 against Moros, and Roosevelt's shameful cable to that horse doctor and favorite of his, Leonard Wood, congratulating the general on his brave feat of arms that was in fact a massacre from a cratertop of 900 men, women, and children penned below and effectively weaponless. There was the Brownsville business of later that year, wherein the President summarily dismissed 167 black soldiers from the service "without honor"—and without evidence—for no better reason than to gain the favor of white southern voters. "He is always vaporing," Roosevelt is, "about purity and righteousness and fairness and justice, just the same as if he really respected those things and regards himself as their pet champion, whereas there is little or nothing in his history to show that he even knows the meaning of those words." Recall Order 78, which exposed the politician in full cry: giving the public's money away to Civil War veterans on no better pretext than that they've managed to reach age sixty-two, or sixty-five, or seventy. Award them pensions for surviving, then collect their vote. And the Rough Rider's constant harassing of corporations, especially H. H. Rogers's and John Archbold's Standard Oil. "Mr. Roosevelt has done what he could to destroy the industries of the country, and they all stand now in a half-wrecked condition and waiting in an ague to see what he will do next." As for the Constitution, "Hasn't he tunneled so many subways under the Constitution," Clemens figured, "that the transportation facilities through that document are only rivaled, not surpassed, by those now enjoyed by the City of New York?"

Some of this sounds like the ranting of an aged widower with a gift for vituperation that he likes to exercise, drawling dictations for Miss Lyon and Mr. Paine to admire. Clemens was too close to the scene and misled by the clamor in the daily papers, although he knew very well how deceptive the press's outrages can be: how this week's uproar—about underlings escorting a respectable but overimportunate lady petitioner from the White House right out to the street—can have sunk into oblivion two weeks on. And being so close to the unfolding of an administration filled with novelties, one led by a chief magistrate different from all his predecessors, the humorist, like his industrialist friends, often underrated, overreacted, or misinterpreted.

Brownsville, to be sure, was far from Roosevelt's finest moment; yet the President stood by his decision to punish the innocent many for shielding the guilty few—would have behaved (he said) precisely the same if the defendants had been white. As for Foraker of Ohio, who had condemned Roosevelt's action while eloquently defending the culprits on the Senate floor, Foraker was a tool of Wall Street, bought with Standard Oil money, so that in the senator's attack on Roosevelt, J. D. Rockefeller was merely getting what he paid for. California's dealing with its abundant immigrant population by segregating Japanese schoolchildren posed a thornier issue, which the President dealt with differently. He cajoled the Californians and talked to the Japanese—for Roosevelt admired the Japanese and could talk to them; one of their principal emissaries to America was a Harvard classmate and friend. Moreover, unlike the Chinese, unlike the Koreans and other Oriental races (as the Colonel regarded those peoples), the Japanese were welcoming of Western ways and full of initiative. So Roosevelt talked with the interested parties and got from them a gentlemen's agreement that satisfied both sides: Japan would restrict emigration to the United States, and California would cease segregating Japanese children. Accordingly, when the Great White Fleet did arrive in Yokohama, it was to a tumultuous welcome, crowds waving American flags and cheering.

So Mark Twain was wrong in asserting that President Roosevelt had behaved provocatively by sending our fleet into Japanese waters. His evaluation of the current chief executive seems faulty on a number of other counts. Roosevelt's self-advertising was no more than what we've come to expect from presidents and their image makers, noteworthy in the earlier instance simply because celebrity culture was only just then getting started. Moreover, Clemens failed to remark on the farsighted policy that posterity now thanks this Wilderness Warrior for day after day: Roosevelt's conservation measures at a time when most people regarded America's resources as both inexhaustible and belonging to *them*, to those alive at the moment and eager to exploit a continent's tremendous natural wealth. President Roosevelt and his forester Gifford Pinchot had other ideas; hence, our national monuments, parks, forests, and sanctuaries that the two men were prescient enough to create and preserve. For that alone, Theodore Roosevelt merits his very high ranking among our presidents. For that and for his enforcing the Sherman Anti-Trust Act. And signing the Food and Drug Act, and the Elkins Act, and the Hepburn Act that forbade railroads discriminating arbitrarily in what they charged their customers.

He did much else during his years in the White House to make America a fairer and better land, not all of it meeting with universal approval at the time. Reform—whether of a coinage redesigned, or the name and appearance of the Executive Mansion, or the rules of football to make the game safer (all of which this versatile president interested himself in)—never meets with universal approval. But most of the changes have worn well and speak loudly to the Colonel's abilities and range, and many of the reforms (the forward pass, for instance) abide to this day.

He did make mistakes, none more glaring than those that arose from his views on race. They were views informed by the brightest scientific light of the time, and views very widely held. Moreover, Roosevelt ameliorated their worst aspects by insisting that each individual, whatever his race, be judged on merit. But even so, he formed from his convictions and his understanding of history certain assumptions on which he acted: that the most savage wars occur when a superior race encounters an inferior one, as in the Indian Wars of the American West; and that the way to peace leads through advanced races policing the less developed. As for the great nations, the secret of keeping peace among them lay in increasing trade and in forging alliances that made their strengths equivalent: a balance of powers. Thus he encouraged Japan privately to assert influence over Korea, an "empire" so primitive, he thought, as to be incapable of governing itself. Japan would stabilize Korea; Russia would stabilize primitive Manchuria; and the two great nations would serve as checks on each other. In fact, as Roosevelt misperceived it, the recipe for world peace would find European powers dominant in Africa, Russia dominant in Asia, Japan dominant on the Asian mainland opposite its home islands, and the United States guaranteeing peace in the Western Hemisphere. Wars henceforth would be fought only among less civilized peoples, brush fires to be put out by the more advanced nations, which, appropriately allied, would have risen above any need or desire to wage war on each other.

But it was all that imperial business, our republic transformed into an empire—a major shift from America's self-contained, continental past—that troubled Mark Twain most in judging Roosevelt the President: our new colonies, ruled without consent of the governed; those overseas entanglements; a new, ubiquitous flagwaving of white South and North reunited; the triumphalist fervor in Roosevelt's Anglo-Saxon "together we can lick the world" swagger. Some of such posturing appeared on display on the morning of February 23, 1909, when Colonel and Mrs. Roosevelt aboard the presidential yacht *Mayflower* joined 2,000 small craft inside the Virginia Capes to watch for the return of the Great White Fleet from its fourteen-month circumnavigation of the globe. The Colonel would later adjudge the cruise his greatest contribution to world peace. Now he was exulting as the huge battleships emerged with their escorts from beneath the horizon, their mission accomplished. "That is the answer to my critics," the President cried out. "Another chapter is complete, and I could not ask a finer concluding scene to my administrations."

One week and two days later, on March 4, William Howard Taft was sworn in as the twenty-seventh president of the United States; and Colonel Roosevelt, promptly and as quietly as possible, left Washington with his family for Oyster Bay. That same day Samuel Clemens wrote from out of town to his friend H. H. Rogers in New York to invite himself to dinner later in the month. On the evening of St. Patrick's Day, the Lotos Club was giving a banquet honoring Andrew Carnegie, and Mark Twain had agreed to attend if he could come late, not to dine (he dined too often at banquets) but for the speeches that followed. So he planned to stay at the Rogerses' up on Seventy-Eighth Street. "In which case, am I going to find," he asked his friend, "eatables, drinkables and lodging at your tavern at reduced rates?—on account of the country having lost the creator and propagator and promoter of its prosperities to-day"—lost, that is, Mr. Roosevelt's loud services with these present inaugural events.

For his part, the now former president would leave after all in fine spirits—or said he did. He and his son Kermit were about to set out on a grand safari in Africa, to gather specimens for the Smithsonian Institution in the course of a scientific expedition that the philanthropist Carnegie was in part subsidizing. "I don't see how any man could have had a happier life than I have had during my fifty years," the ex-chief executive exulted, "and certainly I don't know of any President who has had as happy a time, or who went out of office as pleased and interested as I now feel."

Roosevelt's daughter Alice, meanwhile, living in Washington as Representative Longworth's wife, would remember those same months of 1909,

Figure 44.1. Roosevelt and Taft, Inauguration Day, March
4, 1909.
Courtesy of the Theodore Roosevelt Collection, Harvard College Library.

her father departed on his African adventure. "The great diversion of the
late spring and early summer was to go over to Fort Myer," she looked back
from the 1930s to recall, "to see the Wrights fly. Patiently, day after day, one
would trail across to Arlington, only to be disappointed because a breeze
would spring up, and such a ridiculously light breeze prevented a flight.
When the machine actually left the ground and circled the field, a hundred
feet or so up, it gave us a thrill that no one in this generation will ever have."

CHAPTER **Forty-Five**

Jean

The Great White Fleet promoted global peace by showing the world—in Rio, Callao, Honolulu, Auckland, Sydney, Manila, Colombo, Suez, Gibraltar, and other ports of call—that the United States was now a major seapower, capable of sailing over blue water anywhere on earth. If the Japanese, having demolished two great armadas of imperial Russia, entertained ambitions of dominating the Pacific, this massive American force would give them pause, even as it guaranteed the integrity of Hawaii and the Philippines. A public sensation in transit both at home and abroad, the expedition furnished opportunities for crews to train while at sea; and during their weeks-long layovers in the ports of five continents—the hulls of their vessels painted a peacetime white—the officers and men spread goodwill internationally for more than a year.

Our own peacekeepers, extending the tactical mission of the Great White Fleet (with perhaps somewhat less of the goodwill) into the present, are called carrier battle groups. They evolved out of the flying machine that, when the wind subsided, lifted off in the spring of 1909 to rise precariously a hundred feet in the air and give viewers at Fort Myer below a new kind of thrill. Each battle group comprises at least one cruiser, a destroyer squadron, supply ships as needed, and sometimes a submarine. All are capable of operating anywhere in the world, in confined areas as well as across the open sea. And each group clusters around one of our aircraft carriers, such as the Nimitz-class supercarrier *Theodore Roosevelt*, CVN 71, which accommodates some eighty combat aircraft and 6,000 naval personnel on board. The present total of all U.S. Foreign Service officers is less than the sum of people serving on a single carrier battle group. At present (2012), the United States has eleven such groups; no other nation has more than one. Thus has militarism trumped diplomacy in our time, the Pentagon's budget and influence far exceeding the State Department's. And does the enormous outlay buy security? Mark Twain deplored the direction in which Colonel Roosevelt as navy secretary, vice president, and president had been moving the nation; and if he were to see the United States now, with a battle fleet larger than the next thirteen navies of the world combined (eleven of which are our allies or partners), would he find his worst fears about Roosevelt as president confirmed?

Be that as it may, by June 1908 the humorist was commenting on current affairs less often than formerly. During that month, in which the Republican convention in Chicago nominated William Howard Taft for president, Clemens moved out of his Fifth Avenue home and into the country. Albert Bigelow Paine, at work on Mark Twain's authorized biography, had earlier called his subject's attention to land available near property of his own in Connecticut, close to Redding, by a depot a convenient hour's train ride from New York City. Windfall money was on hand from the sale of generous portions of Mark Twain's autobiography that had run in the *North American Review*, with more money arriving from "Captain Stormfield's Visit to Heaven" in *Harper's*, funds enough to allow for purchasing the acreage and erecting on it a rural home that Clemens ended up living in year round. He had got his friend Howells's son, John Mead Howells (who would later design the Beekman Tower in New York and the Tribune Tower in Chicago), to draw up plans, and Miss Lyon was put in charge of choosing interior decorations.

The future homeowner didn't want to have anything to do with the project, didn't even want to look at the rising structure, he said, until it was finished and the cat was purring at the hearth. However: "The moment I saw the house," he exclaimed soon after that day arrived, "I was glad I built it." Clemens came to Redding in the early evening of June 18, 1908, moved in, and at once loved everything around him. If only Livy could have lived here! In August he wrote a friend to share his delight. "I realize," he told Mrs. Rogers, "that I haven't had a real home, until now, since we left the Hartford one 17 years ago. It is a long, long time to be homeless. I can hardly bear to go a mile from this one." And he lived there the rest of his life.

Situated at the crest of a knoll, it was a handsome Italianate villa, white stucco with a red tile roof, guest rooms upstairs and a suite for Clara, downstairs a living room of large proportions with the organ-like orchestrelle dominating one wall, French doors giving onto an arched loggia open on three sides, a brick terrace the length of the back of the house, with a graded lawn sloping down past a garden to a pergola at a distance, offering grand views of the hills beyond. Yet if this lifelong wanderer in his new abode had finally found a place that he was disinclined to leave, he didn't feel alone out there, not like in the gothic pile he had moved from on Fifth Avenue. Visitors back in New York came only for lunch or dinner, but at Redding they come "and bring a trunk, and stay from two days to eight. Already we have had 21 in the 7 weeks that I have been here, and the guestrooms are fast being taken for August and September." Howells visited, and relished his son's handiwork and the pleasure the client was deriving from it; and Twichell came down from Hartford, and other guests rode up from the city. "The distance from New York is so easy that the friends do not mind the journey. I wish you and Mr. Rogers had elected to come here for a few weeks' rest," he gently chided the wife of that other intimate, "for this is the very quietest place outside the dungeon of St. Peter and St. Paul; no strangers, no crowds, no fashion, only one neighbor within three quarters of a mile—Miss Lyon's mother."

Figure 45.1. William Dean Howells visits Clemens at Stormfield, 1908.

Courtesy of the Mark Twain House & Museum, Hartford.

Miss Lyon, his secretary, was given an outbuilding on the property to refurbish as her own. Of his dear friends, circumstances prevented the Rogerses from ever making the train ride up. Girls, however, between the ages of eleven to sixteen did arrive regularly at Mark Twain's invitation; for Clemens had revived the pleasures he took earlier, in the early months of 1906, when he entertained and was entertained by Gertrude Natkin— "Marjorie"—until she was unlucky enough to turn sixteen and thus effectively end their brief friendship. Later, Clemens on his way to Oxford in June 1907 to receive his honorary degree had met an English child and her mother on shipboard and was charmed. And charmed by an eleven-year-old, Dorothy Quick, aboard the *Minetonka* on the way home. "Dorothy dear," he wrote to that second young friend after they landed in New York, "Will you come and make me a visit? Do you think your Mother could spare you a week? Will you come? If you can't come for a whole week, will you come for half a week?"

At the time, he had been escaping urban heat at Tuxedo Park, an exclusive community in the Ramapo Hills forty miles northwest of Manhattan. The responsible Miss Lyon, forty-three years old and formerly a governess, would pick up the little girl, Clemens assured Mrs. Quick, and return her to her home in Plainfield at the end of the visit. Dorothy did come, and was looked after by Catherine the maid and Claude the butler. She heard Mark Twain dictating in the morning—"The sentences came one after the other, with scarcely a pause between"—enjoyed the fresh fruit, took photographs, and with her host formed The Authors' League for Two to benefit her writing. For Dorothy wanted to be a writer (and became one, and in maturity wrote of her friendship with Mark Twain as unalloyed joy, in a book she called *Enchantment*). While the old man and the young girl listened in the evening, Miss Lyon played the orchestrelle; and there were card games, delightful conversation, kittens to pet, and books galore. Too soon Miss Lyon took the child home, and her host wrote at once to Dorothy dear: "I went to bed as soon as you departed, there being nothing to live for after that, and the sunshine all gone. How do you suppose I am going to get along without you? For five hours this has been a dreary place, a sober and solemn place, a hushed and brooding and lifeless place, for the blessed spirit of youth has gone out of it and left nothing that's worthwhile."

Dorothy came back for several other visits, when her friend returned to Fifth Avenue in October, and later out to Redding to stay with her beloved SLC (the name they had agreed on) after Clemens moved to the country. There were, she tells us, "no rules for little girls at Mark Twain's house. And that wasn't the least of its charms." But the rules did come, in good humor, when her elderly host regularized his attachment to such girls as this by creating—under the inspiration of Bermuda's tropical beauty—"the Aquarium," each member of which new club was denominated an "angelfish." Besides Dorothy Quick, they included Dorothy Butes, Carlotta Welles, Frances Nunnally, Margaret Blackmer, Irene Gerken, Dorothy Sturgis, Helen Martin, Helen Allen, Dorothy Harvey, Marjorie Breckenridge, and Albert Bigelow Paine's daughter Louise. People collect all sorts of things: andirons, stamps. "As for me," Clemens said, "I collect pets: young girls—girls from ten to sixteen years old; girls who are pretty and sweet and naive and innocent—dear young creatures to whom life is a perfect joy and to whom it has brought no wounds, no bitterness, and few tears." They served as the grandchildren he didn't have, only better; for he got to pick his, whereas other grandfathers had to take what came along. By 1908, his letters to and from the girls had become, he said, the "chief occupation and delight" of his days. Some 300 of them survive. To Dorothy Quick, for instance, he wrote from Bermuda when his plans for a club were forming, in mid-March 1908. "Dear child, I am taking the liberty of appointing you to membership in my 'Aquarium' if you will let me. It consists of five angel fishes and one shad. I am the shad. The device of the club is a very small angel fish pin to be worn on the breast. I will fetch it when I come. I have to wear a flying fish pin until I can get a shad made." Tiffany crafted the small, brilliantly colored enamel jewelry, and Dorothy was thrilled to wear hers: "Dorothy Quick, M.A." Member of the Aquarium. She must now, however, abide by the rules and secrets of the order. "Members of the Aquarium are forbidden to divulge its affairs to any but their parents & guardians. Members desiring to conspire must give notice to the Admiral & tell him what it is about." Unless the conspiracy is against the Admiral himself, Mr. Clemens; "in that case notice must be given to the Official Legal Staff," which included Miss Lyon. The Admiral is obliged to replace lost angelfish badges; "Members need only give him notice." And portraits of non-members are not allowed in the billiard room. Dorothy arriving at SLC's country home in Connecticut was especially curious about the billiard room, "for I had never met any of the other members of the club"; and there she found them all: photographs of children around her age that hung among framed pictures of real angelfish. Soon the little girl learned to play billiards herself, her host even seeing that she won sometimes.

The whole thing made Clemens's daughter Clara uneasy. It may make us uneasy, but more than one of the angelfish looked back in maturity to recall an old gentleman's attentions in nothing but the most gratefully pleasurable terms. Despite what we in a more candid era have learned about pedophilia's doleful extent—and making due allowance for the constancies in human behavior from age to age—it seems inconceivable that more was involved in Clemens's preoccupation than a flight from his embittered present back to what he saw as a simpler, happier past: to Hartford, when his own daughters were young and romping with Papa in the library; or back farther still to a platonic sweetheart of his youth, unforgotten (and written about) even this late; or to a blue-eyed, pigtailed little girl in Hannibal, Laura Hawkins, who became Tom Sawyer's Becky Thatcher before turning at last into Mrs. Frazer, an old woman paying the celebrated author a visit the other week here in Redding. But childhood is the golden time. Don't grow old, Marjorie. Don't grow old, Dorothy, and Frances, and Helen, and the other children whose company the widower had come to depend on and cherish.

After her father died, Clara Clemens did what she could to hide his aquarium of angelfish from public awareness. More generally, she strove with his biographer Albert Bigelow Paine to accentuate the benign aspects of Mark Twain's genius: his humor, his generosity of spirit, his stature as a serious author, his kindliness and the range of his friendships, and the love worldwide that was showered upon him. Yet in life, markedly after Livy's death in 1904, Clemens and his daughter Clara had trouble getting along. She knew her father—when he wasn't being utterly delightful (as he often was)—to be moody, irascible, short-tempered, and vain. In fact, after the mourning family's return from Italy, Clara took pains to stay away from him more often than not; and when she did visit, it was for days more likely than weeks, and was all but invariably followed by sojourns in rest homes before she resumed the pursuit of her musical career in the East and overseas.

In Redding on rare visits, involving herself with Miss Lyon's duties of furnishing the new home, Clara soon found matter to criticize. She had liked the Lyoness very well at the start and had written warmly to thank the Hartford friend who had recommended her. Miss Lyon in turn had exulted in Miss Clemens's goodness: Santa Clara in the diary, Clarissima. But what Clara learned now, as the house rose through the spring of 1908 and after, stirred suspicions and objections. In a play on *The Innocents Abroad* Clemens called his new residence "Innocents at Home," and had stationery printed with the name at the top. But was that too suggestive of the little girls often in attendance there? Clara objected, and the mansion thenceforth became "Stormfield." Stormfield sounded more appropriate anyway, on its hilltop as dark clouds gathered. Clara had expected more than a guest room upstairs, wanted a suite; so the architectural plans were altered, and a suite installed. Occupying it, she grew to suspect that Miss Lyon was diverting money meant for Stormfield's beautification to furnishing her own cottage elsewhere on the property, and before long she sensed that the secretary was aspiring to become the second Mrs. Clemens. Finally Clara discovered to her horror that her father had signed a power of attorney giving Miss Lyon and Mr. Ashcroft control of his assets.

The case of Isabel Van Kleek Lyon remains a vexed one. Was she the selfless (and drastically underpaid) gratifier of Mark Twain's every reasonable desire in his bereft old age, managing his social and financial affairs, handling his correspondence, seeing to details of his grooming, his shopping needs, the logistics of his travels, the dealings with architect and contractors, dealing with the household staff, greeting and caring for his visitors, providing her employer with music in the evening and her full attention to his conversation and his readings aloud? She lived into her mid-nineties and, all that while, kept Mark Twain's memory enshrined, untarnished, alone in a Greenwich Village apartment. Mementoes of her service in his household cluttered her living quarters, her recollections of those years vivid to the last as the supreme happiness of her life. Books and articles have been written that present Miss Lyon as devotedly loyal to Mark Twain, who, by the end, shamefully, woefully abused her.

Books have also been written that portray her in darker hues. For Clara grew convinced that her father's secretary was a schemer, angling to wed the great Mark Twain or, failing that, to squeeze whatever she could out of her privileged relationship. The slick Frank Ashcroft, co-holder of Clemens's power of attorney (which the humorist professed to having had no recollection of signing), appeared in an even more sinister light, possessed as he was of a canniness in business practices. Suddenly, in March 1909, Ashcroft and Lyon (twelve years his senior) got married. Clemens attended their Fifth Avenue wedding, but what was that all about? Was it to lay to rest any fears that the bride aspired to be Mrs. Clemens? On her occasional visits Clara went on voicing alarm; so that in April, after six and a half years of diligent service, Miss Lyon was fired, abruptly evicted from her cottage—her Lobster Pot—and sent on her way. Ashcroft, too. They both were fired that April of 1909, the power of attorney revoked; and Clemens set about writing, initially in the form of a letter to William Dean Howells, what turned into a 426-page manuscript excoriating the two and setting down the "facts" to use against them if they tried to cause legal troubles later. Her former employer ended by characterizing Miss Lyon, in a letter to Clara, as "a liar, a forger, a thief, a hypocrite, a drunkard, a sneak, a humbug, a traitor, a conspirator, and a filthy-minded & salacious slut pining for seduction."

The woman's greatest offense by far, her King adjudged, had been her keeping him away from his younger daughter, Jean. Clara was often out of the father's presence anyhow, by choice; but Jean remained under a doctor's care and longing for home. Yet Miss Lyon had conspired (or had she?) with Dr. Peterson (or was it Dr. Quintard?) to keep Jean secluded, under extended treatment for epilepsy long after the young woman appeared well enough to rejoin the family.

Presumably Jean's absence from Stormfield had left the secretary free to pursue her schemes of exploiting the ingenuous Clemens. That youngest daughter's was a sad case from every point of view. As a child Jean had exhibited a lovely disposition, bright, friendly, wonderful with animals of all kinds. Then at eight or nine her head "got a bad knock" from a fall. At thirteen, she grew unaccountably moody; and three years later, in 1896, "the New York experts pronounced her case *epilepsy*. This we learned," Clemens confided to his close friend Rogers, "when we got back from around the world." At the very time of Susy's death, this other tragedy fell on the family. It kept them in Europe longer than they had planned, pursuing the best care they could find for Jean's hushed-up malady. Over five years Clemens had witnessed only three of his daughter's many frightening convulsions; but his wife had had to deal with numbers of them, so that her husband was sure Livy's death was hastened thereby. Jean for her part felt the full force of her predicament. "Why must I live on aimlessly," she wrote in her diary, "with nothing to do, utterly useless, all my life? I who long so for the love and companionship that only a man can give, and that man a husband." Because she was an epileptic "and shouldn't marry if I had the chance," did that condemn her never to know love?

Then, in April 1909, Lyon and Ashcroft were sent on their way; and scarcely a week later, Jean Clemens came to Stormfield to live. She and her father got to know each other all over again. He gave her some land on the property to farm, and she thrived outdoors with her orchard and animals, and at Stormfield took up some of the duties that Miss Lyon had formerly discharged: typing manuscripts, managing Mark Twain's correspondence, directing household staff. Clemens soon found in his grown youngest daughter, at twenty-nine, unsuspected reserves of merit: "Wisdom, judgment, penetration, practical good sense, like her mother," he wrote to the other daughter, Clara, "character, courage, definiteness, decision; also goodness, a human spirit, charity, kindliness, pity; industry, perseverance, intelligence, a clean mind, a clean soul, dignity, honesty, truthfulness, high ideals, loyalty, faithfulness to duty—she is everything that Miss Lyon isn't."

Figure 45.2.   The wedding of Clara Clemens and Ossip Gabrilowitsch, October
1909. Twichell is on the far right, beside the bride and groom; Jean stands next to
her father and her cousin, Charley Langdon's son Jervis.
Courtesy of the Mark Twain Project, The Bancroft Library, University of California, Berkeley.

Father and daughter lived happily together that summer and fall, both
of them relishing the revived affection. In October, Clara, now in her mid-
thirties, returned to Stormfield to wed a suitor whom she had known since
Vienna days and had earlier refused, the musician Ossip Gabrilowitsch.
Jean served as bridesmaid, Charley Langdon's son was best man, the Reverend Joseph Twichell performed the ceremony, and Clemens in his Oxford
gown gave the bride away. Afterward, the new Mr. and Mrs. Gabrilowitsch
returned to Europe, to their musical life, leaving a father and his youngest
daughter to resume their rediscoveries of each other's sterling qualities.

Ill health drove Clemens to Bermuda for a month in the fall of 1909,
but he wanted to be in Stormfield for Christmas. On December 20 he
came back to New York, disembarking, reporters noted, "somewhat out
of sorts physically and even disinclined to jest." The shift from a warm,
sunny isle to frigid Manhattan had proved disagreeable; but after a night
in the city, he rode up to Redding and, once home with Jean, was soon
in better spirits. She had been making much of the season, buying and
wrapping gifts for some fifty friends and servants. Two evenings later
father and daughter spent a particularly pleasant interlude together,

Christmas preparations about done by then. They dined, after which they walked hand in hand to the library—Jean "all flushed with splendid health, and I the same, from the wholesome effects of my Bermuda holiday"—and sat chatting and making plans until nine—"which is late for us—then went upstairs, Jean's friendly German dog following. At my door Jean said, 'I can't kiss you good night, father: I have a cold, and you could catch it.' I bent," he recalled, "and kissed her hand. She was moved—I saw it in her eyes—and she impulsively kissed my hand in return. Then with the usual gay 'Sleep well, dear!' from both, we parted."

CHAPTER **Forty-Six**

Funerals

S ounds of voices beyond his bedroom door awakened the late riser early next day, at seven-thirty. His daughter was up, getting ready for her usual horseback ride to fetch the mail first thing from the depot. "When I heard the door open behind the bed's head without a preliminary knock, I supposed it was Jean coming to kiss me good morning, she being the only person who was used to entering without formalities."

But it wasn't Jean. It was Katy. For a moment the servant stood at Mr. Clemens's bedside quaking, gasping, unable to speak, before she cried out: "Miss Jean is dead!"

Stunned, the father rose and was led to his daughter's bathroom. She lay on the floor covered with a sheet, "looking so placid, so natural, and as if asleep. We knew what had happened," he wrote later that day in the midst of his grief, trying to deal with it in the only way he was able to, pen in hand. "She was an epileptic: she had been seized with a convulsion and heart failure in her bath. The doctor had to come several miles. His efforts, like our previous ones, failed to bring her back to life."

Jean was dead. Christmas exertions must have brought on the seizure, her first in months. In those initial dark hours a father stumbling about the house—*Jean is dead!*—kept encountering evidence of his daughter's late happy labors. Just last night in the library she had cautioned him not to look in the loggia, for there were Christmas surprises out there. Disloyally he had peeked when he could, and had seen a tree "drenched with silver film in a most wonderful way; and on a table was prodigal profusion of bright things which she was going to hang upon it today." And today, upstairs in her parlor, her father discovered the many presents she had wrapped, as yet unaddressed. She had meant to label them this morning; now there would be no way of knowing for whom the gifts were intended.

In a closet he did find the present she had bought for him: a terrestrial globe, something he had often wished for. "I couldn't see it for the tears. She will never know the pride I take in it, and the pleasure."

Arrangements were made to transport the body to Elmira. Katy Leary dressed Jean in her white silk dress, "the one she wore at Clara's wedding," the maid recalled later. "It fell to me to do it, as I had done it for her mother and little Susy. And I put the pretty buckle on her dress that day, that her father had brought her from Bermuda for Christmas, that she had never seen." Christmas afternoon it snowed; Jean always loved the snow. At six that evening the hearse pulled up to the door. Jervis Langdon had arrived from Elmira: "Jervis, the cousin she had played with when they were babies together—he and her beloved old Katy—were conducting her to her distant childhood home, where she will lie by her mother's side once more, in the company of Susy and Langdon," that other Clemens child, who had died at a year and a half, soon after Susy was born, in 1872.

The father remained at Stormfield. His health was not good; and besides, he had vowed when he saw Livy laid in the earth five years ago never to witness such a moment again. Now through Stormfield's windows "I saw the hearse and the carriages wind along the road and gradually grow vague and spectral in the falling snow, and presently disappear. Jean was gone out of my life, and would not come back any more."

Howells, in their many conversations together—so often laughter-filled—had spoken with Clemens, wonderingly, about old age as well, and death, and the loss of children: of Winny Howells, of Susy Clemens, now Jean. He had written wryly of his distaste for the ugliness old age brought with it—how physically ugly it made one; that was what galled him about being old. And a few years back, in early 1906, Howells had written to his friend of realizing in those latter months "that I shall die, hitherto having regarded it as problematical, and the sense of it is awful. I do not see how so many people stand it. That is nonsense, but the notion does not present itself conceivably. My wife does not let me discuss these ideas with her, and so I keep them for my own edification. When my father was 87 he once said to me that the night before he had thought it all out, and now he was satisfied. Perhaps," he concluded, "each has to come to some such settlement with himself."

After her father's recent return from Bermuda, Jean had been troubled by messages of concern that began arriving at Stormfield, prompted by the news reports from New York of the humorist's languidness upon disembarking. You must reassure your public, she insisted. So to please her, Mark Twain had issued a statement to the press that he wasn't dying; "I would not do such a thing at my time of life." By ill luck the blithe dismissal appeared just as news of his daughter Miss Jean Clemens's sudden untimely death was broadcast in the nation's newspapers, an apparent insensitivity of tone on the father's part that added its small weight to his anguish.

Having written of her death himself in these bleak hours and days of the Christmas season, Clemens gave his pages to Paine to use as the final entry of the *Autobiography*, "The Death of Jean," if the biographer saw fit to include them. Mark Twain would write no more. The humorist was weary, and in truth not in good health. A while back, in 1906, his friend Rogers and he had been talking. "Well, Rogers," Clemens remarked, "I don't know what you think of it, but I think I have had about enough of this world, and I wish I were out of it." To which the other—tycoon with all his millions—replied, "I don't say much about it, but that expresses my view." A couple of old gentlemen amid their triumphs, possessed of every comfort and solace that success such as theirs could provide. Perhaps the sentiment reflected no more than a passing mood; yet griefs mount with age, and the ills of the body are relentless. More so then: all those Victorian ailments of dyspepsia, neuralgia, cephalalgia, dysentery, lumbago, catarrh, carbuncles, rheumatism, apoplexy, nervous prostration, gout. Clemens had suffered from most of them and watched loved ones suffer: wracking coughs on and on, the sharp pains, the pus, the diarrhea, the exhaustion, the weeks stretching to months bedridden. Journals and letters of the time impress on us how medicines and diet developed since then have spared the comfortably off so much that bore upon our aching forebears with a doleful regularity.

During the same year that Jean died over the Christmas season, earlier, in the springtime, on Thursday morning, May 20, 1909, Clemens had set out from Redding to meet with his friend Rogers in New York on business having to do with the firing of Lyon and Ashcroft. The magnate had assured Clara that he would look over aspects of those ex-employees' financial behavior; so Clemens was not surprised to find her at Grand Central waiting to meet him. She was there, however, not to accompany her father to Mr. Rogers's Broadway offices; rather, Clara had come to tell him the sad news that his dear friend had died the morning before. Reporters pressed Mark Twain for comment. "Mr. Clemens was too moved to fully express his feelings. 'It is terrible, terrible,' he said. 'I am inexpressibly shocked.'" He couldn't talk about it. "Mr. Rogers was my dearest and closest friend for years. And I only heard of his death a few minutes ago, when I got off the train at the Grand Central." Tears streamed down his face. "I can't talk any more. Mr. Rogers was as close to me as a brother."

The papers that May were full of the news of Henry Huttleston Rogers's sudden death; for the titan of Standard Oil was far better known back then than now, one of America's great capitalists and among the wealthiest. The final weekend of his life Rogers had spent at Fairhaven, and the last full day in his usual manner: leaving his residence at 3 East Seventy-Eighth Street for a morning of work on lower Broadway. Later he visited the homes of two of his children. In the evening he returned uptown in good spirits, chatting with his wife about how bright the grandchildren were. Next morning, a Wednesday, he woke feeling some nausea and an ache in his left arm. At 7 A.M., Rogers abruptly lost consciousness and was dead before either the doctor or his children could reach him.

Clemens went at once to the Rogerses' home, but was unable to attend the interment at Fairhaven, couldn't put himself where he would have to converse with friends on the way up and back. And anyway, he would not stand beside another loved one's coffin as it descended into the grave. Instead, he remained in a Manhattan hotel with the faithful Albert Bigelow Paine, who had hurried down as soon as the news reached Redding. The two read through the long day, each on his side of the room, and spoke very little. Once, checking the time, Clemens remarked, "Mr. Rogers is under the ground now."

And at peace. Death was God's gift to humanity. When Susy died, her grieving father, left alone in England, had sought to console Livy with all that their daughter had been spared. If he knew the word that would bring Susy back to life, he wrote to his wife while she was en route to America, he wouldn't say it. Nor, later, would he for anything have brought Livy back, for all his grief at her loss. And when, after Rogers's death, Jean died those seven months on, at Christmastime, he again felt envy—"I always envy the dead"—for the trouble-free peace she had found. "The funeral has begun. Four hundred miles away"—in Elmira—"but I can see it all," he wrote from Stormfield, "just as if I were there. The scene is the library in the Langdon homestead. Jean's coffin stands where her mother and I stood, forty years ago, and were married; and where Susy's coffin stood thirteen years ago; where her mother's stood five years and a half ago; and where mine will stand after a little time."

Only a little time now. In July Clemens had responded to an inquiry from an angelfish, Frances Nunnally: "I can answer your question definitely now, Francesca Dear. It is heart-disease. Not the best kind, but good enough for the purpose. It is decided that I have what is technically termed a 'tobacco heart.'" People will laugh about that, of course, "for in my vanity I have often bragged that tobacco couldn't hurt me. Privately & between you & me, I am well aware that I ought to laugh at *myself*—& would if I were a really honest person." But there wasn't much for others to gloat over after all, "for it has taken 63 years to build this disease. I was immune *that* long, anyway."

For relief, he went with his angina pectoris back to Bermuda early in January of the new year 1910. On the last evening of Jean's life, father and daughter had sat together in the library at Stormfield planning just such a voyage. Katy would go with them to the happy isles in the early spring, as soon as Jean had attended to matters at home. Now, with her gone, there was no need to linger in wintry New England. But how this father had worried after Clara's wedding—and the bride and groom returned to their life far off in Europe—about what would become of Jean if anything happened to him, as in the nature of things it very soon would. He need worry about that no longer. Or about Susy. Or about Livy. Here at the last, his designated biographer Paine tells us, "peace came more and more to him each day with the thought that Jean and Susy and their mother could not be troubled any more."

Claude Beuchotte, Clemens's butler and valet, accompanied him to Bermuda on this, the final trip there. They reached the island on January 11, and as late as mid-March Clemens was writing with good cheer to a friend in the States who had shared such days with him earlier. "You ought to be here *now*! The weather is divine, and you know what it is to drive along the North Shore in such weather and watch the sun paint the waters. We had that happiness today. The joy of it never stales." That, and the peace of the place: "no newspapers, no telegrams, no mobiles, no trolleys, no trains," he reminded her, "no tramps, no railways, no theatres, no noise, no lectures, no riots, no murders, no fires, no burglaries, no politics, no offenses of any kind, no follies but church, and I don't go there."

He told this friend, Betsy Wallace, that he could live in Bermuda forever. "You go to heaven if you want to—I'd druther stay here."

Earlier, in February and already well ensconced on the island, he had written to H. H. Rogers's daughter-in-law, the enchanting Mary Rogers, his fellow yachtsman on *Kanawha* cruises. "My health is blemishless," he sought to reassure her, "except for the pain in my breast. That is permanent, I suppose. It doesn't allow me to work, and it doesn't allow me to walk even so much as a hundred yards; but as it lets me do all the things I want to do, it is not an incumbrance."

Yet he found ever more difficult this keeping his spirits up. Paine back in Redding grew alarmed and in early April took ship for Bermuda. At Hamilton the biographer came upon his friend "not yet shaven, and he seemed unnaturally pale and gray; certainly he was much thinner." They must get him in physical shape to make the trip home. The voyage itself, as soon as Clemens was able to undertake it, proved dreadful from the moment the vessel entered the humid Gulf Stream. His breathing became increasingly difficult, so much so that Paine felt sure the end would come within minutes. "It was impossible for him to lie down, even to recline, without great distress"—as with Livy in those last horrible months of her life. "I am sorry for you, Paine," the sufferer murmured, "but I can't help it—I can't hurry this dying business."

They did make it to shore. As in the autumn of 1900, a decade earlier, when the expatriate Mark Twain returned home to New York to the warmest of welcomes, now—at this sadder return in the spring of 1910—a crowd, a smaller crowd, awaited him: "relatives, physicians, and news-gatherers."

Figure 46.1.   Mark Twain returns to New York, April 1910.
Courtesy of the Mark Twain Project, The Bancroft Library, University of California, Berkeley.

Always the news-gatherers. Seated, bowler hat on his head, Mark Twain was borne down the gangway, put in an invalid carriage, transferred to a special compartment on an afternoon express to Redding, met at the depot, and taken to Stormfield, where the patient insisted on descending from the carriage and with his usual courtliness greeting the household gathered at the door. Then, on that evening of April 14, 1910, they got him, finally, to his room upstairs and in his own bed.

He lived a week longer. Clara arrived from Europe before he died and was at his bedside while he was conscious. She was pregnant by then, although there is no evidence that she told her father so. Perhaps she did—why wouldn't she?—yet neither Paine, that meticulous observer, nor any other source who might know speaks of it. And if she didn't, was it overfastidiousness? Or bitterness, or spite? Perhaps she didn't want to excite the patient in his extremity.

Dorothy Quick, M.A., Member of the Aquarium, now fourteen, had come to Bermuda with her mother in early spring and seen her beloved SLC for the first time in a year and a half. He who had always appeared so youthful—two steps at a time up stairs—now looked old to this maturing angelfish; but before long they both were on their former affectionate footing. Until suddenly Dorothy was gone. "Yesterday you did not come to us, and we wondered if something was wrong." Clemens had dispatched his servant Claude to find out, without enlightenment. Soon a letter explained. A cable reporting the death of Mrs. Quick's brother had obliged mother and daughter to set out at once for New York. Later, in her grief, Mrs. Quick fell ill. A restorative trip to Europe was called for. And in London, the papers screamed forth the news for young Dorothy Quick to read that Mark Twain was dead. "While the whole world mourned his passing," she wrote years afterward, "a little girl shed bitter tears, bitter tears for the SLC she had loved with all her heart."

He had died on April 21, 1910, at Stormfield, at half past six in the evening. On the twenty-third, in the open coffin, the body in its white suit was put on view at the Brick Church on Fifth Avenue and Thirty-Seventh Street, where three thousand people paid their last respects in gazing a final time on the familiar features. Voice breaking, his friend Joe Twichell had offered a prayer in the course of the simple ceremony, which Howells attended alongside the surviving family: the Langdons, the Gabrilowitsches. And in Elmira on the twenty-fourth, after a brief service in the Langdon mansion, the mortal remains of Samuel Langhorne Clemens were laid to rest beside his wife Olivia and three of his children while the rain poured down on the tree-shaded plot in nearby Woodlawn Cemetery.

A week and more passed. Not quite two weeks—when, 3,500 miles away, at Sandringham House in Norfolk, ninety miles north of London, Edward VII, King of Great Britain and Ireland and of the British Dominions and Emperor of India—sometime dinner companion of Mark Twain and guest at Andrew Carnegie's Skibo Castle—died in his sixty-ninth year.

King Edward's funeral took place on May 20. It was everything such an event should be. Alice Roosevelt Longworth saw the pagentry—she of the long memory who could recall sitting as a teenager in New Haven beside Samuel Clemens (Alice's father, the new president, "made a speech about which I have no memory whatever. I only remember sitting in a box with silver-haired Mark Twain") during the festivities, in 1901, that had celebrated the bicentennial of the founding of Yale College. This later pageantry of 1910 she recalled more vividly. "We went," she wrote two decades farther along, "to Lady Herbert's house in Carlton House Terrace to see the procession, when the King's body was taken from Buckingham Palace to lie in state at Westminster Hall. It was an impressive sight: a leaden-gray day, the line of march packed with huge silent crowds; bells slowly tolling, the weird music of the pipes, the shuddering rumble of the drums; then the band playing the 'Chopin Funeral March,' the King's horse, saddled, the stirrups reversed, and a man leading his little pet terrier"—King Edward's beloved Caesar. Nine monarchs were in attendance, three by three on horseback in the grand procession. The new king, George V, was there, and at his right was Kaiser Wilhem II, emperor of Germany. Haakon VII of Norway, Ferdinand I of Bulgaria, Manuel II of Portugal, George I of Greece, Albert I of Belgium, Alphonso XIII of Spain, and Frederick VIII of Denmark, all in full uniform, splendid in their helmets and epaulettes, their sashes and bejeweled medals, sat astride chargers ramrod straight, as the procession made its slow way between the crowds on either side. Nicholas II, Czar of all the Russias, did not attend, busy with pogroms at home; but his brother the Archduke Michael represented him. And standing in for the ancient Franz Josef of Austria (already fifty years on his throne when he had received Mark Twain in Vienna in private audience back in 1898) was the emperor's heir apparent these twelve years later, the Archduke Franz Ferdinand, whom an assassin would shoot dead on the Latin Bridge at Sarajevo four years on. As for the United States, that new world power was represented by President Taft's designated emissary, Theodore Roosevelt. His African safari and a triumphal tour of Europe just behind him, the former president, in top hat and civilian evening attire, had taken his unpretentious place amid all those resplendent princes, counts, dukes, sultans, pashas, and envoys from every nation on earth, in order to help bury England's stout sovereign at what proved to be the end of an era.

CHAPTER Forty-Seven

Bull Moose

In the month after King Edward's funeral, Colonel Roosevelt returned home to New York, on June 18, 1910, to a tumultuous welcome. Crowds had been gathering since dawn of that summer day, and by 7:30 they were lining the parade route from Battery Park north five miles along Broadway and Fifth Avenue as far uptown as Fifty-Ninth Street. Amid the horns and whistles of small craft and the boom of cannon from Fort Wadsworth on Staten Island, the Colonel, who had been out of the country for fourteen months, disembarked in the harbor and, coming ashore in midmorning, took part with his family in a grand celebration. Dignitaries in fourteen open carriages rolled slowly uptown, preceded and followed by mounted police, marching bands, Rough Riders on horseback, and Spanish-American War veterans afoot, Roosevelt as honoree showered with confetti and ticker tape and engulfed in the cheers of nearly a million fellow citizens.

For the Colonel, it was the capstone of more than a year of glory. As African big-game hunter he had bagged among much else nine lions, thirteen rhinos, seven giraffes, eight elephants, twenty zebras, and six fearsome water buffaloes, and had sent back to the Smithsonian 3,000 skins and 13,000 specimens to augment the holdings of that scientific repository. Once arrived in Europe, in early April 1910, the hunter had metamorphosed into world statesman, a former president of the United States honored wherever he went: in Rome, Vienna, Budapest, Paris (where he delivered a rapturously received address at the Sorbonne, "The Man in the Arena," among his most characteristic and frequently cited), on to Brussels, Amsterdam, Copenhagen, Christiania in Norway (now Oslo, where, as recipient of the Nobel Prize, he spoke appropriately of attaining world peace), to Stockholm, to Berlin (where Kaiser Wilhelm, whom he was meeting for the first time, honored the distinguished American by having him review units of the German army), and finally to England (where Mr. Roosevelt not only represented the United States at King Edward VII's funeral but also delivered the prestigious Romanes Lecture at Oxford and was awarded honorary degrees both there and at Cambridge University).

Now he was home, to the cheers and good wishes of huge numbers of his countrymen—merely a private citizen, however, author of the recent bestselling *African Game Trails* and under contract to furnish the journal *Outlook* with regular commentary on matters of his own choosing.

As for political affairs, the Colonel had vowed to write nothing on that subject for at least these first couple of months back at Sagamore Hill. Let President Taft discharge his duties without any second-guessing from his still enormously popular predecessor. Yet it was hard to keep quiet. To Roosevelt's way of thinking, Taft's presidency had been a disaster. The Colonel would hold his peace for now, but it pained him to see how an old friend elevated to the White House was betraying causes that the two had fought for when Roosevelt was president and Taft his able governor of the Philippines and secretary of war. For example, this current chief executive had let himself be persuaded to fire from his cabinet Gifford Pinchot, one-time head of the forestry service with whom Roosevelt had worked closely ever since his days as governor of New York: the most valuable man in his own administration, the Colonel had come to believe, and the author of Roosevelt's conservation program that had awakened Americans to the need to preserve their unique natural heritage. In Pinchot's place, the new president was supporting a complacent functionary much more to the liking of greedy timber and mining interests out West. By doing so, as well as through various other presidential decisions, Taft appeared meekly to be delivering Republican leadership back into the hands of the Old Guard, the party of Lincoln thus wrenched from the plain people whom Roosevelt had championed, in order—as in the bygone Gilded Age—to make it once more the servant of the wealthy few.

"Taft, who is such an admirable fellow, has shown himself," according to his mentor, who had got the man the presidency in the first place, "such an utterly commonplace leader; good-natured; feebly well-meaning; but with plenty of small motive, and totally unable to grasp or put into execution any great policy." The Cincinnati judge raised to the top job in the land appeared to be supporting whatever in the law protected property. Which was all well and good: Roosevelt believed in the sanctity of property, too; but he also believed in those parts of the Constitution that speak of providing for and promoting the general welfare. His idol Lincoln had put the matter succinctly: "Labor is prior to, and independent of, capital. Capital is only the fruit of labor, and could never have existed if labor had not first existed. Labor is the superior of capital, and deserves much the higher consideration." To be sure, that was but one side of the argument—the side, however, that capitalists should be heeding. The working man for his part should keep in mind the other side: "Capital has its rights"—again quoting Lincoln—"which are as worthy of protection as any other rights." For property is the fruit of labor, and "a positive good in the world." But, as Roosevelt insisted in a speech he delivered at Osawatomie, Kansas, in late August 1910, scarcely two months after his return from Europe, those who own property should expect no governmental favors merely for being rich.

History through the ages records an ongoing conflict, he said on that same occasion, "between the men who possess more than they have earned and the men who have earned more than they possess." At present the conflict takes the form of a "struggle of freemen to gain and hold the right of self-government as against the special interests, who twist the methods of free government into machinery for defeating the popular will." What the current strife is about, then, according to Roosevelt (energized, as ever, by strife), is the effort "to equalize opportunity, destroy privilege, and give to the life and citizenship of every individual the highest possible value both to himself and to the commonwealth." At Osawatomie, outdoors, standing on a kitchen table, the speaker made clear to his large audience, many of them veterans of an earlier great conflict, that he sought no more than "what you fought for in the Civil War. I ask that civil life be carried on according to the spirit in which the army was carried on. You never get perfect justice, but the effort in handling the army was to bring to the front the men who could do the job. Nobody grudged promotion to Grant, or Sherman, or Thomas, or Sheridan, because they earned it. The only complaint was when a man got promotion which he did not earn."

Give everybody a chance: our great republic was founded on that principle. No aristocracy, no established church, no entrenched privilege. For the first time a nation of continental extent was exhibiting "the triumph of a real democracy," one based on merit, by means of "an economic system under which each man shall be guaranteed the opportunity to show the best that there is in him." That ideal, of no privileged favorites and opportunity for all, must be lived up to. Yet President Taft's policies were too often indulging special interests—the well connected, the powerful few—at the expense of Lincoln's plain people and the Constitution's general welfare.

If anyone else could have restored the Great Emancipator's party to its original purposes, Roosevelt would have given such a one his full support.

But nobody adequate to the task came forward. Only Colonel Roosevelt (he convinced himself, encouraged by many of his fellow citizens) was sufficiently selfless, large of motive, full of vigor, and ready to reenter the political fray in the service of the nation by taking up the cudgels against his former dear friend Will Taft. As for his earlier, two-term pledge, the Colonel now explained that he had meant all along two *successive* terms, one after the other, uninterrupted. This late—and him years out of the White House—the pledge about not running again no longer applied. Thus, in February 1912, Theodore Roosevelt told the press that he was stripped to the buff, and his hat was in the ring. The image evokes a makeshift boxing ring roped off in some village square, a roaming pugilist on hand to fight whoever in town is willing to stand up to him for a bit of prize money. Anybody so inclined tosses his hat in the ring, takes off his shirt, climbs between the ropes—and may the better man win. So our Teddy would be coming to fisticuffs with Big Bill Taft. The contest promised tension and rollicking excitement; yet Roosevelt's determining to seek the presidency in 1912 came near to breaking his old friend's heart.

Even so, in the end Taft resolved to fight back. Shortly before, twelve states had introduced the novelty of primaries as a way to let voters have a say in choosing nominees. Roosevelt entered all the primaries, campaigning flat out and ending by winning nine of the twelve, including the one in Taft's own state of Ohio. Accordingly, when delegates met in Chicago that summer to pick the Republican candidate, the Roosevelt faction had amassed impressive support among the populace at large. But the convention machinery remained in the hands of the Old Guard, who managed to disqualify most of Roosevelt's delegates in favor of the regulars, pledged to Taft. Charging theft, TR's supporters stormed out, held their own convention, and nominated their man for president at the head of a new, third party—the National Progressives—which chose as its emblem a bull moose, its candidate in the course of the fight proclaiming himself as fit as a bull moose to lead.

A three-ring circus, then: elephant, bull moose, and donkey. The Bull Moose platform was designed to curb the power of big business in national affairs. Thus, one plank demanded that lobbyists be registered, another that campaign contributions be limited and amounts disclosed. Further, the platform called for constitutional amendments providing for a national income tax and for the election of senators directly by the people (rather than by state legislators, as the Constitution stipulated). And an inheritance tax would be set up to frustrate any burgeoning aristocracy's passing of its wealth down through the generations. This same platform went on to advocate a national health service, the vote for women, a minimum wage for women in the workforce, an eight-hour workday, compensation for work-related injuries, limits on the use of injunctions to break up strikes, relief for farmers, and insurance for the disabled, the elderly, and the unemployed.

In effect, the Progressive platform of 1912 provided specifics to flesh out Lincoln's earlier praise of labor in general. Business of course denounced the document as communistic, the moneyed classes loath to support any such radical program. Most of their funds flowed the other way, into the Taft campaign. Democrats, meanwhile, sensing the nation's current progressive mood, had nominated as their candidate the former president of Princeton University, now reform governor of New Jersey, Woodrow Wilson, who ended by campaigning as an alternative for liberals and—with Roosevelt poised to split the Republican vote—a leader who could win.

When the ballots were counted that November of 1912, Roosevelt had brought about the only instance in American history where a third-party candidate outpolled the nominee of one of the two major parties at the national level. Taft the Republican received 23 percent of the popular vote; Roosevelt the Progressive won 27 percent. But the Democrat Wilson captured 42 percent—and the election—with a crushing majority in the electoral college, of 435 for Wilson, 88 for Roosevelt, and a measly 8 for the incumbent, Mr. Taft.

"Well, we have gone down in a smashing defeat," Roosevelt remarked of his loss. "Whether it is a Waterloo or a Bull Run, time only can tell." As matters turned out, it was a Waterloo. Denied the power he so ardently craved—not for its own sake (he insisted) but for what he could do with it for the nation's benefit and the world's—Theodore Roosevelt, just turned fifty-four, found himself at loose ends. By the next presidential campaign his Progressives had dwindled into irrelevancy; and TR was back in the Republican fold supporting New York's governor Charles Evans Hughes, a presidential candidate he felt no affection for, against the incumbent President Wilson, a politician he despised. But by that later summer and fall, of 1916, Roosevelt was a changed man, prematurely aged, in a world that had altered drastically as well.

After losing his 1912 presidential bid, the Colonel had gone to South America—he and his wife Edith—to visit a continent they had never seen, to fulfill lucrative speaking engagements, and to be with son Kermit, approaching his mid-twenties that fall of 1913 and building railroads in Brazil. Kermit had accompanied his father on the African safari four years earlier, a young man apparently unacquainted with fear and thus, perhaps, the Colonel's favorite son. They planned an adventure now—Roosevelt's last chance to be a boy, he said—so after seeing Mrs. Roosevelt off in Valparaiso on her return home, he and Kermit (following a spell of jaguar-hunting in Uruguay) joined twenty others on an exploring expedition deep in the Brazilian rainforest. There was a river in there whose source was known but its course uncharted—the River of Doubt it was called, *Rio da Dúvida*—and the expedition meant to follow that river down, gathering specimens along the way, and discover where it came out. On February 27, 1914, the party got under way in seven heavy, awkward dugout canoes: a former president and his son, a physician, an ornithologist, a professional explorer, his assistant, and sixteen Brazilian porters and paddlers, all ill-equipped, as it happened, for the ordeal that lay before them.

Roosevelt very nearly died. It was a horrible journey, two months of heat and relentless rain, of rapids innumerable, of portages around those rapids one after another, each track through the jungle taking eight or ten hours to hack clear, log rollers made and laid down to drag the one-ton dugouts overland, supplies borne the distance around falls and the impassably swollen rapids to be reloaded for the brief stretches where the river leveled out before raging impassably again. Natives lurked in the woods, and the rains poured down. Fire ants, sandflies, bees, wasps in great numbers, ticks, incessant gnats, poisonous snakes, mosquitoes, piranhas, malaria—and the unforeseen mishaps: a dugout dislodged and carried irretrievably downriver, causing a perilous delay while a new one was gouged out as supplies ran low. It was on the occasion of trying to retrieve another dugout wedged in boulders that Roosevelt at work in the swirling current banged his knee and opened a wound from a carriage accident years before. The abscess grew inflamed. The sufferer lapsed into delirium, helpless, his life in jeopardy. All of their lives were jeopardized as the journey lengthened, their ill-chosen food about exhausted, any hunting for game impossible in the thick growth on shore, and the question pressing: would they get out at all? At last, at long last, they did come upon a rubber-porter's solitary hut at the water's edge and realized they had drifted, just barely in time, to safety. After two months and nearly a thousand miserable miles of exploration the exhausted team emerged at the Madeira, a tributary of the Amazon—earth's greatest river—the raging stream just traversed having proved to be as long as the Rhine.

When he got back to the States, Roosevelt weighed fifty-five pounds less than when he set out, limping, severely weakened; and thereafter he never fully recovered from what the adventure had put him through.

The diminished former president landed in New York on May 19, 1914. A month later, on June 28, Archduke Franz Ferdinand, heir to the

Austro-Hungarian throne, and his consort Sophie, Duchess of Hohenberg, were shot dead in the Serbian city of Sarajevo. Outraged, the Austrian government issued a July ultimatum that set impossible demands on Serbia as retribution. In addressing those demands, the Serbs came up short. Austria, followed by its ally Germany, broke off relations and mobilized its armed forces. Russia came to the defense of fellow Slavs. France, in alliance with Russia, felt obliged to honor its treaty; and England, allied with France, entered the conflict as well.

Thus, in August 1914, the First World War—the so-called Great War—began. Above all else, Roosevelt wanted to get into it. He loathed what he saw as President Wilson's dithering early on. Germany violated Belgium's neutrality to strike at France, and Wilson did nothing about it. How different the response would have been had Roosevelt been president! Then in May 1915, a German U-boat sank the British liner *Lusitania* off the Irish coast. One hundred twenty-eight Americans drowned; and again, the professor-president did nothing beyond dispatching protests to the German government. Words, words. "There's such a thing," President Wilson said, "as a man being too proud to fight"; and for that craven sentiment, as for the coward who uttered it, Roosevelt felt only contempt. In months ahead, he reached in private for the most egregious epithets to describe this current leader: a "wretched creature," a "white rabbit," "yellow all through," "the lily-livered skunk in the White House."

Wilson ran for a second term in the fall of 1916 on the slogan "He kept us out of war." If earlier, back from his African safari and his triumphal tour of Europe six years before, in 1910, Roosevelt had been willing to wait—leave Taft alone and wait until now, till 1916, to declare his candidacy—this time he would almost surely have won. Even Governor Hughes of New York, that gray iceberg of a nominee, came within a shadow's breadth of defeating Wilson. Out of nearly 18 million votes cast, the incumbent was reelected by a majority of just over 600,000—a mere whisper—277 electoral votes to Hughes's 254. One or two states going the other way would have been enough to let even the starchy Charles Evans Hughes prevail.

Roosevelt all this while, in the pages of the *Outlook*, the *Metropolitan*, and the *Kansas City Star*, went on writing blisteringly of the academic returned to the White House. Some of it was envy, recalling his own time as chief executive and not a shot fired except for that skirmishing in the Philippines—persuaded, too, that only the crisis of war makes for the greatest presidencies, above all for Lincoln's. Yet this current commander in chief, given a just war to fight, would do nothing. And when at last Wilson, even the timorous Wilson, was pushed so far by Germany's unrestricted submarine warfare as to enter the European conflict, he denied Colonel

Roosevelt—who went personally to him and pleaded his case—the privilege of organizing a division of volunteers and leading it into early combat on the western front. That had been the Colonel's burning desire; but he apparently was judged too old, too enfeebled, and the times were passing him by. President Wilson graciously thanked the petitioner for his offer, yet nothing came of it. Roosevelt must leave America's fighting to younger men.

Young Kermit, unwilling to wait for his country to enter the conflict, had already joined the British army to do battle against the Turk in Mesopotamia. His three brothers got into the fight as soon as they could, to their father's infinite gratification. In March 1918 Archie Roosevelt suffered severe wounds in combat and was hospitalized in France. Ted was wounded in July; and in that same summer month, five days earlier, flying in the skies over Belleau Wood, Quentin Roosevelt had dived into aerial combat with German pilots and was shot down. Hope flickered, then went out, as word arrived at Sagamore Hill that the Colonel's aviator son, his youngest, had not survived.

Roosevelt never recovered from Quentin's death, although he bore it stoically. To Kermit soon after, he wrote, "No man could have died in finer or more gallant fashion; and our pride equals our sorrow." And he phrased an oblique tribute: "Only those are fit to live who do not fear to die; and none are fit to die who have shrunk from the joy of life and the duty of life. Both life and death are part of the same Great Adventure." Yet privately, alone, the father felt the loss of poor Quinikens to his core, and to the very last.

Even then, however, even toward the end, despite the conflict's appalling human cost, the foul trenches, the mud, the mustard gas that son Ted had breathed in, despite the utter futility and waste in a new, horrendous type of war on a world scale that was mere butchery, Theodore Roosevelt clung to talk of sacrifice, gallantry, and glory, and to battle as something grand, noble, and sublime. That February of 1918 he had gone into the hospital with a persistence of jungle fever, an ear abscess, and the Amazon rainforest leg-wound still troublesome, needing tissue to be cut away. The patient was back home at Sagamore Hill in March, but returned to the hospital on Armistice Day, November 11, 1918, and was there until Christmas. Yet despite such late grave illnesses and his grievous loss, these closing days of a supremely busy life held consolations: Roosevelt's deep love for Edith, for his new grandchildren, for his children and their spouses. "I don't believe in all the United States," he said, "there is any father who has quite the same right that I have to be proud of his four sons." And there was talk of his running for president again, in 1920, to retrieve the Republican Party

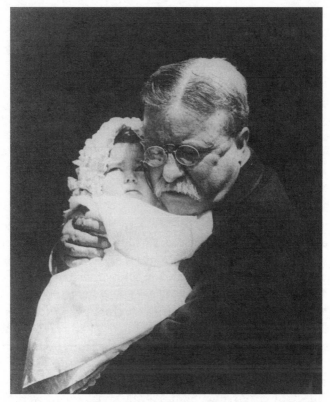

Figure 47.1. TR with Edith Derby, his daughter Ethel's second child, born in 1917. This is among the last pictures taken of the Colonel.

Courtesy of the Theodore Roosevelt Collection, Harvard College Library.

from the Old Guard's iron grip and restore it to the service of Lincoln's kind of people.

But that didn't come to pass. At Sagamore Hill, at age sixty, on the evening of January 15, 1919, Theodore Roosevelt bade an affectionate goodnight to Edith and went to bed feeling a bit odd, short of breath. Before dawn he was dead—found lying as though "just asleep, only he could not hear"—dead of what was revealed to be malignant endocarditis and an embolism in the coronary arteries. His simple burial service occurred two days later in Christ Episcopal Church at Oyster Bay, where ex-President Taft, now a professor of law at Yale University, was among the mourners. Later, at the snowy gravesite in nearby Youngs Cemetery, Mr. Taft was observed standing alone, head bowed in grief, lingering longer than all the others with his thoughts and his tears.

CHAPTER Forty-Eight

Afterward

Roosevelt had professed an indifference to fame. "I am not in the least concerned as to whether I will have any place in history," he said, "and, indeed, I do not remember ever thinking about it." It was enough to lead a full, decent life and be of some use. Of course he would want his family to be proud of him, and his friends to remember him and respect the way he lived. "But aside from this it does not seem to me that after a man is dead it matters very much whether it is a little longer or a little shorter before the inevitable oblivion, steadily flooding the sands of time, effaces the scratches on the sand which we call history." In a geologic sense, "as the ages roll by in the life of this globe," what difference can it make: "the few weeks' remembrance of the average hard-working, clean-living citizen, and the few years, or few hundreds of years, or few thousands of years, before the memory of the mighty fades into the dim gray of time and then vanishes into the blackness of eternity"?

Well, in our later century, on Mount Rushmore, Roosevelt abides like some benign Ozymandias recently sculpted, his sixty-foot-high granite face betraying little of time's wear, alongside the scarcely worn faces of Washington, Jefferson, and Lincoln. Conceived originally as a South Dakota tourist attraction (which it quite successfully has become), the monument was to represent the first 150 years of United States history up to 1926. In 1927, President Coolidge, Republican, approved the massive undertaking, with the stipulation that his colleague Washington be represented, and that the other three chief executives comprise two Republicans and one Democrat. Hence, Jefferson for the latter, and Lincoln as one of the Republicans. That Roosevelt was chosen for the second may have been owing partly to the sculptor Gutson Borglum's having known our twenty-sixth president personally, having stayed at Roosevelt's White House, and having been, like many Americans, utterly taken with the man. But part of what the monument set out to commemorate was America's expansion across a continent, with Jefferson's purchase of Louisiana and Roosevelt's acquisition of Panama enough in themselves to justify including those two. No doubt Roosevelt's love of the West added to a sense of fitness in situating the Dakota rancher alongside three statesmen of such lofty attainments. And, on reflection, what other Republican between Andrew Johnson and Calvin Coolidge might more suitably have been carved up there?

In any case, the passing years have confirmed the wisdom of the choice. Authorities who have spent their professional lives studying American history rate our chief executives periodically from best to worst; and for a half century those ratings have placed Theodore Roosevelt among the top four or five presidents, with—of those who have followed in the office since TR's death—only the other Roosevelt, Franklin Delano, being judged to rank alongside Lincoln and Washington, and ahead both of Jefferson and of that Democratic Roosevelt's fifth cousin, uncle-by-marriage, and mentor whom Franklin idolized.

Theodore for his part holds his high standing even though he led no precedent-setting administration like Washington's, wrote no Jeffersonian founding document, triumphed over no Lincolnian rebellion, and dealt with no Rooseveltian crises of massive economic depression and global war. Yet at the start of the twentieth century, the bellicose colonel, in a time of peace, was nevertheless able to compile a record from the White House that leaves his name shining among the brightest in our presidential firmament, and this despite his goodly share of human flaws and misjudgments. Roosevelt felt sure, for instance, that "every expansion of a great civilized power means a victory for law, order, and righteousness," as when we expanded roughshod westward, or Europe intruded to form British East Africa and German South-West Africa and French Indochina, or when Russia expanded into Manchuria, and Japan into Korea. We've learned to be far less certain of the benefits of such incursions than he was. Again, Roosevelt was convinced that "With civilized powers there is but little danger of our getting into war"—until the Marne and Ypres and Verdun proved him wrong. And despite the 37.5 million casualties of that bloodletting over the face of Europe from 1914 to 1918, to the end the Colonel clung to a romantic view of warfare that was more fitting, perhaps, to pikes, swords, and maces than to the industrialized weaponry of flamethrowers, poison gas, machine guns, tanks, and Big Berthas that stunned and devastated Europe, scythed through the broad swath of a generation, and led to the horrors of World War II. Carnegie, who died in the same year as Roosevelt, seven months afterward, in August 1919, was—like other sensitive souls—so appalled by the abominations of World War I that he lived his final years virtually in a stupor of mental prostration, able to do little beyond sit in his garden and brood.

Earlier in that same 1919, on the way to Europe to help negotiate the terms of peace among nations that had recently laid down their arms, President Woodrow Wilson performed a sad duty on January 7, proclaiming "officially the death of Theodore Roosevelt, President of the United States," at Sagamore Hill on the morning preceding. According to the proclamation, America had lost with his passing "one of its most distinguished and patriotic citizens, who had endeared himself to the people by his strenuous devotion to their interest and the public interests of his country." The achievements of the deceased were enumerated, including his "singular initiative and energy" in our war with Spain, as well as his dedicated service as president. In that office, "Colonel Roosevelt awoke the nation to the dangers of private control which lurked in our financial and industrial systems. It was by thus arresting the attention and stimulating the purpose of the country that he opened the way for subsequent necessary and beneficent reforms" (among them three amendments to the Constitution during this current president Wilson's time in office, reforms that instituted an income tax, provided for the direct election of senators, and gave women the vote). As for Roosevelt as exemplum: "His private life was characterized by a simplicity, a virtue and an affection worthy of all admiration and emulation by the people of America."

For, for all the complexities of his learning and the elaborations of his wealth, Theodore Roosevelt was at heart a simple man, relishing life in the rough, the rounding up of cattle, the rowing for miles in and around Oyster Bay harbor, exulting in the primitiveness of Edith's cabin in the Virginia woods as much as in his own cabin out West. On hikes he was joyful, and on the trail, under the stars, loving to camp with his family and get his hands dirty. He cared little for pomp or the trappings of power, only for what power could let him do to fill his days worthily. Hardly surprising, then, that such a one loathed Jane Austen's novels as much as Mark Twain did (novels that the cultured Edith Roosevelt adored): frivolities—as it must have seemed to him—among all those idling English effetes forever preoccupied with class, gossip, whist, and each other's incomes.

Roosevelt expressed his dislikes forcefully, and his likes as well. For of affection he had vast quantities: for his wife, his children, his children's spouses, for his grandchildren, for friends, for books and birds and nature and hunting and horses and guns and sports and history, and inexhaustibly for challenge—ever alive to striving. From strife grew the virtues that his life exemplified, and that he passed on to his children as his father had passed them to him. Simple virtues: get joy out of life; do your duty; play hard and play fair; be decent; stand up for yourself, and for the weak and the vulnerable; judge a man on his merits; love your country; be proud to be an American. All of which may sound like windy Polonius speaking; yet Theodore Roosevelt thrived on such maxims, and surely one secret of his popularity lay in the congruence of those beliefs with the intuitive faith that so many of his fellow citizens lived by.

He instilled his values in his children, who followed them as best they could. One life, that of the youngest, Quentin, was cut short in air combat over France at age twenty. The other three boys lived on as hunters like their father, and strivers, and lovers of nature and of combat. Ted, the oldest, earned both the Distinguished Service Cross and the Silver Star for bravery in World War I. Afterward, between the wars, he entered business, politics, and public service, then fought with exceptional bravery in World War II, in Africa, Italy, and as the only general to land with the first wave of troops on the beaches of D-Day. On that day he conducted himself with a heroism that won him the Medal of Honor; but only weeks after his brigade came ashore Ted—Brigadier General Theodore Roosevelt Jr.—died of a heart attack near the front lines at age fifty-six.

Like their brother, Kermit and Archie fought in both wars. As a civilian, Archie had been a fervent critic of the New Deal, and after the second war a vigorous anti-communist, helping to found the arch-conservative John Birch Society. Archibald Roosevelt died at eighty-five, in 1979. The middle son, Kermit, an explorer and (like his brothers) a businessman, suffered in late years from depression and alcoholism—all three sons had problems with alcohol; it can't have been easy living in their father's giant shadow. Kermit's mental woes grew acute during World War II. To help him regain his health he was posted to the quietudes of Alaska, near Anchorage, at Fort Richardson. He died there in 1943, a suicide, at age fifty-three.

All the boys except for Quentin—slumbering in the fields of Normandy—as well as Roosevelt's two daughters Alice and Ethel and his wife Edith were still alive, and astonished, and hurt to hear Mark Twain speak from beyond the grave in 1940. The author and lecturer had done what he said he would, although not one hundred years after his death, but rather no more than thirty years later, scarcely more than twenty since the death of Colonel Roosevelt. For near the start of World War II appeared a volume of posthumous writings assembled from previously unpublished papers and entitled *Mark Twain in Eruption*. Looking into it, the surviving

Roosevelts were left to wonder: why had Mr. Clemens recorded such ill-tempered thoughts about their father? Theodore Roosevelt had always loved Mark Twain, as a senior at Harvard had laughed himself purple in the face over *A Tramp Abroad*, and as late as 1909, in the bookbag of choice titles that he brought along on his African safari, had included *Huckleberry Finn* to read yet again. Newly sworn in as president, Roosevelt had sought Mark Twain's advice while attending Yale's bicentennial, and had grieved with the rest of the world at the death of Mark Twain's eldest daughter and of his wife. He had entertained the humorist at the White House, and had exulted with readers the world over on the occasion of Mark Twain's seventieth birthday. True, the President was once overheard—at the Yale bicentennial—saying he would like to skin Mark Twain alive (unsettling perhaps, from one with TR's taxidermic skills) for what he wrote about missionaries, Clemens never having cared for missionaries, whom he saw as meddling in foreign lands and preying on the unformed minds of children. But the Colonel's remark was hardly personal; and anyway, the vitriol in this posthumous volume went beyond any pique from one offhand, overheard comment.

Mark Twain had erupted—and posterity would read—that Father was far and away the worst president we've ever had, that he was showy, bombastic, self-advertising, lacking in presidential dignity, ill-mannered, abusive, provocative, and that invariably the Rough Rider, the Great Hunter, played for the gallery's applause. But didn't Mark Twain do that, too? Isn't that last what just about every celebrity does? And indeed, some of Clemens's irritation with his younger contemporary may have arisen from their similarities. Both, after all, were on the public stage and liked it there. Both were internationally famous, citizens of the world. Both were democrats at heart, friends alike of the exalted and the humble. And both were restless and impulsive, omnivorous in their curiosity, raconteurs who were listened to raptly, both given to hyperbole, able to go shrill with colorful invective. Both, moreover, were uxorious, and both stayed young in spirit almost to the end. Come to that, maybe such lifelong youthfulness is a trait of the genius that Clemens and Roosevelt shared: seeing every day freshly, through a child's eyes, differently from how the habituated multitudes greet their future, each day making them a little bit older, tireder, and more conventional.

Yet for all their similarities, these two public figures differed from one another, and not only in age—Clemens the senior by nearly a quarter century—although age was crucial to what separated them. For the elderly Mark Twain, young Mr. Roosevelt appeared hardly mature enough to be presidential. But then, this twentieth wasn't the humorist's century anyhow, even as he wished it well. His was the nineteenth, and his heart lingered in the agrarian America of that earlier time. Or so it would appear from the best of his writing—though the man was protean, even more so than Roosevelt. Sam Clemens was out of agrarian America, yet he exulted in the urban East's technologies of typewriters, telephones, water closets, electric lights, bicycles, and miraculous typesetters. Satirist of the Gilded Age, he was an avid speculator himself, who relished his friendships with the captains of American industry and grumbled when President Roosevelt hectored them. He was a man of the people who built two mansions and enjoyed a leased third overlooking the Hudson, an idealist who insisted on the material comfort of first-class travel even as his wife strived to economize. He was the imaginative, free-thinking iconoclast who urged on his daughters the most conventional Victorian behavior, the loving husband and father who spent weeks in travel away from home and didn't always get along with his children once they were grown, the humorist vexed when reviewers refused to take him seriously, the entirely original author out of the frontier West who coveted the approval of the modish, genteel East, the artist of some of America's supreme literature who kept one eye ever fixed on ways to maximize sales and profits. And he could bear a grudge and be unforgiving, toward Dan Slote, toward Charley Webster, toward James W. Paige—and finally toward Theodore Roosevelt, not as a person (the person of Roosevelt striking him face-to-face as irresistible) but as a politician, the bumptious politician Roosevelt at the helm of our ship of state, who had steered America off its steady course pointing toward democracy in order to follow Europe's lead on the way to empire.

Perhaps the determinist that Mark Twain became could have been made to understand that it was not TR who changed our course. It was the time, after the Civil War, which brought industrialism, wealth, corporations, factories requiring raw materials and markets, and a rapidly growing population that exulted in its newfound power even as it needed to be fed. It was all that together that had led even the placid McKinley to accede to America's ventures in imperialism. And maybe Mark Twain's looking back to earlier times, when the United States stayed home and abided by the unique tenets of its founding documents, its citizens created equal and giving their consent to be governed, leaving other countries alone and setting an example—Switzerland on a continental scale—for the rest of the world to follow: maybe any such dream of clinging to that while these industrial decades advanced was naive. Roosevelt, looking forward, thought so, although that statesman did come early to regret our involvement in the Philippines, our Achilles' heel (he judged them), all but impossible for a democracy with a federal legislature, of necessity poorly informed from across an ocean, to govern.

That was the point: democracy and empire didn't mix. As Clemens understood it, when the young Roosevelt pushed us into empire, he disabled democracy. The humorist growing old in a new century took it hard, as Howells had noted—took this new America hard—and the results were bitterness and carping, ranting and near despair. Much of such writing Clemens himself suppressed, ever mindful of sales and of what Mark Twain's public expected from him. And after the author's death Clara Clemens, his surviving daughter, did what she could to withhold the late, darker writings and to protect her father's image as America's drawling, kindhearted humorist, lecturer, and author beloved the world over.

At Stormfield, which she inherited, Clara Clemens Gabrilowitsch gave birth in mid-August 1910, four months after her father's death, to a daughter, Nina, Mark Twain's only grandchild. The Gabrilowitsches returned to Europe; and in 1918 Clara's pianist husband, Ossip, was named founding director of the Detroit Symphony Orchestra, a position he held until shortly before his death of cancer, in 1936. He was fifty-eight. His widow moved west, and in time, in her seventies, she married a musician of sorts twenty years her junior, Jacques Samossoud, addicted to gambling, who went through much of her money. Clara died in San Diego in 1962, at eighty-eight.

By then her only child was in her fifties. Not until the teenage years had Nina Gabrilowitsch been told who her grandfather was; presumably the parents had reasons for their reticence. Nina's adulthood was plagued with depression, alcoholism, and drugs. Alone in a Los Angeles hotel room, she died of an overdose at fifty-five, in 1966, four years after her mother and in the same year as her stepfather Samossoud. With that, Samuel Langhorne Clemens's line of direct descendants came to an end.

The Roosevelt progeny were far more prolific, all but two of them. Quentin perished affianced but unmarried, but the other three boys and their sister Ethel had families from whom have descended numerous great-grandchildren of Theodore Roosevelt, he who loved large families and had feared race suicide. Son Ted and wife Eleanor had three sons and a daughter, as did Kermit and his wife Belle. Archie and Grace had three daughters and a son, and Ethel—the Queen of Oyster Bay—and her surgeon husband Dick Derby had three daughters who grew to adulthood, as well as a son who died young, of septicemia. Their grandmother, Edith Roosevelt, lived to hold and love many of those children; she survived her husband Theodore through twenty-nine years of widowhood, dying at eighty-seven, in 1948.

Only Edith's stepdaughter, Alice Lee Roosevelt Longworth, limited her maternity to a single child, a daughter, Paulina. The Longworth marriage had proved shaky, husband Nick an industrious womanizer. Moreover, as far back as 1912, Colonel Roosevelt's failed attempt to regain the presidency on the Progressive ticket had not only delivered the Republican Party once and for all to the Old Guard and business and wealth. It had also added its strains to his daughter's marriage, Alice enthusiastically supporting her father's bid, while Nicholas, from Taft's home district in Cincinnati, felt obliged to throw his weight behind the incumbent. Although Mr. and Mrs. Longworth kept up appearances more or less thereafter, often they went their separate ways. On February 14, 1925, just after her forty-first birthday, Alice gave birth to her only child. Her husband took little Polly in and loved her and always treated her as his own, although Senator Borah of Idaho was the child's natural father. The convivial Nicholas, after distinguished service as speaker of the House (the Longworth Office Building in Washington is named in his honor), died at sixty-one, in 1931. Having earlier attempted suicide—alas, the sadness inherent in endings—Paulina died of a drug overdose in 1957. She was thirty-one.

Her mother Alice, however, the celebrated Mrs. L, lived on: witty, admired, envied, once so beautiful and for long afterward a social force, her invitations coveted, she the other Washington Monument, in attendance at quadrennial presidential nominating conventions into old age, friend of chief executives as late as Richard Nixon, tart-tongued and ever quotable, dying at ninety-six, not before 1980. How bright it all shone once, this image of Alice now fading. As finally Mark Twain's image will fade, one supposes, and Roosevelt's will fade—even as Pharaoh Nectanebo's image has faded, even as the Holy Roman Emperor Conrad II's and—nearer home—the Bay Colony's imposing Puritan worthies have. At last, even Mark Twain's and the inextinguishable Roosevelt's renown will fade. But at present, a century after their deaths and unlike so many of their contemporaries—the Josh Billingses, the Artemus Wards, the Petroleum V. Nasbys, the Chester A. Arthurs, the Benjamin Harrisons, the Warren G. Hardings, all those crowding figures fading into the dim gray of time before vanishing (in Roosevelt's own stark image) into the blackness of eternity—unlike those, these two uniques, these mighties of our politics and our culture, the one who strove in the arena, the other who wryly observed, leave us rejoicing in how lifelike both of them linger among us, how high they tower still.

Chronology

1835	Samuel Clemens is born in Florida, Mo., November 30. Andrew Carnegie born in Scotland five days earlier.
1839	Clemens family moves to Hannibal, Mo., on Mississippi River.
1840	Henry Huttleston Rogers born in Fairhaven, Mass.
1845	Olivia Langdon born November 27, in Elmira, N.Y.
1847	Clemens's father dies, leaving family in straitened circumstances.
1848	Carnegie family emigrates from Scotland, joins relatives in Pittsburgh; Andrew is twelve.
1851	In Hannibal, young Sam begins work as journeyman printer, publishing his earliest sketches.
1853	Clemens leaves Hannibal for good at age seventeen. Sees Crystal Palace in New York City, then Washington, D.C., and Philadelphia.
1856	Booker T. Washington born to slave mother in Franklin County, Va.
1857	Clemens becomes cub pilot on Mississippi River under tutelage of Horace Bixby.
1858	Clemens's brother Henry badly scalded in steamboat explosion; dies in Memphis. Theodore Roosevelt born on October 28 in New York City.
1861	Start of Civil War in April halts civilian riverboat traffic on Mississippi. In June Clemens joins Confederate militia unit briefly, and in July sets out with brother Orion for Nevada, reaching Carson City on August 15. Mines unsuccessfully for silver.
1862	Clemens goes to work for Virginia City's *Enterprise*.
1863	In February, for the first time, Clemens uses pen name Mark Twain in article in the *Enterprise*.
1865	Gen. Lee surrenders in April, effectively ending the Civil War. Mark Twain's "Jumping Frog" sketch published in eastern newspapers in late fall.
1866	Clemens sails for Sandwich Islands (Hawaii), returning to San Francisco in late summer. In the fall, as Mark Twain, he lectures successfully on his travels. Sails for the East in December.
1867	In June Clemens sails from New York aboard *Quaker City* on five-month cruise to Holy Land, returning in late November. In NYC meets Olivia Langdon, sister of a fellow passenger.

1868   Mark Twain signs contract to write a book about his travels. He meets Joseph Twichell on visit to Hartford, Conn. Lectures throughout eastern United States. In November, Olivia Langdon agrees to marry Clemens.

1869   In May, when Theodore is ten, Roosevelt family sails for year of travel in Europe. The same month sees completion of transcontinental railroad. Mark Twain's *The Innocents Abroad* published in August, to great success. Favorably reviewed in *Atlantic*. Clemens meets William Dean Howells.

1870   Sam Clemens and Olivia Langdon are married in February, move to Buffalo. Livy's father dies in August. Childhood friend of Livy's dies in September while visiting the Clemenses. Clemenses' first child, Langdon, born prematurely in November. Returned from Europe, young Theodore Roosevelt, now eleven, sets about at father's urging to build himself up physically.

1871   Clemenses move from Buffalo to Elmira in March. In October, family moves permanently to Hartford, leasing Hooker home in Nook Farm. Fire destroys much of Chicago that month. Young Theodore Roosevelt dons spectacles, seeing the world adequately for the first time.

1872   Mark Twain's *Roughing It* published in February, sells well. Daughter Susy born March 19. Son Langdon dies June 2. Clemens to Liverpool in August to write book on England (never undertaken). Roosevelt family sails for Europe and Mideast in October. Clemens returns home in November. Roosevelts on voyage along the Nile at year's end.

1873   Roosevelt children spend five months with German family in Dresden. Clemens buys a lot in Hartford on which to build home for his family. With neighbor C. D. Warner he finishes *The Gilded Age*, then travels with his family to England in May and remains there and on Continent through rest of the year. Roosevelt family returns to NYC in November, moves into new mansion uptown. *The Gilded Age* published in December.

1874   Clara Clemens born June 8, in Elmira. Her father is working there on *Tom Sawyer*. *Atlantic* publishes Mark Twain's "A True Story" in November. Clemenses move into their Hartford home, where they will live until 1891.

1875   The Clemenses entertain lavishly in new Hartford mansion. "Old Times on the Mississippi" appears in installments in *Atlantic*.

1876   Centennial Exposition in Philadelphia. In September, Roosevelt
        enters Harvard College. *Tom Sawyer* published in December.
1877   To settle disputed presidential election of 1876, Republicans
        agree to withdraw federal troops from the South, ending Recon-
        struction. Clemens travels with Twichell to Bermuda. Works on
        writing plays.
1878   In February, Roosevelt's father dies at forty-six. Clemens family
        sails for Europe in April, with contract to make a book of the
        experience. Young Roosevelt, still at Harvard, meets Alice Lee in
        October.
1879   Clemenses continue to travel in Europe and England, returning to
        America in September. Roosevelt enters his senior year at Harvard.
1880   Mark Twain's *A Tramp Abroad* published in March. In June, Roo-
        sevelt graduates from Harvard. Jean Clemens born in July. Roo-
        sevelt with brother Elliott travels west during summer to hunt.
        Marries Alice Lee in Brookline, Mass., in October.
1881   Booker Washington arrives in Tuskegee, Ala., as new head of
        school he must build from scratch. Theodore and Alice Roosevelt
        travel in Europe, returning to NYC in October. The following
        month Roosevelt wins election to NY Assembly. Mark Twain's *The
        Prince and the Pauper* published in December.
1882   In spring, Clemens travels down and up the Mississippi, preparing
        to expand his *Atlantic* articles on steamboat days into a book. Roo-
        sevelt's *The Naval War of 1812*, begun at Harvard, is published to fa-
        vorable reviews. He wins reelection to NY Assembly in November.
1883   Mark Twain's *Life on the Mississippi* published in May. In September,
        Roosevelt travels to Dakota Territory to hunt buffalo, ends by buy-
        ing two cattle ranches. Reelected to third term in NY Assembly.
        Brother Elliott marries Anna Hall in December.
1884   Roosevelts' first child, Alice, born February 12. New father returns
        from Albany to family mansion, where, on February 14, he wit-
        nesses death of his mother and his wife less than twelve hours
        apart. Declines running for another term in Assembly. Daughter
        Alice is left in care of Theodore's sister Bamie (Anna). He attends
        1884 Republican convention in Chicago, then journeys to Dakota
        in July and builds ranch house near Medora. Clemens starts on
        lucrative four-month lecture tour with author George Washington
        Cable in November.
1885   *Adventures of Huckleberry Finn* published by Webster & Co., Mark
        Twain's own publishing firm, in February. Webster & Co. signs

contract that month to publish Gen. Grant's memoirs. Susy Clemens at thirteen begins writing biography of her father. Roosevelt in Badlands in April, spends summer with sister Bamie and daughter Alice in newly finished home at Oyster Bay. His *Hunting Trips of a Ranchman* published in July. Gen. Grant dies July 23. Roosevelt encounters old friend Edith Carow in New York in September. Two months later they become secretly engaged. First volume of Grant's *Memoirs* published to enormous success.

1886   Elaborate amateur performance in Clemens home of *Prince and Pauper*, adapted by Mrs. Clemens. Second and final volume of Grant's *Memoirs* appears; together the two volumes earn Grant's family over $400,000. Roosevelt spends April at his ranch. Runs for mayor of New York in fall; comes in third in field of three. Sails for England and marries Edith Carow in London on December 2. Mark Twain at work writing *A Connecticut Yankee in King Arthur's Court*.

1887   On honeymoon, Roosevelts travel widely in Europe, returning to New York in March. Half of Roosevelt's herd of cattle perish in brutal winter on the plains. After spring visit there, he returns to Sagamore Hill and sets about writing to earn a living. Daughter Alice comes to Sagamore Hill to live. Son Theodore Jr. born September 13. Clemens busy with his publishing company, speaking engagements, and interest in Paige typesetter, in which he has invested heavily.

1888   Charles Webster takes sick leave from Webster & Co., replaced by Fred Hall. Roosevelt begins work on multivolume *The Winning of the West* and writes numerous magazine articles. His *Ranch Life and the Hunting Trail* published in November.

1889   Republican President Harrison appoints Roosevelt to civil service commission in Washington. First two volumes of *The Winning of the West* published in June. On October 10, son Kermit born. Mark Twain's *A Connecticut Yankee in King Arthur's Court* appears in December.

1890   Roosevelt reads and reviews Capt. Mahan's *Influence of Sea Power*. Brother Elliott succumbing to alcoholism. Susy Clemens enters Bryn Mawr in October. Clemens's financial problems intensify, as Paige overrefines his typesetter and Webster & Co. overextends.

1891   Susy leaves Bryn Mawr in April. Charles Webster dies the same month. Clemenses close Hartford house and sail for Europe June 6. Roosevelt's daughter Ethel born August 13.

1892   In January, Roosevelt travels to France to deal with Elliott's drinking problems. After frequent moves around western Europe, Clemens settles with family in Florence in September. Works on *Pudd'nhead Wilson* and *Joan of Arc*. Democrat Cleveland reelected to presidency in November.

1893   Cleveland retains Republican Roosevelt in civil service post. World's Columbian Exposition opens in Chicago in May, runs to November. Clemens returns to America to deal with business problems. Meets H. H. Rogers, who agrees to help. Clemens and Rogers travel to Chicago to consult with Paige about typesetter.

1894   Archie Roosevelt born April 9. On Rogers's advice, Webster & Co. declares bankruptcy. Elliott Roosevelt dies in August, age thirty-four. Clemens back in Europe with family, awaiting Rogers's advice. *Pudd'nhead Wilson* published in United States in November. In December, Clemens learns from Rogers that typesetter has failed test in Chicago pressroom. Third volume of Roosevelt's *Winning of the West* published.

1895   Roosevelt becomes NYC police commissioner in May. Clemens and family sail for America that month, proceeding to Elmira. In mid-July, Clemens, wife, and daughter Clara set out on trip west to Pacific Coast and around the world, Mark Twain intending to pay Webster & Co. creditors with profits from lecturing; they reach Australia by year's end.

1896   Clemens family touring India in January, sail for South Africa at end of March, arrive in England at end of July. In mid-August, family learns of Susy Clemens's death in Hartford, on way to rejoin them in England. Daughter Jean diagnosed with epilepsy. Fourth volume of Roosevelt's *Winning of the West* published. He campaigns in fall for Gov. McKinley's election to presidency. McKinley defeats Bryan decisively in November.

1897   Pres. McKinley appoints Roosevelt assistant secretary of the Navy in April. Naval War College speech in June. In July Clemenses leave England for Switzerland, then to Vienna for twenty-two-month stay. Quentin Roosevelt born November 19. Mark Twain's *Following the Equator* is published that same month.

1898   In February, USS *Maine* explodes in Havana harbor. Spanish-American War begins in April. On July 1 Rough Riders under Col. Roosevelt take San Juan Heights in Cuba. Armistice signed in mid-August. Back in civilian life, Roosevelt wins election in November for governor of New York. Peace treaty with Spain signed in Paris in mid-December.

1899 Clemens family leaves Vienna for England in May, and from there to Sweden in July for treatment of Jean's epilepsy. Roosevelt's *Rough Riders* published. Back in London in October, Clemens is disillusioned with America's purposes in recent Spanish-American War and with England's in ongoing Boer War.

1900 Mark Twain sympathizes with Chinese Boxers, who are seeking to throw foreigners out of their country. In June, Roosevelt is chosen as vice presidential nominee in Chicago. He campaigns extensively for McKinley against Bryan through the autumn. Clemens family returns to U.S. in mid-October, settles in rented home on Tenth St., NYC. Roosevelt publishes *The Strenuous Life*. McKinley reelected president November 6.

1901 McKinley takes oath of office March 4, Roosevelt as his vice president. Judge Taft becomes civil governor of Philippines July 4. McKinley shot in Buffalo September 6, dies eight days later. Roosevelt sworn in and assumes presidential duties. Booker T. Washington dines with President at White House. Clemenses lease mansion on Hudson River, shortly before Yale's bicentennial celebration in October, where both Roosevelt and Mark Twain receive honorary degrees. Roosevelt's first message to Congress delivered in early December.

1902 In January, young Alice Roosevelt debuts. Justice department files antitrust suit against Northern Securities in March. Mark Twain receives honorary degree from University of Missouri; visits Hannibal for the last time. Clemenses spend summer in York Harbor, Maine. Livy desperately ill in August, returns to Riverdale-on-Hudson as invalid in October. Roosevelt intervenes that month to settle Pennsylvania coal strike, persuading both sides to arbitrate differences; miners go back to work late that month. Presidential hunting trip to Mississippi results in incident that leads to first marketing of Teddy Bears. Over protests of white southerners, Roosevelt appoints William Crum collector of customs in Charleston. Isabel Lyon serving as Clemens's secretary.

1903 U.S. signs isthmus treaty with Colombia in January. At Roosevelt's insistence, Germany lifts blockade of Venezuela in February and submits the issue of debts owed to its nationals to arbitration. Alaska-Canada border dispute settled in United States' favor. Roosevelt signs Elkins Act, prohibiting railroad rebates, and creates first wildlife refuge. Leaves on two-month western trip in April. Mrs. Clemens's health improving. Hartford house sold at loss in May. On doctors' advice, Clemenses leave Hudson River home for good in July, bound for Elmira for Livy's final visit there. Colombians reject canal treaty in August. In October, Clemens signs lucrative contract that lets Harper's publish all his works. Family sails late that month for Europe, settling in rented villa outside Florence. Panama declares its independence from Colombia and, on November 14, is formally recognized by United States, which signs treaty four days later confirming zone in which to construct isthmian canal. Wright brothers get their flying machine airborne at Kitty Hawk in December.

1904　　Russo-Japanese War begins February 8. Roosevelt nominated by acclamation to his own term as president in June. Olivia Clemens dies in Florence on June 5. Surviving Clemenses sail for America at end of month, attend Livy's funeral in Elmira in July. Clara retires to rest home; Clemens takes lease on Fifth Avenue home and moves in near year's end. In November, Roosevelt wins reelection and pledges not to seek another term. His annual message to Congress in December promulgates corollary to Monroe Doctrine.

1905　　United States signs protocol to collect Dominican customs that will be used to pay its foreign debts (operative over the next year and a half). Roosevelt sworn in on March 4, soon after gives away his niece Eleanor in marriage to cousin Franklin Roosevelt. Clemens, Jean, and Miss Lyon summer in Dublin, N.H. In August, he visits Clara at rest home in Connecticut, first visit in a year. Japan asks Roosevelt to mediate peace with Russia. Talks begin at Portsmouth, N.H.; treaty ending Russo-Japanese War signed September 5. Mark Twain's gala seventieth birthday party at Delmonico's on December 5. He meets and befriends fifteen-year-old Gertrude Natkin later that month.

1906　　Albert Bigelow Paine moves into Clemens's home in January to write Mark Twain's biography. The humorist participates at Carnegie Hall in twenty-fifth-anniversary celebration of Tuskegee's founding. Alice Roosevelt marries Rep. Nicholas Longworth at White House February 17. Gertrude Natkin turns sixteen, effectively ending her friendship with Mark Twain. Algeciras Conference involving European powers ends April 6, settling issues of

Moroccan sovereignty. Earthquake destroys much of San Francisco on April 18. Selections from Mark Twain's autobiography appear in *North American Review* beginning in September (continuing to December 1907). Jean Clemens enters sanitarium at Katonah, N.Y. Mark Twain's *What Is Man?* published in private edition. In November, Roosevelt orders discharge of 167 black soldiers from the army, in wake of incident at Brownsville, Tex., in August. Roosevelt and wife travel to Panama in mid-November. Clemens, dressed in white (as he will be publicly from now on), lobbies for copyright reform in Washington in December. Roosevelt awarded Nobel Peace Prize.

1907   Clemens spends week with Twichell in Bermuda, in spring attends Jamestown Exposition with H. H. Rogers. San Francisco ceases segregating Japanese school children when Japan agrees to restrict emigration. Mark Twain goes to England in June to receive honorary degree from Oxford; encounters great warmth and affection. Meets Dorothy Quick, age eleven, on shipboard returning, and later entertains her at Tuxedo Park and at Fifth Avenue home. Roosevelt supports Taft as his successor in White House. Knickerbocker Trust Co. collapses in October, intensifying financial panic. Great White Fleet of sixteen battleships sets out in December to circumnavigate the globe.

1908   Mark Twain travels to Bermuda with Rogers and Miss Lyon. Creates "Aquarium" for schoolgirl friends, whom he calls angelfish. House at Redding, Conn., designed by John Howells, is ready for occupancy in June. Clemens moves in by end of month, names it "Stormfield" in October, and lives there for the rest of his life. On June 18 Republicans nominate for president William Howard Taft, who defeats Bryan in November.

1909   At Hampton Roads, Va., February 22, Roosevelt welcomes return of Great White Fleet as fitting end to his presidency. Taft inaugurated as twenty-seventh president on March 4. Roosevelt and son Kermit sail for Africa three weeks later on long-planned, extended safari. At Stormfield, Clara Clemens shares with her father her suspicions of Isabel Lyon, who has married Ralph Ashcroft on March 18. Clemens fires both Ashcroft and Lyon in April, and Jean returns to live with him in Redding before the month is out. H. H. Rogers dies in May; Clemens shocked and heartsick. Is diagnosed with angina pectoris in July. In October, Clara marries Ossip

Gabrilowitsch at Stormfield. Clemens sails to Bermuda in November, returning to Redding for Christmas. Jean Clemens dies on Christmas Eve morning. Her father writes "Death of Jean," his final composition; he is unable to attend Elmira funeral. Roosevelt's hunting safari has reached Uganda by year's end.

1910   Declining in health, Clemens returns to Bermuda in early January. Sees Dorothy Quick there. Roosevelt, joined by wife Edith and daughter Ethel, lands in Naples April 2, at start of triumphal tour of European cities. Suffering chest pains, Clemens leaves Bermuda on April 12, reaching NYC on the 14th. Dies at Stormfield April 21. Edward VII's funeral in London on May 10 is attended by Roosevelt as Pres. Taft's representative. On June 18 huge crowds greet Roosevelt's return to NYC. Delivers speech advocating progressive views at Osawatomie, Kans., in late August. At Stormfield, Clara gives birth that month to Clemens's only grandchild, Nina. Roosevelt publishes *African Game Trails* and writes articles on current affairs.

1912   Having grown increasingly critical of Taft's presidency, Roosevelt announces his candidacy for president in February. He campaigns vigorously through the spring. Despite wide popular support for him, his delegates are disqualified at convention in Chicago, resulting in Taft's renomination on June 22. Roosevelt nominated as Progressive ("Bull Moose") candidate in August. Outpolls Taft in the general election on November 5, but loses to Democratic candidate Woodrow Wilson.

1913   Roosevelt's *Autobiography* published. With Edith, he sails in October for South America, where he gives speeches in four countries, hunts jaguars with son Kermit, and joins expedition to explore uncharted river in Brazilian rainforest.

1914   On February 2, Roosevelt and son Kermit, with a party of twenty others, begin descent of the River of Doubt. Injures his leg severely on March 27. After life-threatening ordeals, party reaches Amazon April 30. Roosevelt returns to NYC much enfeebled on May 19. He never fully recovers from this adventure. Travels to Europe for Kermit's wedding in Spain; visits France and England and is home to stay in June. Archduke Franz Ferdinand assassinated at Sarajevo late that month, leading to major European powers declaring war in August.

1915   Roosevelt sharply critical of Pres. Wilson for acceding to Germany's violation of Belgian neutrality and for his failure to prepare United States for war. German U-boat sinks British liner *Lusitania* on May 7, drowning 128 Americans. Wilson's inaction stirs Roosevelt to launch vigorous protests; privately he calls the President a coward.

1916   Roosevelt endorses and campaigns for Republican Charles Evans Hughes against Wilson for president, the Democratic incumbent winning the election in November by a narrow margin.

1917   Germany's resumption of unrestricted submarine warfare leads Pres. Wilson to declare war in early April. Roosevelt unsuccessful in seeking permission to lead division of volunteers to western front. Kermit has already entered the war in British army, in Mesopotamia; Ted and Archie as officers sail for France with American expeditionary force. Quentin trains as pilot and sails in late July. Roosevelt criticizes Wilson administration for inadequately equipping American troops.

1918   In February, Roosevelt is hospitalized for ear surgery and illnesses lingering from Amazon exploration. Son Archie severely wounded on March 11. In mid-July, German fighters shoot down Quentin's aircraft near Reims. He perishes; and five days later, Ted is wounded. Roosevelt appears for last time in public on November 2. Enters hospital in NYC on Armistice Day, November 11, returning to Sagamore Hill in time for Christmas.

1919   On January 6, Roosevelt dies in his sleep at age sixty, at Sagamore Hill, and is buried two days later in Oyster Bay. In August, in Lenox, Mass., Andrew Carnegie dies at eighty-three.

Notes

MT is Mark Twain; SLC is Samuel Langhorne Clemens; TR is Theodore Roosevelt. Full titles of works cited are on pages 469–76.

Epigraphs: "a fine thing." Ray Stannard Baker quoting TR at a Sagamore Hill luncheon on 7-15-03. E. Morris, *Theodore Rex*, 258.

"sardonic times." MT to Howells, 2-23-97. Smith and Gibson, *MT-Howells Letters*, 2:665.

Preface: "worst President." DeVoto, *MT in Eruption*, 34.

"best friend." L. Leary, *MT's Correspondence with H.H. Rogers*, 38 (3-4-94).

WAR

1. Return to America

5   "harmless-looking man." C. Clemens, *My Father*, 190, 191.

6   "second U.S. Embassy." Ibid., 193.

6   "self-appointed Ambassador." From MT's notebooks, as quoted in Dolmetsch, *"Our Famous Guest,"* 111.

7   "famous in all countries." C. Clemens, *My Father*, 96.

7   "d——d good!" Ibid., 202.

7   "Dinner at the Embassy." MT's notebooks, as quoted in Dolmetsch, *"Our Famous Guest,"* 155.

8   MT's creativity in Vienna. Ibid., 242: "the last great creative surge of Mark Twain's long career."

8   "series of farewells?" C. Clemens, *My Father*, 214.

8   *"Mann kann nicht."* Dolmetsch, *"Our Famous Guest,"* 17.

9   "our beloved friends." C. Clemens, *My Father*, 214.

10   "courtesy of the port." This and the remaining citations in the chapter are from the article on p. 3 of *New York Times* for 10-16-00, reporting on the Clemenses' return to America.

2. Celebrity

11   "great festive occasion." C. Clemens, *My Father*, 217. Among books about Mark Twain that focus on his late years are, notably, Hamlin

Hill's *Mark Twain: God's Fool* (1973), William R. Macnaughton's *Mark Twain's Last Years as a Writer* (1979), and Karen Lystra's *Dangerous Intimacy* (2004), as well as Michael Shelden's *Mark Twain: Man in White* and Laura Skandera Trombley's *Mark Twain's Other Woman* (both 2010).

12   The earliest, *The Innocents Abroad*. Some of Mark Twain's western sketches, including "The Jumping Frog," had been published two years before, in 1867, to very modest success.

12   "to his chin." "Jim Smiley and His Jumping Frog." MT, *Collected Tales 1852–1890*, 176.

12   "literally purple." Corinne Roosevelt to Douglas Robinson, 2-10-81; quoted in McCullough, *Mornings*, 232.

12–13 *Huckleberry Finn*. The author's opinion of this book varied. By 1902, he could write a young correspondent, in answer to her question, that his favorites among his works were, first, *Joan of Arc*, and second, *Huckleberry Finn*. Paine, *MT's Letters*, 2:719 (2-22-02).

13   "have an opinion." C. Clemens, *My Father*, 217.

15   "won't it be nuts?!" Salsbury, *Susy and MT*, 368–69.

15   "*do* belong together." Quoted in Willis, *Mark and Livy*, 234.

16   "released today." MT, *Autobiography*, 1:324.

16   "misfortune and sorrow." Wecter, *Love Letters*, 320–21.

17–18 America in 1900. The evocation is principally from Wagenknecht, *American Profile*, and Sullivan, *Our Times*, vol. 1, passim.

18   "look over the field." Scharnhorst, *MT: The Complete Interviews*, 358.

3. Vice Presidential Candidate

19   "The Democratic idea." Bryan, *First Battle*, 205.

20   Deflation after the Civil War. The account is adapted from Sullivan, *Our Times*, 1:153–82.

21   "find its way up." Bryan, *First Battle*, 205.

22   "nearly a thousand strong." The details of that day's rallies in Canton are from *LA Times*, 9-13-96.

23   "I drowned him out." Quoted in Dalton, *TR: A Strenuous Life*, 195.

25   "vote as he chooses." *New York Times*, 10-16-00: "Roosevelt at Covington," 3.

27   "a grand demonstration." Ibid.

4. Warfare

28   "no one looking." Quoted in Kerr, *Bully Father*, 15. See Hagedorn, *Roosevelt Family*, for a full description of the home and its surroundings.

29   "love a great many things." TR, *Autobiography*, 584.

31   "worst misgovernment." Gould, *Spanish-American War*, 40.
32   "vulture or buzzard." Foner, *Spanish-Cuban-American War*, 1:117.
33   "a thirst for adventure." Roosevelt, *Rough Riders*, 24–25. The citations that follow, into [34], are from the same source: 21 ("carbines, saddles"), 55 ("Ship after ship"), 58 ("deeds of violence").
35   "the great day." To Hermann Hagedorn, 8-14-17, in E. Morris, *Rise of TR*, 681.
35   "magnificent soldier." Quoted in ibid., 674.
35   "waiting for the command." Hall, *Fun and Fighting*, 194.
35   "the Spaniards ran." Roosevelt, *Rough Riders*, 112.
37   "in a common grave." Ibid., 90.

5. Imperialist America

40   "your officers cannot eat." E. Morris, *Rise of TR*, 678.
41   "God's country." Silbey, *War of Frontier and Empire*, 49, quoting from Lewis O. Saum, "The Western Volunteer and 'The New Empire,'" *Pacific Northwest Quarterly* 57, no. 1 (1996): 18–27.
41   "Russia in Turkestan." From an interview in *New York Tribune*, 10-10-00; quoted in Beale, *TR and the Rise*, 72.
42   "our duty in the Philippines?" Ibid.
42   "dominant power." To John Barrett, 10-29-00; quoted in Beale, *TR and the Rise*, 76.
42   "race of national greatness." Ibid., 77, from *Fargo Morning Call*, 9-15-00.
43   "factors of incalculable moment." TR, "Address at Mechanics' Pavilion, San Francisco," 5-15-03, in TR, *California Addresses*, 95.
43   "do all I could." Roosevelt, *Rough Riders*, 11.
43   "misery at our doorsteps." To Elihu Root, 4-5-98, in Morison, *Letters*, 2:813.
44   "waters at Europe and Asia." TR, "Address before the Society of Naval Architects and Marine Engineers," *New York Sun* 11-13-97; quoted in Beale, *TR and the Rise*, 293.
46   "his glorious prime." Ibid., 67.

6. Anti-Imperialist

47   "fight for another man's." To Twichell, from Kaltenleutgeben, 6-17-98, in Paine, *MT's Letters*, 2:663.
48   Notebook entry after Sampson's victory. At Kaltenleutgeben, 7-4-98. "News that Sampson has destroyed the Spanish fleet in the Harbor of Santiago de Cuba. . . . Dr. E. S. Parker and Cornell Dunham are here to enjoy the news with us." Paine, *MT's Notebook*, 343.

48   "war for coaling stations." Smith and Gibson, *MT-Howells Letters*, 2:673.

48   "borne by wireless." *New York Times*, 1-14-10.

50   "no more business in China." "Mark Twain, the Greatest American Humorist, Returning Home, Talks at Length to *The World*," *New York World*, 10-14-00; Scharnhorst, *MT: The Complete Interviews*, 350.

51   "Boxer is a patriot." Gibson, "MT and Howells," 447.

52   "no idea of surrendering." *New York Tribune*, 6-2-98, quoted in Gould, *Spanish-American War*, 64.

52   Roosevelt nor Lodge nor Hay. Thomas's *War Lovers* describes the maneuverings in their "rush to empire," of these three expansionists and others in high places before and during crucial months in 1898.

52   "duty and humanity." Gould, *Spanish-American War*, 108.

53   "benevolent assimilation." Ibid., 115–16 (12-21-98).

54   "I am an anti-imperialist." "Mark Twain Home, an Anti-Imperialist," *New York Herald*, 10-16-00. Scharnhorst, *MT: Complete Interviews*, 353.

7. Election Results

55   "manifest destiny." Diary of McKinley's secretary, George Cortelyou, 6-8-98. Quoted in Gould, *Spanish-American War*, 14.

56   "Then you're for Bryan?" Interview with MT in *Chicago Tribune*, 10-15-00. Zwick, *MT's Weapons of Satire*, 4.

56   "don't ask political questions." *New York World*, 10-16-00. Ibid., 358.

57   "best thought of the country." Sullivan, *Our Times*, 1:534.

57   "turn green in bed." Adams to Elizabeth Cameron, 1-22-99, in Adams, *Letters 1892–1918*, 208.

57   "the sacredest thing." William James to *Boston Evening Transcript*, 3-1-99; quoted in Perry, *Thought and Character of William James*, 246.

57   "the Negro and Indian problems." Quoted in Gatewood, *Black Americans*, 187.

59   "Bryan's dominant note." Speech to American Republican College League, 10-15-96. Williams, *William Jennings Bryan*, 184, 185.

61   "like beasts of prey." Ibid., 227.

61   "attack on civilization." Quoted in Kazin, *Godly Hero*, 105.

62   "under a polluted flag." Gibson, "MT and Howells," 453.

8. The Strenuous Life

65   "justify that compliment." Speech to the Lotos Club, 11-10-00, in Zwick, *MT's Weapons of Satire*, 7.

66   "I wish to preach." TR, *Strenuous Life*, 1. Citations that follow, into 71, are from the same source: 21 ("shrink from no strife"), 4 ("rotten to

the heart's core"), 3 ("cumberer of the earth's surface"), 8 ("great captains of industry"), 5 ("ignoble counsels of peace"), 9 ("well-to-do hucksters"), 19 ("they are despicable"), 20 ("domination of the world").

71 "stronger, manlier power." In "Expansion and Peace," from *The Independent*, 12-21-99, as reprinted in TR, *Strenuous Life*, 34, 35.

72 Mark Twain's Salutation. The *New York Herald* first published the message, in MT's handwriting, dated "New York, Dec. 31, 1900." A facsimile of the greeting as printed on a widely disseminated card of the time appears in Zwick, *Confronting Imperialism*, 114.

WEST
9. Rural Upbringing

75 Clemens was born . . . Among recent single-volume biographies of Mark Twain are Andrew Hoffman, *Inventing Mark Twain* (1997); Fred Kaplan, *The Singular Mark Twain* (2003); Ron Powers, *Mark Twain: A Life* (2005); and Jerome Loving, *Mark Twain: The Adventures of Samuel L. Clemens* (2010). Justin Kaplan's *Mr. Clemens and Mark Twain* (1966) remains simply the best single volume ever written about its subject—and one of the great biographies in American letters.

75 "armed neutrality." The recollection appeared in the *Galaxy*, to which MT contributed regularly from Buffalo in 1870–1871, in the months just after his marriage. Quoted in Sanborn, *Mark Twain: The Bachelor Years*, 32.

76 "champagne and charm." To Mary Benjamin Rogers, 8-14-06, in L. Leary, *MT's Letters to Mary*, 42.

76 "sunniest temperament." Quoted in Wecter, *Sam Clemens*, 86.

77 "not all comedy." Neider, *Autobiography of MT*, 40.

77 "her warm-heartedness." Autobiographical dictation, 12-29-06, in Wecter, *Sam Clemens*, 20.

77 "Cling to the land." Neider, *Autobiography of MT*, 19.

78 "found him asleep on the floor." Wecter, *Sam Clemens*, 204. The two citations that follow are from the same source: 262 ("drunkenness and debauching") and 263 ("APPLY SOON").

79 "a glorious sight." MT, *Letters*, 1:13 (9-3?-53). The citations that follow, into 80, are from the same source: 16 (Forrest in "The Gladiator," 10-8-53), 10 (crossing Broadway; to Jane Lampton Clemens, 8-31-53), 29 ("write for the paper," to Orion Clemens, 11-28-53), 21 ("the first bridge"), 20 ("'Downhearted,' the devil!" 10-26-53), 65 ("in *six weeks*," from Keokuk to Henry Clemens, 8-5-56).

81 "mote-magnifying tyrant." MT, *Life on Mississippi*, 344.

82   "hurts were past help." Ibid., 359. In his account of the accident in *Life on the Mississippi* (p. 356), MT has Henry swimming back to the steamboat to help others, but the victim was likely too scalded to have done that. See Loving, *MT: Adventures of SLC*, 63–64.

82   "call me '*lucky*.'" To Mollie Clemens (Orion's wife), 6-18-58, in MT, *Letters*, 1:81.

82   "my poor sinless brother." Ibid., 82.

82   "capacity of suffering." Paine, *MT: Biography*, 3:1592.

10. Urban Upbringing

83   Theodore Roosevelt was born . . . Recent single-volume biographies of TR include Nathan Miller, *Theodore Roosevelt: A Life* (1992); H. W. Brands, *TR: The Last Romantic* (1997); and Kathleen Dalton, *Theodore Roosevelt: A Strenuous Life* (2002). Edmund Morris's superb three-volume narrative (1979–2010) is vivid from the opening paragraph through nearly 2,000 pages, year by year, that carry the fascinated reader on to its moving conclusion.

83   "absolutely commonplace." Quoted in Wagenknecht, *Seven Worlds*, 149.

83   "full of mischief." Dalton, *TR: A Strenuous Life*, 26 (12-9-61).

84   "walking up and down." TR, *Autobiography*, 266.

84   "entirely 'unreconstructed.'" Ibid., 263.

85   "delicate fingers." TR, *Diaries of Boyhood*, 74–75 (10-10-69).

85   "best man." TR, *Autobiography*, 258. Citations that follow, through 88, are from the same source: 258 ("ever really afraid"), 262 ("every spare halfhour"), ("joy out of living"), 257 ("always wildly eager," "cats, dogs, rabbits," "enthralling pleasures"), 267 ("encouraged me warmly"), 271 ("it puzzled me").

88   "against her brothers." Dalton, *TR: A Strenuous Life*, 26.

89   "cordially hated it." TR, *Autobiography*, 266.

89   "saw our cousins." TR, *Diaries of Boyhood*, 15 (5-22-69).

11. Clemens Goes West

90   "follow the river." MT, *Life on Mississippi*, 360.

90   "incapacitated by fatigue." Neider, *Autobiography MT*, 102.

91   "complete and satisfying happiness." MT, *Roughing It*, 548. Citations that follow, into 93, are from the same source: 576 ("man and horse burst past"), 561 ("things new and strange"), 751–52 ("nowhere to be seen"). Grant H. Smith, in his *History of the Comstock Lode*, records that

the "yield of the Comstock mines increased from $6,000,000 in 1862 to $12,400,000 in 1863 and $16,000,000 in 1864." Smith, *MT of the Enterprise*, 209, n. 3.

93   "lay up $100 or $150." MT, *Letters*, 1:186 (4-13-62).

93   "never look upon Ma's face again." To Orion Clemens, 4-24/25-62, in Ibid., 195.

93   "I must have something to do." Ibid., 228–29 (7-23-62).

94   "the wine of life." Paine, *MT's Letters*, 2:773 (5-24-05).

94   "I fare like a prince." MT, *Letters*, 1:264 (8-19-63).

95   "I had the 'spring fever.'" MT, *Roughing It*, 826. Part 3 of Smith, *MT of the* Enterprise, explores a different reason for Clemens's departure: in haste, to escape the consequences of having involved himself in a duel, which Nevada ordinances prohibited.

95   "all New York in a roar." MT, *Letters*, 1:328 (1-20-66).

95   "pistols or poisons for one." Ibid., 1:324 (10-19/20-65). Late in life SLC, not always rigorous about adhering to historical truth, spoke of once having attempted suicide, in 1866; he hadn't been able to pull the trigger. This would have been the interval when the event played itself out. See MT, *Roughing It*, 849 (ch. 59); Shelden, *MT: Man in White*, 348–49; Hill, *MT: God's Fool*, 223–24.

95   "temperance virtue was temporarily upon him." Autobiographical dictation, 4-5-06; MT, *Letters*, 1:327.

96   "cant about law & religion." MT, *Notebooks I*, 112 ("At Sea, March 9 [1866]").

96   "a perfect jubilee to me." Frear, *MT in Hawaii*, 55.

96   "a 'call' to literature." To Orion and Mollie Clemens, 10-19-65, in MT, *Letters*, 1:322–23.

96   "No—*not* home again." Notebook entry on day of arrival in San Francisco, 8-13-66, in MT, *Notebooks I*, 163.

97   Responses to first lecture. Fatout, *MT on the Lecture Circuit*, 40.

97   despite shipboard terrors. These, which included passengers at sea dying of cholera with horrifying randomness and speed, are vividly described in Walker and Dane, *MT's Travels with Mr. Brown*, 67 ff.

98   "Isn't it a most attractive scheme?" MT, *Letters*, 2:15 (3-2-67).

98   "Mark Twain's quaint remarks last evening." *New York Times*, 5-7-67; quoted in MT, *Letters*, 2:43.

98   "the sunny lands of the Mediterranean!" MT, *Letters*, 2:58.

12. Grand Tours

99   opportunity "waiting on the pier." "The Turning Point of My Life," in MT, *Collected Tales 1891–1910*, 935.

99   "deviled the life out of those girls." MT, *Letters*, 2:144 (1-8-68).

100   "a visiting *Spirit* from the upper air." SLC to Olivia Langdon, 1-6-69, in Wecter, *Love Letters*, 43.

100   "we can give an author as favorable terms." MT, *Letters*, 2:120 (11-21-67). Hill, *MT and Elisha Bliss*, provides a full account of the often fretful dealings between author and publisher that were to follow, up to and beyond Bliss's death in 1880.

100   "beyond my own comprehension." MT, *Letters*, 2:119 (12-2-67). McKeithan, *Traveling*, reprints the letters MT wrote from aboard the *Quaker City* and the changes he made shaping them into *The Innocents Abroad*.

101   "made a splendid contract." MT, *Letters*, 2:160 (1-24-68).

101   "affections in kisses and caresses." Neider, *Autobiography of MT*, 185 (dictated 2-1-06).

102   "For I *do* love you, Livy." Wecter, *Love Letters*, 79.

104   "*It shan't cost you a cent.*" J. Kaplan, *Mr. Clemens*, 113–14.

104   "We played on the beach." TR, *Diaries of Boyhood*, 16. Citations that immediately follow are from the same source: 17 ("galloped so funnily"), 22 ("the river ouse"), 43 ("such a kind sister"), 70–71 ("slide down it"), 105 ("verry dull time"), 105–6 ("cried for homesickness").

105   "make your body." Robinson, *My Brother*, 50.

105   "useful part of my education." TR, *Autobiography*, 271.

106   "Egypt, the land of my dreams." TR, *Diaries of Boyhood*, 276 (11-28-72). The citations that immediately follow are from the same source: 299 ("Father and I") and 300 ("only small waders").

107   "capacity for hard work." TR, *Autobiography*, 274.

107   "the eight subjects I tried." Cowles, *Letters*, 5 (7-25-75).

13. Western Writings

108   "a son of so little worth." TR's private diary, 7-11/14-78, quoted in E. Morris, *Rise of TR*, 72.

109   "so pure and holy." Ibid., 112.

109   "an awful cropper." Kerr, *Bully Father*, 9–10.

110   TR's memorial of Alice. *In Memory of My Darling Wife* . . . Privately printed, 1884. Cordery, *Alice*, 17–18.

110   "extreme of every feeling." Paine, *MT: Biography*, 3:1592.

110   "Black care rarely sits." *Ranch Life and the Hunting Trail* (1888); TR, *Works*, 1:329.

111   "hens in a barn-yard." Roosevelt, *Hunting Trips*, 72. Citations that follow, into 113, are from the same source: 315 ("grand elk lying dead"), 174–75 ("days of sunny weather"), 230 ("in fairy-land"), 282–84 (the mud-pool), 231 ("grumbling and bad temper"), 33 ("I suppose it is right"), 211 ("strong fascination").

113   "very most perfect gem." To Will Bowen, 2-6-70; MT, *MT's Letters to Bowen*, 20.

113   "mar our joy." Quoted in Steinbrink, *Getting to Be MT*, 111 (4-16-70).

113   "in our own bedroom." To Mary Fairbanks, 10-13-70, in ibid., 136.

114   "the new state of things." TR, *Roughing It*, 559.

114   "sparkling Krug." Ibid., 560.

115   "vials of hellfire." MT, *Letters to Publishers*, 60 (3-17-71).

115   "loathe the very sight." To Orion in early 1871. Fatout, *MT on the Lecture Circuit*, 148.

115   "what a pity I can't." Wecter, *Love Letters*, 159 (8-10-71).

116   A plank with holes. Ibid., 165–66 (11-27-71). Like a brook, a narrative properly has "its course changed by every bowlder it comes across and by every grass-clad gravelly spur that projects into its path . . . but always going, and always following at least one law . . . the law of narrative, which has no law." Paine, *MT's Autobiography*, 1:237

118   whatever Mark Twain touched. Paine, *MT: Biography*, 2:830.

14. Continental America

119   cougars and grizzlies. TR, *Hunting Trips*, 27, 320.

120   "perfect fairy palace." MT, *Letters*, 1:13 (9-3?-53).

124   "the need of a history." TR to F. J. Turner, 2-10-94, in Billington, *Frederick Jackson Turner*, 130.

124   "a frontier line." The essay appears in Turner, *Early Writings*, 183–229.

125   "some first class ideas." Bogue, *Frederick Jackson Turner*, 113.

126   "the horse well ridden." TR, *The Wilderness Hunter*, "Author's Preface"; *Works*, 2:xxix–xxx.

127   "can possibly atone." Ibid., xxix.

15. The Philippines

128   "rash prophet." Turner, *Early Writings*, 228.

131   "a mess, a quagmire." Zwick, *MT's Weapons of Satire*, 3–4.

132   "lesser breeds." "Recessional" (1897). *Rudyard Kipling's Verse: Inclusive Edition, 1884–1932* (London, 1933), 325–26.

132   "give those poor things a rest." "Person Sitting in Darkness"; MT, *Collected Tales 1891–1910*, 461. Citations that follow, through 135, are from the same source: 462 ("it is pie"), 463 ("the Kaiser went to playing"), 464 ("holier and higher and nobler?"), 462–63 ("nest of field mice"), 465 ("regular *American* game"), 466 ("Rich winnings," "not have been molested," "prevail in Europe or America"), 469 ("through the woods and swamps"), 471 ("debauched America's honor").

135   "the lousy McKinley." To Twichell, 1-24-01, in Zwick, *MT's Weapons of Satire*, 18.

16. Pan-American Exposition

136 "we have backers." To Edmund B. Kirby, 1-22-01, in Zwick, *MT's Weapons of Satire*, 20.

136 "a most right-minded man." Howells to his sister Aurelia, in M. Howells, *Life in Letters*, 2:142.

137 "rough-riding up San Juan hills." *Harper's Weekly*, 46 (7-12-02), 907.

137 "might have mobbed him." Dr. Frank Van Fleet of NY Medical Society, speaking on 2-27-01. Zwick, *MT's Weapons of Satire*, 67.

137 "they are despicable." TR, *Strenuous Life*, 19.

138 "tell which from which." MT responding in speech to Lotos Club, 3-23-01. Zwick, *MT's Weapons of Satire*, 69.

138 "superior as a people." Gould, *Spanish-American War*, 103 (8-98).

138 "a set of desperadoes." E. Morris, *Rise of TR*, 336 (8-86).

139 "declare war himself." Hay, *Letters and Extracts*, 2:235–36 (1-6-92).

139 "cities are bombarded." To Henry Cabot Lodge, 12-20-95, in Morison, *Letters*, 1:500.

141 "their wants increase." Chauncey Depew speaking at Youngstown during presidential campaign; *New York Times*, 9-9-00. Pringle, *Theodore Roosevelt*, 225.

143 "report last night." L. Leary, *MT's Correspondence with H.H. Rogers*, 470 (9-7-01).

144 "that damned cowboy." Kohlsaat, *McKinley to Harding*, 101.

RACE
17. Yale Bicentennial

147 "public employment." From the original charter. *Record of Celebration*, 380. Citations through 149 are from the same source: 54–55 ("years gone by"), 406 ("work of supererogation").

149 "this splendid compliment." Wecter, *Love Letters*, 179 (9-28-72).

150 "not at all agree." Paine, *MT: Biography*, 3:1143.

151 "crowning moment." *Record of Celebration*, 414.

151 "thank you from my heart." Ibid., 415.

151 "never speak one word." Robinson, *My Brother*, 240–41.

152 "continue, absolutely, unbroken." Quoted in N. Miller, *Theodore Roosevelt: A Life*, 352.

153 "your invitation for dinner." Washington, *My Larger Education*, 175–76.

153 "President asked me." DeVoto, *MT in Eruption*, 30–31.

18. Racial America

155 "discouraging surroundings." Washington, *Up from Slavery*, 1. The citations that follow, into 158, are from the same source: 25 ("Drinking,

gambling, quarrels"), 52 ("equal of General Armstrong"), 16 ("badge of degradation"), 195 ("true philanthropist"). See Harlan's two volumes, *The Making of a Black Leader* and *The Wizard of Tuskegee*, for a full account of Washington's extraordinary life.

158　"how do you like it?" *New York Times*, 10-19-01. Sullivan, *Our Times*, 3:133–35. Pringle, *Theodore Roosevelt*, 248. Grantham provides a detailed account of the episode and its aftermath in "Dinner at the White House."

160　"separate as the fingers." Washington, *Up from Slavery*, 210.

161　"old bag of beef." Simkins, *Pitchfork Ben*, 315.

161　"A more loyal friend." Quoted in ibid., 403–4. The citations that follow, into 162, are from the same source: 394 ("barbarism, savagery, cannibalism"), 399 ("virtues of the negro race"), 397 ("jewel of her womanhood").

163　"learn their place." Kantrowitz, *Ben Tillman*, 259.

19. Back to Hannibal

164　"They love him." Simkins, *Pitchfork Ben*, 395.

165　"Sectional feeling." Quoted in Gould, *Spanish-American War*, 111 (12-14-98).

166　"turn the boys loose." Silbey, *War of Frontier and Empire*, 68.

166　"It all seems so small." Paine, *MT: Biography*, 3:1167–68.

167　"Court House in Syracuse." MT, *Letters*, 1:4 (8-24-53).

168　"my schoolboy days." Neider, *Autobiography of MT*, 6.

168　"unwarrantable usurpation." "Jane Lampton Clemens." MT, *Huck and Tom Among the Indians*, 87, 88.

168　"liking for his race." Neider, *Autobiography of MT*, 6.

169　"our Missourians." Smith chronicles Clemens's shift of loyalties toward Unionism in *MT of the Enterprise*, 19. And see Lynn, *MT and Humor*, 144.

169　"I only have one trouble." To Jane Clemens and family, 8-25-68, in MT, *Letters*, 2:244.

170　"splendidest man." Steinbrink, *Getting to MT*, 41 (12-2-68).

171　"sauciness and irreverence." Howells, *My Mark Twain*, 108, 111.

171　"red in the face." C. Clemens, *My Father*, 43.

171　"ashamed of ourselves." "American Authors and British Pirates," *New Princeton Review* 5 (January 1888), 50–51. Quoted in Budd, *MT: Social Philosopher*, 94.

20. Roosevelt and Race

172　"various races of men" TR, *Diaries of Boyhood*, 289 (12-7-72).

174　"whip the world." To Cecil Spring Rice, 8-11-99, in Morison, *Letters*, 2:1053. TR is passing along, approvingly, what he overheard a naval friend telling a Russian observer in Santiago, that the two branches of the Anglo-Saxon race were coming together, "and that together we can whip the world, Prince, we can whip the world!"

175   "extraordinary panic." To Robert J. Fleming, 5-21-00, in Morison, *Letters*, 2:1305. For a fuller discussion see Dyer, *TR and Race*, 100–101.

176   "last man in the world." Dyer, *TR and Race*, 101.

177   "Chinaman is kept out." "National Life and Character," in TR, *American Ideals*, 280.

177   "a new race, a new type." To Edward Grey, 12-18-06, in Morison, *Letters*, 5:529.

177   "most honorable of titles." TR, *American Ideals*, 28; TR, *Works*, 13:24–26; Dyer, *TR and Race*, 133.

179   "his merits as a man." To Albion Winegar Tourgée, 11-8-01, in Morison, *Letters*, 3:190–91.

21. Livy

180   "not *in* New York." Olivia Clemens's Guest Book; Willis, *Mark and Livy*, 262.

180   Guests at Riverdale. Paine, *MT: Biography*, 3:1152.

181   Subsisting more on nerves. Trombley, *MT in the Company of Women*, 83–84. The correspondent, writing to her husband in mid-July 1860, is Harriet Beecher Stowe's sister Isabella Hooker, for her health attending the Gleasons' hydropathic sanitarium in Elmira and rooming with young Olivia, then fourteen. Trombley here adjudges Livy's frequent and severe illnesses in adolescence and afterward to have been "almost certainly organic in nature," rather than psychosomatic or hysterical, as commentators looking back have sometimes charged (see, for example, Hill, *MT: God's Fool*, xxiv).

181   "at family worship." Ibid., 94.

181   "honored this anniversary alone." C. Clemens, *My Father*, 19.

182   "perfectly at rest in you." Quoted in Wecter, *Love Letters*, 120 (11-69).

182   Nook Farm. The Clemenses' near-idyllic Hartford surroundings—lovely setting, congenial friendships, appealing social routines—are described with great attractiveness in Andrews, *Nook Farm*.

183   "quite an ideal life." Smith and Gibson, *MT-Howells Letters*, 1:16.

183   "the loveliest person." Howells, *My Mark Twain*, 10. Our more skeptical age has produced a few less enraptured appraisals of Clemens's wife these several years after her death: in Brooks's *Ordeal of Mark Twain*, for instance, passim, and in Hill's *MT: God's Fool*, summing up at xxiv–xxv.

183   "sensitiveness and self-control." Salsbury, *Susy and MT*, 53.

185   "most noble example of woman." C. Clemens, *My Father*, 83, 84.

185 "women must be everything." Trombley, *MT in the Company of Women*, 59 (11-30-79).

185 "so very far short." Harris, *Courtship*, 135 (1-19-72).

186 "we glided back and forth." C. Clemens, *My Father*, 8.

186 "tremendous comforts." Olivia Clemens's journal, 6-8-85, in Salsbury, *Susy and MT*, 201.

186 "ten chapters in Elmira." MT, *MT to Mrs. Fairbanks*, 191.

187 "An' no *joy!*" MT, *Collected Tales 1852–1890*, 578, 582.

188 "no humor in it." Smith and Gibson, *MT-Howells Letters*, 1:22–23.

188 "whatever I touch." Paine, *MT: Biography*, 2:830.

188 "out of our lives forever." Autobiographical dictation, 4-17-08; quoted in Trombley, *MT in the Company of Women*, 155.

188 O Death in Life. Tennyson, "Tears, Idle Tears." Song from *The Princess* (1847). *The Poems of Tennyson* (3 vols., Berkeley, 1987), 2:232–33.

22. *Huckleberry Finn*

189 "A happy, happy home." K. Leary, *Lifetime with MT*, 73. The two citations that follow, into 190, are from the same source: 58–59 ("so sweet and true") and 84 ("laughing out loud").

190 "talking & *talking.*" Smith and Gibson, *MT-Howells Letters*, 1:26 (9-20-74).

190 "a number of dialects." MT, *Huckleberry Finn*, 620.

191 "You don't know about me." Ibid., 625.

191 "Tom Blankenship!" Webster, *MT, Business Man*, 265.

191 "ignorant, unwashed." Neider, *Autobiography of MT*, 68 (dictated 3-8-06).

191 "good citizen and greatly respected." Clemens may have been told this, but see explanatory notes in MT, *Autobiography* 1:609-10: "No evidence has been found that [Blankenship] went to Montana." Rather, he appears to have remained in Hannibal, been arrested frequently for stealing food, and died there of cholera in 1889.

191 "rotten glad of it." MT, *Huckleberry Finn*, 912. The seven citations that follow, through 194, are from the same source: 688–89 ("things of that kind"), 675 ("there'd be some fun"), 708 ("I did dream it"), 709 ("all safe en soun'"), 833 ("done me no harm"), 834 ("how good it was"), 834–35 ("and tore it up").

194– High-school students and *Huck Finn*. See Lorrie Moore's concurrence with
96   this view in "Send Huck Finn to College," *New York Times*, 1-15-2011.

196 "pernicious stuff." *New York World* on Mark Twain's new novel, under the headline: "Wit and Literary Ability Wasted on a Pitiable Exhibition of Irreverence and Vulgarity." Budd, *Our Mark Twain*, 109–10.

196 "best book we've had." Hemingway, *Green Hills*, 22. See Fishkin, *Lighting Out*, 111.

23. Roosevelt and the Philippines

198   "I's gwyne to *leave*." MT, *Huckleberry Finn*, 882.
198   "Whoosh! Dem's de ticket." "Tom Sawyer's Conspiracy." Blair, *Mark Twain's Hannibal*, 37.
199   "Don't you *dare*." K. Leary, *Lifetime with MT*, 84.
199   "noblest of the five races." Simkins, *Pitchfork Ben*, 396.
200   "the new world's surface." TR, *American Ideals*, 280.
200   "a nation of pioneers." "National Duties," delivered at the Minnesota State Fair, St. Paul, 9-2-01, in TR, *Letters and Speeches*, 767, 775, 776.
201   "enslave the world." Rydell, *All the World's a Fair*, 161.
202   "ten years and older." Karnow, *In Our Image*, 191. The two citations that follow ("growing hard-hearted" and "brainless monkeys") are from the same source, 154.
202–3 Waterboarding insurgents. See S. Miller, *Benevolent Assimilation*, 125 and passim.
203   "I walked away." Silbey, *War of Frontier and Empire*, 157.
204   "peace has been established." Speech at Arlington National Cemetery, 5-30-02. Quoted in Bradley, *Imperial Cruise*, 127.

24. Placating the South

205   "bitter against us." MT, "Comments on the Moro Massacre." Zwick, *MT's Weapons of Satire*, 170. The three citations that follow, through 206—("Christian butchers," "If I know President Roosevelt," and "in a hole like rats")—are from the same source.
208   "we can never mingle." Quoted in Beale, *TR and the Rise*, 240 (12-13-05).
208   "this great National highway." Griswold, *Work of Giants*, 144.
208   "utterly underdeveloped." Scheiner, "President TR and the Negro," 170.
209   "inferior to the whites." To Owen Wister, 4-27-06, in Morison, *Letters*, 5:226. The long communication, 221–30, contains a detailed statement of TR's political dealings with African-Americans and his views on race. He writes, "I do not know a white man of the South who is as good a man as Booker Washington" (227), and "I am not satisfied that I acted wisely in either the Booker Washington dinner or the Crum appointment, though each was absolutely justified from every proper standpoint save that of expediency" (227). On that page and into 228 TR provides the background for the actions he took regarding Indianola's postmistress, shutting down the mail service when town hoodlums drove Mrs. Cox from office while respectable white citizens looked on, deplored, and did nothing to intervene.
209   "not worthy to untie." DeVoto, *MT in Eruption*, 30.
209   "destiny of the race." "The Education of the Negro," address at Tuskegee Institute, 10-24-05. *American Problems*, in TR, *Works*, 16:354.

209   "industrial uplifting." Scheiner, "President TR and the Negro," 181.

210   "indulging in hysterics." To Henry Smith Pritchitt, 12-14-04, in Morison, *Letters*, 4:1068–71.

210   "still further reduced." Ibid., 1068.

210   Cockfight. MT, *Life on Mississippi*, 493. Pettit, *MT and the South*, discusses SLC's feelings in enlightening detail.

211   17 percent of lynchings. Newby, *Jim Crow's Defense*, 138.

211   "his inhuman crime." Wagenknecht, *Seven Worlds*, 89.

211   "very aged ones." "United States of Lyncherdom" in *Collected Tales, 1891–1910*, 480.

211   "cases of 'the usual crime.'" Ibid. Remaining citations in the paragraph are from the same source.

211   *"procure coal oil."* Ibid., 485.

212   "Other friends are silent." F. Kaplan, *Singular MT,* 585.

213   "Why always dwell on the evil" Wecter, *Love Letters*, 333.

OIL

25. The *Kanawha*

217   "Bring it back!" Wecter, *Love Letters*, 333.

218   "not all comedy." Neider, *Autobiography of MT*, 40.

218   "healthy as granite." Quoted in F. Kaplan, *Singular MT*, 591.

220   "holding his train." Howells to Thomas Bailey Aldrich, 12-8-02, in Smith and Gibson, *MT-Howells Letters*, 2:735.

220   "Goodness, who is there." Paine, *MT: Biography*, 3:1215.

220   Howells and Stoddard's "visit." Smith and Gibson, *MT-Howells Letters*, 2:763–64.

221   Clemens's reply. Ibid., 767–68.

222   "It is friends." L. Leary, *MT's Correspondence with H.H. Rogers*, 452. The citations that follow, into 224, are from the same source: 401 ("a berth for me," 7-3-99), 464 ("make him roar," 7-5-01), 482 ("go as Sundayschool Supt," 3-8?-02), 488 ("if you get stuck," 5-26-02).

225   "heroic measures." F. Kaplan, *Singular MT*, 596.

225   "saw Livy 5 minutes." MT notebook, 12-30-02, in Smith and Gibson, *MT-Howells Letters*, 2:759.

225   "why didn't you ever tell her?" Howells, *My Mark Twain*, 87.

26. Corporate America

228   "We will take your burdens." Sullivan, *Our Times*, 2:292. Chernow's *Titan* describes Rockefeller's life in full and absorbing detail.

231   "timekeepers of progress." McKinley's phrase. Leech, *In the Days of McKinley*, 584.

232 "as natural as the sun." Henry Adams, *Education*, 1033, 1032.

233 "swam far out." Quoted in F. Kaplan, *Singular MT*, 592.

27. Roosevelt as Reformer

235 "weakness of the weak." Gossett, *Race*, 159.

236 "benevolence of a stranger." Fishkin, *Lighting Out*, 101.

236 "one of the greatest lawyers." Ibid., 106.

237 "untrustworthy in every way." Kaneko Kentaro, "The Russo-Japanese War: Its Causes and Its Results," *International Quarterly* 10, no. 1 (1904), 53; cited in Bradley, *Imperial Cruise*, 205. Baron Kaneko, a contemporary of Roosevelt's at Harvard, was special envoy from Japan to Washington during the Russo-Japanese War; he was among those urging TR to persuade the Russians to enter into peace negotiations.

238 "wish I wasn't a reformer." Quoted in Hofstadter, *American Political Tradition*, 203.

239 "of all dangerous classes." Wagenknecht, *Seven Worlds*, 217 (1883).

241 "Chicago dynamiters." Quoted in Ginger, *Age of Excess*, 61.

242 "keeper of the brother." To Philander C. Knox, 11-10-04; TR, *Letters and Speeches*, 359.

28. The Gilded Age

243 "nothing in the collection plate." Martin, *Things I Remember*, 239. The description of the ball, with citations, is from this source, by Bradley-Martin's brother, who was in attendance. Of course, New York newspapers of the time covered the event thoroughly.

247 "reverence for the old." MT, *MT to Mrs. Fairbanks*, 174–75 (7-6-73).

247 "what amount of money." MT, *Letters*, 2:119 (12-2-67).

248 "the gladdest man." Salsbury, *Susy and MT*, 35.

249 "An inventor is a poet." To his sister, Pamela, from Buffalo, 6-12-70, in Webster, *Mark Twain, Business Man*, 114. The two citations that follow are from the same source: 172 ("world has got to buy them" 10-25-81) and 338 ("send a check," 11-10-85).

29. Bankruptcy

252 "papa and I were promonading." S. Clemens, *Papa*, 187.

253 "and, tear-blinded, passed." C. Clemens, *My Father*, 87–88.

253 "*that God damned house.*" Quoted in F. Kaplan, *Singular MT*, 603.

254 "great and genuine poet." Paine, *MT: Biography*, 2:903–4.

254 "I always believe him." Ibid., 2:956.

255   "about 1000 of those machines." Webster, *MT, Business Man*, 331 (7-28-85). The intricate, exasperating story of MT's descent into bankruptcy is the subject of Gold's book-length study *"Hatching Ruin."*

255   "speak out the big secret." Paine, *Letters*, 2:508 (1-5-89).

255   "Machine O.K." to MT in New York, 1-2-89, in J. Kaplan, *Mr. Clemens*, 292.

256   "Compositor marches alone." Paine, *MT: Biography*, 2:910.

256   "the work of six men." Ibid., 909.

256   "Esquimaux Girl's Romance," in Wecter, *Love Letters*, 267 (9-7-93).

256   "for lack of $8,000." Ibid., 270.

257   "friends when we parted." Neider, *Autobiography of MT*, 259.

258   Mark Twain told the press. The interview at Vancouver, which appeared in the *San Francisco Examiner* for 8-17-95 ("Mark Twain to Pay All"), is in Scharnhorst, *MT: The Complete Interviews*, 185–86.

258   "I have seen them do it." L. Leary, *MT's Correspondence with H.H. Rogers*, 90 (11-2-94).

259   "Look out for good news." Wecter, *Love Letters*, 293.

259   "our troubles are over!" Ibid. (1-15-94).

259   "what is the matter with it?" Paine, *MT: Biography*, 2:991.

259   "it was not practical." Ibid.

259   "like a thunder-clap." L. Leary, *MT's Correspondence with H.H. Rogers*, 108 (12-22-94).

260   "reading the creditors' letters." Paine, *Letters*, 2:654 (3-7-98).

260   "knocked the gloom out." Leary, *MT's Correspondence with H.H. Rogers*, 384 (1-3-99). Cf. from London, 1-4-97, after Susy's death: "You guessed rightly as to Xmas. It was a desolate time. It was the first, since our marriage, that the day came and went without mention. No presents were exchanged, and we studiously pretended to be unaware of the day." Ibid., 259.

260   "no hurt to my pride." Neider, *Autobiography of MT*, 259 (1909).

30. In the White House

261   "certain strong convictions." Dalton, *TR: A Strenuous Life*, 209.

261   "without nervous prostration." M. Howells, *Life in Letters*, 2:264 (3-14-09).

263   "more marked in the House." Lodge, *Selections*, 1:512 (12-3-01).

263   "bitter animosities." TR, *Works*, 15:81–83. Citations that follow, to 267, are from the same source: 84 ("symbol of government"), 86 ("band against the anarchist"), 95 ("present immigration laws"), 95–96 ("a stout heart, a good head"), 96 ("act sanely as . . . citizens"), 94 ("excluding Chinese laborers"), 110 ("more friendly relations with us"), 112 ("banditti and marauders"), 117 ("international duties" and "upbuilding the navy"), 114 ("prospects of success").

267– Roosevelt and conservation. Brinkley's *Wilderness Warrior* provides a
  68 comprehensive, engrossing account of Roosevelt as conservationist.

31. Trustbusting

269   "known as 'trusts.' " TR, *Works*, 15:90. Citations that follow, to the top
      of 273, are from the same source: 87 ("complex industrial develop-
      ment"), 88 ("rewards of success"), 91 ("work in harmony").
273   "we will not surrender." E. Morris, *Theodore Rex*, 133.
273   "interests of the laboring man." Ibid., 137
275   first such action. Earlier, in 1895, the Supreme Court had ruled, in the
      Knight case, that the federal government could not use the Sherman
      Anti-Trust Act of 1890 against a monopoly engaged in manufactur-
      ing—in this instance the refining of sugar—inasmuch as no crossing of
      state lines was involved. Thereafter, until TR's move against Northern
      Securities, the Sherman Act was invoked principally against unions,
      charged with restraining interstate commerce when their members
      struck. Trachtenberg's *The Incorporation of America* (originally 1982),
      Beatty's *Age of Betrayal* (2007), and Weinberg's *Taking on the Trust* (2008)
      are three readable studies that deal with the rise of corporate America.
275   "attack my other interests?" Bishop, *TR and His Times*, 1:184–85. Morris
      identifies Morgan's "man" as Francis Lynde Stetson, his personal at-
      torney. E. Morris, *Theodore Rex*, 600 (n. to p. 91).

32. Our Life Is Wrecked

278   "one of the most likable men." MT, *Autobiography*, 1:259 (1-10-06).
278   "the worst President." DeVoto, *MT in Eruption*, 34. The two citations
      that follow are from the same source: 25 ("do not despise him") and 29
      ("strong and outspoken praises").
279   "controvert some previous act." MT, *Autobiography*, 1:259. "I always
      enjoy his society," SLC writes here; "he is so hearty, so straightforward,
      outspoken, and so absolutely sincere." Such qualities are endearing in
      a private citizen, but the same impulses, according to this observer,
      "make of him a sufficiently queer president."
279   "not so fast." Quoted in Wagenknecht, *Seven Worlds*, 210.
279   "with incredible dispatch." MT, *Autobiography*, 1:259.
279   lowering the dignity of the office. DeVoto, *MT in Eruption*, 22.
279   "envy the hugged." Ibid., 12.
279   "the jelly McKinley." To Twichell, 6-24-05; quoted in Messent, *MT and
      Male Friendship*, 75.
279   "I took Panama." Abbott, *Impressions*, 67.

279   "insane in several ways." DeVoto, *MT in Eruption*, 8.

280   "also the most admired." Ibid., 34.

280   "anything I could do for you." Paine, *MT: Biography*, 2:981.

280   "to write a veritable history." L. Leary, *MT's Correspondence with H.H. Rogers*, 478 (12-26-01).

281   "hostility to the corporations." DeVoto, *MT in Eruption*, 97.

281   "Man with the Muck-rake." The passage occurs some twenty pages into the second part, alongside the marginal note, "The man with the Muck-rake expounded," p. 164 in the World's Classics edition of *The Pilgrim's Progress* (Oxford, 1984).

282   Livy "mostly very gay." Paine, *MT's Letters*, 2:741 (7-21-03).

283   Its terms *"guarantee* me." L. Leary, *MT's Correspondence with H. H. Rogers*, 540.

283   "always live at Florence." To his sister, Aurelia, 10-18-03; M. Howells, *Life in Letters*, 2:178.

284   "now she is at rest." To Twichell, 6-8-04, in Wecter, *Love Letters*, 348.

284   "Five times in 4 months." Ibid.

284   "chatting cheerfully." L. Leary, *MT's Correspondence with H. H. Rogers*, 571 (6-8-04).

284   "Our life is wrecked." Ibid., 569 (6-6-04).

284   "'I don't want to die.'" To Howells, 6-12-04, in Smith and Gibson, *MT-Howells Letters*, 349.

285   "down below & lonely." Wecter, *Love Letters*, 349.

285   "all ranks in life." To Thomas R. Lounsbury, 7-21-04, in ibid., 350.

285   "benediction & farewell." Ibid.

285   "it was my very best." Quoted in Trombley, *MT's Other Woman*, 42.

285   "capacity of suffering." Paine, *MT: Biography*, 3:1592.

285   took things "intensely hard." M. Howells, *Life in Letters*, 2:178.

CHILDREN

33. A Seventieth Birthday

289   "deep & honest curses." Wecter, *Love Letters*, 272 (9-21-93).

289   "looked for the last time." C. Clemens, *My Father*, 253.

290   "I said I hated him." Trombley, *MT's Other Woman*, 35–36.

291   "most grim and unhappy." Quoted in Hoffman, *Inventing MT*, 460.

292   "procession of remorses." To Twichell, 7-28-04, in Lystra, *Dangerous Intimacy*, 42.

292   "full of unworthy conduct." MT, *Letters*, 2:58 (6-7-67).

293   "My dear darling child." Quoted in Willis, *Mark and Livy*, 206 (4-19-93).

293   "two thousand incidents." Neider, *Autobiography of MT*, 224 (4-6-06).

293   "artist of uncommon power." Howells, *My Mark Twain*, 135, 139, 141, 143.

294   "sting or blush of shame." *St Louis Star*, 5-29-02; Scharnhorst, *MT: The Complete Interviews*, 412.

294   "the best we have." Paine, *MT's Letters*, 2:742–44. In this same year, 1903, Merwin, who had been born in Evanston, Illinois, in 1874, published *His Little World* and *Whip Hand: A Tale of the Pine Country*. He would continue writing novels and plays, some quite successful, until his death in 1936. See *A Chat about Samuel Merwin*, by Robert Cortes Holliday (in the public domain and available online).

295   "no words could be said." Paine, *MT's Letters*, 2:744.

296   "abiding and permanent value." TR's remarks were reprinted in the *New York Times* the following day, 12-6-05, and in a special illustrated supplement to *Harper's Weekly* of 12-23-05: *Mark Twain's Seventieth Birthday Record of a Dinner Given in His Honor* . . . See Smith and Gibson, *MT-Howell Letters*, 2:798–99; Wagenknecht, *Seven Worlds*, 63.

297   "the worm turned." Fatout, *MT Speaking*, 463 (12-5-05). The speech is given in its entirety here, at 462–67.

34. Susy

299   "lengthen the lives." The birthday tributes appear in *The Critic* for 9-28-85.

300   "no praise, no tribute." MT, *Autobiography*, 1:337.

300   "*has* got a temper." S. Clemens, *Papa*, 83–84. The three citations that follow are from the same source: 101 ("could listen to himself talk"), 110 ("Grandma released him"), 116 ("has told me the story").

301   "happy, happy home." K. Leary, *Lifetime with MT*, 73.

302   "in a happy heaven of excitement." Salsbury, *Susy and MT*, 189–90.

302   "looked brilliant and lovely!" K. Leary, *Lifetime with MT*, 30–31.

302   "enjoyed 'Huckelberry Finn.'" S. Clemens, *Papa*, 106-7.

303   "means a deep thinker." K. Leary, *Lifetime with MT*, 289.

303   "crawl on his hands and knees." Ibid., 72.

303   "never see her at her best." Salsbury, *Susy and MT*, 354.

303   "I can see her yet." MT, *Autobiography*, 1:580.

304   "the most interesting person." S. Clemens, *Papa*, 67.

304   "a rattle-brained girl." C. Clemens, *My Father*, 65 (Susy was born 3-19-72).

304   "frail, attractive, charming." Salsbury, *Susy and MT*, 281. The citations that follow, to the top of 306, are from the same source: 309 ("emotional, high-strung"), 283 ("*does* not, *can* not compare"), 351 ("a beautiful slender girl").

306   "waiting in the house." To Henry C. Robinson, 9-28-96, in Paine, *MT's Letters*, 2:636. The citations that end the chapter are from the same source, in a letter to Twichell of 1-19-97: 641 ("treasure in the bank") and 642 ("She sits solitary").

35. America at Home

308   "one of the great marriages." E. Morris, *Colonel Roosevelt*, 570.

310   "a visiting *Spirit*." SLC to Olivia Langdon, 1-6-69, in Wecter, *Love Letters*, 43.

310   "not grace her to know." To Will Bowen, 2-6-70, in MT, *MT's Letters to Will Bowen*, 20.

310   Knowledge was for men. See Welter, *Dimity Convictions*, 38 and passim, for an enlightening discussion of late-nineteenth-century domestic life in America.

311   "an inimical mimic." King, *Memories*, 174.

311   "'the rage of *living*.'" Salsbury, *Susy and MT*, 312.

311   "I hate that name!" King, *Memories*, 173-74.

311   "creating day or night." Salsbury, *Susy and MT*, 312.

312   "whether I am embarrassed." Ibid., 314.

312   "refreshing little naps." S. Clemens, *Papa*, 15. The citation appears in Neider's introduction, which provides the earliest account of the relationship. See also L. Morris, *Gender Play*, 11–20, for additional information on Louise Brownell, and, at 132, for a sensitive consideration of lesbianism as understood in the late nineteenth century: "There was as yet no clear notion in the 1890s of a fixed gender identity determined by the object of one's desire. A young woman could enter into a Boston marriage, and schoolgirls and college girls could develop 'smashes' on one another and have intimate romantic relationships, without such choices or activities constituting an 'identity' as we have come to know it in the twenty-first century."

313   "What shall I do if you do?" S. Clemens, *Papa*, 28 (Neider's introduction).

313   "such a congenial family." Harnsberger, *MT, Family Man*, 151.

314   "athletics nor good works." Quoted in S. J. Morris, *Edith*, 197.

314   only a moderately good time. Longworth, *Crowded Hours*, 47.

315   "Father doesn't care for me." Quoted in Cordery, *Alice*, 70 (1-27-03).

36. Bully Father

317   The Race Suicide Club. Despite its name, the club, which is described in Cordery, *Alice*, 77-78, sounds prim enough by our laxer social standards.

318   "greatest duty of womanhood." "The Woman and the Home," address to National Congress of Mothers, 3-13-05, in TR, *Works*, 16:165. Citations immediately following are from the same source.

320   "submissive and repentant." S. J. Morris, *Edith*, 141. Citations immediately following ("as gay as a butterfly," "it was absolutely useless," "if only he could have died") are from the same source, 141-43.

321   "one great comfort." To Corinne Roosevelt Robinson, 8-29-94, in TR, *Letters and Speeches*, 61.

322   "coyotes with the greyhounds." Kerr, *Bully Father*, 169 (4-20-05). Citations to the end of the chapter are from the same source: 171 ("the little prairie girl," 4-26-05, and "hard time in mathematics," 5-2-05); 221 ("ask . . . about Mark Twain," 10-1-07); 203–4 ("a great variety of books," 11-13-06); 123 ("found him a handful," 8-25-03); 131 ("they were in ambush," 10-19-03); 197–98 ("I know just what it is," 6-17-06); 136 ("scramble down Rock Creek," 11-15-03); 151 ("Mother walked behind," 5-28-04); 191–92 ("I love you very much," 4-1-06); 161 ("Don't get cast down").

37. President in His Own Right

324   "perpetuate myself in power." TR, *Autobiography*, 644. Citations that immediately follow are from the same source, 644–45.

325   "took Panama." Abbot, *Impressions*, 67.

325   "give away Eleanor." To Kermit, 3-20-05, in Kerr, *Bully Father*, 166.

325   "flamboyant President." MT, *Autobiography*, 1:462 (3-30-06).

326   "Have pity, sir." DeVoto, *MT in Eruption*, 11.

326   "a hereditary monarchy." Ibid., 3.

327   "through God's mercy." MT, *Autobiography*, 1:442 (3-26-06).

327   "hysterical, unbalanced." To William Allen White, 7-31-06, in Morison, *Letters*, 5:340–41.

328   Some unimaginable ass. DeVoto, *MT in Eruption*, 31.

328   "friction, race riot, butchery." Quoted in Lane, *Brownsville Affair*, 8.

328   "entertain race hatred." Weaver, *Brownsville*, 77.

328   "fling this firebrand." DeVoto, *MT in Eruption*, 31.

329   "look to you for relief." Quoted in Weaver, *Brownsville*, 75–76.

329   "wooden, stolid look." Lane, *Brownsville Affair*, 22.

329   "anxious to convict." DeVoto, *MT in Eruption*, 32.

330   "lend no assistance whatever." TR, *Works*, 15:352.

330   "my dear Mr. Washington." Lane, *Brownsville Affair*, 93 (8-3-07).

331   "honor of the American army." To Curtis Guild, 11-7-06, in TR, *Letters and Speeches*, 507.

38. Global Visions

332   "in his happiest vein." MT, *Autobiography*, 1:548.

333   "the mob, the mob." Clark, *Quarter Century*, 1:443–48. A longtime Democratic representative from Missouri, Champ (Beauchamp) Clark was present at the dinner; his memoir provides a vivid account of the clash. Foraker's version, in *Notes*, 2:249–57, includes a long descriptive letter

that the senator wrote to his son at the time, as well as press comment on the day after the exchange. See also Dunn, *Gridiron Nights*, 185.

333   "take orders from anybody." Clark, *Quarter Century*, 447.

334   "because they are men." Foraker, *Speech of . . . April 14, 1908*, 45.

335   "a little corn and oil." DeVoto, *MT in Eruption*, 69, 68.

335   "benevolent assimilation." Pres. McKinley's term. Gould, *Spanish-American War*, 115–16 (12-21-98).

335   "I congratulate you." MT, "Comments on the Moro Massacre," in Zwick, *MT's Weapons of Satire*, 168–78.

336   "the price of national honor." Naval War College Address ("Washington's Forgotten Maxims"), 6-2-97. TR, *Works*, 13:184.

337   "infernal little Cuban republic." To Henry White, 9-13-06; quoted in E. Morris, *Theodore Rex*, 456.

337   "to give you your Independence." Mrs. Campbell Dauncey, *An Englishwoman in the Philippines* (New York, 1906), 326. Quoted in ibid., 253.

338   800 permanent . . . bases . . . in foreign countries. Recent books critical of America's present worldwide imperial role include Judis's *The Folly of Empire* (2004), Johnson's *Dismantling the Empire* (2010), and Pfaff's *The Irony of Manifest Destiny* (2010).

339   "I wish it well." Paine, *MT's Notebook*, 372.

39. Bereft and Adrift

341   "'have I got to leave now?'" K. Leary, *Lifetime with MT*, 136. Powers, *Mark Twain*, describes Susy's pitiful last days fully and feelingly, 576–79.

342   "poor troubled head!" Wecter, *Love Letters*, 320 (8-19-96).

342   "the darkness universal." Ibid., 319.

342   "the release came." Ibid.

342   "call up a single instance." C. Clemens, *My Father*, 175. The two citations that follow are from the same source: 180 ("I hate Him for that") and 179 ("before anyone laughed").

344   "The Enchanted Sea-Wilderness." Tuckey, *Devil's Race-Track*, 28–38.

345   "death was everywhere." Ibid., 34.

345   "Which Was the Dream?" Tuckey, *Devil's Race-Track*, 39–79.

346   "she is a reality." Paine, *MT's Notebook*, 351.

346   "freed from clogging flesh." Ibid., 350.

346   "The Great Dark." Tuckey, *Devil's Race-Track*, 80–128.

347   "most magnificent imagination." C. Clemens, *My Father*, 102.

347   one amazing effort. "3,000 Years Among the Microbes, by a Microbe, B. b. Bkshp, With Notes Added by the Same Hand 7,000 Years Later, Translated from the Original Microbic by Mark Twain," in Tuckey, *Devil's Race-Track*, 161–281.

347   "man is himself a microbe." Ibid., 182.

40. Young People

348–51 Roosevelt's children. Renehan, *Lion's Pride*, relates the considerable roles TR's children played in the two world wars, as well as Quentin's brief life and his death in the first of those.

350 "a mighty bad master." Kerr, *Bully Father*, 126–27 (10-4-03).

351 "I am a fortunate person." MT, "What Ought He to Have Done?" *Christian Union*, 7-16-85; quoted in Salsbury, *Susy and MT*, 201.

351 "a lovely woman." Trombley, *MT's Other Woman*, 90.

352 "forlorn sea of banquets." Dictation, 4-17-08; quoted in Cooley, *MT's Aquarium*, xix.

353 "never on sea or shore." Lystra, *Dangerous Intimacy*, 58.

353 "all my days are hallowed." Quoted in Rafferty, "Lyon of St. Mark," 46.

353 "Oh, the richness of his nature." Lystra, *Dangerous Intimacy*, 52 (1-06). Citations that follow are from the same source: 58 ("full of repetitious adoration") and 101 ("nothing I love so much").

353 "she struck Katie." Did Miss Lyon fabricate this encounter to get rid of Jean and clear the way for her schemes to marry SLC? Scholars of Mark Twain's late years unsympathetic to Isabel Van Kleek Lyon point out that there were no corroborating witnesses at the event and that Clemens's daughter, before and after, was innocent of any such behavior. Those taking Miss Lyon's side insist that her private diary musings, although laden with sentimental romanticizing, are generally both accurate and candid, and that epileptics were regarded at the time as susceptible to violent actions before the onset of seizures. See on that last point Lystra, *Dangerous Intimacy*, 54.

354 "When would you like to begin?" Paine, *MT's Biography*, 3:1264.

354 "Dear Mrs. Saunders." S. Clemens, *Papa*; quoted in Neider's introduction, 40.

355 "must have companionship." Hoffmann, *MT in Paradise*, 69.

355 "hate his life." Hill, *MT: God's Fool*, 123 (3-24-06).

355 "*Aren't* you dear!" Cooley, *MT's Aquarium*, 21 (3-18-06). Citations that immediately follow are from the same source

356 "as long as you wish it." Ibid., 29 (5-06).

PEACE
41. Carnegie

359 "blude-reid wine." "Sir Patrick Spens," Percy's *Reliques* (1765), 1:71.

359 hard times came. The United States constituted the primary market for fine Scottish linens. During the Panic of 1837 and its aftermath luxury linens were among the first purchases that customers in America could forgo. Hand weavers in Scotland, including Will Carnegie, found them-

selves out of work, and their families suffering accordingly. See Nasaw, *Andrew Carnegie*, 19–21. Nasaw's detailed study is an informative pleasure throughout.

360 "mysterious golden visitor." Carnegie, *Gospel of Wealth*, xviii ("How I Served My Apprenticeship").

361 "holy name!" Ibid., xii.

364 the man who dies rich. Rich people were merely temporary stewards of their wealth. Thus, Carnegie favored substantial estate taxes, the more so because handing down wealth through families and generations was both antidemocratic and harmful to the character of beneficiaries.

365 "as modest a man." DeVoto, *MT in Eruption*, 36–37. The citations that follow to the end of the chapter are from the same source: 37 ("forever and ever and ever"), 38 ("a happy hummingbird" and "reverence for his moneybags"), 45 ("There is an American here"), 41 ("He sent for me").

42. America at Peace

368 "the calamitous conditions." DeVoto, *MT in Eruption*, 41.

368 "he knew that I knew." Ibid., 42.

368 "improved by almsgiving." "Wealth," in Carnegie, *Gospel of Wealth*, 17.

368 apprenticeship in industry. "How I Served My Apprenticeship," ibid., vii–xxii.

369– Homestead strike. Among the numerous recountings, the clash is de-
70 scribed concisely and stirringly in Brands, *Reckless Decade*, 130–42.

370 "real and lasting peace." Russian notes inviting representatives to participate were issued on 12-30-98 and 1-11-99.

371 "busy night and day." "Americanism and Imperialism," in Carnegie, *Gospel of Wealth*, 169.

372 "distinctively the best." Quoted in Brands, *Reckless Decade*, 294.

374 "a war to the death." To John Hay, 4-2-05; Beale, *TR and the Rise*, 439–40. The two citations that follow, into 375, are from the same source: 352 ("feel an increasing horror") and 339 ("rail at the manly virtues," 9-11-05).

375 "Who is to decide?" Wagenknecht, *Seven Worlds*, 163; Beale, *TR and the Rise*, 459–60.

43. Late Pleasures

377 "sword girt on thigh." TR, "Expansion and Peace," first published in the *Independent*, 12-21-99; reprinted in TR, *Strenuous Life*, 30.

377 "swords of a million men." Raymond Esthus, *Double Eagle and the Rising Sun* (Chapel Hill, 1988), 174; quoted in Bradley, *Imperial Cruise*, 305.

378   "revolution its death-blow." MT, *Autobiography*, 1:462–63.

378   "get pleasure out of them." To Thomas Bailey Aldrich, 10-2-06, in L. Leary, *MT's Correspondence with H. H. Rogers*, 617.

379   "jolly and darling." Isabel Lyon's Journal, 8-24-06; ibid., 616.

379   "a magnificent *coup*." Howells, *My Mark Twain*, 96.

380   "world and the devil." Hoffmann, *MT in Paradise*, 26.

381   "to see the naval review." "Mark Twain Is Going to Be a Buccaneer," in *New York American*, 4-23-07; Scharnhorst, *MT: The Complete Interviews*, 583–84.

382   "grimy sons of labor." Paine, *MT's Biography*, 3:1382.

382   "greatest American writer." *Westminster Gazette*, 6-18-07; Scharnhorst, *MT: The Complete Interviews*, 612.

383   "amiable and charming sir." Paine, *MT's Biography*, 3:1394.

383   "I have changed my mind." "Twain Postpones Funeral," *New York Times*, 7-13-07. Scharnhorst, *MT: The Complete Interviews*, 837.

44. TR Steps Down

385   "a straitjacket cunningly fashioned." TR, *Autobiography*, 643.

385   "malefactors of great wealth." At Pilgrim Memorial Monument, Provincetown, Massachusetts, 8-20-07; TR, *Works*, 16:84.

385   "most dangerous of all classes." E. Morris, *Rise of TR*, 177.

386   "crimes by the well off." To S. S. McClure, 10-4-05; TR, *Letters and Speeches*, 420.

386   "so well fitted to be President." Pringle, *Life and Times of William Howard Taft*, 2:356.

386   "accept another nomination." TR, *Autobiography*, 646.

386   "dexterity and sincerity." Norman Hapgood in *Collier's Weekly*, 7-11-08, as quoted by MT in autobiographical dictation of 7-14-08. DeVoto, *MT in Eruption*, 25–26. Citations that follow, through 388, are from the same source: 28 ("example for the other burglars"), 20–21 ("measurelessly impossible"), 17 ("all for advertisement"), 18 ("most formidable disaster"), 28–29 ("always vaporing"), 17 ("waiting in an ague"), 20 ("tunneled so many subways"). An additional reason for keeping his criticism of TR out of the public prints arose from an earlier request that MT made on Howells's behalf, to which TR had responded promptly and favorably, the petitioner no doubt recalling that kindness as well as presidential instructions to pass the grieving Clemenses undelayed through New York customs after Livy's death in 1904.

391   "answer to my critics." Butt, *Letters*, 354 (2-23-09).

391   "eatables, drinkables." L. Leary, *MT's Correspondence with H. H. Rogers*, 659–60 (3-4-09).

391   "went out of office as pleased." Wagenknecht, *Seven Worlds*, 190.

392   "it gave us a thrill." Longworth, *Crowded Hours*, 167.

45. Jean

394   next thirteen navies. Speech by Robert M. Gates, Secretary of Defense, at the Naval War College in Newport, 4-17-2009. Available online.

394   "I haven't had a real home." To Mrs. H. H. Rogers, 8-6-08, in L. Leary, *MT's Correspondence with H. H. Rogers*, 650. The two citations that follow are from the same letter, same page.

396   "come and make me a visit?" Quick, *Enchantment*, 38. The three citations that immediately follow are from the same source: 62 ("with scarcely a pause"), 79 ("nothing to live for after that"), 114 ("no rules for little girls").

397   "I collect pets." Autobiographical dictation, 2-12-08. Quoted in Cooley, *MT's Aquarium*, xvii.

397   "chief occupation and delight." Autobiographical dictation, 4-17-08, in ibid., ix.

397   "appointing you to membership." Quick, *Enchantment*, 165.

397   "the Official Legal Staff." "Rules & Regulations" governing the club as written by Clemens appear in Cooley, *MT's Aquarium*, 191–95.

397   "never met any of the other members." Quick, *Enchantment*, 186.

399   Books and articles have been written. See, for instance, the generally wary portrayal of Miss Lyon in Lystra, *Dangerous Intimacy*. More sympathetic treatments appear in Trombley, *MT's Other Woman*; Rafferty, "Lyon of St. Mark"; and Hill, *MT: God's Fool*.

399   "a sneak, a humbug, a traitor." Quoted in J. Kaplan, *Mr. Clemens*, 386.

400   "got a bad knock." L. Leary, *MT's Correspondence with H. H. Rogers*, 430 (from London, 2-5-00).

400   epileptic "and shouldn't marry." Quoted in Hill, *MT: God's Fool*, 148.

400   "everything that Miss Lyon isn't." To Clara, 7-18-09, in Lystra, *Dangerous Intimacy*, 181.

401   "out of sorts physically." *New York Sun*, 12-21-09; Scharnhorst, *MT: The Complete Interviews*, 692.

402   "flushed with splendid health." "Death of Jean," in Neider, *Autobiography of MT*, 371. The document is reprinted in its entirety as chapter 79, 371–80.

46. Funerals

403   "I heard the door open." "Death of Jean," in Neider, *Autobiography of MT*, 371, 373. Citations immediately following are from the same source.

404   "the pretty buckle." K. Leary, *Lifetime with MT*, 322.

404   "lie by her mother's side." "Death of Jean," in Neider, *Autobiography of MT*, 379.

404   "that I shall die." Smith and Gibson, *MT-Howells Letters*, 2:802 (2-28-06).

405   "at my time of life." Paine, *MT's Biography*, 3:1549.

405   "I have had about enough." Ibid., 1337.

405   "as close to me as a brother." *Boston Herald*, 5-20-09; Scharnhorst, *MT: The Complete Interviews*, 678.

406   "under the ground now." Paine, *MT's Biography*, 3:1492.

406   "I always envy the dead." Ibid., 3:1549.

406   "funeral has begun." "Death of Jean," in Neider, *Autobiography of MT*, 379.

407   "has taken 63 years." To Frances Nunnally, 7-15-09; Cooley, *MT's Aquarium*, 261–62.

407   "could not be troubled any more." Paine, *MT's Biography*, 3:1554.

407   "The joy of it never stales." Wallace, *MT and the Happy Island*, 138–39.

407   "I'd druther stay here." Ibid.

407   "My health is blemishless." L. Leary, *MT's Letters to Mary*, 133 (2-21-10, from Hamilton, signed "with all the love permissible by the statutes. Affectionately, SL. Clemens").

408   "he was much thinner." Paine, *MT's Biography*, 3:1564. The citations immediately following are from the same source: 1570 ("impossible for him to lie down"), 1571 ("I can't help it"), 1573 ("physicians, and news-gatherers").

409   Clara's pregnancy. Trombley, in *MT's Other Woman*, 224–33, assembles what evidence survives to indicate that Clara was having an affair with her accompanist, Charles Wark, a married man, and that the wedding with Gabrilowitsch was rushed forward to avoid scandal. See also Shelden, *MT: Man in White*, 261–65 and passim.

409   "you did not come to us." Quick, *Enchantment*, 215 (3-10-10).

409   "shed bitter tears." Ibid., 217.

410   "silver-haired Mark Twain." Longworth, *Crowded Hours*, 43.

410   "It was an impressive sight." Ibid., 177.

47. Bull Moose

411   TR's New York reception. E. Morris, *Colonel Roosevelt*, 82–87. This, the third volume of Edmund Morris's monumental biography of TR, covers the post-presidential years virtually month by month in lively detail. Patricia O'Toole's fine *When Trumpets Call* considers the same years from, inevitably, a different vantage point. Cooper's *The Warrior and the Priest* describes the period by focusing on TR's vexed relations with Woodrow Wilson.

411   nine lions, thirteen rhinos, 3,000 skins, and 13,000 specimens. The statistics are from Brands, *TR*, 652, and S. J. Morris, *Edith*, 353.

412   "utterly commonplace leader." To Arthur Hamilton Lee, 8-16-10, in Morison, *Letters*, 7:112.

413   "only the fruit of labor." TR, "The New Nationalism," in TR, *Letters and Speeches*, 801. Citations that immediately follow are from this remarkable speech given at Osawatomie, Kansas, on 8-31-10.

414   his hat was in the ring. Pringle, *Theodore Roosevelt*, 556.

415   "a Waterloo or a Bull Run." To Kermit, 11-5-12; quoted in Brands, *TR*, 725.

416   TR and River of Doubt. The adventure is retold compellingly in Millard's *River of Doubt*. Firsthand accounts include Roosevelt's own *Through the Brazilian Wilderness* (New York, 1914) and Kermit Roosevelt's *The Long Trail* (New York, 1921), in which see 74 ff for the "particularly black night" when his father almost died.

417   "too proud to fight." "Address to Newly Naturalized Citizens," in Link, *Papers of Woodrow Wilson*, 33:149 (5-10-15).

417   egregious epithets. These appear in letters to Lodge, 2-20-17, in Morison, *Letters*, 8:1156, and to Kermit (3-1-17, 9-16-17), as quoted in Brands, *TR*, 788, 776.

418   "finer or more gallant fashion." TR to Kermit, 7-21-18. Quoted in Brands, *TR*, 800.

418   "the same Great Adventure." TR, *Works*, 19:243.

418   "proud of his four sons." To R. Derby (Ethel's husband, TR's son-in-law), 7-1-18; quoted in Brands, *TR*, 793.

419   "he could not hear." Edith Roosevelt to son Kermit, 1-12-19. S J. Morris, *Edith*, 433.

419   Cause of TR's death. Wagenknecht, *Seven Worlds*, 30.

419   Taft at TR's graveside. See S. J. Morris, *Edith*, 436–37. For Taft's feelings about TR then and afterward, Pringle, *Life and Times of William Howard Taft*, 2:913.

48. Afterward

420   "have any place in history." To William Allen White, 11-28-06, in TR, *Letters and Speeches*, 514.

421   "a victory for law, order." Roosevelt, *Strenuous Life*, 32.

421   "our getting into war." Ibid., 36.

422   "death of Theodore Roosevelt." Link, *Papers of Woodrow Wilson*, 53:635 (1-17-19).

423   like windy Polonius. Hofstadter makes the comparison with Polonius in his stimulating if by no means entirely sympathetic essay on Roosevelt in *American Political Tradition*, 203-33.

423   the Roosevelt children. Renehan, *Lion's Pride*, passim.

424   skin Mark Twain alive. Smith and Gibson, *MT-Howells Letters*, 2:743.

426   our Achilles' heel. "The Philippines form our heel of Achilles." To Taft, 8-21-07, in Morison, *Letters*, 5:762.

427   Roosevelt's own stark image. To William Allen White, 11-28-06, in TR, *Letters and Speeches*, 514.

Works Cited

Abbot, Lawrence. *Impressions of Theodore Roosevelt*, Garden City, N.Y., 1919.

Adams, Henry. *The Education of Henry Adams*. In *Henry Adams: Novels, Mont Saint Michel, The Education*. Library of America. New York, 1983.

——. *Letters 1892–1918*. Worthington C. Ford, ed. Boston, 1938.

Andrews, Kenneth R. *Nook Farm: Mark Twain's Hartford Circle*. Cambridge, Mass., 1950.

Beale, Howard K. *Theodore Roosevelt and the Rise of America to World Power*. Baltimore, 1956.

Beatty, Jack. *Age of Betrayal: The Triumph of Money in America, 1865–1900*. New York, 2007.

Billington, Ray Allen. *Frederick Jackson Turner: Historian, Scholar, Teacher*. New York, 1973.

Bishop, Joseph Bucklin. *Theodore Roosevelt and His Times, Shown in His Own Letters*. 2 vols. New York, 1920.

Blair, Walter, ed. *Mark Twain's Hannibal, Huck & Tom*. Berkeley, 1969.

Bogue, Allan G. *Frederick Jackson Turner: Strange Roads Going Down*. Norman, Okla., 1998.

Bradley, James. *The Imperial Cruise: A Secret History of Empire and War*. New York, 2009.

Brands, H. W. *TR: The Last Romantic*. New York, 1997.

——. *The Reckless Decade: America in the 1890s*. New York, 1995.

Brinkley, Douglas. *The Wilderness Warrior: Theodore Roosevelt and the Crusade for America*. New York, 2009.

Brooks, Van Wyck. *The Ordeal of Mark Twain*. New York, 1933.

Bryan, William Jennings. *The First Battle: A Story of the Campaign of 1896*. Chicago, 1896.

Budd, Louis J. *Mark Twain: Social Philosopher*. Bloomington, Ind., 1962.

——. *Our Mark Twain: The Making of His Public Personality*. Philadelphia, 1983.

Butt, Archibald. *The Letters of Archie Butt, Personal Aide to President Roosevelt*. Lawrence F. Abbott, ed. Garden City, N.Y., 1924.

Carnegie, Andrew. *The Gospel of Wealth and Other Timely Essays*. New York, 1901.

Chernow, Ron. *Titan: The Life of John D. Rockefeller, Sr.* New York, 1998.

Clark, Champ [James Beauchamp]. *My Quarter Century of American Politics*. 2 vols. New York, 1920.

Clemens, Clara. *My Father Mark Twain*. New York, 1931.

Clemens, Susy. *Papa: An Intimate Biography of Mark Twain by His Daughter, Thirteen*. Charles Neider, ed. Garden City, N.Y., 1985.

Cooley, John. *Mark Twain's Aquarium: The Samuel Clemens Angelfish Correspondence, 1905–1910*. Athens, Ga., 1991.

Cooper, John Milton, Jr. *The Warrior and the Priest: Woodrow Wilson and Theodore Roosevelt*. Cambridge, Mass., 1983.

Cordery, Stacy A. *Alice: Alice Roosevelt Longworth, from White House Princess to Washington Power Broker*. New York, 2007.

Cowles, Anna Roosevelt. *Letters from Theodore Roosevelt to Anna Roosevelt Cowles, 1870–1918*. New York, 1924.

Dalton, Kathleen. *Theodore Roosevelt: A Strenuous Life*. New York, 2002.

DeVoto, Bernard, ed. *Mark Twain in Eruption*: *Hitherto Unpublished Pages about Men and Events*. New York, 1940.

Dolmetsch, Carl. *"Our Famous Guest"*: *Mark Twain in Vienna*. Athens, Ga., 1992.

Dunn, Arthur Wallace. *Gridiron Nights: Humorous and Satirical Views of Politics and Statesmen as Presented by the Famous Dining Club*. New York, 1915.

Dyer, Thomas G. *Theodore Roosevelt and the Idea of Race*. Baton Rouge, 1980.

Fatout, Paul. *Mark Twain on the Lecture Circuit*. New York, 1962.

——, ed. *Mark Twain Speaking*. Iowa City, 1976.

Fishkin, Shelley Fisher. *Lighting Out for the Territory: Reflections on Mark Twain and American Culture*. New York, 1997.

Foner, Philip. *The Spanish-Cuban-American War and the Birth of American Imperialism, 1895–1902*. 2 vols. New York, 1972.

Foraker, Joseph Benson. *Notes on a Busy Life*. 2 vols. Cincinnati, 1916.

——. *Speech of Hon. Joseph B. Foraker of Ohio in the Senate of the United States, April 14, 1908*. Washington, D.C., 1908 (available online; search "Black Battalion Foraker").

Frear, Walter Francis. *Mark Twain in Hawaii*. Chicago, 1947.

Gatewood, William B., Jr. *Black Americans and the White Man's Burden*. Urbana, Ill., 1975.

Gibson, William M. "Mark Twain and Howells: Anti-Imperialists." *The New England Quarterly* 20 (1947), 435–70.

Ginger, Ray. *Age of Excess: The United States from 1877 to 1914*. New York, 1965.

Gold, Charles H. *"Hatching Ruin," or Mark Twain's Road to Bankruptcy*. Columbia, Mo., 2003.

Gossett, Thomas F. *Race: The History of an Idea in America*. Dallas, 1963.

Gould, Lewis L. *The Spanish-American War and President McKinley*. Lawrence, Kans., 1980.

Grantham, Dewey W., Jr. "Dinner at the White House: Theodore Roosevelt, Booker T. Washington, and the South." *Tennessee Historical Quarterly* 128 (June 1958), 112–30.

Griswold, Wesley S. *A Work of Giants: Building the First Transcontinental Railroad.* New York, 1962.

Hagedorn, Hermann. *The Roosevelt Family of Sagamore Hill.* New York, 1954.

Hall, Tom. *The Fun and Fighting of the Rough Riders.* New York, 1899.

Harlan, Louis R. *Booker T. Washington: The Making of a Black Leader: 1856–1901.* New York, 1972.

——. *Booker T. Washington: The Wizard of Tuskegee: 1901–1915.* New York, 1983.

Harnsberger, Caroline Thomas. *Mark Twain, Family Man.* New York, 1960.

Harris, Susan K. *The Courtship of Olivia Langdon and Mark Twain.* New York, 1996.

Hay, John. *Letters of John Hay and Extracts from Diary.* 3 vols. Henry Adams and Clara Hay, eds. Printed but not published. Washington, D.C., 1908.

Hemingway, Ernest. *Green Hills of Africa.* New York, 1935.

Hill, Hamlin. *Mark Twain: God's Fool.* New York, 1973.

——. *Mark Twain and Elisha Bliss.* Columbia, Mo., 1964.

Hoffman, Andrew. *Inventing Mark Twain: The Lives of Samuel Langhorne Clemens.* New York, 1997.

Hoffmann, Donald. *Mark Twain in Paradise: His Voyages to Bermuda.* Columbia, Mo., 2006.

Hofstadter, Richard. *The American Political Tradition and the Men Who Made It.* New York, 1948.

Howells, Mildred. *Life in Letters of William Dean Howells.* 2 vols. Garden City, N.Y., 1928.

Howells, William Dean. *My Mark Twain: Reminiscences and Criticisms.* New York, 1910.

Johnson, Chalmers. *Dismantling the Empire: America's Last Best Hope.* New York, 2010.

Judis, John. *The Folly of Empire: What George W. Bush Could Learn from Theodore Roosevelt and Woodrow Wilson.* New York, 2004.

Kantrowitz, Stephen. *Ben Tillman & the Reconstruction of White Supremacy.* Chapel Hill, 2000.

Kaplan, Fred. *The Singular Mark Twain.* New York, 2003.

Kaplan, Justin. *Mr. Clemens and Mark Twain.* New York, 1966.

Karnow, Stanley H. *In Our Image: America's Empire in the Philippines.* New York, 1989.

Kazin, Michael. *A Godly Hero: The Life of William Jennings Bryan.* New York, 2006.

Kerr, Joan Paterson, ed. *A Bully Father: Theodore Roosevelt's Letters to His Children.* New York, 1995. An introduction, illustrations, and commentary accompany this reprinting of *Theodore Roosevelt's Letters to His Children,* which was first published posthumously in 1919, the year of the Colonel's death.

King, Grace. *Memories of a Southern Woman of Letters.* New York, 1932.

Kohlsaat, H. H. *From McKinley to Harding: Personal Recollections of Our Presidents.* New York, 1923.

Lane, Ann J. *The Brownsville Affair: National Crisis and Black Reaction.* Port Washington, N.Y., 1971.

Leary, Katy. *A Lifetime with Mark Twain: The Memories of Katy Leary, for Thirty Years His Faithful and Devoted Servant.* Transcribed by Mary Lawton. New York, 1925.

Leary, Lewis, ed. *Mark Twain's Correspondence with Henry Huttleston Rogers, 1893–1909.* Berkeley, 1969.

——. *Mark Twain's Letters to Mary.* New York, 1961.

Leech, Margaret. *In the Days of McKinley.* New York, 1959.

Link, Arthur S., et al., eds. *The Papers of Woodrow Wilson.* 69 vols. Princeton, 1966–1994.

Lodge, Henry Cabot. *Selections from the Correspondence of Theodore Roosevelt and Henry Cabot Lodge, 1884-1918.* 2 vols. New York, 1925.

Longworth, Alice Roosevelt. *Crowded Hours, Reminiscences.* New York, 1933.

Loving, Jerome. *Mark Twain: The Adventures of Samuel L. Clemens.* Berkeley, 2010.

Lynn, Kenneth. *Mark Twain and Southwestern Humor.* Boston, 1959.

Lystra, Karen. *Dangerous Intimacy: The Untold Story of Mark Twain's Final Years.* Berkeley, 2004.

Macnaughton, William R. *Mark Twain's Last Years as a Writer.* Columbia, Mo., 1979.

Mark Twain. *Adventures of Huckleberry Finn.* In *Mississippi Writings*, Library of America. New York, 1982.

——. *Autobiography of Mark Twain.* Vol. 1. Harriet Elinor Smith, ed. Berkeley, 2010.

——. *Collected Tales, Sketches, Speeches, & Essays, 1852–1890.* Library of America. New York, 1992.

——. *Collected Tales, Sketches, Speeches, & Essays, 1891–1910.* Library of America. New York, 1992.

——. *Huck Finn and Tom Sawyer Among the Indians and Other Unfinished Stories.* Dahlia Armon and Walter Blair, eds. Berkeley, 1989.

——. *Letters to His Publishers, 1867–1894.* Hamlin Hill, ed. Berkeley, 1967.

——. *Letters, Volume I: 1853–1866.* Edgar Marquess Branch et al., eds. Berkeley, 1988.

——. *Letters, Volume II: 1867–1868.* Harriet Elinor Smith et al., eds. Berkeley, 1990.

——. *Letters, Volume III: 1869.* Victor Fischer and Michael B. Frank, eds. Berkeley, 1992.

——. *Life on the Mississippi.* In *Mississippi Writings*, Library of America. New York, 1982.

——. *Mark Twain's Letters to Will Bowen: "My First, & Oldest & Dearest Friend."* Theodore Hornberger, ed. Austin, 1941.

——. *Mark Twain to Mrs. Fairbanks.* Dixon Wecter, ed. San Marino, Calif., 1949.

——. *Notebooks & Journals, Volume I (1855–1873).* Frederick Anderson et al., eds. Berkeley, 1975.

——. *Roughing It.* In *The Innocents Abroad. Roughing It.* Library of America. New York, 1984.

Martin, Frederick Townsend. *Things I Remember.* London, 1913 (reprint, New York, 1975).

McCullouch, David. *Mornings on Horseback.* New York, 1981.

McKeithan, Daniel Morley, ed. *Traveling with the Innocents Abroad: Mark Twain's Original Reports from Europe and the Holy Land.* Norman, Okla., 1958.

Messent, Peter. *Mark Twain and Male Friendship: The Twichell, Howells, and Rogers Friendships.* New York, 2009.

Millard, Candice. *The River of Doubt: Theodore Roosevelt's Darkest Journey.* New York, 2005.

Miller, Nathan. *Theodore Roosevelt: A Life.* New York, 1992.

Miller, Stuart Creighton. *Benevolent Assimilation: The American Conquest of the Philippines, 1899–1903.* New Haven, 1982.

Morison, Elting, et al. *The Letters of Theodore Roosevelt.* 8 vols. Cambridge, Mass., 1951–54.

Morris, Edmund. *Colonel Roosevelt.* New York, 2010.

——. *The Rise of Theodore Roosevelt.* Revised Edition. New York, 2001.

——. *Theodore Rex.* New York, 2002.

Morris, Linda A. *Gender Play in Mark Twain: Cross-Dressing and Transgression.* Columbia, Mo., 2007.

Morris, Sylvia Jukes. *Edith Kermit Roosevelt: Portrait of a First Lady.* New York, 1980.

Nasaw, David. *Andrew Carnegie.* New York, 2006.

Neider, Charles, ed. *The Autobiography of Mark Twain, Including Chapters Now Published for the First Time.* New York, 1959.

Newby, Idus A. *Jim Crow's Defense: Anti-Negro Thought in America, 1900–1930.* Baton Rouge, 1965.

O'Toole, Patricia. *When Trumpets Call: Theodore Roosevelt after the White House.* New York, 2005.

Paine, Albert Bigelow. *Mark Twain: A Biography.* 3 vols. New York, 1912.

——, ed. *Mark Twain's Autobiography.* 2 vols. New York, 1924.

——, ed. *Mark Twain's Letters,* 2 vols. New York, 1917.

——, ed. *Mark Twain's Notebook: Prepared for Publication with Comments by Albert Bigelow Paine.* New York, 1935.

Perry, Ralph Barton. *The Thought and Character of William James*. Cambridge, Mass., 1948.

Pettit, Arthur G. *Mark Twain and the South*. Lexington, Ky., 1974.

Pfaff, William. *The Irony of Manifest Destiny: The Tragedy of America's Foreign Policy*. New York, 2010.

Powers, Ron. *Mark Twain: A Life*. New York, 2005.

Pringle, Henry F. *The Life and Times of William Howard Taft*. 2 vols. New York, 1939.

——. *Theodore Roosevelt: A Biography*. New York, 1931.

Quick, Dorothy. *Enchantment: A Little Girl's Friendship with Mark Twain*. Norman, Okla., 1961.

Rafferty, Jennifer L. "'The Lyon of St. Mark': A Reconsideration of Isabel Lyon's Relationship to Mark Twain." *Mark Twain Journal* (Fall 1996), 43–55.

The Record of the Celebration of the Two Hundredth Anniversary of the Founding of Yale College, Held at Yale University, in New Haven, Connecticut, October the Twentieth to October the Twenty-Third, A. D. Nineteen Hundred and One. New Haven, 1902.

Renehan, Edward J., Jr. *The Lion's Pride: Theodore Roosevelt and His Family in Peace and War*. New York, 1998.

Robinson, Corinne Roosevelt. *My Brother, Theodore Roosevelt*. New York, 1921.

Roosevelt, Theodore. *American Ideals*. New York, 1920.

——. *An Autobiography*. In *The Rough Riders* and *An Autobiography*. The Library of America. New York, 2004.

——. *California Addresses*. San Francisco, 1903.

——. *Diaries of Boyhood and Youth*. New York, 1928.

——. *Hunting Trips of a Ranchman: Sketches of Sport on the Northern Cattle Plains*. New York, 1885.

——. *Letters and Speeches*. The Library of America. New York, 2004.

——. *The Rough Riders*. In *The Rough Riders* and *An Autobiography*. The Library of America, New York, 2004.

——. *The Strenuous Life: Essays and Addresses*. New York, 1900.

——. *The Wilderness Hunter: An Account of the Big Game of the United States and Its Chase with Horse, Hound, and Rifle*. New York, 1893.

——. *The Works of Theodore Roosevelt*. National Edition. Hermann Hagedorn, ed. 20 vols. New York, 1926.

Rydell, Robert W. *All The World's a Fair: Visions of Empire at American International Expositions, 1876–1916*. Chicago, 1984.

Salsbury, Edith Colgate, compiler. *Susy and Mark Twain: Family Dialogues*. New York, 1965.

Sanborn, Margaret. *Mark Twain: The Bachelor Years*. New York, 1990.

Scharnhorst, Gary, ed. *Mark Twain: The Complete Interviews*. Tuscaloosa, Ala., 2006.

Scheiner, Seth M. "President Theodore Roosevelt and the Negro, 1901–1908." *The Journal of Negro History*, 47, no. 3, 169–82.

Shelden, Michael. *Mark Twain, Man in White: The Grand Adventure of His Final Years*. New York, 2010.

Silbey, David J. *A War of Frontier and Empire: The Philippine-American War, 1899–1902*. New York, 2007.

Simkins, Francis Butler. *Pitchfork Ben Tillman, South Carolinian*. Baton Rouge, 1944.

Smith, Henry Nash, ed. *Mark Twain of the Enterprise: Newspaper Articles and Other Documents, 1862–1864*. Berkeley, 1957.

Smith, Henry Nash, and William M. Gibson, eds. *Mark Twain–Howells Letters: The Correspondence of Samuel L. Clemens and William D. Howells*. 2 vols. Cambridge, Mass., 1960.

Steinbrink, Jeffrey. *Getting to Be Mark Twain*. Berkeley, 1991.

Sullivan, Mark. *Our Times: The United States 1900–1925*. Volume 1: *The Turn of the Century*. New York, 1926. Volume 2: *America Finding Herself*. New York, 1927. Volume 3: *Pre-War America*. New York, 1930.

Thomas, Evan. *The War Lovers: Roosevelt, Lodge, Hearst, and the Rush to Empire, 1898*. New York, 2010.

Trachtenberg, Alan. *The Incorporation of America: Culture and Society in the Gilded Age*. 25th anniversary edition. New York, 2007.

Trombley, Laura Skandera. *Mark Twain in the Company of Women*. Philadelphia, 1994.

——. *Mark Twain's Other Woman: The Hidden Story of His Final Years*. New York, 2010.

Tuckey, John S., ed. *The Devil's Race-Track: Mark Twain's Great Dark Writings*. Berkeley, 1966.

Turner, Frederick Jackson. *The Early Writings of Frederick Jackson Turner*. Fulmer Mood, ed. Madison, Wisc., 1938.

Twain, Mark. See Mark Twain.

Wagenknecht, Edward. *American Profile 1900–1909*. Amherst, Mass., 1982.

——. *The Seven Worlds of Theodore Roosevelt*. New York, 1958.

Walker, Franklin, and G. Ezra Dane. *Mark Twain's Travels with Mr. Brown*. New York, 1940.

Wallace, Elizabeth. *Mark Twain and the Happy Island*. Chicago, 1913.

Washington, Booker T. *My Larger Education: Being Chapters from My Experience*. New York, 1911.

——. *Up from Slavery*. New York, 1902. Facsimile in *Uncle Tom or Negro? African Americans Reflect on Booker T. Washington and* Up from Slavery *One Hundred Years Later*. Rebecca Carroll, ed. New York, 2006.

Weaver, John D. *The Brownsville Raid*. New York, 1970.

Webster, Samuel Charles. *Mark Twain, Business Man*. Boston, 1946.

Wecter, Dixon, ed. *The Love Letters of Mark Twain*. New York, 1949.

——. *Sam Clemens of Hannibal*. Boston, 1952.

Weinberg, Steve. *Taking on the Trust: The Epic Battle of Ida Tarbell and John D. Rockefeller*. New York, 2008.

Welter, Barbara. *Dimity Convictions: The American Woman in the Nineteenth Century*. Athens, Ohio, 1976.

Williams, Wayne C. *William Jennings Bryan*. New York, 1936.

Willis, Resa. *Mark and Livy: The Love Story of Mark Twain and the Woman Who Almost Tamed Him*. New York, 1992.

Zwick, Jim. *Confronting Imperialism: Essays on Mark Twain and the Anti-Imperialist League*. West Conshohocken, Penn., 2007.

——. *Mark Twain's Weapons of Satire: Anti-Imperialist Writings on the Philippine-American War*. Syracuse, N.Y., 1992.

Index

Progressive Platform. *See* Bull-Moose
(Progressive) Platform
Promontory Summit (Utah), 91
Puerto Rico, 30, 37, 43, 129, 174
Pullman Strike, 241
Pure Food and Drug Act, 327, 385,
390

Quaker City, 98, 101–3, 169, 181–82,
249, 380
Quarry Farm, 186–87, 189, 282–83,
313
Quick, Dorothy: and angelfish,
397; in Bermuda, 409; learns of
Clemens's death, 409; meets Mark
Twain, 396

race: and Anglo-Saxons, 200; and
Aryan history, 200; and black
"inferiority," 199; classifications
of, 155; Clemens's evolving views
on, 168–69, 171; and colored
races as unassimilable, 199, 208;
and evolution of races, 176–77,
209; extremist views on, 160;
"historical" development of, 159,
200; and miscegenation, 199–200;
moderate southern views on, 159–
60; and northern attitudes toward
blacks, 164–65; Roosevelt's views
on, 176, 178–79, 452n. *See also*
bigotry, racial
railroads: building the
transcontinental railroad, 91,
208, 230; Central Pacific, 91; as
early corporations, 270; effects
of transcontinental railroad,
114, 177; Erie Railroad, 229, 256;
and Northern Pacific, 256; and
Northern Securities, 274–76;
and Pennsylvania Railroad, 229,

360; and rebates, 228–29, 273;
speculation regarding, 275, 361;
and Trans-Siberian Railway,
372; and Union Pacific, 274; and
World's Columbian Exposition,
121
Raymond, John T., 186
Reconstruction, 159–60; and
election of 1876, 160, 161–62;
and Freedmen's Bureau, 156, 164;
and *Huckleberry Finn*'s ending as
comment on, 197–98; reasons for
abandonment of, 164–65; South's
resistance to, 160, 162, 164–65
Reed, Thomas, 223–24, 233
Republican Old Guard, 385, 412–15
Rhodes, James Ford, 56
Rice, Cecil Spring, 384
Rice, Dr. Clarence, 233, 257, 341
Riverdale-on-Hudson, 224, 260;
Clemenses departing from there
for good, 282; and Clemens
family leasing of, 180; Roosevelts'
use of as summer home, 180
Robinson, Edwin Arlington, 56
Rockefeller, John D., Sr., 158, 251,
389; and Civil War, 228; and
competition, 228, 369; early life,
228–29; and Standard Oil, 228,
269–70, 280–81
Rodin, Auguste, 383
Rogers, Henry Huttleston, 296,
382; birth of, 222; and the
Civil War, 226; and Clemens's
financial affairs, 257–58, 260,
283; Clemens's opinion of, 260,
405; and Fairhaven, 222, 280,
406; as family man, 223, 406;
and favors asked of Clemens,
280; at Gridiron dinner, 332; and
Helen Keller, 236; and *Kanawha*,

About the Author

Philip McFarland has written two works of fiction and six of nonfiction, among the latter most recently *Hawthorne in Concord* (2004) and *Loves of Harriet Beecher Stowe* (2007). The father of two grown sons, he lives with his wife in Lexington, Massachusetts. For more information, please visit www.philipmcfarland.com.